BANKRUPTCY
MATERIALS AND CASES

Third Edition

■ ■ ■

By

David G. Epstein
George E. Allen Chair Professor of Law
University of Richmond

Bruce A. Markell
United States Bankruptcy Judge
District of Nevada
Senior Fellow, Bankruptcy and Commercial Law
William S. Boyd School of Law
University of Nevada, Las Vegas

Steve H. Nickles
C.C. Hope Chair in Law and Management
Wake Forest University

Elizabeth L. Perris
United States Bankruptcy Judge
District of Oregon

AMERICAN CASEBOOK SERIES®

WEST®

A Thomson Reuters business

Mat #40785224

American Casebook Series is a trademark registered in the U.S. Patent and Trademark Office.

© West, a Thomson business, 2005, 2006
© 2010 Thomson Reuters

    610 Opperman Drive
    St. Paul, MN 55123
    1–800–313–9378

Printed in the United States of America

ISBN: 978–0–314–91155–1

DEDICATION

To Louis Higgins,

Whom faculty everywhere know as a genuine friend
and a real mensch

David, Bruce, Steve, and Liz

PREFACE TO THE THIRD EDITION

1. Who We Are

David G. Epstein

Bruce A. Markell

Elizabeth L. Perris

Steve H. Nickles

Obviously, all of us are prime candidates for one of the reality-television "makeover" shows. Two of us—David and Steve—are now law professors; two of us—Liz and Bruce—are now bankruptcy judges. Among the four of us, we have taught bankruptcy courses at more than 20 different law schools.

2. Why We Wrote this Book

While we have had different professional experiences, we have a common understanding about how to learn and how to "do" bankruptcy law. There are a handful of basic bankruptcy building blocks. Learn the building blocks; see the relationship among the building blocks; find how these building blocks affect the legal issues that arise in consumer bankruptcy cases and in business bankruptcy cases.

3. *How the Book Works (And How You Will Work with this Book)*

In a sense, this book starts in the middle of a story. It is a story that had a happy beginning. C thought well enough of D to extend credit to D. Now there are problems with D and C's debtor-creditor relationship: D is not paying C, or C is concerned about whether D will be able to continue paying it. This book is about what lawyers can do to fix the problems.

In the "real world," these problems are typically fixed without litigation or other formal recourse to the legal process, and without lawyers. D pays C or D and C work out some sort of alternative payment plan. Sometimes, however, lawyers' help is needed. But lawyers can be helpful in resolving debtor-creditor problems, with or without recourse to bankruptcy and other legal process, only if they know the legal rights and remedies of debtors and creditors.

And, except for the "lawyers" on *The Good Wife* (or whatever lawyers show is currently popular) or a John Grisham novel, most lawyers spend most of their time in the office working on their clients' problems. So, you will spend most of your time in this book working on your clients' problems.

All of the problems in the book can be understood and discussed from materials already considered in the book. We have made a special effort to design problems that could be discussed on the basis of the materials surrounding them.

Bankruptcy impacts so many aspects of what lawyers do, from business transactions to consumer protection to litigation of domestic relations matters. Understanding bankruptcy is thus critically important for almost every lawyer. To meet this challenge, we want you to learn the basics of debtor-creditor law, to become familiar with the issues of debtor-creditor law that you are likely to encounter in practice, and to think about the policy questions that underlie those issues. While policy questions are consistently and constantly raised, the book does not espouse any particular theory or philosophy of debtor-creditor law. You are left to develop your own opinions on these policy issues. The only "message" that we are trying to convey is that this stuff is important, interesting and intellectually challenging.

A couple of notes before we get to the "fun stuff." Bankruptcy law is largely statutory law; to be more precise, it is largely federal statutory law. The main text of statutes is the "Bankruptcy Code," found in title 11 of the United States Code. When we refer to the "Code" in this book, it is to the Bankruptcy Code as found in title 11. In addition, there are rules that govern the day-today practice and procedure in bankruptcy courts. They are the Federal Rules of Bankruptcy Procedure, which should be in your statutory supplement. We refer to them as the "Rules" or cite to them as "Bankr. R. XXX."

We do think bankruptcy law is fun. Fun because it can be intellectually challenging; fun because it can be helpful in solving problems that really matter to the people involved. We had fun working together on this book. We hope you'll have fun working through it.

DGE
Richmond, Virginia

BAM
Las Vegas, Nevada

SHN
Winston–Salem, North Carolina

ELP
Portland, Oregon

June 2010

Summary of Contents

TABLE OF CONTENTS

TABLE OF CASES

The principal cases are in bold type. Cases cited or discussed in the text are in roman type. References are to pages. Cases cited in principal cases and within other quoted materials are not included.

TABLE OF STATUTES

BANKRUPTCY
MATERIALS AND CASES

Third Edition

UNIT 1

WHAT IS THIS COURSE ABOUT?

■ ■ ■

This course is about the legal questions that arise when a business or individual does not pay debts owed to creditors. The answers to these legal questions are found primarily in the Bankruptcy Code. And so, we will be looking at the Bankruptcy Code A lot. To make that "easier" for you, there is a lot of the Bankruptcy Code in this book.

A. JUST ENOUGH BANKRUPTCY HISTORY FOR YOU TO BE ABLE TO DEVELOP A NEW BRAVO NETWORK REALITY SERIES, "I WANT TO BE A ROMAN BANKRUPT"

Nothing new about people not paying their debts.[1] And nothing new about bankruptcy being the legal "answer."

Historically, the purposes of bankruptcy were to force debtors into a court proceeding in which their assets were divided up among claimants in some form of collective setting in which all creditors participated, or to criminalize insolvency, or both. Beyond those general purposes, however, outcomes varied.

For example, if a debtor's assets were insufficient to pay all creditors ancient Romans gave themselves the power to dismember and distribute a debtor's body to creditors in proportion to the amount of debts owed each.[2] Medieval Italians, who gave us the term "bankruptcy,"[3] remitted

---

1. I realize that this is a sentence fragment. Miss Lindemann, my eleventh grade "Language Arts" teacher, told me that I could use sentence fragments when I got a book published. DGE

2. *See* 2 WILLIAM BLACKSTONE, COMMENTARIES 472 (1766) ("[Under Roman law], creditors might cut the debtor's body into pieces, and each of them take his proportionate share. . . ."). *See also* Vern Countryman, *Bankruptcy and the Individual Debtor—and a Modest Proposal to Return to the Seventeenth Century*, 32 CATH. U.L. REV. 809, 810 (1983).

3. From the concatenation of "banca"—bench or table—and "rotta,"—broken or ruptured. Medieval merchants traded from benches or tables in a common area, and the breaking of such a bench signaled the revocation of the merchant's trading privileges or his banishment from the city. ["Concatenation?" This is Markell's footnote.]

criminal penalties for those who could not pay all their debts if they exposed their naked bodies in public, and people then banged the bankrupts' "backsides"[4] on a public post while the bankrupts loudly proclaimed "I am bankrupt" three times.[5] In France, those who could not pay their debts were made to wear a "Green Cap" at all times so that others would know that they had stiffed their creditors.[6]

B. WHAT YOU SHOULD CARE ABOUT IN THIS COURSE

Even if you really don't care about this history, in this course, you have to care about the 21st Century questions: (1) what can an individual debtor accomplish in bankruptcy, (2) what can a business debtor accomplish in bankruptcy, (3) what can creditors accomplish in bankruptcy, and (4) what are the roles of lawyers in bankruptcy. These questions, like others that judges or law professors ask, lead to other, more specific questions. The two specific questions that we will be considering most often in this course are (1) what are the possible decisions and (2) who decides.

C. THE NATIONAL BANKRUPTCY REVIEW COMMISSION'S OVERVIEW OF BANKRUPTCY

In 1994, Congress enacted legislation establishing a commission to review business and consumer bankruptcy. In 1997, the Commission submitted a report (that looks a lot like the Greater Las Vegas Smart Yellow Pages) with 170 individual recommendations.

Congress has ignored this big yellow book. You shouldn't. As law students, you get it free and "un-yellow" on Westlaw: "NBRCR" database. Hundreds of pages of helpful explanations of bankruptcy concepts and discussions of bankruptcy problems. Look at it!

For now, please look at the Commission's Report's overview of business bankruptcy and consumer bankruptcy:

1. Business Bankruptcy

"Business bankruptcies are only a small fraction of all filings—about 4% overall—but the bankruptcy system is a critical part of the cycle of business life and death in the American economy. Principally through Chapter 11, business bankruptcy creates the opportunity to restructure failing businesses, to preserve jobs, to prevent the spread of economic failure to smaller suppliers and other dependent busi-

---

4. Nickles vetoed our use of the more descriptive term "butts" but was oblivious to today's use of the term "bang."

5. *See* James Q. Whitman, *The Moral Menace of Roman Law and the Making of Commerce: Some Dutch Evidence,* 105 YALE L.J. 1841, 1872–73 (1996).

6. Id. at 1874.

nesses, and to permit communities to retain their tax base. Liquidation is also an important part of the business bankruptcy system, providing an efficient and orderly way to dissolve a business and to distribute its assets equitably among parties who might otherwise see no recovery at all."

NAT'L BANKRUPTCY REV. COMM'N, BANKRUPTCY: THE NEXT TWENTY YEARS, THE NATIONAL BANKRUPTCY REVIEW COMMISSION FINAL REPORT 303 (1997).

2. Consumer Bankruptcy

"Consumer bankruptcy has become part of America's economic landscape. Once regarded as an unlikely legal alternative chosen by only a few desperate families, bankruptcy had become a refuge for one in every 96 American families by the time the National Bankruptcy Review Commission filed its report. . . .

As bankruptcy filings increase, creditors justifiably worry whether a promise to repay has any meaning, while consumer advocates express concern that the financial distress of more than a million American families each year foreshadows a larger economic problem. The inherent conflict between the twin goals of bankruptcy—appropriate relief for those in trouble and equitable treatment for their creditors—ensures that it always will be an area of contention. To deal with financial loss, the bankruptcy system necessarily embraces competing interests. Recommendations fully endorsed by either debtors or by creditors would not maintain the balance essential to any consumer bankruptcy system. Bankruptcy is a system born of conflict and competing values. To function well, it must remain unpopular and controversial. No area of bankruptcy law is more complex than consumer bankruptcy."

NAT'L BANKRUPTCY REV. COMM'N, BANKRUPTCY: THE NEXT TWENTY YEARS, THE NATIONAL BANKRUPTCY REVIEW COMMISSION FINAL REPORT 77–78 (1997).

D. A CLOSER VIEW OF AN ACTUAL BUSINESS BANKRUPTCY CASE AND AN ACTUAL CONSUMER CASE

1. CIRCUIT CITY BANKRUPTCY

On November 10, 2008, Circuit City Stores, Inc. and affiliates (hereafter "Circuit City") filed for Chapter 11 relief in the bankruptcy court for the Eastern District of Virginia in Richmond, Virginia. Circuit City was founded in 1949 and headquartered in Richmond. Prior to its bankruptcy filing, Circuit City was a specialty retailer of consumer electronics, operating 712 superstores and 9 outlet stores, with a workforce of approximately 39,600 full and part-time employees, with an additional 11,000 part-time employees anticipated for the Christmas season.

The schedules Circuit City filed with the bankruptcy court showed $3.4 billion in assets and $2.3 billion in liabilities. Hewlett–Packard was listed as Circuit City's largest creditor—$118.8 million. Samsung was a close second at $116 million.

Circuit City's last pre-bankruptcy quarterly report, issued in late September, 2008, reported a quarterly loss of nearly $240 million. Circuit City had lost more than $5 billion in stock market value in the two years before bankruptcy.

There was news of Circuit City's bankruptcy filing in newspapers such as the Wall Street Journal, International Herald Tribune, and, of course, the Richmond Times Dispatch. In covering the first hearing in the Circuit City bankruptcy, the Richmond paper reported, "The chain's attorneys, company executives, and lawyers packed the courtroom in the new federal courthouse in downtown Richmond ... Gregg Galardi, a partner in the Delaware [office of the] law firm of Skadden, Arps, Slate, Meagher & Flom LLP that is representing the chain, said repeatedly that Circuit City's goal is to come out of the bankruptcy reshaped and ready to do business by the end of April."[7]

Well, Circuit City did not realize this goal. Faced with weak Christmas sales, no lender willing to provide enough new funding to enable it to continue operating, and no buyer for the company, Circuit City decided on January 16, 2009, with court approval, to close its stores and liquidate its assets. Circuit City hired four independent liquidation companies to handle the liquidation of store assets and sent 60–day pink slips to more than 34,000 employees.

On March 11, 2009, the Subcommittee on Commercial and Administrative Law of the House Judiciary Committee held hearings on "Circuit City Unplugged: Why Did Chapter 11 Fail to Save 34,000 Jobs"?

The Circuit City bankruptcy did create jobs for lawyers, some of whom billed Circuit City at $995 an hour. Current estimates are that, before the bankruptcy case is over, Circuit City will pay lawyers and other professionals more than $37,000,000 and will pay its unsecured creditors 10 to 14% on pre-bankruptcy debts. People who bought Circuit City stock will get nothing.

2.   MR. 64 AND MRS. 64 BANKRUPTCY

The Circuit City bankruptcy petition was not the only bankruptcy petition filed on November 10, 2008. That day, like every other day, hundreds of bankruptcy petitions were filed in Richmond, Virginia, and around the country by business entities and individuals.

One such petition was Case Number 08–64496, a Chapter 13 petition, filed by a husband and wife in Oregon. There was no news of this bankruptcy in the Wall Street Journal, International Herald Tribune, or even the local Portland newspaper. We will also respect the privacy of the debtors in this case and simply refer to them at "Mr. 64 and Mrs. 64."

7. Louis Llovio and Michael Martz, Circuit City Files for Bankruptcy,11/11/08 Richmond Times–Dispatch, 2008 WLNR 21819682.

Mr. 64 and Mrs. 64 are no more the typical individuals unable to pay their debts than Circuit City is the typical business unable to pay its debts. Their schedules filed with the bankruptcy court show (1) total assets of $522,185 with two houses, a 2004 Ford F250 truck and a 2006 Ford Fusion, $20 in cash, and $115 in various savings and checking accounts; (2) total debts of $504,813, and (3) monthly income of $8,486.

At the time of their bankruptcy filing, Mr. 64 worked as an electrician for a construction company. Mrs. 64 worked as an apprentice electrician for a different employer. For the first nine months of 2008, Mr. 64 and Mrs. 64 had owned a tanning salon.

In February, 2009, the bankruptcy court approved a plan of repayment by Mr. 64 and Mrs. 64 that would, over a five-year period, pay 35% to Mr. 64 and Mrs. 64's unsecured creditors and pay $4,000 to their bankruptcy attorney "through the plan." Shortly thereafter, Mrs. 64 lost her job, and the child support payments she was receiving from a former husband were reduced because of his financial problems. In May, 2009, Mr. 64 and Mrs. 64 filed a modified plan that reduced Mr. 64 and Mrs. 64's monthly payments to creditors by $400 and thus reduced the total payment to unsecured creditors to 8%.

There are a couple of reasons that we wanted you to have this early look at a real business bankruptcy case and a real individual bankruptcy case.

First reason. While, like Emmy Lou Harris, "We Believe in Happy Endings", there are not always (or even often) "happy endings" in bankruptcy stories. More specifically,

- bankruptcy *cannot* fix all problems—can't even fix all debt problems;

- in bankruptcy, most creditors do *not* get paid most of what they are owed;

The ending of a bankruptcy case depends in the main on (1) the liquidation and going concern values of the debtor's assets; (2) the debtor's ability to generate cash flow i.e., the debtor's ability to make money that can be used to pay creditors; (3) creditors' interests and needs; and (4) the "bankruptcy" attorneys' and bankruptcy judge's ability to work creatively and effectively with the bankruptcy concepts covered in this book

Second reason. It is mistake to think that lawyers think of looking to the Bankruptcy Code only when dealing with "bankrupts" like Circuit City or Mr. 64 and Mrs. 64.

It is a mistake because there is no longer any such person as a "bankrupt." Circuit City is not a "bankrupt." Nor are Mr. 64 and Mrs. 64. The 1978 Bankruptcy Code eliminated the use of the term "bankrupt." A person who has filed a bankruptcy petition with the bankruptcy court for bankruptcy relief is supposed to be called a "debtor", not a "bankrupt."

More important, it is a mistake to think that bankruptcy law questions only arise when a debtor has filed for bankruptcy relief. Increasingly, lawyers and law students need to consider bankruptcy law questions in connection with transactions. Obviously, when C makes a loan to D, C needs to consider the possible effects of D's later filing for bankruptcy. And when S sells B goods on credit, S needs to think about the possible effects of B's filing for bankruptcy, and B needs to think about the possible effects of S's filing for bankruptcy. And, when L leases a building to T, L needs to consider the possible effects of T's filing for bankruptcy and T needs to consider the possibility of L's filing for bankruptcy.

E.   THIS COURSE AND CONSTITUTIONAL LAW AND CONTRACTS LAW AND PROPERTY LAW AND MORE CONSTITUTIONAL LAW

While this course is primarily about bankruptcy law, this course also covers constitutional law concepts not "covered"[8] in your constitutional law course, and contract law concepts not covered in your contracts course, and property concepts not covered in your property course.

First, constitutional law. The United States Constitution delegates to Congress the exclusive power to establish "uniform laws on the subject of Bankruptcies" in Article 1, section 8, clause 4.

Now, constitutional law and contracts. Article I, section 10 of the Constitution bars states (not the federal government) from impairing contract obligations. When read together, Article 1, section 8, and Article 1, section 10, mean that Congress may enact "uniform laws on the subject of Bankruptcies" which impair the obligation of contracts. As the Seventh Circuit explained: "All parties to a contract are, of necessity, aware of the existence of, and subject to, the power of Congress to legislate on the subject of bankruptcies. They were and are chargeable with knowledge that their rights and remedies ... are affected by existing bankruptcy laws and all future bankruptcy legislation which might be enacted." *In re Prima Co.*, 88 F.2d 785, 788 (7th Cir. 1937).

Now property law and con law. A mortgage, security interest or other lien is a property interest. A creditor who has a lien on the debtor's property has a property interest. The Fifth Amendment prohibits taking private property without just compensation. And, the Article 1 Congressional power to enact bankruptcy laws is "subject to the Fifth Amendment's prohibition against taking private property without compensation." United States v. Security Indus. Bank, 459 U.S. 70, 75 (1982). Accordingly, the Bankruptcy Code [and this book] regularly distinguishes between what bankruptcy can do to a creditor's right to payment (which is in the nature of a contract right) and what bankruptcy can do to a creditor's lien (which is in the nature of a property right).

---

8. "Not covered" is, of course, law students' way of saying "We don't remember our professors' covering."

Unit 2

Why Are There So Many Bankruptcy Cases?

■ ■ ■

More than a million individuals and business entities file a petition for bankruptcy relief each year.[1]

A legitimate question is why there are so many filings. An equally legitimate question is why there are so few.

The point of these two "questions" is that you should approach the investigation of bankruptcy with an open mind; to label the numbers above too many (or too few) means that you have already made some assumptions about bankruptcy relief. Before those assumptions harden, let us first explore the alternatives to bankruptcy.

A. WHAT CAN CREDITORS DO OUTSIDE OF BANKRUPTCY?

Creditors are generally happy to do nothing. More specifically, creditors are happy to do nothing so long as their debtors are paying them.

When debtors default in paying an obligation, creditors will first attempt through "persuasion" to get the debtor to pay "voluntarily." The creditor may even hire a collection agency or attorney to help persuade the debtor.[2] If these nonjudicial collection efforts are unsuccessful, the creditor can resort to the debt collection remedies provided by either (i) law of creditors' remedies or (ii) the creditor's contract with the debtor to seize and sell the debtor's assets to satisfy the debt.

Let's consider the law of creditors' remedies first. At the broadest level, the law of creditors' remedies involves only two issues: (1) when and how a creditor gets a lien on property of the debtor (or the property itself), and (2) the lien's priority in relation to third parties' rights to the

---

1. You can look up the official bankruptcy statistics on line. *See* http://www.uscourts.gov/bnkrpctystats/bankruptcystats.htm.

2. When the debt is a consumer debt, these nonjudicial persuasion efforts are controlled by the federal Fair Debt Collection Practices Act and various state consumer protection statutes.

7

property, including other creditors' liens and the claims of transferees. These two issues are common to every kind of creditors' remedy.

Why the focus on "liens"? A creditor cannot seize and sell its debtor's property unless it has some property interest in the debtor's property, and the principal way to obtain such an interest is to obtain a "lien" on that property.

Say for example that Perris claims that Epstein owes her $1,000. Perris can't simply come over to Epstein's house and take his stuff. She needs to establish her legal right to be paid $1,000. She needs to establish her right to Epstein's property. This example illustrates the most general rule of the law of creditors' remedies: generally a creditor does not acquire or retain a lien or other property interest in the debtor's property until the creditor reduces her claim to judgment and enforces this judgment through the appropriate postjudgment process, execution.[3]

You should now be asking the questions: (1) why is action beyond a judgment necessary and (2) what is execution?

The answer to the first question that you should be asking is that a judgment is no more than another form of debt; it is a new form of the obligation that the debtor owes the creditor. A judgment does, however, differ from the original obligation in that a judgment is the State's recognition of the legitimacy of the creditor's claim against the debtor. Along with this recognition comes (1) a judgment lien, which attaches by force of law to the debtor's real property once the judgment is appropriately recorded, and also (2) a willingness by the state to use its coercive power to enforce this lien and otherwise collect the amount of the judgment forcibly from the debtor's property (both real and personal) if the judgment debtor does not pay "voluntarily." This coercive power is brought to bear through the process of execution which is triggered simply by a judgment creditor requesting it.

Now, to answer the second question: what is execution? A creditor with a judgment initiates the execution process by applying to the court that issued the judgment for a *writ of execution*. The writ of execution is ordinarily issued from the court that rendered the judgment and is directed to a sheriff. The writ orders the sheriff to seize property of the debtor, sell it, and apply the proceeds in satisfaction of the judgment.

To reach tangible property of a debtor held by third persons, and to collect debts owed to the debtor, there is a special proceeding at law in the nature of an adversary suit against the person who holds the debtor's property or owes the debtor money: *garnishment*. Garnishment is in essence a special form of execution—designed for reaching property of the debtor held by a third party.

---

3. There is a small exception to the rule that a creditor cannot seize property of the debtor except through postjudgment execution. In a narrow class of cases, property sufficient to satisfy a creditor's claim can be impounded by judicial lien at the time suit is filed. The means is a provisional remedy known as *prejudgment attachment* or, when the property is held by a third person, *prejudgment garnishment*.

The most common example of garnishment is garnishment of bank accounts. When a creditor tries to collect its judgment against the debtor from funds in the debtor's bank account, it seeks to obtain property of the debtor's held by a third person. In this context, the proper terminology regarding what occurs when, for example, the IRS tries to seize a bank account of delinquent taxpayer, is that the IRS is garnishing the bank account.

Most lawyers do not like to do debt collection work; most creditors do not like to pay for this kind of legal work. Obtaining a judgment and getting a sheriff to seize and sell property of a debtor can be difficult, time consuming and expensive. And, most important, obtaining a judgment and getting a sheriff to seize and sell property of a debtor is often unsuccessful.

Why? One of the largest roadblocks to collection of debts through this legal process is that there is no guarantee that the debtor will have property that can be seized and sold, or that the property will be in the place that the creditor told the sheriff to go look.

Second, even if the debtor has property, that property may be encumbered by other creditors' liens that have priority. These other liens may have been created because of (i) a prior judicial collection effort, or (ii) statute, or (iii) agreement.

Tax liens, mechanics' liens and landlords' liens are examples of statutory liens. These are liens that arise by operation of law–arise if the debtor fails to pay a debt protected by the statute.

While statutory liens are important, consensual liens are the most common liens. Most debt deals which are large enough to involve lawyers also involve consensual liens

We are going to spend a lot of time in this course talking about consensual liens—property rights that creditors obtain by contract. For now, you need to understand that (1) by contract, a creditor can obtain rights in addition to the rights available to a creditor under creditors' remedies law, (2) these rights, i.e., consensual liens, have the effect of limiting the rights of other creditors under creditors' remedies law, and (3) these consensual liens are property rights and so enjoy the constitutional protection afforded to property rights.

Federal bankruptcy law does not govern the creation of these consensual liens. Instead, state law controls here, and state law tends to categorize the types of consensual liens by the type of property involved, The two basic types of property in this regard are real property (that is, dirt and things built on and attached to the dirt) and personal property (that is, things that are not real property).

There are various devices for creating consensual liens on real property—the mortgage, the deed of trust, and the land-sale contract. The differences in these devices largely concern the procedures for (a) applying the collateral in satisfaction of the secured obligation, and (b) safeguarding the debtor's rights and interests.

When the creditor and debtor create a consensual lien on personal property or fixtures, the governing law is Uniform Commercial Code Article 9, the subject of another course in law school sometimes called "Secured Transactions" or "Commercial Law." Article 9 provides for only one kind of consensual lien on personal property, the Article 9 security interest.

"Security interest" is Article 9's term for a consensual lien on personal property. Other Article 9 terms that are you will encounter in this course are "secured party" and "collateral." A "secured party'" is a creditor with a security interest. The property subject to the secured party's security interest is the "collateral."

Problem 2–1:   What Can a Creditor's Attorney Do Without Bankruptcy?

Your firm's client, C, has a $1,000,000 judgment against Nick's Chicks, Inc. (N), a chicken farm operating adjacent to C's property. What can you do to collect this judgment if N's assets include:

(i) chicken houses,

(ii) 25,000 chickens,

(iii) equipment,

(iv) accounts receivable, and

(v) various bank accounts in S Bank.

And, N's other creditors include:

(i) S Bank,

(ii) IRS,

(iii) trade creditors, and

(iv) employees who are to be paid $70,000 in wages, benefits, etc. at the end of the week

Problem 2–2: How Much Can the Creditor's Attorney "Bill?"

How much should your firm charge C for collecting the $1,000,000 judgment? How much should your firm charge if C's judgment is only a $100,000 judgment? How much should you charge if, at the end of the day, you collect nothing for C despite good faith and reasonable attempts to do so?

B.   WHAT CAN A DEBTOR DO OUTSIDE OF BANKRUPTCY?

There is not much a debtor can do outside of bankruptcy to fix its debt problems. At least not much that a debtor can do without the help and support of its creditors.

Recall that when a debtor does not pay a debt despite the requests (and then demands) of a creditor, the creditor can go to court and sue on the debt. Such a suit usually results in a default judgment; that is, in most cases the debtor will not defend or show up, and the creditor will get everything it asked for in its complaint "by default."

Remember, that a creditor with a judgment can then obtain an "execution lien" from the court that issued the judgment. And, with an execution lien, the creditor can get the sheriff to "levy on," or take physical possession of, the debtor's property. The sheriff will then sell the property at an execution sale, the terms of which will be set by state statute.

A debtor can try to work out some sort of debt repayment agreement with its creditors. Professors who teach first year contracts courses call these agreements "compositions" and "extensions." Real lawyers call these agreements "workout agreements."

Whatever you call these agreements, they are "agreements" and only bind the creditors who agree. If even one creditor refuses to participate in the workout agreement, that dissenting creditor, can in essence, "blow up" any deal by suing on its debt and using the execution process to seize and sell assets of the debtor that are essential to the debtor's performing its workout obligations to the assenting creditors.

Assume, for example, that Perris Printing Company has reached an agreement with nine out of ten of its largest creditors to pay 90% of its debts over three years at a new, higher interest rate. The tenth, non-assenting creditor is not bound by that agreement. And, that creditor can sue on its debt, obtain a judgment and a writ of execution and seize and sell the equipment essential to Perris Printing's continued business operations.

Problem 2–3: What Can a Debtor's Attorney Do Without Bankruptcy?

Same facts as Problem 2–1 except that you represent Nick's Chicks, Inc. What can you do for Nick's Chicks outside of bankruptcy?

———————

If the debtor is an individual, state and federal laws exempt certain property of the debtor from the collection efforts of certain creditors. At most, these exemption statutes enable a debtor to keep some of his or her property from some of his or her creditors. Exemption statutes do not enable a person with debt problems to "fix" the problems.

State exemption laws vary significantly from state to state. In most states, the amount of property that a debtor can designate as exempt is very limited. And, in all states, creditors with a mortgage or security interest in property that is designated as exempt can still seize and sell that property. If, for example, First Bank has a mortgage on Epstein's house and Epstein defaults, First Bank can seize and sell Epstein's house even if Epstein has designated the house as his exempt homestead.

C. BUT WHY BANKRUPTCY?

Again, more than one million bankruptcy petitions are filed each year. More than 99% of these petitions are filed by debtors, less than 1% are filed by creditors against debtors.

Why? "Inquiring minds want to know." These guys must know something we don't. But not for long.

Unit 3

What Happens in a Bankruptcy Case?

■ ■ ■

A great bankruptcy teacher, Stefan Riesenfeld, accurately (and repeatedly) observed, "Bankruptcy is not mashed potatoes. You need to study it a lump at a time."

If this book is anything, it is very "lumpy" [big on lumps]. We have tried to isolate bankruptcy concepts and introduce you to one concept at a time. Nonetheless, it is important that you understand what happens in a bankruptcy case, that you "see the big picture". [This book is also big on trite expressions.]

A. BASIC STRUCTURE OF THE BANKRUPTCY CODE

The Bankruptcy Code may initially seem daunting, but a little knowledge of how it is put together can "un-daunt."

1. THE BANKRUPTCY CODE AS A "CODE"

The first thing to realize is that the Bankruptcy Code is, well, a code. What does that mean? That means that it is an integrated and comprehensive approach to a particular statutory problem. Ideally, the Bankruptcy Code is not supposed to have outright conflicts, and it is supposed to contain a balance of interests reached through legislative compromise. Supposed to.

There is structure to the Bankruptcy Code. It may not be readily apparent, but it is there.

2. THE UNDERLYING STRUCTURE

The underlying structure of the Bankruptcy Code is fairly simple. It consists of one title of the United States Code (title 11), and within title 11 are nine chapters. Each of these chapters has a different function, outlined as follows:

Chapter 1—Definitions

Chapter 3—Administration

Chapter 5—Claims and Creditors

Chapter 7—Liquidation

Chapter 9—Municipal Bankruptcy

Chapter 11—Reorganization

Chapter 12—Family Farmer Rehabilitation

Chapter 13—Rehabilitation of Individuals with Income

Chapter 15—Ancillary and Other Cross–Border Cases

Of these, Chapters 1, 3 and 5 apply in all bankruptcy cases.

The titles of the various chapters are helpful. For example, the most important part of Chapter 1 is its definitions. That is to say, there are a lot of definitions in Chapter 1, especially in section 101.[1] So many, in fact that Congress has lost the ability to consecutively number the definitions in section 101 correctly.[2]

The general structure of bankruptcy administration—what happens between the time the bankruptcy case is filed and the time that the bankruptcy case is over—is found in Chapter 3. The way in which the Code collects and distributes assets to creditors is found in Chapter 5.

Chapters 7, 9, 11, 12, 13, and 15 each deal with a different type of debtor or a different type of relief. A bankruptcy case will be either a Chapter 7 case, a Chapter 9, a Chapter 11 case, a Chapter 12 case, a Chapter 13 case, or a Chapter 15 case. The person filing the bankruptcy petition chooses whether the bankruptcy case will begin as a Chapter 7 case, or a Chapter 11 case, or . . .

This book deals primarily with Chapter 7 cases, Chapter 11 cases and Chapter 13 cases. And, remember, that in a Chapter 7 case or a Chapter 11 case or a Chapter 13 case, you will also be using Chapters 1, 3 and 5. Again, Chapters 1, 3 and 5 apply in all cases.

As among Chapters 7, 11 and 13, Chapter 7 is the easiest and the most important. Most persons filing a bankruptcy petition choose Chapter 7. And, most cases that are filed as Chapter 11 cases or Chapter 13 cases are later converted, i.e. changed into, Chapter 7 cases.

As its title indicates, Chapter 7 is about liquidation: the forced sale of the assets of the debtor and distribution of the sale proceeds pro rata to creditors in accordance with statutory guidelines and priorities. In Chapter 7 cases, most of the important decisions—decisions such as what is the source for payment of creditors and how the payment is to be allocated among creditors—have been made by Congress and set out in the Bank-

---

1. Some specific sections have their own internal definitions, applicable only within that section. *See* 11 U.S.C. § 547(a), which contains definitions that are applicable only to preference actions governed by Section 547.

2. Check out 11 U.S.C. § 101(53), which is followed by Section 101(53A), 101(53B), 101(53C), 101(53D), and then 101(54). Which would be fine, except that 101(55) is followed by 101(56A); there is no 101(56).

ruptcy Code. In the typical Chapter 7 case, there is no real opportunity for creative lawyering—not much for lawyers to do.

There is much more for lawyers to do in Chapter 11 cases. Chapter 11 contemplates that the debtor and creditors will negotiate a plan for payment of creditors that is to be approved by the bankruptcy court. Chapter 11 also allows the debtor to remain in possession of assets and become a "debtor in possession," or "DIP."

Chapter 13 is in some ways like Chapter 11. Chapter 13, like Chapter 11, allows the debtor to remain in possession of assets. And, in Chapter 13, like Chapter 11, it is the court-approved plan that governs payment of creditors.

A Chapter 13 case is also in some ways like a Chapter 7 case. Essentially, Congress has decided the source of payment of creditors—the debtor's "disposable income"—and the allocation of that payment—pro rata among creditors.

Chapter 12 allows Chapter 13 type relief for "family farmers." Remember that it is section 101 that you will look to find the definition of important Bankruptcy Code terms such as "family farmer."

Chapter 15 provides an alternative to a debtor with a bankruptcy case pending in some other country. Instead of commencing a full bankruptcy case in the United States, a "foreign representative" of the debtor may file a petition under Chapter 15. Upon the issuance of an order for recognition under section 1517, certain provisions of the Bankruptcy Code become effective. Most basic bankruptcy courses do not cover Chapter 15. Nonetheless, we cover Chapter 15 in the last unit in the book.

Set out below, in an altered print format, is the explanation of chapters 7, 11, and 13 that Mr. 64 and Mrs. 64 (and all individual debtors) receive "before the commencement of a case."

UNITED STATES BANKRUPTCY COURT
DISTRICT OF OREGON

NOTICE TO INDIVIDUAL CONSUMER DEBTOR UNDER § 342(b) OF THE BANKRUPTCY CODE

In accordance with § 342(b) of the Bankruptcy Code, this notice: (1) Describes briefly the services available from credit counseling services; (2) Describes briefly the purposes, benefits and costs of the four types of bankruptcy proceedings you may commence; and (3) Informs you about bankruptcy crimes and notifies you that the Attorney General may examine all information you supply in connection with a bankruptcy case. You are cautioned that bankruptcy law is complicated and not easily described. Thus, you may wish to seek the advice of an attorney to learn of your rights and responsibilities should you decide to file a petition. Court employees cannot give you legal advice.

1. Services Available from Credit Counseling Agencies

With limited exceptions, § 1.09(h) of the Bankruptcy Code requires that all individual debtors who file for bankruptcy relief on or after October 17, 2005, receive a briefing that outlines the available opportunities for credit counseling and provides assistance in performing a budget analysis. The briefing must be given within 180 days before the bankruptcy filing. The briefing may be provided individually or in a group (including briefings conducted by telephone or on the Internet) and must be provided by a nonprofit budget and credit counseling agency approved by the United States trustee or bankruptcy administrator. The clerk of the bankruptcy court has a list that you may consult of the approved budget and credit counseling agencies.

In addition, after filing a bankruptcy case, an individual debtor generally must complete a financial management instructional course before he or she can receive a discharge. The clerk also has a list of approved financial management instructional courses.

2. The Four Chapters of the Bankruptcy Code Available to Individual Consumer Debtors

Chapter 7: Liquidation ($345 filing fee, $39 administrative fee, $15 trustee surcharge: Total Fee $399)

1. Chapter 7 is designed for debtors in financial difficulty who do not have the ability to pay their existing debts. Debtors whose debts are primarily consumer debtors are subject to a "means test" designed to determine whether the case should be permitted to proceed under chapter 7. If your income is greater than the median income for your state of residence and family size, in some cases, creditors have the right to file a motion requesting that the court dismiss your case under § 707(b) of the Code. It is up to the court to decide whether the case should be dismissed.

2. Under chapter 7, you may claim certain of your property as exempt under governing law. A trustee may have the right to take possession of and sell the remaining property that is not exempt and use the sale proceeds to pay your creditors.

3. The purpose of filing a chapter 7 case is to obtain a discharge of your existing debts. If, however, you are found to have committed certain kinds of improper conduct described in the Bankruptcy Code, the court may deny your discharge and, if it does, the purpose for which you filed the bankruptcy petition will be defeated.

4. Even if you receive a general discharge, some particular debts are not discharged under the law. Therefore, you may still be responsible for most taxes and student loans; debts incurred to pay nondischargeable taxes; domestic support and property settlement obligations; most fines, penalties, forfeitures, and criminal restitution obligations; certain debts which are not properly listed in your bankruptcy papers; and debts for death or personal injury caused by operating a motor vehicle, vessel, or aircraft while intoxicated from alcohol or drugs. Also, if a creditor can prove that a debt arose from fraud, breach of fiduciary duty, or theft, or

from a willful and malicious injury, the bankruptcy court may determine that the debt is not discharged.

Chapter 13: Repayment of All or Part of the Debts of an Individual with Regular Income ($235 filing fee, $39 administrative fee: Total fee $274)

1.   Chapter 13 is designed for individuals with regular income who would like to pay all or part of their debts in installments over a period of time. You are only eligible for chapter 13 if your debts do not exceed certain dollar amounts set forth in the Bankruptcy Code.

2.   Under chapter 13, you must file with the court a plan to repay your creditors all or part of the money that you owe them, using your future earnings. The period allowed by the court to repay your debts may be three years or five years, depending upon your income and other factors. The court must approve your plan before it can take effect.

3.   After completing the payments under your plan, your debts are generally discharged except for domestic support obligations; most student loans; certain taxes; most criminal fines and restitution obligations; certain debts which are not properly listed in your bankruptcy papers; certain debts for acts that caused death or personal injury; and certain long term secured obligations.

Chapter 11: Reorganization ($1000 filing fee, $39 administrative fee: Total fee $1039)

Chapter 11 is designed for the reorganization of a business but is also available to consumer debtors. Its provisions are quite complicated, and any decision by an individual to file a chapter 11 petition should be reviewed with an attorney.

Chapter 12: Family Farmer or Fisherman ($200 filing fee, $39 administrative fee: Total fee $239)

Chapter 12 is designed to permit family farmers and fishermen to repay their debts over a period of time from future earnings and is similar to chapter 13. The eligibility requirements are restrictive, limiting its use to those whose income arises primarily from a family-owned farm or commercial fishing operation.

3.   Bankruptcy Crimes and Availability of Bankruptcy Papers to Law Enforcement Officials

A person who knowingly and fraudulently conceals assets or makes a false oath or statement under penalty of perjury, either orally or in writing, in connection with a bankruptcy case is subject to a fine, imprisonment, or both. All information supplied by a debtor in connection with a bankruptcy case is subject to examination by the Attorney General acting through the Office of the United States Trustee, the Office of the United States Attorney, and other components and employees of the Department of Justice.

WARNING: Section 521(a)(1) of the Bankruptcy Code requires that you promptly file detailed information regarding your creditors, assets, liabilities, income, expenses and general financial condition. Your bankruptcy case may be dismissed if this information is not filed with the court within the time deadlines set by the Bankruptcy Code, the Bankruptcy Rules, and the local rules of the court.

Certificate of Attorney

I hereby certify that I delivered to the debtor this notice required by § 342(b) of the Bankruptcy Code.

_____

Certificate of Debtor

I (We), the debtor(s), affirm that I (we) have received and read this notice.

_____

3. THE ROLE OF NON–BANKRUPTCY LAW

Bankruptcy law is federal law. There are no state bankruptcy laws. Article I of the Constitution empowers Congress to enact bankruptcy laws, and Congress has enacted bankruptcy laws.

Under the Constitution's Supremacy Clause found in Article VI, federal law preempts contrary state law. So a state that passes a law that says "Debts owed to the health care providers shall not be subject to a bankruptcy discharge" has passed a nullity; such a state "bankruptcy law" will not be enforced.

While there are no state bankruptcy laws, state law is often important in bankruptcy cases. There are times—actually many, many times-when the Bankruptcy Code alone is not enough.

A truly complete bankruptcy code would contain all sorts of definitions of property and regulate priorities with respect to the property interests so defined. The United States Bankruptcy Code does not do this. Rather, in most situations, the Bankruptcy Code tries not to change the result under non-bankruptcy law, so as to minimize litigants' strategic reasons to seek bankruptcy relief.

The interface between federal bankruptcy law and non-bankruptcy law consists of a zone that is well-defined in the main, but fuzzy and contentious at the edges. Many of the issues in this book will draw on non-bankruptcy law for their resolution.

4. TIPS FOR READING THE BANKRUPTCY CODE

One of the early mentors for one of the junior authors of this book once took that author aside and pointed to the Code. He then said the following magic words: "There are two rules for reading this or any other Code. Number 1: Read carefully. Number 2: Read on."

With respect to Rule #1, there is, of course, no substitute for careful textual reading of any statute. In the case of a code such as the Bankruptcy Code, careful textual reading is especially important because the Bankruptcy Code was drafted, at least initially, as an integrated whole, with care toward the consequences of the application of one part of the Code on other parts of the Code. Look for the connections among the various Bankruptcy Code sections.

Connections among sections is just one of the reason for the admonition of "Read on." The integrated nature of the Bankruptcy Code's text, and the style of its drafting, require you to read more than just part of the text you may initially focus upon.

A general rule is often stated at the beginning of a section of the Code, only to be gutted by the exceptions that follow. Worse, in some sections, the exceptions are stated at the beginning of the section and the general rule at the end. In a dispute over the application of a section, one side will often champion the general rule, while the other side will champion the exception. And, the "champion" will often be the one who understands how the two are supposed to fit together.

B.   TYPICAL PLAYERS IN A BANKRUPTCY CASE

1.   BANKRUPTCY AS LITIGATION

In the real world, most lawyers use bankruptcy mostly in negotiating in doing new deals and in "re-doing" troubled deals. In a law school basic bankruptcy course, law students see bankruptcy primarily in litigation.

Bankruptcy litigation takes place in a court. There are rules of procedure, and a person in a black robe presides. There are usually two tables.

Other parallels to typical civil litigation are few. Part of this comes from the fact that in bankruptcy, disputes are generally resolved by negotiation rather than litigation, Part of this comes from the fact that a debtor may have many different types of creditors with different interests: secured or unsecured, vendor or lender, friendly or unfriendly. Bankruptcy litigation is generally more like chess than checkers—more complicated than debtor v. creditor or plaintiff v. defendant.

2.   PLAYERS AND ROLES IN BANKRUPTCY CASES

We won't be using the litigation terms "plaintiff" and "defendant" in talking about bankruptcy. Here is a short listing of the major players that we will encounter in this book:

- *Debtor.* Most simply, the person, individual or business entity that is the subject of the bankruptcy case. Put another way, it is the person who owes money and is seeking some form of relief under the Bankruptcy Code. *See* § 101(13).

- *Debtor in Possession.* A special type of debtor that only appears in Chapter 11 cases and Chapter 12 cases. A debtor in possession (or "DIP") is the debtor, but with expanded duties as a representative of the bankruptcy estate. A DIP has fiduciary duties to the estate that the debtor does not. *See* § 1101(1).

- *Creditor.* Again, most simply, a person to whom the debtor owes a monetary obligation. "Creditor" is defined at § 101(10) in a way that may be more expansive than your general understanding of the word "creditor." We will explore this more when we talk about "claims" in Unit 4.

- *Creditors' Committee.* Most generally, this refers to a committee of unsecured creditors in a Chapter 11 case. Such committees are recognized by statute, § 1102, and are given statutory duties, § 1103(c). A committee may hire its own professionals, who will be paid from the estate and not by the individual members of the committee (a mixed blessing, because it also means that the professionals for any committee serve the estate and not the individual interests of the committee members).

- *"Professionals."* This is more a term of art, and refers to the lawyers, accountants and sometimes the investment bankers hired to assist the bankruptcy estate or a committee. In many cases, in order to be paid from the estate, these professionals have to seek permission from the bankruptcy court to be employed, must not have any conflicts or adverse interests with respect to the estate, and must apply publicly for payment of their fees (which means that their time sheets become a matter of public record).

- *Trustee.* This term has different meanings in different bankruptcy cases. It refers to the representative of the estate charged with administering the case, but there are different types of trustees in bankruptcy cases.

  - *Chapter 7 Trustee* (also of "panel" trustees). A person who represents the estate in a Chapter 7 case, collects and liquidates the debtor's assets, and distributes the proceeds to creditors. An interim trustee is appointed upon the filing of the bankruptcy case, § 701, and creditors can then vote for a permanent trustee at the first meeting of creditors. § 702. Most of the time, the interim trustee becomes the "trustee" for the Chapter 7 case.

    Chapter 7 trustees more often than not are drawn from a "panel" of individuals qualified under 28 U.S.C. § 586(a)(1) maintained by the Office of the United States Trustee (see below).

The three most important things to remember about Chapter 7 trustees are that (1) trustees are required by the Code in all Chapter 7 cases, and (2) these Chapter 7 trustees "work for" the debtor's unsecured creditors and (3) Chapter 7 trustees do most of the "work" in most Chapter 7 cases.

- *Chapter 11 Trustee.* A person who represents the estate in a Chapter 11 case. Unlike Chapter 7, Chapter 11 does not provide for the automatic appointment of a trustee; instead, the debtor in possession is the norm. Only when the debtor is unwilling to serve as the debtor in possession, or when the court is convinced that a Chapter 11 trustee should be appointed, will a Chapter 11 case be administered by a trustee. The appointment of a trustee in a Chapter 11 case is unusual, if not rare.

- *Chapter 12 and 13 Trustees.* Trustees in Chapter 12 and 13 cases perform administrative functions; they monitor the debtor's development and performance of his or her plan, they collect and disburse plan payments and occasionally object to plan confirmation if they believe that the debtor has not complied with the requirements of confirming a plan. *See* §§ 1202; 1302. Chapter 12 trustees or Chapter 13 trustees are called "standing" trustees because in most judicial districts Chapter 12 trustees or Chapter 13 trustees are one or more individuals who undertake the duties of the office as a full-time job and serve as trustees in all Chapter 12 or Chapter 13 cases in the district.

- ***United States Trustee*** (or sometimes, the Office of the United States Trustee, or just "OUST"). The Attorney General appoints a "United States Trustee" for various regions (consisting of one or more judicial districts) across the country; at present there are twenty-one regions nationwide. The OUST is a representative of the executive branch of government. He or she employs counsel, financial analysts and case administrators. He or she also appoints trustees under the various chapters (such as Chapter 7 and Chapter 13 trustees), and monitors all cases for debtor compliance (for such things as whether the debtor has filed schedules, operating reports and similar required information). The OUST also monitors the retention of, and fee requests by, professionals.

- ***Examiner.*** In Chapter 11 cases only, an examiner may be appointed to investigate the pre-petition activities of the debtor. For example, in the Enron and Lehman Brothers bankruptcy cases, examiners were appointed and authored lengthy and expensive reports. More than $100,000,000 in Enron.

- *Bankruptcy Judge.* The judicial officer that presides over a bankruptcy case. Although federal judges, bankruptcy judges are appointed under Article I of the Constitution, not Article III. Accordingly, bankruptcy judges do not have life tenure; they serve 14–year terms, for pay that equals 92% of what an Article III federal judge makes. 28 U.S.C. § 153(a). Congress has determined that Circuit Judges shall select the bankruptcy judges for the circuits in which they sit. 28 U.S.C. § 152. Appeals from decisions of bankruptcy judges are to Article III district judges, or in some circuits, to Bankruptcy Appellate Panels (also know as "BAPs") which consist of three bankruptcy judges. *See* 28 U.S.C. § 158(b). Appeals from the district court or BAP are to the Circuit Courts of Appeal. 28 U.S.C. § 158(d).

- *Clerk of the Court.* In most districts, the bankruptcy court is a separate court, with separate records maintained by a separate person known as the clerk of the court. 28 U.S.C. § 156.

C. PROCEDURE AND PROCEDURAL TERMS IN A BANKRUPTCY LITIGATION

Bankruptcy procedure is somewhat like Russian *matryoshka,* the nesting dolls that fit one within the other. All litigation revolves in some way around the debtor, and we start with the basic unit of bankruptcy procedure involving the debtor, the bankruptcy case.

1. THE BASIC RULES OF THE GAME (HEREIN OF THE FEDERAL RULES OF BANKRUPTCY PROCEDURE)

As we have indicated before, bankruptcy litigation is federal litigation. It happens in a federal courthouse.

As such, you might initially suspect that procedure within bankruptcy is governed by the Federal Rules of Civil Procedure that you studied in your Civil Procedure class. That suspicion, however, would prove (mostly) wrong.

Bankruptcy has its own rules of procedure, known as the Federal Rules of Bankruptcy Procedure. We refer to them in this book as "Bankr. R. XXX."[3]

To complicate matters, the Federal Rules of Bankruptcy Procedure incorporate parts of (or even whole rules found in) the Federal Rules of Civil Procedure. Bankr. R. 9016, for example, simply states that "Rule 45 F.R.Civ.P. applies in cases under the Code." F.R.Civ.P. 45, in turn, refers

---

3. Although not particularly important for law students in basic bankruptcy course, local bankruptcy rules are very important for practitioners. These rules are authorized by Bankr. R. 9029, and often govern things such as number of copies of documents to file, and the amount of time a party has to respond to a motion.

to subpoenas, and so Bankr. R. 9016 means that the general federal rule on subpoenas applies in bankruptcy "cases." But what is a case?

2. THE CASE (HEREIN OF "IN RE DEBTOR")

The debtor files a petition with the clerk of the bankruptcy court and commences a bankruptcy *case*.[4] The case is a unified piece of litigation, in which all other actions, motions and the like relate. To use the metaphor of the Russian *matryoshka* again, it is the main outside nesting doll.

The general way bankruptcy practitioners refer to litigation is that they have filed it "in" the debtor's case. The caption of the case on the pleading filed which initiated the case, and hence the way most case reporting services such as West's *Bankruptcy Reporter* pick up and index the case, is usually just *"In re* Debtor," where "Debtor" is the name of the person about whom the case is filed.[5] Since many different types of litigation and issues can be resolved within a debtor's case, the simple designation *"In re* Debtor" does not tell you much.

3. THE ADVERSARY PROCEEDING (HEREIN OF "X v. Y (IN RE DEBTOR)")

The Federal Rules of Bankruptcy Practice acknowledge that some types of litigation which occur in bankruptcy court are more like typical civil litigation. The rules specify what types of litigation are in this "special" class, and label them "adversary proceedings." That is, some litigation has to proceed by "adversary proceeding," which means that Part VII of the Bankruptcy Rules will apply, and that the litigation will have to be commenced by summons and complaint, just like an ordinary piece of civil litigation.

The rules for adversary proceedings for the most part incorporate the Federal Rules of Civil Procedure. The types of litigation that are to be prosecuted by adversary proceeding are found in Bankr. R. 7001, which states that adversary proceedings include: "a proceeding (1) to recover money or property, ... (2) to determine the validity, priority, or extent of a lien or other interest in property, ... (3) to obtain approval pursuant to § 363(h) for the sale of both the interest of the estate and of a co-owner in property, (4) to object to or revoke a discharge, (5) to revoke an order of confirmation of a Chapter 11, Chapter 12, or Chapter 13 plan, (6) to determine the dischargeability of a debt, (7) to obtain an injunction or other equitable relief, (8) to subordinate any allowed claim or interest, ... (9) to obtain a declaratory judgment relating to any of the foregoing, or

---

4. In an involuntary case, the petition is filed by creditors, but it does not change the naming conventions except that until the involuntary case is decided, the debtor is referred to as the "alleged debtor."

5. There is no distinction made in citation form between the debtor and the debtor in possession. On the caption, the convention is to state the debtor's name, and then follow it with "debtor and debtor in possession."

(10) to determine a claim or cause of action removed pursuant to 28 U.S.C. § 1452.''

Again, the traditional caption of an adversary proceeding determines how the case is cited. When an adversary proceeding is filed, the pleading notes the case to which it refers—it has ''In re Debtor'' at the beginning. But then, since the relief requested typically involves less than all of the debtor's creditors, the pleading will also have a traditional caption indicating a plaintiff and a defendant, along the lines of ''X v. Y.'' The convention that has evolved is to combine these two designations when referring to an adversary proceeding. As a consequence, the citation form for an adversary proceeding is usually ''X v. Y *(In re* Debtor),'' where X is the plaintiff, Y the defendant and ''Debtor'' is the debtor.[6]

4. THE CONTESTED MATTER

Some disputes are very important to a bankruptcy case, yet are not resolved in full-blown adversary proceedings. For example, the confirmation [court approval] of a Chapter 11 plan is not among the actions or proceedings listed in Bankr. R. 7001. These proceedings have a name nonetheless. They are called ''contested matters.'' They differ from adversary proceedings in that they may be initiated by motion, and are heard on a much faster time schedule. Contested matters are much more common than adversary proceedings.

Bankr. R. 9014 governs the conduct of contested matters, although the rule leaves much to local rules of procedure, including the minimum time upon which a motion may be heard. It also permits, in appropriate cases, the bankruptcy judge to incorporate some of the adversary proceeding rules (such as discovery rules). The general convention in citation form is to cite to a contested matter the same way that you would cite to a case, *i.e.,* ''*In re* Debtor.''

5. THE CONCEPT OF ''NOTICE AND A HEARING''

Notice has a key role in bankruptcy. Because of the power of the bankruptcy court to affect debtor-creditor relations, creditors' finding out about what is happening in a bankruptcy case is important. At the start of the case, for example, all creditors receive notice of the case based on a list filed initially by the debtor.

After a case commences, the Code conditions many actions taken in bankruptcy court on giving ''notice and a hearing.'' The obvious reading of that phrase would seem to require both notice *and* a hearing. But the Code is not always obvious.

11 U.S.C. § 102(1)

''after notice and a hearing'', or a similar phrase—

---

6.   Note that often the debtor is also one of the litigants, so that you will often see ''X v.Y (*In re* X).''

(A) means after such notice as is appropriate in the particular circumstances, and such opportunity for a hearing as is appropriate in the particular circumstances; but

(B) authorizes an act without an actual hearing if such notice is given properly and if—

(i) such a hearing is not requested timely by a party in interest; or

(ii) there is insufficient time for a hearing to be commenced before such act must be done, and the court authorizes such act....

Read this statute carefully. It actually authorizes action *without* a hearing if no one objects, or if "there is insufficient time for a hearing to be commenced." In other words, the court the bankruptcy court can conclude that the Code's requirement of "notice and hearing" does not require an actual hearing.

6. ELECTRONIC FILING

As of January 1, 2005, all filings with the bankruptcy court are supposed to be made by electronic means. This means that you can access all the "papers" filed in the Circuit City bankruptcy, Mr. and Mrs. 64's bankruptcy or any other bankruptcy case.

To gain access to the electronic filing system, you'll need to register and be prepared to pay for each page you view. The web site for access is called PACER, and can be found at: http://pacer.psc.uscourts.gov/.

UNIT 4

WHAT ARE THE BASIC BANKRUPTCY BUILDING BLOCKS?

■ ■ ■

A. "EQUALITY OF DISTRIBUTION"

Equality of distribution is consistently described as an important, even the most important, purpose of bankruptcy. The Supreme Court in *Bailey v. Glover*, 88 U.S. 342, 346 (1874), stated: "It is obviously one of the purposes of the Bankruptcy law that there should be a speedy disposition of the bankrupt's assets. This is second only in importance to securing equality of distribution." (emphasis added).

Similar statements can be found in more recent Supreme Court opinions and in reported cases from other courts. No such statement, however, can be found in the Code. No Code section mentions or directly requires equality of distribution. *But cf.* section 726(b)(distribution should be "pro rata among claims of the kind specified in each such particular paragraph").

As we will see, most provisions in the Code and most court orders in bankruptcy cases are consistent with a policy of equality of distribution. However, we will also see provisions in the Code and court orders in bankruptcy cases that are consistent with the policy of equality of distribution only in the *"Animal Farm"* sense of that phrase. Cf. George Orwell, *Animal Farm* 133 (Signet 1996) (1946) ("All animals are equal but some animals are more equal than others").

B. "FRESH START" AND THE DISCHARGE

The Supreme Court has also stated, "The federal system of bankruptcy is designed not only to distribute the property of the debtor, not by law exempted, fairly and equally among his creditors, but as a main purpose of the act, intends to aid the unfortunate debtor by giving him a fresh start in life, free from debts, except of a certain character, after the property which he owned at the time of bankruptcy has been administered for the benefit of creditors. Our decisions lay great stress upon this feature of the law—as one not only of private but of great public interest in that it secures to the unfortunate debtor, who surrenders his property for distribution, a new opportunity in life." *Stellwagen v. Clum*, 245 U.S. 605, 616 (1918).

And, the phrase "fresh start" nowhere appears in the Code. Courts and commentators however consistently connect the bankruptcy "fresh start" policy with the bankruptcy discharge. The term "discharge" does appear in the Code. A lot.

A debtor who receives a bankruptcy discharge is relieved from any further personal, legal liability on her dischargeable debts. Reread this sentence and notice the three limitations on the concept of discharge.

First, limitation on discharge. Not every person who is a debtor in a bankruptcy case receives a discharge. The tests for whether a debtor receives a discharge vary from chapter to chapter.

In Chapter 7 cases, debtors that are corporations and other business entities cannot receive a discharge. With respect to humans, section 727(a) lists eleven other bases for withholding a discharge from an individual debtor in a Chapter 7 case. Most of these "objections" to discharge are based on a debtor's misdeeds before or during the bankruptcy case.

In Chapter 11 cases involving debtors who are business entities such as corporations or limited liability companies or partnerships, the biggest hurdle for obtaining a discharge is court approval of the plan of reorganization. Under section 1141(d), a business entity in Chapter 11 generally receives a discharge on the "confirmation of a plan." The business debtor's completion of payments under the plan is not a condition precedent to a Chapter 11 discharge.

By contrast, in Chapter 13 cases, individual debtors receive discharges only if there has been both (1) confirmation of the plan and (2) payments under the plan have been made or judicially excused. Similarly, in Chapter 11 cases involving individual debtors, there will generally be no discharge until payments under the plan have been made.

Second limitation on discharge. A discharge does not make a debt disappear; it does not vaporize or obliterate it. The discharge only relieves the debtor from personal liability on the debt. Accordingly, if D's debt is guaranteed by X, D's discharge does not affect X's guarantee. The creditor can sue X on the guaranty and not worry about D's discharge. And, if D's debt to M is secured by a mortgage on Blackacre, then D's discharge does not affect M's rights as a mortgage holder with respect to Blackacre. This means that, if done correctly, M may foreclose and evict D regardless of D's discharge.

Section 524 of the Code governs the effect of a discharge.

11 U.S.C. § 524(a), (e)

(a) A discharge in a case under this title—

(1) voids any judgment at any time obtained, to the extent that such judgment is a determination of the personal liability of the debtor with respect to any debt discharged under section 727, 944, 1141, 1228, or 1328 of this title, whether or not discharge of such debt is waived;

(2) operates as an injunction against the commencement or continuation of an action, the employment of process, or an act, to collect, recover or offset any such debt as a personal liability of the debtor, whether or not discharge of such debt is waived; . . .

(e) [D]ischarge of a debt of the debtor does not affect the liability of any other entity, or the property of any other entity for such debt.

Third limitation on discharge. A discharge does not relieve the debtor from personal liability on all debts. A discharge only affects "dischargeable" debts. Whether a debt is dischargeable depends on:

— whether the case is a 7, 11 or 13 case;

— when the debt arose; and

— whether the debt is excepted from discharge.

We consider exceptions from discharge later in Unit 9.

Problem 4–1: Discharge and What Creditors Can Do to the Debtor

1.   D owes C $10,000. D files a Chapter 7 petition. C receives $500 from D's Chapter 7 trustee as its Chapter 7 distribution. D receives a discharge. Can C sue D for the other $9,500?

2.   Same facts. Can C call D and politely ask D to pay the other $9,500?

3.   D Corp. owes C $100,000. D Corp. files a Chapter 11 petition. D Corp.'s Chapter 11 plan is confirmed and D Corp. obtains a discharge, 11 U.S.C. § 1141(d). The plan provides for 10 monthly payments of $5,000 to C. D Corp. makes two of the monthly payments and then fails to make the other 8 monthly payments of $5,000. Can C sue D Corp. for $40,000? For $90,000?

Problem 4–2: Discharge and What a Secured Creditor Can Do

D owes S $20,000. The debt is secured by a lien on D's truck. D files a Chapter 7 petition, claims the truck as exempt, receives a discharge, and retains the truck. Can S still repossess the truck?

Problem 4–3: Discharge and What a Creditor Can Do to Third Parties

1. D owes C $30,000. The debt is guaranteed by G. D files a Chapter 7 petition. C receives $3,000 from D's Chapter 7 trustee. D receives a discharge. Can C sue G for the other $27,000?

2. C has a $1,000,000 malpractice judgment against Dr. D. Dr D files a Chapter 7 petition and receives a discharge. Can C recover from Dr. D's malpractice insurer?

Problem 4–4: Discharge and What the Debtor Can Do

1. D owes various credit card issuers $40,000. D files a Chapter 7 petition. D gets a discharge. Her creditors get nothing—a no asset case. Can D still voluntarily pay the card credit debts?

2. D borrows $4,000 from C. In the loan agreement, D agrees to pay the debt even if she later files for bankruptcy and gets a discharge. D later files for bankruptcy and gets a discharge. Is the waiver enforceable? *Cf.* sections 727(a)(10), 524(c); 524(d).

3. Same facts except that D agrees to pay C the $4,000, after she files for bankruptcy but before she receives a discharge. Why would a debtor make such an agreement? Should such an agreement be enforceable? *Cf.* section 524(c). [We will see, not just *cf*, section 524 in Unit 9]

Now, see the title of section 525: "Protection against discriminatory treatment." When you see and apply the language of section 525, you will see that the title of section 525 "promises" more than the language of section 525 "delivers."

11 U.S.C. § 525

§ 525.   Protection against discriminatory treatment

(a)   ... [A] governmental unit may not deny, revoke, suspend, or refuse to renew a license, permit, charter, franchise, or other similar grant to, condition such a grant to, discriminate with respect to such a grant against, deny employment to, terminate the employment of, or discriminate with respect to employment against, a person that is or has been a debtor under this title ... or another person with whom such ... debtor has been associated, solely because such ... debtor is or has been a debtor under this title ... has been insolvent before the commencement of the case under this title, or during the case but before the debtor is granted or denied a discharge, or has not paid a debt that is dischargeable in the case under this title ...

(b) No private employer may terminate the employment of, or discriminate with respect to employment against, an individual who is or has been a debtor under this title . . . ,or an individual associated with such debtor . . . , solely because such debtor—

(1) is or has been a debtor under this title . . . ;

(2) has been insolvent before the commencement of a case under this title or during the case but before the grant or denial of a discharge; or

(3) has not paid a debt that is dischargeable in a case under this title . . .

Problem 4–5: Discharge and What Governmental Entities Can Do

State S requires licensing of operators of driver training schools. D has such a license and operates a driver training school. D has consulted your firm about his filing for bankruptcy to discharge debts, most of which arose from D's operation of his driver training school. If D files for bankruptcy and receives a discharge, can State S revoke D's license to operate a driver training school? See section 525(a).

Problem 4–6: Discharge and What an Employer Can Do

D files for bankruptcy and receives a discharge. D applies for a job with your client, T Trust Co. ("T") as a cashier. T wants to know if it can tell D that T has decided to hire someone other than D because of D's bankruptcy. See section 525(b).

Problem 4–7: Discharge as a "Fresh Start" or a "Head Start"

X Airline and Y Airline both have the same unfavorable labor contracts; both have the same unfavorable airplane leases. X files for bankruptcy and eliminates the unfavorable labor contracts and leases. Did X receive a "fresh start" or the unfair advantage of a "head start"?

C. CLAIMS

In a Chapter 7 case, property of the estate is liquidated and the proceeds are used to pay "claims," section 726. In a case under Chapter 11 or Chapter 13, the plan provides for distributions to "claims," sections

1123, 1322. Similarly section 362 stays actions to recover a "claim." (The discharge provisions of the Code generally use the word "debt" rather than the word "claim." Section 101(12) defines "debt" as "liability on a claim.")

The term "claim" is defined in section 101(5). Please section 101(5). Note that a claim can be "unliquidated", "contingent", "unmatured", and "disputed."

---

11 U.S.C. § 101(5)

(5) "claim" means—

(A) right to payment, whether or not such right is reduced to judgment, liquidated, unliquidated, fixed, contingent, matured, unmatured, disputed, undisputed, legal, equitable, secured, or unsecured; or

(B) right to an equitable remedy for breach of performance if such breach gives rise to a right to payment, whether or not such right to an equitable remedy is reduced to judgment, fixed, contingent, matured, unmatured, disputed, undisputed, secured, or unsecured;

. . . .

1. SECTION 101(5)'S ADJECTIVES

Problem 4–8: Disputed Claims

P sues D for $100,000. D files an answer denying liability. D later files a bankruptcy petition. Does P have a claim?

Problem 4–9: Contingent Claims

1. C loans D $200,000. G guarantees payment. D files for bankruptcy. Does C have a claim against D? Does G?

2. C gets her car painted by D, Inc. The paint job has a five-year, no crack, no peel warranty. Two years after the paint job, D, Inc. files for bankruptcy. Does C have a claim? Does it matter if the paint shows no sign of cracking or peeling?

Problem 4–10: Unmatured Claims

L leases a building to D on a 25–year lease. Two years later, D files a bankruptcy petition. At the time of the bankruptcy filing, D is current on its rent obligations to L. Does L have a claim?

---

2. SECTION 101(5)'S REQUIREMENT OF "RIGHT TO PAYMENT"

Please re-read section 101(5). Note that a claim must be a "right to payment." Obviously, if D is arrested for driving while intoxicated and ordered by the court to attend drunk driving school, then D's later bankruptcy will not affect D's obligation to attend drunk driving school. While drunk driving school is a legal obligation, there is no "claim"—there is no "right to payment." Similar issues arise with respect to certain types of government regulation—such as antitrust injunctions.

Some of the questions of as to whether there is a "right to payment," and thus a claim that can be affected by the bankruptcy, are much less obvious. The question in the *Kovacs* case, which follows, was sufficiently "non-obvious" that answering it divided the Supreme Court.

OHIO v. KOVACS

469 U.S. 274 (1985)

JUSTICE WHITE delivered the opinion of the Court.

Petitioner, State of Ohio, obtained an injunction ordering respondent William Kovacs to clean up a hazardous waste site. A receiver was subsequently appointed. Still later, Kovacs filed a petition for bankruptcy. The question before us is whether, in the circumstances present here, Kovacs' obligation under the injunction is a "debt" or "liability on a claim" subject to discharge under the Bankruptcy Code. . . .

Kovacs was the chief executive officer and stockholder of Chem–Dyne Corp., which with other business entities operated an industrial and hazardous waste disposal site in Hamilton, Ohio. In 1976, the State sued Kovacs and the business entities in state court for polluting public waters, maintaining a nuisance, and causing fish kills, all in violation of state environmental laws. In 1979, both in his individual capacity and on behalf of Chem–Dyne, Kovacs signed a stipulation and judgment entry settling the lawsuit. Among other things, the stipulation enjoined the defendants from causing further pollution of the air or public waters, forbade bringing additional industrial wastes onto the site, required the defendants to remove specified wastes from the property, and ordered the payment of $75,000 to compensate the State for injury to wildlife.

Kovacs and the other defendants failed to comply with their obligations under the injunction. The State then obtained the appointment in state court of a receiver, who was directed to take possession of all property and other assets of Kovacs and the corporate defendants and to implement the judgment entry by cleaning up the Chem–Dyne site. The receiver took possession of the site but had not completed his tasks when Kovacs filed a personal bankruptcy petition.

Seeking to develop a basis for requiring part of Kovacs' postbankruptcy income to be applied to the unfinished task of the receivership, the State then filed a motion in state court to discover Kovacs' current income and assets. Kovacs requested that the Bankruptcy Court stay those proceedings, which it did. The State also filed a complaint in the Bankruptcy Court seeking a declaration that Kovacs' obligation under the stipulation and judgment order to clean up the Chem–Dyne site was not dischargeable in bankruptcy because it was not a "debt," a liability on a "claim," within the meaning of the Bankruptcy Code. In addition, the complaint sought an injunction against the bankruptcy trustee to restrain him from pursuing any action to recover assets of Kovacs in the hands of the receiver. The Bankruptcy Court ruled against Ohio, as did the District Court. The Court of Appeals for the sixth circuit affirmed, holding that Ohio essentially sought from Kovacs only a monetary payment and that such a required payment was a liability on a claim that was dischargeable under the bankruptcy statute. We granted certiorari to determine the dischargeability of Kovacs' obligation under the affirmative injunction entered against him.

III

Except for the nine kinds of debts saved from discharge by § 523(a) for re-expenses, a discharge in bankruptcy discharges the debtor from all debts that arose before bankruptcy. § 727(b). It is not claimed here that Kovacs' obligation under the injunction fell within any of the categories of debts excepted from discharge by § 523. Rather, the State submits that the obligation to clean up the Chem–Dyne site is not a debt at all within the meaning of the bankruptcy law.

For bankruptcy purposes, a debt is a liability on a claim. § 101(11). A claim is defined by § 101(4) as follows:

"(4) 'claim' means—

"(A) right to payment, whether or not such right is reduced to judgment, liquidated, unliquidated, fixed, contingent, matured, unmatured, disputed, undisputed, legal, equitable, secured, or unsecured; or

"(B) right to an equitable remedy for breach of performance if such breach gives rise to a right to payment, whether or not such right to an equitable remedy is reduced to judgment, fixed, contingent, matured, unmatured, disputed, undisputed, secured, or unsecured."

The provision at issue here is § 101(4)(B). For the purposes of that section, there is little doubt that the State had the right to an equitable remedy under state law and that the right has been reduced to judgment in the form of an injunction ordering the cleanup. The State argues, however, that the injunction it has secured is not a claim against Kovacs for bankruptcy purposes because (1) Kovacs' default was a breach of the statute, not a breach of an ordinary commercial contract which concededly would give rise to a claim; and (2) Kovacs' breach of his obligation under the injunction did not give rise to a right to payment within the meaning of § 101(4)(B). We are not persuaded by either submission.

There is no indication in the language of the statute that the right to performance cannot be a claim unless it arises from a contractual arrangement. The State resorted to the courts to enforce its environmental laws against Kovacs and secured a negative order to cease polluting, an affirmative order to clean up the site, and an order to pay a sum of money to recompense the State for damage done to the fish population. Each order was one to remedy an alleged breach of Ohio law; and if Kovacs' obligation to pay $75,000 to the State is a debt dischargeable in bankruptcy, which the State freely concedes, it makes little sense to assert that because the cleanup order was entered to remedy a statutory violation, it cannot likewise constitute a claim for bankruptcy purposes. Furthermore, it is apparent that Congress desired a broad definition of a "claim" and knew how to limit the application of a provision to contracts when it desired to do so.

The injunction surely obliged Kovacs to clean up the site. But when he failed to do so, rather than prosecute Kovacs under the environmental laws or bring civil or criminal contempt proceedings, the State secured the appointment of a receiver, who was ordered to take possession of all of Kovacs' nonexempt assets as well as the assets of the corporate defendants and to comply with the injunction entered against Kovacs. As wise as this course may have been, it dispossessed Kovacs, removed his authority over the site, and divested him of assets that might have been used by him to clean up the property. Furthermore, when the bankruptcy trustee sought to recover Kovacs' assets from the receiver, the latter sought an injunction against such action. Although Kovacs had been ordered to "cooperate" with the receiver, he was disabled by the receivership from personally taking charge of and carrying out the removal of wastes from the property. What the receiver wanted from Kovacs after bankruptcy was the money to defray cleanup costs. At oral argument in this Court, the State's counsel conceded that after the receiver was appointed, the only performance sought from Kovacs was the payment of money. Had Kovacs furnished the necessary funds, either before or after bankruptcy, there seems little doubt that the receiver and the State would have been satisfied. On the facts before it, and with the receiver in control of the site, we cannot fault the Court of Appeals for concluding that the cleanup order had been converted into an obligation to pay money, an obligation that was dischargeable in bankruptcy.

IV

It is well to emphasize what we have not decided. First, we do not suggest that Kovacs' discharge will shield him from prosecution for having violated the environmental laws of Ohio or for criminal contempt for not performing his obligations under the injunction prior to bankruptcy. Second, had a fine or monetary penalty for violation of state law been imposed on Kovacs prior to bankruptcy, § 523(a)(7) forecloses any suggestion that his obligation to pay the fine or penalty would be discharged in bankruptcy. Third, we do not address what the legal consequences would have been had Kovacs taken bankruptcy before a receiver had been appointed and a trustee had been designated with the usual duties of a bankruptcy trustee. Fourth, we do not hold that the injunction against bringing further toxic wastes on the premises or against any conduct that will contribute to the pollution of the site or the State's waters is dischargeable in bankruptcy; we here address, as did the Court of Appeals, only the affirmative duty to clean up the site and the duty to pay money to that end. Finally, we do not question that anyone in possession of the site- whether it is Kovacs or another in the event the receivership is liquidated and the trustee abandons the property, or a vendee from the receiver or the bankruptcy trustee-must comply with the environmental laws of the State of Ohio. Plainly, that person or firm may not maintain a nuisance, pollute the waters of the State, or refuse to remove the source of such conditions. As the case comes to us, however, Kovacs has been dispos- sessed and the State seeks to enforce his cleanup obligation by a money judgment.

The judgment of the Court of Appeals is

Affirmed.

JUSTICE O'CONNOR, concurring.

I join the Court's opinion and agree with its holding that the cleanup order has been reduced to a monetary obligation dischargeable as a "claim" under § 727 of the Bankruptcy Code. I write separately to address the petitioner's concern that the Court's action will impede States in enforcing their environmental laws.

To say that Kovacs' obligation in these circumstances is a claim dischargeable in bankruptcy does not wholly excuse the obligation or leave the State without any recourse against Kovacs' assets to enforce the order. Because "Congress has generally left the determination of property rights in the assets of a bankrupt's estate to state law," the classification of Ohio's interest as either a lien on the property itself, a perfected security interest, or merely an unsecured claim depends on Ohio law. That classifi- cation-a question not before us-generally determines the priority of the State's claim to the assets of the estate relative to other creditors. Cf. § 545 (trustee may avoid statutory liens only in specified circumstances). Thus, a State may protect its interest in the enforcement of its environ- mental laws by giving cleanup judgments the status of statutory liens or secured claims.

The Court's holding that the cleanup order was a "claim" within the meaning of § 101(4) also avoids potentially adverse consequences for a State's enforcement of its order when the debtor is a corporation, rather than an individual. In a Chapter 7 proceeding [sic] under the Bankruptcy Code, a corporate debtor transfers its property to a trustee for distribution among the creditors who hold cognizable claims, and then generally dissolves under state law. Because the corporation usually ceases to exist, it has no postbankruptcy earnings that could be utilized by the State to fulfill the cleanup order. The State's only recourse in such a situation may well be its "claim" to the prebankruptcy assets.

For both these reasons, the Court's holding today cannot be viewed as hostile to state enforcement of environmental laws.

QUESTIONS ABOUT *KOVACS*

1. Facts

   1.1   Who is the "debtor" in this case? Is that fact important in this case?

   1.2   Are there any other facts that were important to the Court's concluding that Kovacs' obligation to remove wastes from the property is a "claim"?

   1.3   Who is arguing that Kovacs' obligation to remove wastes from the property is not a "claim" under section 101?

2. Law

   2.1   What language in section 101 did the majority rely on in concluding that Kovacs' obligation to remove wastes from the property is a "claim"?

   2.2   What is the point of Justice O'Connor's point about a State's protecting its interest by giving cleanup judgments the status of statutory liens?

   2.3   Apex Oil's predecessor created environmental hazards. The predecessor filed a Chapter 11 petition, included the government's environmental release related claim in its bankruptcy case and received a discharge of all claims. Years later, the EPA filed a court action for a mandatory injunction to require Apex to participate in remediation of the environmental hazards created by its predecessor. To clean up the contaminated site, Apex would have to hire an independent contractor at an estimated cost of $150,000,000. The Seventh Circuit concluded that EPA's entitlement to a mandatory injunction was not a "claim" that was discharged as part of the predecessor's bankruptcy case. Judge Posner, writing for the Seventh Circuit, reasoned that the reference to "right to payment" in section 101(5)(B) focuses on the claimant's right to payment not the debtor's obligation to incur monetary costs to comply with the equitable remedy. Judge Posner distinguished *Kovacs:* "It is true that in *Ohio v. Kovacs,*, the Supreme Court allowed the discharge in bankruptcy of an equitable obligation to clean up a contaminated site owned by the debtor. An injunction ordering the cleanup had been issued before the bankruptcy. The debtor had failed to comply with the injunction and a receiver had been appointed to take possession of his assets and obtain from them the money needed to pay for the cleanup. The receiver thus was seeking money rather than an order that the debtor clean up the contaminated site. That was a claim to a 'right to payment.' The plaintiff in our case (the government) is not seeking a payment of money and the injunction that it has obtained does not entitle it to payment." *United States v. Apex Oil Co.*, 579 F.3d 734, 737 (7th Cir, 2009). Judge Posner is really smart. Do you agree with his reasoning? Do you agree that *Apex* is distinguishable from *Kovacs*?

3. "FUTURE CLAIMS"

Remember, a discharge only affects "claims." In the *Kovacs* case, the State of Ohio argued (unsuccessfully) that the right created by an injunction compelling the debtor to clean up environmental violations was not a "claim" because that right was not "a right to payment" as required by section 101(5) and so was not discharged. A creditor can "win" by establishing that it does not hold a "claim" as defined in the Code. No claim, no discharge.

Also remember that only holders of claims are paid in a bankruptcy case. In the next case, the senior bankruptcy author of this book argued unsuccessfully that people who would in the future fall out of the sky because the Piper aircraft that they were flying in was negligently designed or manufactured prior to July 1, 1991, had section 101(5) claims in the Piper Aircraft Corporation Chapter 11 bankruptcy case. Shortly after losing this case, he returned to full-time teaching.

IN RE PIPER AIRCRAFT CORPORATION

58 F.3d 1573 (11th Cir. 1995)

BLACK, CIRCUIT JUDGE:

This is an appeal by David G. Epstein, as the Legal Representative for the Piper future claimants (Future Claimants), from the district court's order of June 6, 1994, affirming the order of the bankruptcy court entered on December 6, 1993. The sole issue on appeal is whether the class of Future Claimants, as defined by the bankruptcy court, holds claims against the estate of Piper Aircraft Corporation (Piper), within the meaning of § 101(5) of the Bankruptcy Code. After review of the relevant provisions, policies and goals of the Bankruptcy Code and the applicable case law, we hold that the Future Claimants do not have claims as defined by § 101(5) and thus affirm the opinion of the district court.

I. FACTUAL AND PROCEDURAL BACKGROUND

For purposes of this appeal, the relevant facts are as follows. Piper has been manufacturing and distributing general aviation aircraft and spare parts throughout the United States and abroad since 1937. Approximately 50,000 to 60,000 Piper aircraft still are operational in the United

States. Although Piper has been a named defendant in several lawsuits based on its manufacture, design, sale, distribution and support of its aircraft and parts, it has never acknowledged that its products are harmful or defective.

On July 1, 1991, Piper filed a voluntary petition under Chapter 11 of Bankruptcy Code in the United States Bankruptcy Court for the Southern District of Florida. Piper's plan of reorganization contemplated finding a purchaser of substantially all of its assets or obtaining investments from outside sources, with the proceeds of such transactions serving to fund distributions to creditors. On April 8, 1993, Piper and Pilatus Aircraft Limited signed a letter of intent pursuant to which Pilatus would purchase Piper's assets. The letter of intent required Piper to seek the appointment of a legal representative to represent the interests of future claimants by arranging a set-aside of monies generated by the sale to pay off future product liability claims.

On May 19, 1993, the bankruptcy court appointed Appellant Epstein as the legal representative for the Future Claimants. The Court defined the class of Future Claimants to include:

> All persons, whether known or unknown, born or unborn, who may, after the date of confirmation of Piper's Chapter 11 plan of reorganization, assert a claim or claims for personal injury, property damages, wrongful death, damages, contribution and/or indemnification, based in whole or in part upon events occurring or arising after the Confirmation Date, including claims based on the law of product liability, against Piper or its successor arising out of or relating to aircraft or parts manufactured and sold, designed, distributed or supported by Piper prior to the Confirmation Date.

This Order expressly stated that the court was making no finding on whether the Future Claimants could hold claims against Piper under § 101(5) of the Code.

On July 12, 1993, Epstein filed a proof of claim on behalf of the Future Claimants in the approximate amount of $100,000,000. The claim was based on statistical assumptions regarding the number of persons likely to suffer, after the confirmation of a reorganization plan, personal injury or property damage caused by Piper's pre-confirmation manufacture, sale, design, distribution or support of aircraft and spare parts. The Official Committee of Unsecured Creditors (Official Committee), and later Piper, objected to the claim on the ground that the Future Claimants do not hold § 101(5) claims against Piper. After a hearing on the objection, the bankruptcy court agreed that the Future Claimants did not hold § 101(5) claims, and, on December 6, 1993, entered an Order Sustaining the Committee's Objection and Disallowing the Legal Representative's Proof of Claim. In a Memorandum Opinion dated January 14, 1994, that court entered final findings of fact and conclusions of law to support its December Order. Epstein, as Legal Representative, then appealed from the bankruptcy court's order. On June 6, 1994, the district court affirmed and accepted the decision of the bankruptcy court. Epstein now appeals from the district court's order, challenging in particular its use of the prepetition relationship test to define the scope of a claim under § 101(5).

II.   DISCUSSION

The sole issue on appeal, whether any of the Future Claimants hold claims against Piper as defined in § 101(5) of the Bankruptcy Code, is one of first impression in this Circuit.

A.   Statute

Under the Bankruptcy Code, only parties that hold preconfirmation claims have a legal right to participate in a Chapter 11 bankruptcy case and share in payments pursuant to a Chapter 11 plan. 11 U.S.C.A. §§ 101(10), 501, 502 In order to determine if the Future Claimants have such a right to participate, we first must address the statutory definition of the term "claim." The Bankruptcy Code defines claim as:

(A) right to payment, whether or not such right is reduced to judgment, liquidated, unliquidated, fixed, contingent, matured, unmatured, disputed, undisputed, legal, equitable, secured, or unsecured; or

(B) right to an equitable remedy for breach of performance if such breach gives rise to a right to payment, whether or not such right to an equitable remedy is reduced to judgment, fixed, contingent, matured, unmatured, disputed, undisputed, secured, or unsecured.

11 U.S.C.A. § 101(5). The legislative history of the Code suggests that Congress intended to define the term claim very broadly under § 101(5), so that "all legal obligations of the debtor, no matter how remote or contingent, will be able to be dealt with in the bankruptcy case."

B.   Case Law

Since the enactment of § 101(5), courts have developed several tests to determine whether certain parties hold claims pursuant to that section: the accrued state law claim test, the conduct test, and the prepetition relationship test. The bankruptcy court and district court adopted the prepetition relationship test in determining that the Future Claimants did not hold claims pursuant to § 101(5).

Epstein primarily challenges the district court's application of the prepetition relationship test. He argues that the conduct test, which some courts have adopted in mass tort cases, is more consistent with the text, history, and policies of the Code. Under the conduct test, a right to payment arises when the conduct giving rise to the alleged liability occurred. Epstein's position is that any right to payment arising out of the prepetition conduct of Piper, no matter how remote, should be deemed a claim and provided for, pursuant to § 101(5), in this case. He argues that the relevant conduct giving rise to the alleged liability was Piper's prepetition manufacture, design, sale and distribution of allegedly defective aircraft. Specifically, he contends that, because Piper performed these acts prepetition, the potential victims, although not yet identifiable, hold claims under § 101(5) of the Code.

The Official Committee and Piper dispute the breadth of the definition of claim asserted by Epstein, arguing that the scope of claim cannot extend so far as to include unidentified, and presently unidentifiable, individuals with no discernible prepetition relationship to Piper. Recognizing, as Appellees do, that the conduct test may define claim too broadly in certain circumstances, several courts have recognized "claims" only for those individuals with some type of prepetition relationship with the debtor. The prepetition relationship test, as adopted by the bankruptcy court and district court, requires "some prepetition relationship, such as contact, exposure, impact, or privity, between the debtor's prepetition conduct and the claimant" in order for the claimant to hold a § 101(5) claim.

Upon examination of the various theories, we agree with Appellees that the district court utilized the proper test in deciding that the Future Claimants did not hold a claim under § 101(5). Epstein's interpretation of "claim" and application of the conduct test would enable anyone to hold a claim against Piper by virtue of their potential future exposure to any aircraft in the existing fleet. Even the conduct test cases, on which Epstein relies, do not compel the result he seeks. In fact, the conduct test cases recognize that focusing solely on prepetition conduct, as Epstein espouses, would stretch the scope of § 101(5). Accordingly, the courts applying the conduct test also presume some prepetition relationship between the debtor's conduct and the claimant.

While acknowledging that the district court's test is more consistent with the purposes of the Bankruptcy Code than is the conduct test supported by Epstein, we find that the test as set forth by the district court unnecessarily restricts the class of claimants to those who could be identified prior to the filing of the petition. Those claimants having contact with the debtor's product post-petition but prior to confirmation also could be identified, during the course of the bankruptcy proceeding, as potential victims, who might have claims arising out of debtor's prepetition conduct.

We therefore modify the test used by the district court and adopt what we will call the "Piper test" in determining the scope of the term claim under § 101(5): an individual has a § 101(5) claim against a debtor manufacturer if (i) events occurring before confirmation create a relationship, such as contact, exposure, impact, or privity, between the claimant and the debtor's product; and (ii) the basis for liability is the debtor's prepetition conduct in designing, manufacturing and selling the allegedly defective or dangerous product. The debtor's prepetition conduct gives rise to a claim to be administered in a case only if there is a relationship established before confirmation between an identifiable claimant or group of claimants and that prepetition conduct.

In the instant case, it is clear that the Future Claimants fail the minimum requirements of the Piper test. There is no preconfirmation exposure to a specific identifiable defective product or any other preconfirmation relationship between Piper and the broadly defined class of Future Claimants. As there is no preconfirmation connection established between Piper and the Future Claimants, the Future Claimants do not hold a § 101(5) claim arising out of Piper's prepetition design, manufacture, sale, and distribution of allegedly defective aircraft.

III. CONCLUSION

For the foregoing reasons, we hold that the Future Claimants do not meet the threshold requirements of the Piper test and, as a result, do not hold claims as defined in § 101(5) of the Bankruptcy Code.

QUESTIONS ABOUT PIPER

1. Why did the Official Committee of Unsecured Creditors take the position that the future claims were not section 101(5) claims?

2. Why did Epstein take the position that the future claims were section 101(5) claims? If Piper sold all of its assets to Pilatus, would Pilatus be liable for damages from planes that Piper manufactured before the bankruptcy sale to Pilatus that crashed after the bankruptcy sale to Pilatus?

3. "The *Piper* test" for the existence of a claim requires that "there is a relationship established before confirmation between an identifiable claimant or group of claimants and that prepetition conduct." What does that mean? What is the statutory basis for any such requirement?

4. Recently a judge from the same bankruptcy court that decided *Piper*, concluded "the analysis set out by the Eleventh Circuit in *Piper Aircraft* to be useful in asbestos cases.... The end result of strictly applying the ruling in *Piper Aircraft* would essentially deny personal injury asbestos claimants (due to the extremely latent nature of their injuries) recovery from debtors, absent the debtor's choice to channel its asbestos liabilities to a trust pursuant to section 524(g) or its common-law predecessors or to otherwise provide for such claimants in a confirmed plan. Congress and the courts did not intend that asbestos claimants should have no ability to recover from a bankruptcy debtor simply because the debtor did not avail itself of the mechanisms for obtaining a channeling injunction or because, at the time it confirmed its plan, the debtor saw no need to otherwise provide for such asbestos claims by payment or other form of compensation. It seems much more plausible that Congress intended that debtors who have no reason to believe they will face significant, if any, asbestos-related liabilities will not be able to discharge those potential future asbestos claims without providing for such class of claims in a confirmed plan." In re Evans Products Co., 2009 WL 2448145 (Bankr. S.D. Fla. 2009). Is there a statutory basis for a different definition of "claim" in asbestos cases?

D. PROPERTY OF THE ESTATE

1. WHY IS "PROPERTY OF THE ESTATE" AN IMPORTANT CONCEPT?

The filing of a bankruptcy petition automatically creates an estate, section 541(a).

In a Chapter 7 case, the bankruptcy trustee is charged with collecting and selling "property of the estate"; the proceeds from the sale of the property of the estate are then distributed to creditors. In other words, the loss of property of the estate to the bankruptcy trustee is the primary cost of Chapter 7 bankruptcy to the debtor; the receipt of the proceeds from the sale of property of the estate is the primary benefit creditors derive from a Chapter 7 bankruptcy.

In most Chapter 11 and 12 cases, the debtor will remain in possession of "property of the estate" as "debtor-in-possession." However, the Chapter 11 or Chapter 12 debtor-in-possession's use of the property of the estate will be subject to bankruptcy court supervision. Consider the example of Chapter 11 cases involving business debtors. Successful rehabilitation of a business generally requires continued operation of the business. Continued operation of the business generally requires continued possession of the business property. A debtor will continue to operate its business in Chapter 11 as debtor-in-possession unless a request is made by a "party in interest" for the appointment of a trustee, and the bankruptcy court, after notice and hearing, grants the request. (When a trustee is appointed in a Chapter 11 case, she takes possession of property of the estate.) Even if a trustee is not appointed in a Chapter 11 case, the debtor-in-possession's use and sale of the property of the estate is subject to the supervision of the bankruptcy judge as provided in section 363, which is considered later.

Similarly, in Chapter 12 cases, the debtor will generally retain possession of the property and continue to operate the farm. As in Chapter 11, a "party in interest" can request that the debtor-in-possession be dispossessed and a trustee takeover. And, again as in Chapter 11, if a trustee is not so installed, the Chapter 12 debtor in possession's use and sale of the property of the estate is subject to the supervision of the bankruptcy court as provided in sections 363 and 1206.

While Chapter 13 contemplates that there will be a trustee in every case, a Chapter 13 trustee does not take possession of property of the estate. A debtor who files for Chapter 13 relief retains possession of his property, section 1306(b). Again, however, the use and sale of "property of the estate" is subject to the supervision of the bankruptcy court as section 363 provides.

In both Chapter 12 and Chapter 13 cases, the value of the property of the estate determines the minimum amount that must be offered to holders of unsecured claims in the debtor's plan of repayment, sections 1225(a)(4); 1325(a)(4). Chapter 11 imposes a similar requirement as to non-assenting holders of unsecured claims, section 1129(a)(7)(A)(ii).

Finally, a number of general provisions in Chapters 3 and 5 that are applicable in all bankruptcy cases use the phrase "property of the estate." For example, the automatic stay bars a creditor from collecting a claim from property of the estate, section 362(a)(3) and(4).

In short, in all bankruptcy cases and in all bankruptcy classes, it is necessary to be able to answer the question what does property of the estate include?

2. WHAT DOES "PROPERTY OF THE ESTATE" INCLUDE?

With specific exceptions set out in section 541(b) and 541(c)(2), property of the estate includes all property of the debtor as of the time of the filing of the bankruptcy petition.

The seven numbered paragraphs of section 541(a) specify what property becomes property of the estate. Paragraph one is by far the most comprehensive and significant part of section 541(a).

Section 541(a)(1) provides that property of the estate includes "all legal or equitable interests of the debtor in property as of the commencement of the case." This is a very broad statement. Property of the estate thus includes both real property and personal property, both tangible and intangible property, both property in the debtor's possession and property that is held by others in which the debtor has an interest.

The application of section 541(a)(1) requires answering these three questions:

#1. Is the item in question "property" for purposes of section 541(a)(1)?

#2. If so, what is the debtor's interest in that property? [Note that section 541(a)(1) reaches merely the debtor's interest in property rather than simply the debtor's property.]

#3. If so, did the debtor have this interest in the property as of the time of the commencement of the bankruptcy case?

11 U.S.C. § 541. Property of the Estate

(a) The commencement of a case under section 301, 302, or 303 of this title creates an estate. Such estate is comprised of all the following property, wherever located and by whomever held:

(1) Except as provided in subsections (b) and (c)(2) of this section, all legal or equitable interests of the debtor in property as of the commencement of the case. . . .

(6) Proceeds, product, offspring, rents, or profits of or from property of the estate, except such as are earnings from services performed by an individual debtor after the commencement of the case.

---

11 U.S.C. § 1306. Property of the Estate

(a) Property of the estate includes, in addition to the property specified in section 541 of this title,

(1) all property of the kind specified in such section that the debtor acquires after the commencement of the case but before the case is closed, dismissed, or converted to a case under Chapter 7, 11, or 12 of this title, whichever occurs first; and

(2) earnings from services performed by the debtor after the commencement of the case but before the case is closed, dismissed, or converted to a case under Chapter 7, 11, or 12 of this title, whichever occurs first.

(b) Except as provided in a confirmed plan or order confirming a plan, the debtor shall remain in possession of all property of the estate.

Section 1115 adopts a "section 1306" type approach to property of the estate for Chapter 11 individual debtor cases.

Problem 4–11: "As of The Commencement of the Case"

1.   D is paid every Friday. D files a bankruptcy petition on Friday, April 1. Is the paycheck that she receives on April 8th property of the estate?

2.   D owns a rental house. She files a Chapter 7 petition on September 30. Is the October rent from D's house property of the estate?

3.   ANC Rental Corp., files a Chapter 11 petition on November 13 and continues to rent cars and operate its business. Are rentals received after November 13 property of the estate?

4.   Circuit City filed its Chapter 11 petition on November 10, 2008. Are the cash and credit card receipts its post-November 10, 2008, sales "property of the estate"? Is "as of the commencement of the case" a significant limitation on property of the estate in a business Chapter 11 case?

5. How do you know what the debtor's interests in property are? See section 521.

Problem 4–12: *"All Legal or Equitable Interests"*

T tortuously injures P. P sues T for damages for her personal injuries. While the law suit is pending, P files for bankruptcy. Is the pending law suit "property of the estate"? If so, so what? Would T care? P? P's creditors? P's personal injury attorney?

Problem 4–13: *"Interests of the Debtor in Property"*

1. D and T each own an undivided 50% interest in Blackacre. D files for bankruptcy. Is Blackacre property of the estate?

2. D is leasing Blackacre for ten years. D files for bankruptcy. Is Blackacre property of the estate?

3. F loaned D $100,000 to buy Blackacre and retained a mortgage on Blackacre as security. D later files for bankruptcy. Is Blackacre property of the estate?

Again, section 541(c)(2) and section 541(b) contain some specific exclusions from property of the estate. Most importantly, a debtor's interest in an ERISA-qualified plan is excluded from the bankruptcy estate under section 541(c)(2), *Patterson v. Shumate*, 504 U.S. 753, 112 S.Ct. 2242 (1992). If your bankruptcy prof thought that *Patterson* or section 541(b) was important enough to discuss in a basic bankruptcy class and you did not understand that discussion, go to Westlaw and read 4 Norton Bankr. L. & Prac. 3d § 61:1.

E.   SECURED CLAIMS

Under nonbankruptcy law, certain creditors have greater rights than other creditors because they have liens or a right of setoff. For now, let's focus on liens. These liens are property interests in the debtor's property.

Some creditors obtain liens by judicial proceedings Law professors who teach civil procedure regularly assure us that their students are also familiar with execution liens, garnishment liens, judgment liens, i.e., liens created by judicial proceedings. And, some creditors are granted liens by statute: federal tax liens and mechanics' liens are examples.

The most common form of a consensual lien is a consensual lien—a lien created by contract. Perhaps the most familiar example of a lien is a real estate mortgage. Students who have taken a secured credit course (or read and remember Unit 2) are also familiar with consensual liens on personal property called security interests.

When the debtor defaults, these creditors with liens (also known as secured creditors) have all of the rights of other creditors (also known as unsecured creditors). Lien creditors also have additional rights because of their property interests.

Under non-bankruptcy law, a secured creditor has greater rights than unsecured creditors have in both the property subject to its lien and the proceeds from any disposition thereof. More specifically, under nonbankruptcy law, a secured creditor can seize and sell the property subject to its lien and use the proceeds to satisfy its claim.

Somewhat similar rights exist under the Code. First, bankruptcy law does not eliminate the right of a holder of a secured claim to seize and to sell the property subject to its lien. However, bankruptcy law makes such seizure and sale subject to the automatic stay: the creditor with a lien must obtain relief from the automatic stay before seizing its collateral, before selling its collateral.

Second, bankruptcy law, in its own way, recognizes that the holder of a lien enjoys special rights in the property subject to its lien and in the proceeds from any disposition thereof. When we study what happens in Chapter 7, 11, and 13 cases we will see that in all forms of bankruptcy cases better things happen to holders of secured claims than to holders of unsecured claims.

While law professors and even courts often use the terms "secured creditor" and "secured claim" interchangeably, law students need to see the difference between being a secured creditor outside of bankruptcy and being the holder of a secured claim in bankruptcy.

Outside of bankruptcy, if S is owed 100 and that debt is secured by a mortgage on Blackacre, S retains its mortgage on Blackacre until the 100 has been paid—regardless of the value of Blackacre.

In bankruptcy, the rights of holders of secured claims are more limited. If 100 is owed on a claim secured by a mortgage on Blackacre and Blackacre has a value of 60, there are provisions in Chapters 7, 11 and 13 empowering a debtor to extinguish the mortgage by paying 60.[1] For now, we need to understand section 506(a)(set out below) because the first step to understanding the difference between being a secured creditor outside of bankruptcy and the holder of a secured claim in bankruptcy is understanding section 506(a)

---

11 U.S.C. § 506(a)(1)

(a)(1) An allowed claim of a creditor secured by a lien on property in which the estate has an interest, or that is subject to setoff under

---

1. Later we will learn that in Chapter 11 or Chapter 13 cases, a nonconsensual change in the payment rights of the holder of a secured claim is called a cram down.

section 553 of this title, is a secured claim to the extent of the value of such creditor's interest in the estate's interest in such property, or to the extent of the amount subject to setoff, as the case may be, and is an unsecured claim to the extent that the value of such creditor's interest or the amount so subject to setoff is less than the amount of such allowed claim. Such value shall be determined in light of the purpose of the valuation and of the proposed disposition or use of such property, and in conjunction with any hearing on such disposition or use or on a plan affecting such creditor's interest.

Problem 4–14:   First Sentence of Section 506(a)(1)

[Note the phrase in the first sentence of section 506(a)(1): "to the extent of the value of such creditor's interest in the estate's interest in such property." Apply that phrase to the following simple (we hope) problems.]

1. D owes M $100,000. D owns Blackacre. M has a first mortgage on Blackacre. Blackacre has a value of $60,000. What is the amount of M's secured claim?

2. D owes M $100,000. D only has a 50% ownership interest in Blackacre. M has a first mortgage on Blackacre. Blackacre has a value of $60,000. What is the amount of M's secured claim?

3. D owes M $100,000. D owns Blackacre. M has a second mortgage on Blackacre. F has a first mortgage for $20,000. Blackacre has a value of $60,000. What is the amount of M's secured claim?

4. D owes M $100,000. M has a mortgage on Blackacre. D files for bankruptcy. M obtains relief from the stay and forecloses on Blackacre. M sells Blackacre for $40,000. Does M still have a secured claim? Does M still have a claim?

5. Review question: In the above problems, is Blackacre "property of the estate"?

---

1. DETERMINATION OF "VALUE OF SUCH CREDITOR'S INTEREST" AND *RASH*

The problems above were unrealistic. Too simple. In the problems, we simply "made up" the value of Blackacre. In the "real world", the difficult problem presented by the language of section 506 is determining the value of Blackacre or whatever the collateral is.

In the next case, the collateral was a tractor truck, not Blackacre. The question of how to value tractor trucks and similar collateral was so "valuable" to secured creditors that they appealed an unfavorable bankruptcy court decision to the district court, then to the Fifth Circuit, and then to the Supreme Court.

ASSOCIATES COMMERCIAL CORP. v. RASH

520 U.S. 953 (1997)

JUSTICE GINSBURG delivered the opinion of the Court.

We resolve in this case a dispute concerning the proper application of 11 U.S.C. § 506(a) of the Bankruptcy Code when a bankrupt debtor has exercised the "cram down" option for which 11 U.S.C. § 1325(a)(5)(B) provides. Specifically, when a debtor, over a secured creditor's objection, seeks to retain and use the creditor's collateral in a Chapter 13 plan, is the value of the collateral to be determined by (1) what the secured creditor could obtain through foreclosure sale of the property (the "foreclosure-value" standard); (2) what the debtor would have to pay for comparable property (the "replacement-value" standard); or (3) the midpoint between these two measurements? We hold that 506(a) directs application of the replacement-value standard.

In 1989, respondent Elray Rash purchased for $73,700 a Kenworth tractor truck for use in his freight-hauling business. Rash made a down-payment on the truck, agreed to pay the seller the remainder in 60 monthly installments, and pledged the truck as collateral on the unpaid balance. The seller assigned the loan, and its lien on the truck, to petitioner Associates Commercial Corporation (ACC).

In March 1992, Elray and Jean Rash filed a joint petition and a repayment plan under Chapter 13 of the Bankruptcy Code (Code), 11 U.S.C.§§ 1301–1330. At the time of the bankruptcy filing, the balance owed to ACC on the truck loan was $41,171. Because it held a valid lien on the truck, ACC was listed in the bankruptcy petition as a creditor holding a secured claim. Under the Code, ACC's claim for the balance owed on the truck was secured only to the extent of the value of the collateral; its claim over and above the value of the truck was unsecured. See 11 U.S.C. § 506(a).

To qualify for confirmation under Chapter 13, the Rashes' plan had to satisfy the requirements set forth in 11 U.S.C. § 1325(a) of the Code. The Rashes' treatment of ACC's secured claim, in particular, is governed by subsection (a)(5).Under this provision, a plan's proposed treatment of secured claims can be confirmed if one of three conditions is satisfied: The secured creditor accepts the plan, see 11 U.S.C. § 1325(a)(5)(A) ; the debtor surrenders the property securing the claim to the creditor, see 1325(a)(5)(C); or the debtor invokes the so-called "cram down" power, see 1325(a)(5)(B). Under the cram down option, the debtor is permitted to keep the property over the objection of the creditor; the creditor retains the lien securing the claim, see 1325(a)(5)(B)(i), and the debtor is required to provide the creditor with payments, over the life of the plan, that will total the present value of the allowed secured claim, i.e., the present value of the collateral, see 1325(a)(5)(B)(ii). The value of the allowed secured claim is governed by § 506(a) of the Code.

The Rashes' Chapter 13 plan invoked the cram down power. It proposed that the Rashes retain the truck for use in the freight-hauling business and pay ACC, over 58 months, an amount equal to the present value of the truck. That value, the Rashes' petition alleged, was $28,500. ACC objected to the plan and asked the Bankruptcy Court to lift the automatic stay so ACC could repossess the truck. ACC also filed a proof of claim alleging that its claim was fully secured in the amount of $41,171. The Rashes filed an objection to ACC's claim. The Bankruptcy Court held an evidentiary hearing to resolve the dispute over the truck's value. At the hearing, ACC and the Rashes urged different valuation benchmarks. ACC maintained that the proper valuation was the price the Rashes would have to pay to purchase a like vehicle, an amount ACC's expert estimated to be $41,000. The Rashes, however, maintained that the proper valuation was the net amount ACC would realize upon foreclosure and sale of the collateral, an amount their expert estimated to be $31,875. The Bankruptcy Court agreed with the Rashes and fixed the amount of ACC's secured claim at $31,875; that sum, the court found, was the net amount ACC would realize if it exercised its right to repossess and sell the truck. The Bankruptcy Court thereafter approved the plan, and the United States District Court for the Eastern District of Texas affirmed. A panel of the Court of Appeals for the Fifth Circuit reversed.

On rehearing en banc, however, the Fifth Circuit affirmed the District Court, holding that ACC's allowed secured claim was limited to $31,875, the net foreclosure value of the truck. . . .

The Code provision central to the resolution of this case is 506(a), which states:

> "An allowed claim of a creditor secured by a lien on property in which the estate has an interest . . . is a secured claim to the extent of the value of such creditor's interest in the estate's interest in such property, . . . and is an unsecured claim to the extent that the value of such creditor's interest . . . is less than the amount of such allowed claim. Such value shall be determined in light of the purpose of the valuation and of the proposed disposition or use of such property. . . . " 11 U.S.C. § 506(a).

Over ACC's objection, the Rashes' repayment plan proposed, pursuant to 1325(a)(5)(B), continued use of the property in question, i.e., the truck, in the debtor's trade or business. In such a "cram down" case, we hold, the value of the property (and thus the amount of the secured claim under 506(a)) is the price a willing buyer in the debtor's trade, business, or situation would pay to obtain like property from a willing seller. Rejecting this replacement-value standard, and selecting instead the typically lower foreclosure-value standard, the Fifth Circuit trained its attention on the first sentence of 506(a). In particular, the Fifth Circuit relied on these first sentence words: A claim is secured "to the extent of the value of such creditor's interest in the estate's interest in such property." The Fifth Circuit read this phrase to instruct that the "starting point for the valuation [is] what the creditor could realize if it sold the estate's interest in the property according to the security agreement," namely, through "repossess[ing] and sell [ing] the collateral."

We do not find in the 506(a) first sentence words—"the creditor's interest in the estate's interest in such property"—the foreclosure-value meaning advanced by the Fifth Circuit. Even read in isolation, the phrase imparts no valuation standard: A direction simply to consider the "value of such creditor's interest" does not expressly reveal how that interest is to be valued.

Reading the first sentence of 506(a) as a whole, we are satisfied that the phrase the Fifth Circuit considered key is not an instruction to equate a "creditor's interest" with the net value a creditor could realize through a foreclosure sale. The first sentence, in its entirety, tells us that a secured creditor's claim is to be divided into secured and unsecured portions, with the secured portion of the claim limited to the value of the collateral. To separate the secured from the unsecured portion of a claim, a court must compare the creditor's claim to the value of "such property," i.e., the collateral. That comparison is sometimes complicated. A debtor may own only a part interest in the property pledged as collateral, in which case the court will be required to ascertain the "estate's interest" in the collateral. Or, a creditor may hold a junior or subordinate lien, which would require the court to ascertain the creditor's interest in the collateral. The 506(a) phrase referring to the "creditor's interest in the estate's interest in such property" thus recognizes that a court may encounter, and in such instances must evaluate, limited or partial interests in collateral. The full first sentence of 506(a), in short, tells a court what it must evaluate, but it does not say more; it is not enlightening on how to value collateral.

The second sentence of 506(a) does speak to the how question. "Such value," that sentence provides, "shall be determined in light of the purpose of the valuation and of the proposed disposition or use of such property." 11 U.S.C. § 506(a) . By deriving a foreclosure-value standard from 506(a)'s first sentence, the Fifth Circuit rendered inconsequential the sentence that expressly addresses how "value shall be determined." As we comprehend 506(a), the "proposed disposition or use" of the collateral is of paramount importance to the valuation question. If a secured creditor does not accept a debtor's Chapter 13 plan, the debtor has two options for handling allowed secured claims: surrender the collateral to the creditor, see § 1325(a)(5)(C); or, under the cram down option, keep the collateral over the creditor's objection and provide the creditor, over the life of the plan, with the equivalent of the present value of the collateral, see 1325(a)(5)(B). The "disposition or use" of the collateral thus turns on the alternative the debtor chooses—in one case the collateral will be surrendered to the creditor, and in the other, the collateral will be retained and used by the debtor. Applying a foreclosure-value standard when the cram down option is invoked attributes no significance to the different consequences of the debtor's choice to surrender the property or retain it. A replacement-value standard, on the other hand, distinguishes retention from surrender and renders meaningful the key words "disposition or use."

Tying valuation to the actual "disposition or use" of the property points away from a foreclosure-value standard when a Chapter 13 debtor, invoking cram down power, retains and uses the property. Under that option, foreclosure is averted by the debtor's choice and over the creditor's objection. From the creditor's perspective as well as the debtor's, surrender and retention are not equivalent acts. When a debtor surrenders the property, a creditor obtains it immediately, and is free to sell it and reinvest the proceeds. We recall here that ACC sought that very advantage.

If a debtor keeps the property and continues to use it, the creditor obtains at once neither the property nor its value and is exposed to double risks: The debtor may again default and the property may deteriorate from extended use. Adjustments in the interest rate and secured creditor demands for more "adequate protection," 11 U.S.C. § 361 , do not fully offset these risks.

Of prime significance, the replacement-value standard accurately gauges the debtor's "use" of the property. It values "the creditor's interest in the collateral in light of the proposed [repayment plan] reality: no foreclosure sale and economic benefit for the debtor derived from the collateral equal to . . . its [replacement] value." The debtor in this case elected to use the collateral to generate an income stream. That actual use, rather than a foreclosure sale that will not take place, is the proper guide under a prescription hinged to the property's "disposition or use."

In sum, under § 506(a), the value of property retained because the debtor has exercised the § 1325(a)(5)(B) "cram down" option is the cost the debtor would incur to obtain a like asset for the same "proposed . . . use."

For the foregoing reasons, the judgment of the Court of Appeals is reversed, and the case is remanded for further proceedings consistent with this opinion. It is so ordered.

QUESTIONS ABOUT RASH

1. What fact was most important to the Court's decision to look to the replacement value standard?

2. Did the Court base its decision on language in the Code? If so, what words?

3. Courts and commentators have paid at lot of attention to the words in footnote 6 of Justice Ginsburg's decision:

"Our recognition that the replacement-value standard, not the foreclosure-value standard, governs in cram down cases leaves to bankruptcy courts, as triers of fact, identification of the best way of ascertaining replacement value on the basis of the evidence presented. Whether replacement value is the equivalent of retail value, wholesale value, or some other value will depend on the type of debtor and the nature of the property. We note, however, that replacement value, in this context, should not include certain items. For example, where the proper measure of the replacement value of a vehicle is its retail value, an adjustment to that value may be necessary: A creditor should not receive portions of the retail price, if any, that reflect the value of items the debtor does not receive when he retains his vehicle, items such as warranties, inventory storage, and reconditioning. Nor should the creditor gain from modifications to the property—*e.g.*, the addition of accessories to a vehicle—to which a creditor's lien would not extend under state law."

How does footnote 6 affect how you would represent a Chapter 13 debtor who wants to keep her car?

Problem 4–15:   *Rash and Issues in a Business Case*

D Furniture Stores, Inc. (D) is in Chapter 11. S Bank (S) has a first mortgage on D's building. D owes S $3,200,000. D's Chapter 11 plan provides for D to continue operating as a furniture store in the same building. How should the court determine the amount of S's secured claim?

------

2. DETERMINATION OF "VALUE OF SUCH CREDITOR'S INTEREST" AND SECTION 506(A)(2)

11 U.S.C. § 506(a)(2)

(a)(2) If the debtor is an individual in a case under Chapter 7 or 13, such value with respect to personal property securing an allowed claim shall be determined based on the replacement value of such property as of the date of the filing of the petition without deduction for costs of sale or marketing. With respect to property acquired for personal, family, or household purposes, replacement value shall mean the price a retail merchant would charge for property of that kind considering the age and condition of the property at the time value is determined.

Section 506(a)(2) was added by the 2005 amendments. Why did your professor ask you to read both *Rash* and section 506(a)(2)? Is *Rash* of any practical significance after 2005?

F. AUTOMATIC STAY

After the filing of a bankruptcy petition, a debtor usually needs immediate protection from the collection efforts of creditors. If the petition is a voluntary Chapter 7, the bankruptcy trustee needs time to collect the "property of the estate" and make pro rata distributions to creditors. If the petition is a voluntary Chapter 11 or Chapter 12, the debtor needs time to prepare a plan. And, if the petition is an involuntary Chapter 7 or Chapter 11, the debtor needs time to controvert the petition.

Accordingly, the filing of a voluntary petition under Chapter 7, Chapter 11, Chapter 12 or Chapter 13, or the filing of an involuntary petition under Chapter 7 or Chapter 11 automatically "stays," i.e., restrains, creditors from taking further action against the debtor, the property of the debtor, or the property of the estate to collect their claims or enforce their liens, section 362.

With respect to section 362, there are five questions that lawyers (and law students) are asked:

(1) When does the automatic stay become effective?

(2) What is covered by the automatic stay?

(3) When does the automatic stay end?

(4) How can a creditor obtain relief from the stay?

(5) What are the consequences of violating the stay?

The fifth question is the easiest (and least important to most law professors) so let's get that one out of the way. There are two major consequences of violating the stay. First, action in violation of the stay has no legal effect as against the debtor and bankruptcy estate. Courts disagree as to whether actions in violation of the stay are "void", or merely "voidable." Second, "[a]n individual injured by any willful violation of a stay provided by this section shall recover actual damages, including costs and attorneys' fees, and, in appropriate circumstances, may recover punitive damages," section 362(h). Courts disagree as to whether debtors who are not individuals can also recover actual or punitive damages because of a stay violation.

The first two of the remaining four stay questions are answered by section 362(a) below.

----

11 U.S.C. § 362(a)

(a) Except as provided in subsection (b) of this section, a petition filed under section 301, 302, or 303 of this title, ... operates as a stay, applicable to all entities, of—

(1) the commencement or continuation, including the issuance or employment of process, of a judicial, administrative, or other action or proceeding against the debtor that was or could have been commenced before the commencement of the case under this title, or to recover a claim against the debtor that arose before the commencement of the case under this title;

(2) the enforcement, against the debtor or against property of the estate, of a judgment obtained before the commencement of the case under this title;

(3) any act to obtain possession of property of the estate or of property from the estate or to exercise control over property of the estate;

(4) any act to create, perfect, or enforce any lien against property of the estate;

(5) any act to create, perfect, or enforce against property of the debtor any lien to the extent that such lien secures a claim that arose before the commencement of the case under this title;

(6) any act to collect, assess, or recover a claim against the debtor that arose before the commencement of the case under this title;

(7) the setoff of any debt owing to the debtor that arose before the commencement of the case under this title against any claim against the debtor; and

---

1. TIME STAY ARISES

The automatic stay is triggered by the filing of a bankruptcy petition. No court action at all is needed for the stay to be created. The filing itself "operates as a stay."

Note that the stay dates from the time of the filing, not from the time that a creditor receives notice of or learns of the bankruptcy. If D files a voluntary bankruptcy petition on April 5, the stay becomes effective April 5. If D's creditors file an involuntary bankruptcy petition on April 5, the stay becomes effective on April 5. The stay dates from April 5 even if creditors do not learn of the bankruptcy until much later.

---

2. SCOPE OF THE STAY

Paragraph (a) of section 362 defines the scope of the automatic stay by listing all of the acts and actions that are stayed by the commencement of a bankruptcy case. It is comprehensive and includes virtually all creditor collection activity. Creditors commonly summarize the scope of section 362(a) in terms similar to the following: "If something is worth doing, you can't do it because it will be stayed by section 362(a)."

While paragraph (a) of section 362 indicates what is stayed, paragraph (b) lists actions that are not stayed, i.e., exceptions to the automatic stay. For example, section 362(b)(2) (a)(iv) provides a limited stay exception for "domestic support obligations." Notwithstanding bankruptcy and the automatic stay, such claims can be collected from property that is not property of the estate.

Most of the section 362(b) exceptions to stay are narrowly drawn. In other words, most of the automatic stay exceptions in section 362(b) apply in relatively few bankruptcy cases.

There is an important limitation on the scope of section 362 that is not dealt with in paragraph (b) of section 362. The automatic stay of section 362(a) only covers the debtor, property of the debtor, and property of the estate. It does not protect third parties. Assume, for example, that D borrows $30,000 from C and G guarantees repayment. If D files for bankruptcy, section 362(a) will stay C from attempting to collect from D. Section 362(a) will not, however, protect G.

While section 362 does not protect third parties such as guarantor G, section 1301 might. When a debtor files for relief under Chapter 13, section 1301 expands the protection of the automatic stay to certain third parties such as Momma who guarantees payment of the note on Bubba's pickup truck.

a. Protection of the Debtor, Property of the Debtor, Property of the Estate

Problem 4–16:   Collection of Prepetition Judgment

On January 15, D borrows $10,000 from C. On February 22, D defaults. On June 6, C files a collection action. On August 8, C obtains a default judgment. On September 9, D files a bankruptcy petition. What is the effect of the automatic stay on the pending collection action?

Problem 4–17:   Pending Litigation

P brings a civil antitrust action against D Corp. After the second week of what is projected to be a seven week trial, D Corp. files for bankruptcy. What is the effect of the automatic stay?

Problem 4–18:   Litigation of Postpetition Debt

On April 5, D files a bankruptcy petition. On June 1, D negligently injures X. Does the automatic stay prevent X from commencing an action in state court against D? Does the automatic stay prevent X from enforcing a judgment entered in such a state court action?

Problem 4–19:   Lien Enforcement

When D defaulted on her debt, C foreclosed its mortgage on D's building. C's foreclosure sale is scheduled for Thursday afternoon. If D files for bankruptcy on Thursday morning, will the foreclosure sale be stayed?

Problem 4–20:   Informal Collection Efforts

On April 10, D filed a voluntary petition for protection under Chapter 7 of the Code. D attended a meeting of creditors on May 8. Following the meeting, American General Finance's representative stopped her in the courthouse's hallway, repeatedly asking her why she was not going to pay the debt she owed American General Finance. Any violation of the automatic stay?

---

b.   Protection of Third Parties

Problem 4–21:   Stay and Third Parties

C makes a loan to D. G guarantees D's payment. D later files for bankruptcy. Does the automatic say bar C from suing G?

The automatic protection of section 362 is limited to the debtor, property of the debtor and property of the estate. The automatic stay does not extend to third parties who are not "debtors" such as the chief executive officer of the debtor corporation. Courts, including the district court in the next case, have used section 105 to enter orders providing injunctive relief to parties other than the debtor.

11 U.S.C. § 105. Power of Court

(a) The court may issue any order, process, or judgment that is necessary or appropriate to carry out the provisions of this title. . . .

SAS OVERSEAS CONSULTANTS AND ASIA CONTRACTING, LTD. v. BENOIT

2000 Westlaw 140611 (E.D. La., Feb. 7, 2000)

ORDER AND REASONS

VANCE, J.

Before the Court is the motion of defendant, Michael M. Benoit, to stay this matter pending the resolution of bankruptcy proceedings filed by Offshore Consultants U.S.A., Ltd....

I. BACKGROUND

On November 4, 1997, plaintiffs, SAS Overseas Consultants and Asia Trading & Contracting, Ltd., filed suit in this Court against Offshore Consultants U.S.A., Ltd. SAS–ATAC sought to recover damages for the purported breach of an Agreement executed on September 12, 1996 between Offshore and SAS–ATAC. Pursuant to the Agreement, SAS–ATAC was to recruit foreign-national workers and arrange for their transportation to the United States. Offshore was then to employ the foreign-national workers and provide their services to third-party customers in return for compensation. SAS–ATAC and Offshore pledged to divide equally the net profits from the third-party customers. The Agreement also required Offshore to render to SAS–ATAC a contemporaneous accounting for its receipts with respect to each payroll for the foreign workers. In their suit against Offshore, SAS–ATAC argued that Offshore failed to pay after employing these workers. When Offshore filed for relief under Chapter 11 of the Bankruptcy Code after nearly two years of litigation, this Court stayed that action on May 17, 1999.

Two weeks after Offshore filed under Chapter 11, SAS–ATAC filed this suit against Michael M. Benoit, Offshore's president and majority stockholder. The complaint asserts the following theories of liability against Benoit: tortuous interference with contract; breach of personal duties owed to SAS–ATAC under LA C.C. article 2315 ; and fraud. SAS–ATAC also claims that Benoit is Offshore's alter ego, which justifies piercing the corporate veil to impose liability on Offshore's shareholders, including Benoit, for Offshore's breach of contract.

II. DISCUSSION

A. Motion to Stay

Benoit requested a stay of this matter pending the outcome of Offshore's bankruptcy proceedings under either the automatic stay provided in Bankruptcy Code section 362 or under Bankruptcy Code section 105.... The Court does not reach the applicability of the automatic stay, however, because it finds that the facts here clearly warrant a discretionary stay under section 105(a).

This Court has the inherent power to stay any matter pending before it in the interests of justice and "economy of time and effort for itself, for counsel and for litigants.". To determine whether to grant a discretionary stay of this matter pending the outcome of Offshore's bankruptcy proceedings, the Court will look to the standard used by the bankruptcy courts to resolve this issue.

A bankruptcy court has broader authority under section 105 of the Bankruptcy Code to grant a stay than it does under the automatic stay provisions of section 362, and may use its equitable powers to ensure the orderly resolution of reorganization proceedings. In pertinent part, section 105 allows a bankruptcy court to "issue any order, process, or judgment that is necessary or appropriate to carry out the provisions of this title." 11 U.S.C. § § 105(a) .

The Fifth Circuit has held that a court may temporarily enjoin actions against a nondebtor under "unusual circumstances." See In re Zale Corp., 62 F.3d 746, 761 (5th Cir.1995). Stays under section 105(a) are also subject to the usual rules for the issuance of an injunction under Federal

Rule of Civil Procedure 65. Accordingly, the Court must examine whether both "unusual circumstances" and the prerequisites to issuance of an injunction exist so as to stay this litigation against Benoit.

1. "Unusual Circumstances"

As referenced above, this Court may issue a temporary stay of the action against Benoit, a nondebtor, if "unusual circumstances" exist. These circumstances include 1) when the nondebtor and the debtor enjoy such an identity of interests that the suit against the nondebtor is essentially a suit against the debtor, and 2) when the third-party action will have an adverse impact on the debtor's ability to accomplish reorganization. In re Zale Corp., 62 F.3d 761 .

The test is disjunctive and an injunction may be warranted under either set of circumstances. Here, the suit against Benoit is clearly a suit against Offshore for breach of the Agreement. SAS–ATAC filed this action against Offshore's president and controlling shareholder less than two weeks after this Court stayed the action against Offshore as a result of its bankruptcy filing. Although SAS–ATAC has recast their allegations against Benoit personally, they ultimately seek to pierce the corporate veil and to hold Benoit liable for breach of a contract by Offshore. Additionally, the rights and liabilities of SAS–ATAC under the Agreement with Offshore will necessarily have to be determined before SAS–ATAC can prevail on their claims against Benoit.

Furthermore, permitting this action to continue will have an adverse impact on Offshore's ability to accomplish reorganization. Offshore has the right to have the bankruptcy court adjudicate claims to its corporate assets, including the Agreement in this case. Nothing in the record indicates that Offshore misused the bankruptcy process or that it is not entitled to the normal considerations of a debtor in bankruptcy.

Proceeding with this action would divert Offshore's president and controlling shareholder from assisting in his company's reorganization efforts. Moreover, the suit against Benoit, if successful, might prejudice Offshore's future defense against identical claims based upon identical facts. For the foregoing reasons, the Court finds that this case meets the "unusual circumstances" identified by In re Zale Corp., and the Court may therefore temporarily stay the proceedings against the nondebtor, Benoit, provided the prerequisites for issuance of a preliminary injunction are met.

2.   Merits of Injunctive Relief

The four prerequisites to issuance of a preliminary injunction are: (1) a substantial likelihood of success on the merits; (2) a substantial threat of irreparable injury if the injunction is not granted; (3) that the threatened injury to the movant outweighs the threatened harm an injunction may cause the party opposing the motion; and (4) that the granting of the injunction will not disserve the public interest. The Fifth Circuit employs a sliding scale when analyzing the degree of "success on the merits" a movant must demonstrate to justify injunctive relief. This involves "balancing the hardships associated with the issuance or denial of a preliminary injunction with the degree of likelihood of success on the merits." Moreover, when the other factors weigh in favor of an injunction, a showing of some likelihood of success on the merits will justify temporary injunctive relief. Bankruptcy courts have defined success on the merits as "the probability of a successful plan or reorganization."

At the outset, the Court finds it more likely that Offshore will successfully reorganize if this action is stayed and Benoit is permitted to give his full attention to developing and implementing a viable plan of reorganization. The Court now examines the potential harms to the debtor, creditor and the public to determine if this showing of success on the merits is sufficient.

When assessing the nature of irreparable harm in a proceeding against a nondebtor, as is the case here, the Court focuses on whether the debtor will suffer irreparable harm if the proceedings against the nondebtor go forward. Bankruptcy courts have repeatedly found irreparable harm warranting a stay under section 105(a) when actions brought against nondebtor officers and principals would distract them from the debtor's daily business affairs and divert resources from the debtor's reorganization efforts. As discussed above, the Court finds that Offshore's reorganization efforts would be seriously impaired if its president and controlling shareholder were forced to defend himself in ancillary proceedings in this Court. Additionally, because the rights and liabilities of Offshore and SAS–ATAC under the Agreement will also be addressed by the bankruptcy court, proceeding with the Benoit case could produce inconsistent results on the same issues. SAS–ATAC have also directed discovery at Benoit, much of which involves records of Offshore. The privileges applicable to these materials are Offshore's, and such discovery may force Offshore to intercede to protect its interests. Based on all of these facts, the Court concludes that the reorganization efforts of the debtor, Offshore, will suffer irreparable harm if this action is not stayed.

Furthermore, there is no evidence that SAS–ATAC will suffer any harm if this litigation is stayed. SAS–ATAC is a creditor in the bankruptcy proceeding by virtue of the Agreement with Offshore. The bankruptcy court will determine the rights and liabilities of the parties under that Agreement. The resolution of those issues are central to this case. The Court also notes that no discovery has been conducted to date. A temporary stay will not prejudice SAS-ATAC's ability to proceed against Benoit in this Court but merely delays the litigation temporarily.

Finally, it is clear that the public interest will be served by promoting Offshore's successful reorganization.

After reviewing all of the foregoing considerations, the Court finds that Benoit has satisfied all of the elements necessary for the Court to issue a stay of SAS–ATAC's action against him. The facts of this case demonstrate that continuation of this litigation would adversely effect the debtor's estate and interfere with the debtor's ability to formulate and implement a plan of reorganization. The Court notes that granting a stay here also comports with the general policies underlying the Bankruptcy Code. In particular, a stay of this litigation will give the debtor and its control persons the breathing room necessary to reorganize its finances. For the foregoing reasons, the Court hereby grants Benoit's motion to stay this litigation pending the outcome of the bankruptcy proceedings involving Offshore Consultants U.S.A., Ltd.

The Court finds that Benoit has satisfied all of the elements necessary for the Court to issue a stay of SAS–ATAC's action against him. The facts of this case demonstrate that continuation of this litigation would adversely effect the debtor's estate and interfere with the debtor's ability to formulate and implement a plan of reorganization. The Court notes that granting a stay here also comports with the general policies underlying the Bankruptcy Code. In particular, a stay of this litigation will give the debtor and its control persons the breathing room necessary to reorganize its finances. For the foregoing reasons, the Court hereby grants Benoit's motion to stay this litigation pending the outcome of the bankruptcy proceedings involving Offshore Consultants U.S.A., Ltd.

QUESTIONS ABOUT BENOIT

1. In which court did SAS file its law suits? In which court did Benoit file his motion for relief?

2. What did Judge Vance mean by her statement "this Court stayed that action . . ."?

3. Did Judge Vance rely on section 105 in deciding to "issue a stay"? What is the statutory basis for the "unusual circumstances" test?

Problem 4–22: Arguing for Bankruptcy Court's Protection of Person Who Is Not a Party in the Bankruptcy Case

Your client, D, Inc. has filed a Chapter 11 petition. D, Inc.'s debt to C is guaranteed by G, who is the CEO and principal stockholder of D, Inc. C has sued G in state court on the guarantee. G has "asked" you to do something about this. What, if anything, can you do? Can you represent G? Can D, Inc's attorney ask the bankruptcy court to protect G? What are the reasons that a bankruptcy court might protect a person who is not a party in the bankruptcy case?

---

3. TERMINATION OF THE STAY

Remember that the automatic stay begins when the bankruptcy petition is filed and generally bars a creditor from taking any action to collect its debt from the debtor or the debtor's property.

Section 362(c) describes situations in which the automatic stay ends automatically. Section 362(c)(1) provides that the automatic stay ends as to particular property when the property ceases to be property of the estate. Assume, for example, that M has a mortgage on D Corp.'s office building. D Corp. Files a bankruptcy petition. M is stayed from foreclosing on its mortgage. The bankruptcy trustee then sells the building to X. M is no longer stayed from foreclosing its lien.

Under section 362(c)(2), the automatic stay ends when the bankruptcy case is closed or dismissed or the debtor who is an individual receives a discharge. Remember that the typical Chapter 7 is completed in a matter of months, but Chapter 11 cases and Chapter 13 cases can take years to complete.

The 2005 legislation added two grounds for automatic termination of the automatic stay based on the debtor's recent bankruptcy history. Usual "caveat": this stuff is important in a basic bankruptcy course only if your professor thinks it is. If you did not fully understand her thinking on section 362(c)(3), go to Westlaw and access 2009 Ann. Sur. of Bankr. Law Part III.section 6.

4. RELIEF FROM THE STAY

Creditors in a Chapter 11 case or a Chapter 12 case often would have to wait several years for an automatic stay to terminate automatically. Is there any affirmative action that a creditor can take to obtain earlier relief from the stay?

A creditor can file a motion requesting relief from the automatic stay, Bankruptcy Rule 4001. The bankruptcy court can order the end of the automatic stay or place conditions on continuation of the stay. Paragraphs (d) through (g) of section 362 deal with the grounds for relief from stay.

Bankr. R. 4001. Relief From Automatic Stay

(a) Relief from stay; . . .

(1) Motion

A motion for relief from an automatic stay provided by the Code . . . shall be made in accordance with Rule 9014 . . .

———————

11 U.S.C. § 362(d)(1) and (2)

(d) On request of a party in interest and after notice and a hearing, the court shall grant relief from the stay provided under subsection (a) of this section, such as by terminating, annulling, modifying, or conditioning such stay—

(1) for cause, including the lack of adequate protection of an interest in property of such party in interest'

(2) with respect to a stay of an act against property under subsection (a) of this section, if—

(A) the debtor does not have an equity in such property; and

(B) such property is not necessary to an effective reorganization; . . . .

[There are two other grounds for relief from stay in section 362(d). We do not think that section 362(d)(3) or 362(d)(4) merit coverage in a basic bankruptcy course. If your bankruptcy professor thinks otherwise but the merit of her thinking is not clear to you, again go to Westlaw (which is free for you) and find 2 Norton Bankr. L. & Prac. 3d § 43:48]

———————

Problem 4–23: Cause for Relief From Stay

P files a civil suit against D and D's insurer for injuries from an automobile accident. D files a bankruptcy petition the day that closing arguments are scheduled in that civil suit. Is P's civil suit subject to the automatic stay? Can P obtain relief from the automatic stay? If so, what relief?

Problem 4–24: Pre–Bankruptcy Loan Restructuring Agreements as Cause for Relief From Stay

D owns and operates a tavern. S has a mortgage on the tavern building. After D defaults on the mortgage payments, D and S negotiate changes in the mortgage loan terms, reducing the amount of monthly payments and the interest rate. Their new mortgage agreement provides that if D files for bankruptcy, S's concessions in the loan restructuring are "cause" for relief from stay so that S can foreclose on its mortgage.

D files for bankruptcy. S files a motion for relief from stay under section 362(d)(1) so that it can foreclose. Should the court grant S such relief from the stay? Will other holders of claims in D's bankruptcy be adversely affected by the court's grant of relief from stay to S? Should that be relevant?

Problem 4–25: "Effective Reorganization"

Your client, C, has a mortgage on the buildings of Community Hospital, Inc. (D) to secure a $19,000,000 debt. D has just filed a Chapter 11 petition. What do you have to prove in order to obtain relief from stay under section 362(d)(2) and how do you prove it?

The most frequently invoked ground for relief from stay is "lack of adequate protection of an interest in property of such party in interest." What does this mean? Who is "such party in interest" with "an interest in property"? What is "adequate protection"?

The answers to these questions are important not only in working with the automatic stay in section 362 but also in working with other bankruptcy concepts in other Bankruptcy Code sections. Accordingly, we will consider "adequate protection" separately below.

G. ADEQUATE PROTECTION

"Adequate protection" is a basic bankruptcy concept, an important part of several Code provisions Section 361 describes adequate protection. Understanding "adequate protection" is critical to understanding what happens to holders of secured claims during the course of a bankruptcy case. And the course of many Chapter 11 and 13 cases is longer than this course in bankruptcy.

Recalling the nature of a lien and recalling some of the stuff that you learned in constitutional law is critical to understanding "adequate protection." A creditor with a lien or a right of setoff has not only a right to payment but also an interest in property of the debtor securing that right to payment.

The Fifth Amendment protects interests in property: Federal law cannot deprive a person of her interest in property without due process or without just compensation. Congress's exercise of its bankruptcy powers under Article I, section 8, clause 4 of the Constitution is subject to this Fifth Amendment prohibition on taking property. In general, the Fifth Amendment requires that the value of the creditor's collateral be maintained during the course of the bankruptcy case or that the creditor be compensated for any decline in the value of its collateral.

11 U.S.C. § 361. Adequate Protection

When adequate protection is required under section 362, 363, or 364 of this title of an interest of an entity in property, such adequate protection may be provided by—

(1) requiring the trustee to make a cash payment or periodic cash payments to such entity, to the extent that the stay under section 362 of this title, use, sale, or lease under section 363 of this title, or any grant of a lien under section 364 of this title results in a decrease in the value of such entity's interest in such property;

(2) providing to such entity an additional or replacement lien to the extent that such stay, use, sale, lease, or grant results in a decrease in the value of such entity's interest in such property; or

(3) granting such other relief, other than entitling such entity to compensation allowable under section 503(b)(1) of this title as an administrative expense, as will result in the realization by such entity of the indubitable equivalent of such entity's interest in such property.

Problem 4–26:   *What Is Adequately Protected?*

D owes C $100,000. C has a lien on D's equipment worth $40,000. What right of C qualifies for adequate protection: C's contract right to be paid $100,000 or C's property rights in equipment worth $40,000? Who cares?

Problem 4–27:   *Depreciation Payments as Adequate Protection*

D owes C $200,000. C has a lien on equipment worth $180,000. If the value of this equipment is declining by $5,000 a month, can D provide adequate protection by paying C $5,000 a month? Should any such "adequate protection" payments reduce the amount of C's claim?

Problem 4–28: "Equity Cushion" as Adequate Protection

D owes C $200,000. C has a lien on equipment worth $250,000. The value of the equipment is declining by $5,000 a month. Under these facts, can C's "equity cushion" be the adequate protection? What if D's debt to C is based on a note which provides for interest of 10% per year? Reconsider your answer after considering section 506(b) in *Timbers* below.

UNITED SAVINGS ASSOCIATION OF TEXAS v. TIMBERS OF INWOOD FOREST ASSOCIATES, LTD.

484 U.S. 365 (1988)

JUSTICE SCALIA delivered the opinion of the Court.

Petitioner United Savings Association of Texas seeks review of an en banc decision of the United States Court of Appeals for the Fifth Circuit, holding that petitioner was not entitled to receive from respondent debtor, which is undergoing reorganization in bankruptcy, monthly payments for the use value of the loan collateral which the bankruptcy stay prevented it from possessing.

. . .

On June 29, 1982, respondent Timbers of Inwood Forest Associates, Ltd., executed a note in the principal amount of $4,100,000. Petitioner is the holder of the note as well as of a security interest created the same day in an apartment project owned by respondent in Houston, Texas. The security interest included an assignment of rents from the project. On March 4, 1985, respondent filed a voluntary petition in the United States Bankruptcy Court for the Southern District of Texas.

On March 18, 1985, petitioner moved for relief from the automatic stay of enforcement of liens triggered by the petition, see 11 U.S.C. §§ 362(a), on the ground that there was lack of "adequate protection" of its interest within the meaning of 11 U.S.C. §§ 362(d)(1). At a hearing before the Bankruptcy Court, it was established that respondent owed petitioner $4,366,388.77, and evidence was presented that the value of the collateral was somewhere between $2,650,000 and $4,250,000. The collateral was appreciating in value, but only very slightly. It was therefore undisputed that petitioner was an undersecured creditor.

Respondent had agreed to pay petitioner the postpetition rents from the apartment project (covered by the after-acquired property clause in the security agreement), minus operating expenses. Petitioner contended, however, that it was entitled to additional compensation. The Bankruptcy Court agreed and on April 19, 1985, it conditioned continuance of the stay on monthly payments by respondent, at the market rate of 12% per annum, on the estimated amount realizable on foreclosure, $4,250,000— commencing six months after the filing of the bankruptcy petition, to reflect the normal foreclosure delays .. The court held that the postpetition rents could be applied to these payments.... The District Court affirmed but the Fifth Circuit en banc reversed.

We granted certiorari to determine whether undersecured creditors are entitled to compensation under 11 U.S.C. §§ 362(d)(1) for the delay caused by the automatic stay in foreclosing on their collateral.

II

When a bankruptcy petition is filed, § 362(a) of the Bankruptcy Code provides an automatic stay of, among other things, actions taken to realize the value of collateral given by the debtor. The provision of the Code central to the decision of this case is § 362(d), which reads as follows:

"On request of a party in interest and after notice and a hearing, the court shall grant relief from the stay provided under subsection (a) of this section, such as by terminating, annulling, modifying, or conditioning such stay—

"(1) for cause, including the lack of adequate protection of an interest in property of such party in interest; or

"(2) with respect to a stay of an act against property under subsection (a) of this section, if—

"(A) the debtor does not have an equity in such property; and

"(B) such property is not necessary to an effective reorganization."

The phrase "adequate protection" in paragraph (1) of the foregoing provision is given further content by § 361 of the Code, which reads in relevant part as follows:

"When adequate protection is required under section 362 ... of this title of an interest of an entity in property, such adequate protection may be provided by—

"(1) requiring the trustee to make a cash payment or periodic cash payments to such entity, to the extent that the stay under section 362 of this title ... results in a decrease in the value of such entity's interest in such property;

"(2) providing to such entity an additional or replacement lien to the extent that such stay ... results in a decrease in the value of such entity's interest in such property; or

"(3) granting such other relief ... as will result in the realization by such entity of the indubitable equivalent of such entity's interest in such property."

It is common ground that the "interest in property" referred to by § 362(d)(1) includes the right of a secured creditor to have the security applied in payment of the debt upon completion of the reorganization; and that that interest is not adequately protected if the security is depreciating during the term of the stay. Thus, it is agreed that if the apartment project in this case had been declining in value petitioner would have been entitled, under § 362(d)(1), to cash payments or additional security in the amount of the decline, as § 361 describes. The crux of the present dispute is that petitioner asserts, and respondent denies, that the phrase "interest in property" also includes the secured party's right (suspended by the stay) to take immediate possession of the defaulted security, and apply it in payment of the debt. If that right is embraced by the term, it is obviously not adequately protected unless the secured party is reimbursed for the use of the proceeds he is deprived of during the term of the stay.

. . .

Section 506 of the Code defines the amount of the secured creditor's allowed secured claim and the conditions of his receiving postpetition interest. In relevant part it reads as follows:

> "(a) An allowed claim of a creditor secured by a lien on property in which the estate has an interest . . . is a secured claim to the extent of the value of such creditor's interest in the estate's interest in such property, . . . and is an unsecured claim to the extent that the value of such creditor's interest . . . is less than the amount of such allowed claim. . . .

> "(b) To the extent that an allowed secured claim is secured by property the value of which . . . is greater than the amount of such claim, there shall be allowed to the holder of such claim, interest on such claim, and any reasonable fees, costs, or charges provided for under the agreement under which such claim arose."

In subsection (a) of this provision the creditor's "interest in property" obviously means his security interest without taking account of his right to immediate possession of the collateral on default. If the latter were included, the "value of such creditor's interest" would increase, and the proportions of the claim that are secured and unsecured would alter, as the stay continues—since the value of the entitlement to use the collateral from the date of bankruptcy would rise with the passage of time. No one suggests this was intended. The phrase "value of such creditor's interest" in § 506(a) means "the value of the collateral." We think the phrase "value of such entity's interest" in § 361(1) and (2), when applied to secured creditors, means the same.

Even more important for our purposes than § 506's use of terminology is its substantive effect of denying undersecured creditors postpetition interest on their claims—just as it denies over secured creditors postpetition interest to the extent that such interest, when added to the principal amount of the claim, will exceed the value of the collateral. Section 506(b) provides that "[t]o the extent that an allowed secured claim is secured by property the value of which ... is greater than the amount of such claim, there shall be allowed to the holder of such claim, interest on such claim." (Emphasis added.) Since this provision permits postpetition interest to be paid only out of the "security cushion," the undersecured creditor, who has no such cushion, falls within the general rule disallowing postpetition interest. See 11 U.S.C. §§ 502(b)(2) . If the Code had meant to give the undersecured creditor, who is thus denied interest on his claim, interest on the value of his collateral, surely this is where that disposition would have been set forth, and not obscured within the "adequate protection" provision of § 362(d)(1). Instead of the intricate phraseology set forth above, § 506(b) would simply have said that the secured creditor is entitled to interest "on his allowed claim, or on the value of the property securing his allowed claim, whichever is lesser." Petitioner's interpretation of § 362(d)(1) must be regarded as contradicting the carefully drawn disposition of § 506(b).

. . .

Section 362(d)(2) also belies petitioner's contention that undersecured creditors will face inordinate and extortionate delay if they are denied compensation for interest lost during the stay as part of "adequate protection" under § 362(d)(1). Once the movant under § 362(d)(2) establishes that he is an undersecured creditor, it is the burden of the debtor to establish that the collateral at issue is "necessary to an effective reorganization." See § 362(g). What this requires is not merely a showing that if there is conceivably to be an effective reorganization, this property will be needed for it; but that the property is essential for an effective reorganization that is in prospect. This means, as many lower courts, including the en banc court in this case, have properly said, that there must be "a reasonable possibility of a successful reorganization within a reasonable time." 808 F.2d, at 370–371. The cases are numerous in which § 362(d)(2) relief has been provided within less than a year from the filing of the bankruptcy petition. And while the bankruptcy courts demand less detailed showings during the four months in which the debtor is given the exclusive right to put together a plan, see 11 U.S.C. §§ 1121(b), (c)(2), even within that period lack of any realistic prospect of effective reorganization will require § 362(d)(2) relief....

The Fifth Circuit correctly held that the undersecured petitioner is not entitled to interest on its collateral during the stay to assure adequate protection under 11 U.S.C. §§ 362(d)(1).... Accordingly, the judgment of the Fifth Circuit is

Affirmed.

QUESTIONS ABOUT *TIMBERS*

1.   What facts are important in *Timbers*? Is it important that the value of the collateral is less than the amount of the debt? Is it important that the

note secured by the mortgage provided for interest? Is it important that "the collateral was appreciating in value"?

2. What provision of the Code was important in *Timbers*? Do you agree with Justice Scalia's statement that "the provision of the Code central to the decision of this case is section 362(d)"? With his statement "Even more important for our purposes than section 506's use of terminology is its substantive effect of denying undersecured creditors postpetition interest on their claims? Is the petitioner asking for interest on its $4,366,338.77 claim?

Problem 4–29: Relief From Stay After Timbers

D owes your client C $3,000,000. The debt is secured by a first mortgage on Blackacre. D files a Chapter 11 petition. You have credible appraisals of Blackacre ranging from $2,500,000 to $3,500,000. What, if any action, do you recommend to C? What, if any, additional facts would be helpful to you in deciding what to recommend to C?

Problem 4–30: Relief From Stay Under Section 362(d)(2) Review

D, a Chapter 11 debtor owns a ski resort—Colorado Outdoor Lodge (COL). D owes F $4,000,000; F has a first mortgage on COL that provides for 5% interest. D also owes S $2,000,000; S has a second mortgage on COL that provides for 10% interest. The value of COL is no more than $5,500,000 and not less than $5,000,000.

1. If S moved for relief from stay under section 362(d)(2), could S satisfy the burden of proof under section 362(d)(2)(A)?

2. If F moved for relief from stay under section 363(d)(2), could F satisfy the burden of proof under section 362(d)(2)(A)?

3. Would F be allowed interest on its secured claim under section 506(b)?

4. Would S be allowed interest on its secured claim under section 506(b)?

5. To the extent that either F or S would be allowed interest on its claim under section 506(b), does section 506(b) require that the interest be paid monthly? Quarterly? Annually?

6. If F was allowed interest on its secured claim and that interest accrued, what is S's strongest argument for relief from stay under section 362(d)(1)?

UNIT 5

ISSUES THAT CAN (BUT GENERALLY DON'T) ARISE IN CASES UNDER ANY CHAPTER: ELIGIBILITY AND DISMISSAL

Recall that a bankruptcy case begins with the filing of a bankruptcy petition, and that more than 99% of the bankruptcy petitions are filed by the person seeking bankruptcy relief, by the "debtor." These bankruptcy cases are called "voluntary cases" by both section 301 and the lawyers and judges who work with section 301.

Less than one percent of the bankruptcy petitions are filed by creditors against a debtor. These bankruptcy cases are called "involuntary cases" by both section 303 and the lawyers and judges who work with section 303. Both sections 301 and 303 provide that the case is "commenced" when a petition is filed by or against an eligible debtor.

Section 301 requires that a "petition" be used by a debtor to commence a "voluntary" case, and section 303 requires that a "petition" be used by creditors to file an involuntary case. Form 1 (titled "Voluntary Petition") contains the information required by section 301 for a "voluntary" case, and Form 5 (titled "Involuntary Petition") contains the allegations required by section 303 for an involuntary case.

Section 301 provides that the filing of the petition both commences the bankruptcy case and operates as "an order for relief", i.e., no formal adjudication of bankruptcy is necessary. While section 303 provides that the filing of the creditors' petition commences the case, a bankruptcy petition filed by creditors does not operate as an order for relief. Adjudication of bankruptcy is necessary. The debtor has a right to file an answer. If the debtor does not timely answer the petition or if the debtor answers the petition and the creditors are able to establish one of the grounds for relief in section 303(h)—generally "the debtor is generally not paying his debts as such debts become due," then the bankruptcy court shall enter an order for relief.

Problem 5–1: Involuntary Petitions

On January 15, Markell, Nickles and Perris file a bankruptcy petition against Epstein. Epstein files a pro se answer with the simple argument "I don't belong here." What are the litigable issues?

Remember, more than 99% of the bankruptcy cases are filed by the debtor. Is the argument the debtor "don't [sic] belong here" relevant in voluntary bankruptcy cases?

A. OVERVIEW OF ELIGIBILITY

There are two different "eligible debtor questions": (1) whether the debtor is eligible for any form (7, 9, 11, 12 or 13) of bankruptcy relief and (2) whether the debtor is eligible for the form of bankruptcy relief selected. This unit considers only the first of the two questions. The second question of whether a debtor is eligible for relief under the particular chapter of the Bankruptcy Code she, he or it selected, a question which arises primarily when an individual debtor selects Chapter 7, will be considered in the units dealing with Chapter 7 and Chapter 13.

As the title to this unit indicates, the question of whether the debtor is eligible for any form of bankruptcy relief rarely arises. Virtually any "person" eligible for some form of relief under the Bankruptcy Code.

Section 109 focuses on the person who is the debtor and provides the statutory basis for answering the question, is this person eligible to be a debtor in a case under the Code. As you read section 109 set out below, think not only about what it says but also about what it does not say.

---

11 U.S.C. § 109. Who May Be a Debtor?

(a) Notwithstanding any other provision of this section, only a person that resides or has a domicile, a place of business, or property in the United States, or a municipality, may be a debtor under this title....

(h)(1) Subject to paragraphs (2) and (3), and notwithstanding any other provision of this section, an individual may not be a debtor under this title unless such individual has, during the 180–day period preceding the date of filing of the petition by such individual, received from an approved nonprofit budget and credit counseling agency described in section 111(a) an individual or group briefing (including a briefing conducted by telephone or on the Internet) that outlined the opportunities for available credit counseling and assisted such individual in performing a related budget analysis....

(3)(A) Subject to subparagraph (B), the requirements of paragraph (1) shall not apply with respect to a debtor who submits to the court a certification that—

(i) describes exigent circumstances that merit a waiver of the requirements of paragraph (1);

(ii) states that the debtor requested credit counseling services from an approved nonprofit budget and credit counseling agency, but was unable to obtain the services referred to in paragraph (1) during the 5–day period beginning on the date on which the debtor made that request; and

(iii) is satisfactory to the court.

Problem 5–2: An Individual

D, a self-employed long distance trucker, tells you that the finance company is "fixing to" repossess his tractor and trailer and that he is "maxed out" on his credit cards, and has doctor bills, and ... If D files for bankruptcy, the automatic stay will provide at least short-term protection. What, if anything, do you have to do **before** filing a bankruptcy petition for D? See section 109(h); see also sections 342(b); 521(a), 526, 527, 528.

Problem 5–3: Sole Proprietorship

Epstein owns a bar (Eppie's Bar), a barbershop (Eppie's Barbershop) and a barbecue stand (Eppie's Barbecue). Epstein is the only owner; each of the businesses is a sole proprietorship. Epstein keeps a separate set of books for each business. Eppie's Bar and Eppie's Barbecue are profitable. Epstein is losing money on the barbershop. Can Epstein file a bankruptcy petition for Eppie's Barbershop?

Problem 5–4: Recidivism

Nickles filed for bankruptcy in 2010. Can Nickles file for bankruptcy again in 2011? *Cf.* section 727(a)(8). Can his creditors file a bankruptcy petition against him in 2011? *Cf.* section 303.

Problem 5–5: Insolvency

EMNP, Inc. has "liquidity" problems. While the market value of its assets exceeds its debt, its current earnings are not sufficient to satisfy its current payment obligations. Is EMNP, Inc. eligible for bankruptcy? *Cf.* section 101(32).

Problem 5–6:   Prebankruptcy Agreement

In 2008, C makes a real estate loan to L Limited Partnership (L). In 2010, L is in default. C and L agree to restructure the loan. The workout agreement reduces the interest rate, extends the payment period, forgives default interest that had accrued, eliminates some of the financial covenants and operational restrictions, and provides that L will not file a bankruptcy petition for three years. L files a bankruptcy petition in 2012. What result? Should a business be able to enter into a legally enforceable agreement that it will not file for bankruptcy?

Problem 5–7:   Bankruptcy–Proof Entity

In 2010, C makes a secured loan to L Limited Partnership (L). The loan agreement provides inter alia that:

(i) GP, Inc., shall be the sole general partner of L,

(ii) GP, Inc., shall at all times have an "independent director", acceptable to C;

(iii) L can not file a bankruptcy petition without the affirmative vote of all of the directors of GP, Inc;

(iv) L can not incur more than $13, 474 of debt other than its debt to C without the affirmative vote of all of the directors of GP, Inc.

In 2012, L is in default, and C commences foreclosure procedures. Can L file a bankruptcy petition?

B.   DISMISSAL OF CASES

Dismissal of bankruptcy cases—particularly cases under either Chapter 11 or Chapter 13—are common, and, commonly are uncontested. When there is a legal challenge to a motion to dismiss a Chapter 7, 11, 12, or 13 case, the challenge is typically based on the dismissal provision for that particular chapter. Accordingly, the units on Chapter 7, Chapter 11 and Chapter 13 cover dismissal.

Section 305, which as a Chapter 3 provision is of course applicable to all bankruptcy cases, also empowers the bankruptcy court to dismiss a case if "the interests of creditors and the debtor would be better served by such dismissal." Bankruptcy judges seldom use this power to dismiss.

Think about the statutory requirement of "interests of creditors AND THE DEBTOR" and think about what you know about who commences most bankruptcy cases. If , as in 99% of the cases, the debtor has filed the bankruptcy petition, how does a judge substitute her judgment for the debtor's about what better serves that debtor's interests and dismiss a bankruptcy case that the debtor filed?

UNIT 6

ISSUES THAT CAN ARISE IN CASES UNDER ANY CHAPTER: CLAIMS

We have already looked at "claims" in Unit 4 and learned that claims are what get (1) paid from bankruptcy distributions, (2) discharged after a bankruptcy discharge, and (3) stayed during a bankruptcy case. And, we saw the broad definition of "claim" in section 101.

Lawyers generally see issues relating to claims more than once in a bankruptcy case. In our second, closer look at claims, we are going to focus on three questions that can arise in cases under any chapter: (1) which claims get kicked out or reduced (disallowed) , (2) which claims get paid before other claims (priority) and (3) which claims get paid after other claims (subordination).

A. AVOIDING OR REDUCING CLAIMS

1. DISALLOWANCE UNDER § 502

In a sense, bankruptcy is a "zero-sum" game. In Chapter 7 cases, creditors are limited to the proceeds from the liquidation of the property of the estate. In Chapter 13 cases, creditors' recoveries are limited to the debtor's disposable income. In Chapter 11, the creditors are limited to payments as provided in the proposed plan.

The larger the claims that are made against the Chapter 7 liquidation proceeds or the Chapter 11, or 13 plan payments, the smaller the distribution to a particular claim. To use a familiar metaphor, the size of the pie is finite so that a claimant gets a bigger share of the pie by reducing the other claims on that pie. And, to mix metaphors, a claimant can reduce the other claims to the bankruptcy pie—win the zero sum game—by successfully objecting to the allowance of other claims.

An unsecured claim must go through the allowance process in order to participate in the bankruptcy distribution. Section 502 governs allowance.

The first step in the allowance process is the filing of a proof of claim. And the first step to understanding the proof of claim process is to recall how creditors learn about a bankruptcy.

Section 521 requires the debtor to file a "list of creditors." Creditors on the list receive a notice of the bankruptcy pursuant to Rule 2002.

The Bankruptcy Rules and Official Forms prescribe the time for filing a proof of claim and the contents of the filing. In Chapter 11 cases, certain claims listed on the debtor's schedules are deemed filed, section 1111(a).

Once a claim is filed or deemed filed, it is automatically deemed allowed unless a "party in interest" objects. We are not making this up— *see* see section 502(a); Bankr. R. 3001(f). Grounds for objection to the allowance of a claim are set out in section 502(b), (d), (e), and (k).

The most frequently invoked ground for disallowance of a claim is section 502(b)(1): "The claim is unenforceable ... under any agreement or applicable law for a reason other than because such claim is contingent or unmatured." In other words, a defense that the debtor would have had to the enforceability of the claim outside of bankruptcy is a defense to the allowance of the claim in bankruptcy. Statute of limitations, statute of frauds, and failure of consideration are examples of such defenses.

There are also section 502 grounds for disallowance that are unique to bankruptcy. The following excerpt from section 502(b) contains two such grounds: (1) 502(b)(2)(disallowance of postpetition interest) and (2) 502(b)(6)(disallowance in part of future rents).

---

11 U.S.C. § 502(a), (b)

(a) A claim or interest, proof of which is filed under section 501 of this title, is deemed allowed, unless a party in interest, ... , objects.

(b) [I]f such objection to a claim is made, the court, after notice and a hearing, shall determine the amount of such claim in lawful currency of the United States as of the date of the filing of the petition, and shall allow such claim in such amount, except to the extent that—

(1) such claim is unenforceable against the debtor and property of the debtor, under any agreement or applicable law for a reason other than because such claim is contingent or unmatured;

(2) such claim is for unmatured interest;[1]

(6) if such claim is the claim of a lessor for damages resulting from the termination of a lease of real property, such claim exceeds—

(A) the rent reserved by such lease, without acceleration, for the greater of one year, or 15 percent, not to exceed three years, of the remaining term of such lease, following the earlier of—

(i) the date of the filing of the petition; and

(ii) the date on which such lessor repossessed, or the lessee surrendered, the leased property; plus

(B) any unpaid rent due under such lease, without acceleration, on the earlier of such dates;

---

1. *But cf.* 11 U.S.C. §§ 506(b), 726(a)(5).

Bankr. R. 3007

An objection to the allowance of a claim shall be in writing and filed. A copy of the objection with notice of the hearing thereon shall be mailed or otherwise delivered to the claimant, the debtor or debtor in possession and the trustee at least 30 days prior to the hearing.

Problem 6–1: Loans and Unmatured Interest

D owes C $200,000 on an unsecured basis. The D–C contract provides for interest-only payments of $1,100 a month. D files a Chapter 11 petition on January 15. D's Chapter 11 plan is confirmed later that year, on December 7. Does C have an allowable claim for the interest that accrued between January 15 and December 7?

Problem 6–2: Leases and Unmatured Rent

D rents a building from L in April 2010. The term of the lease is 32 years; the lease terms call for monthly rental payments of $20,000 a month. In April 2011, D files a Chapter 7 bankruptcy petition. At the time of D's bankruptcy filing, D owes L $60,000 in back rent.

What is the amount of L's maximum allowable claim?

What additional information is needed to determine the amount of L's actual allowable claim?

What additional information is needed to determine the amount of the actual payment on L's allowable claim?

What are the consequences of determining that only part of L's claim is allowable?

Re-read the last part of section 502(b)(1): "other than because such claim is contingent or unmatured." The fact that a claim is speculative or contingent or that its amount is difficult to ascertain is not a basis for disallowance. In these circumstances, the court can either estimate the amount of the claim or delay distribution and closing of the bankruptcy case until the amount of the claim has been determined, See section 502(c)(1) ("There shall be estimated for purposes of allowance under this section . . . any contingent or unliquidated claim, the fixing or liquidation of which . . . would unduly delay the administration of the case.")

Problem 6–3: Contingent Claim for Reimbursement

D Co. has filed for bankruptcy. The Environmental Protection Agency has filed a proof of claim in the D Co. bankruptcy stating that the basis of the claim is that D Co. and T Corp. (which is not in bankruptcy) are jointly and severally liable for the pollution of Walden Pond and indicating that the amount of the claim is "still unknown." Does the Environmental Protection Agency have a section 101(5) claim? An allowable claim? Does T Corp. have a section 101(5) claim? If both the Environmental Protection Agency and T Corp. have claims, should both claims be allowable? See section 502(e)(1)(B)("the court shall disallow any claim for reimbursement or contribution of an entity that is liable with the debtor or has secured the claim of a creditor to the extent that .. such claim for reimbursement or contribution is contingent as of the time of allowance or disallowance of such claim for reimbursement or contribution.")

You have just learned about disallowance of a claim under section 502. Disallowance affects bankruptcy distributions. A claim that is disallowed will not receive a distribution from the liquidation of the property of the estate in a Chapter 7 case, or from the confirmed plan in a Chapter 11 or Chapter 13 case.

Disallowance does not however affect discharge. Even though a claim is disallowed in whole or in part, it will still be subject to any discharge resulting from a Chapter 7 case, a Chapter 11 case, or a Chapter 13 case.

In sum, to a creditor, the disallowance of a claim is a "lose-lose" proposition. The creditor loses in bankruptcy—no distribution on its *disallowed* claim. The creditor loses after bankruptcy—discharge of its disallowed *claim*. A creditor will never make the argument that its own claim should be disallowed.

---

2. TRADING CLAIMS

LYNETTE WARMAN, *LET'S MAKE A DEAL*, BUSINESS CREDIT

May 1, 2009, 2009 WLNR 9459221

To sell or not to sell your claim. That is often the issue confronting unsecured creditors in medium to large corporate bankruptcies. The buying and selling of claims is often referred to as "claims trading." This somewhat hidden and virtually unregulated market has evolved into a lucrative, billion dollar industry since the early 1990s. Its key players are banks, hedge funds, claims traders and other sophisticated vendors on the one hand, and lots of ordinary creditors on the other hand.

What Makes Trading Claims Against a Corporate Bankrupt Debtor So Attractive?

Why would a creditor sell its claim? Immediate access to cash, while lowering the risk of receiving no payment. Given the costs, delays and risks inherent in a Chapter 11 bankruptcy case, the ability to sell claims allows creditors to cash out now at a fixed price without having to wait several years for confirmation of a plan of reorganization and a speculative payout.

Creditors often ask, when should I sell my claim? Attempts to buy claims by investors and other financial institutions in the business of trading claims in bankruptcy often occur at various times throughout a bankruptcy case. There may be a flurry of solicitation and offers to purchase claims by investors and other financial institutions at the beginning of the bankruptcy case, and then waves of solicitation as the bankruptcy case progresses. Waiting to sell a claim can be beneficial or detrimental to a creditor depending on how the market views the debtor's reorganization progress. Sometimes the most optimistic purchase offers are at the beginning of the case. Other times, the purchase offers get better once a plan of reorganization is on file and it appears that there is less risk.

Why is buying the debt of a corporate bankrupt debtor attractive to investors? Profit, control and competition. Although it is a risky proposition, significant value can be realized through the reorganization and/or asset sale of a bankrupt entity. Thus, some buyers seek to recover a profit that far exceeds the discounted price at which they purchased the claims from creditors who prefer immediate cash. Other buyers seek to acquire a large block of claims and use it to veto the vote of dissenting creditors on a self-favored plan of reorganization.

Problem 6–4: Trading Claims

D Co. files a Chapter 11 petition. V, one of D Co.'s vendors has an unsecured claim against D Co. for $600,000 and has filed its proof of claim for $600,000. T has offered to buy V's claim for $50,000. Can V sell its claim? If V sells the claim to T, should the claim now be treated by the bankruptcy court as a $600,000 claim or as a $50,000 claim?

B. INCREASING PAYMENT ON A CLAIM BY REASON OF PRIORITIES

In virtually all bankruptcy cases, the amount of claims exceeds the amount available to be distributed to claims. It is kind of like that first Madison Square Garden Phish concert after the first Phish "hiatus"—the one on December 31, 2002. More people wanting seats than seats.

Some people got seats for the Madison Square Garden Phish concert because of a past intimate relationship with Trey or some other Phish members. *Cf.* section 507(a)(1). Other people got seats (albeit less desirable seats) because they worked on making the concert happen. *Cf.* section 507(a)(2). In "bankruptcy talk," these were people with priorities.

There are a number of statements in reported cases, books, and articles about equality of distribution to creditors in bankruptcy cases. Such statements must be using the term "equality" in the Phish concert sense or perhaps the *Animal Farm* sense.

In bankruptcy cases, some claims are "more equal" than others. Secured claims are "more equal" than unsecured claims. And, some unsecured claims are "more equal" than other unsecured claims. More specifically, in a bankruptcy case, certain allowed unsecured claims are entitled to priority in distribution over other unsecured claims. Section 507(a) sets out the levels of priorities.

In a Chapter 7 case, section 726(a)(1) requires that the various priority classes are paid in the order in which they are listed in section 507. In other words, each first priority claim is to be paid in full before any second priority claim is paid at all. If there are not sufficient funds to pay all claims within a particular priority class, then generally all claims entitled to that priority are paid pro rata.

Chapter 11, Chapter 12, and Chapter 13, require that the plan provide for payment in full of all priority claims, although the payments of claims within some of the priority classes may be stretched over a period of time, sections 1129(a)(9); 1222(a)(2), 1322(a)(2).

In its proof of claim form, a creditor can assert a priority and state the amount and basis therefore. Most of the litigation over whether a "claim" is entitled to a priority involve assertions of administrative "expense" status, under section 507(a)(2).

---

1. ADMINISTRATIVE PRIORITY

11 U.S.C. § 507. Priorities

(a) The following expenses and claims have priority in the following order:

(1) First,

(A) Allowed unsecured claims for domestic support obligations ...

(2) Second, administrative expenses allowed under section 503(b) of this title, and any fees and charges assessed against the estate under chapter 123 of title 28.

---

11 U.S.C. § 503. Allowance of Administrative Expenses

(b) After notice and a hearing, there shall be allowed, administrative expenses, other than claims allowed under section 502(f) of this title, including—

>(1)(A) the actual, necessary costs and expenses of preserving the estate, including—

>>(i) wages, salaries, and commissions for services rendered after the commencement of the case; and

* * *

Problem 6–5: Administrative Expenses in a Liquidation Case

D, a cigar store, files for Chapter 7. Are the costs that the Chapter 7 trustee incurs in advertising the sale of D's assets an administrative expense? Are the costs that the Chapter 7 trustee incurs in storing the cigars an administrative expense?

Problem 6–6: Administrative Expenses in an Operating Case

D, a cigar store, files for Chapter 11 on June 30.

1. Is the July salary for its store manager an administrative expense?

2. The store manager's June salary?

3. The tort claim of a customer who slipped, fell, and hurt herself in D's store in July, after D had filed its Chapter 11 petition?

IN RE OLD CARCO LLC, F/K/A CHRYSLER LLC, ET AL.

2010 WL 22426 (Bankr.S.D. N.Y. 2010)

OPINION DENYING MOTION OF RAMIREZ CHRYSLER JEEP DODGE, INC. FOR ALLOWANCE OF ADMINISTRATIVE EXPENSES PURSUANT TO 11 U.S.C. §§ 503(b)(1) AND 507(a)(2)

ARTHUR J. GONZALEZ, BANKRUPTCY JUDGE.

Before the Court is a motion seeking administrative expense priority for damages sustained by an automobile dealer as a result of the voluntary termination by the dealer of its sales and service agreements with the automobile manufacturer.

The Court concludes that any claim for damages sustained by the dealer stems from the applicable pre-petition executory contracts. Therefore, any such claim is a pre-petition general unsecured claim not entitled to administrative expense priority.

FACTS

On April 30, 2009, Old Carco LLC f/k/a Chrysler LLC and 24 of its domestic direct and indirect subsidiaries . . .

Prior to the filing by the Debtors for bankruptcy protection, Ramirez Chrysler Jeep Dodge, Inc. (the "Dealer") operated as a dealer for each of the Debtors' three separate lines of automobiles. In 2002, the Dealer entered into separate sales and servicing agreements (the "Dealer Agreements") with Chrysler Motors for each of those lines of automobiles. Paragraph 28(a) of each of the separate Dealer Agreements provided that the Dealer could "terminate this Agreement on not less than 30 days written notice." Each Dealer Agreement also provided that, for certain delineated reasons, Chrysler Motors could terminate the Dealer Agreement on 60 days' notice. Although Chrysler Motor's right to terminate was limited to certain situations, the Dealer's right to terminate was not restricted, other than with respect to the requirement that it provide at least 30 days' notice. The Dealer Agreements also provided that within ninety days of any effective termination under paragraph 28 of the applicable Dealer Agreement, Chrysler Motors would buy, and the dealer would sell, among other things, vehicle inventory and automobile parts, signs, tools, and equipment (the "Repurchase Obligations").

On March 31, 2009, the Dealer sent a Notice of Termination of Dealer Sales and Service Agreement by Ramirez Chrysler Jeep Dodge, Inc. (the "Termination Notice"). In the Termination Notice, the Dealer expressly referenced its claim based upon Chrysler Motor's Repurchase Obligations.

In response to the Termination Notice, Chrysler Motors sent a letter, dated May 4, 2009, to the Dealer acknowledging the termination and stating that such termination was "effective April 30, 2009." In the letter, Chrysler Motors also acknowledged that the termination imposed certain Repurchase Obligations upon it. In addition, Chrysler Motors sought certain details concerning the vehicles subject to the Repurchase Obligations. The Dealer replied by sending an e-mail, dated May 15, 2009, with a chart attached providing information concerning the vehicles.[3]

On August 27, 2009, the Dealer filed a motion in these bankruptcy cases seeking administrative expense priority, pursuant to sections 503(b)(1) and 507(a)(2) of the Bankruptcy Code, for its claim for $1,310,060 allegedly arising from the Repurchase Obligations. The Debtors oppose the Dealer's motion. A hearing on this matter was held before the Court on October 22, 2009.

---

3. At the time of the May 15, 2009 e-mail, the amount of vehicle inventory for which the Dealer was asserting a claim was $1,879,963. Since that date, the Dealer has sold various portions of the automobile inventory to other dealers. At the time it filed its motion on August 27, 2009, the Dealer alleged that the vehicle inventory claim had been reduced to $810,060. In addition, as of August 27, 2009, the Dealer asserts that its claim for the Repurchase Obligations related to automobile parts, signs, tools, and equipment is approximately $500,000, resulting in a total alleged claim of approximately $1,310,060.

Parties' Contentions

The Dealer argues that it is entitled to an administrative expense priority for its claim arising from the termination of the Dealer Agreements and the resulting Repurchase Obligations imposed on Chrysler Motors by the Dealer Agreements.... Dealer asserted that the claim was entitled to priority under traditional administrative expense priority standards, arguing that the Dealer bestowed a benefit upon the estates.... Dealer argued that the estates received a separate benefit because the Dealer worked diligently to continue to sell inventory to reduce the Debtors' Repurchase Obligations. The Dealer also argued that the vehicles were property of the Debtors' estates, which estates were benefitted when the Dealer preserved such property. . . .

DISCUSSION

Administrative Expense Priority

Traditional Criteria

Section 503(b)(1)(A) of the Bankruptcy Code provides a priority for "the actual, necessary costs and expenses of preserving the estate ... for services rendered after the commencement of the case." Pursuant to section 507(a)(1)[sic] of the Bankruptcy Code, these expenses for administering the estate are afforded a first priority. Thus, expenses incurred by the debtor-in-possession during the reorganization effort are afforded a first priority. *See In re Jartran, Inc.,* 732 F.2d 584, 586 (7th Cir.1984).

This priority is based upon the premise that the operation of the business by a debtor-in-possession benefits pre-petition creditors; therefore, any claims that result from that operation are entitled to payment prior to payment to "creditors for whose benefit the continued operation of the business was allowed." *Cramer v. Mammoth Mart, Inc. (In re Mammoth Mart, Inc.),* 536 F.2d 950, 954 (1st Cir.1976)....

Administrative expenses are afforded this priority to facilitate the reorganization effort by encouraging third parties, who might otherwise be reluctant to deal with a debtor-in-possession, to transact such business. Absent this incentive, third parties would refrain from dealing with the debtor-in-possession, thereby inhibiting the reorganization effort and harming pre-petition creditors. . . .

Ordinarily, an expense will be accorded administrative status

    1) if it arises out of a transaction between the creditor and the bankrupt's trustee or debtor-in-possession; and

    2) only to the extent that the consideration supporting the claimant's right to payment was both supplied to and beneficial to the debtor-in-possession in the operation of the business.

The services performed by the claimant must have been "induced" by the debtor-in-possession, not the pre-petition debtor. Considering inducement by the debtor-in-possession to be a crucial element comports with the policy reason for allowing the priority, which is to encourage third parties to supply the debtor-in-possession with goods and services with the goal of achieving a reorganization to benefit all creditors .. Thus, benefit to the debtor-in-possession alone, without its having induced the performance, is not sufficient to warrant entitlement to an administrative claim priority, as it would contradict this policy reason for allowing the priority.

Priority ... is not afforded a claim merely because the right to payment arises post-petition. Thus, where there is a pre-petition contract or lease, and the consideration supporting the claim is supplied prepetition, court have determined that those claims are not entitled to administrative priority, even if the right to payment arises post-petition.

The Reading Line of Cases

An exception to the requirement that there be an actual benefit to the estate before a claim can be accorded administrative priority has developed in the context of torts committed by the trustee or debtor-in-possession during the course of a chapter 11 proceeding. See *Reading Co. v. Brown,* 391 U.S. 471, 482, 88 S.Ct. 1759, 1765, 20 L.Ed.2d 751 (1968)).

In *Reading,* which concerned an arrangement under Chapter XI of the Bankruptcy Act, the Supreme Court reasoned that if a party were injured by negligence in the operation of an "insolvent business thrust upon it by operation of law," it was "fairer" to compensate the injured party upon whom the arrangement had been imposed before compensating those for whose benefit the arrangement was being effected. Thus, the Supreme Court held that a tort arising during the arrangement is treated as an "actual and necessary expense[ ]" of the estate. The concept has since been applied in chapter 11 reorganization cases under the Bankruptcy Code. The justification is that it is "more natural and just" to compensate those who were injured by the operation of the business during the reorganization effort ahead of those for whose benefit the business was allowed to continue to operate....

Applying Law to the Dealer's Claim

The Dealer's claim arises out of the terms of the pre-petition Dealer Agreements. The claim does not arise from a transaction between the Dealer and the Debtors. Further, the Dealer did not provide any benefit to the Debtors' estates. The Debtors correctly assert that the Dealer had an obligation to continue to sell inventory to mitigate damages against the estates and, in addition, that the Dealer itself benefitted from any such sales. Whatever benefit the Debtors' estates received in terms of a reduction of the Repurchase Obligations, the Dealer was fully compensated as it received payment in that amount. Moreover, the Dealer was preserving its own property, not the Debtors' property; otherwise, the Debtors would not have had an obligation to "repurchase" such property. Indeed, paragraph 29(a) of each Dealer Agreement provides that Chrysler Motors' Repurchase Obligations applied to vehicles that were "purchased" by the Dealer from Chrysler Motors and "that are on the effective date of termination the property of . . . Dealer." In addition, if the property at issue were the Debtors' property, the Dealer would have been subject to the section 362 automatic stay. Nor was any meaningful benefit conferred upon the estates as a result of the elimination of the obligation to reject the contract.

The traditional standard for administrative claim priority as set forth in *Mammoth Mart* is not met because the claim did not arise out of a transaction between the Dealer and the Debtors; nor was a benefit conferred upon the estates in the operation of their businesses. . . .

The Court recognizes that the Dealer has a claim against the Debtors based upon the Repurchase Obligations contained in Dealer Agreements and relevant state law. However, because that claim arises out of the pre-petition contracts, and because no cognizable benefit was conferred on the Debtors' estates in connection therewith, any such claim is a pre-petition general unsecured claim.

[T]he reasoning of the *Reading* line of cases has been applied in the context of a debtor's negligence, a debtor's intentional misconduct, or injury to an innocent third party with no prior relationship to the debtor. There is no allegation that the Debtors were negligent or that they committed an intentional tort. Further, in the instant case, the Dealer was not an unrelated third party adversely affected by the Debtors' actions. Instead, it had a pre-petition contractual relationship with the Debtors and its claim stems from the breach of the very contracts that engendered that relationship. Although the due date for payment of the Repurchase Obligations may occur post-petition, the obligations stem from a pre-petition relationship. The *Reading* exception does not include a right to payment emanating from a pre-petition contract with a debtor. The Court reiterates that the Dealer is allowed a claim against the Debtors' estates for any entitlement it may have to payment of the Reimbursement Obligations. That claim, however, is a general unsecured claim, similar to that of other claimants who have claims against the Debtors arising from the breach of a pre-petition contract. . . .

CONCLUSION

Any claim that the Dealer has against the Debtors' estates based upon the Repurchase Obligations arises out of the pre-petition Dealer Agreements. Inasmuch as any such claim arises out of the pre-petition contracts, and because no benefit was conferred on the Debtors' estates, that claim is a pre-petition general unsecured claim that is, therefore, not entitled to administrative expense priority.

The rationale of the *Reading* line of cases does not justify affording this claim administrative priority . . . . Nor is the language of the *Reading* line of cases concerning "costs incident to operation of a business" implicated. . . .

The Debtors are to submit a proposed order, consistent with this Opinion.

QUESTIONS ABOUT CARCO

1. What was Dealer's best fact? Dealer's best legal argument?

2. What were Judge Gonzales' reasons for denying Dealer's motion for administrative expense priority under section 507(a)(2)? Judge Gonzales' most persuasive reason?

3. Note the first phrase in Judge Gonzales' conclusion, "Any claim that the Dealer has." Does the Dealer have a claim? In light of footnote 3 above (and common sense), is it a $1,310,060 claim?

In 2005, Congress added section 503(b)(9), a new administrative expense priority for goods delivered on credit within 20 days before the bankruptcy filing. Section 503(b)(9) is set out below and below that is a problem applying section 503(b)(9) and then, below that, an excerpt from Congressional testimony by the counsel for the creditors' committee in the Circuit City case about what a problem section 503(b)(9) was for Circuit City.

11 U.S.C. § 503(b)(9)

After notice and a hearing, there shall be allowed administrative expenses, ... including

(9) the value of any goods received by the debtor within 20 days before the date of commencement of a case under this title in which the goods have been sold to the debtor in the ordinary course of such debtor's business.

Problem 6–7: Recovering for Goods Delivered Within 20 Days Before Bankruptcy

D, a chain of convenience stores, files a Chapter 11 petition. In the 20 days before D's bankruptcy filing, D obtained the following:

A. New software from A,

B. Inventory from B,

C. Equipment from C.

Before its bankruptcy filing, D did not make any payments to A or B or C. Are the amounts owed to A, B, and C administrative expenses under section 503(b)(9)?

"In the case of Circuit City—filed Section 503(b)(9) claims of approximately $359 million.... In the event that allowed Section 503(b)(9) claims were, for example, $215 million, at least that amount would have to have been available on the effective date of any Circuit City plan of reorganization, to pay Section 503(b)(9) claims, instead of those monies being used for distribution to similarly situated creditors who gave trade credit more than 20 days before the petition date for needed capital expenditures, labor upgrades, and other necessary costs to effectuate a successful reorganization.

In conclusion, while Circuit City may have been bigger than any other retailer to have been forced to liquidate in 2008, the major factors that caused the liquidation are presently inherent in all retail bankruptcies. A difficult economy, risk-averse lenders facing their own financial struggles, and Section 503(b)(9) claims, making virtually any Chapter 11 more problematic.''

Testimony of Richard M. Pachulski before the Subcommittee on Commercial and Administrative Law of the House Judiciary Committee, 11 Cong. 1st Sess., for Hearings on ''Circuit City Unplugged: Why Did Chapter 11 Fail To Save 34,000 Jobs'', March 3, 2009.

2. SOME OTHER PRIORITIES

Problem 6–8: Priority for Domestic Support Obligation

W comes to you for advice. Her husband, H, who just graduated from medical school, has filed for divorce. H and W have no children. They were married during H's first year of medical school, and W worked two jobs to pay H's medical school tuition and their living costs. H has offered to make monthly payments to W for four years measured by 75% of W's earnings during the four years he was in medical school. What is the relevance, if any, of section 507(a)(1)(A)(''allowed unsecured claims for domestic support obligations'') to this problem?

Problem 6–9: Priority for Pre–Bankruptcy Taxes

On April 15, 2010 T filed her Form 1040 U.S. Individual Income Tax Return. T's tax return showed that she owed $165,000 in taxes for 2009. T made a $2,000 payment with her return and made a $2,000 payment each month until March 1, 2011, when she filed a bankruptcy petition. Why did Congress relegate tax claims to an 8th priority? See section 507(a)(8); cf section 523(a)(1)(A). What if prior to T's bankruptcy filing, the IRS had obtained a federal tax lien?

3. REVIEW: PRIORITIES, AND LIEN PRIORITY

The Code uses the term ''priorities'' to identify those administrative expenses and **UNSECURED** claims that are to be satisfied before other **UNSECURED** allowable claims. One more time, **UNSECURED** allowable claims. In bankruptcy, priorities are unsecured allowable claims and administrative expenses.

Outside of bankruptcy, laws and lawyers use the term "priority" to identify those liens that are to be satisfied over other liens. A first mortgage has priority over a second mortgage, a purchase money security interest in equipment that complied with UCC § 9–324(a) has priority over other security interests in the same equipment.

In general, the Bankruptcy Code does not change the priority among liens outside of bankruptcy. If, outside of bankruptcy, P's purchase money security in D's equipment has priority over S's security interest in D's equipment, then, in bankruptcy, P's security interest will still have priority over S's. If the value of the equipment is more than the amount owed to P but less than the total amount owed to both P and S, then P's secured claim will be satisfied first.

And, in general,[2] in bankruptcy, even the lowest priority secured claim will be satisfied from collateral proceeds before unsecured claims with section 507 priorities will be paid from any collateral proceeds. In the hypothetical in the previous paragraph, S's secured claim will be satisfied before proceeds from S's collateral will be used to pay section 507 priorities.

Problem 6–10: Liens, Lien Priority and Section 507 Priorities

D Corporation is in Chapter 11 bankruptcy. D Corporation owns Blackacre. D Corporation's creditors include F, S, T, U, V, W, X, Y and Z. F has a $700,000 first mortgage on Blackacre; S has a $500,000 second mortgage on Blackacre. Blackacre has a value of $1,000,000. X, Y and Z are asserting section 507 priorities. Is that important to F? To S?

C.   DECREASING (OR, MORE LIKELY, ELIMINATING) PAYMENT ON A CLAIM BECAUSE OF SUBORDINATION

Think again about that Phish Madison Square Garden concert. If you are a Phish fan, you don't want to be at the end of the line—even if you

---

2. Section 506(c) codifies an exception to this rule. Administrative expenses that benefit a holder of a secured claim can be recovered first from that claimant's collateral. Assume, for example, that (i) D owes S $1000, (ii) the debt is secured by D's Eppielator, (iii) after D's bankruptcy filing, the trustee spends $20 in storing the Eppielator, and (iv) the Eppielator is later sold for $600. Under section 506, the trustee could recover the $20 from the $600 sale proceeds. *See generally* Hartford Underwriters Insurance Company v. Union Planters Bank N.A., 530 U.S. 1 (2000).

have a ticket (think allowable claim). If you are at the end of the line, there probably will not be any seats left. Even if there are still seats, it is highly unlikely that the seats available to the guy at the end of the line will be as good as the seats that the guys at the middle of the line have.

How can a person wind up at the end of the line at a Phish concert? It might be because of an agreement. Epstein agrees to buy the tickets if Nickles will get in line a day earlier and then yield that spot in line to Epstein 15 minutes before the doors open. *Cf.* section 510(a). Or, it might be because of bad behavior. Markell and Perris get in line earlier but because of their bad behavior, the New York security guards move them to the end of the line. *Cf.* section 510(c).

1. CONTRACTUAL SUBORDINATION AND SECTION 510(A)

As a part of a financing deal, creditors sometimes agree that some creditors will be paid before other creditors. The business reasons creditors enter into such agreements can be complicated. Perhaps, the junior (subordinated) creditors receive a higher interest rate in return for their risk. Perhaps, the junior creditors preceded the senior creditors and agree to the subordination to induce new creditors to fund their borrower who needs the additional funding to continue business operations.

The legal effect of such a pre-bankruptcy subordination agreement in bankruptcy is not complicated. Section 510(a) provides "A subordination agreement is enforceable in a case under this title to the same extent that such an agreement is enforceable under applicable nonbankruptcy law."

Problem 6–11: The "Whys" and "What Ifs" of Contractual Subordination

D Co. meets with its major creditors to try to work out its financial problems without having to file for bankruptcy. D Co. proposes three alternatives for creditors to choose among:

(1) get paid 10% of what is owed now and agree to defer the payment of the remaining 90% of what is owed now until all other creditors are paid in full;

(2) get collateral valued at 20% of what is owed now and agree to defer payment of the balance of the claim until creditors who receive neither part payment nor collateral get paid;

(3) get neither part payment nor collateral but get paid principal and 8% interest before creditors who received either part payment or collateral are paid anything.

Your client C is one of the major creditors of D Co. Do you have any helpful advice for C?

Problem 6–12: The "Hows" of Contractual Subordination— A Simple Story

X and Y are both unsecured creditors of D Corp. X agreed to subordinate the payment of its $100,000 claim to the payment of Y's $100,000 claim. In D Corp.'s bankruptcy, unsecured creditors are receiving 60%. How much does X receive and how much does Y receive?

2.   EQUITABLE SUBORDINATION

11 U.S.C. § 510(c)

(c) Notwithstanding subsections (a) and (b) of this section, after notice and a hearing, the court may—

> (1) under principles of equitable subordination, subordinate for purposes of distribution all or part of an allowed claim to all or part of another allowed claim or all or part of an allowed interest to all or part of another allowed interest; . . .

In the next excerpt from a reported case, a Southern District of New York bankruptcy judge explains "equitable subordination" (with some "help" from some of your favorite authors.)

"The doctrine of equitable subordination is codified in section 510(c) of the Code. It empowers the Bankruptcy Court, under 'principles of equitable subordination,' to subordinate, for purposes of distribution, claims to other claims, and interests to other interests, and to transfer the lien securing the subordinated claim to the estate.

The power to subordinate a claim derives from the Bankruptcy Court's general equitable power to adjust equities among creditors in relation to the liquidation results. It involves viewing claims "through the eyes of equity and dealing with them on the basis of equitable considerations to prevent injustice or unfairness in the bankruptcy situation."

The doctrine is limited to reordering priorities, and does not permit disallowance of claims. It requires the court to consider whether, notwithstanding the apparent legal validity of a particular claim, the conduct of the claimant in relation to other creditors is or was such that it would be unjust or unfair to permit the claimant to share pro rata with the other claimants of equal status.

In considering the applicability of the doctrine, courts have uniformally[sic] applied the three-pronged test:

a) The claimant engaged in some type of inequitable conduct;

b) The misconduct caused injury to the creditors or conferred an unfair advantage on the claimant;

c) Equitable subordination of the claim is consistent with bankruptcy law.

Equitable subordination requires proof of "inequitable conduct" which, one commentator has noted, is a "very slippery concept with little predictive value." 2 David G. Epstein et al., Bankruptcy, § 6–93, at 256 (1992) ("Epstein")...."

In re 80 Nassau Associates, 169 B.R. 832, 836 (Bankr. S.D.N.Y. 1994).

———

Problem 6–13: Simple Equitable Subordination Story

Epstein is the principal shareholder in and creditor of Eppie's, Inc. Epstein invested $1,000 and loaned $700,000 to Eppie's Inc.

Eppie's, Inc. is in financial trouble. Epstein tells all of Eppie's, Inc vendors that he intends to loan Eppie's, Inc. another $500,000. Relying on this statement from Epstein, the vendors continue to sell on credit to Eppie's, Inc. Epstein does not make the new loan. Eppie's, Inc. files for bankruptcy. Epstein files a proof of claim for the $700,000 he loaned Eppie's, Inc. Should Epstein's claim be disallowed under section 502(b)? Should Epstein's claim be subordinated under section 510(c) to the claims of the vendors who relied on his representation? In this case (and most cases), what is the practical difference between disallowance and subordination?

———

UNIT 7

ISSUES THAT CAN ARISE IN CASES UNDER ANY CHAPTER: AVOIDING POWERS

■ ■ ■

A. INCREASING PROPERTY OF THE ESTATE OR DECREASING THE PAYMENT TO A CLAIM THROUGH THE AVOIDING POWERS: AN OVERVIEW

Some property transfers can be undone or "avoided" under state law. For example, if Jack, an insolvent person, gives all of his property to Jill to prevent his creditors from seizing the property to satisfy their claims, then Jack's gift to Jill can be invalidated under state laws, such as state fraudulent conveyance laws. Jill has to return the property that Jack gave her.

The Code incorporates these state laws in section 544(b). A transfer of a debtor's property that can be invalidated under state law in the absence of bankruptcy can be invalidated under section 544(b) in the event of bankruptcy.

Chapter 5 of the Code also contains several other "avoidance" provisions that are unique to bankruptcy. Accordingly, some payments, sales, exchanges, judicial liens, security interests and other transfers that are valid under state law can be avoided in bankruptcy.

The Code's avoidance provisions reach both "voluntary" transfers such as a debtor's making a gift to a relative or granting a mortgage to a creditor and "involuntary" transfers such as a creditor's garnishing the debtor's bank account or subjecting the debtor's real property to a judgment lien. See 101 (54) (definition of "transfer"). Note also that the Code's avoidance provisions reach both "absolute" transfers such as gifts, payments and sales, and "security transfers" such as mortgages and judgment liens. Id.

In working with these avoidance provisions, law students and lawyers are called on to answer three basic questions:

(1) What are the consequences of avoiding a transfer? and

(2) Which transfers can be avoided? and

(3) How does avoidance of a transfer happen?

The last of these three questions is the easiest—at least for a law student. Avoidance does not occur by operation of law. Avoidance requires litigation [or the threat of litigation] and involves all of the usual litigation questions such as who can sue, who can be sued, when the suit has to be brought, where the suit can be brought and what can be recovered.

The avoidance statutes generally use the phrase "the trustee may avoid." Recall that in Chapter 11 cases without a trustee, the debtor in possession has the rights of a trustee, section 1107(a). This means that any transfer that can be avoided by a trustee can be avoided by a debtor in possession in a Chapter 11 case. For example, D pays C $600,000. D then files for Chapter 11. If D's $600,000 payment to C is covered by one of the Code's avoiding powers, then D as the Chapter 11 debtor in possession can recover the $600,000 it earlier transferred to C.

Section 546 deals with the question of when an avoidance action must be brought. It is in essence a statute of limitations which generally requires that legal action be initiated within two years after the order for relief.

Sections 541(a)(3), 502(d) and 550 deal with the first of the three questions—(1) What are the consequences of avoiding a transfer?

1. Increase in Property of the Estate

In the main, the consequence of avoiding a transfer is an increase in property of the estate. The avoiding powers are a part of a subchapter of the Code entitled "The Estate."

When the bankruptcy trustee avoids an absolute transfer of property, that property then becomes property of the estate. Assume that D owes C $25,000. D repays C $12,000 of that debt. D later files for bankruptcy. At the time of D's bankruptcy filing, the $12,000 D paid to C is not property of D's estate. If, however, the bankruptcy trustee is able to invoke one of the Code's avoidance provisions to avoid D's payment to C and recover the $12,000, the $12,000 will then become property of D's estate, sections 541(a)(3), 550.

The consequences of avoiding a security transfer such as the debtor's grant of a mortgage are similar. Assume, for example, that D borrows $77,000 from C and grants C a mortgage on Blackacre which is worth $120,000. D later files for bankruptcy. Absent the trustee's use of one of the avoidance powers, C has a $77,000 secured claim.

[Recall that under section 541, Blackacre itself is not property of the estate. The estate's interest in Blackacre is only D's limited equity and other rights in Blackacre.]

Accordingly, in a Chapter 7 case for example, if the Chapter 7 trustee is not able to avoid D's transfer granting the mortgage on Blackacre, C has a property right to $77,000 of the value of Blackacre. and D's other creditors share in the $43,000 balance, pro rata. If, however, the Chapter 7 trustee is able to avoid the grant of the mortgage on Blackacre, then Blackacre without any encumbrance will be property of the estate, and all unsecured creditors, including C, will share pro rata in the $120,000 value of Blackacre.

In the two examples, the consequences of avoidance were the recovery of the property interest transferred from the party to whom it had been transferred. Under section 550, the consequences of avoidance are not limited to recovery of the property transferred, or to the person to whom the transfer was made.

Under section 550(a), the court can order the recovery of the "value of the property" transferred, rather than the property. And, section 550 permits recovery not only from (i) the initial transferee but also (ii) from the later transferees or (iii) from a person who was not a transferee but benefitted from the transfer. Finally, section 550 provides protection for certain transferees.

11 U.S.C. § 550. Liability of Transferee of Avoided Transfer

(a) ... [T]he trustee may recover, for the benefit of the estate, the property transferred, or, if the court so orders, the value of such property, from—

(1) the initial transferee of such transfer or the entity for whose benefit such transfer was made; or

(2) any immediate or mediate transferee of such initial transferee.

(b) The trustee may not recover under section (a)(2) of this section from—

(1) a transferee that takes for value, including satisfaction or securing of a present or antecedent debt, in good faith, and without knowledge of the voidability of the transfer avoided; or

(2) any immediate or mediate good faith transferee of such transferee.

Problem 7–1: Recovery Of What, From Whom

D transfers real property to X. At the time of the transfer, the property was worth $400,000. X later sells the property to Y for $500,000 .. Still later, D later files for bankruptcy. Y still owns the real property. Because of declining property values, the property is now worth only $220,000. If the trustee is able to avoid the transfer, what can she recover under section 550? From whom?

---

2. DECREASE IN ALLOWABLE CLAIMS

The avoidance of an absolute transfer can also affect the amount of a creditor's claim. Recall the above hypothetical, in which (i) D owed C $25,000; (ii) D paid C $12,000 and (iii) D then filed for bankruptcy. C thus had a $13,000 claim at the time of D's bankruptcy filing. If the bankruptcy trustee is able to avoid the payment and recover the $12,000 D paid C, then C will have a $25,000 claim against D, section 502(h). If, however, the bankruptcy trustee is able to establish a legal basis for avoiding the transfer but is unable to recover the payment, then C's claim for $13,000 will be disallowed under section 502(d), set out below

11 U.S.C. § 502(d)—Disallowance

(d) Notwithstanding subsections (a) and (b) of this section, the court shall disallow any claim of any entity from which property is recoverable under section 542, 543, 550, or 553 of this title or that is a transferee of a transfer avoidable under section 522(f), 522(h), 544, 545, 547, 548, 549, or 724(a) of this title, unless such entity or transferee has paid the amount, or turned over any such property, for which such entity or transferee is liable under section 522(i), 542, 543, 550, or 553 of this title.

B. INCREASING PROPERTY OF THE ESTATE OR DECREASING THE PAYMENT TO A CLAIM THROUGH AVOIDANCE OF FRAUDULENT TRANSFERS AND FRAUDULENT OBLIGATIONS

For more than four hundred years, there have been statutes that empower creditors to avoid transfers that "hinder, delay or defraud creditors." Every state has such a fraudulent conveyance law. A bankruptcy trustee can use these state laws by invoking section 544(b) as indicated earlier in this unit and considered later in this unit.

Additionally, the bankruptcy trustee can avoid fraudulent transfers by invoking section 548 set out below. For the most part, the requirements of section 548 are the same as the requirements of most state fraudulent conveyance laws.

Section 548(a)(1)(A) empowers the bankruptcy trustee to avoid transfers made and obligations incurred with "actual intent" to hinder, delay or defraud creditors. There is rarely direct evidence of actual intent. Instead, there are certain facts recognized as strong indicia of actual fraudulent intent which are called "badges of frauds." Some of these "badges of fraud" are (i) the existence of a family or other close relationship between the transferor and the transferee, (ii) the absence or inadequacy of consideration, and (iii) secrecy of the transfer.

The classic illustration of "badges of fraud", *Twyne's Case*, involves sheep. Assume for example that Epstein and Perris are suing Markell, and Markell is concerned that Epstein and Perris will get a judgment against him and collect that judgment by having the sheriff seize and sell his prized sheep. Accordingly, Markell enters into a contract with his close friend Nickles, selling the sheep to Nickles.

Notwithstanding the sale, Markell keeps possession of the sheep. And, Markell continues to shear the sheep and whatever. When, however, Epstein and Perris get their judgments against Markell and get the sheriff out to levy on the sheep to satisfy what Markell owes them, Markell tells the sheriff that "The sheep are Nickles', not mine, and so sheriff, you can't take these sheep—Nickles' sheep—to satisfy Epstein and Perris' judgments against me, Markell."

Under the rule of *Twyne's Case*, Epstein and Perris get the sheep. More precisely, Epstein and Perris can avoid Markell's sale of the sheep to Nickles because of the "badges of fraud" that indicate Markell's actual fraudulent intent.

We have not included *Twyne's Case* or even a citation to *Twyne's Case* in this book because most lawyers don't have a sheep case over the course of their careers. More important, most cases under section 544(b) or section 548 do not involve actual fraudulent intent.

Instead, most cases under section 544(b) or 548 involve what is called "constructive fraud." That word "constructive" does not appear in section 544(b) or 548 but is used throughout the law: "constructive" adverse possession, "constructive" eviction, "constructive" trespass. According to Bryan Garner's Black's Law Dictionary, "constructive" is an adjective meaning "legally imputed, having an effect in law though not necessarily in fact."

In short, "constructive" means "let's pretend." And when a transfer is constructively fraudulent, section 544 or section 548 pretends it is a fraudulent transfer and treats it as a fraudulent transfer even though there is nothing fraudulent about it.

Section 548(a)(1)(B) provides for avoidance of transfers and obligations that are constructively fraudulent. Please read section 548(a)(1)(B) carefully. Note the two big "litigable" issues:

    1. Adequacy of what the debtor received in return for the transfer, section 548(a)(1)(B)(ii)

    2. Financial condition of the debtor at the time of the transfer, section 548(a)(1)(B)(ii)

1. SECTION 548: BANKRUPTCY'S FRAUDULENT CONVEYANCE LAW

11 U.S.C. § 548. Fraudulent Transfers and Obligations

(a)

(1) The trustee may avoid any transfer of an interest of the debtor in property, or any obligation incurred by the debtor, that was made or incurred on or within two years before the date of the filing of the petition, if the debtor voluntarily or involuntarily—

(A) made such transfer or incurred such obligation with actual intent to hinder, delay, or defraud any entity to which the debtor was or became, on or after the date that such transfer was made or such obligation was incurred, indebted; *or* [emphasis added]

(B)

(i) received less than a reasonably equivalent value in exchange for such transfer or obligation; **and** [emphasis added]

(ii)(I) was insolvent on the date that such transfer was made or such obligation was incurred, or became insolvent as a result of such transfer or obligation;

(II) was engaged in business or a transaction, or was about to engage in business or a transaction, for which any property remaining with the debtor was an unreasonably small capital; or

(III) intended to incur, or believed that the debtor would incur, debts that would be beyond the debtor's ability to pay as such debts matured.

. . .

(c) Except to the extent that a transfer or obligation voidable under this section is voidable under section 544, 545, or 547 of this title, a transferee or obligee of such a transfer or obligation that takes for value and in good faith has a lien on or may retain any interest transferred or may enforce any obligation incurred, as the case may be, to the extent that such transferee or obligee gave value to the debtor in exchange for such transfer or obligation.

---

11 U.S.C. § 101(32)(A)—Insolvent

(32) "insolvent" means—

(A) with reference to an entity other than a partnership and a municipality, financial condition such that the sum of such entity's debts is greater than all of such entity's property, at a fair valuation, exclusive of—

> (i) property transferred, concealed, or removed with intent to hinder, delay, or defraud such entity's creditors; and

> (ii) property that may be exempted from property of the estate under section 522 of this title;

Problem 7–2: Insolvency And Cash Flow

D Ltd is a limited partnership that owns and develops real estate. Most of D Ltd's land is still undeveloped. The market value of D Ltd's land is $4,000,000. Its debts are $3,000,000. D Ltd's monthly payment obligations to creditors—$200,000—is much greater than D Ltd's monthly earnings—$100,000. In other words, D Ltd is not able to pay its debts as they mature. Is D Ltd "insolvent" as that term is used in the Code?

Problem 7–3: Gift To Relative

D's creditors are threatening to repossess his boat. D, who is insolvent, gives the boat to his father, F. Within two years, D files for bankruptcy. Can the trustee avoid the gift of the boat as a fraudulent transfer?

Problem 7–4: Gift To Charity

Epstein's creditors are threatening to garnish his bank account. Epstein, who is insolvent, makes a gift of $20,000 to the Jewish Community Federation of Richmond. Within two years, Epstein files for bankruptcy. Can the trustee avoid the gift as a fraudulent transfer?

Problem 7–5: Sale For Less Than Reasonably Equivalent Value

D's creditors are threatening to repossess his boat. D, who is insolvent, sells the boat to his friend F for $3,000. Within two years, D files for bankruptcy. Can the bankruptcy trustee avoid the sale if she can establish that the value of the boat at the time of the sale was $7,000? If so, what are F's rights?

Problem 7–6: Judicial Sale And Reasonable Equivalent Value

One of D's creditors with a judgment against D, who is insolvent, obtains an execution lien, and has the sheriff seize and sell D's boat. The judicial sale of the boat for $3,000 completely complies with state law. Within two years, D files for bankruptcy. Can the bankruptcy trustee avoid the sale by establishing that the value of the boat at the time of the sale was $7,000? *Cf. BFP v. Resolution Trust Corp.*, 511 U.S. 531, 545 (1994)("We deem, as the law has always deemed, that a fair and proper price, or a 'reasonably equivalent value', for foreclosed property is the price in fact received at the foreclosure sale, so long as all of the requirements of the State's foreclosure law have been complied with.")

Loan guarantees raise more challenging issues of constructive fraud. An unsecured guarantee of a loan by a person who is insolvent can result in an avoidable, fraudulent obligation. A secured guarantee by such a person can result in both an avoidable, fraudulent obligation and an avoidable fraudulent transfer.

The key to applying section 548(b)(1)(B) to loan guarantees that the debtor made before filing for bankruptcy is remembering that the word "debtor" precedes the phrase "received less than reasonably equivalent value in exchange" in section 548(b)(1)(B). Accordingly, the test is not whether someone in the world received "reasonably equivalent value in exchange" but whether the debtor, i.e., the person in bankruptcy, received "reasonably equivalent value."

Apply this test to the next problem and case.

Problem 7–7: Guarantee And Reasonable Equivalent Value To Whom

National, TWO, Propper, USN and UMO are separate but related business entities. MHT loans $6,660,000 to National, TWO and Propper. USN and UMO, which are insolvent, guarantee the payment of this loan to National, TWO and Propper, and mortgage their assets to MHT to secure payment of the loan. Within a year, USN and UMO file for bankruptcy. Can USN and UMO avoid the mortgage on their assets as a fraudulent transfer and the guarantee as a fraudulent obligation?

Rubin v. Manufacturers Hanover Trust Co., 661 F.2d 979 (2d Cir. 1981), set out below, dealt with a similar question under the Bankruptcy Act of 1898.

RUBIN v. MANUFACTURERS HANOVER TRUST CO.

661 F.2d 979 (2d Cir. 1981)

KEARSE, Circuit Judge.

. . .

On appeal, the trustees renew their contentions that the obligations to repay the debts of National, TWO, and Propper assumed by USN and UMO under the system of guarantees were not supported by fair consideration, that these obligations were incurred at a time when USN and UMO were insolvent, and that MHT must therefore return to the trustees, pursuant to § 67(d) [section 548 of the Bankruptcy Code] of the Bankruptcy Act, the value of the collateral given by the bankrupts that was applied to the debts of National, TWO, and Propper. For the reasons below we conclude that the district court's rulings as to fair consideration and insolvency were based on erroneous legal principles, and that the judgment must be vacated and the matter remanded for further proceedings.

III.   DISCUSSION

When an overburdened debtor perceives that he will soon become insolvent, he will often engage in a flurry of transactions in which he transfers his remaining property, either outright or as security, in exchange for consideration that is significantly less valuable than what he has transferred. Although such uneconomical transactions are sometimes merely final acts of recklessness, the calculating debtor may employ them as a means of preferring certain creditors or of placing his assets in friendly hands where he can reach them but his creditors cannot. Whatever the motivation, the fraudulent conveyance provisions of § 67(d) [section 548] of the Bankruptcy Act recognize that such transactions may operate as a constructive fraud upon the debtor's innocent creditors, for they deplete the debtor's estate of valuable assets without bringing in property of similar value from which creditors' claims might be satisfied. In addition, § 67(d) recognizes that the incurring of an obligation chargeable against the debtor's property, as distinguished from the actual grant of an interest in that property, may unfairly deplete the debtor's estate if the debtor does not receive in exchange a consideration roughly equal in value to the obligation incurred. Thus, § 67(d)(2) provides in relevant part as follows:

> Every transfer made and every obligation incurred by a debtor within one year prior to the filing of a petition initiating a proceeding under this title by or against him is fraudulent (a) as to creditors existing at the time of such transfer or obligation, if made or incurred without fair consideration by a debtor who is or will be thereby rendered insolvent, without regard to his actual intent; or (b) as to then existing creditors and as to other persons who become creditors during the continuance of a business or transaction, if made or

incurred without fair consideration by a debtor who is engaged or is about to engage in such business or transaction, for which the property remaining in his hands is an unreasonably small capital, without regard to his actual intent. . . .

Section 67(d)(6) of the Act empowers the bankruptcy trustee to set aside transfers made or obligations incurred on uneconomical terms, and to recover for the benefit of creditors the value of the property removed from the debtor's estate through such transactions.

In the present case, in order to prove their claims that UMO's and USN's guarantees of the obligations of National, TWO, and Propper were constructively fraudulent, and therefore voidable under criteria set forth in '67(d)(2)(a) and (b), the trustees were required to show: (1) that USN and UMO made transfers or incurred obligations to MHT within one year of the January 1977 filings of their bankruptcy petitions, (2) that these transactions were entered into without "fair" consideration to USN and UMO, and (3) that the bankrupts were, or were rendered, insolvent or insufficiently capitalized as a result. We discuss these issues in turn.

A.   The Timing of the Transactions

Subsections 67(d)(2)(a) and (b) apply only to transfers and obligations made or incurred "within one year prior to the filing" of bankruptcy petition. . . .

USN and UMO "incurred" "obligation(s)" within the meaning of the Act when MHT loaned money to National, TWO, and Propper in December 1976. This event of course occurred within the one-year period dealt with by the statute.

B.   "Fair" Consideration

Even if the debtor has transferred property or incurred an obligation within one year of filing a bankruptcy petition, the trustee cannot set aside the transaction under § 67(d)(2), (a), (b) if the debtor received "fair" consideration for his property or obligation. "Fair" consideration under the Bankruptcy Act, which is defined in § 67(d)(1)(e), means more than just the "good and valuable" consideration needed to support a simple contract:

> (C)onsideration given for the property or obligation of a debtor is "fair" (1) when, in good faith, in exchange and as a fair equivalent therefor, property is transferred or an antecedent debt is satisfied, or (2) when such property or obligation is received in good faith to secure a present advance or antecedent debt in an amount not disproportionately small as compared with the value of the property or obligation obtained.

The reason for this requirement is obvious: if the debtor receives property or discharges or secures an antecedent debt that is substantially equivalent in value to the property given or obligation incurred by him in exchange, then the transaction has not significantly affected his estate and his creditors have no cause to complain. By the same token, however, if the benefit of the transaction to the debtor does not substantially offset its cost to him, then his creditors have suffered, and, in the language of § 67(d), the transaction was not supported by "fair" consideration.

Three-sided transactions such as those at issue here present special difficulties under the § 67(d)(1)(e) definition of fair consideration. On its face, the statute appears to sanction, as supported by "fair" consideration, a transaction in which the debtor transfers property or incurs an obligation as security for the debt of a third person, provided that the debt is "not disproportionately small" in comparison to that property or obligation. Nonetheless, if the debt secured by the transaction is not the debtor's own, then his giving of security will deplete his estate without bringing in a corresponding value from which his creditors can benefit, and his creditors will suffer just as they would if the debtor had simply made a gift of his property or obligation. Accordingly, courts have long recognized that "(t)ransfers made to benefit third parties are clearly not made for a 'fair' consideration," and, similarly, that "a conveyance by a corporation for the benefit of an affiliate (should not) be regarded as given for fair consideration as to the creditors of the conveying corporations."

The cases recognize, however, that a debtor may sometimes receive "fair" consideration even though the consideration given for his property or obligation goes initially to a third person. As we have recently stated, although "transfers solely for the benefit of third parties do not furnish fair consideration" under § 67(d)(1)(e), the transaction's benefit to the debtor "need not be direct; it may come indirectly through benefit to a third person." If the consideration given to the third person has ultimately landed in the debtor's hands, or if the giving of the consideration to the third person otherwise confers an economic benefit upon the debtor, then the debtor's net worth has been preserved, and § 67(d) has been satisfied-provided, of course, that the value of the benefit received by the debtor approximates the value of the property or obligation he has given up. For example, fair consideration has been found for an individual debtor's repayment of loans made to a corporation, where the corporation had served merely as a conduit for transferring the loan proceeds to him.

Thus the simple fact that National, TWO, and Propper, rather than USN and UMO, received the loan line advances need not compel a ruling in favor of the trustees on this point. The relationships among the Trent/Skowron firms and Propper were such that the advances to National, TWO, and Propper very likely did facilitate transfers of funds from those firms to the bank account shared by USN and UMO, benefitting each of those firms to some degree. Accordingly, the district court did not err in rejecting the trustees' argument that the corporate separateness of the loan recipients from their guarantors necessarily precluded a finding of fair consideration.

On the other hand, the district court did err in accepting MHT's argument that the existence of any indirect benefit whatever to USN and UMO from the advances to National, TWO, and Propper meant that the issuers' obligations as guarantors were necessarily supported by fair consideration. In a transfer for security, § 67(d)(1)(e) requires that the present advance or antecedent debt be "not disproportionately small as compared with the value of the property or obligation" given by the bankrupt to secure it. In a three-sided transaction such as that presented here, it is not enough merely to compare the absolute amount of the third person's debt with the amount of security given by the bankrupt. The trustee, who has the burden of proving that the transaction was "without fair consideration," could establish lack of fair consideration under § 67(d) by proving that the value of what the bankrupt actually received was disproportionately small compared to the value of what it gave. Accordingly, the court must attempt to measure the economic benefit, if any, that accrued to each bankrupt as a result of the third person's indebtedness, and it must then determine whether that benefit was "disproportionately small" when compared to the size of the security that that bankrupt gave and the obligations that it incurred.

The district court did not undertake such an analysis. The court observed that both USN and UMO "had a vital interest in inducing MHT to make ... loans to (National, TWO, and Propper)," and it stated that the issuers' "receipt of indirect benefits because of (their) affiliation and identity of interest with the direct recipients of the loans was receipt of fair consideration"; but it did not attempt to quantify the indirect benefits to either issuer or to compare those benefits with the obligations assumed by the issuers under the guarantees. Without such an analysis, it was impossible for the court to determine whether the estate of either issuer had been conserved in accordance with the principles of § 67(d), and it was therefore error for the court to conclude that those purposes had been satisfied.

Given the complexity of the transactions and relationships at issue here, we think it advisable to detail the inquiry to be pursued on remand. First, the court must attempt to determine the extent to which the December 1976 loans to National and TWO increased remittances from those firms to USN, their principal in the money order business. Next, it must attempt to determine the extent to which UMO shared in the increased remittances to USN by virtue of the pooling of the issuers' funds. Similarly, it must attempt to determine the extent to which the December 1976 loans to Propper increased remittances from Propper to UMO, and the extent to which USN shared in any such increases by virtue of the pooling arrangement. The court must then compare its estimate of the value thus received by each issuer with the magnitude of the obligation charged against that issuer under its guarantee. If the value received by either issuer is found to be disproportionately small as compared with its obligation, then, to that extent, the trustee for that issuer will have proved lack of fair consideration, and the court must proceed to consider the insolvency issue, discussed below.[1] However, if

---

1. Section 67(d)(1)(e) also requires that the consideration be given in good faith. The district court found that MHT acted in good faith. On the present record, we see no reason to disturb this finding.

either trustee fails to establish that the value is disproportionately small, the court must rule for MHT against that trustee.

In making the determinations and comparisons called for above, the court need not strive for mathematical precision. Section 67(d) requires only "fair" consideration, not a penny-for-penny exchange. At the same time, however, the court must keep the equitable purposes of the statute firmly in mind, recognizing that any significant disparity between the value received and the obligation assumed by either issuer will have significantly harmed the innocent creditors of that firm. Given the financial weakness of National and TWO revealed by the present record, it may well be that the trustees will be able to show that those firms absorbed much of the money provided them under the loan lines, remitting little or nothing to their principal, USN. Or it may be that USN received the lion's share of any remittances, perhaps even an amount properly proportionate to its obligations as guarantor, but that UMO's benefit from the loans was "disproportionately small." Of course, we leave these factual questions to the district court.

C.   Insolvency or Insufficiency of Capital

As the third principal element of their causes of action under § 67(d)(2)(a), (b), the trustees were required to show that USN and UMO were, or were rendered, insolvent or insufficiently capitalized when they incurred obligations under their guarantees in September or December 1976. Under § 67(d)(1)(d), a person is insolvent "when the present fair salable value of his property is less than the amount required to pay his debts." The statute does not define insufficiency of capital, and the amount of capital deemed sufficient under § 67(d)(2)(b) for the carrying on of a particular business will of course depend on its nature and size. [Discussion of financial status of UMO and USN omitted.]

.   .   .

We vacate the judgment of the district court and remand the matter for further consideration of the issues of fair consideration and insolvency in accordance with this opinion.

———————

QUESTIONS ABOUT RUBIN

1. Questions about the facts:
    1.1 Who was indebted to MHT?
    1.2 Who received funding from MHT?
    1.3 Who made a transfer to MHT?
    1.4 Who filed for bankruptcy?
2. Questions about the law:
    2.1 As the term "debtor" is used in the Code, who is the debtor?

2.2   Would this case be decided differently under section 548 of the Code?

3.   Do you agree with Professor Tabb's observation: "The real problem then, in cases such as intercorporate guaranties, where the value flows directly to a third party and only indirectly to the debtor, is to make the mathematical comparison between the value given and received. Often neither is readily measurable.?" Charles Jordan Tabb, The Law of Bankruptcy 615 (2d ed 2009). Do you understand his observation?

Problem 7–8: Distribution To Owners Of Business

In January 15, D Corp., which is insolvent, pays a dividend to its shareholders. On April 5, D Corp. files for bankruptcy. Can the debtor in possession recover the dividend from the shareholders under sections 548 and 550?

Problem 7–9: Proof Of Insolvency

In all of the preceding problems, the insolvency of the debtor/transferor has been assumed. In the "real world," a party invoking section 548(a)(1)(B) has to prove that the debtor transferor was "insolvent on the date that such transfer was made." What sort of evidence would a trustee introduce to establish "insolvency" on the date of the transfer? Cf. § 101(32).

Problem 7–10: LBO "Lite"

O owns 100% of the stock of D, Inc. E, a long-time employee, wants to buy D, Inc. from O for $700,000. E does not have $700,000. Nonetheless, through the following transactions, E becomes the owner of D. Inc. (1) E borrows $700,000 from C. (2) E then uses the $700,000 to pay O for O's stock so that E now owns 100% of the stock of D, Inc. (3) As owner of D, Inc., E then causes D, Inc. to borrow another $700,000 from C and grant C a mortgage on D, Inc's real property and a security interest on D, Inc's personal property to secure repayment of the second $700,000 loan. (4) D, Inc. then loans the $700,000 obtained from C in (3) to E. (5) E uses this $700,000 to repay his loan in (1) from C. D, Inc. files for bankruptcy less than two years after (1). Is there a section 548 fraudulent transfer? If so, which transfer? And, if there is a section 548 fraudulent transfer, what can the bankruptcy trustee recover from whom?

MOODY v. SECURITY PACIFIC
BUSINESS CREDIT, INC.

971 F.2d 1056 (3d Cir. 1992)

SCIRICA, Circuit Judge.

This bankruptcy case requires us to address, once again, the application of the fraudulent conveyance laws to a failed leveraged buyout. This case raises several questions about the application of this Act to the failed leveraged buyout of Jeannette Corporation.

On July 31, 1981, a group of investors acquired Jeannette in a leveraged buyout. Less than a year and a half later, Jeannette, which had been profitable for many years, was forced into bankruptcy. The bankruptcy trustee brought this action to set aside the advances made and obligations incurred in connection with the acquisition. The trustee alleges that the leveraged buyout constitutes a fraudulent conveyance under the UFCA and is voidable under the Bankruptcy Code. After a bench trial, the district court entered judgment for defendants. We will affirm.

Founded in 1898, Jeannette Corporation manufactured and sold glass, ceramic, china, plastic, and candle houseware products in the United States and Canada. For many years, Jeannette was a profitable enterprise.

In 1978, the Coca–Cola Bottling Company of New York, Inc. acquired Jeannette for $39.6 million.

In late 1979, Coca–Cola decided to sell Jeannette and focus attention on its core bottling business. In June 1981, John P. Brogan expressed an interest in acquiring Jeannette. Brogan was affiliated with a small group of investors in the business of acquiring companies through leveraged buyouts, the hallmark feature of which is the exchange of equity for debt.[2] On July 22, 1981, Coca–Cola agreed to sell Jeannette for $12.1 million on condition that Brogan complete the transaction by the end of the month. Brogan contacted Security Pacific Business Credit Inc., a lending group that had financed one of his prior acquisitions, about obtaining financing. He submitted one year of monthly projections, based in large part on Jeannette's 80-page business plan for 1981, which showed that Jeannette would have sufficient working capital under the proposed financing arrangement in the year following the acquisition. Before agreeing to finance the transaction, however, Security Pacific undertook its own investigation of Jeannette. Security Pacific assigned this task to credit analyst Stephen Ngan. Based on his discussions with Jeannette personnel and a review of the company's financial records, Ngan made his own set of projections. He concluded that Jeannette would earn a pre-tax profit of $800,000 after interest expenses in its first year of operation, and recom-

---

2. As this court recently explained: A leveraged buyout refers to the acquisition of a company ("target corporation") in which a substantial portion of the purchase price paid for the stock of the target corporation is borrowed and where the loan is secured by the target corporation's assets. Commonly, the acquirer invests little or no equity. Thus, a fundamental feature of leveraged buyouts is that equity is exchanged for debt.

mended that Security Pacific finance the acquisition. He thought Jeannette was a "well-established" company with "a good track record for growth and earnings."

After reviewing Ngan's recommendation, together with an inventory report, the 1978 appraisal of Jeannette's PP & E, Brogan's projections, and a 55-page report on Jeannette prepared by another bank, Security Pacific decided to finance the acquisition. At that point, Coca–Cola formally approved the sale of Jeannette to J. Corp., which had been incorporated for the purpose of acquiring Jeannette.

The acquisition of Jeannette was consummated on July 31, 1981. J. Corp. purchased Jeannette with funds from a $15.5 million line of credit Security Pacific extended Jeannette secured by first lien security interests on all Jeannette's assets. J. Corp. never repaid Jeannette any portion of, or executed a promissory note for, the amount ($11.7 million) Security Pacific initially forwarded to J. Corp. on behalf of Jeannette to finance the acquisition. Other than new management, the only benefit Jeannette received was access to credit from Security Pacific.[3]

As with most leveraged buyouts, the acquisition left Jeannette's assets fully encumbered by the security interests held by Security Pacific. Jeannette could not dispose of its assets, except in the ordinary course of business, without the consent of Security Pacific, and was prohibited from granting security interests to anyone else. As a result, Jeannette's sole source of working capital after the transaction was its line of credit with Security Pacific.

Although Jeannette's performance initially tracked expectations, its financial condition deteriorated steadily in 1982. Jeannette experienced a shrinking domestic glassware market, a marked increase in foreign competition, dramatic price slashing and inventory dumping by its domestic competitors, and a continued nationwide recession. In January 1982, orders for Jeannette products fell to 86% of projected levels and in February orders fell to 70%.

On October 4, 1982, an involuntary bankruptcy petition was filed under Chapter 7 of the Bankruptcy Code.

On September 22, 1983, plaintiff James Moody, the trustee of the bankruptcy estate of Jeannette, filed this action in federal district court

---

3. The transaction comprised the following steps, which were deemed by the parties to have taken place at once: (1) J. Corp. entered into an agreement with Coca–Cola and KNY Development Corporation, a wholly owned subsidiary of Coca–Cola, to purchase all outstanding stock of Jeannette; (2) J. Corp. obtained a $12.1 million unsecured loan from Security Pacific and executed a demand note therefor; (3) these funds were transferred from Security Pacific to Coca–Cola to fund the purchase of Jeannette stock, which was transferred from KNY Development to J. Corp.; (4) upon acquisition of the stock, J. Corp. appointed a new board of directors for Jeannette and named Brogan chairman; (5) Jeannette entered into a $15.5 million revolving credit arrangement with Security Pacific, in exchange for which it granted Security Pacific first lien security interests in all its assets; (5) on behalf of Jeannette, Brogan directed Security Pacific to remit $11.7 million from the revolving credit facility to J. Corp., which was used to repay all but $400,000 of the demand note to Security Pacific; and (6) Jeannette and Security Pacific entered into a "lock box" agreement, whereby Jeannette's accounts receivable would be forwarded to the Mellon Bank and credited against the outstanding balance on Jeannette's line of credit.

against defendants Security Pacific, Coca-Cola, KNY Development, J. Corp., M-K Candle, Brogan, and other individuals. He alleges that the leveraged buyout constitutes a fraudulent conveyance under the UFCA, 39 Pa.Cons.Stat.Ann. §§ 354–57, and is voidable under § 544(b) of the Bankruptcy Code, 11 U.S.C. § 544(b).[5] After a bench trial, the district court made findings of fact and conclusions of law and entered judgment for defendants.

According to the district court, the leveraged buyout was not intentionally fraudulent because it was "abundantly clear" that defendants expected the transaction to succeed and hoped to profit from it. Likewise, although the leveraged buyout was made for less than fair consideration to Jeannette, the district court held that it was not constructively fraudulent.

Because the leveraged buyout was made for less than fair consideration, the district court placed on defendants the burden of proving solvency by clear and convincing evidence. The court, however, concluded that defendants met this burden. Jeannette was not rendered insolvent in the "bankruptcy sense" because the "present fair salable value" of Jeannette's assets immediately after the leveraged buyout exceeded total liabilities by at least $1–2 million. In making this determination, the district court valued assets on a going concern basis.

Nor was Jeannette rendered insolvent in the "equity sense" or left with an unreasonably small capital. Based on the parties' projections, which it found "reasonable and prudent when made," and the availability on Jeannette's line of credit with Security Pacific, the district court found that Jeannette was not left with an unreasonably small capital after the acquisition. Rather than a lack of capital, the district court attributed Jeannette's demise to intense foreign and domestic competition, a continued recession, and, to a lesser degree, mismanagement, which led to a drastic decline in sales beginning in early 1982.

The UFCA proscribes both intentional and constructive fraud. Under the Act's intentional fraud provisions, any conveyance made or obligation incurred either without fair consideration by one who "intends or believes that he will incur debts beyond his ability to pay as they mature," or with an "actual intent ... to hinder, delay, or defraud ... creditors" is fraudulent. Actual intent to defraud may be inferred from the circumstances surrounding a transfer.

---

5. Section 544(b) of the Bankruptcy Code provides that "[t]he trustee may avoid any transfer of an interest of the debtor in property or any obligation incurred by the debtor that is voidable under applicable law by a creditor holding an unsecured claim ..." 11 U.S.C. § 544(b) (emphasis added). The "applicable law" here is the UFCA, and it is clear that there is an unsecured creditor into whose shoes plaintiff trustee may step. Plaintiff also alleges that the leveraged buyout is voidable under the fraudulent conveyance provisions of the Bankruptcy Code, 11 U.S.C. § 548. After concluding that the transaction did not constitute a fraudulent conveyance under the UFCA, however, the district court summarily rejected these claims. It reasoned that, because the fraudulent conveyance provisions of the Bankruptcy Code are modeled after and typically interpreted in conjunction with those of the UFCA, it follows that if the leveraged buyout is not fraudulent under the UFCA, it is not fraudulent under § 548 of the Bankruptcy Code.

The UFCA's constructive fraud provisions operate without regard to intent. Under § 4, any conveyance made or obligation incurred "by a person who is or will be thereby rendered insolvent" is fraudulent if it is made or incurred for less than fair consideration. Insolvency has two components under Pennsylvania law: insolvency in the "bankruptcy sense" (a deficit net worth immediately after the conveyance), and insolvency in the "equity sense" (an inability to pay debts as they mature). Fair consideration requires a "good faith" exchange of "a fair equivalent."

Under § 5, any conveyance made or obligation incurred by a person engaged in "a business or transaction" is fraudulent if it is made or incurred without fair consideration and leaves that person with an "unreasonably small capital." The relationship between "insolvency" under § 4 of the UFCA and "unreasonably small capital" under § 5 is not clear. However, as we discuss below, the better view would seem to be that "unreasonably small capital" denotes a financial condition short of equitable insolvency. The UFCA's constructive fraud provisions furnish a standard of causation that attempts to link the challenged conveyance with the debtor's bankruptcy.

At first, the applicability of the UFCA's fraudulent conveyance provisions to leveraged buyouts was a matter of some dispute. However, we think it settled, as a general matter at least, that the fraudulent conveyance provisions of the UFCA extend to leveraged buyouts, and defendants do not contest their applicability here.

Because of the difficulty in proving intentional fraud, challenges to leveraged buyouts tend to be predicated on the constructive fraud provisions of the UFCA.

With these general principles in mind, we turn now to an analysis of the leveraged buyout of Jeannette under the constructive and then intentional fraud provisions of the UFCA.

According to the district court, the leveraged buyout was without fair consideration to Jeannette because, in exchange for granting Security Pacific security interests in all its assets and undertaking an $11.7 million demand obligation at 3 1/4% above prime, all Jeannette received was new management and access to credit. Defendants do not challenge this finding, and we accept it for purposes of our analysis here.

We turn now to the thrust of plaintiff's attack, the district court's solvency and adequacy of capital analyses. As we have discussed, under § 4 of the UFCA a conveyance is fraudulent if it is made without fair consideration and renders the transferor insolvent. "A person is insolvent when the present, fair, salable value of his assets is less than the amount that will be required to pay his probable liability on his existing debts as they become absolute and matured." The Pennsylvania Supreme Court has interpreted this provision as requiring solvency in both the "bankruptcy" and "equity" sense. Insolvency is determined "as of the time of the conveyance."

The district court valued Jeannette's assets on a going concern basis and found that immediately after the leveraged buyout the present fair salable value of Jeannette's total assets was at least $26.2–$27.2 million. It then found that the company's total liabilities were $25.2 million. Thus, the district court concluded that Jeannette was solvent in the bankruptcy sense "by at least $1–2 million and most probably by more."

At trial, plaintiff argued that Jeannette was rendered insolvent in the bankruptcy sense because the present fair salable value of Jeannette's total assets could not have exceeded the $12.1 million J. Corp. paid for Jeannette's stock. The district court rejected this argument and undertook its own valuation of Jeannette's assets. We find no error here. Although purchase price may be highly probative of a company's value immediately after a leveraged buyout, it is not the only evidence. The parties here viewed the $12.1 million purchase price as a "significant bargain," made possible by Coca–Cola's decision to focus attention on its bottling business and Brogan's ability to close the deal quickly.

Plaintiff argues that valuation on a going concern basis fails to give effect to "present" in the UFCA's "present fair salable value" language, and the district court should have calculated the amount the company would have received had it attempted to liquidate its PP & E on the date of the acquisition or immediately thereafter. We disagree. Where bankruptcy is not "clearly imminent" on the date of the challenged conveyance, the weight of authority holds that assets should be valued on a going concern basis.

Accordingly, we conclude that the district court did not err in finding that Jeannette was solvent in the bankruptcy sense after the leveraged buyout.

Next, we look at whether the leveraged buyout either rendered Jeannette insolvent in the equity sense or left it with an unreasonably small capital. Although it recognized that these issues were "conceptually distinct," the district court considered them together. Plaintiff contends this was improper because "unreasonably small capital" denotes a financial condition short of equitable insolvency.

As we have discussed, under § 5 of the UFCA any conveyance made or obligation incurred by a person engaged in "a business or transaction" is fraudulent if it is made or incurred without fair consideration and leaves that person with an "unreasonably small capital." Unlike "insolvency," "unreasonably small capital" is not defined by the UFCA. This has engendered confusion over the relationship between these concepts: some courts have equated a finding of equitable insolvency with that of unreasonably small capital, whereas others have said that unreasonably small capital encompasses financial difficulties short of equitable insolvency.

We believe the better view is that unreasonably small capital denotes a financial condition short of equitable insolvency.

We think it telling that having adopted § 4 of the UFCA, which proscribes conveyances made without fair consideration that render the debtor "insolvent," the drafters saw fit to add § 5, which proscribes conveyances made without fair consideration that leave the debtor with an "unreasonably small capital." If the drafters viewed these concepts interchangeably, one would expect them to have employed the same language.

In undertaking its adequacy of capital analysis, the district court focused on the reasonableness of the parties' projections, but also considered the availability on Jeannette's line of credit with Security Pacific. It found the parties' projections reasonable and, based on the availability of credit as well as the company's historical cash flow needs, determined that Jeannette was not left with an unreasonably small capital under the circumstances. Rather than a lack of capital, the district court attributed Jeannette's demise to the "substantial drop in orders and sales that began in 1982," which it attributed in turn to increased foreign and domestic competition and the continued recession.

Because projections tend to be optimistic, their reasonableness must be tested by an objective standard anchored in the company's actual performance. Among the relevant data are cash flow, net sales, gross profit margins, and net profits and losses. However, reliance on historical data alone is not enough. To a degree, parties must also account for difficulties that are likely to arise, including interest rate fluctuations and general economic downturns, and otherwise incorporate some margin for error.

Defendants here relied on two sets of one-year projections, one prepared by Brogan and the other by Ngan. Brogan's projections were based on a month-by-month analysis of Jeannette's balance sheet, income statement, and resulting credit availability. Ngan's projections were grounded in his interviews with Jeannette personnel and examination of the company's financial records for the year and a half preceding the acquisition. The district court found these projections reasonable and prudent when made. We agree.

The district court properly found that Jeannette's failure was caused by a dramatic drop in sales due to increased foreign and domestic competition, rather than a lack of capital. Plaintiff plausibly contends that defendants should have anticipated some of these problems and incorporated a margin for error. But we cannot say the district court erred in finding that the drastic decline in sales was unforeseeable as of the date of the leveraged buyout. Therefore, we conclude that the district court properly determined that the leveraged buyout did not leave Jeannette with an unreasonably small capital.

Because we assume the notion of unreasonably small capital denotes a financial condition short of equitable insolvency, it follows that the transaction did not render Jeannette equitably insolvent either. And because the leveraged buyout neither left Jeannette with an unreasonably small capital nor rendered it equitably insolvent, we agree with the district court that the acquisition does not constitute a fraudulent conveyance under either §§ 4 or 5 of the UFCA.

All that remains to be decided is whether the district court properly determined that the leveraged buyout did not violate the UFCA's intentional fraud provisions. As we have discussed, a conveyance is intentionally fraudulent if it is made either without fair consideration by one who "intends or believes that he will incur debts beyond his ability to pay as they mature," or with an "actual intent . . . to hinder, delay, or defraud either present or future creditors."

The district court found that "defendants did not know or believe that Jeannette's creditors could not be paid, and did not intend to hinder, defraud, or delay creditors." This conclusion followed from the absence of any direct evidence of fraud, as well as defendants' profit motives, the parties' awareness of the transaction's leveraged nature, and Jeannette's operation as a going concern for at least five months following the acquisition.

We conclude, then, that the district court properly held that the leveraged buyout was not intentionally fraudulent.

In sum, we will affirm the district court's conclusions that the leveraged buyout does not constitute a fraudulent conveyance under either the constructive or intentional fraud provisions of the UFCA.

QUESTIONS ABOUT *MOODY*

1. Why does *Moody* focus on section 544(b) instead of section 548? Why does *Moody* discuss provisions of the UFCA?

2. Footnote 3 provides a helpful summary of the various transactions. Both section 548 and section 544(b) refer to a "transfer." What is the transfer that the trustee alleges is voidable under section 544(b)?

3. What is the basis for the courts statement "the leveraged buyout was made for less than fair consideration"? Did Coca-Cola get fair consideration? Is that relevant? Did Jeannette get fair consideration when it entered into a $15.5 million revolving credit arrangement with Security Pacific?

4. In Boyer v. Crown Stock Distribution, Inc., 587 F.3d 787, 791–92 (7th Cir. 2009), Judge Posner provides the following analysis of LBO's: "In a conventional LBO, an investor buys the stock of a corporation from the stockholders with the proceeds of a loan secured by the corporation's own assets. It follows that if all the assets are still fully secured when the corporation declares bankruptcy, the unsecured creditors cannot satisfy any part of their claims from a sale of the assets. . . .

Should the acquired company be doomed to go broke after and because of the LBO—if the burden of debt created by the transaction was so heavy that the corporation had no reasonable prospect of surviving—the payment to the shareholders by the buyer of the corporation is deemed a fraudulent conveyance because in exchange for the money the shareholders received they provided no value to the corporation but merely increased its debt and by doing so pushed it over the brink. A corporate transfer is 'fraudulent' within the meaning of the Uniform Fraudulent Transfer Act, even if there is no fraudulent intent, if the corporation didn't receive "reasonably equivalent value" in return for the transfer and as a result was left with insufficient assets to have a reasonable chance of surviving indefinitely.

Some courts have been reluctant to apply the Act as written to leveraged buyouts.... They may also agree with the scholars who have argued that many LBOs are welfare-enhancing transactions because by making the managers owners (managers are often the buyers in an LBO) and thus fusing ownership with control, an LBO increases the managers' incentive to operate the corporation with a view to maximizing its value rather than their salaries and perks. These scholars also argue that devices that facilitate transfers of corporate control increase the mobility of capital.

LBOs, ... can indeed have redeeming economic value when the corporation is publicly held and the managers have a low equity stake prior to the transaction. In a publicly held corporation there is a separation of ownership from control, and the managers may use their control to manage the company in a way that will increase their personal wealth rather than maximize the profits of the corporation; the conflict of interest is eliminated by making the managers the owners. But this rationale for an LBO is missing from this case because both old and new Crown were closely held corporations. And while the economic literature also argues that the increased risk of bankruptcy that an LBO creates concentrates the minds of the managers (just as, according to Samuel Johnson, the prospect of being hanged concentrates the mind of the condemned person), this is hard to take seriously in the present case; for the owner-manager had only a $500 stake in the company.

But the critical difference between the LBO in this case and a bona fide LBO is that this LBO was *highly* likely to plunge the company into bankruptcy. There was scant probability that the transaction would increase the firm's value; on the contrary, it left the firm with so few assets that it would have had to be extremely lucky to survive." How would Judge Posner have decided *Moody*?

5. What is the difference between insolvency in the bankruptcy sense and insolvency in the equity sense? How would the trustee prove that Jeannette was insolvent in the bankruptcy sense? Insolvent in the equity sense? What does the court mean by the statement "unreasonably small capital denotes a financial condition short of equitable insolvency"?

6. "Those who structure LBO's work tirelessly to avoid the provisions of section 548 and the UFTA. To a large degree, these efforts, at least insofar as they apply to reasonably equivalent value, have been unsuccessful, It is very difficult to convince a court that new or rejuvenated management constitutes a measurable, reasonably equivalent value. * * * More important as a defense to fraudulent conveyance attack is ensuring that when the transaction is complete, the leveraged entity is not left insolvent or with unreasonably small

capital." Jeff Ferriell & Edward J. Janger, *UNDERSTANDING BANKRUPTCY* 596 (2d ed. 2007) Do you agree with the last sentence of this excerpt?

11 U.S.C. § 544(b)—State Fraudulent Conveyance Law in Bankruptcy

(b)(1) Except as provided in paragraph (2), the trustee may avoid any transfer of an interest of the debtor in property or any obligation incurred by the debtor that is voidable under applicable law by a creditor holding an unsecured claim that is allowable under section 502 of this title or that is not allowable only under section 502(e) of this title.

Problem 7–11: Transfers More Than Two Years Before Bankruptcy

D, <u>while insolvent</u>, transfers Greenacre to T for less than reasonably equivalent value. Three years later, D files for bankruptcy. Can the trustee avoid the transfer of Greenacre? What additional information do you need?

Problem 7–12: Payment Of A Debt And Fraudulent Transfer Law

D is insolvent and unable to pay all of its creditors which include A, B and C. C obtains a judgment against D. Before C is able to levy on and sell Ds assets, D sells its assets to X at a reasonable price and uses the proceeds from this sale to pay creditors A and B, but not creditor C. If D files for bankruptcy six months later, what, if anything, can the bankruptcy trustee do? See §§ 548(d)(2)(A), 547.

Looking back at the material on fraudulent transfers, the essence of an argument that a transfer is a fraudulent transfer avoidable under section 548 or section 544(b) is that stuff (i.e., an interest of the debtor in property) that but for the transfer would be property of the estate was transferred before bankruptcy (1) to someone who is almost always not a creditor (2) for less than reasonably equivalent value so that ALL creditors got less.

Looking ahead to the material on preferential transfers, the essence of an argument that a transfer is avoidable under section 547 is that "stuff" that but for the transfer would be property of the estate was transferred before bankruptcy (1) to someone who was a creditor (2) for a prior debt so that creditor got more but all OTHER creditors got less.

C. INCREASING PROPERTY OF THE ESTATE BY AVOIDING PREFERENTIAL TRANSFERS

As we have just seen, the Code provisions relating to fraudulent transfers are very similar to state statutes. As we will now see, the Code provisions relating to preferential transfers are different from both (i) the Code fraudulent conveyance provision and (ii) state statutes.

In looking for a fraudulent transfer, we looked for what the debtor/transferor received—we were concerned that a transferee who was not a creditor benefitted from the transfer to the disadvantage of creditors generally. In looking for a preference, we will look at to whom the transfer was made rather than what the debtor/transferor received for the transfer, and we will be concerned about whether one creditor transferee benefitted from a transfer to the disadvantage of other similar creditors.

There is no state law counterpart to the Code's preference provisions. State creditors rights law does not "condemn" a preference.[6] Outside of bankruptcy, a debtor, even an insolvent debtor, can treat some creditors more favorably than other similar creditors. Although D owes X, Y, and Z $1,000 each, D can pay X in full before paying Y or Z anything.

Bankruptcy law *does* "condemn" *certain* preferences. A House report that accompanied a draft of the Code explained the rationale for such a bankruptcy policy as follows:

> The purpose of the preference section is two-fold. First, by permitting the trustee to avoid pre-bankruptcy transfers that occur within a short period before bankruptcy, creditors are discouraged from racing to the courthouse to dismember the debtor during his slide into bankruptcy. The protection thus afforded the debtor often enables him to work his way out of a difficult financial situation through cooperation with all of his creditors. Second, and more important, the preference provisions facilitate the prime bankruptcy policy of equality of distribution among creditors of the debtor. Any creditor that received a greater payment than others of his class is required to disgorge so that all may share equally.

H. REP. NO. 595, 95TH CONG., 1st Sess. 117–18 (1977).

1. REQUIREMENTS FOR A PREFERENCE

Section 547(b) sets out an initial unnumbered requirement of a "transfer of an interest of the debtor in property" and then five additional numbered requirements. Looking to the numbered requirements, the bankruptcy trustee may void a transfer of property of the debtor if she can establish:

---

6. Some state statutes void certain transfers because of their preferential character. The trustee may take advantage of such statutes by virtue of his powers under section 544(b): if the state anti-preference provision protects any actual creditor with an allowable claim, it protects the bankruptcy trustee. under section 544(b).

- first, the transfer was "to or for the benefit of a creditor"; *and*

- second, the transfer was made for or on account of an "antecedent debt", i.e., a debt owed prior to the time of the transfer; *and*

- third, the debtor was insolvent at the time of the transfer; *and*

- fourth, the transfer was made within 90 days before the date of the filing of the bankruptcy petition, *or*, was made between 90 days and 1 year before the date of the filing of the petition to an "insider"; *and*

- fifth, the transfer has the effect of increasing the amount that the transferee would receive in a Chapter 7 case.

The first two numbered requirements of section 547(b) will usually be easy to apply. To illustrate, a true gift is not a preference—not to or for the benefit of a creditor. A pledge of stock to secure a new loan is not a preferential transfer—not for or on account of antecedent debt.

The third numbered requirement or element—insolvency of the debtor at the time of the transfer—requires a showing that debts exceed assets at fair valuation, 11 U.S.C. § 101(32). At first blush, this would seem to present significant problems of proof. Proving insolvency requires establishing the value[7] of the assets and the the amount of the debts as of the time of the transfer.[8]

Proof of insolvency for the limited purpose of establishing that a pre-bankruptcy transfer is a section 547(b) preference has been made much easier under the Bankruptcy Code by section 547(f) which creates a rebuttable presumption[9] of insolvency for the 90 days immediately preceding the filing of the bankruptcy petition.

Section 547(b)(4) establishes the preference period as 90 days, or one year for an insider. In determining whether the transfer was made within 90 days of the filing of the petition, look to Federal Rule of Civil Procedure 6(a) which provides that the day on which the transfer occurred is not included.[10] In determining whether the transfer was made to an "insider" so that the relevant time period is 1 year, not merely 90 days, look to Code section 101(31)'s explanation of who is an "insider."

---

7. Courts generally have valued assets at so-called "fair value" or "intrinsic value"—what a willing buyer would pay a willing seller within a reasonable time.

8. Note that under Section 101(32) exempt property is not considered as an asset in determining solvency. The result is that many consumers are insolvent in the bankruptcy sense.

9. The Federal Rules of Evidence are incorporated by sections 251 and 252 of Title II of the Bankruptcy Reform Act of 1978. Rule 301 of the Federal Rules of Evidence provides:

A presumption imposes on the party against whom it is directed the burden of going forward with the evidence to rebut or meet the presumption, but does not shift to such party the burden of proof in the sense of the risk of nonpersuasion, which remains throughout the trial upon the party on whom it was originally cast.

10. If under state law, a transfer is not fully effective against third parties until public notice of the transfer has been given and such public notice is not timely given, then section 547(e) deems the transfer to have occurred at the time public notice was given. The use of section 547 to invalidate transfers not recorded in a timely fashion is considered infra.

Remember that the presumption of insolvency for the limited purpose of section 547 is limited to the 90 days immediately preceding the bankruptcy petition. Accordingly, in order to invalidate as a preference a transfer that occurred more than 90 days before the filing of the bankruptcy petition the trustee must establish both that the transferee was an "insider" and the debtor was insolvent at the time of the transfer.

Section 547(b)'s fifth numbered element essentially tests whether the transfer enabled the creditor/transferee to get more than she would have received if (a) the transfer had taken place and (b) the case was a Chapter 7 case. This fifth element is generally satisfied unless (i) the creditor/transferee has a claim secured by property worth more than the amount of its claim or (ii) the creditor/transferee has a secured claim and all that is transferred to it is part or all of the collateral that secured the claim or (iii) the estate is sufficiently large to pay all unsecured claims in full.

In (i), (ii), and (iii) above,, a prebankruptcy transfer does not result in the creditor/transferee receiving more than she would have received in a Chapter 7 case if the transfer had not been made. The creditor/transferee is simply receiving earlier what she ultimately would have received in the Chapter 7 case. Earlier is not "more" for purposes of section 547(b)(5).

11 U.S.C. § 547(b), (f), (g)

(b) Except as provided in subsection (c) of this section, the trustee may avoid any transfer of an interest of the debtor in property—

(1) to or for the benefit of a creditor;

(2) for or on account of an antecedent debt owed by the debtor before such transfer was made;

(3) made while the debtor was insolvent;

(4) made—

(A) on or within 90 days before the date of the filing of the petition; or

(B) between ninety days and one year before the date of the filing of the petition, if such creditor at the time of such transfer was an insider; and

(5) that enables such creditor to receive more than such creditor would receive if—

(A) the case were a case under chapter 7 of this title;

(B) the transfer had not been made; and

(C) such creditor received payment of such debt to the extent provided by the provisions of this title. . . .

(f) For the purposes of this section, the debtor is presumed to have been insolvent on and during the 90 days immediately preceding the date of the filing of the petition.

(g) For the purposes of this section, the trustee has the burden of proving the avoidability of a transfer under subsection (b) of this section, and the creditor or party in interest against whom recovery or avoidance is sought has the burden of proving the nonavoidability of a transfer under subsection (c) of this section.

———————

Problem 7–13: "Interest Of The Debtor In Property"

Bubba is in default on his payment obligations to 26 different creditors: A to Z. On January 15, Bubba's, mother, Momma, pays $3,300 to C, one of Bubba's creditors. Neither Momma nor Bubba pays any of the other creditors. On April 5, Bubba files a bankruptcy petition. Is the January 15 payment a section 547(b) preference?

———————

Problem 7–14: An "Earmarked Loan"

Same facts as 7–13 above except Momma was unable to find C, and so she gave the $3,300 to Bubba with the specific direction to Bubba to use that $3,300 only to pay C. Bubba did indeed pay the $3,300 to C. Is the payment to C a section 547(b) preference?

———————

Problem 7–15: Another "Earmarked Loan"

D Corp. is in debt to 26 different creditors, from A Bank to Z Supplies. A Bank, D's largest creditor, makes an additional $330,000 loan to D Corp. to be used to pay Z Supplies so that Z Supplies will continue to supply D Corp. The D Corp./A Bank loan agreement expressly provides that D Corp. will use the loan proceeds only to pay Z Supplies. D Corp. does indeed use the $330,000 loaned by A Bank to pay Z Supplies. Eighty days later, D Corp. files for bankruptcy. Is the $330,000 payment to Z Supplies a preference?

———————

Problem 7–16: "Enable Such Creditor To Receive More" And Unsecured Creditors

1. D owes $100,000 to X and hundreds of thousands of dollars to other unsecured creditors. On January 15, D makes a $15,000 payment to X. D does not make a payment to any other creditors. On April 5, D files for Chapter 11 bankruptcy. If "the case were a case under Chapter 7 "and" "the transfer had not been made" holders of unsecured claims would be paid 15% from D's bankruptcy. Why was the $15,000 payment to X a section 547(b) preference?

2.   D owes $100,000 to X and hundreds of thousands of dollars to other unsecured creditors. On January 15, D grants X a first mortgage on Black-acre, property valued at $15,000. D does not make any transfers to any other unsecured creditors. On April 5, D files for Chapter 11 bankruptcy. If "the case were a case under chapter 7" and "if the transfer had not been made" holders of unsecured claims would be paid 15% from D's bankruptcy. Was the January 15th mortgage a section 547(b) preference?

Problem 7–17: "Enable Such Creditor To Receive More: And Fully Secured Claims"

D owes S $600,000. The debt to S is secured by a first mortgage on Greenacre, real property owned by D that is valued at $800,000. On January 15, D pays S $300,000. On April 5, D files a bankruptcy petition. Was the $300,000 payment to S a section 547(b) preferential transfer? What, if any, additional information do you need to answer this question?

Problem 7–18: "Enable Such Creditor To Receive More: And A Partly Secured Claim"

1.   D owes C $100,000. C has a first lien on collateral worth $60,000. D surrenders the collateral to C, and C reduces the debt from $100,000 to $40,000. Two months later, D files for bankruptcy. Was the transfer of the collateral to C a preference?

2.   D owes C $100, 000. C has a first lien on collateral worth $60,000. D pays C $30,000. Two months later, D files for bankruptcy. If "the case were a case under chapter 7" and "the transfer had not been made", holders of unsecured claims would receive 10% of their claims. Was the payment of $30,000 to C a preference?

3.   D owes C $100,000. C has a first lien on collateral worth $60,000. D pays C $50,000. Two months later, D files for bankruptcy. If "the case were a case under Chapter 7" and "the transfer had not been made", holders of unsecured claims would receive 10% of their claims. How much of the $50,000 payment to C was a preference?

The next case provides a review of the elements of a preference.

IN RE PYSZ

2008 WL 2001753 (Bkrtcy.D.N.H.)
United States Bankruptcy Court, D. New Hampshire

VAUGHN, Chief Judge.

The Court has before it the motion for summary judgment pursuant to 11 U.S.C. § 547(b) filed by Andrew E. Pysz (the "Debtor") and Lawrence P. Sumski, as Chapter 13 trustee (together, the "Plaintiffs"), and James M. Hawkins' (the "Defendant") objection thereto. The Defendant is the holder of a judicial lien in the amount of $43,723.14. This lien arose from a post-judgment attachment the Defendant obtained in the Sullivan County Superior Court. The Superior Court entered a judgment for unpaid professional services in favor of the Defendant against the Debtor and subsequently issued a writ of attachment on January 18, 2007. The attachment was on certain logging equipment and real property located at 415 E. Mountain Road in Newport (the "Newport Property") belonging to the Debtor. On January 19, 2007, the Defendant recorded the attachment in the Sullivan County Register of Deeds. The Debtor owns a fifty percent interest in the Newport Property, and his mother owns the other fifty percent interest.

On April 5, 2007, the Debtor filed for protection under chapter 13 of the Bankruptcy Code. In his schedules, the Debtor lists the Newport Property's fair market value as $300,000. The Defendant offered a separate appraisal report that values the Newport Property at $443,000 as of April 5, 2007.

Discussion

The Plaintiffs move for summary judgment seeking to avoid the Defendant's judicial lien as a preference under 11 U.S.C. § 547(b). * * *

Section 547(b) provides:

Except as provided in subsections (c) and (i) of this section, the trustee may avoid any transfer of an interest of the debtor in property-

(1) to or for the benefit of a creditor;

(2) for or on account of an antecedent debt owed by the debtor before such transfer was made;

(3) made while the debtor was insolvent;

(4) made—

(A) on or within 90 days before the date of the filing of the petition; or

(B) between ninety days and one year before the date of the filing of the petition, if such creditor at the time of such transfer was an insider; and

(5) that enables such creditor to receive more than such creditor would receive if—

(A) the case were a case under chapter 7 of this title;

(B) the transfer had not been made; and

(C) Such creditor received payment of such debt to the extent provided by the provisions of this title.

11 U.S.C. § 547(b). "[T]he trustee has the burden of proving the avoidability of a transfer under subsection (b) of this section[.]" *Id.* § 547(g).

First, there is no issue that the obtainment of the attachment was a transfer of the Debtor's interest in property. [section 101(54)(A) "The term 'transfer' means (A) the creation of a lien"] Second, three of the five elements required to avoid a transfer under section 547(b) are unequivocally present here. It is undisputed that the subject lien was for the benefit of a creditor. It is also undisputed that the subject lien was for or on account of an antecedent debt. Finally, the attachment occurred during the ninety-day preference period. The Defendant obtained and recorded the writ of attachment on January 18th and 19th, respectively, in 2007, and the Debtor filed his voluntary petition on April 5, 2007. As such, the issues in this preference action are whether the Debtor was insolvent at the time of the attachment and whether the Defendant would receive more with the judicial lien than he would without the lien in a Chapter 7 case.

A. *Insolvency under Section 547(b)(3)*

The term "insolvent" means "financial condition such that the sum of such entity's debts is greater than all of such entity's property, at a fair valuation[,]" excluding property that may be exempt under section 522. 11 U.S.C. § 101(32)(A). "For the purposes of this section, the debtor is presumed to have been insolvent on and during the 90 days immediately preceding the date of the filing of the petition." *Id.*§ 547(f). The creditor bears the burden of overcoming this presumption.

The Defendant attempts to rebut this presumption by alleging that the fair market value of the Newport Property is $443,000 ..... [The following is a balance sheet of the Debtor's assets and liabilities, which incorporates the Defendant's fair market value for the Newport Property.]

ASSETS		LIABILITIES	
Newport Property	$443,000	Lake Sunapee Bank	$166,516
Cash	$500	Bank of NH 2002 Chevy 4x4	$14,000
Household Goods	$1,000	Capital One Auto Finance 2005 Chevy 4x4	$21,850
Wearing Apparel	$2,000	Capital One Auto Finance 2002 Escalade	$14,179
Fishing Equipment	$100	Internal Revenue Service	$11,253
2006 Federal Tax Refund	$4,172	Schedule F Debt	$126,044
2005 Chevy 4x4	$23,075	DSO	$3,175
2002 Chevy 4x4	$12,000	Town of Newport	$12,042
2002 Cadillac Escalade	$20,000	Creative Capital Arrearage	$12,555
1970 One–Ton Truck	$1,200	**Total Liabilities:**	**$381,614**
Computer & Desk	$1,000		
10 Chainsaws and MISC Hand Tools	$6,000		
1997 Timberjack 240 Skidder	$3,500		
Dog	$100		
Subtotal	$517,647		
Less the Mother's 50% interest in the Newport Property[1]	$126,242		

---

1. The Court derived the mother's interest in the Newport Property by dividing the net equity in the Newport Property ($252,484) by two ($126,242). The Court determined the net equity by subtracting the total liens, not including the Defendant's judicial lien, from the Defendant's proposed fair market value of the Property ($443,000–$190,516). The liens comprising the

Less Homestead Exemption	$100,000
Less Personal Property Exemptions[2]	–20,000

Total Assets: $271,405

As indicated above, the Debtor's liabilities exceed his assets. Thus, the Court finds that the Defendant fails to rebut the presumption, and the Debtor was insolvent during the ninety days preceding his bankruptcy in accordance with section 547(b)(3).

B.   *"Receive More" Analysis under Section 547(b)(5)*

The final element to avoid the Defendant's judicial lien as a preference under section 547(b) is a showing that the judicial lien "enables such creditor to receive more than such creditor would receive if-(A) the case were a case under chapter 7 of this title; (B) the transfer had not been made; and (C) such creditor received payment of such debt to the extent provided by the provisions of this title." § 547(b)(5). Whether section 547(b)(5) "is met turns on the status of the creditor to whom the transfer was made." With respect to unsecured creditors, " '[a]s long as the distribution in bankruptcy is less than one-hundred percent, any payment 'on account' to an unsecured creditor during the preference period will enable that creditor to receive more than he would have received in liquidation had the payment not been made.' "(citation omitted). "[A]s a matter of law, whenever a general unsecured creditor obtains, within the preference period, a judicial lien against a debtor who cannot fully repay his unsecured creditors, he has received a preference." *4 In the instant case, the Debtor's liabilities exceed his assets. As such, under a hypothetical Chapter 7 liquidation analysis, the Debtor cannot repay his general unsecured creditors 100%.[3] The Defendant's judgment is for unpaid professional services, which, absent the attachment, is a general unsecured debt. By obtaining and recording the attachment, the Defendant converted an otherwise unsecured claim to a secured one. Thus, the lien enables the Defendant to receive more than he would without the lien in a Chapter 7 case. Therefore, the Court finds that section 547(b)(5) is satisfied.

In sum, the Court finds that there is no genuine issue that the Debtor was insolvent in accordance with section 547(b)(3), and the Defendant stands to receive more with the judicial lien in accordance with section 547(b)(5). Accordingly, the Court finds that all the preferential elements exist in the instant case, and the judicial lien is a preferential transfer subject to avoidance under section 547(b).

$190,516 total are Lake Sunapee mortgage for $166,516, Town of Newport tax lien for $12,000, and Creative Capital Arrearage for $12,000. (*See* Debtor's Mot. to Avoid Lien 1.)

2. The total exemptions does not include the Debtor's recent Schedule C amendments, in which he claims an exemption for the 1997 Timberjack skidder and 1970 one-ton truck.

3. Under a Chapter 7 liquidation analysis, general unsecured creditors stand to receive a 7.96% dividend. The Debtor's total liabilities less Schedule F debts is $255,570 ($381,614–$126,044). The Debtor's assets total $271,405, leaving $15,835 ($271,405–$255,570) or a 7.96% dividend ($126,044/$15,835) to pay general unsecured creditors.

Conclusion

For the reasons set out herein, the Court grants summary judgment in favor of the Plaintiffs.

QUESTIONS ABOUT PYSZ

1. Who are the winners and the losers in this case? How much would the Defendant have received in this Chapter 13 case if its judicial lien had not been avoided under section 547? How much will the Defendant now receive in this Chapter 13 case? ·

2. This is a Chapter 13 case. Why does the court discusses Chapter 7? Why is a Chapter 13 trustee bringing an avoidance action? Who benefits from a Chapter 13 trustee's bringing an avoidance action?

3. "Insolvent" is defined in section 101. What language in that definition was important to the holding in the *Pysz* case?

2. AVOIDING THIRD PARTY PREFERENCES AND THE *DEPRIZIO* PROBLEM

Most of the above preference problems involve two parties: the debtor transferor and the creditor transferee. The phrase "to or for the benefit of a creditor" in section 547(b)(1) includes three-party transactions in which D makes a transfer to C that is preferential as to S. *See also* § 550(a)(1) ("or the entity for whose benefit the transfer was made.")

Assume, for example, Firm borrows money from Lender, with payment guaranteed by Firm's officer (Guarantor). It is obvious from reading the hypothetical that Lender is a creditor of Firm, and, while it is not obvious from reading the hypothetical or the Code's definition of creditor,[11] Guarantor is also a "creditor" of Firm—at least for purposes of section 547. As the Seventh Circuit explained,

> "Suppose Firm borrows money from Lender, with payment guaranteed by Firm's officer (Guarantor).... Guarantor is not Firm's creditor in the colloquial sense, but under § 101[10] of the Code any person with a 'claim' against Firm is a 'creditor,' and anyone with a contingent right to payment holds a 'claim' under § 101[5]. A guarantor has a contingent right to payment from the debtor: if Lender collects from Guarantor, Guarantor succeeds to Lender's entitlements and can collect from Firm. So Guarantor is a 'creditor' in Firm's bankruptcy. A payment (transfer) by Firm to Lender is 'for the benefit of' Guarantor under § 547(b)(1) because every reduction in the debt to Lender reduces Guarantor's exposure. Because the pay-

---

11. Section 101(10) of the Code defines a creditor as an "entity that has a claim against the debtor...." Section 101(5) of the Code defines claim as a "right to payment, whether or not such right is ... contingent, matured...."

ment to Lender assists Guarantor, it is avoidable under § 547(b)(4)(B) unless one of the exemptions in § 547(c) applies."

Levit v. Ingersoll Rand Fin. Corp., (*In re* V.N. Deprizio Constr. Co.), 874 F.2d 1186, 1190 (7th Cir. 1989)("*Deprizio*").

Finding such an "indirect" preference can be important to Firm's bankruptcy trustee where the transferee, Lender, is also now in financial distress and not able to repay what it was paid by the Firm, The transfer is also a preference as to Guarantor under section 547(b), and the bankruptcy trustee for the Firm can recover from Guarantor under section 550(a)(1).

Finding such an indirect preference can also be important where the transfer is not avoidable as to the actual transferee. Assume that Firm does not file for bankruptcy until six months after it paid Lender. If Lender is not an "insider," the payment is not a preference as to Lender. If Guarantor, like virtually all guarantors, is an "insider," then the payment to Lender would still be a preference as to Guarantor. Under these facts, courts have consistently held that Firm's bankruptcy trustee can recover from Guarantor. Until *Deprizio*, courts generally held that the bankruptcy trustee could not recover from Lender under these facts.

Deprizio held that a payment to a noninsider creditor where there is an insider guarantor could be recovered from that noninsider creditor even though it occurred more than ninety days before the bankruptcy filing. The methodology of *Deprizio* can be outlined as follows:

- First, look at section 547(b) and determine if there has been a preference to anybody.

- Second, if there has been a preference as to anybody, look at section 550(a)(1) and determine the possible responsible parties.

In essence, *Deprizio* views sections 547 and 550 as independent provisions to be applied independently. The party responsible under section 550 does not have to be the same party as to whom the transfer was preferential.

After *Deprizio*, law professors spent thousands of hours working on articles explaining, attacking or defending *Deprizio*. Practitioners spent even more hours trying to solve possible *Deprizio* problems in transactions involving an insider guarantee and finding possible *Deprizio* problems in very different transactions such as transactions involving a fully secured first mortgage and a partly secured second mortgage. Lenders spent even more time and dollars lobbying Congress. And, Congress added section 550(c) to fix the *Deprizio* problem.

And then in 2005, Congress added section 547(i) to insure that the *Deprizio* problem—lenders would have longer greater vulnerability under section 547(b) if they obtained loan guarantees from insiders—was fully fixed. Please read sections 547(i), and section 550(c). Are all indirect preference problems now fixed?

---

11 U.S.C. § 547(i)

If the trustee avoids under subsection (b) a transfer made between 90 days and 1 year before the date of the filing of the petition, by the debtor to an entity that is not an insider for the benefit of a creditor that is an insider, such transfer shall be considered to be avoided under this section only with respect to the creditor that is an insider.

11 U.S.C. § 550(a)(1), (c)

(a) ...[T]he trustee may recover...from

(1) the initial transferee of such transfer or the entity for whose benefit such transfer was made ...

(c) If a transfer made between 90 days and one year before the filing of the petition—

(1) is avoided under section 547(b) of this title; and

(2) was made for the benefit of a creditor that at the time of such transfer was an insider; the trustee may not recover under subsection (a) from a transferee that is not an insider.

Problem 7–19: Indirect Preferences

1. D borrows $100,000 from C. G, an "insider" of D, guarantees D's payment to C and secures its guarantee by granting C a security interest in equipment worth more than $100,000. D later pays C the $100,000. One hundred days after paying C, D files for bankruptcy. Can D's bankruptcy trustee recover anything from anybody?

2. D owes F $300,000. D owes S $400,000. Both F and S have security interest in all of D's equipment. The equipment has a value of $500,000. D pays F in full. Thirty days after paying F in full, D files for bankruptcy. Can D's bankruptcy trustee recover anything from anybody?

3. D owed C $2,000,000 on an unsecured loan. On January 15, D gets B Bank (B) to issue a $2,000,000 standby letter of credit, naming C as beneficiary. Under this letter of credit, C can draw on the letter of credit on March 1 and receive $2,000,000 from B by establishing unpaid obligations of D. B is willing to issue this letter of credit because D grants B a security interest in collateral worth more than $2,000,000. On March 1, C draws on the letter of credit and receives $2,000,000 from B. On April 5, D files for bankruptcy. What can the trustee recover from whom?

---

3.   EXCEPTIONS

Recall that section 547(b) sets out the elements of a preference. In order to avoid a transfer as a preference, the trustee must allege and establish each of the elements of section 547(b).

Even if the trustee proves her entire case under section 547(b), she may not be able to avoid the transfer. Section 547(c) contains nine exceptions from section 547(b): a creditor/transferee can prevent avoidance of the transfer by proving that the transfer is covered by section 547(c).

Remember the relationship between paragraphs (b) and (c) of section 547(b). "B" not only comes before "C" in the alphabet but also in section 547 of the Code. There is a reason that the elements of a preference are set out in section 547(b) before the exceptions are set out in section 547(c). Do section 547(b) first.

Section 547(c) protects transfers that would otherwise be avoidable by the trustee under section 547(b). Section 547(c) applies only in concert with section 547(b). If the trustee fails to establish a preference under section 547(b), it is not necessary to look to section 547(c). It is only after the trustee has proved her entire case under section 547(b) that it becomes necessary to look to whether one of the section 547(c) exceptions protects all or part of the transfer from avoidance.

We will only look at the two most important such exceptions: section 547(c)(2) and 547(c)(4). If your professor looks at others, you might want to look (for free) on Westlaw for 4 Norton Bankr. L. & Prac.3d § 66:15

The key word to understanding section 547(c)(2) is the word "ordinary." When individuals pay their ordinary bills in the ordinary way— rent, cell phone, childcare, they are paying antecedent debts. When individuals file for bankruptcy, those ordinary payments of ordinary bills within 90 days before bankruptcy. are section 547(b) preferences. Similarly, when businesses pay their ordinary bills in the ordinary way and file for bankruptcy within 90 days thereafter, the ordinary payments of ordinary bills are section 547(b) preferences.

In the view of Congress, these ordinary payments of ordinary bills are part of "normal financial relations" and "do not offend the objectives of section 547(b)—do not detract from the general policy of the preference section to discourage unusual action by either the debtor or his creditors during the debtor's slide into bankruptcy." To protect ordinary payments of ordinary debts, Congress enacted section 547(c)(2). One more time–the key to understanding section 547(c)(2) is focusing on the word "ordinary."

---

11 U.S.C. § 547(c)(2)

(c) The trustee may not avoid under this section a transfer—

(2) to the extent that such transfer was in payment of a debt incurred by the debtor in the ordinary course of business or financial affairs of the debtor and the transferee, and such transfer was—

(A) made in the ordinary course of business or financial affairs of the debtor and the transferee; or

(B) made according to ordinary business terms;

Problem 7–20: Late Payment As "Ordinary Course"

Tolona, a maker of pizza, issued eight checks to Rose, its sausage supplier [and your client], within 90 days before being thrown into bankruptcy by its creditors. The checks, which totaled a shade under $46,000, cleared and as a result Tolona's debts to Rose were paid in full. Tolona's other major trade creditors stand to receive only 13 cents on the dollar under the plan approved by the bankruptcy court, if the preferential treatment of Rose is allowed to stand. Tolona, as debtor in possession, brought an adversary proceeding against Rose to recover the eight payments as voidable preferences.

Rose's invoices recited "net 7 days," meaning that payment was due within seven days. For years preceding the preference period, however, Tolona rarely paid within seven days; nor did Rose's other customers. Most paid within 21 days.

The eight payments at issue were made between 12 and 32 days after Rose had invoiced Tolona, for an average of 22 days. In the 34 months before the preference period, the average time for which Rose's invoices to Tolona were outstanding was 26 days and the longest time was 46 days. The trustee offers to settle her claim against Rose for $25,000. Do you settle?

As the next problem illustrates, the words that are key to understanding section 547(c)(4) are "after such transfer."

11 U.S.C. § 547(c)(4)

(4) to or for the benefit of a creditor, to the extent that, after such transfer, such creditor gave new value to or for the benefit of the debtor—

(A) not secured by an otherwise unavoidable security interest; and

(B) on account of which new value the debtor did not make an otherwise unavoidable transfer to or for the benefit of such creditor

---

Problem 7–21: Subsequent Advances

D owes C $100,000. On January 15. D pays C $60,000. On March 3, C loans D an additional $90,000. On April 5, D files a bankruptcy petition. Was the $60,000 payment a section 547(b) preference? If so, can the trustee recover the $60,000 from C?

2.   D owes C $100,000. On January 15, C loans D an additional $90,000. On March 3, D pays C $60,000. On April 5, D files a bankruptcy petition. Was the $60,000 payment a section 547(b) preference? If so, can the trustee recover the $60,000 from C?

3.   D Community Hospital, Inc., (D) filed for bankruptcy. D has approximately $900,000 to pay unsecured claims exceeding $4,500,000.

Before bankruptcy, C shipped drugs to D on credit. At the beginning of the 90 day preference period, D owed C $42,791. At the date of bankruptcy, D owed C $44,541.96.

During that 90 day period, C shipped D $76,459.04 of drugs on credit, and D made payments to C totaling $76,944.93. A comparison of the amounts invoiced by C with the amounts paid by D shows that each of the payments was on account of an invoice at least two months old.

A chart setting out the timing of the payments and shipments is set out below: The first column shows the dates that C received payments from D; the third column shows the net value of shipments by C to D between checks:

Check Date	Check Amount	Goods Shipped
11/15/89	$12,318.81	
		$21,416.10
11/30/89	$21,813.79	
		$9,752.18
12/15/89	$11,644.11	
		$12,190.38
12/29/89	$21,416.10	
		$14,821.70
1/15/90	$9,752.12	
		$17,529.88
		$748.80
Total:	$76,944.93	$76,459.04

You represent the trustee. Do you accept C's offer to withdraw its proof of claim for $44,541.96 in exchange for your releasing any preference causes of action,? *Cf.* section 547(c)(4)

D. INCREASING PROPERTY OF THE ESTATE BY AVOIDING OR PREVENTING SETOFFS

1. WHAT IS A RIGHT OF SETOFF (A/K/A OFFSET)?

Under nonbankruptcy law, certain creditors have a right of setoff. The Supreme Court in *Citizens Bank of Maryland v. Strumpf,* 516 U.S. 16 (1995) described the right of setoff as follows. "The right of setoff (also called 'offset') allows entities that owe each other money to apply their mutual debts against each other, thereby avoiding 'the absurdity of making A pay B when B owes A.'"

The most common setoff situation involves a person who has borrowed money from the same bank in which she deposits funds. For example, D owes S Bank $600,000 and is in default. D has an account at S Bank with a $400,000 balance. D and S Bank thus owe each other money. Obviously, D owes S Bank $600,000 because of the loan. And, it should be equally obvious that S Bank owes D $400,000 because of D's deposits to her account. Under these facts, S Bank has the right to setoff the $400,000 balance in D's account against the delinquent loan so that the balance owed on the loan is reduced by $400,000 to $200,000 and that the balance in the account is reduced by $400,000 to 0.

The use of setoffs is not limited to banks. The following hypothetical illustrates a setoff by a creditor other than a bank. D regularly buys goods from S. D files for bankruptcy in December. D has not paid S's $400,000 invoice for goods delivered in November because $600,000 of the goods delivered on the October and September orders were defective. D owes S $400,000 and S owes D $600,000. Why should D have to pay $400,000 to S and then S pay $600,000 to D? Setoff, as described by the *Strumpf* case, allows them to "apply their mutual debts against each other."

The Code does not create any new right of setoff. Instead, the Code generally recognizes whatever rights of setoff a creditor would have had outside of bankruptcy. As the introductory language of section 553 states, "this title [title 11, *i.e.*, the Bankruptcy Code] does not affect any right of a creditor to offset."

---

11 U.S.C. § 553—Setoff

(a) Except as otherwise provided in this section and in sections 362 and 363 of this title, this title does not affect any right of a creditor to offset a mutual debt owing by such creditor to the debtor that arose before the commencement of the case under this title against a claim of such creditor against the debtor that arose before the commencement of the case, except to the extent that—

(1) the claim of such creditor against the debtor is disallowed;

(2) such claim was transferred, by an entity other than the debtor, to such creditor—

(A) after the commencement of the case; or

(B)(i) after 90 days before the date of the filing of the petition; and

(ii) while the debtor was insolvent; or

(3) the debt owed to the debtor by such creditor was incurred by such creditor—

(A) after 90 days before the date of the filing of the petition;

(B) while the debtor was insolvent; and

(C) for the purpose of obtaining a right of setoff against the debtor.

(b)(1) if a creditor offsets a mutual debt owing to the debtor against a claim against the debtor on or within 90 days before the date of the filing of the petition, then the trustee may recover from such creditor the amount so offset to the extent that any insufficiency on the date of such setoff is less than the insufficiency on the later of—

(A) 90 days before the date of the filing of the petition; and

(B) the first date during the 90 days immediately preceding the date of the filing of the petition on which there is an insufficiency.

(2) In this subsection, ''insufficiency'' means amount, if any, by which a claim against the debtor exceeds a mutual debt owing to the debtor by the holder of such claim.

(c) For the purposes of this section, the debtor is presumed to have been insolvent on and during the 90 days immediately preceding the date of the filing of the petition.

---

2. OVERVIEW OF BANKRUPTCY LAW ON SETOFF

The bankruptcy law of setoff is primarily sections 506(a), 362(a)(7) and 553.

First, second 506(a) and the secured claim status of setoff. As section 506(a) states, bankruptcy law equates the right of setoff with a lien. S Bank, the creditor with a $400,000 right of setoff gets the same recovery in bankruptcy as Z, the creditor with a lien on property valued at $400,000.

Second, 362(a)(7) and the stay of setoff. A creditor who did not do its setoff prior to the debtor's filing for bankruptcy cannot exercise the right of setoff after the bankruptcy filing without first obtaining relief from the stay from the bankruptcy court.

Third, section 553 and the recognition of and limitations on a non-bankruptcy right of setoff. Again, neither section 553 nor any other provision of the Code creates a right of setoff. Instead, section 553 does three things:

- first, section 553 generally recognizes a nonbankruptcy right of setoff;

- second, section 553 protects any prebankruptcy setoff from avoidance under sections 545–548 and any postbankruptcy setoff from avoidance under section 549;

- third, section 553 provides a basis, in section 553(b), for avoiding a prebankruptcy setoff in which the creditor improved its position within 90 days of bankruptcy and provides bases in section 553(a) for limiting the amount that can be setoff prepetition or postpetition.

Problem 7–22: Applying Section 553(b) To A Prebankruptcy Setoff

1. D files for bankruptcy. 90 days before bankruptcy, D owes C Bank $100,000 and has $20,000 on deposit in C Bank. 10 days before bankruptcy, C Bank exercised its right of setoff. At that time, D owed C Bank $90,000 and its account in C Bank had a $50,000 balance. Can the trustee recover any part of the $50,000 under section 553(b)? If so, what are C Bank's rights? See section 502(h).

2. Note that section 553(b) applies only to prebankruptcy setoffs. Should C Bank in problem 1 wait until after the bankruptcy petition is filed to setoff? *Cf.* 362(a)(7), 553(a).

Problem 7–23: Applying Section 553(a) To A Prebankruptcy Setoff

D owes Acme $100,000 for goods bought on open account. Baker owes D $120,000 for services rendered. Acme sells its $100,000 account receivable to Baker. Ten days later, D files for bankruptcy. When the trustee demands Baker pay the estate the $120,000 for services rendered, Baker asserts a right of setoff and pays only $20,000. Advise the bankruptcy trustee as to her rights, if any, under section 553.

Problem 7–24: The "Arose Before" Requirements Of Section 553(a)

TLC Hospitals, Inc. (TLC) was the operator of skilled nursing facilities that provided many of their services subject to reimbursement by Medicare, a health insurance program administered by the United States Department of Health and Human Services (HHS). In June 1994, TLC filed a petition to reorganize its business under Chapter 11 of the Code. TLC thereafter continued to operate the skilled nursing facilities and participate in the Medicare program until it later converted its petition to a Chapter 7 liquidation case. Audits then revealed that HHS had overpaid TLC for services rendered prepetition and underpaid TLC for services rendered postpetition. Can HHS exercise its right of setoff to deduct prepetition overpayments HHS made to TLC from the sums it owes to TLC for postpetition services?

3. DISTINGUISHING SETOFF FROM RECOUPMENT

The following law review article excerpt and edited case re-introduce (introduce?) you to recoupment and explain why (1) it is important to be able distinguish setoff from recoupment and (2) it is sometimes difficult to distinguish setoff from recoupment.

> Much like setoff, the doctrine of recoupment is a common law concept which dates to legal antiquity. Unlike a setoff, however, recoupment requires that the defense asserted arise out of the same transaction upon which plaintiff bases his claim.

> The value of recoupment is grounded in the Code's treatment, or more accurately, nontreatment, of recoupment rights. Specifically, the Code fails to provide mention of, much less a system for dealing with, common law recoupment rights. Nonetheless, courts have virtually uniformly agreed that the Code preserves the right of a creditor to claim, and unilaterally exercise, any common law recoupment rights available against the debtor. As such, the 'same transaction' requirement within the context of bankruptcy provides the foundation for the equitable right of recoupment against the debtor: [A]llowing the creditor to recoup damages simply allows the debtor precisely what is due when viewing the transaction as a 'whole.'

> Recall that sections 362(a)(7), 506 and 553 expressly deal with setoffs. Recoupment is not mentioned in any of these three sections of the Bankruptcy Code; recoupment is not mentioned in any section of the Bankruptcy Code.

Gary E. Sullivan, *In Defense of Recoupment*, 15 Bankr. Dev. J. 63 (1998).

IN RE HOLYOKE NURSING HOME, INC.

372 F.3d 1 (1st Cir. 2004)

CYR, Senior Circuit Judge:

Chapter 11 debtor Holyoke Nursing Home, Inc. ("Holyoke") and its official unsecured creditors committee challenge a bankruptcy court ruling which awarded summary judgment to the Health Care Financing Administration ("HCFA") on Holyokes adversary proceeding complaint that HCFA's postpetition efforts to collect prepetition Medicaid overpayments to Holyoke either constituted preferential transfers or violated the automatic stay. We affirm the judgment.

BACKGROUND

In 1990, Holyoke became a participant in the Medicare Reimbursement Program pursuant to a Provider Agreement whereby HCFA periodically reimburses health care providers like Holyoke for the estimated costs of services they have provided to Medicare patients subject to an annual audit aimed at determining the reasonableness of the costs of those services. In the event HCFA determines that the costs of a providers past reimbursement requests were either overstated or understated, HCFA is authorized by statute to make "necessary adjustments [to the providers current reimbursement requests] on account of previously made overpayments or underpayments."

In 2000, HCFA determined that it had overpaid Holyoke $373,639 for cost years 1997 and 1998, and proceeded to deduct a portion of the overpayment and interest—viz., $177.656.25—from Holyoke's pending reimbursement requests for cost-year 2000. In late 2000, Holyoke filed a voluntary chapter 11 petition, and thereupon commenced the instant adversary proceeding against HCFA, contending that HCFA's prepetition deductions ($99,965.97) constituted voidable preferential transfers, see 11 U.S.C. § 547(b), and that its postpetition deductions ($77,690.28) were effected in violation of the automatic stay, see id. § 362(a)(7).

In due course, the bankruptcy court entered summary judgment for HCFA, holding that the HCFA deductions from current reimbursement requests were in the nature of recoupment, and constituted neither voidable preferences nor violations of the automatic stay. The district court denied Holyokes intermediate appeal in an unpublished opinion.

DISCUSSION

The lone issue on appeal-one of first impression in this circuit—is whether the HCFA deductions for a portion of the 1997–98 overpayments it made to Holyoke are more akin to a setoff, whose collection normally is barred by the automatic stay, see 11 U.S.C. § 362(a)(7) (staying "the setoff of any debt owing to the debtor that arose before the commencement of the [bankruptcy] case"), or to a recoupment, which normally is not barred.

The pertinent distinction between a setoff and a recoupment is whether the debt owed the creditor (viz., HCFA) arose out of the "same transaction" as the debt the creditor owes the debtor. For example, if A were to buy a truck worth $1,000 from B, but A finds that he must expend

$100 to put the truck back into working condition, A might send B a check for only $900, rather than pay B $1,000 and await a $100 refund from B. The $100 A recovers by deducting it from the amount he owes B constitutes a recoupment because the reciprocal obligations arose out of the same transaction, viz., the purchase-sale of the truck. Had B filed for bankruptcy protection, A could recoup the $100 prepetition debt from B without violating the automatic stay because "it would be inequitable for [B] to enjoy the benefits of that transaction without also meeting its obligations." Univ. Med. Ctr. v. Sullivan (In re Univ. Med. Ctr.), 973 F.2d 1065, 1081 (3d Cir.1992) (emphasis added). Thus, in essence the recoupment doctrine constitutes an equitable exception to the Bankruptcy Code § 362(a)(7) prohibition against offsetting reciprocal debts.

However, were A to buy the same truck from B, but instead of sending a $1,000 check to B, sends a $900 check (deducting the $100 B still owes him for a bicycle A sold B earlier), the $100 which A has deducted constitutes a setoff because the mutual obligations did not arise out of the same transaction, but from different transactions, viz., the sale of the bicycle and the sale of the truck. Upon the intervention of B's bankruptcy proceeding, Bankruptcy Code § 362(a)(7) would prohibit A from effecting such a deduction, and A's claim for $100 would be collectible (if at all) through the normal distributive mechanisms prescribed by the Bankruptcy Code. Neither the Medicare statute, the Bankruptcy Code, nor their respective legislative histories expressly treats the issue before us, and other courts of appeals have split on the issue.

We accept the majority view, and hold that the HCFA recovery of the $177,656.25 in overpayments previously made to Holyoke constituted a transaction in the nature of a recoupment, rather than a setoff. As such, it was neither a voidable preferential transfer nor a violation of the automatic stay. Both the Medicare statute and the provider agreement—by contemplating HCFA's payment of estimated costs, corrective audits, and retroactive adjustments or partial adjustments for overpayments and underpayments in determining HCFA's net liability for current cost-year services—strongly indicate that the contractual relationship between HCFA and Holyoke constitutes one, ongoing, integrated transaction.

Holyoke further contends that, even if HCFA's overpayment adjustments constitute recoupments, recoupment is an equitable doctrine, and therefore the case should be remanded to the bankruptcy court to determine the appropriate equitable balance to be struck as between itself and HCFA. Holyoke notes, for instance, that such recoupments for prepetition overpayments may either cut off or drastically reduce a bankruptcy providers most prominent cash flow, thereby diminishing the prospects for a successful chapter 11 reorganization, and jeopardizing the availability of healthcare to Medicare recipients. Holyoke argues, on the other hand, that HCFA will not be deprived of all recovery, but likely will be able to recover (albeit partially) on its overpayment claims under Holyokes chapter 11 Plan.

We perceive no need for equitable balancing. First, the recoupment doctrine is equitable for the very reason that "it would be inequitable for [Holyoke] to enjoy the benefits of [the same] transaction without also meeting its obligations." Thus, HCFA was *overcharged* for the services provided by Holyoke in 1997 and 1998, and in equity, Holyoke should not be allowed to retain the windfall. Moreover, to allow these overpayments to become property of the Holyoke bankrupt estate would mean that its estate might apply a portion of those government-provided funds to satisfy Holyokes other debts, thus violating the manifest congressional intent that HCFA expend such funds only to defray the costs of services provided to Medicare beneficiaries.

Second, even assuming *arguendo* that further equitable balancing is permissible, the equitable powers of the bankruptcy court do not accord it "a roving commission to do equity," nor "authorize courts to create substantive rights that are otherwise, unavailable under the Code, or to expand the contractual obligations of parties." As we conclude that Congress contemplated that the Medicare provider agreements would constitute a single, ongoing, and integrated transaction, the equitable powers of the bankruptcy court do not entitle it to second-guess Congress's implicit policy choices. Both by statute and by contract, the HCFA has the unqualified right to recoup these overpayments *in full*, and to return the funds to the public fisc, where they can be used to fund other facilities providing care to Medicare beneficiaries. In our view, public policy would be ill-served by permitting insolvent providers—like Holyoke—a windfall at the expense of other Medicare providers which have managed their facilities prudently to avoid chapter 11. Accordingly, we conclude that a remand to the bankruptcy court for a balancing of the equities is not warranted.

AFFIRMED.

QUESTIONS ABOUT HOLYOKE NURSING

1. Is there a Bankruptcy Code basis for HCFA's right of recoupment? Does the Bankruptcy Code even mention recoupment?

2. Is there a Bankruptcy Code basis for the *Holyoke* decision?

3. Is a creditors exercise of its right of recoupment subject to the automatic stay? Should creditor's have based its argument on section 362(a)(3)?

4. According to In re Lincoln–Gerard USA, Inc., 2002 WL 1676564 (Bankr. M.D.N.C. 2002):

    "Because it is based upon the same transaction, recoupment is essentially a defense to the debtor's claim against the creditor. See Epstein, Nickles & White, BANKRUPTCY § 6–45 (1992). Although recoupment is not expressly recognized in the Bankruptcy Code, recoupment nonetheless is allowed in bankruptcy cases when the requisite circumstances are present. Because recoupment works a preference not provided for in the Bankruptcy Code, the bankruptcy courts have been careful to limit the application of recoupment to situations in which the subject matter of the creditor's claim arises from the same transaction or contract as the debtor's claim against the creditor.... In determining whether conflicting claims arose from the same transaction or contract for purposes of recoupment, the courts generally have focused on the facts and the equities of each case, rather than resorting to a precisely defined test or standard.''

Do you agree with the statement that recoupment works a preference?

E. INCREASING PROPERTY OF THE ESTATE BY AVOIDING UNRECORDED TRANSFERS

State law and federal law requires recordation or other public notice of many kinds of liens. For example,

- Real estate recording statutes require the recording of real property transfers (including mortgages).

- Article 9 of the Uniform Commercial Code provides for similar public notice, i.e., perfection, of liens on personal property.

- The Federal Tax Lien Act provides for public filing of federal tax liens.

The Code does not have not its own public notice requirements. The Code does not impose any new, additional recordation requirements. Rather, the Code through provisions such as section 544(a) and 545 incorporates these non-bankruptcy recordation requirements.

A bankruptcy trustee [or Chapter 11 debtor in possession] can avoid certain pre-petition liens that are not recorded or otherwise perfected. A creditor's failure to give the required public notice of its lien can adversely affect other creditors. If creditor X does not record its lien on D's property, other creditors might not know that D's property is encumbered. Relying on the mistaken belief that D holds property free from liens, other creditors might extend credit, refrain from obtaining a lien, or forbear from instituting collection proceedings.

Section 544(a) empowers the bankruptcy trustee to invalidate any transfer that under non-bankruptcy law is voidable as to a creditor who extended credit and obtained a lien on the date of the filing of the bankruptcy petition, or is voidable as to a bona fide purchaser of real property, whether or not such a creditor or purchaser actually exists. In applying section 544(a), it is thus necessary to determine whether:

- non-bankruptcy law public notice requirements have been timely satisfied; and

- a creditor who extended credit and obtained a lien on the date that the petition was filed or a bona fide purchaser of real property on the date of the bankruptcy petition comes within the class of persons protected by such state law.

In applying section 544(a), it is not necessary to determine "whether or not such a creditor actually exists." Section 544(a) gives the trustee the status and rights of a hypothetical creditor who extends credit as of the date of the bankruptcy petition.

---

11 U.S.C. 544(a). Trustee as Lien Creditor and as Successor to Certain Creditors and Purchasers

(a) The trustee shall have, as of the commencement of the case, and without regard to any knowledge of the trustee or of any creditor, the rights and powers of, or may avoid any transfer of property of the debtor or any obligation incurred by the debtor that is voidable by—

(1) a creditor that extends credit to the debtor at the time of the commencement of the case, and that obtains, at such time and with respect to such credit, a judicial lien on all property on which a creditor on a simple contract could have obtained such a judicial lien, whether or not such a creditor exists;

(2) a creditor that extends credit to the debtor at the time of the commencement of the case, and obtains, at such time and with respect to such credit, an execution against the debtor that is returned unsatisfied at such time, whether or not such a creditor exists; or

(3) a bona fide purchaser of real property, other than fixtures, from the debtor, against whom applicable law permits such transfer to be perfected, that obtains the status of a bona fide purchaser and has perfected such transfer at the time of the commencement of the case, whether or not such a purchaser exists.

Problem 7–25: Unrecorded Mortgage

On January 15, D borrows $600,000 from M. M obtains a mortgage. M improperly records the mortgage. On April 5, D files for bankruptcy. Will the trustee be available to avoid M's mortgage under section 544(a)? If so, what are M's rights?

Problem 7–26: Unperfected Security Interest

On January 15, D borrows $600,000 from S. S obtains a security interest on D's inventory. S fails to perfect its security interest. *Cf.* UCC § 9–

317(a)(1). On April 5, D files for bankruptcy. Will the trustee be able to avoid S's security interest under section 544(a)?

Problem 7–27: Snidely Whiplashs Delayed Recordation

On January 10, Dudley Doright, D, borrows $10,000 from Snidely Whiplash, S, and gives S a security interest in his horse, Horse. Later that year, on December 29, S properly files the financing statement. On December 30, D files a bankruptcy petition. Will D's bankruptcy trustee be able to invalidate S's security interest UNDER SECTION 544?

F. INCREASING PROPERTY OF THE ESTATE BY AVOIDING TRANSFERS THAT ARE RECORDED, BUT NOT "TIMELY" RECORDED

In the Doright/Snidely Whiplash problem above, Doright's bankruptcy trustee cannot invalidate Snidely's security interest under section 544(a): Section 544(a)(1) gives the bankruptcy trustee the rights and powers of a creditor that obtained a lien on the date of bankruptcy. The security interest was perfected on the date of bankruptcy. A perfected security interest is effective as against a lien creditor and so is valid against a bankruptcy trustee invoking the avoiding power of section 544(a).

While you can now see why Doright's bankruptcy trustee can not avoid Snidely's late-perfected security interest under section 544(a), you should also see why a bankruptcy trustee should be able to avoid transfers like the Snidely security interest—transfers of interests that are recorded but are not timely recorded.

Remember the reasons for invalidating unfiled liens. Creditors of Doright may have been misled by Snidely Whiplash's failure to record. Unaware of this "secret," unrecorded lien, a creditor might extend credit to Doright that it would not extend if aware of the lien. Unaware of a "secret," unrecorded lien, a creditor might delay in collecting a delinquent debt from Doright that it would try to collect if aware of the lien. Accordingly, the Code invalidates liens that are not recorded.

The same reasons apply for invalidating liens that are not timely recorded. The Bankruptcy Code should invalidate liens that are not timely recorded. And it does. In section 547.

Although it is easy to see the reason for invalidating liens that are not timely perfected, it is difficult to understand why section 547 should be the mechanism for invalidating such liens. The easy way to invalidate such secret liens would be to add a section to the Code to the effect that any lien required to be recorded by state law must be recorded within 10 (21? 30?) days after it is obtained in order to be valid in bankruptcy. While that is the "easy way," it is not the way of the Code.

Basically, the Code's method is to "deem" that, for purposes of applying the requirements of section 547(b), the date of transfer is the date of recordation or perfection, not the actual date of transfer. Thus, a transfer for new consideration that is not timely recorded or perfected will be treated as a transfer for antecedent debt.

The Doright/Snidely Whiplash hypothetical illustrates the practical significance of treating the recordation date as the transfer date. Remember, Doright borrowed $10,000 from Snidley Whiplash on January 10 and gave Snidely a security interest in equipment which Snidely perfected on December 29. Doright filed a bankruptcy petition on December 30. At first, it might seem that section 547 is not applicable—that the January 10 security "transfer" from Doright to Snidely Whiplash was not for an antecedent indebtedness and did not occur within 90 days of the bankruptcy petition. For purposes of section 547, however, the transfer will be deemed made on December 29, not January 10. [Under section 9–301, Snidely Whiplash's security interest would not be effective as against subsequent judicial lien creditors until that date. Accordingly, by reason of section 547(e), the transfer will not be deemed made until that date.] Thus, the "December 29 transfer" would be within 90 days of the bankruptcy petition. Thus, the "December 29 transfer" would be for an antecedent indebtedness, i.e., the $100,000 loaned on January 10. Thus, the trustee would be able to invalidate S's security interest under section 547.

The above hypothetical illustrates that a delay in perfection can result in a security interest actually given for present consideration being deemed made for an antecedent indebtedness and thus a section 547 preference. The Snidely Whiplash problem is an easy one—delay of more than 11 months in filing and then filing just before the debtor's bankruptcy. What if the creditor's delay in recording is a matter of days, instead of months? Section 547(e) does not require immediate perfection—it instead provides a grace period. Originally ten days, now thirty days.

---

11 U.S.C. § 547(e)

(e)(1) For the purposes of this section

(A) a transfer of real property other than fixtures, but including the interest of a seller or purchaser under a contract for the sale of real property, is perfected when a bona fide purchaser of such property form the debtor against whom applicable law permits such transfer to be perfected cannot acquire an interest that is superior to the interest of the transferee; and

(B) a transfer of a fixture or property other than real property is perfected when a creditor on a simple contract cannot acquire a judicial lien that is superior to the interest of the transferee.

(2) For the purposes of this section, except as provided in paragraph (3) of this subsection, a transfer is made—

(A) at the time such transfer takes effect between the transferor and the transferee, if such transfer is perfected at, or within 30 days after, such time, except as provided in subsection (c)(3)(B);

(B) at the time such transfer is perfected, if such transfer is perfected after such 30 days; or

(C) immediately before the date of the filing of the petition, if such transfer is not perfected at the later of—

(i) the commencement of the case; or

(ii) 30 days after such transfer takes effect between the transferor and the transferee.

Problem 7–28: Snidely Whiplash And 547(E)(2)(B)

One more time: On January 10, Dudley Doright, D, borrows $10,000 from Snidely Whiplash, S. And, on January 10, at the very same time D signs a note promising to repay the $10,000, D also signs a security agreement, granting S a security interest in his horse. Horse. On December 29, S properly files the financing statement. On December 30, D files a bankruptcy petition. Will D's bankruptcy trustee be able to avoid S's security interest under section 547?

Problem 7–29: Snidely Whiplash And 547(E)(2)(A)

Same facts as above except that (i) Snidely filed his financing statement on January 19, and (ii) Dudley filed his bankruptcy petition on April 15.

It is not just your authors' favorite childhood cartoon characters that screw up and delay in recording their liens. As the next case illustrates, real financial institutions make the same mistake. In reading *Lee*, constantly keep in mind (1) the date that Lee signed the refinanced mortgage agreement, (2) the date that Chase finally recorded the refinanced mortgage and (3) the date that Lee filed his Chapter 13 bankruptcy petition.

IN RE LEE

530 F.3d 458 (6th Cir. 2008)

COLE, JR., CIRCUIT JUDGE

Approximately six months before he filed a voluntary Chapter 7 bankruptcy petition, David Scott Lee ("Lee" or "Debtor") refinanced a residential mortgage loan with Chase Manhattan Mortgage Corporation ("Chase"), which was both the holder of the original mortgage and the refinanced mortgage. Seventy-seven days before Lee filed his bankruptcy case, and seventy-two days after Chase had distributed the funds that were used to discharge the original mortgage, a new mortgage on his residential real estate was recorded in favor of Chase to secure Lee's obligation to repay the new loan. At issue in this appeal is whether Chase's new mortgage lien may be avoided as a preferential transfer under 11 U.S.C. § 547. For the reasons below, we hold that the earmarking doctrine does not provide a refuge for late-perfecting secured creditors and thus does not shield Chase from preference exposure. We also reject Chase's contention that perfection of its mortgage during the 90–day preference period did not result in diminution of Lee's bankruptcy estate. * * *

Under § 547 of the Bankruptcy Code, a trustee may avoid certain transfers made to creditors within 90 days prior to the commencement of the bankruptcy case.[1] The section serves two purposes. First, it fosters equality of distribution among creditors, which is one of the primary goals of the Bankruptcy Code. See Begier v. I.R.S., 496 U.S. 53, 58, 110 S.Ct. 2258, 110 L.Ed.2d 46 (1990)("Equality of distribution among creditors is a central policy of the Bankruptcy Code * * * Section 547(b)furthers this policy by permitting a trustee in bankruptcy to avoid certain preferential payments made before the debtor files for bankruptcy."). Second, it "discourages 'secret liens' upon the debtor's collateral which are not perfected until just before the debtor files for bankruptcy." Grover v. Gulino (In re Gulino), 779 F.2d 546, 549 (9th Cir.1985).

The elements of a preferential transfer are set forth in § 547(b), * * *

The other provision of the Bankruptcy Code before us is § 547(e). Prior to BAPCPA, § 547(e) provided as follows:

(e)(1) For the purposes of this section—

(A) a transfer of real property other than fixtures ... is perfected when a bona fide purchaser of such property from the debtor against whom applicable law permits such transfer to be perfected cannot acquire an interest that is superior to the interest of the transferee....

---

1. Because the Debtor filed his bankruptcy case prior to the effective date of The Bankruptcy Abuse Prevention and Consumer Protection Act of 2005 ("BAPCPA"), the pre-amendment law applies, and references in this opinion to the Bankruptcy Code, unless otherwise noted, are to the pre-amendment version.

(2) For the purposes of this section, except as provided in paragraph (3) of this subsection, a transfer is made—

(A) at the time such transfer takes effect between the transferor and the transferee, if such transfer is perfected at, or within 10 days after, such time, except as provided in subsection (c)(3)(B);

(B) at the time such transfer is perfected, if such transfer is perfected after such 10 days; or

(C) immediately before the date of the filing of the petition, if such transfer is not perfected at the later of—

(i) the commencement of the case; or

(ii) 10 days after such transfer takes effect between the transferor and the transferee.

(3) For the purposes of this section, a transfer is not made until the debtor has acquired rights in the property transferred.

11 U.S.C. § 547(e) (2004).

In examining the rationale behind § 547(e), we return briefly to § 547(b), specifically § 547(b)(2), under which a trustee must demonstrate that the transfer was made "for or on account of an antecedent debt owed by the debtor before such transfer was made." 11 U.S.C. § 547(b)(2). A debt is antecedent if it is incurred before the transfer in question. In the context of a loan, the borrower incurs the debt at the time the lender disburses the loan proceeds. Therefore, lenders who advance loan proceeds prior to the recording of the mortgage are undertaking "a transfer of an interest in the subject property for purposes of § 547." Superior Bank, FSB v. Boyd (In re Lewis), 398 F.3d 735, 746 (6th Cir.2005). Such transfers are subject to preferential transfer liability.

[5] Under this scenario, a borrower who later becomes a debtor incurs an antecedent and, at the time the mortgage is recorded, a transfer occurs for or on account of the debt that could be challenged as preferential by a trustee. Section 547(e) addresses this potential problem for lenders by providing a grace period for perfecting a security interest. As long as the mortgage is recorded within the 10–day time period,[2] the associated * * * On the other hand, if perfection occurs more than ten days after the transfer takes effect, the transfer occurs at the time of the perfection, and the debt thus will be an antecedent one. * * *

Applying § 547(e) to the facts of this case, we first note that the Debtor incurred his obligation under the New Loan when Chase disbursed the loan proceeds on October 6, 2003. Next, we must determine when the New Mortgage was perfected and whether the perfection occurred within pre-BAPCPA's 10–day grace period. Under § 547(e)(1)(A), the New Mortgage was perfected "when a bona fide purchaser of [the Property] from the debtor against whom applicable law permits such transfer to be

---

2. BAPCPA increased the grace period from 10 days to 30 days. The New Mortgage was recorded well outside even the new 30–day grace period and, thus, the result would be the same under either version of the law.

perfected cannot acquire an interest that is superior to the interest of the transferee." Here, the "applicable law" referenced in § 547(e)(1)(A) is the law of Michigan. Under Michigan law, perfection occurs upon recording. Therefore, a bona fide purchaser of the Property from the Debtor could have acquired an interest superior to the interest of Chase up until the date that the New Mortgage was recorded. It is undisputed that the New Mortgage was recorded on December 17, 2003, which was 72 days after the loan proceeds were disbursed-well outside the 10–day grace period. As a result, under § 547(e)(2)(B), a transfer of the Debtor's interest in the Property occurred "at the time such transfer [was] perfected," on December 17, 2003, and was accordingly made on account of an antecedent debt.

* * *

Under § 547(e)(2), if Chase had taken steps to ensure that the New Mortgage was perfected within 10 days of the Debtor's granting it, the date on which the transfer would have been considered made would have been October 6, 2003—the date that the transfer "[took] effect between the transferor and the transferee." If Chase had done so, the New Mortgage would not have been for or on account of an antecedent debt. The New Mortgage, however, was recorded 72 days after the Debtor gave Chase the mortgage and thus constituted a transfer for or on account of an antecedent debt. Therefore the date the transfer was made is December 17, 2003.

3. The Other Elements of Preference Liability

Chase does not dispute that the Trustee has established the elements of an avoidable preference set forth in subsections (b)(1), (b)(3) and (b)(4) of § 547. The only issues before us, then, are: (i) whether the earmarking doctrine applies-if so, the grant of the New Mortgage to Chase would not be deemed to be a transfer of an interest of the Debtor in property; and (ii) whether Chase's recording of the New Mortgage during the preference period resulted in diminution of the Debtor's bankruptcy estate.

B. The Earmarking Doctrine—Transfer of an "Interest of the Debtor in Property"

1. Development and Elements of the Earmarking Defense

[8] When the other elements of a preferential transfer are established, § 547(b)'s prefatory language sweeps into the bankruptcy estate any transfer "of an interest of the debtor in property." Although this provision has a potentially expansive reach, it is not without limits. In addition to the exceptions to preference liability set forth in § 547(c)—none of which are at issue here—this Court adopted another limitation on § 547(b), the judicially-crafted "earmarking doctrine":

> [T]here is an important exception to the general rule that the use of borrowed funds to discharge the debt constitutes a transfer of property of the debtor: where the borrowed funds have been specifically earmarked by the lender for payment to a designated creditor, there is

held to be no transfer of property of the debtor even if the funds pass through the debtor's hands in getting to the selected creditor.

When applying the earmarking doctrine in the context of a refinancing transaction, courts have split * * * [W]e conclude that the earmarking doctrine does not protect the late-perfecting refinancer from preference exposure. [A]pplying the earmarking doctrine to insulate Chase from preference liability would essentially write § 547(e) out of the Bankruptcy Code and, in the process, defeat the sound policy the statute was intended to promote—the discouragement of secret liens. By enacting § 547(e) and establishing a definite and firm 10–day time period for lien perfection (now expanded to 30 days by BAPCPA), Congress sought to promote the Bankruptcy Code's policy of discouraging secret liens on property of the estate.

C. Diminution—§ 547(b)(5)

Chase contends, and the Trustee concedes, that § 547(b)(5) requires that the Trustee establish diminution in order to prevail. [T]he lapsed perfection of the Original Mortgage and Chase's late perfection of the New Mortgage diminished the Debtor's estate. That is, Chase's security interest in the Property was released and re-perfected, and diminution occurred when Lee's unencumbered, non-exempt equity in the Property once again became subject to a perfected lien when the New Mortgage was recorded.* * *

Chase argues that imposing preference liability on it would be unfair and against public policy because the refinancing transaction involved a mere substitution of its New Mortgage for the Original Mortgage and ultimately benefitted the Debtor's other creditors, not Chase. According to Chase, the refinancing reduced the amount of the Debtor's monthly mortgage payments, causing more funds to be available for other creditors. Moreover, Chase argues, it derived no benefit from the refinancing transaction and should not be penalized for assisting the Debtor in his attempt to avoid bankruptcy. However, "whatever equitable powers remain in the bankruptcy courts must and can only be exercised within the confines of the Bankruptcy Code." Norwest Bank Worthington v. Ahlers, 485 U.S. 197, 206, 108 S.Ct. 963, 99 L.Ed.2d 169 (1988). * * *

Congress, by enacting § 547(e)(2), has determined the appropriate length of time between a creditor's transfer of value and perfection: originally 10 days, now expanded to 30 days by BAPCPA. By hewing to the plain meaning of the Code and respecting Congress's judgment in enacting § 547(e)(2), our holding today fosters predictability in the law of preferences.

Moreover, the result in this case, although arguably harsh, could have readily been prevented by Chase. * * * Chase is a sophisticated lender well aware of the consequences of failing to perfect its security interest within the grace period afforded by § 547(e)(2)—a deadline in effect since the enactment of the Bankruptcy Code more than a quarter century ago. We simply are not at liberty to rewrite the Code's preference provision under the rubric of doing equity to protect late-perfecting secured creditors.

III. CONCLUSION

For the foregoing reasons, we hold that the recording of the New Mortgage is a preferential transfer under § 547(b).

QUESTIONS ABOUT LEE

1. Did Chase improve its position within 90 days of bankruptcy? Is that a relevant question?

2. Judge Cole, a bankruptcy judge before his appointment to the Sixth Circuit (and a really good guy) rejected Chase's earmarking argument. Was Chase's failing to perfect within the section 547(e) grace period relevant to this ruling?

3. Judge Cole also rejected Chase's no diminution defense. Again, was Chase's failing to perfect within the section 547(e) grace period relevant?

G. INCREASING PROPERTY OF THE ESTATE BY TURNOVER

Usually property of the estate will be in the possession of the debtor at the time of the bankruptcy. Property of the estate, however, is not limited to property in the possession of the debtor. "Interests of the debtor in property" "wherever located and by whomever held" are "property of the estate." Sections 542 and 543 govern the turnover of property of the estate in possession of a third party at the time of bankruptcy.

---

11 U.S.C. § 543(a), (b)(1)—Turnover of Property by a Custodian

(a) A custodian with knowledge of the commencement of a case under this title concerning the debtor may not make any disbursement from, or take any action in the administration of, property of the debtor, proceeds, product, offspring, rents, or profits of such property, or property of the estate, in the possession, custody, or control of such custodian, except such action as is necessary to preserve such property.

(b) A custodian shall—

(1) deliver to the trustee any property of the debtor held by or transferred to such custodian, or proceeds, product, offspring, rents, or profits of such property, that is in such custodian's possession, custody, or control on the date that such custodian acquires knowledge of the commencement of the case; ...

Problem 7–33: Effect Of Bankruptcy On Receivership

Debtor owns and operates the New Society Court Apartments (the "Apartments") upon which WRH Mortgage, Inc. ("WRH") holds a note and mortgage. Upon debtor's default under the mortgage, WRH instituted state foreclosure proceedings. The state court enters its order appointing you receiver to take possession of and operate the Apartments. A day after your taking possession of the Apartments, Debtor files a Chapter 11 petition. What do you do?

More common that a state court's appointment of a receiver who takes possession of all of the debtor's property is a mortgagee or secured party's taking possession of its collateral. Section 542 and the *Whiting Pools* case are relevant when a secured creditor takes possession of its collateral and then the debtor files for bankruptcy before that collateral is sold.

11 U.S.C. § 542(a)—Turnover of Property to the Estate

[A]n entity, other than a custodian, in possession, custody, or control, during the case, of property that the trustee may use, sell, or lease under section 363 of this title, or that the debtor may exempt under section 522 of this title, shall deliver to the trustee, and account for, such property or the value of such property, unless such property is of inconsequential value or benefit to the estate.

UNITED STATES v. WHITING POOLS, INC.

462 U.S. 198 (1983)

JUSTICE BLACKMUN delivered the opinion of the Court.

Promptly after the Internal Revenue Service (IRS or Service) seized respondent's property to satisfy a tax lien, respondent filed a petition for reorganization under the Bankruptcy Reform Act of 1978, hereinafter referred to as the "Bankruptcy Code." The issue before us is whether 542(a) of that Code authorized the Bankruptcy Court to subject the IRS to a turnover order with respect to the seized property.

Respondent Whiting Pools, Inc., a corporation, sells, installs, and services swimming pools and related equipment and supplies. As of January 1981, Whiting owed approximately $92,000 in Federal Insurance Contribution Act taxes and federal taxes withheld from its employees, but had failed to respond to assessments and demands for payment by the IRS. As a consequence, a tax lien in that amount attached to all of Whiting's property.[1]

---

1. Section 6321 of the Internal Revenue Code of 1954, 26 U.S.C. § 6321, provides: "If any person liable to pay any tax neglects or refuses to pay the same after demand, the amount ...

On January 14, 1981, the Service seized Whiting's tangible personal property—equipment, vehicles, inventory, and office supplies—pursuant to the levy and distraint provision of the Internal Revenue Code of 1954. According to uncontroverted findings, the estimated liquidation value of the property seized was, at most, $35,000, but its estimated going-concern value in Whiting's hands was $162,876. The very next day, January 15, Whiting filed a petition for reorganization, under the Bankruptcy Code's Chapter 11, in the United States Bankruptcy Court for the Western District of New York. Whiting was continued as debtor-in-possession.

The United States, intending to proceed with a tax sale of the property,[4] moved in the Bankruptcy Court for a declaration that the automatic stay provision of the Bankruptcy Code, § 62(a), is inapplicable to the IRS or, in the alternative, for relief from the stay. Whiting counterclaimed for an order requiring the Service to turn the seized property over to the bankruptcy estate pursuant to § 542(a) of the Bankruptcy Code.[5] Whiting intended to use the property in its reorganized business.

The Bankruptcy Court determined that the IRS was bound by the automatic stay provision. Because it found that the seized property was essential to Whiting's reorganization effort, it refused to lift the stay. Acting under § 543(b)(1) of the Bankruptcy Code, rather than under § 542(a), the court directed the IRS to turn the property over to Whiting on the condition that Whiting provide the Service with specified protection for its interests.[7]

The United States District Court reversed, holding that a turnover order against the Service was not authorized by either § 542(a) or § 543(b)(1). The United States Court of Appeals for the Second Circuit, in turn, reversed the District Court. It held that a turnover order could issue against the Service under § 542(a), and it remanded the case for reconsideration of the adequacy of the Bankruptcy Court's protection conditions. The Court of Appeals acknowledged that its ruling was contrary to that reached by the United States Court of Appeals for the Fourth Circuit. We

---

shall be a lien in favor of the United States upon all property and rights to property, whether real or personal, belonging to such person."

4. Section 6335, as amended, of the 1954 Code, 26 U.S.C. § 6335, provides for the sale of seized property after notice. The taxpayer is entitled to any surplus of the proceeds of the sale. § 6342(b).

5. Section 542(a) provides in relevant part: "[A]n entity, other than a custodian, in possession, custody, or control, during the case, of property that the trustee may use, sell, or lease under section 363 of this title, or that the debtor may exempt under section 522 of this title, shall deliver to the trustee, and account for, such property or the value of such property, unless such property is of inconsequential value or benefit to the estate."

7. Section 363(e) of the Bankruptcy Code provides: "Notwithstanding any other provision of this section, at any time, on request of an entity that has an interest in property used, sold, or leased, or proposed to be used, sold, or leased by the trustee, the court shall prohibit or condition such use, sale, or lease as is necessary to provide adequate protection of such interest. In any hearing under this section, the trustee has the burden of proof on the issue of adequate protection." Pursuant to this section, the Bankruptcy Court set the following conditions to protect the tax lien: Whiting was to pay the Service $20,000 before the turnover occurred; Whiting also was to pay $1,000 a month until the taxes were satisfied; the IRS was to retain its lien during this period; and if Whiting failed to make the payments, the stay was to be lifted.

granted certiorari to resolve this conflict in an important area of the law under the new Bankruptcy Code.

By virtue of its tax lien, the Service holds a secured interest in Whiting's property. We first examine whether § 542(a) of the Bankruptcy Code generally authorizes the turnover of a debtor's property seized by a secured creditor prior to the commencement of reorganization proceedings. Section 542(a) requires an entity in possession of "property that the trustee may use, sell, or lease under § 363" to deliver that property to the trustee. Subsections (b) and (c) of § 363 authorize the trustee to use, sell, or lease any "property of the estate," subject to certain conditions for the protection of creditors with an interest in the property. Section 541(a)(1) defines the "estate" as "comprised of all the following property, wherever located: (1) . . . all legal or equitable interests of the debtor in property as of the commencement of the case." Although these statutes could be read to limit the estate to those "interests of the debtor in property" at the time of the filing of the petition, we view them as a definition of what is included in the estate, rather than as a limitation.

In proceedings under the reorganization provisions of the Bankruptcy Code, a troubled enterprise may be restructured to enable it to operate successfully in the future. Until the business can be reorganized pursuant to a plan under 11 U.S.C. §§ 1121–1129, the trustee or debtor-in-possession is authorized to manage the property of the estate and to continue the operation of the business. By permitting reorganization, Congress anticipated that the business would continue to provide jobs, to satisfy creditors' claims, and to produce a return for its owners. Congress presumed that the assets of the debtor would be more valuable if used in a rehabilitated business than if "sold for scrap." The reorganization effort would have small chance of success, however, if property essential to running the business were excluded from the estate. Thus, to facilitate the rehabilitation of the debtor's business, all the debtor's property must be included in the reorganization estate.

This authorization extends even to property of the estate in which a creditor has a secured interest. § 363(b) and (c). Although Congress might have safeguarded the interests of secured creditors outright by excluding from the estate any property subject to a secured interest, it chose instead to include such property in the estate and to provide secured creditors with "adequate protection" for their interests. § 363(e). At the secured creditor's insistence, the bankruptcy court must place such limits or conditions on the trustee's power to sell, use, or lease property as are necessary to protect the creditor. The creditor with a secured interest in property included in the estate must look to this provision for protection, rather than to the nonbankruptcy remedy of possession.

Both the congressional goal of encouraging reorganizations and Congress' choice of methods to protect secured creditors suggest that Congress intended a broad range of property to be included in the estate.

The statutory language reflects this view of the scope of the estate. As noted above, § 541(a) provides that the "estate is comprised of all the following property, wherever located: . . . all legal or equitable interests of the debtor in property as of the commencement of the case."[8] The House and Senate Reports on the Bankruptcy Code indicate that § 541(a)(1)'s scope is broad. Most important, in the context of this case, § 541(a)(1) is intended to include in the estate any property made available to the estate by other provisions of the Bankruptcy Code. Several of these provisions bring into the estate property in which the debtor did not have a possessory interest at the time the bankruptcy proceedings commenced.[10]

Section 542(a) is such a provision. It requires an entity (other than a custodian) holding any property of the debtor that the trustee can use under § 363 to turn that property over to the trustee. Given the broad scope of the reorganization estate, property of the debtor repossessed by a secured creditor falls within this rule, and therefore may be drawn into the estate. While there are explicit limitations on the reach of § 542(a), none requires that the debtor hold a possessory interest in the property at the commencement of the reorganization proceedings.

As does all bankruptcy law, § 542(a) modifies the procedural rights available to creditors to protect and satisfy their liens.[14] In effect, § 542(a) grants to the estate a possessory interest in certain property of the debtor that was not held by the debtor at the commencement of reorganization proceedings. The Bankruptcy Code provides secured creditors various rights, including the right to adequate protection, and these rights replace the protection afforded by possession.

This interpretation of § 542(a) is supported by the section's legislative history.

Moreover, this interpretation of § 542 in the reorganization context is consistent with judicial precedent predating the Bankruptcy . Under Chapter X, the reorganization chapter of the Bankruptcy Act of 1878, the bankruptcy court could order the turnover of collateral in the hands of a

---

8. Section 541(a)(1) speaks in terms of the debtor's "interests . . . in property," rather than property in which the debtor has an interest, but this choice of language was not meant to limit the expansive scope of the section. The legislative history indicates that Congress intended to exclude from the estate property of others in which the debtor had some minor interest such as a lien or bare legal title.

10. See, e.g., §§ 543, 547, and 548. These sections permit the trustee to demand the turnover of property that is in the possession of others if that possession is due to a custodial arrangement, § 543, to a preferential transfer, § 547, or to a fraudulent transfer, § 548. We do not now decide the outer boundaries of the bankruptcy estate. We note only that Congress plainly excluded property of others held by the debtor in trust at the time of the filing of the petition.

14. One of the procedural rights the law of secured transactions grants a secured creditor to enforce its lien is the right to take possession of the secured property upon the debtor's default. A creditor's possessory interest resulting from the exercise of this right is subject to certain restrictions on the creditor's use of the property. Here, we address the abrogation of the Service's possessory interest obtained pursuant to its tax lien, a secured interest. We do not decide whether any property of the debtor in which a third party holds a possessory interest independent of a creditor's remedies is subject to turnover under § 542(a). For example, if property is pledged to the secured creditor so that the creditor has possession prior to any default, § 542(a) may not require turnover.

secured creditor. Nothing in the legislative history evinces a congressional intent to depart from that practice. Any other interpretation of § 542(a) would deprive the bankruptcy estate of the assets and property essential to its rehabilitation effort and thereby would frustrate the congressional purpose behind the reorganization provisions.

We conclude that the reorganization estate includes property of the debtor that has been seized by a creditor prior to the filing of a petition for reorganization.

We see no reason why a different result should obtain when the IRS is the creditor. The Service is bound by § 542(a) to the same extent as any other secured creditor. The Bankruptcy Code expressly states that the term "entity," used in § 542(a), includes a governmental unit. § 101(14).

When property seized prior to the filing of a petition is drawn into the Chapter 11 reorganization estate, the Service's tax lien is not dissolved; nor is its status as a secured creditor destroyed. The IRS, under § 363(e), remains entitled to adequate protection for its interests, to other rights enjoyed by secured creditors, and to the specific privileges accorded tax collectors. Section 542(a) simply requires the Service to seek protection of its interest according to the congressionally established bankruptcy procedures, rather than by withholding the seized property from the debtor's efforts to reorganize.

The judgment of the Court of Appeals is affirmed.

It is so ordered.

Questions About *Whiting Pools*

1. What facts were important in this case? Was it important that the creditor was the IRS instead of a private secured creditor? Was it important that Whiting Pools filed for Chapter 11, instead of Chapter 7? Was it important the IRS had not yet sold the property it had taken from Whiting Pools?

2. What Code provisions were important to the Court's decision in this case? Why does the Court quote from section 541? What does this quotation from *Whiting Pools* mean:

Although these statutes could be read to limit the estate [property of the estate] to those interests of the debtor in property at the time of the filing of the petition, we view them as a definition of what is included in the estate, rather than as a limitation.

3. At the time of the filing of the petition, did Whiting Pools have "interests" in the property that the IRS had seized? What if the IRS sale of the property is conducted by a dedicated agent such as Jim Prufrock[2] and nets an amount greater than the amount of the tax liability?

---

2. Have you already forgotten *Push, Nevada*, http://us.imdb.com/title/tt0315701/?

Problem 7–34: Prepetition Repossession Of Motor Vehicle

In January, D purchased a new Volvo for $35,700. The major part of the purchase price was financed by Southern Financial Corporation ("S"). The finance contract between D and S sets out the terms of repayment and grants S a security interest in D's Volvo. By December D has missed three monthly payments to S. On December 7, S exercised its rights under its contract and under the Uniform Commercial Code and (i) repossessed the Volvo and (ii) sent D a notice of a pending private sale. D's response was to file both a Chapter 13 petition and an adversary proceeding seeking the turnover of the Volvo under section 542 and a determination that S was violating the automatic stay of section 362 by its continued possession of the Volvo. Advise S. What, if any, additional information do you need to advise S?

UNIT 8

ISSUES THAT CAN ARISE IN CASES UNDER ANY CHAPTER: LEASES AND EXECUTORY CONTRACTS

■ ■ ■

Section 365 of the Code treats prebankruptcy unexpired leases and "executory contracts" differently than other prebankruptcy transactions. Since there is a general understanding of how section 365 works and a general confusion over what a section 365 "executory contract" is, this book deals first with how section 365 works and then with the scope of section 365.

Recall that bankruptcy involves both the assets and the obligations of the debtor. Bankruptcy deals with these assets and obligations through the creation of a fictional estate. The assets of the debtor become property of the estate. The estate is administered by a trustee or debtor in possession to satisfy the secured and unsecured payment obligations of the debtor, i.e., the "claims." In the course of administration, the estate will incur its own obligations; these administrative expenses are given priority over the debtor's unsecured obligations.

Generally, the Code's provisions dealing with the debtor's assets are separate from the Code's provisions dealing with the debtor's obligations and the estate's obligations. A lease or executory contract involves potentially both property of the estate and a claim against the debtor or the estate.

This hybrid nature of a lease or executory contract is most apparent in lease situations in which the debtor is the lessee. Assume, for example, that D Store, Inc. (D) leases its store in the mall from L. D later files for bankruptcy. By reason of the lease, D has section 541 "interests ... in property." D's right to use the space in the mall is property of the estate. D's lease, however, involves burdens as well as benefits. D has performance obligations under the lease such as paying rent. Accordingly, by reason of the lease, L has a "right to payment," i.e., a section 101(5) claim.

For over seventy years American bankruptcy statutes have had special sections for leases and executory contracts. In 1938 the Chandler Act

Amendments added section 70b and 63c. In 1978, the Code replaced these provisions with section 365 and 1110. And, later, section 1113. And, still later, section 1114. While there are now several pages of bankruptcy statutes on leases and executory contracts instead of a couple of paragraphs, the core concepts from the Chandler Act have been retained.

A. WHAT ARE THE CHOICES, CONSEQUENCES OF CHOICES, AND TIME TO CHOOSE?

1. CHOICES IN THE CODE

In section 365, the bankruptcy treatment of a lease or executory contract can take one of three possible forms:

1. Rejection

2. Assumption

3. Assignment

Assumption and rejection are both mentioned in section 365(a) and throughout section 365. Assignment is not mentioned in section 365(a); assignment is, however, provided for in section 365(f).

In comparing rejection, assumption, and assignment, it is important to keep in mind that the lease or contract involves potentially both property of the estate and a claim against the estate. The following chart provides a general view of the effect of rejection, assumption, and assignment on property of the estate and claims against the estate.

	REJECTION	**ASSUMPTION**	**ASSIGNMENT**
Property of the estate	No property of the estate	Debtor's rights under contract or lease	Proceeds, if any, from assignment of debtor's rights under contract or lease
Claims	Unsecured claim for (1) pre-petition defaults and (2)breach resulting from rejection; administrative expense priority claim for post-petition obligations, if any.	Administrative expense priority claim for all obligations under contract or lease, post-petition or pre-petition.	No claim against the estate. Nondebtor party to an assigned contract or lease looks solely to the assignee.

Rejection, assumption, and assignment are the only three elections available to the debtor under the Code. A debtor does not have a statutory right to modify or change the terms of an unexpired lease or an executory contract.

To illustrate, assume that D Stores, Inc., (D) leases a space in a mall from L for $200,000 a year. D owes $600,000 to unsecured trade creditors and $3,000,000 to secured lenders. D files a Chapter 11 petition. D wants to continue operating in the mall and wants to retain the leasehold. D will have to assume the lease payment as is: $200,000 a year, no change. In its Chapter 11 plan, D will be able to alter its payment obligation to lenders and trade creditors, secured and unsecured. D cannot, however, use bankruptcy to effect a modification in its obligations under its leases or executory contracts. Rejection, assumption, or assignment. *No modification.*

The italicized statement in the prior paragraph is both correct and misleading. A debtor does not have a right under the Code to change the terms of an unexpired lease or executory contract. Nonetheless, a debtor is often able to use its bargaining power and other legal rights under the Code to "persuade" the other party to the lease or contract to "agree" to modifications in the lease or contract. For example, D is leasing a building from L. D files for bankruptcy. D wants L to reduce her rent. D presents L with the choice that either D will reject the lease which will leave L with an empty building and a general claim in D's bankruptcy case or L will agree to modifications in the lease. L will often "choose" to modify the lease.

2. CHOICES IN KMART CHAPTER 11 CASE

6/24/02 CRAIN'S DET. BUS. 3

Monday, June 24, 2002 Vol: 18 Num: 25
2002 WL 10365602

Slow auction leads Kmart to give up on sale of most leases:
Less than 25% of closed stores are claimed

Brent Snavely & Jennette Smith

. . . Kmart, which filed for Chapter 11 bankruptcy protection Jan. 22, sold 59 leases and raised at least $46.6 million at the auction.

Some say the auction results were fairly good for a company that was selling the rights to occupy buildings that it does not own and no longer wants to occupy. But Kmart got rid of less than 25 percent of the 278 it tried to sell, leaving the retailer with more than 200 leases to deal with. . . .

"We are going to move forward on rejecting a number of these leases," said Michael Freitag, a partner with the New York City public-relations firm Kekst and Co. and a spokesman for Kmart. "But we have some where we might see if there is still some value to be maintained."
. . .

Kmart needed to act swiftly to save money. Earlier this year it told the court that it was costing more than $11 million a month in rent and other fees to hold on to the leases, said Fred Ringel, an attorney who represents several landlords and a partner at New York City-based Robinson Brog Leinwand Green Genovese & Gluck P.C.

When Kmart announced plans to close 283 stores, the theory was that the unexpired leases would be desirable to other retailers because many offered low rent with multiyear terms. But a depressed economy, an excess supply of empty sites left over from other recent retail bankruptcies and the undesirable characteristics of the Kmart sites caused many potential buyers to turn away, retail experts say.

Plus, much of the interest in Kmart's leases ended before the auction began. That's because a motion submitted by Cleveland-based Developers Diversified Realty Corp. to change the bidding process was defeated at a hearing just before the auction. Developers Diversified argued that a bid on 53 stores submitted by a joint venture led by New Hyde Park, N.Y.-based Kimco Realty Group unfairly chilled the bidding. The bid was structured so that anyone bidding on any of the leases Kimco wanted had to bid on all 53 sites.

Developers Diversified said Kmart could get more money if it auctioned the stores individually. About a dozen other landlords made that argument, Ringel said.

But Kimco guaranteed Kmart $43 million and might pay more in the future, because Kimco agreed to share profits. And both of Kmart's creditors committees told the judge that they supported Kmart's argument that a store-by-store auction wasn't worth the risk of ending up with less money. The judge ruled against Developers Diversified....

Kimco Vice President Ray Edwards said he wasn't surprised at the lack of interest shown in the majority of Kmart's leases. "This was the bottom group on a performance level. It was 300 stores, but it was the 300 bottom stores in a 2,100–store chain," Edwards said.

Many of the landlords are hoping Kmart terminates more leases.

Scott Campbell, vice president of equity research at Raymond James Financial Inc. in St. Petersburg, Fla., said having a center anchored by a closed Kmart store makes neighboring tenants and landlords anxious. In fact, Ringel said, some landlords are better off if Kmart terminates its leases. "They have stores that are empty, and rather than have continued uncertainty, they'd like to be able to move forward," he said.

In other Kmart news last week: Lead law firm Skadden, Arps, Slate Meagher & Flom asked the U.S. Bankruptcy Court in Chicago for $9.48 million in fees for work done in the first three months of the retailer's bankruptcy ... The firm also sought reimbursement of $1.17 million for expenses incurred while working on Kmart's Chapter 11 case from Jan. 25 to April 30.

QUESTIONS ABOUT KMART'S LEASES

1. Why was the Kimco joint venture willing to pay $43 million for the 54 leases? Who gets the $43 million? What do the landlords get? *See* section 365(f).

2. If Kimco defaults on a lease, can the landlord still recover from Kmart? *See* section 365(k).

3. The article refers to Kmart's terminating leases. Is a section 365 rejection the same as a termination? *Cf.* sections 365(g)("constitutes a breach"), 365(h)("may treat such lease as terminated by the rejection"). The article also suggests that some landlords are "better off if Kmart terminates [sic] its leases." What will a landlord get if its lease is rejected? *Cf.* sections 365(g), 502(g), 502(b)(6) and ... What additional information do you need to be able to tell a landlord how much it will receive from Kmart if its lease is rejected in the Kmart bankruptcy?

The excerpt from the article notes that Kmart has 1,800 other stores. Reading this should raise the question how soon does a debtor like Kmart have to decide whether to assume or reject more than 2,000 leases.

3. TIME TO "CHOOSE"

Prior to the 2005 legislation, the Bankruptcy Code provided that (1) a Chapter 11 debtor had to decide whether to assume or reject leases of commercial real estate within 60 days after filing for bankruptcy, but (2) the bankruptcy court could extend the time period "for cause." While there was no limit on the number of extensions or the duration of the extension, the common bankruptcy court practice was to extend the debtor's decision period until plan confirmation.

This bankruptcy court practice was prompted in substantial part by an opinion written by Judge Calabresi in In re Klein Sleep Prods., Inc., 78 F.3d 18 (2d Cir. 1996). There, Klein Sleep Products, Inc. (Klein) assumed a commercial lease early in its Chapter 11 case. When the Chapter 11 reorganization efforts were unsuccessful, Klein surrendered the leasehold and moved to reject the lease. The landlord successfully sued the bankruptcy estate for the payment of all rent over the life of the lease. According to Judge Calabresi, "we hold that claims for future rent arising out of assumed leases are administrative expenses, regardless of whether they are subsequently rejected, and that they are not capped at a year's worth of unpaid rent under section 502(b)(6). We reach this conclusion in light of the prior practice under the Bankruptcy Act, the timing provisions of the Code, and an understanding that debtors generally benefit from court-approved assumption of executory contracts and unexpired leases."

The 2005 legislation changed the initial 60–day decision period to 120 days but allows the court to grant only a single 90–day extension "for cause." Any additional extension beyond 210 days (120 + 90) requires consent of the landlord. The new law also limits administrative expense priority claims arising from the later rejection of previously assumed leases to monetary obligations due in the two years following rejection.

Note that the article refers to the bankruptcy court's approval of Kmart's assignment of leases, and Judge Calabresi also refers to the bankruptcy court's approval of Klein Sleep's assumption of lease. This raises the question . . .

B. WHO MAKES THE CHOICE OF REJECTION, ASSUMPTION OR ASSIGNMENT?

Section 365(a) refers to the "trustee." "The trustee . . . may assume or reject." And section 1107 gives a Chapter 11 debtor in possession a trustee's powers.

Section 365(a) also requires court approval of assumption or rejection of leases or executory contracts. Section 365(a) does not indicate what standard the bankruptcy court should apply in determining whether to approve the assumption or rejection of a lease or executory contract. Bankruptcy judges generally apply a business judgment test and give great weight to the business judgment of the debtor. Should the Tampa bankruptcy judge grant Sabal Hotel's motion to reject its franchise contract with Holiday Inns set out below?

11 U.S.C. § 365(a)—Executory Contracts and Unexpired Leases

(a) Except as provided in section 765 and 766 of this title and in subsections (b), (c), and (d) of this section, the trustee, subject to the court's approval, may assume or reject any executory contract or unexpired lease of the debtor.

Sabal Hotel Motion to Reject Executory Contract

IN THE UNITED STATES BANKRUPTCY COURT
FOR THE MIDDLE DISTRICT OF FLORIDA
TAMPA DIVISION

IN RE:	)	
	)	CASE NO. 91–91–3599813
SABAL HOTEL, LTD.,	)	
	)	CHAPTER 11
Debtor.	)	

MOTION TO REJECT EXECUTORY CONTRACT

SABAL HOTEL, LTD., as Debtor and Debtor-in-Possession, by its undersigned attorneys, moves, pursuant to 11 U.S.C. 365, to reject its executory contract with Holiday Inns Inc. on the following grounds:

1. The Debtor has filed a voluntary Petition under Chapter 11 of the Bankruptcy Code and has been retained in possession of its assets as

Debtor-in-Possession. No committee of creditors has been appointed in this case.

2.   The Debtor owns and operates a hotel facility located in the Sabal Park industrial-business area in the eastern suburbs of Tampa, Florida. The Debtor's facility is a multi-story hotel comprising of 265 guest rooms and suites as well as various public areas, function rooms, restaurants, and the like. The Debtor's hotel facility is four years old, and can be described a "first rate" hotel facility.

3.   On March 6, 1987, Debtor entered into a Holiday Inn License Agreement ("Contract") with Holiday Inns, Inc. The Contract expires on March 5,2007. The Contract is an "executory contract" for purposes of section 365.

4.   The Contract provides for termination by the Debtor on twelve months notice. Because it was the Debtor's business judgment that its Contract costs exceeded its Contract benefits, Debtor sent a termination notice to Holiday Inns, Inc. on or about March 7, 1991.

5.   Similarly, it is the business judgment of the Debtor as Debtor-in-Possession that the costs of the Contract to the estate exceed the benefits to the estate from the Contract and that the Contract inhibits rather than enhances the prospects of an effective reorganization.

WHEREFORE, SABAL HOTEL, LTD. prays this Court to enter an order authorizing it to reject its executory contract with Holiday Inns Inc.

JOHNSON, BLAKELY, POPE, BOKOR,
RUPPEL & BURNS, P.A.

Problem 8–1: Objection to Rejection by Non–Debtor Party

Should the bankruptcy court approve the rejection if Holiday Inns objects? What if the License Agreement provides for liquidated damages of $100,000.00 if the License Agreement is rejected in a bankruptcy case?

Problem 8–2: Objection to Rejection by Other Creditors in the Case

Should the bankruptcy court approve the rejection if the bank that has a mortgage on the hotel objects?

Problem 8–3: Objection to Assumption

Assume that the debtor Sabal Hotel was moving for court approval of an assumption of its contract with Holiday Inns. As attorney for the creditors' committee, would you object?

C. CAN A CLAUSE IN A PRE-BANKRUPTCY LEASE OR CONTRACT CONTROL THE CHOICE IN BANKRUPTCY?

Understandably, landlords want to be able to terminate leases when tenants file for bankruptcy. And as the Stones have long understood, "you can't always get what you want."

1. BANKRUPTCY TERMINATION CLAUSES

11 U.S.C.§ 365(e)(1)

(e)(1) Notwithstanding a provision in an executory contract or unexpired lease, or in applicable law, an executory contract or unexpired lease of the debtor may not be terminated or modified, and any right or obligation under such contract or lease may not be terminated or modified, at any time after the commencement of the case solely because of a provision in such contract or lease that is conditioned on—

(A) the insolvency or financial condition of the debtor at any time before the closing of the case;

(B) the commencement of a case under this title; or

(C) the appointment of or taking possession by a trustee in a case under this title or a custodian before such commencement.

You need to understand this provision. Lawyers who are primarily "dirt" lawyers will insist that bankruptcy termination clauses are valid And will show you their form books.

Problem 8–4: Effectiveness of Bankruptcy Termination Clause

Would you use the following clause in a real estate lease?

ARTICLE 20. DEFAULT.

20.1.   Event of Default.

The occurrence of any of the following constitutes a material default and breach of this **Lease** by Tenant (an "Event of Default") * * * (iii) any action taken or suffered by Tenant under any insolvency act or the **Bankruptcy** Reform Act of 1978 as amended from time to time;

20.2.   Remedies on Default

In addition to any other remedies available at Law or in equity, Landlord will have the following rights: (a) to terminate this Lease and Tenant's right to possession of the Premises

2 Cal. Real Est. Forms § 2:19, Miller & Starr California Real Estate Forms (Database updated June 2009)

2. SECTION 365(F) AND CONTRACTUAL PROHIBITIONS ON ASSIGNMENT

And, understandably, landlords don't want their tenants to be able to assign a lease that has become a below market lease and keep the premium paid by the assignee. And, again, "you can't always get what you want."

11 U.S.C. § 365(f)

(f)

(1) Except as provided in subsections (b) and (c) of this section, notwithstanding a provision in an executory contract or unexpired lease of the debtor, or in applicable law, that prohibits, restricts, or conditions the assignment of such contract or lease, the trustee may assign such contract or lease under paragraph (2) of this subsection. * * *

(3) Notwithstanding a provision in an executory contract or unexpired lease of the debtor, or in applicable law that terminates or modifies, or permits a party other than the debtor to terminate or modify, such contract or lease or a right or obligation under such contract or lease on account of an assignment of such contract or lease, such contract, lease, right, or obligation may not be terminated or modified under such provision because of the assumption or assignment of such contract or lease by the trustee.

Problem 8–5: Effectiveness of Lease Clauses Requiring Lessor's Consent to Assignment

L leases a building to T. The lease contains the following provision: "The lessee shall not sell or assign this lease or sublet said premises or any part thereof without first obtaining the written consent of the lessor." T files for bankruptcy. What is the effect of this lease provision?

D.   WHEN? WHAT HAPPENS DURING THE "GAP" BETWEEN THE FILING OF THE PETITION AND THE CHOICE?

The business decision whether to assume or reject a lease or executory contract will not always be obvious .. Obviously, you need to know how long the debtor has to make that business decision whether to assume or reject leases or executory contracts and what happens during that "gap" period.

U.S.C. § 365(d)(1)–(4)

(d)

(1) In a case under chapter 7 of this title, if the trustee does not assume or reject an executory contract or unexpired lease of residential real property or of personal property of the debtor within 60 days after the order for relief, or within such additional time as the court, for cause, within such 60–day period, fixes, then such contract or lease is deemed rejected.

(2) In a case under chapter 9,11,12, or 13 of this title, the trustee may assume or reject an executory contract or unexpired lease of residential real property or of personal property of the debtor at any time before the confirmation of a plan but the court, on the request of any party to such contract or lease, may order the trustee to determine within a specified period of time whether to assume or reject such contract or lease.

(3) The trustee shall timely perform all the obligations of the debtor, except those specified in section 365(b)(2), arising from and after the order for relief under any unexpired lease of nonresidential real property, until such lease is assumed or rejected, notwithstanding section 503(b)(1) of this title. The court may extend, for cause, the time for performance of any such obligation that arises within 60 days after the date of the order for relief, but the time for performance shall not be extended beyond such 60–day period. This subsection shall not be deemed to affect the trustee's obligations under the provisions of subsection (b) or (f) of this section. Acceptance of any such performance does not constitute waiver or relinquishment of the lessor's rights under such lease or under this title.

(4)

(A) Subject to subparagraph (B), in any case under any chapter of this title, an unexpired lease of nonresidential real property under which the debtor is the lessee shall be deemed rejected, and the trustee shall immediately surrender that nonresidential real property to the lessor, if the trustee does not assume or reject the unexpired lease by the earlier of

(i) the date that is 120 days after the date of the order for relief; or

(ii) the date of the entry of an order confirming a plan.

(B)

(i) The court may extend the period determined under subparagraph (A), prior to the expiration of the 120–day period, for 90 days upon motion of the trustee or lessor for cause.

(ii) If the court grants an extension under clause (i), the court may grant a subsequent extension only upon prior written consent of the lessor in each instance.

Problem 8–6: Deciding On Commercial Real Estate Leases

Gap, Inc. (GAP, Banana Republic, and Old Navy) has more than 3,000 stores in the United States, UK, France, and Japan. If Gap, Inc. files for bankruptcy, how long will Gap, Inc., have to decide whether to assume or reject its U.S. leases? *See* (again, we hope) section 365(d)(4). Is Gap, Inc. required to continue making monthly rent payments until it decides whether to assume or reject these U.S. leases? *See* section 365(d)(3).

Problem 8–7: Deciding On Equipment Leases

Gap, Inc. also leases equipment from L. Gap, Inc. is uncertain how much of the leased equipment it will need in its "reorganized" business. How long can Gap, Inc. delay the decision to assume or reject equipment leases? What if any action can L take? *See* section 365(d)(2). Is Gap, Inc. required to continue making monthly rent payments until it decides whether to assume or reject? *See* section 365(d)(5) [formerly section 365(d)(10)] set out below.

> (5) The trustee shall timely perform all of the obligations of the debtor, except those specified in section 365(b)(2), first arising from or after 60 days after the order for relief in a case under chapter 11 of this title under an unexpired lease of personal property (other than personal property leased to an individual primarily for personal, family, or household purposes), until such lease is assumed or rejected notwithstanding section 503(b)(1) of this title, unless the court, after notice and a hearing and based on the equities of the case, orders otherwise with respect to the obligations or timely performance thereof. This subsection shall not be deemed to affect the trustee's obligations under the provisions of subsection (b) or (f). Acceptance of any such performance does not constitute waiver or relinquishment of the lessor's rights under such lease or under this title.

E. WHAT ARE THE REQUIREMENTS FOR ASSUMING A LEASE OR EXECUTORY CONTRACT?

Assume that the debtor decides to assume. Section 365(b) (set out below) sets out the requirements for assumption. While any of the words in section 365(b) can be important, the first six words in section 365(b) are the most important for most law school exam questions.

11 U.S.C. § 365(b)

(b)

(1) If there has been a default in an executory contract or unexpired lease of the debtor, the trustee may not assume such contract or lease unless, at the time of assumption of such contract or lease, the trustee—

(A) cures, or provides adequate assurance that the trustee will promptly cure, such default other than a default that is a breach of a provision relating to the satisfaction of any provision (other than a penalty rate or penalty provision) relating to a default arising from any failure to perform nonmonetary obligations under an unexpired lease of real property, if it is impossible for the trustee to cure such default by performing nonmonetary acts at and after the time of assumption, except that if such default arises from a failure to operate in accordance with a nonresidential real property lease, then such default shall be cured by performance at and after the time of assumption in accordance with such lease, and pecuniary losses resulting from such default shall be compensated in accordance with the provisions of this paragraph;

(B) compensates, or provides adequate assurance that the trustee will promptly compensate, a party other than the debtor to such contract or lease, for any actual pecuniary loss to such party resulting from such default; and

(C) provides adequate assurance of future performance under such contract or lease

(2) Paragraph (1) of this subsection does not apply to a default that is a breach of a provision relating to—

(A) the insolvency or financial condition of the debtor at any time before the closing of the case;

(B) the commencement of a case under this title;

(C) the appointment of or taking possession by a trustee in a case under this title or a custodian before such commencement; or

(D) the satisfaction of any penalty rate or penalty provision relating to a default arising from any failure by the debtor to perform nonmonetary obligations under the executory contract or unexpired lease.

1. REQUIREMENTS FOR ASSUMPTION IF DEFAULT

Problem 8–8: Past Payment Defaults

A. Cure. Your client D has filed for Chapter 11 bankruptcy and has decided to assume all of its leases. One of the landlords, L, sends you a letter demanding immediate payment of $40,000 rent due for the four months preceding D's bankruptcy filing. Advise D.

B. Compensate. AL, another of D's landlord's, is demanding not only past due rent but (i) interest and (ii) attorney's fees. Again, advise D.

C. Adequate assurance. How can D provide "adequate assurance of future performance"?

Problem 8–9: Past Covenant Defaults

Your client L owns a building. D, a tenant, operates the only restaurant in the building. D is in bankruptcy and has filed a motion to assume the lease.

One of the many covenants in the lease is a "going dark" clause. Under this clause, D covenants that the restaurant will not be closed for more than 72 consecutive hours. D breached this covenant before filing for bankruptcy. Advise L.

2. REQUIREMENTS FOR ASSUMPTION IF NO DEFAULT

Problem 8–10: Assumption And No Default

L leases a building to D. D files for bankruptcy. If D is not in default under the lease, would D have to provide adequate assurance of future performance in order to obtain a court order approving its assumption of the lease?

F. WHAT ARE ADDITIONAL ISSUES WHEN THE CHOICE IS ASSIGNMENT?

As the term "additional" in the heading suggests (and, more importantly, as section 365(f)(2) expressly states and the next case explains), assignment involves all of the requirements of assumption plus a possible additional requirement. The next case shows why people care about section 365(f)(2)'s requirements for assignment. In *U.L. Radio*, if the section 365(f)(2) requirements are satisfied, then (i) the bankruptcy court will approve the assignment (ii) landlord Jemrock will continue to receive only the (now below market) monthly rental payment from its new tenant Just Heaven and (iii) U.L. Radio's other creditors will receive $200 a month from that new tenant .

1. CHANGE IN USE

MATTER OF U.L. RADIO CORP.

19 B.R. 537 (Bankr. S.D.N.Y. 1982)

JOHN J. GALGAY, Bankruptcy Judge.

Debtor, U.L. Radio Corp., has moved for an order, pursuant to Bankruptcy Code section 365(f), authorizing it to assume its lease ("Lease") with Jemrock Realty Company ("Jemrock"), the landlord, and authorizing U.L. Radio to assign the Lease to Just Heaven Restaurant, Ltd. ("Just Heaven"). U.L. Radio operates the leasehold as a television sales and service store. Just Heaven, the prospective assignee, will operate the premises as a small bistro. Jemrock opposes such an assignment, citing a use clause in the Lease which provides that the lessee shall use the premises only for television service and sale of electrical appliances. Jemrock asserts that the assignment of the Lease to Just Heaven would unlawfully modify the Lease by violating the use clause. Such modification, Jemrock avers, is not permitted under section 365 without the landlord's consent, which consent Jemrock withholds.

After a hearing, the Court ordered the parties to submit proposed findings of fact and conclusions of law (hereinafter "Findings and Conclusions"). The Court has considered all the papers submitted by the parties, the oral arguments and the applicable law and legislative history. The Court grants debtor's motion to assume and assign the Lease to Just Heaven.

I. Background

On September 17, 1979, the debtor entered into the Lease with Jemrock for a store located at 2656 Broadway, New York, New York. The store is located in a building which is also occupied by a grocery store, a Chinese restaurant, a liquor store, and 170 apartments. The term of the Lease is for ten years.... Paragraph 43 of the Rider to the Lease provides that the tenant may assign the Lease with the written consent of the Landlord, which consent is not to be unreasonably withheld.

On May 20, 1981, the debtor filed an original petition under Chapter 11 of the Bankruptcy Code and continues to operate its business as debtor in possession. No creditors' committee has been formed. The debtor intends to propose a liquidation plan of reorganization. The debtor is current in the payment of rent and related charges required by the terms of the Lease and is not in default of any of the Lease terms.

In furtherance of its intention to liquidate all of its assets and to propose a plan of reorganization, the debtor, subject to the approval of this Court, entered into an assignment of the Lease to Just Heaven. The proposed assignment provides, inter alia, that Just Heaven will pay to the Debtor as consideration for the assignment as follows: for the period commencing three months after this Court's approval of the assignment to October 31,1988, the sum of $2000 per month. Such payments will fund a plan paying unsecured creditors 100 percent of their claims. Rockwell International, the largest creditor, recommends the assignment.

The president of Just Heaven has executed a personal guarantee for the payment of rent in favor of the landlord for the first two years of the assignment, together with a statement that her net worth exceeds $50,000.

The Lease provides in paragraph 45 of the rider to the Lease that "any noise emanating from said premises shall be deemed a breach of the terms and conditions of this Lease." Just Heaven has allocated $20,000 for construction, including soundproofing. David Humpal St. James, Vice President and Secretary as well as a director and a shareholder of Just Heaven, is a noted interior designer including the design of commercial restaurants. His design work has involved soundproofing.

II. Issues

Two issues confront this Court: (1) Have the provisions of section 365, regarding assumption and assignment of leases, been satisfied? (2) Can deviation from a use clause prevent the assignment of a lease, when the assumption and assignment otherwise comport with the requirements of section 365?

III.   Assumption and Assignment Under Section 365

Code section 365 governs the assumption and assignment of executory contracts, providing broad authority to a trustee or debtor in possession[15] to assume and assign an unexpired lease. 11 U.S.C. § 365(a). The aim of this statutory authority to assume a lease is to "assist in the debtor's rehabilitation or liquidation."

Assignment of a lease, which is at issue here, must comply with section 365(f), which states:

> (f)(1) Except as provided in subsection (c) of this section, notwithstanding a provision in an executory contract or unexpired lease of the debtor, or in applicable law, that prohibits, restricts, or conditions the assignment of such contract or lease, the trustee may assign such contract or lease under paragraph (2) of this subsection.
>
> (2) The trustee may assign an executory contract or unexpired lease of the debtor only if—
>
>> (A) the trustee assumes such contract or lease in accordance with the provisions of this section; and
>>
>> (B) adequate assurance of future performance by the assignee of such contract or lease is provided, whether or not there has been a default in such contract or lease.
>
> (3) Notwithstanding a provision in an executory contract or unexpired lease of the debtor, or in applicable law that terminates or modifies, or permits a party other than the debtor to terminate or modify, such contract or lease or a right or obligation under such contract or lease on account of an assignment of such contract or lease, such contract, lease right, or obligation may not be terminated or modified under such provision because of the assumption or assignment of such contract or lease by the trustee.

A.   Requirements of Assumption

The first requirement of assignment under section 365(f)(2) is proper assumption under section 365. The broad authority of a trustee or debtor in possession to assume is limited in Code section 365 by subsections (b), (c), and (d).

Section 365(b)(1) and (2) prescribe conditions to assumption of a lease if a default has occurred. "Subsection (b) requires the (debtor) to cure any default in the . . . lease and to provide adequate assurance of future performance . . . before he may assume." No default exists under the Lease before this Court; therefore, the subsection (b) requirements for assignment are not applicable.

---

15. Code section 1107 vests the rights, powers, and duties of a trustee in a debtor in possession.

Section 365(c) prohibits a debtor from assuming a lease if applicable nonbankruptcy law "independent of any language in the contract or Lease itself" excuses the other party from giving performance to or receiving performance from someone other than the debtor. Such "nondelegable" and, therefore, non-assumable contracts and leases include those for unique personal services, as well as those to extend credit, to make loans, and to issue securities. The Lease before this Court does not fall under the prohibition of section 365(c).

Section 365(d) sets time limits on the assumption of unexpired leases. The time requirements of subsection (d) have been met and are not at issue.

B.   Adequate Assurance of Future Performance

The second requirement of assignment under section 365(f)(2) is adequate assurance of future performance ("adequate assurance"). Adequate assurance also appears in section 365(b) as a requirement of assumption if an executory contract is in default. The phrase "adequate assurance of future performance" is not found in the Bankruptcy Act.

Adequate assurance is not defined in section 365(f) nor in the legislative history of section 365(f), but "(t)he definition should generally be the same as in section 365(b)." In the legislative history of section 365(b), Congress while discussing assumption under section 365(b) and the bankruptcy clause under section 365(f), provided this explanation of adequate assurance: "If a trustee is to assume a contract or lease, the courts will have to insure that the trustee's performance under the contract or lease gives the other contracting party the full benefit of the bargain."

Beyond equating adequate assurance with the full benefit of the bargain, Congress offers no definition of adequate assurance except in the case of real property leases in shopping centers. The Lease at issue here is not located in a shopping center. Congress [House Report] described a shopping center as "often a carefully planned enterprise, and though it consists of numerous individual tenants, the center is planned as a single unit, often subject to a master lease or financing agreement." The building in which U.L. Radio is located is primarily a residential apartment building, with a liquor store, a grocery store, a restaurant, and U.L. Radio on the first floor. Thus the specific provisions of adequate assurance in the shopping center case do not apply to the assignment at issue here.

Apart from shopping center leases, Congress "entrusted the courts with the definition of adequate assurance of the performance of contracts and other leases." Adequate assurance of future performance are not words of art, but are to be given practical, pragmatic construction. What constitutes "adequate assurance" is to be determined by factual conditions. The broad authorization of the trustee or debtor to assume or assign unexpired leases, notwithstanding anti-assignment or bankruptcy clauses, prompted the admonition from Congress that the courts must "be sensitive to the rights of the nondebtor party to ... unexpired leases."

The phrase "adequate assurance of future performance" was adopted from Uniform Commercial Code section 2–609. U.C.C. section 2–609 . . . indicates that "adequate assurance" focuses on the financial condition of a contracting party and his ability to meet his financial obligations. ** * * "

Thus, the primary focus of adequate assurance is the assignee's ability to satisfy financial obligations under the lease. In this case, the president of the assignee has executed a personal guarantee of the payment of rent in favor of the landlord for the first two years of the assignment, together with a statement that her net worth exceeds $50,000. The assignee has budgeted $20,000 for construction, enhancing the chances of success of the assignee's enterprise. The assignee will have operating capital of an additional $30,000. Upon these facts, the Court rules that adequate assurance of future financial performance has been provided by the assignee.

IV. Use Clause

However, adequate assurance of future financial performance is not the complete statutory requirement; adequate assurance of future performance is. The financial capability of an assignee may be sufficient for a finding of adequate assurance under an executory sales contract or a similar commercial transaction. In a landlord-tenant relationship, more than an assignee's ability to comply with the financial provisions of a lease may be required. More particularly, will compliance with a use clause be required in order to provide adequate assurance?

Congress indicates that adequate assurance will give the landlord the full benefit of his bargain. In its case-by-case determination of those factors, beyond financial assurance, which constitute the landlord's bargain, the Court will generally consider the provisions of the lease to be assigned.

However, it is equally clear that, by requiring provision of adequate assurance under section 365, i.e., "the lessor's receipt of the 'full benefit of his bargain'," Congress did not require the Court to assure "literal fulfillment by the lessee of each and every term of the bargain." Section 365, by its own terms, empowers the court to render unenforceable bankruptcy clauses and anti-assignment clauses which permit modification or termination of a lease for filing in bankruptcy or assignment of the lease. 11 U.S.C. § 365(e), (f)(3). Section 365(k) relieves the estate of liability for future breaches of a lease after assignment, notwithstanding lease provisions to the contrary.

Section 365 expresses a clear Congressional policy favoring assumption and assignment. Such a policy will insure that potential valuable assets will not be lost by a debtor who is reorganizing his affairs or liquidating assets for distribution to creditors. This policy parallels case law which disfavors forfeiture. To prevent an assignment of an unexpired lease by demanding strict enforcement of a use clause, and thereby contradict clear Congressional policy, a landlord or lessor must show that actual and substantial detriment would be incurred by him if the deviation in use was permitted.

In this case, the contemplated deviation in use is from an appliance store to a small bistro. The building in which the unexpired leasehold is located already contains a restaurant, a laundry, and a liquor store. The landlord has failed to demonstrate any actual and substantial detriment which he would incur if the proposed deviation in use is permitted. The Court also notes that the contemplated use, along with the planned soundproofing, will have no adverse effect on other tenants in the building. Thus, this Court rules that the use clause may not be enforced so as to block assignment of this lease to Just Heaven.

Congress, in section 365, has stated a general policy favoring assignment. Balanced against this general policy is the requirement that the non-debtor contracting party receive the full benefit of his bargain. Jemrock Realty will receive the full benefit of its bargain under the proposed assignment of the leasehold from U.L. Radio to Just Heaven. No defaults exist under the lease. The lease has properly been assumed and Just Heaven has provided adequate assurance of future performance. The landlord has shown no actual or substantial detriment to him from the proposed assignment. The statutory requirements have been satisfied. The assignment is authorized.

It is so ordered.

QUESTIONS ABOUT *U.L. RADIO* CASE

1. The opinion states that the debtor was "not in default on any of the Lease terms." Note the prefatory language in section 365(b)—"If there has been a default .. " Since there was no default, why did the court require adequate assurance of future performance? Remember section 365(f)(2)(B)?

2. Why did Jemrock, the landlord, object to the assignment?

3. Note that in the last paragraph, the court finds that "the landlord has shown no actual or substantial detriment to him from the proposed assignment." How could the landlord show such detriment? Compare section 365(k) with section 365(f)(2)(B). If the landlord had shown that other tenants were moving out because of a bistro in the building, would Judge Galgay have reached a different decision?

4. The court mentions that "the lease at issue here is not located in a shopping center." Why is that relevant? *Cf.* section 365(b)(3).

2. SPECIAL REQUIREMENTS FOR ASSIGNING SHOPPING CENTER LEASES

Problem 8–11: Shopping Center Lease Assignment

Your client L owns and operates shopping centers. The "tenant mix" at its shopping center is important. More specifically, L wants one home improvement center at each of its shopping malls. L has agreed to lease space in

11 malls to Rickel Home Centers, Inc. and has employed your firm to prepare the leases. A senior lawyer seeks your advice as to whether the following language will effectively ensure that the leased space can only be used for a home improvement center:

> 2.08(b): Tenant's business operation in the Store shall be limited to a home improvement center. ["Home improvement center" is defined in paragraph 1 of the lease.]

> 10. The Store shall not be used by Tenant or its successors or assigns for any purpose other than a home improvement center.

3. "APPLICABLE LAW" PROHIBITIONS ON ASSIGNMENTS AND DELEGATION

Even if you didn't "cover" the common law of assignments in contracts class and so don't know the "applicable law", common sense should tell you that not all contracts can be assigned. For example,

Problem 8–12: Assignment and Contract Law as "Section 365(c)(1)(A) "Applicable Law"

1. Ron Jeremy ("RJ") http://www.time.com/time/arts/article/0,8599, 1836153,00.html has a contract for two more films with Caballero Films (CF). Under non-bankruptcy contract law, can RJ "assign" the contract to Steve Nickles ("SN") so that SN not RJ, performs and SN not RJ gets paid by CF?

2. Same facts as (1) except that RJ has filed for bankruptcy. Under section 365, can RJ assign the contract to SN?

---

11 U.S.C. § 365(c) and "Applicable Law"

(c) The trustee may not assume or assign any executory contract or unexpired lease of the debtor, whether or not such contract or lease prohibits or restricts assignment of rights or delegation of duties, if-

(1)(A) applicable law excuses a party, other than the debtor, to such contract or lease from accepting performance from or rendering performance to an entity other than the debtor or the debtor in possession, whether or not such contract or lease prohibits or restricts assignment of rights or delegation of duties; and

(B) such party does not consent to such assumption or assignment; or

(2) such contract is a contract to make a loan, or extend other debt financing or financial accommodations, to or for the benefit of the debtor, or to issue a security of the debtor;

In the next case, the "applicable law" is a state statute.

IN RE PIONEER FORD SALES

729 F.2d 27 (1st Cir. 1984)

BREYER, Circuit Judge.

The Ford Motor Company appeals a federal *district* court decision, allowing a bankrupt Ford dealer (Pioneer Ford Sales, Inc.) to assign its Ford franchise over Ford's objection to a Toyota dealer (Toyota Village, Inc.). The district court decided the case on the basis of a record developed in the bankruptcy court. The bankruptcy court had approved the transfer, which ran from Pioneer to Fleet National Bank (Pioneer's principal secured creditor) and then to Toyota Village. Fleet sought authorization for the assignment because Toyota Village will pay $10,000 for the franchise and buy all parts and accessories in Pioneer's inventory at fair market value (about $75,000); if the franchise is not assigned, Ford will buy only some of the parts for between $45,000 and $55,000. Thus, the assignment will increase the value of the estate. Fleet is the appellee here.

The issue that the case raises is the proper application of § 365(c)(1)(A), an exception to a more general provision, § 365(f)(1), that allows a trustee in bankruptcy (or a debtor in possession) to assign many of the debtor's executory contracts even if the contract itself says that it forbids assignment.

The words "applicable law" in this section mean "applicable non-bankruptcy law." Evidently, the theory of this section is to prevent the trustee from assigning (over objection) contracts of the sort that contract law ordinarily makes nonassignable, *i.e.* contracts that cannot be assigned when the contract itself is silent about assignment. At the same time, by using the words in (1)(A) 'whether *or not* the contract prohibits assignment,' the section prevents parties from using contractual language to prevent the trustee from assigning contracts that (when the contract is silent) contract law typically makes assignable. *Id.* Thus, we must look to see whether relevant nonbankruptcy law would allow Ford to veto the assignment of its basic franchise contract "whether or not" that basic franchise contract itself specifically "prohibits assignment."

The nonbankruptcy law to which both sides point us is contained in Rhode Island's "Regulation of Business Practices Among Motor Vehicle Manufacturers, Distributors and Dealers" Act, R.I.Gen.Laws § 31–5.1–4(C)(7). It states that

> [N]o dealer ... shall have the right to ... assign the franchise ... without the consent of the manufacturer, except that such consent shall not be unreasonably withheld.

The statute by its terms, allows a manufacturer to veto an assignment where the veto is reasonable but not otherwise. The statute's language also indicates that it applies "whether or not" the franchise contract itself restricts assignment. Thus, the basic question that the case presents is whether Ford's veto was reasonable in terms of the Rhode Island law.

Neither the district court nor the bankruptcy court specifically addressed this question. Their failure apparently arose out of their belief that § 365(c)(1)(A) refers only to traditional personal service contracts. But in our view they were mistaken. The language of the section does not limit its effect to personal service contracts. It refers *generally* to contracts that are not assignable under nonbankruptcy law. State laws typically make contracts for personal services nonassignable (where the contract itself is silent); but they make other sorts of contracts nonassignable as well. The legislative history of § 365(c) says nothing about "personal services." To the contrary, it speaks of letters of credit, personal loans, and leases—instances in which assigning a contract may place the other party at a significant disadvantage. The history thereby suggests that (c)(1)(A) has a broader reach.

The source of the "personal services" limitation apparently is a bankruptcy court case, *In re Taylor Manufacturing, Inc.,* 6 B.R. 370 (Bkrtcy.N.D.Ga.1980), which other bankruptcy courts have followed. The *Taylor* court wrote that (c)(1)(A) should be interpreted narrowly, in part because it believed that (c)(1)(A) conflicted with another section, (f)(1), which states in relevant part:

> Except as provided in subsection (c) . . . , notwithstanding a provision . . . in applicable law that prohibits . . . the assignment of [an executory] contract . . . the trustee may assign [it] . . .

As a matter of logic, however, we see no conflict, for (c)(1)(A) refers to state laws that prohibit assignment "whether or not" the contract is silent, while (f)(1) contains no such limitation. Apparently (f)(1) includes state laws that prohibit assignment only when the contract is *not* silent about assignment; that is to say, state laws that enforce contract provisions prohibiting assignment. The section specifically excepts (c)(1)(A)'s state laws that forbid assignment even when the contract *is* silent; they are to be heeded. Regardless, we fail to see why a "conflict" suggests that (c)(1)(A) is limited to "personal services."

Indeed, since it often is difficult to decide whether or not a particular duty can be characterized by the label "personal service," it makes sense to avoid this question and simply look to see whether state law would, or would not, make the duty assignable where the contract is silent. We therefore reject the district court's conclusion in this respect.

Although the district court did not explicitly decide whether Ford's veto was reasonable, it decided a closely related question. Under other provisions of § 365 a bankruptcy court cannot authorize assignment of an executory contract if 1) the debtor is in default, unless 2) there is "adequate assurance of future performance." § 365(b)(1)(C). Pioneer is in default, but the bankruptcy and district courts found "adequate assurance." For the sake of argument, we shall assume that this finding is equivalent to a finding that Ford's veto of the assignment was unreasonable. On these assumptions, favorable to Fleet, we nonetheless must reverse the district court, for, in our view, any finding of unreasonableness, based on this record, is clearly erroneous.

Our review of the record reveals the following critical facts. First, in accordance with its ordinary business practice and dealer guidelines incorporated into the franchise agreement, Ford would have required Toyota Village, as a dealer, to have a working capital of at least $172,000, of which no more than half could be debt. Toyota Village, however, had a working capital at the end of 1981 of $37,610; and its net worth was $31,747. . . .

Second, at a time when Japanese cars have sold well throughout the United States, Toyota Village has consistently lost money. . . .

. . . In these circumstances, Ford would seem perfectly reasonable in withholding its consent to the transfer. Thus, Rhode Island law would make the franchise unassignable . . .

Therefore, neither the bankruptcy court nor the district court had the power to authorize the transfer.

QUESTIONS ABOUT PIONEER FORD

1. Who would benefit from Pioneer Ford's assignment of its franchise to Toyota Village?

2. Did the Ford contract with Pioneer Ford prohibit assignments? Is that relevant?

3. Do you agree with Professor Bussel's observation "Pioneer Ford invites state legislatures to override bankruptcy's pro-assignment policy to protect favored constituencies thereby undermining the uniformity and coherence of federal bankruptcy law on an ad hoc and state-by-state basis." Daniel J. Bussel & Edward A. Friedler, *The Limits on Assuming and Assigning Executory Contracts* 74 Am. BANKR. L.J. 321, 328 (2002).

4. "APPLICABLE LAW" PROHIBITIONS ON ASSIGNMENTS AFFECTING ASSUMPTION

Recall the practical differences between assumption and assignment. If D tenant assumes a lease, she remains as tenant and remains legally obligated to pay the rent. If D tenant assigns the lease to X, then X becomes the tenant and only X is legally obligated to pay the rent.

Similarly, if D franchisee assumes a franchise agreement, it remains as franchisee and remains obligated to make payments and otherwise perform under the franchise agreement. And, if D franchisee assigns its rights under a franchise agreement to X, then X becomes the franchisee and only X is legally obligated to pay and otherwise perform under the franchise agreement

In summary, the effect on the nondebtor party of a debtor's assignment is very different from the effect of a debtor's assumption.

The next case considers the question: is the law on whether a debtor can assign a contract the same as the law on whether a debtor can assume a contract.

IN RE CATAPULT ENTERTAINMENT, INC.

165 F.3d 747 (9th Cir. 1999)

FLETCHER, Circuit Judge:

Appellant Stephen Perlman ("Perlman") licensed certain patents to appellee Catapult Entertainment, Inc. ("Catapult"). He now seeks to bar Catapult, which has since become a Chapter 11 debtor in possession, from assuming the patent licenses as part of its reorganization plan. Notwithstanding Perlman's objections, the bankruptcy court approved the assumption of the licenses and confirmed the reorganization plan. The district court affirmed the bankruptcy court on intermediate appeal. Perlman appeals that decision. We are called upon to determine whether, in light of § 365(c)(1) of the Bankruptcy Code, a Chapter 11 debtor in possession may assume certain nonexclusive patent licenses over a licensor's objection. We conclude that the bankruptcy court erred in permitting the debtor in possession to assume the patent licenses in question.

I.

Catapult, a California corporation, was formed in 1994 to create an online gaming network for 16–bit console videogames. That same year, Catapult entered into two license agreements with Perlman, wherein Perlman granted to Catapult the right to exploit certain relevant technologies, including patents and patent applications.

In October 1996, Catapult filed for reorganization under Chapter 11 of the Bankruptcy Code. . . .

On October 24, 1996, as part of the reorganization plan, Catapult filed a motion with the bankruptcy court seeking to assume some 140 executory contracts and leases, including the Perlman licenses. Over Perlman's objection, the bankruptcy court granted Catapult's motion and approved the reorganization plan. The district court subsequently affirmed the bankruptcy court. This appeal followed. . . .

II.

Section 365 of the Bankruptcy Code gives a trustee in bankruptcy (or, in a Chapter 11 case, the debtor in possession) the authority to assume, assign, or reject the executory contracts and unexpired leases of the debtor, notwithstanding any contrary provisions appearing in such contracts or leases. See 11 U.S.C. § 365(a) & (f). This extraordinary authority, however, is not absolute. Section 365(c)(1) provides that, notwithstanding the general policy set out in § 365(a):

(c) The trustee may not assume or assign any executory contract or unexpired lease of the debtor, whether or not such contract or lease prohibits or restricts assignment of rights or delegation of duties, if

(1)(A) applicable law excuses a party, other than the debtor, to such contract or lease from accepting performance from or rendering performance to an entity other than the debtor or the debtor in possession, whether or not such contract or lease prohibits or restricts assignment of rights or delegation of duties; and (B) such party does not consent to such assumption or assignment . . .

11 U.S.C. § 365(c). Our task, simply put, is to apply this statutory language to the facts at hand and determine whether it prohibits Catapult, as the debtor in possession, from assuming the Perlman licenses without Perlman's consent.

While simply put, our task is not so easily resolved; the proper interpretation of § 365(c)(1) has been the subject of considerable disagreement among courts and commentators. On one side are those who adhere to the plain statutory language, which establishes a so-called "hypothetical test" to govern the assumption of executory contracts. On the other side are those that forsake the statutory language in favor of an "actual test" that, in their view, better accomplishes the intent of Congress. We hold that we are bound by the plain terms of the statute and join the Third and Eleventh Circuits in adopting the "hypothetical test."

We begin, as we must, with the statutory language. The plain language of § 365(c)(1) "link[s] nonassignability under 'applicable law' together with a prohibition on assumption in bankruptcy." 1 *David G. Epstein, Steve H. Nickles & James J. White, Bankruptcy* § 5–15 at 474 (1992). In other words, the statute by its terms bars a debtor in possession from assuming an executory contract without the nondebtor's consent where applicable law precludes assignment of the contract to a third party. The literal language of § 365(c)(1) is thus said to establish a "hypothetical test": a debtor in possession may not assume an executory contract over the nondebtor's objection if applicable law would bar assignment to a hypothetical third party, even where the debtor in possession has no intention of assigning the contract in question to any such third party.

Before applying the statutory language to the case at hand, we first resolve a number of preliminary issues that are either not disputed by the parties, or are so clearly established as to deserve no more than passing reference. First, we follow the lead of the parties in assuming that the Perlman licenses are executory agreements within the meaning of § 365. Second, it is well-established that § 365(c)'s use of the term "trustee" includes Chapter 11 debtors in possession. Third, our precedents make it clear that federal patent law constitutes "applicable law" within the meaning of § 365(c), and that nonexclusive[17] patent licenses are "personal and assignable only with the consent of the licensor."

---

17. One of the two Perlman licenses began its life as an exclusive license. Perlman in a sworn declaration stated that, pursuant to its terms, the license has since become nonexclusive. Because Catapult has not offered any rebuttal evidence, and because neither party raised the issue in connection with the issues raised in this appeal, we will assume that the Perlman licenses are nonexclusive. Accordingly, we express no opinion regarding the assignability of exclusive patent

When we have cleared away these preliminary matters, application of the statute to the facts of this case becomes relatively straightforward:

> (c) Catapult may not assume ... the Perlman licenses, ... if

> (1)(A) federal patent law excuses Perlman from accepting performance from or rendering performance to an entity other than Catapult ... ; and (B) Perlman does not consent to such assumption....

11 U.S.C. § 365(c) (substitutions in italics). Since federal patent law makes nonexclusive patent licenses personal and nondelegable, § 365(c)(1)(A) is satisfied. Perlman has withheld his consent, thus satisfying § 365(c)(1)(B). Accordingly, the plain language of § 365(c)(1) bars Catapult from assuming the Perlman licenses.

IV.

Catapult urges us to abandon the literal language of § 365(c)(1) in favor of an alternative approach, reasoning that Congress did not intend to bar debtors in possession from assuming their own contracts where no assignment is contemplated. In Catapult's view, § 365(c)(1) should be interpreted as embodying an "actual test": the statute bars assumption by the debtor in possession only where the reorganization in question results in the nondebtor actually having to accept performance from a third party. Under this reading of § 365(c), the debtor in possession would be permitted to assume any executory contract, so long as no assignment was contemplated. Put another way, Catapult suggests that, as to a debtor in possession, § 365(c)(1) should be read to prohibit assumption and assignment, rather than assumption or assignment.

Catapult has marshalled considerable authority to support this reading. The arguments supporting Catapult's position can be divided into three categories: (1) the literal reading creates inconsistencies within § 365; (2) the literal reading is incompatible with the legislative history; and (3) the literal reading flies in the face of sound bankruptcy policy. Nonetheless, we find that none of these considerations justifies departing from the plain language of § 365(c)(1).

Policy arguments cannot displace the plain language of the statute; that the plain language of § 365(c)(1) may be bad policy does not justify a judicial rewrite....

V.

Because the statute speaks clearly, and its plain language does not produce a patently absurd result or contravene any clear legislative history, we must "hold Congress to its words." Accordingly, we hold that, where applicable nonbankruptcy law makes an executory contract nonassignable because the identity of the nondebtor party is material, a debtor in possession may not assume the contract absent consent of the nondebt-

---

licenses under federal law, and note that we expressed no opinion on this subject in Everex. See Everex, 89 F.3d at 679 ("Federal law holds a nonexclusive patent license to be personal and nonassignable....") (emphasis added).

or party. A straightforward application of § 365(c)(1) to the circumstances of this case precludes Catapult from assuming the Perlman licenses over Perlman's objection. Consequently, the bankruptcy court erred when it approved Catapult's motion to assume the Perlman licenses, and the district court erred in affirming the bankruptcy court.

QUESTIONS ABOUT CATAPULT ENTERTAINMENT

1. In *Pioneer Ford,* the debtor wanted to assign an executory contract. In *Catapult,* the debtor wanted to assume an executory contract. What are the practical differences between assumption and assignment? The "policy differences"? According to Professor Bussel, "Section 365 gets off on the wrong foot by equating assumption and assignment notwithstanding sharp policy distinctions between the two." Daniel J. Bussel & Edward Friedler, *The Limits on Assuming and Assigning Executory Contracts,* 74 AM. BANKR. L.J. 321, 323 (2000).[18]

2. Why did Catapult want to assume the Perlman licenses? Do we know why Perlman opposed the assumption? Is that relevant?

3. What was the "applicable law"?

4. In the *Catapult* opinion, the Ninth Circuit states that it is joining the Third Circuit and Eleventh Circuit in applying the "hypothetical" test. What is the "hypothetical" test and how is it different from the "actual test"? Which test is more consistent with the language of section 365? Which test is more consistent with bankruptcy policy?

Two Justices addressed these questions in explaining the denial of a writ of certiorari in a recent case. "According to the Court of Appeals for the Ninth Circuit, this language means that a debtor-in-possession may assume an executory contract only if hypothetically it might assign that contract to a third party. That is to say, if the debtor-in-possession lacks hypothetical authority to assign a contract, then it may not assume it-even if the debtor-in-possession has no *actual* intention of assigning the contract to another. *In re Catapult Entertainment, Inc.,* 165 F.3d 747 (C.A.9 1999). The so-called "hypothetical test" is preferred by a majority of the other Courts of Appeals that have addressed this question.

The hypothetical test is not, however, without its detractors. One arguable criticism of the hypothetical approach is that it purchases fidelity to the Bankruptcy Code's text by sacrificing sound bankruptcy policy. For one thing, the hypothetical test may prevent debtors-in-possession from continuing to exercise their rights under nonassignable contracts, such as patent and copyright licenses. Without these contracts, some debtors-in-possession may be unable to effect the successful reorganization that Chapter 11 was designed to promote. For another thing, the hypothetical test provides a windfall to nondebtor parties to valuable **executory contracts**: If the debtor is outside of bankruptcy, then the nondebtor does not have the **option** to renege on its agreement; but if the debtor seeks bankruptcy protection, then the nondebtor

---

18.   This article is quoted from again because it refers to a treatise co-authored by two of your authors as a "leading treatise", 74 AM. BANKR. L.J.329.

obtains the power to reclaim-and resell at the prevailing, potentially higher market rate-the rights it sold to the debtor.

To prevent § 365(c) from engendering unwise policy, one Court of Appeals, and a number of Bankruptcy Courts, reject the hypothetical test in favor of an "actual test," under which a Chapter 11 debtor-in-possession may assume an executory contract provided it has no actual intent to assign the contract to a third party. Of course, the actual test may present problems of its own. It may be argued, for instance, that the actual test aligns § 365(c) with sound bankruptcy policy only at the cost of departing from at least one interpretation of the plain text of the law.

The division in the courts over the meaning of § 365(c)(1) is an important one to resolve for Bankruptcy Courts and for businesses that seek reorganization. This petition for certiorari, however, is not the most suitable case for our resolution of the conflict. Addressing the issue here might first require us to resolve issues that may turn on the correct interpretation of antecedent questions under state law and trademark-protection principles. For those and other reasons, I reluctantly agree with the Court's decision to deny certiorari. In a different case the Court should consider granting certiorari on this significant question." *N.C.P. Marketing Group, Inc. v. BG Star Productions, Inc.* 129 S.Ct. 1577 (2009)

G.   WHAT ARE THE BANKRUPTCY POSSIBILITIES IF THE DEBTOR IS A LANDLORD?

Given the amount of rent that you pay each month for your apartment, condo, or house, you probably find it hard to imagine a landlord filing for bankruptcy but landlords can and do file for bankruptcy and can reject leases.

The effect of a debtor/landlord's rejecting a lease is different from the effect of a debtor/tenant's rejecting a lease. Remember that rejection is in essence a breach. Outside of bankruptcy, breach of a lease by a tenant is grounds for eviction of the tenant. Outside of bankruptcy, breach of a lease by the landlord is not grounds for eviction of the tenant.

Section 365(h) set out below sets out the legal effect of a debtor/landlord's rejecting leases in bankruptcy.

11 U.S.C. § 365(h) And Landlord Bankruptcy

(h)(1)(A) If the trustee rejects an unexpired lease of real property under which the debtor is the lessor and—

> (i) if the rejection by the trustee amounts to such a breach as would entitle the lessee to treat such lease as terminated by virtue of its terms, applicable nonbankruptcy law, or any agreement made by the lessee, then the lessee under such lease may treat such lease as terminated by the rejection; or

(ii) if the term of such lease has commenced, the lessee may retain its rights under such lease (including rights such as those relating to the amount and timing of payment of rent and other amounts payable by the lessee and any right of use, possession, quiet enjoyment, subletting, assignment, or hypothecation) that are in or appurtenant to the real property for the balance of the term of such lease and for any renewal or extension of such rights to the extent that such rights are enforceable under applicable nonbankruptcy law.

(B) If the lessee retains its rights under subparagraph (A)(ii), the lessee may offset against the rent reserved under such lease for the balance of the term after the date of the rejection of such lease and for the term of any renewal or extension of such lease, the value of any damage caused by the nonperformance after the date of such rejection, of any obligation of the debtor under such lease, but the lessee shall not have any other right against the estate or the debtor on account of any damage occurring after such date caused by such nonperformance. . . .

Problem 8–13: Rejection by Debtor Landlord

D owns the office building in which your law firm, Y, has its office. The lease agreement between D and Y provides for:

- payment of rental of $100,000 a month by Y
- exclusive use of floors 7–13 by Y;
- option to rent the 6th floor;
- maintenance and security service by D;

Can D reject the lease with Y? If so, can

- D evict Y?
- D change the amount of rent that Y pays?

If not, why would D reject the lease?

H. WHAT ARE THE BANKRUPTCY POSSIBIL-ITIES IF THE DEBTOR IS A LICENSOR OF INTELLECTUAL PROPERTY?

We will consider what the section 365 term "executory contract" means later in this Unit. However defined, "executory contract" includes intellectual property licenses.

As the *Catapult* case illustrates, a business's intellectual property licenses are often its most important assets. Five years after the *Catapult* decision, Alan Greenspan observed. "Technological advance is continually altering the shape and nature of our economic processes and, in particular, is promoting the trend toward increasing conceptualization of U.S. GDP . . . In recent decades, as the economic product of the United States has become so predominantly conceptual, issues related to the protection of intellectual property rights have come to be seen as significant sources of legal and business uncertainty. In part, this uncertainty derives from the fact that intellectual property is importantly different from physical property. Because they have a material existence, physical assets are more capable of being defended by police, the militia, or private mercenaries. By contrast, intellectual property can be stolen by an act as simple as broadcasting an idea without the permission of the originator. Moreover, one individual's use of an idea does not make that idea unavailable to others for their own simultaneous use. Even more importantly, new ideas—the building blocks of intellectual property—almost invariably build on old ideas in ways that are difficult or impossible to trace." ... http:/www.federalreserve.gov/boarddocs/speeches/2004/200402272/default. htm

Section 365(n) sets out the legal effects of a debtor/licensor's rejecting an intellectual property license. Section 365(n) needs to be read together with section 101(35A) which defines "intellectual property."

Section 365(n) should also be read together with section 365(h). In reading section 365(n) remember 365(h)'s treatment of a debtor/landlord's rejecting leases and remember the parallel between the bankruptcy concept of rejection and the common law concept of breach of contract.

Outside of bankruptcy, a licensee's breach of an intellectual property licensing agreement would be grounds for the licensor's terminating the licensee's rights under the licensing agreement. But, outside of bankruptcy, a licensor's breach of an intellectual property licensing agreement would not be grounds for the licensor's terminating the licensee's rights under the lease.

11 U.S.C. § 365(n)

(n)

(1) If the trustee rejects an executory contract under which the debtor is a licensor of a right to intellectual property,[19] the licensee under such contract may elect—

(A) to treat such contract as terminated by such rejection if such rejection by the trustee amounts to such a breach as would entitle the licensee to treat such contract as terminated by virtue of its own terms, applicable nonbankruptcy law, or an agreement made by the licensee with another entity; or

(B) to retain its rights (including a right to enforce any exclusivity provision of such contract, but excluding any other right under applicable nonbankruptcy law to specific performance of such contract) under such contract and under any agreement supplementary to such contract, to such intellectual property (including any embodiment of such intellectual property to the extent protected by applicable nonbankruptcy law), as

---

19. "Intellectual property" is defined in Section 101 (35A).

such rights existed immediately before the case commenced, for—

(i) the duration of such contract; and

(ii) any period for which such contract may be extended by the licensee as of right under applicable nonbankruptcy law.

(2) If the licensee elects to retain its rights, as described in paragraph (1)(B) of this subsection, under such contract—

(A) the trustee shall allow the licensee to exercise such rights;

(B) the licensee shall make all royalty payments due under such contract for the duration of such contract and for any period described in paragraph (1)(B) of this subsection for which the licensee extends such contract; and

(C) the licensee shall be deemed to waive—

(i) any right of setoff it may have with respect to such contract under this title or applicable nonbankruptcy law; and

(ii) any claim allowable under section 503(b) of this title arising from the performance of such contract.

(3) If the licensee elects to retain its rights, as described in paragraph (1)(B) of this subsection, then on the written request of the licensee the trustee shall—

(A) to the extent provided in such contract, or any agreement supplementary to such contract, provide to the licensee any intellectual property (including such embodiment) held by the trustee; and

(B) not interfere with the rights of the licensee as provided in such contract, or any agreement supplementary to such contract, to such intellectual property (including such embodiment) including any right to obtain such intellectual property (or such embodiment) from another entity.

(4) Unless and until the trustee rejects such contract, on the written request of the licensee the trustee shall—

(A) to the extent provided in such contract or any agreement supplementary to such contract—

(i) perform such contract; or

(ii) provide to the licensee such intellectual property (including any embodiment of such intellectual property to the extent protected by applicable nonbankruptcy law) held by the trustee; and

(B) not interfere with the rights of the licensee as provided in such contract, or any agreement supplementary to such contract, to such intellectual property (including such embodiment), including any right to obtain such intellectual property (or such embodiment) from another entity.

———————

Again, compare section 365(h)(landlord rejection) with section 365(n)(licensor rejection). First, the similarities. Similarities are easy so we will do that part for you. Under section 365(h), the tenant can continue to occupy the leased building or land, notwithstanding the landlord's bankruptcy and rejection of the lease. Under section 365(n), the licensee can continue to use the intellectual property, notwithstanding the licensor's bankruptcy and rejection of the license.

Now, the differences. That is harder. You can do that part. Compare what the tenant gets under section 365(h)(1)(A)(ii) with what the licensee gets under 365(n)(1)(B). Compare what the tenant pays under section 365(h)(1)(B) with what the licensee pays under 365(n)(2)(B).

Problem 8–14: Rejection of Patent License

In 2009, Debtor invented and obtained a patent on a tire shredding machine. Debtor filed a Chapter 13 petition in 2011.

On January 8, 2010, Debtor and Controlled Shredders entered into a twenty-year license agreement which licensed Controlled Shredders to manufacture and sell the tire shredding machine invented by Debtor and covered by his patent. The license to Controlled Shredders was exclusive. The License Agreement gave Controlled Shredders the right to incorporate into its manufacture any improvements or modifications developed by Debtor during the term of the patent. This license was subject to payment of royalties to Debtor on all tire shredders made or sold by Controlled Shredders.

The License Agreement also imposed other rights and obligations on the parties. The agreement required both parties to provide each other with any "assistance, cooperation, know-how, expertise, and information as may be reasonably required or beneficial to facilitating or improving the manufacture, operation, or use of the shredder." Each party was required to share "any improvements, developments, know-how, or information . . . which in any way affects the manufacture, operation, or use of the shredder."

Can the Debtor reject the License? If she does, can Controlled Shredders continue to use the patent? If so, will the Debtor have to provide postpetition modifications and improvements in the intellectual property to Controlled Shredders?

Problem 8–15: Rejection of Trademark License

D grants an exclusive license to use a trademark to S. D files for bankruptcy and rejects the trademark license agreement. Can S still use the trademark? *Cf.* section 101(35A).

I. WHAT IS AN EXECUTORY CONTRACT?

Thomas Jackson, then a professor at the Harvard Law School teaching bankruptcy, provided this explanation of "executory contract", as that term is used in section 365 and other Bankruptcy Code provisions: "Fundamentally, executory contracts ... as the Bankruptcy Code seems to intend, are nothing more than mixed assets and liabilities arising out of the same transaction. This can be seen by considering a simple example. Say Debtor, on December 1, entered into a contract with Supplier for Supplier to ship 1,000 pair of pants on February 1, with payment by Debtor of $10,000 on April 1. From December 1, until February 1, the contract is executory because either side could breach its yet unperformed obligation, giving rise to a power of termination by the other side. Supplier could fail to deliver the pants, for example, in which case Debtor would be relieved of its obligation to pay $10,000. Conversely, Debtor could announce that it would not pay for the pants when delivered, and this 'anticipatory repudiation' would relieve Supplier of its obligation to deliver the pants. Thus, up until February 1, this contract is both an asset of Debtor's (right to receive 1,000 pair of pants) and a liability (the obligation to pay $10,000). This mixture of an unperformed asset and a liability in the same contract is the special attribute of an executory contract. But after February 1, if Supplier meets its obligation to deliver conforming pants, the contract is no longer executory. This is so because once the nonbankrupt party has fully performed, the issue is only one of liability of the debtor–a claim."

THOMAS H. JACKSON, *THE LOGIC AND LIMITS OF BANKRUPTCY LAW* 106 (1986)

Do you think that the attorneys in the next case read Professor Jackson's book?

IN RE ARTS DAIRY, LLC.

2009 WL 3007869 (Bankr. N.D. Ohio 2009)

SPEER, BANKRUPTCY JUDGE.

On April 14, 2009, the Debtor, Arts Dairy, LLC (hereinafter the "Debtor"), filed a voluntary petition in this Court for relief under Chapter 11 of the United States Bankruptcy Code. At the time this case was commenced, the Debtor was engaged in the business of operating a dairy farm with approximately 1,250 cows. The Debtor continues to operate this business as a debtor-in-possession pursuant to 11 U.S.C. §§ 1107 and 1108.

The Plaintiff, Robert McComber (hereinafter the "Plaintiff"), was disclosed by the Debtor as an unsecured creditor, holding a claim in the amount of $95,889.90. The claim was not listed by the Debtor as contingent, unliquidated or disputed. Consideration for the claim was described as "Corn Silage."

It was presented that the claim arose from an agreement, executed on August 29, 2008, between the Debtor and the Plaintiff. (Doc. No. 1, Ex. 1).

This agreement provided that the Plaintiff, as the seller, would deliver to the Debtor "300 acres of Com Silage." *Id*. For this, the Debtor agreed to pay the Plaintiff in 12 monthly installments, beginning in September of 2008. Not long thereafter, in accordance with the agreement, the Plaintiff delivered to the Debtor the required silage. At the time the Debtor filed for bankruptcy relief, however, the Plaintiff had yet to receive full payment for the silage.

In addition to the agreement for silage, the Plaintiff and the Debtor also entered into an undated written arrangement for "Manure application." *Id*. The document evidencing this arrangement scheduled a monthly payment plan, beginning in October of 2008, and extending through September of 2009. Also as to the form of the document, it was set forth at the top: "Agreement: Bob McOmber [sic]" *Id*. After the payment schedule, it was then stated, "If you agree with this payment plan, payments will be sent accordingly." *Id*. Thereafter, the document concluded with the name of the Debtor, "Arts Dairy LLC.".

* * *

LEGAL DISCUSSION

The gravamen of the Plaintiff's first cause of actions seeks a determination that the agreement for corn silage, as executed between himself and the Debtor, be classified as an executory contract for purposes of bankruptcy law.

Under bankruptcy law, a contract which is executory in nature is subject to § 365 of the Code. This section affords the trustee-and by extension, a debtor-in-possession-the power to assume or reject executory contracts (as well as leases) to which the debtor was a party prior to the commencement of the bankruptcy case. 11 U.S.C. § 365(a). The assessment of whether a contract is executory is normally assessed as of the petition date. * * *

The term executory contract is not defined in § 365 nor anywhere in the Bankruptcy Code. To fill the void, courts have often applied the definition formulated by Professor Vern Countryman. This definition provides that an executory contract is "a contract under which the obligation of both the bankrupt and the other party to the contract are so far unperformed that the failure of either to complete performance would constitute a material breach excusing the performance of the other." For this Court, the Countryman definition of an executory contract is generally applicable when determining whether a contract is executory for purposes of § 365. * * *

Countryman's definition of an executory contract cannot be said to be the exclusive method through which the existence of an executory contract is determined. In an earlier decision, captioned *Chattanooga Memorial Park v. Still, Trustee (In re Jolly)*, the Sixth Circuit Court of Appeals held that, while the definition proposed by Professor Vern Countryman is helpful, it is not controlling for purposes of § 365. The Court in *In re Jolly* instead applied a functional approach. Under a functional approach, the Court in *In re Jolly* explained that when assessing whether a contract is executory, one should "work backward, proceeding from an examination of the purposes rejection is expected to accomplish." This decision has never been expressly overturned or otherwise overruled. Consequently, along side the Countryman definition, the functional approach would appear to remain good law in this judicial circuit, the Sixth Circuit.

Regardless of which approach is applied, however, an executory contract will not exist where the only remaining performance to be rendered is the payment of money. As previously noted: "Such contracts have never been treated as executory for bankruptcy purposes and their treatment as such would only cause procedural problems which might perpetrate inequities among creditors." *In re Norquist,* 43 B.R. 224 (Bankr.E.D.Wash. 1984).

When this bankruptcy case was commenced, the Plaintiff had completed his delivery of the corn silage to the Debtor in accordance with their agreement. Thereafter, the only obligation which remained to be performed was for the Debtor to continue to pay the Plaintiff in accordance with their agreement which called for payment on the silage to be made in monthly installments. Accordingly, for this reason, the Parties' agreement for com silage cannot be construed as an executory contract for purposes of § 365.

QUESTIONS ABOUT ARTS DAIRY

1. Why is Plaintiff arguing that the corn silage agreement is an executory contract?

2. Would the corn silage agreement have been an executory contract if Plaintiff had not delivered the required silage to the Debtor prior to Debtor's bankruptcy?

3. Assume that before filing for bankruptcy, D borrowed $300,000 from M and executed a contract that provided that (i) D would repay the $300,000 with 8% interest in 60 equal monthly payments and (ii) M would have have a mortgage on D's farm until the last such payment. Would the bankruptcy court's treating this agreement as an executory contract be beneficial to M? Would the *Arts Dairy* bankruptcy court treat such an agreement as executory contract? Would Professor Jackson?

4. Review question: Use Judge Gropper's description of the facts in *In re Empire Equities Capital Corp.* 405 B.R. 687 (Bankr. S.D.N.Y. 2009) to review this Unit: "The relevant facts are undisputed and uncomplicated. The Debtor entered into an option contract to purchase from the Movants three loans secured by real property located at 423 West Street, New York City. The Debtor initially paid the Movants $100,000 in advance, with this deposit to be applied against the purchase price at the closing or be retained by the sellers if the transaction did not close. The contract, as originally agreed, had a deadline of March 16, 2009. The Debtor obtained two extensions of the

deadline for an additional downpayment of $600,000. The first extension pushed the deadline to April 20, 2009 and the second to April 30, 2009 at 12:00 p.m., time being of the essence. On April 30, 2009, thirty-nine minutes before the closing deadline, the Debtor filed the above-captioned Chapter 11 bankruptcy petition, without having proffered the purchase price to the Movants. The Debtor admits having filed the petition to use the time that it asserts is provided in §§ 365 and 108(b)[1] of the Bankruptcy Code to raise the balance of the purchase price, close the transaction and avoid the forfeiture of its downpayment. The Movants contend that neither §§ 365 nor 108(b) applies under the circumstances of this case." In ruling, Judge Gropper notes that there is a split in the reported cases as to whether "an option contract is executory in nature and thus governed by § 365" and goes on to say "the Court finds that the Debtor has no rights under § 365 for other reasons and thus need not reach these issues."

---

1. 11 U.S.C. § 108(a) provides that [i]f ... an agreement fixes a period within which the debtor may commence an action, and such period has not expired before the date of the filing of the petition, the trustee may commence such action only before the later of—

(1) the end of such period, including any suspension of such period occurring on or after the commencement of the case; or

(2) two years after the order for relief.

UNIT 9

LEGAL ISSUES TO WATCH FOR
IN CHAPTER 7 CASES

■ ■ ■

A. OVERVIEW OF CHAPTER 7

This would be a good time to look at Chapter 7 in your copy of the Bankruptcy Code. Chapter 7 is divided into four subchapters, We will study only the first two in any detail.[1]

Most bankruptcy cases are Chapter 7 cases. Most bankruptcy cases start as Chapter 7 cases, with the debtor selecting Chapter 7 in his or her or its bankruptcy petition. Even more bankruptcy cases end as Chapter 7 cases, with debtors who initially selected Chapter 11 or Chapter 13 electing to convert their case to Chapter 7.

1. CHAPTER 7 PEOPLE

Think again about who works on a Chapter 7 case. The attorney for the debtor (or that attorney's paralegal staff) does most of the pre-bankruptcy work, preparing the petition and accompanying schedules. *See* Official Forms 1, 6, 7, and 8.

After a Chapter 7 petition has been filed, most of the work is done by the bankruptcy trustee. She collects and sells "property of the estate." *See* section 704. Then she distributes the proceeds from the sale of property of the estate to creditors in the manner set out in section 726, if there are any such proceeds. In more than 90% of Chapter 7 cases there are no distributions to holders of unsecured claims.

2. CHAPTER 7 COSTS AND BENEFIT

For most individual debtors, Chapter 7 cases end in a discharge. We covered discharge generally in Unit 4 and will cover discharge in Chapter 7 cases later in this Court. For now, it should be obvious that discharge is a benefit to the debtor and a cost to creditors.

And, for now, think about the other costs and benefits of a Chapter 7 case to both the debtor and to the creditors. In every bankruptcy case the

---

1. We will not be looking at Subchapter III which applies only if the debtor is a "stockbroker" as defined in section 101 or Subchapter IV which applies only if the debtor is a "commodity broker" as defined in section 101.

delay provided by the automatic stay is a cost to creditors and a benefit to the debtor. In every Chapter 7 case the costs to the debtor include (i) the debtor's paying attorney's fees, and (ii) the debtor's losing "property of the estate." In every Chapter 7 case the benefit to creditors is the trustee's distribution of the money received from the sale of property of the estate in the manner set out in section 726 which is set out below

(a) Except as provided in section 510 of this title, property of the estate shall be distributed—

(1) first, in payment of claims of the kind specified in, and in the order specified in, section 507 of this title . . . ;

(2) second, in payment of any allowed unsecured claim, other than a claim of a kind specified in paragraph (1), (3), or (4) of this subsection . . . ;

(5) fifth, in payment of interest at the legal rate from the date of the filing of the petition, on any claim paid under paragraph (1), (2) . . . ;

(b) Payments on claims of a kind specified in paragraph (1), . . . of section 507(a) of this title, . . . shall be made pro rata among claims of the kind specified in each such particular paragraph, *except that in a case that has been converted to this chapter [from another chapter such as Chapter 11], a claim allowed under section 503(b) of this title incurred under [Chapter 7] after such conversion has priority over a claim allowed under section 503(b) of this title incurred under any other chapter of this title . . . .* (emphasis added)

Problem 9–1: Chapter 7 Distribution

The Chapter 7 trustee sells the property of the estate for $220,000. The costs of administering and selling the property of the estate are $20,000. There are the following "allowed unsecured claims":

- A, $30,000
- B, $40,000
- C, $50,000
- D, $60,000
- E, $70,000
- F, $150,000 (Total allowed unsecured claims equals $400,000)

How should the trustee distribute the $220,000?

Section 726 distribution is a part of the end game in every Chapter 7 case—Chapter 7 cases involving debtors who are individuals and Chapter 7 cases involving debtors who are corporations or other business entities. Remember that the debtor in a Chapter 7 case can be a corporation or other business entity. However, most Chapter 7 cases involve individual debtors.[2]

3. PREVIEW OF LEGAL ISSUES THAT CAN ARISE IN CHAPTER 7 CASES INVOLVING INDIVIDUAL DEBTORS

Most of the rest of the legal issues to watch for in Chapter 7 cases and most of the legal issues in this unit of the book arise only in Chapter 7 cases involving individual debtors. More specifically, most of the "legal issues" that arise in a Chapter 7 case involve either disputes with respect to an individual debtor's (1) exemptions or (2) her eligibility for discharge or (3) debts not covered by her discharge or (4) secured claims against her or (5) her eligibility for Chapter 7.[3]

B. EXEMPTIONS

While exemptions are limited to individuals. exemptions are not limited to individuals who are in Chapter 7 bankruptcy. And, while section 522 issues on exemptions can arise in a Chapter 13 case or a Chapter 11 case in which the debtor is an individual, exemption issues arise most frequently in Chapter 7 cases.

There are three exemption questions that a law student or lawyer doing bankruptcy work needs to be able to answer: first, what is exempt property, second, what law determines what property is exempt, and third what important bankruptcy law issues are implicated[4] by exempt property.[5]

1. WHAT IS EXEMPT PROPERTY?

Exempt property is property that an individual can keep free from the claims of <u>certain creditors</u>, even though those creditors have not been

---

2. Obviously, there are more individuals than business entities. And, it should already be obvious why "the vast majority [more than 80%] of small businesses resolve financial distress under state law." Edward R. Morrison, *Bargaining Around Bankruptcy: Small Business Workouts And State Law*, 38 J.Legal Stud. 25 (2009) Is it obvious to you? Have you already taken your law school's basic course covering corporations and other limited liability business structures?

3. In terms of the "life cycle" of a Chapter 7 case, eligibility for Chapter 7 is the first possible issue. Nonetheless, we are covering eligibility for Chapter 7 as the last of our possible Chapter 7 issues. There are several reasons we do this. First. the section 707 "means test" for eligibility for Chapter 7 is the most complicated and most boring part of Chapter 7. Second, understanding the section 707(b)(2) "means test" will help you in understanding section 1322(d), which we will be covering in the next unit. The final reason we are covering the beginning of a Chapter 7 at the end of the unit on Chapter 7 is that your senior author grew up with prayer books that had page 1 at the "back of the book." http://www.nytimes.com/2007/09/03/us/03prayerbook.html

4. "Implicate" is Liz's word. Great law school word. Did you ever use the word "implicate" before law school?

5. These exemption questions can only arise is cases in which the debtor is an individual. No exemptions for business entity debtors. While these exemption questions can arise in a Chapter 13 case or a Chapter 11 case in which the debtor is an individual, exemption questions arise most frequently in Chapter 7 cases.

paid. If, for example, D's home is exempt, then even though D has not paid her credit card bill owing to C or the hospital bill owing to H, neither C nor H can seize and sell D's home.

Recall the underlined words "certain creditors" in the preceding paragraph. An individual debtor's exempt property is protected from the claims of most, but not all, creditors, In the above example involving D's exempt home, if D defaults on her obligations to F, the creditor with a mortgage on D's home, then F can still seize and sell D's home.

2. WHAT LAW DETERMINES WHAT PROPERTY IS EXEMPT?

Statutes determine what property is exempt. More specifically, exempt property law is primarily state statutory law.

Every state has exemption statutes—statutes which identify property that an individual is able to retain even if she is unable to pay her creditors. These state statutes typically exempt certain tangible person property such as automobiles and home furnishings, intangible property such as life insurance and retirement benefits, and, most important for most individual debtors, the debtor's home (commonly referred to as the "homestead.")

These statutes vary significantly from state to state with respect to the amount of property that is exempt. Particularly with respect to the homestead. Compare the relevant New York and Florida homestead exemption provisions:

New York McKinney's CPLR § 5206

§ 5206. Real property exempt from application to the satisfaction of money judgments

(a) Exemption of **homestead.** Property of one of the following types, not exceeding fifty thousand dollars in value above liens and encumbrances, owned and occupied as a principal residence, is exempt from application to the satisfaction of a money judgment, unless the judgment was recovered wholly for the purchase price thereof:

1. a lot of land with a dwelling thereon,
2. shares of stock in a cooperative apartment corporation,
3. units of a condominium apartment, or
4. a mobile home

Florida Constitution, Article X, section 4,

SECTION 4. Homestead; exemptions.-

(a) There shall be exempt from forced sale under process of any court, and no judgment, decree or execution shall be a lien thereon, except for the payment of taxes and assessments thereon, obligations contracted for the purchase, improvement or repair thereof, or obligations contracted for house, field or other labor performed on the realty, the following property owned by a natural person:

(1) a homestead, if located outside a municipality, to the extent of one hundred sixty acres of contiguous land and improvements thereon, which shall not be reduced without the owner's consent by reason of subsequent inclusion in a municipality; or if located within a municipality, to the extent of one-half acre of contiguous land, upon which the exemption shall be limited to the residence of the owner or the owner's family;

There are also some federal statutes that exempt certain property—primarily specific federal benefits such as Social Security payments—from creditors claims. In the main, however, state exemption statutes determine what property is exempt.[6]

Even in bankruptcy, in the main, state exemption laws determine what property is exempt.

In section 522(b)(1), Congress seems to give individual debtors[7] a choice of what law determines exempt property. Under section 522(b)(1), individual debtors seemingly can chose the exemptions provided in section 522(d) or can choose the exemptions provided in state law and federal non-bankruptcy law.

Section 522(b)(1) needs to be read together with section 522(b)(2). In section 522(b)(2), Congress gives states legislatures a choice—the choice of eliminating the choice that section 522(b)(1) gives individual debtors. More than ¾ of the state legislatures have made this choice by enacting what is generally referred to as "opt-out legislation" so that most debtors have no choice other than state exemption law and non-bankruptcy federal exemption law.

Accordingly, we have "opted out" of coverage of section 522(d) to cover section 522(b) more thoroughly. Please read the except from section 522(b) set out below, especially section 522(b)(3)(A).

11 U.S.C. § 522(b)(1) Through 522(b)(3)(C)

(b)(1) Notwithstanding section 541 of this title, an individual debtor may exempt from property of the estate the property listed in either paragraph (2) or, in the alternative, paragraph (3) of this subsection. . . .

(2) Property listed in this paragraph is property that is specified under subsection (d), unless the State law that is applicable to the debtor under paragraph (3)(A) specifically does not so authorize;

---

6. Title III of the Consumer Credit Protection Act, 15 USCA sections 1671 et seq, limits the amount of a debtor's wages that a creditor can garnish. Its primary purpose is to protect employers from the hassles associated with garnishment of their employees' wages. Once an employee receives wages, Title III no longer protects them.

7. Only an individual can claim exempt property under section 522. In Chapter 11, only an individual debtor is subject to the section 523 exceptions to discharge, *see* section 1141. And, of course, only an individual debtor can use Chapter 13.

(3) Property listed in this paragraph is—

(A) subject to subsections (*o*) and (p) any property that is exempt under Federal law, other than subsection (d) of this section, or State or local law that is applicable on the date of the filing of the petition at the place in which the debtor's domicile has been located for the 730 days immediately preceding the date of the filing of the petition, or if the debtor's domicile has <u>not been located at a single State for such 730–day period,</u> the place in which the debtor's domicile was located for <u>180 days immediately preceding the 730–day period</u> or for a longer portion of such 180–day period than in any other place;

(B) any interest in property in which the debtor had, immediately before the commencement of the case, an interest as a tenant by the entirety or joint tenant to the extent that such interest as a tenant by the entirety or joint tenant is exempt from process under applicable nonbankruptcy law; and

(C) retirement funds to the extent that those funds are in a fund or account that is exempt from taxation under section 401, 403, 408, 408A, 414,457, or 501(a) of the Internal Revenue Code of 1986.

If the effect of the domiciliary requirement under subparagraph (A) is to render the debtor ineligible for any exemption, the debtor may elect to exempt property that is specified under subsection (d). (emphasis added)

***

Recall that exemption laws vary significantly from state to state. Congress was concerned that individuals would move to states with more generous exemptions before filing for bankruptcy. Section 522(b)(3)(A) is one of the provisions Congress added in 2005 to address that concern. Please apply section 522(b)(3)(A) in the next problem.

Problem 9–2: Determining State That Determines Exemptions

1. D lived for more than 50 years in Virginia, a state with very limited exemptions. D then moved to Florida, a state with very generous exemptions, and lived in Florida for a year. D then moved back to Virginia. 727 days after returning to Virginia D filed a bankruptcy petition. Under section 522(b)(3) which state is the state whose exemption laws control what property is exempt in D's bankruptcy case?

2. D lived in State X until 2009. That year, D sold her house in State X, moved to State Y, and bought a house in State Y. Six months later, D filed for bankruptcy. State X provides for an unlimited homestead, so long as the home is located in State X. State X has also enacted opt out legislation. Is D's home exempt?

3. WHAT IMPORTANT BANKRUPTCY LAW ISSUES ARE IMPLICATED BY EXEMPT PROPERTY?

To the extent that a Chapter 7 debtor is able to win a battle of whether property is exempt, he will be able to keep more and his creditors get less. While creditors are directly affected by the result of a legal battle over what property of the Chapter 7 debtor is exempt, individual creditors are generally not directly involved in legal battles over exemptions. Rather, exemption litigation in Chapter 7 cases typically involves the attorney for the debtor and the attorney for the Chapter 7 trustee who acts as representative of the creditors.[8]

a. Increasing Exempt Property Before Bankruptcy

The 2005 amendments also added two specific limitations on a a debtor's increasing his or homestead before bankruptcy. section 522(o)(4) and 522(p)(1)(D). Please read and apply these provisions

11 U.S.C. § 522(o)(4)

(o) For **purposes** of **subsection (b)(3)(A)**, and notwithstanding subsection (a), the value of an interest in—

> (4) real or personal property that the debtor or a dependent of the debtor claims as a homestead;

> shall be reduced to the extent that such value is attributable to any portion of any property that the debtor disposed of in the 10–year period ending on the date of the filing of the petition with the intent to hinder, delay, or defraud a creditor and that the debtor could not exempt, or that portion that the debtor could not exempt

11 U.S.C. § 522(p)(1)(D)

(p)(1) ... [A] debtor may

> not exempt any amount of interest that was acquired by the debtor during the 1215–day period preceding the date of the filing of the petition that exceeds in the aggregate $125,000 in value in— ...

> (D) real or personal property that the debtor or dependent of the debtor claims as a homestead.

Problem 9–3: Section 522(o) and (p) Limitations on Amount of Exempt Homestead

D has lived all of his life in Texas, a state with a virtually unlimited homestead. D is retired, living off his investments, in a $1,500,000 home, encumbered by a $700,000 mortgage. Because of some bad investment decisions, D is considering filing for bankruptcy. D has $650,000 in his bank

---

8. Judge Conrad Cyr, a distinguished bankruptcy judge before appointment to the United States Court of Appeals for the First Circuit, described a Chapter 7 trustee as 'the representative of all unsecured creditors.' *In re* Thompson, 965 F.2d 1136, 1145 (1st Cir. 1992).

account. If D used that $650,000 to reduce his $700,000 mortgage and later files for bankruptcy, would that be another bad investment decision?

The phrase "intent to hinder, delay. or defraud" appears not only in section 522(*o*)(4) but also appears in sections 548 and 727 and those sections have also been involved in cases involving a prebankruptcy increase in exempt property. The next case, *In re Tveten*, is probably the most cited such case. *Tveten* is probably most remembered for dictum in Judge Arnold's dissenting opinion (which is dictum from a New Mexico bankruptcy court opinion): "when a pig becomes a hog it is slaughtered." In reading *Tveten*, please think about whether you agree with the majority's conclusion that "the bankruptcy court was not clearly erroneous in inferring fraudulent intent" or whether you agree with Judge Arnold's conclusion: "Tveten did nothing more fraudulent than seek to take advantage of a state law of which the federal courts disapprove."

IN RE TVETEN

848 F.2d 871 (8th Cir. 1988)

TIMBERS, Circuit Judge.

Appellant Omar A. Tveten, a physician who owed creditors almost $19,000,000, mostly in the form of personal guaranties on a number of investments whose value had deteriorated greatly, petitioned for Chapter 11 bankruptcy. He had converted almost all of his non-exempt property, with a value of about $700,000, into exempt property that could not be reached by his creditors. The bankruptcy court, on the basis of its findings of fact and conclusions of law, entered an order on February 27, 1987, denying a discharge in view of its finding that Tveten intended to defraud, delay, and hinder his creditors. The district court affirmed the bankruptcy court's order. On appeal, Tveten asserts that his transfers merely constituted astute pre-bankruptcy planning. We hold that the bankruptcy court was not clearly erroneous in inferring fraudulent intent on the part of Tveten.

We affirm.

I.

We shall summarize only those facts and prior proceedings believed necessary to an understanding of the issues raised on appeal.

Tveten is a 59 year old physician in general practice. He is the sole shareholder of Omar A. Tveten, P.A., a professional corporation. He has no dependents. He began investing in various real estate developments. These investments initially were quite successful. Various physician friends of Tveten joined him in organizing a corporation to invest in these ventures. These investments were highly leveraged.

The physicians, including Tveten, personally had guaranteed the debt arising out of these investments. In mid–1985, Tveten's investments began to sour. He became personally liable for an amount close to $19,000,000—well beyond his ability to pay. Appellees became creditors of Tveten as a result of his various investment ventures.

Tveten filed a Chapter 11 petition on January 7, 1986.... On the date the Chapter 11 petition was filed, Tveten owed his creditors close to $19,000,000. Before filing for bankruptcy, Tveten consulted counsel. As part of his pre- bankruptcy planning, he liquidated almost all of his non-exempt property, converting it into exempt property worth approximately $700,000. All of the liquidated property was converted into life insurance or annuity contracts with the Lutheran Brotherhood, a fraternal benefit association, which, under Minnesota law, cannot be attached by creditors. Tveten concedes that the purpose of these transfers was to shield his assets from creditors. Minnesota law provides that creditors cannot attach any money or other benefits payable by a fraternal benefit association. Unlike most exemption provisions in other states, the Minnesota exemption has no monetary limit. Indeed, under this exemption, Tveten attempted to place $700,000 worth of his property out of his creditors' reach.

Tveten sought a discharge with respect to $18,920,000 of his debts. Appellees objected to Tveten's discharge. In its order of February 27, 1987, the bankruptcy court concluded that, although Tveten's conversion of non-exempt property to exempt property just before petitioning for bankruptcy, standing alone, would not justify denial of a discharge, his inferred intent to defraud would.[2] The bankruptcy court held that, even if the exemptions were permissible, Tveten had abused the protections permitted a debtor under the Bankruptcy Code (the "Code"). His awareness of a judgment against him and of several pending lawsuits, his rapidly deteriorating business investments, and his exposure to extensive liability well beyond his ability to pay, all were cited by the court in its description of the circumstances under which Tveten converted his property. Moreover, the court concluded that Tveten intended to hinder and delay his creditors. Accordingly, the bankruptcy court denied Tveten a discharge.

Tveten appealed from the bankruptcy court order to the federal district court. In a memorandum opinion and order entered July 10, 1987, the district court affirmed the denial of a discharge, concluding that the bankruptcy court's finding as to Tveten's intent was not clearly erroneous.[3]

---

2. Several creditors also objected to Tveten's claimed exemptions. In response, the bankruptcy court, by order entered September 16, 1986, certified the question to the Minnesota Supreme Court. The bankruptcy court decided that it need not wait for the Supreme Court's decision, since the determinative factor on the issue of discharge was Tveten's intent.

3. Before the district court entered its order, the Supreme Court of Minnesota held in a decision entered March 27, 1987, that annuities and life insurance contracts issued by a fraternal benefit society were exempt under Minnesota law, but that these statutory provisions violated the Minnesota Constitution. In re Tveten, 402 N.W.2d 551 (Minn.1987). Accordingly, Tveten no

The instant appeal followed. Basically, Tveten asserts on appeal that as a matter of law we should reject the factors relied on by the bankruptcy court to infer that Tveten intended to delay, hinder and defraud creditors. We disagree. We affirm.

II.

The sole issue on appeal is whether Tveten properly was denied a discharge in view of the transfers alleged to have been in fraud of creditors.

At the outset, it is necessary to distinguish between (1) a debtor's right to exempt certain property from the claims of his creditors and (2) his right to a discharge of his debts. The Code permits a debtor to exempt property either pursuant to the provisions of the Code if not forbidden by state law, 11 U.S.C. § 522(b) & (d), or pursuant to the provisions of state law and federal law other than the minimum allowances in the Code. 11 U.S.C. § 522(b)(2). When the debtor claims a state-created exemption, the scope of the claim is determined by state law . . .

A debtor's right to a discharge, however, unlike his right to an exemption, is determined by federal, not state, law. The Code provides that a debtor may be denied a discharge under Chapter 7 if, among other things, he has transferred property "with intent to hinder, delay, or defraud a creditor" within one year before the date of the filing of the petition. 11 U.S.C. § 727(a)(2) Although Tveten filed for bankruptcy under Chapter 11, the proscription against discharging a debtor with fraudulent intent in a Chapter 7 proceeding is equally applicable against a debtor applying for a Chapter 11 discharge. The reason for this is that the Code provides that confirmation of a plan does not discharge a Chapter 11 debtor if "the debtor would be denied a discharge under section 727(a) of this title if the case were a case under chapter 7 of this title." 11 U.S.C. § 1141(d)(3)(C)

Although the determination as to whether a discharge should be granted or denied is governed by federal law, the standard applied consistently by the courts is the same as that used to determine whether an exemption is permissible, i.e. absent extrinsic evidence of fraud, mere conversion of non-exempt property to exempt property is not fraudulent as to creditors even if the motivation behind the conversion is to place those assets beyond the reach of creditors.

As the bankruptcy court correctly found here, therefore, the issue in the instant case revolves around whether there was extrinsic evidence to demonstrate that Tveten transferred his property on the eve of bankruptcy with intent to defraud his creditors. The bankruptcy court's finding that there was such intent to defraud may be reversed by us only if clearly erroneous. . . .

---

longer will be able to claim these exemptions. Following the opinion of the Supreme Court of Minnesota, Tveten claimed an exemption for his pension in the amount of approximately $200,000. He and his creditors settled this issue before the bankruptcy court. He will retain this property as exempt.

[T]his case presents a situation in which the debtor liquidated almost his entire net worth of $700,000 and converted it to non-exempt property in seventeen transfers on the eve of bankruptcy while his creditors, to whom he owed close to $19,000,000, would be left to divide the little that remained in his estate. Borrowing the phrase used by another court, Tveten "did not want a mere fresh start, he wanted a head start." His attempt to shield property worth approximately $700,000 goes well beyond the purpose for which exemptions are permitted. Tveten's reliance on his attorney's advice does not protect him here, since that protection applies only to the extent that the reliance was reasonable. The bankruptcy court, as affirmed by the district court, examined Tveten's entire pattern of conduct and found that he had demonstrated fraudulent intent. We agree. While state law governs the legitimacy of Tveten's exemptions, it is federal law that governs his discharge. Tveten still is entitled to retain, free from creditors' claims, property rightfully exempt under relevant state law. . . .

To summarize:

We hold that the bankruptcy court was not clearly erroneous in inferring fraudulent intent on the part of the debtor, rather than astute pre-bankruptcy planning, with respect to his transfers on the eve of bankruptcy which were intended to defraud, delay and hinder his creditors.

Affirmed.

ARNOLD, Circuit Judge, dissenting.

The Court reaches a result that appeals to one's general sense of righteousness. I believe, however, that it is contrary to clearly established law, and I therefore respectfully dissent.

Dr. Tveten has never made any bones about what he is doing, or trying to do, in this case. He deliberately set out to convert as much property as possible into a form exempt from attachment by creditors under Minnesota law. Such a design necessarily involves an attempt to delay or hinder creditors, in the ordinary, non-legal sense of those words, but, under long-standing principles embodied both in judicial decisions and in statute, such a purpose is not unlawful. . . .

A debtor's right to make full use of statutory exemptions is fundamental to bankruptcy law. To unsecured creditors, a debtor's conversion of his assets into exempt categories of property will always appear unfair, but this apparent unfairness is simply a consequence of the existence of exemptions under the jurisdiction's bankruptcy law. . . .

The same principle was confirmed by Congress when it enacted the Bankruptcy Code of 1978. The report of the House Judiciary Committee states as follows:

As under current law, the debtor will be permitted to convert nonexempt property into exempt property before filing a bankruptcy petition. See Hearings, Pt. Ill, at 1355–58. The practice is not fraudulent as to creditors, and permits the debtor to make full use of the exemptions to which he is entitled under the law.

... The House Report's language plainly says that debtors may convert nonexempt property into exempt property, that doing so is not fraudulent, and that debtors may make "full use" of any applicable exemption.

To be sure, if there is extrinsic evidence of fraud, or of a purpose to hinder or delay creditors, discharge may and should be denied, but "extrinsic," in this context, must mean something beyond the mere conversion of assets into exempt form for the purpose of putting them out of the reach of one's creditors. If Tveten had lied to his creditors or misled them in some way, or transferred property for less than fair value to a third party, we would have a very different case. There is absolutely no evidence of that sort of misconduct in this record, and the Court's opinion filed today cites none.

One is tempted to speculate what the result would have been in this case if the amount of assets converted had been $7,000, instead of $700,000. Where courts punish debtors simply for claiming exemptions within statutory limits, troubling problems arise in separating judicial from legislative power. As Judge Kishel explained in his excellent opinion in In re Johnson, 80 B.R. 953 (Bankr.D.Minn.1987):

> The legislative branch alone determines what is necessary ... to meet a debtor's needs, by establishing the nature and value of the property subject to claims exemption.... To deny discharge for a debtor's non-fraudulent invocation of these protections is, overtly or covertly, to make a political and/or value judgment on these legislative determinations. To equate a non-fraudulent intent to 'place assets beyond the reach of creditors' with an invidious intent to 'hinder or delay creditors' is ultimately to frustrate statutory exemption rights by causing a chilling effect on the full exercise of those rights. A court which causes such a chilling effect is, in a very real sense, invading legislative prerogatives by substituting its own judgment for that of the legislature.

If there ought to be a dollar limit, and I am inclined to think that there should be, and if practices such as those engaged in by the debtor here can become abusive, and I admit that they can, the problem is simply not one susceptible of a judicial solution according to manageable objective standards. A good statement of the kind of judicial reasoning that must underlie the result the Court reaches today appears in In re Zouhar, 10 B.R. 154 (Bankr.D.N.M.1981), where the amount of assets converted was $130,000. The Bankruptcy Court denied discharge, stating, among other things, that" 'there is a principle of too much; phrased colloquially, when a pig becomes a hog it is slaughtered.' " Id. at 157. If I were a member of the Minnesota Legislature, I might well vote in favor of a bill to place an over-all dollar maximum on any exemption.[3] But sitting as a judge, by what criteria do I determine when this pig becomes a hog? If $700,000 is too much, what about $70,000? Would it matter if the debtor were a farmer, as in Forsberg, rather than a physician? (I ask the question because the appellee creditor's brief mentions the debtor's profession, which ought to be legally irrelevant, several times.)

Debtors deserve more definite answers to these questions than the Court's opinion provides. In effect, the Court today leaves the distinction between permissible and impermissible claims of exemption to each bankruptcy judge's own sense of proportion. As a result, debtors will be unable to know in advance how far the federal courts will allow them to exercise their rights under state law.

Where state law creates an unlimited exemption, the result may be that wealthy debtors like Tveten enjoy a windfall that appears unconscionable, and contrary to the policy of the bankruptcy law. I fully agree with Judge Kishel, however, that [this] result ... cannot be laid at [the] Debtor's feet; it must be laid at the feet of the state legislature. Debtor did nothing more than exercise a prerogative that was fully his under law.

It cannot be said that his actions have so tainted him or his bankruptcy petition as to merit denial of discharge.

I submit that Tveten did nothing more fraudulent than seek to take advantage of a state law of which the federal courts disapprove.

I would reverse this judgment and hold that the debtor's actions in converting property into exempt form do not bar a discharge in bankruptcy.

QUESTIONS ABOUT TVETEN

1. According to the majority opinion, "absent extrinsic evidence of fraud, mere conversion of nonexempt property to exempt property is not fraudulent." What was the extrinsic evidence of fraud in this case?

2. Did this case answer the question whether Tveten's Lutheran Brotherhood annuities purchased on the eve of bankruptcy are exempt? Looking back, does section 522(o) or section 522(p) now answer this question?

3. Looking ahead, who wins because the bankruptcy court denied Tveten a discharge? How much did they win?

4. Looking at the "real world," most individual debtors are not physicians with $700,000 of non-exempt property. More "real world" debtors are

---

3. There is some irony in the fact that the exemption sought by the debtor in this case, that for benefits under annuities or life-insurance policies issued by fraternal associations, has been held unconstitutional under two provisions of the Minnesota Constitution. One such provision, Article 1, Section 12, provides that "[a] reasonable amount of property shall be exempt...." The Supreme Court of Minnesota has held that the exemption statute involved in the present case is unconstitutional precisely because it contains no dollar limit. *In re* Tveten, 402 N.W.2d 551, 556–58 (Minn.1987). So the principle of limitation has been upheld, the debtor has in any event lost the exemption he sought, but he also loses his discharge under today's decision.

moré like the debtor in the next problem than the debtor in *Tveten*. Is *Tveten* helpful in answering the next problem?

Problem 9–3:   Exemption Planning

On March 3, 2009, Curtis Wadley purchased a 2009 Heritage Harley Davidson Motorcycle. By June of 2010, Curtis Wadley realized he could no longer ride the motorcycle due to surgery that limited the use of his hands.

In early August of 2010, Curtis Wadley and his wife, Vickie Wadley, met with attorney Harry Zornow regarding the filing of a bankruptcy petition. After the meeting and with the knowledge that he and his wife were insolvent and would file a petition in the near future, Curtis Wadley sold his motorcycle for $12,000.00 on August 23, 2010. Curtis Wadley made the following payments with the proceeds from the sale:

1.	PERS (Curtis Wadley's retirement)	$3,800
2.	Harry Zornow (bankruptcy attorney)	$600
3.	Doctor's Bills	$200
4.	Glasses Eye Exam	$300
5.	Groceries, etc.	$100
6.	Purchase of Whole Life Insurance Policy (Beneficiary Vickie Wadley)	$7,000

Following the disbursal of the proceeds in the above manner, the Wadleys filed a joint Chapter 7 bankruptcy petition on October 21, 2010. In their schedules, they declared as exempt the whole life insurance policy and Curtis Wadley's retirement account. What, if any action, should the Chapter 7 trustee take?

b.   Avoiding Liens on Exempt Property

If you have bought a house or a car then you can probably recognize a lien on exempt property. And, section 522(c) generally recognizes the validity of such liens in bankruptcy.

There are some liens on exempt property that can be eliminated because of bankruptcy. *Cf.* § 522(c)(2). First, the general avoidance provisions discussed in Unit 7 generally apply to exempt property. Additionally, section 522(f) empowers the debtor to avoid (1) judicial liens on exempt property and (2) security interests that are nonpossessory, nonpurchase money and encumber property of a type identified in section 522(f)(2).

11 U.S.C. § 522(f)

(f)(1) Notwithstanding any waiver of exemptions ..., the debtor may avoid the fixing of a lien on an interest of the debtor in property to the extent that such lien impairs an exemption to which the debtor would have been entitled under subsection (b) of this section, if such lien is—

(A) a judicial lien . . .

(B) a nonpossessory, nonpurchase-money security interest in any—

(i) household furnishings, household goods [defined in section 522(f)(4)], wearing apparel, appliances, books, animals, crops, musical instruments, or jewelry that are held primarily for the personal, family, or household use of the debtor or a dependent of the debtor;

(ii) implements, professional books, or tools, of the trade of the debtor or the trade of a dependent of the debtor; or

(iii) professionally prescribed health aids for the debtor or a dependent of the debtor.

(2)(A) For the purposes of this subsection, a lien shall be considered to impair an exemption to the extent that the sum of—

(i) the lien;

(ii) all other liens on the property; and

(iii) the amount of the exemption that the debtor could claim if there were no liens on the property; exceeds the value that the debtor's interest in the property would have in the absence of any liens.

Problem 9–4:   When Do You Apply Section 522(f)?

Can debtors use section 522(f) to avoid:

1. GMAC's security interest in their car?

2. A second mortgage on their home?

3. Sears' security interest in all furniture that the debtors have purchased on credit from Sears?

Problem 9–5:   How Do You Apply Section 522(f)?

In 2007, D filed a declaration of homestead with the Norfolk Registry of Deeds. In 2010, D filed for relief in the Bankruptcy Court pursuant to Chapter 7 of the Code. D elected the federal exemptions, which limited the homestead to $20,200.

The parties have stipulated that the fair market value of the residential property is $240,200. The property is subject to a mortgage to Randolph Savings Bank in the amount of $200,000 and a judgment lien in favor of Rockland Trust Company ("Rockland") in the amount of $65,000.

D filed a Motion to Avoid Lien pursuant to 11 U.S.C. § 522(f)(1)(A), in which he asserted that the Rockland judgment lien impaired his exemption in his residence. What result?

C.　OBJECTIONS TO DISCHARGE

Recall that (1) in some bankruptcy cases such as *Tveten,* the debtor does not receive a discharge and (2) the availability of a discharge is controlled in Chapter 7 bankruptcy cases by section 727 and Bankr. R. 4004.

Section 727 sets out the twelve grounds for withholding a discharge from a Chapter 7 debtor. These twelve "objections" to discharge are the only statutory grounds for withholding a discharge in a Chapter 7 case.

In Chapter 7 cases, only a individual debtor can receive a discharge. Section 727(a)(1) denies a discharge if "the debtor is not an individual." Section 727(a) then lists eleven grounds for withholding a discharge in a Chapter 7 case even if the debtor is an individual. These section 727(a)(1)–(12) grounds are generally referred to as "objections to discharge."

There are relatively few reported cases applying section 727. A careful review of section 727 is an important part of the pre-bankruptcy work of the debtor's attorney. If the debtor's attorney determines that there is a section 727 basis for objecting to discharge, she will generally recommend that the debtor not use Chapter 7.

Dean Ponoroff of the University of Arizona College of Law provides the following overview of the conceptual basis for and the consequences of these objections to discharge:

> The fresh start is neither a formal legal status nor a cognizable right in the usual sense of the terms. Instead, it represents an aspiration of the bankruptcy system. . . . [T]he defining aspect of the fresh start, and perhaps in the public mind the defining characteristic of the modern bankruptcy system generally, is the discharge from debts. . . .

> In what was even then already a time-worn aphorism, the Supreme Court in 1934 described the primary purpose of the discharge as relieving "the honest debtor from the weight of oppressive indebtedness." One clear implication of this "honest-but-unfortunate debtor" maxim is that the fresh start objectives of the consumer bankruptcy system are not without limits. There is no constitutional right to a discharge in bankruptcy. In fact, most of the grounds on which global denial of an individual's discharge may be ordered are premised upon some type of opprobrious conduct by the debtor. Ultimately, however, the phrase, "honest-but-unfortunate debtor," is itself wholly indeterminate. While it offers the normative ideal of an individual debtor facing dire financial peril through no fault of his own, few debtors actually fit the prototype. Therefore, the phrase only takes on meaning as a practical matter where it finds concrete instantiation in the Bankruptcy Code. The statutory grounds for objection to discharge represent several examples of what is meant by an honest-but-unfortunate debtor because they usually relate to the quality of the debtor's pre-bankruptcy conduct or circumstances.

Outright denial of discharge will ordinarily have ruinous consequences for the debtor, which go considerably beyond the loss of the fresh start. This is due to the fact that the bankruptcy court's refusal to grant a discharge does not trigger automatic dismissal of the case. Rather, subject to the debtor's right to convert the case, the liquidation of the debtor's nonexempt property usually will proceed as in any Chapter 7 case with the notable exception that, after the close of the case, creditors whose claims were not fully satisfied by their dividend in bankruptcy are free to pursue the debtor personally for the unpaid deficiency on their original claims.

Lawrence Ponoroff, *Vicarious Thrills: The Case for Application of Agency Rules in Bankruptcy Dischargeability Litigation,* 70 TULANE L. REV. 2515 (1996).

11 U.S.C. § 727

(a) The court shall grant the debtor a discharge, unless—

(1) the debtor is not an individual;

(2) the debtor, with intent to hinder, delay, or defraud a creditor or an officer of the estate charged with custody of property under this title, has transferred, removed, destroyed, mutilated, or concealed, or has permitted to be, transferred, removed, destroyed, mutilated, or concealed—

    (A) property of the debtor, within one year before the date of the filing of the petition; or . . .

(3) the debtor has concealed, destroyed, mutilated, falsified, or failed to keep or preserve any recorded information, including books, documents, records, and papers, from which the debtor's financial condition or business transactions might be ascertained, unless such act or failure to act was justified under all of the circumstances of the case;

(4) the debtor knowingly and fraudulently, in or in connection with the case—

    (A) made a false oath or account;

    (B) presented or used a false claim;

    (C) gave, offered, received, or attempted to obtain money, property, or advantage, or a promise of money, property, or advantage, for acting or forbearing to act; or

    (D) withheld from an officer of the estate entitled to possession under this title, any recorded information, including books, documents, records, and papers, relating to the debtor's property or financial affairs;

(5) the debtor has failed to explain satisfactorily, before determination of denial of discharge under this paragraph, any loss of assets or deficiency of assets to meet the debtor's liabilities; . . .

(8) the debtor has been granted a discharge under this section, . . . in a case commenced within eight years before the date of the filing of the petition;

(10) the court approves a written waiver of discharge executed by the debtor after the order for relief under this chapter. . . .

(11) after filing the petition, the debtor failed to complete an instructional course concerning personal financial management described in section 111 . . .

(c)(1) The trustee, a creditor, or the United States trustee may object to the granting of a discharge under subsection (a) of this section. . . .

Bankr. R. 4004(a)

(a) Time for filing complaint objecting to discharge; notice of time fixed

In a chapter 7 liquidation case a complaint objecting to the debtor's discharge under § 727(a) of the Code shall be filed no later than 60 days after the first date set for the meeting of creditors under § 341(a).

Problem 9–6: Objections to Discharge Based on What Debtor Has Done Before Bankruptcy

1. Epstein filed for Chapter 7 bankruptcy on October 18, 2008. He received a discharge on January 25, 2009. Epstein is again in financial difficulty and comes to you for advice in February, 2010. Can Epstein file a Chapter 7 bankruptcy petition in 2010? If so, can Epstein obtain a second Chapter 7 discharge? *See* section 727(a)(8)

2. Markell shows up to your office for an initial interview. After discovering that his house is scheduled to be foreclosed upon tomorrow morning at 10:00 a.m., you ask him for a list of his creditors and his debts. Markell then dumps a shoe box full of receipts and other documents on your desk. Rummaging through them, you find payroll stubs, casino matchbooks, and several oily receipts from the local drive-through burger joint. There is no order to the mess. You ask Markell if he has any more papers, and he just shrugs. Before filing the case, what should you discuss with Markell? *See* section 727(a)(3). *See* also section 521.

Problem 9–7: Objection to Discharge Based on What the Debtor Does in the Bankruptcy Case

Dr. Sholdra ("Sholdra") filed a voluntary Chapter 7 petition on January 3. On March 23, Chilmark Financial LLC ("Chilmark") which holds an unsatisfied judgment against Sholdra for more than $1,470,000 filed an adversary proceeding in the bankruptcy court objecting to Sholdra's bankruptcy discharge, alleging that discharge should be denied under section 727(a)(2) for concealing assets, and/or under section 727(a)(4)(A) for making a false oath or account in filing schedules and a statement of financial affairs. Sholdra testified in his deposition that some information in his schedules and statement was false.

One week after the deposition, Sholdra filed amended schedules and statement of financial affairs purporting to correct such false statements. Thereafter, Chilmark filed a motion for summary judgment on June 30 seeking summary judgment for Sholdra's violation of section 727(a)(4)(A), and for a judgment denying discharge. Sholdra argued that there are genuine issues of material fact precluding summary judgment—that the amended schedules and statement of financial affairs create genuine issues of material fact as to his intent to defraud. He also argues that he is merely a medical doctor who is inexperienced with financial affairs and relied on incorrect information from a paralegal employed by his bankruptcy counsel and bad advice from his wife who was his business manager handling his financial affairs. How should the bankruptcy judge rule? *See* also Rule 1008, 18 U.S.C. § 152(a).

Problem 9–8: Settlement of an Objection to Discharge

Your firm represents Chillmark. Your client and Dr. Sholdra have negotiated a settlement under which Dr. Sholdra executes a $500,000 note in favor of Chillmark. The settlement requires Chillmark to dismiss its objection to Dr. Sholdra's discharge. The senior lawyer on the matter tells you to "take care of this." How do you take care of the settlement and dismissal of the discharge complaint?

Problem 9–9: Waiver of Discharge

Seven banks—Bank 1, Bank 2, Bank 3, Bank 4, etc.—have loaned more than $270,000,000 to various real estate development firms controlled by Charlie Croker who has personally guaranteed payment of all of the loans. All of the loans are in default. The banks are willing to restructure all of the loans, extending the time of repayment and reducing the amount of the monthly payments. The banks are insisting that, as a part of this debt restructuring (a/k/a as a "workout") Croker waive his "right" to a discharge in any bankruptcy case that might be filed before the loans are repaid. Can a person waive a discharge? *Cf.* section 727(a)(10).

D. DISCHARGEABILITY OF SPECIFIC DEBTS

1. OVERVIEW OF DISCHARGEABILITY

Even if a Chapter 7 debtor obtains a discharge, that discharge does not always cover all of the Chapter 7 debtor's legal obligations. Certain legal obligations are not affected by a discharge. Issues as to whether a debt is affected by a discharge are commonly referred to as "dischargeability issues."

2. WHAT DEBTS ARE DISCHARGED?

11 U.S.C. § 727(b)

Except as provided in section 523 of this title, a discharge under subsection (a) of this section discharges the debtor from all debts that arose before the date of the order for relief under this chapter ...

Problem 9–10:   Discharge and Post–Petition Debts

D files for Chapter 7 bankruptcy on September 9. On October 10, she incurs hospital bills of $10,000. On November 11, D obtains a discharge in her Chapter 7 bankruptcy case. Is the October 10th medical debt covered by the November 11th discharge? If not, what can D do? Cf sections 707(a)("may dismiss ... only for cause"); and 727(a)(8).

3. WHAT DEBTS ARE EXCEPTED FROM DISCHARGE BY SECTION 523?

Section 523, entitled "Exceptions to discharge" lists the kinds of debt that are not covered by a bankruptcy discharge. The phrase "exceptions to discharge" is unfortunately similar to the phrase "objections to discharge."

It is important to understand the difference between an "objection to discharge" under section 727 and an "exception to discharge" under section 523. Proof of an objection to discharge benefits all of that debtor's creditors. Proof of an exception to discharge benefits only the very creditor that established that its debt was excepted from discharge.[4]

Assume, for example, that Epstein files for bankruptcy and his creditors included Nickles, Markell and Perris. If Perris or any other creditor or, more likely, the Chapter 7 trustee is able to establish a section 727 objection to Epstein's bankruptcy discharge, then Epstein will not receive a discharge. Markell and Nickles as well as Perris will be able to proceed against Epstein personally to collect the remainder of their claims.

If, on the other hand, Perris establishes a section 523 exception to discharge, then Epstein will still receive a discharge. Neither Markell nor Nickles will be able to proceed against Epstein personally to collect the remainder of their claims. Only Perris, whose debt was excepted from the discharge, will be able to proceed against Epstein personally after the bankruptcy discharge.

The previous topic—objections to discharge—like the topic before it, exemptions, affects the Chapter 7 debtor and all holders of unsecured claims. This topic—exceptions to discharge—like the topic after it, reaffirmation—affects only the debtor and a particular creditor.

---

4. There is a second basic difference between sections 727 and 523. Section 727 only applies in Chapter 7 cases and some Chapter 11 cases. Section 523 applies in all cases under Chapters 7 and 12 and all Chapter 11 cases in which the debtor is an individual and to some extent in Chapter 13 cases.

Recall, from reading section 727, that most objections to discharge are based on what the debtor did before filing for bankruptcy or what the debtor has done in the bankruptcy case. In reading section 523 below, notice most exceptions to discharge are based on the nature of the debt.

11 U.S.C. § 523

(a) A discharge under section 727,1141,1228(a), 1228(b), or 1328(b) of this title does not discharge an individual debtor from any debt—

(1) for a tax or a customs duty—

(A) of the kind and for the periods specified in section 507(a)(3) or 507(a)(8) of this title, whether or not a claim for such tax was filed or allowed;

(B) with respect to which a return . . . , if required—

(i) was not filed . . . ; or

(ii) was filed after the date on which such return was last due, under applicable law or under any extension, and after two years before the date of the filing of the petition; or

(C) with respect to which the debtor made a fraudulent return or willfully attempted in any manner to evade or defeat such tax;

(2) for money, property, services, or an extension, renewal, or refinancing of credit, to the extent obtained by

(A) false pretenses, a false representation, or actual fraud, other than a statement respecting the debtor's or an insider's financial condition;

(B) use of a statement in writing—

(i) that is materially false;

(ii) respecting the debtor's or an insider's financial condition;

(iii) on which the creditor to whom the debtor is liable for such money, property, services, or credit reasonably relied; and

(iv) that the debtor caused to be made or published with intent to deceive . . .

(C)

(i) for purposes of subparagraph (A)—

(I) consumer debts owed to a single creditor and aggregating more than $500 for luxury goods or services incurred by an individual debtor on or within 90 days before the order for relief under this title are presumed to be nondischargeable; and

(II) cash advances aggregating more than $750 that are extensions of consumer credit under an open end credit plan obtained by an individual debtor on or within 70 days before the order for relief under this title, are presumed to be nondischargeable; and

    (ii) for purposes of this subparagraph—

    (II) the term luxury goods or services' does not include goods or services reasonably necessary for the support or maintenance of the debtor or a dependent of the debtor.

(4) for fraud or defalcation while acting in a fiduciary capacity, embezzlement, or larceny;

(5) for a domestic support obligation;

(8) unless excepting such debt from discharge under this paragraph would impose an undue hardship on the debtor and the debtor's dependents, for—

    (A)(i) an educational benefit overpayment or loan made, insured or guaranteed by a governmental unit, or made under any program funded in whole or in part by a governmental unit or nonprofit institution, or

    (ii) an obligation to repay funds received as an educational benefit, scholarship or stipend, or . . .

    (B) any other educational loan that is a qualified education loan, as defined in section 221(d)(1) of the Internal Revenue Code of 1986, . . .

(15) to a spouse, former spouse, or child of the debtor and not of the kind described in paragraph (5) that is incurred by the debtor in the course of a divorce or separation or in connection with a separation agreement, divorce decree or other order of a court of record, a determination made in accordance with State or territorial law by a governmental unit—

(c)(1) the debtor shall be discharged from a debt of a kind specified in paragraph (2), (4), or (6) of subsection (a) of this section, unless, on request of the creditor to whom such debt is owed, and after notice and a hearing, the court determines such debt to be excepted from discharge under paragraph (2), (4), or (6), as the case may be, of subsection (a) of this section.

4. RULE 4007 AND DEBT EXCEPTION PROCEDURES

Bankr. R. 4007

(a) **Persons entitled to file complaint**

A debtor or any creditor may file a complaint to obtain a determination of the dischargeability of any debt.

(b) **Time for commencing proceeding other than under § 523(c) of the Code**

A complaint other than under § 523(c) may be filed at any time. A case may be reopened without payment of an additional filing fee for the purpose of filing a complaint to obtain a determination under this rule.

(c) **Time for filing complaint under § 523(c) in a chapter 7 liquidation, . . . notice of time fixed.**

[A] complaint to determine the dischargeability of a debt under § 523(c) shall be filed no later than 60 days after the first date set for the meeting of creditors under § 341(a). The court shall give all creditors no less than 30 days' notice of the time so fixed in the manner provided in Rule 2002. On motion of a party in interest, after hearing on notice, the court may for cause extend the time fixed under this subdivision. The motion shall be filed before the time has expired.

5. EXCEPTIONS TO DISCHARGE BASED ON NATURE OF DEBT

a. Overview

Problem 9–11: Overview of Exceptions to Discharge Based on What the Debt Is

D is considering filing a Chapter 7 bankruptcy petition because he owes $10,000 for taxes for the current year, $200,000 on his educational loans, $3,000 for alimony, and $40,000 for credit card debts. Will Chapter 7 help D?

b. Closer View of "Domestic Support Obligation"

Problem 9–12: Exception to Discharge of Family Obligations

In January 2007, Linda Louise Parnham and Wayne Lee Parnham were divorced. Their final decree of divorce incorporated a negotiated marital dissolution agreement. This agreement disposed of the parties' marital property and debts and made provisions for the custody and support of their sixteen year old child Bubba Sue.

Ms. Parnham received custody of Bubba Sue, and Mr. Parnham agreed to pay $437 monthly child support until Bubba Sue reached eighteen years of age. The agreement also provided that Mr. Parnham would pay Bubba Sue's tuition for college and graduate school and professional school until Bubba Sue was married. In addition, the decree provided that Mr. Parnham would be required to pay Ms. Parnham's attorney's fees, related expenses, and court costs if she was required to return to court to enforce the provisions in the marital dissolution agreement.

In November 2010, Mr. Parnham filed a Chapter 7 bankruptcy petition. On March 21, 2006, he received a Chapter 7 discharge.

In June 2011, Ms. Parnham filed a petition in state court to enforce the support provisions in the parties' marital dissolution agreement. She asserted that:

(i) Bubba Sue decided to transfer from Volunteer State Community College, and

(ii) Bubba Sue had been admitted to Washington & Lee and

(iii) Mr. Parnham refused to pay Bubba Sue's $40,000 W & L tuition.

Mr. Parnham's answer alleges (i) W & L is just a "party school",[5] (ii) his obligation to pay college tuition has been discharged and (iii) the state court lacks subject matter jurisdiction to determine whether his obligation to pay college tuition has been discharged.

What can and should Ms. Parnham's attorney do?

c.   Closer View Credit Card Debt and Dischargeability

According to Travis Plunkett, lobbyist for the nonprofit Consumer Federation of America, "The big winner under the new law (BAPCPA amendments to the Bankruptcy Code) will be the credit card issuers whose reckless and abusive lending practices have driven many American to the brink of bankruptcy." Kathleen Day, *House Passes Bankruptcy Bill,* WASHINGTON POST, April 15, 2005, 2005 WLNR 5853110. Similarly, according to Jonathan Alter *of Newsweek*, "The law was literally written by the credit-card industry, the same folks whose siren-song targeting of high-risk borrowers caused much of the bankruptcy problem in the first place.... History should remember the 109th as the Credit Card Congress." Jonathan Alter, *They're The Credit Card Congress,* NEWSWEEK, April 25, 2005, 2005 WLNR 6098149.

The only 2005 BAPCPA changes affecting the dischargeability of credit card debt were numerical changes to section 523(a)(2)(c). The amount that the debtor must charge for "luxury goods" was reduced from $1,250 to $500 and the time period increased from 60 to 90 days. The amount that the debtor must withdraw in cash advances was reduced from $1,225 to $750 and the time period increased from 60 days to 70 days. Are these significant changes? Reconsider your answer after considering the following credit card problem and reported case.

Problem 9–13:   Credit Card Debt and Section 523(a)(2)

D is a 50 year old paralegal with a junior college degree and a gross annual income of approximately $25,000. In September 2009, C sent D an unsolicited, pre-approved credit card with a $3,000 limit. D used the credit card to obtain 14 separate cash advances totaling more than $3,200 from automatic teller machines in casinos. In January 2010, D filed for Chapter 7 bankruptcy relief. She had lost more than $25,000 gambling in 2009 and owed C more than $3,500 including interest. If D obtains a Chapter 7 discharge, will C's $3,500 claim be excepted from the discharge? Is section 523(a)(2) helpful? Is the *Manriquez* case below helpful?

---

5.   http://talk.collegeconfidential.com/washington-lee-university/459713–party-school.html.

IN RE MANRIQUEZ

2009 WL 3015161 (D.Colo. 2009)

ARGUELLO, District Judge.

This matter is before the Court on appeal from Bankruptcy Judge Michael E. Romero's Order in Case No. 07–1155. In that Order, the Bankruptcy Court considered whether certain credit card debts incurred by Appellee Alfredo Manriquez on a credit card issued by Appellant First National Bank of Omaha were dischargeable in bankruptcy. First National argued that the debts were obtained by fraud and thus not dischargeable. The Bankruptcy Court disagreed, finding insufficient evidence of Mr. Manriquez's intent to deceive. On appeal, First National contends that this finding was based on erroneous findings of fact and misstatements of the law. Taking jurisdiction pursuant to 28 U.S.C. § 1334 and 28 U.S.C. § 158, the Court affirms the order of the Bankruptcy Court.

BACKGROUND

The facts of this case are largely undisputed. Mr. Manriquez and his wife filed for bankruptcy in late 2006, seeking to have discharged, among other debts, the $6,600 balance on his Visa credit card issued by First National. This was one of a number of credit cards held by Mr. Manriquez, all of which were used with some regularity. In the summer and fall of 2006, Mr. Manriquez carried a high balance on most of these cards, often paying only the minimum amount due each month. Mr. Manriquez was sometimes unable to make even these minimum payments; as he testified at trial, bills were paid as he had the resources to pay them.

Even with the use of these credit cards, the Manriquezes' finances grew out of balance. At the time they filed bankruptcy, the Manriquezes' monthly expenses exceeded their monthly income by $1,300. Mr. Manriquez testified that the income and expenditure numbers remained "more or less" the same in the months leading up to their bankruptcy. The one exception was an additional $550 per month in car payments for a Volkswagen Jetta that the Manriquezes purchased just a few months before declaring bankruptcy.

The dispute in this case centers on the charges incurred on the First National credit card in September and October of 2006. As of September 19, the card had only a $1.75 balance, and a $14,700 credit line. Between September 19 and October 10, the Manriquezes made $6,350 in new charges to the card. This included $2,500 for the purchase of a Royal Carribean cruise. These charges appeared on the credit card's October billing statement, which indicated a $147 minimum payment due by November 8, 2006. That minimum payment was not made. Indeed, no additional payments were made on the First National card.

On October 16, 2006, Mr. Manriquez met with a bankruptcy attorney and paid him a $1,300 cash retainer. The attorney prepared the necessary paperwork and, on November 9, faxed that paperwork to the Manriquezes for their signature. The bankruptcy petition was filed in mid-December 2006.

In March 2007, First National filed a complaint seeking to prevent the credit card debt from being discharged. If First National prevailed, it would mean that Mr. Manriquez would still be responsible for the credit card debt notwithstanding his bankruptcy. First National argued that the debt was nondischargeable pursuant to 11 U.S.C. § 523(a)(2)(A), which excepts from discharge debts obtained by fraud, and 11 U.S.C. § 523(a)(2)(C), which excepts debts for "luxury goods." The Bankruptcy Court held a trial on February 13, 2008, after which it issued findings of fact and conclusions of law. As to the Royal Carribean cruise, the Bankruptcy Court found that this was a purchase of a luxury good and thus the debt was not absolved by the bankruptcy filing. As to the remaining debt, however, the Bankruptcy Court found that it was dischargeable. While the use of the card was an implied representation that Mr. Manriquez intended to repay the debt, and while this representation was proved false by virtue of his filing for bankruptcy, the Bankruptcy Court found that the evidence, on balance, did not show the requisite fraudulent intent when the representations were made. Thus, except for the $2,500 for the purchase of the cruise, the credit card debt was discharged. First National appeals that ruling. . . .

First National does not challenge the Bankruptcy Court's ruling on the luxury goods exception, but does seek reversal of the decision that the remaining debt was not dischargeable pursuant to the fraud exception, Section 523(a)(2)(A). To establish nondischargeability under that section, a creditor must prove: (1) the debtor made a false representation; (2) that representation was made with the intent to deceive; (3) the creditor relied on the representation; (4) the creditor's reliance was reasonable; and (5) the creditor suffered a loss therefrom. . . .

In analyzing whether Mr. Manriquez acted with intent to deceive, the Bankruptcy Court noted that a debtor's intent must be determined from the totality of the circumstances. The Bankruptcy Court specifically looked to twelve "non-exclusive" factors that are helpful in that determination. . . .[3]

---

3. As the Bankruptcy Court correctly stated, those factors are:

(1) the length of time between the charges made and the filing of bankruptcy;

(2) whether the debtor consulted an attorney regarding bankruptcy prior to the charges being made;

(3) the number of charges made;

(4) the amount of the charges;

(5) the financial condition of the debtor at the time the charges were made;

(6) whether the charges were above the credit limit of the account;

(7) whether the debtor made multiple charges on any given day;

(8) whether or not the debtor was employed;

(9) the debtor's employment prospects;

(10) the debtor's financial sophistication;

(11) whether there was a sudden change in the debtor's buying habits; and

(12) whether the purchases were made for luxuries or necessities. *In re Kukuk*, 225 B.R. at 786.

In this case, the Bankruptcy Court engaged in a thorough analysis of the totality of the circumstances regarding Mr. Manriquez's intent and found deceptive intent to be lacking . . .

First National also challenges the Bankruptcy Court's ruling that, while use of a credit card gives rise to an implied representation that the debtor intends to repay the charges, it does not impliedly represent that the debtor has the ability to pay. First National contends that Mr. Manriquez's use of the credit card should be deemed a representation as to both intent and ability.

The question of what, if any, representations a debtor makes by the simple act of using a credit card has vexed the courts. Some have endorsed First National's position-that use is an implied representation of an intent and an ability to repay the charges. However, the Tenth Circuit's Bankruptcy Appellate Panel, in a thoughtful opinion, rejected the argument that use implied ability to repay:

> [A]n implied representation regarding the debtor's ability to repay is not grounds for nondischargeability under § 523(a)(2)(A). In particular, § 523(a)(2)(A) expressly modifies the common law definition of "false misrepresentation" by exempting "statement[s] respecting the debtor's or an insider's financial condition[.]" 11 U.S.C. § 523(a)(2)(A). . . . Thus, we hold that, for purposes of dischargeability under § 523(a)(2)(A), the use of a credit card creates an implied representation that the debtor intends to repay the debt incurred thereby, but does not create any representation regarding the debtor's ability to repay the debt.

In re Kukuk, 225 B.R. at 785.

First National notes that its card member agreement expressly provides that "[e]ach time you use your account, you are representing that you intend, and have the ability, to repay all amounts due on your account." (Emphasis added.) First National asserts, with little argument, that this statement somehow alters the *In re Kukuk* principle. . . . But even assuming that the provision in the card member agreement somehow constituted an express representation of ability to repay, First National's argument still fails. In order to except a debt from discharge under Section 523(a)(2)(A), there must not only be a fraudulent representation, but justifiable reliance on that statement by the creditor. First National could not justifiably rely on a statement that, each time Mr. Manriquez used his credit card, he had "the ability[ ] to repay all amounts due on [his] account." As aptly explained by the *In re Kukuk* court,

> it is well-known that credit cards are marketed by issuers and often used by consumers because they lack the ability to pay at the time that they use the card. Thus, sophisticated credit card issuers cannot justifiably rely on a representation that a debtor has the ability to repay at the time that he or she uses the card. *See Field [v. Mans]*, 516 U.S. [59,] 70–71 [1995] (defining "justifiable reliance"); *see also [In re] Kountry Korner [Store],* 221 B.R. [265], 274 [N.D.

Okla.1998] (discussing lack of justifiable reliance on the part of credit card issuers, the court stated: "To ... accuse a customer with fraud for using the card exactly in the manner the Bank permitted, and, in fact, encourages, is audacious, oppressive and hypocritical."); *Chevy Chase Bank v. Briese (In re Briese),* 196 B.R. 440, 448 (W.D.Wis.1996) ("[P]eople use credit cards precisely because they do not have a present ability to pay. It is exactly this reality which makes the credit card industry so profitable, and it is why credit card companies often advertise their cards as just the thing to use in an 'emergency.' ").

For these reasons, the Court finds no legal error in the Bankruptcy Court's holding that Mr. Manriquez's use of the card represented only an intent, not an ability, to repay his debt.

CONCLUSION

Based on the foregoing, the Court ORDERS that the Bankruptcy Court's decision is AFFIRMED.

QUESTIONS ABOUT MANRIQUEZ

1. What fact was most favorable to Mr. Manriquez?

2. What is the statutory basis for requiring that the creditor First National prove (1) the debtor made a false representation; (2) the representation was made with the intent to deceive; (3) the creditor relied on the representation; (4) the creditor's reliance was reasonable; and (5) the creditor suffered a loss therefrom?

3. If you were First National's attorney would you have filed a section 523(a)(2) dischargeability complaint? An appeal from the bankruptcy court's adverse ruling? If you were Mr. Manriquez's attorney would you have invoked section 523(d)?

d. Closer View of Dischargeability of Educational Loans

According to Professor Nathalie Martin, "Student loan obligations are not dischargeable except in very rare situations." Nathalie Martin, The Glannon Guide To Bankruptcy 141 (2d ed 2007). Good book, great prof, but if you are not willing to trust someone whose parents apparently could not spell "Natalie",[11] then read the *Robinson* case below.

IN RE ROBINSON

416 B.R. 275 (E.D. Va. 2009)

MEMORANDUM OPINION

MITCHELL, United States Bankruptcy Judge.

*1 This is an action by a chapter 13 debtor to discharge approximately $143,000 in student loan debt owed to Educational Credit Management

---

11. But cf. http://www.thinkbabynames.com/meaning/0/Nathalie

Corporation. A trial was held on March 26, 2009. The plaintiff was present in person and represented herself. The defendant appeared by its attorney of record. For the reasons stated, the court, although sympathetic to the debtor's situation, concludes that she has not met the high standard required in this Circuit discharging student loans on the ground that payment would constitute an undue hardship. For that reason, discharge of the student loans must be denied. . . .

Background and Findings of Fact

The plaintiff-debtor, Royale Robinson, filed a voluntary petition in this court on January 21, 2005, for relief under chapter 7 of the Bankruptcy Code, . . . Among the liabilities listed on the debtor's schedules is a debt for student loans in the amount of $50,000 held by "Access Group/Education. Mgmt Grp/Key Bank and its Assigns." The debtor incurred that debt, 18 student loans to be exact, while obtaining post-graduate degrees from 1996 to 2002. The debtor filed the present action against Educational Credit Management Corporation ("ECMC") on August 27, 2008, seeking an undue hardship discharge of those student loan debts under § 523(a)(8) of the Bankruptcy Code. ECMC filed an answer on requesting dismissal of the debtor's complaint and a declaration that the student loan debts are non-dischargeable under § 523(a)(8) of the Bankruptcy Code. . . .

The debtor is a 55 year old woman who holds a Juris Doctor (J.D.) degree from Syracuse University, which she received in 1999, and a Master of Laws (LL.M.) in Taxation and Employment Benefits from Georgetown University Law Center, which she received in 2002. She testified that she has not been admitted to the bar in any state. The debtor has no dependents. Since 2002, she has experienced financial difficulties due to unemployment and medical treatment for cancer. Her schedules of monthly income and expenses (Schedules I and J) at the time the petition was filed reflected gross income of $2,200, take home pay of $1,337, and expenses of $1,206, not including any student loan payments. Currently, however, her only sources of income are unemployment benefit payments of $200 per week and $200 in food stamps each month. Her estimated current monthly expenses total $1,879, including $1,079 per month in rent but not including student loan payments, and the debtor does not expect any reduction in expenses over the coming year.

*2 Despite attempts to obtain work in the profession for which she studied, the debtor has held only low paying jobs since receiving her degrees including positions as an airport baggage screener and ramp operator at Dulles International Airport and as a bank teller. In addition, from 2003 to 2006, the debtor lived in various homeless shelters, and she is currently behind on her rent and has been sued for unlawful detainer. She has been unemployed since 2007, when she was diagnosed with cancer and had to undergo three surgeries. The debtor received short-term disability benefits from her employer from April 2007 until September 2007 at her full salary, and was then transferred to long-term disability payments of $1,500 per month until July 2008. At no time since 2003 has the debtor's gross annual income exceeded $32,200. In addition, she is still in treatment for cancer and has been prescribed medication, chemothera-py, and emotional counseling. Although the debtor is actively seeking employment, she testified that any job would have to be on a trial basis due to her medical condition. The debtor's student loans became due in 2003, during the pendency of her prior chapter 7 case, and she has made no payments, which she asserts is because she has been in bankruptcy since the loans became due.

After the debtor filed the present complaint to discharge her student loan debts, ECMC, through its attorney, notified the debtor that she appeared to qualify for several alternative repayment programs through the William D. Ford Direct Loan Program. One program, the Income Contingent Repayment Plan, is based on the borrower's adjusted gross income and family size. *See.* Under the plan, the monthly payment amount is based on the debtor's adjusted gross income from the prior year, and the annual amount paid is twenty percent of the difference between the debtor's adjusted gross income and the federal poverty guidelines for her household size. 3). If the debtor's income is below the federal poverty guidelines, as it currently is, then the required monthly loan payments would be $0, but she would not be considered in default on the obligation. *Id.* The term of the program is 25 years, with monthly payments adjusting each year, and at the end of the term, any remaining debt would be discharged .. The debtor testified that she did not consider the program helpful to her because she would remain liable on the debts, which-because they would be reflected on her credit report-would prevent her from obtaining affordable housing.

Conclusions of Law & Discussion

. . .

Student loan debts are presumptively non-dischargeable in bankrupt-cy. § 523(a)(8), Bankruptcy Code. However, a student loan debt may be discharged if "excepting such debt from discharge ... would impose an undue hardship on the debtor and the debtor's dependents." *Id.* A debtor seeking a discharge of student loan debts has the burden of proving that repayment of the debts would pose an undue hardship by a preponderance of the evidence

A.

In determining whether the repayment of student loan debts would impose an undue hardship, the majority of circuits, including the Fourth Circuit, apply the test first articulated by the Second Circuit in *Brunner v. N.Y. State Higher Educ. Servs. Corp. (In re Brunner)*, 831 F.2d 395, 396 (2d Cir.1987). The *Brunner* test requires the debtor to establish:

> (1) that the debtor cannot maintain, based on current income and expenses, a "minimal" standard of living for herself and her depen-

dents if forced to repay the loans; (2) that additional circumstances exist indicating that this state of affairs is likely to persist for a significant portion of the repayment period of the student loans; and (3) that the debtor has made good faith efforts to repay the loans.

Brunner, 831 F.2d at 396. In this case, ECMC does not dispute that the debtor satisfies the first factor of the *Brunner* test. Thus, the issue here is whether the debtor has demonstrated, by a preponderance of the evidence, the second and third prongs of the test.

B.

The second *Brunner* factor, that the "state of affairs is likely to persist for a significant portion of the repayment period of the student loan," requires the debtor to show "not only . . . current inability to pay but also . . . additional, exceptional circumstances, strongly suggestive of continuing inability to repay over an extended period of time." *Brunner, 831 F.2d at 396.* The Fourth Circuit has determined that the second prong of the *Brunner* test is "a demanding requirement" necessitating the existence of "a certainty of hopelessness" such that the debtor will not be able to repay the student loans. Put another way, it is the rare debtor who satisfies this factor.

In the present case, the debtor testified that she was diagnosed with cancer in 2007 and that she had a total of three surgeries for the cancer in 2007 and 2008. She also testified that she is still being treated for her cancer with medication and prescriptions for chemotherapy, but she is unwilling to follow through with the chemotherapy treatment because she needs a stable housing environment, which she claims she does not currently have. The debtor did not present any further evidence regarding her medical diagnosis, her current condition, her chances for recovery, or the effect of the diagnosis on her ability to be employed in the future.[3]

The court is unable to find that the debtor has shown, by a preponderance of the evidence, the existence of additional circumstances which indicate that her current inability to pay her student loans will continue for a significant portion of the repayment period. While the court is sympathetic to the debtor's current situation, being diagnosed with cancer, without more, does not necessarily mean that the debtor cannot take advantage of the two law degrees she obtained and the excellent education she received. The debtor has provided no evidence, other than her own testimony, that her health problems will prevent her from returning to work, either part-time or full-time, nor has she offered evidence of the

---

3. To be fair, one of the problems with the application of the *Brunner* test is that it places something of an unfair evidentiary burden on debtors who-if they satisfy the first prong-almost by definition do not have the financial resources to obtain the expert testimony that would be needed to satisfy the second prong. That is, because a debtor who does not currently have sufficient income to pay even her basic living expenses, is, as a practical matter, debarred from presenting the type of expert testimony (such as from her treating doctor) that would be required for her to establish that her prognosis for recovery is poor. At the trial, the debtor did offer into evidence a letter from her doctor regarding her medical condition; however, because the letter was clearly hearsay, the court sustained ECMC's objection to its admission.

"certainty of hopelessness" of her circumstances that the Fourth Circuit requires.

C.

The third prong set forth in *Brunner* requires that the debtor show that she "has made good faith efforts to repay the loans." *Brunner,* 831 F.2d at 396. In the Fourth Circuit, the good faith inquiry requires an examination of the debtor's "efforts to obtain employment, maximize income, and minimize expenses." Second, the debtor's hardship must be due to factors over which she had no control. The final consideration is the debtor's efforts to pursue loan consolidation options.

In the present case, . . . the debtor has not demonstrated a good faith effort to maximize her income. While her lack of employment for the past two years is adequately explained by her cancer diagnosis and treatment, there is no real explanation for her why, armed with an LL.M. in Taxation and Employment Benefits from a prestigious law school, she did not work in the field for which she was trained but only in substantially less lucrative jobs such as a baggage screener and a bank teller. The debtor testified that since becoming unemployed, she has sought employment by going to a local workforce center, but she has not sought assistance from the career center at Georgetown University Law Center in finding employment in the legal field. Despite being highly educated and holding marketable degrees and skills, the debtor has seemingly made no efforts to take advantage of those skills in order to maximize her income.

*5 Finally, the debtor did not seriously pursue loan consolidation or repayment plans. The Fourth Circuit has stated that although not dispositive, efforts to seek out loan consolidation or repayment options "illustrate[ ] that the debtor takes her loan obligations seriously, and is doing her utmost to repay them despite her unfortunate circumstances." Indeed, requests for loan deferments and forebearances are insufficient to demonstrate good faith when they are not followed by payments or attempts to work out repayment plans .. Further, the failure to take advantage of loan repayment programs for which the debtor is eligible is indicative of whether "the debtor takes her loan obligations seriously," and is an important component of the analysis of the third *Brunner* factor.

Here, the debtor offered no evidence of attempts to consolidate her loans or seriously consider the Income Contingent Repayment Plan (ICRP) under the William D. Ford Direct Loan Program. There is appears to be no dispute that the debtor is eligible for the program, which would permit her to pay zero dollars per month while her income is below the federal poverty level, with any remaining balance administratively discharged after the 25–year repayment period.

The debtor's sole reason for refusing to consider the ICRP was that such a program was not helpful to her because the debt would still be reflected on her credit report. According to the debtor, landlords look at credit report in determining whether to accept rental applications, and the amount of the debt she owes would almost certainly result in her application being turned down. And without the ability to obtain affordable and stable housing, she was unwilling to undergo the chemotherapy necessary to treat her cancer. For that reason, she argues, her continued liability on the student loan debt would constitute a hardship even if she were not currently required to make payments.

This kind of hardship, however, is not the hardship contemplated by § 523(a)(8) and *Brunner.* . . . While an unfortunate situation, the debtor's justification is insufficient for rejecting a program that would allow her to fulfill her loan obligations in a more reasonable and manageable way.

Conclusion

As the Fourth Circuit has noted, "Congress, in enacting § 523(a)(8), set a high bar for a debtor seeking to discharge government-guaranteed educational loans." While the debtor's situation is compelling, the Fourth Circuit has refused to allow debtors to discharge their student loan obligations in cases where the circumstances were similar. *See e.g., Spence,* 541 F.3d at 542, 544 (denying undue hardship discharge of $161,000 in student loan debts to debtor in her late 60s suffering from diabetes and high blood pressure); *Mosko,* 515 F.3d at 322, 327 (no undue hardship discharge for debtors with one dependent whose combined student loan debts totaled $120,573 despite fact that husband suffered from excessive daytime sleepiness which limited his employment prospects); *Frushour,* 433 F.3d at 396–97, 404 (no undue hardship for single parent debtor with one dependent and $12,149 in student loans); *Ekenasi,* 523 F.3d at 543 (undue hardship discharge more than two years before debtor's scheduled completion of chapter 13 plan premature despite $89,418 in student loan debt and debtor's six dependent children).

Here, the debtor has failed to show additional circumstances indicating the existence of "a certainty of hopelessness" such that the debtor will not be able to repay the student loans in the future. Further, the debtor has not demonstrated efforts to maximize her income or good faith attempts to repay her student loan obligations, and she has refused to consider a loan repayment program that would reduce her monthly payments to zero and would eliminate her debt in 25 years. She has therefore failed to prove that she is entitled to an undue hardship discharge of her student loan debts under § 523(a)(8) of the Bankruptcy Code.

A separate judgment will be entered denying the debtor's request to discharge the student loans on the grounds of undue hardship.

E.   REAFFIRMATION AGREEMENTS

Remember what a discharge is and what a discharge is not. We have just seen that a discharge does not cover all debts—certain debts are excepted from the discharge. And, earlier, in Unit 4, we saw that a discharge does not extinguish the debts that it covers. The discharge merely protects the debtor from any further personal liability on the discharged debts.

Again, a discharged debt does not disappear. A discharged debt can still be enforced against any third party obligors.

Even more important, a discharged secured debt can still be collected from any property that secures its payment. Assume, for example, D financed her purchase of a 2004 Oldsmobile Bravada SUV with GMAC and granted GMAC a security interest in the Bravada. D filed for Chapter 7 bankruptcy. At the close of D's bankruptcy case, she received a discharge and still owed GMAC $10,000. Notwithstanding D's discharge, GMAC can still repossess and resell D's Bravada. D's discharge simply protects her from any further personal liability to GMAC.

Even though a discharge protects a debtor from any further personal liability on discharged debts, a debtor who has received a discharge can still voluntarily repay a discharged debt. Discharge simply means that the discharged debtor is not longer legally obligated to pay discharged debts.

There is a procedure by which a debtor can incur a legal obligation during her bankruptcy case to pay dischargeable debts. This procedure involves an agreement, generally known as a "reaffirmation agreement."

The following problems illustrate some of the reasons that a debtor might want to enter into a reaffirmation agreement.

Problem 9–14:   Reasons for Reaffirmation Agreement

D files for Chapter 7 bankruptcy. Which of the following debts should he decide to reaffirm?

    a. $2,200 to the family orthodontist.

    b. $3,300 debt co-signed by his sister.

    c. $4,444 debt to the credit union at D's employer arising from a loan in which D's credit application was inaccurate and incomplete.

    d. $5,500 debt secured by a security interest in D's car.

A reaffirmation agreement requires more than that the debtor decide to reaffirm. As should be obvious from the term "reaffirmation agreement," it is necessary that both the debtor and the creditor agree.

It is also necessary that the requirements of section 524 be satisfied. Sections 524 requires inter alia that

— the agreement be executed and filed with the bankruptcy court before a discharge is granted;

— the attorney who represented the debtor in the reaffirmation certify inter alia that the agreement does not impose an undue hardship or the debtor;

— the court approve the agreement as not imposing an undue hardship on the debtor if the debtor was not represented by an attorney in the reaffirmation.

Problem 9–15: *Procedures for Reaffirmation*

The new credit manager of a client asks the following questions about reaffirmation procedure:

     1. *Timing:* Can a reaffirmation agreement be entered into before bankruptcy? After the bankruptcy discharge?

     2. *Role of the Bankruptcy Judge:* Does the reaffirmation agreement have to be filed with the bankruptcy judge? Approved by the bankruptcy judge?

     3. *Debtor's Attorney:* Can I deal with the debtor directly or do you have to deal with the debtor's attorney? Will the debtor's attorney care whether his client enters into a reaffirmation agreement?

Problem 9–16: *Reaffirmation and the Automatic Stay*

You file a Chapter 7 petition for Steve and Lynn Jamo ("Debtors"). Kentucky Fried Credit Union ("KFCU") had a first mortgage ("Mortgage") on the Debtors' home. Debtors had missed three Mortgage payments before filing their bankruptcy petition. Debtors also were indebted to KFCU on several unrelated, unsecured loans.

KFCU contacts the Debtors about reaffirming the Mortgage. KFCU tells the Debtors that it is unwilling to agree to reaffirmance of the Mortgage unless the Debtors also agree to reaffirm the unsecured loans. KFCU's attorney tells you that unless the Debtors agree to reaffirm all of their KFCU loans, KFCU will foreclose on the house as soon as the Chapter 7 case ends. WHAT DO YOU DO NEXT?

F. OTHER CHAPTER 7 SECURED DEBT ISSUES

As the above examples (and common sense) suggest, many, if not most, reaffirmation proceedings involve secured debt: Chapter 7 debtors want to keep their homes, cars, and boats and know that notwithstanding any Chapter 7 discharge, the creditor with a lien on the home, car, or boat or home can repossess. To prevent any such repossession, debtors can and do reaffirm the debt by court-approved, post-bankruptcy reaffirmation agreements.

1. REDEMPTION

In some situations, a Chapter 7 can prevent any such post-bankruptcy repossession of cars, bass boats and other personal property by redemption under section 722. In reading section 722, consider the following four questions: (1) when is section 722 redemption a legally available option for Chapter 7 debtors, (2) what does a Chapter 7 debtor have to do in order to "redeem" under section 722, (3) where does a Chapter 7 debtor get the money required for redemption, and (4) how is section 722 redemption different from section 524 reaffirmation.[12]

11 U.S.C. § 722

> An individual debtor may, whether or not the debtor has waived the right to redeem under this section, redeem tangible personal property intended primarily for personal, family, or household use, from a lien securing a dischargeable consumer debt, if such property is exempted under section 522 of this title or has been abandoned under section 554 of this title, by paying the holder of such lien the amount of the allowed secured claim of such holder that is secured by such lien-in full at the time of redemption

Did you notice the phrase "the amount of the allowed secured claim"? Do you remember the Unit 4 discussion of how to determine the amount of a secured claim? Remember section 506(a)(2)("If the debtor is an individual in a case under chapter 7 or 13, such value with respect to personal property securing an allowed claim shall be determined based on the replacement value of such property as of the date of the filing of the petition").

Problem 9–17: Amount and Form of Section 722 Payment

Ballard, a Chapter 7 debtor, owns a 2008 Chevrolet. She owes GMAC $16,000 on her car loan. The interest rate on the loan is 5%. GMAC has a security interest on the car. A standard price guide shows that a used car dealer would pay $9,000 for a 2008 Chevrolet and that a used car dealer would sell such a car for $10,500.

Ballard wants to keep her car.

1. If Ballard decides to redeem, what does she have to do?

2. As Ballard's attorney, what do you tell her about the advantages or disadvantages of redemption as compared with reaffirmation?

3. As Ballard's attorney, what do you tell her about the possible advantages and disadvantages of doing nothing during the bankruptcy and making the usual car payments to GMAC? Reconsider your answer after considering the Ninth Circuit's reconsideration of the court-created concept called "ride through" in the *Dumont* case below.

---

12. Later, when we are doing Chapter 13 in Unit 10, we will compare both reaffirmation and redemption with "cramdown."

2. RIDE THROUGH

IN RE DUMONT

581 F.3d 1104 (9th Cir. 2009)

O'SCANNLAIN, Circuit Judge:

We must decide whether the Bankruptcy Abuse Prevention and Consumer Protection Act of 2005 allows a consumer in bankruptcy to retain personal property subject to a security interest by continuing to make payments under his contract.

I

Antoinette Dumont purchased a car in 2003 from Ford Motor Credit Company ("Ford"). The loan agreement contained a clause stating that Dumont would be in default if she was involved in a bankruptcy proceeding, also known as an "ipso facto" clause.[1] Dumont filed for Chapter 7 bankruptcy protection in 2006, subsequent to the effective date of the Bankruptcy Abuse Prevention and Consumer Protection Act of 2005 ("BAPCPA"), Pub.L. No. 109–8, 119 Stat. 23. The vehicle was listed on the bankruptcy petition as having a value of $5,800. At the time, she owed $8,288 on it and was making payments of $335.78 per month. In her Bankruptcy Statement of Intentions, Dumont stated that she would retain the car and continue to make monthly payments.

Ford's attorney e-mailed Dumont's attorney, asking that Dumont reaffirm the debt. Her attorney declined the offer. It is not clear from the record what the terms of the proposed reaffirmation were.

Ford filed a proof of claim, to which there was no objection; thus Ford's claim was allowed. *See* 11 U.S.C. § 502(a). Dumont received a discharge on August 15, 2006. After the discharge, she continued making payments on the car loan. Without advance notice, Ford repossessed her car on November 14, 2006.

Dumont successfully moved to reopen her bankruptcy case and claimed that Ford had violated the discharge injunction by repossessing her car. The bankruptcy court denied the motion to find Ford in violation of the discharge injunction, and the Bankruptcy Appellate Panel (BAP) unanimously affirmed.

When a debtor files for Chapter 7 bankruptcy, she is required to state her intentions with regard to any property which is subject to a security interest. 11 U.S.C. § 521(a)(2). Prior to BAPCPA, our circuit law allowed the debtor to choose among four options. First, she could merely surrender the collateral. Second, she could redeem such collateral—that is, pay the creditor its present fair market value. *See id.* § 722. The debtor could

---

1. The contract read: "Default means ... [y]ou start a proceeding in bankruptcy or one is started against you or your property." It further states that "[i]f you default, we may take (repossess) the vehicle from you if we do so peacefully."

also reaffirm the debt on terms she and the creditor agreed on. Reaffirmation allowed the debtor to keep her collateral, but re-exposed her to personal liability should she fail to make payments as promised. *See id.* § 524(c) (setting conditions for reaffirmations and exempting them from the discharge injunction). The final option-recognized in only some circuits—was the so-called "ride-through" or "pay and drive." Under this plan, the debtor continued to make payments as if the bankruptcy had never occurred. The creditor was forbidden by the automatic stay (and later, by the discharge injunction) from repossessing the collateral unless the buyer defaulted. If the buyer stopped making payments or otherwise defaulted, then the creditor could reclaim its collateral but could not pursue a deficiency judgment against the debtor.

Unsurprisingly, the ride-through system proved popular for debtors. Debtors usually need a car[3] to travel to and from work, school, medical appointments, and other important activities. Having just filed for bankruptcy, they understandably expect to experience difficulty securing financing for another vehicle. Accordingly, they were often willing to continue payments on loans that were "underwater" (i.e., loans for which the amount due exceeded the value of the collateral)....

Prior to BAPCPA, we had held that ride-through was available to debtors. *McClellan Fed. Credit Union v. Parker (In re Parker)*, 139 F.3d 668 (9th Cir.1998). The Second, Third, Fourth, and Tenth Circuits held likewise. Other circuits rejected ride-through. * * *

BAPCPA wrought several changes in the Code which may be applicable to ride-through. First, it amended section 521(2), which is now section 521(a)(2). Most relevant for our purposes, the savings clause in subparagraph (C) now reads: "[N]othing in subparagraphs (A) and (B) of this paragraph shall alter the debtor's or the trustee's rights with regard to such property under this title, *except as provided in section 362(h).*" (emphasis added). 11 U.S.C. § 362(h), added by BAPCPA, states that the automatic stay is terminated and the "property shall no longer be property of the estate if the debtor fails"

> (A) to file timely any statement of intention required . . . or to indicate in such statement that the debtor will either surrender such personal property or retain it and, if retaining such personal property, either redeem [,reaffirm,] . . .

> (B) to take timely the action specified in such statement, . . . unless such statement specifies the debtor's intention to reaffirm such debt on the original contract terms and the creditor refuses to agree. . . .

We pause to note an exception to section 362(h). A debtor who files an intent to reaffirm on the original contract terms but is unable to complete such a reaffirmation due to the creditor's refusal is not subject to the section. Ride-through is functionally indistinguishable from reaffirmation on the original terms except for the lack of personal liability in the former.

---

3. Ride-through was not limited to automobile loans. However, as the name implies, ride-through was used most frequently to allow debtors to hold on to an automobile.

The careful carve-out of reaffirmation on the contract terms—a return to the status quo ante bankruptcy—implies that debtors who attempt to ride-through are subject to section 362(h). If ride-through existed, any lawyer who advised his client to make a reaffirmation offer on the original contract terms would be guilty of malpractice, and any bankruptcy judge who approved such a reaffirmation from a pro se litigant would be seriously derelict in his duties. For why would one ever choose reaffirmation on such terms and thus incur the risk of personal liability when one could safely achieve the same ends by ride-through? Yet Congress clearly contemplated that offers of reaffirmation on the original terms would be made. If the debtor qualifies for the exception, then it seems that the result would be the same as pre-BAPCPA ride-through. Congress presumably would not have created an "exception" to provide access to an option all debtors had in the first place. If all debtors had the right to elect ride-through in the first instance, the exception would be wholly devoid of content. The traditional rules of statutory construction counsel against that result. This supports a conclusion that ride-through is not available to all. . . .

[A divided Ninth Circuit then holds section 521(a)(2)(C), in conjunction with section 362(h), disallows ride-through].

3. PAYMENT BY THE TRUSTEE OR ABANDONMENT

If a secured creditor's lien is on exempt property, then the secured creditor will be looking to payment from the debtor through a reaffirmation agreement or redemption or will be looking to repossess the encumbered property when the stay is lifted under section 362(d) or ends under section 362(c). If, on the other hand, the encumbered property is not exempt property then the secured creditor will be looking to relief from the stay under section 362(d) or, more likely, payment from the trustee or abandonment by the trustee.

Remember, Chapter 7 contemplates liquidation: the trustee sells the property of the estate and the proceeds from the sale of property of the estate are distributed to creditors. *Cf.* 11 U.S.C. § 726. Recall that property of the estate is limited to the interest of the debtor in property. If D owns Blackacre and M has a mortgage on Blackacre, both D and M have interests in the property and, in the event of D's bankruptcy, only D's interest in the property is property of the estate. Accordingly, if D owed M $100,000 secured by Blackacre and D's bankruptcy trustee's sale of Blackacre netted $125,000, then the trustee would pay M $100,000. *Cf* sections 363(f)(3), 506(c), 506(d).

What if D owed M $200,000 and a sale of Blackacre by the bankruptcy trustee would only net $125,000? How would the bankruptcy estate benefit from the trustee's sale of Blackacre? Why wouldn't the trustee simply let M sell Blackacre? Is anything that simple in bankruptcy? *See* section 554 and Rule 6007(a).

G. COMMENCEMENT AND DISMISSAL

Looking to section 109(b), any person who is not a railroad, or insurance company or bank or saving and loan association can file a Chapter 7 petition. If, however, the person who filed the Chapter 7 petition is an individual with primarily consumer debts, you need to know about the "means test" of section 707.

The words "means test" is not used in section 707 of the Bankruptcy Code. Nonetheless, the words "means test" is is used by lawyers and judges in applying section 707. "Means test" is used when the question is whether an individual debtor can use Chapter 7 or whether she is limited to Chapter 11 or Chapter 13 because she has the "means" to make meaningful payments to creditors. [To complete your understanding of "lawyer talk", a debtor "passes the means test" when she does <u>not</u> have the means to make meaningful payments to creditors.]

The "means test" will appear on your exam if the fact pattern tells you that (1) the debtor is an individual and (2) her debts are primarily consumer debts and (3) she files a Chapter 7 petition, and (4) the fact pattern also gives you detailed information about how much the debtor earned in the six months before filing for bankruptcy and how much she spends. Such a fact pattern raises the question of whether the section 707(b)(2) means test will result in that Chapter 7 bankruptcy case being dismissed or converted to some other chapter.

As amended in 2005, section 707(b)(1) provides for dismissal of a Chapter 7 petition filed by an individual debtor with primarily consumer debts for "abuse." There are three different ways of establishing section 707(b)(1) "abuse":

The first and second ways of establishing section 707 "abuse" require reading section 707(b)(1) together with section 707(b)(3): "abuse" turns on (1) bad faith filing or (2) "totality of the circumstances of the debtor's financial situation."

The third way of establishing section 707 "abuse" requires reading section 707(b)(1) together with section 707(b)(2): "abuse" turns on what is generally referred to as a "means test."

The policy reason for the section 707(b)(2) means test is easy to state in class or on an exam. The section 707(b)(2) means test is based on the premise that if debtors can afford to pay their creditors at least between $6,000 and $10,000 over five years, they should pay creditors in a Chapter 13 plan instead of using Chapter 7 to avoid paying creditors.

However, the particulars of the section 707(b)(2) means test are hard to explain in class or an exam. Before getting into the particulars of the section 707(b)(2) means test, you need to understand that in real bankruptcy cases, most of the particulars of the section 707(b)(2) means test will usually not be applicable.

More specifically, the applicability of the section 707(b)(2) means test turns primarily on a comparison of the debtor's "current monthly income" as defined in section 101 and "median family income" as defined in section 101. If the debtor's "current monthly income" times 12 is less than "median family income," for the state in which the debtor lives, no one can file a motion to dismiss the Chapter 7 case based on the section 707(b)(2) means test, section 707(b)(7). And, in almost all real Chapter 7 bankruptcy cases in which the debtor is an individual whose debts are primarily consumer debts, the debtor's "current monthly income" multiplied by 12 will be less than "median family income" so it will not be necessary to consider the other particulars of the section 707(b)(2) means test.

For those debtors you encounter in the real world or in law school classes with "current monthly income" above "median family income," section 707(b)(2) creates a means test that compares 60 months of "current monthly income" as defined in section 101 with the total of the following:

(1) 60 months of expenses measured by Internal Revenue Service expense standards; and

(2) 60 months of other, actual expenses specified in section 707(b)(2); and

(3) payments due on secured and priority debts for the 60 months after the bankruptcy petition date.

More specifically, subtract the total of (1) and (2) and (3) above from the product of multiplying "current monthly income" by 60. If the difference is greater than either

(1) $10,000 or

(2) the greater of $6,000 or 25% of the debtor's nonpriority unsecured debts, then section 707(b) "abuse" is presumed, section 707(b)(7).

Remember that the section 707(b)(2) computations in the previous paragraph do not conclusively establish "abuse." Rather, these computations establish a presumption of abuse that the debtor can rebut by swearing to and documenting "special circumstances" that increase expenses or decrease "current monthly income" so as to bring the debtor's income after expenses below the $10,000/$6,000 trigger points. More important, remember that these complicated section 707(b)(2) computations will be necessary only if a debtor's "current monthly income" exceeds "median family income."

As we will learn in the next unit on what happens in a Chapter 13 case, debtor's "current monthly income" as compared with "median family income" is also important in determining the Chapter 13 debtor's payment period and plan payment commitment. If the debtor's "current monthly income" exceeds "median family income," then

(1) the Chapter 13 plan payment period is "not less than 5 years" instead of 3 years, section 1325(b)(4) AND

(2) the minimum amount required to be paid under the plan is measured by the "means test" as discussed above instead of the "disposable income" test as applied by courts, section 1325(a)(3).

UNIT 10

LEGAL AND OTHER ISSUES TO WATCH FOR IN CHAPTER 13

■ ■ ■

A. OVERVIEW OF CHAPTER 13 (WHAT IS IN CHAPTER 13 OF THE BANKRUPTCY CODE?)

In Chapter 13, an individual debtor with a regular source of income proposes and performs a payment plan. During the year ending September 30, 2008, 34% of all bankruptcy debtors chose to file under Chapter 13 (approximately 354,000 Chapter 13 cases). Chapter 13 trustees disbursed approximately $5 billion to creditors that same year.

As will be discussed in greater detail later in this unit, Chapter 7 and Chapter 13 are quite different. For now,

- **What the debtor gives up.** In Chapter 7, the debtor surrenders his nonexempt assets, which are liquidated for the benefit of the debtor's creditors. In Chapter 13, the debtor commits part of her future income which, along with any other assets the debtor has committed to the plan, is distributed to creditors

- **What the debtor gets.** The ability of a Chapter 7 debtor to deal with a secured creditor whose debt is in default and who does not want to make a deal with the debtor is limited. In Chapter 13, the debtor has the right to cure defaults over a period of time, even if the secured creditor does not agree, and, in the case of some undersecured creditors, to reduce the debt that has to be paid to the value of the collateral. In addition, the Chapter 13 debtor will be able to discharge a few debts that are nondischargeable in Chapter 7 and, with respect to those debts not dischargeable in Chapter 13, will be able to impose payment terms on those creditors.

- **How long it takes.** Obtaining a discharge in Chapter 7 is relatively quick; it usually takes four to six months. In Chapter 13, obtaining a discharge takes much longer, usually three to five years.

- **Who gets what.** In Chapter 7, the Code determines what is distributed and to whom. Central to Chapter 13 is a plan that establishes how much and when creditors will be paid. The following Model Chapter 13 Plan developed by practitioners at Advanced Consumer Bankruptcy Practice Institutes sponsored by the National Association of Chapter 13 Trustees and modified by the bankruptcy court in the Middle District of Tennessee shows you what a typical plan may cover. Many courts prescribe the form of the plan.

CHAPTER 13. PLAN AND RELATED MOTIONS
United States Bankruptcy Court
Middle District of Tennessee

IN RE:

_____   Case No. _____
_____   Chapter 13
_____

SSN: XXX–XX-_____ SSN: XXX–XX-_____

CHAPTER 13 PLAN AND MOTIONS   _____ Original _____ Amended   Date_____

YOUR RIGHTS WILL BE AFFECTED BY THIS PLAN. You should read this and other documents sent to you carefully and discuss them with your attorney. Any party opposing any provision of this plan or any motion below must file a written objection by the date first set for the meeting of creditors or raise such objection orally before the conclusion of the meeting of creditors.

THIS PLAN MAY REQUEST THAT YOU ACCEPT ITS TERMS. If you are listed in Paragraph 4 below and you DO NOT ACCEPT the plan provisions listed in 4(a), the provisions of 4(b) will be your treatment under the plan. If you DO NOT ACCEPT the provisions of 4(a), you must file a statement that you DO NOT ACCEPT the plan either in writing prior to the meeting of creditors, or orally before the conclusion of the meeting of creditors, and the provisions of 4(b) will be part of the plan. The filing of a statement or orally making such statement at the meeting of creditors that you DO NOT ACCEPT the plan will not be deemed an objection to confirmation; it will be deemed an election to be treated as provided in Paragraph 4(b).

IF YOU OBJECT TO CONFIRMATION, you must either file a written objection to confirmation or orally object before the conclusion of the meeting of creditors as set by separate notice. This plan may be confirmed and the motions below granted WITHOUT FURTHER NOTICE unless timely objection to the motion(s) or confirmation is filed. If you hold a secured claim, this Plan is notice that your lien may be voided or modified as herein noted if you do not object.

THIS PLAN DOES NOT ALLOW CLAIMS. You must file a proof of claim to be paid under any plan that may be confirmed.

1. **PAYMENT AND LENGTH OF PLAN**

(a) Debtor shall pay $_____ per _____ to the Chapter 13 trustee starting _____ for approximately _____ months. This date can be no later than 30 days after filing of the petition. This amount may be altered if a creditor rejects the plan. See Paragraph 4.

☐ A payroll deduction order will issue to the Debtor's employer: _____
                                                                          _____
☐ Debtor will pay directly to the trustee.   (Name & Address of Employer)

(b) Joint Debtor shall pay $_____ per _____ to the Chapter 13 Trustee starting _____ for approx. _____ months. This date can be no later than 30 days after filing of the petition. The amount may be altered if a creditor rejects the plan. See Paragraph 4 below.

☐ A payroll deduction order will issue to the Joint Debtor's employer: _____
                                                                                _____
☐ Joint Debtor will pay directly to the trustee.   (Name & Address of Employer)

(c) Other payments to the Trustee: _____
_____
_____

(d) Total amount to be paid to Trustee shall not be less than $_____ ("Base"). This amount may be altered if a creditor rejects the plan.

2. PRIORITY CLAIMS (INCLUDING ADMINISTRATIVE EXPENSES AND SUPPORT) [See § 1322(a)(2)]

The following priority claims, if allowed, will be paid in full unless creditor agrees otherwise:

CREDITOR	TYPE OF PRIORITY	SCHEDULED AMOUNT	MONTHLY PAYMENT

☐ The Trustee ☐ The Debtor shall pay Domestic Support Obligations that become due after filing of the petition as follows:

DSO CREDITOR	SCHEDULED AMOUNT	MONTHLY PAYMENT

3. PRIORITY CLAIMS SUBJECT TO SUBORDINATION

Pursuant to § 1322(a)(4), the following priority creditors shall not be paid in full:

CREDITOR	REASON FOR SUBORDINATION	SCHEDULED AMOUNT

4. SECURED CLAIMS NOT SUBJECT TO § 506

The following debts were either (1) incurred within 910 days before the petition date and secured by a purchase money security interest in a motor vehicle or (2) incurred within one year before the petition date and secured by a purchase money security interest in any other thing of value.

(a) The Plan DOES propose to limit the secured claims listed below to the following amounts (cramdown). THIS WILL BE THE TREATMENT OF THE CREDITORS LISTED BELOW UNLESS THE LISTED CREDITOR FILES A STATEMENT BEFORE THE MEETING OF CREDITORS THAT IT DOES NOT ACCEPT THE PLAN OR ORALLY MAKES SUCH STATEMENT AT THE MEETING OF CREDITORS.

CREDITOR	COLLATERAL	SCHEDULED AMT.	VALUE	INTEREST RATE	MONTHLY PAYMENT

(b) If a creditor noted above DOES NOT ACCEPT the plan, the collateral listed above for that creditor will be surrendered and the payments to the Trustee will be reduced by the amount listed under "Per Mo." for that creditor in 4(a) above, and the "base" reduced accordingly.

(c) Debtor proposes to pay the claims not subject to § 506 as listed below in full.

CREDITOR	COLLATERAL	SCHEDULED AMT.	INTEREST RATE	MONTHLY PAYMENT

5. PRECONFIRMATION ADEQUATE PROTECTION PAYMENTS AND PAYMENTS TO LESSORS

The Debtor proposes that the trustee make adequate protection payments, or payments to lessors prior to the confirmation of the plan, pursuant to § 1326(a)(1) as follows:

CREDITOR	AMOUNT OF MONTHLY PAYMENT

The Trustee shall commence making such payments to creditors holding allowed claims secured by a purchase money security interest in personal property or leases of personal property as soon as practicable after the filing of a proof of claim by such creditor. The Trustee shall receive the percentage fee fixed under 28 U.S.C. § 586(e) on such payments. Upon confirmation the treatment of such claims will be governed by Paragraph 4 or 6 as appropriate.

6. SECURED CLAIMS AND MOTION TO VALUE COLLATERAL.

Debtor moves to value the collateral as indicated below. Trustee shall pay allowed secured claims the value indicated or the amount of the claim, whichever is less. The excess of creditors claim shall be treated as an unsecured claim. Any claim listed as "NO VALUE" in the value column below will be treated as an unsecured claim, and the lien avoided pursuant to § 506.

CREDITOR	COLLATERAL	SCHEDULED AMOUNT	VALUE	INTEREST RATE	MONTHLY PAYMENT

7. SURRENDERED PROPERTY.

In addition to any property surrendered under 4(b), Debtor surrenders the following collateral. Upon confirmation, the stay is lifted as to surrendered collateral. Any claim submitted by such creditor will receive no distribution under the plan until an amended proof of claim is filed by such creditor, reflecting any deficiency balance remaining following surrender.

CREDITOR	COLLATERAL

8. UNSECURED CLAIMS

Allowed non-priority unsecured claims shall be paid as follows:

☐ The Debtor shall pay sufficient funds to provide a pool to unsecured creditors of $_____ ("Unsecured Pool"). Payments to unsecured priority and general creditors will be made from this pool. The unsecured creditors will receive all funds remaining in the Unsecured Pool after satisfaction of all allowed priority claims.

☐ Not less than _____ percent.

☐ Funds that the Trustee receives which exceed the total allowed priority unsecured claims, the total secured claims plus interest, long term claims, and the Unsecured Pool shall increase the Unsecured Pool until the Debtor has paid the total Base amount indicated in Paragraph 1(d).

Separately Classified Unsecured Claims
    (1) Cosigned claims shall be treated as follows:

CREDITOR	COSIGNER	TREATMENT	AMOUNT

    (2) Other classified unsecured claims:

CREDITOR	REASON FOR CLASSIFICATION	TREATMENT	AMOUNT

9. CURING DEFAULT AND MAINTAINING PAYMENTS

(a) Trustee shall pay the allowed claims for arrearages, and Trustee shall pay the postpetition monthly payments to creditor.

CREDITOR	COLLATERAL	ESTIMATED ARREARAGE	LAST MONTH IN ARREARS	INTEREST RATE	REGULAR PAYMENT AMOUNT

(b) Trustee shall pay the allowed claims for arrearages, and Debtor shall pay the postpetition monthly payments to creditor.

CREDITOR COLLATERAL	EST. ARREARAGE	LAST MONTH IN ARREARS	INTEREST RATE	REGULAR PAYMENT AMOUNT

10. EXECUTORY CONTRACTS AND UNEXPIRED LEASES

All executory contracts and leases are rejected, except the following are assumed and treated under the plan as noted:

CREDITOR	PROPERTY DESCRIPTION	TREATMENT UNDER PLAN

11. OTHER PLAN PROVISIONS AND MOTIONS

(a) **Motion to Avoid Lien under § 522(f)**.
Debtor moves to avoid the following liens that impair exemptions:

CREDITOR	COLLATERAL

(b) **Lien Retention and Motions to Avoid Liens**
Except as provided above in Paragraph 7 and 10(a), allowed secured claim holders retain liens until liens are released upon completion of all payments under the plan.

(c) **Debtors Certificate of Compliance with § 521 and Motion for Order Acknowledging Compliance**
Debtors Counsel (or debtor, if not represented by counsel) certifies that all information required under § 521(a)(1) has been filed and /or submitted to the trustee and moves the court for an order that such information satisfied the requirements of § 521 and that the case is not dismissed under § 521(i).

(d) ☐   **Debtors move the Court to substantively consolidate the joint estates.**

       ☐   **Debtors move the Court to NOT substantively consolidate the joint estates.**

(e) **Vesting of Property of the Estate**
Property of the estate shall revest in the Debtor:
_____ Upon confirmation _____ Upon discharge or dismissal _____ Other_____

(f) **Direct Payment by Debtor**
☐   Secured creditors and lessors to be paid directly by the Debtor shall continue to mail to Debtor the customary monthly notices or coupons notwithstanding the automatic stay.

(g) **Order of Distribution**
Trustee shall pay allowed claims in the following disbursement priority :
(1) _____
(2) _____
(3) _____
(4) _____
(5) _____
(6) _____

(h) **Other, Special Provisions of the Plan Not Elsewhere Described:**

_____
_____

_____
DEBTOR'S ATTORNEY SIGNATURE

● **The Chapter 13 participants.** Several "players" have a role in administering the Chapter 13 plan.

---

1. ROLE OF THE CHAPTER 13 TRUSTEE

Each judicial district has one or more standing Chapter 13 trustees whose job is to administer the Chapter 13 cases in the district. Unlike the Chapter 7 trustee, the Chapter 13 trustee does not take possession of or liquidate the nonexempt property of the estate. Rather, the Chapter 13 trustee acts as a disbursing agent, collecting and distributing the plan payments to creditors. Before confirmation Chapter 13 trustees review the plans proposed by debtors to determine both whether they are feasible and whether they comply with the legal requirements of Chapter 13. If there are any questions in that regard, the Chapter 13 trustee asks the debtor the pertinent questions during the § 341(a) meeting of creditors, which the Chapter 13 trustee conducts. At the confirmation hearing, the Chapter 13 trustee advises the court whether the plan should be confirmed. When a debtor fails to make plan payments as required, the Chapter 13 trustee takes appropriate remedial action. You can find out more about the Chapter 13 trustees in your area by using the web site http://www.bestcase.com/trustees13.htm, which provides links to the web sites of Chapter 13 trustees throughout the United States.

2. ROLE OF THE BANKRUPTCY JUDGE IN CHAPTER 13

Bankruptcy judges have a more active role in most Chapter 13 cases than they do in Chapter 7 cases. To obtain a discharge, the Chapter 13 debtor must have a plan specifically confirmed by a bankruptcy judge.

There are more disputes requiring judicial resolution in Chapter 13 cases than there are in Chapter 7 cases.

The judge presides at the confirmation hearing and resolves any disputes. After confirmation, if the debtor gets behind in plan payments, the judge will often hear motions for relief from stay filed by lessors or creditors with secured claims, motions to dismiss or convert the case to Chapter 7, and requests for a hardship (early) discharge by debtors who are unable to fully perform their plan. The judge will also consider confirmation of any modified plan proposed by the debtor, the Chapter 13 trustee or an unsecured creditor.

3. ROLE OF THE DEBTOR'S ATTORNEY IN CHAPTER 13

Initially the debtor's attorney helps the debtor decide which chapter of the Code will best provide the relief the debtor needs. After the debtor decides to file Chapter 13, the lawyer has a lot of work to do. In addition to completing the bankruptcy schedules and statement of financial affairs, in most districts the lawyer has to help the debtor to develop and draft the payment plan, such as the one included above.

In order to draft a feasible and confirmable plan, the lawyer has to analyze the following questions, which are discussed in greater detail later in this unit: (1) what is the debtor's disposable income that is available for plan payments; (2) how much must be paid into the plan (this is usually an amount not less than the amount necessary to satisfy priority and secured claims being paid through the plan, amounts necessary to cure defaults on secured debt and leases being cured through the plan, amounts necessary to pay the costs of administering the Chapter 13 plan, and amounts necessary to pay the nonpriority unsecured claims being paid under the plan); and (3) how much would creditors receive if the debtor filed a Chapter 7 case.

Once the plan is drafted and filed, the lawyer attends the § 341(a) meeting of creditors with the debtor and responds to any concerns or objections that the Chapter 13 trustee and/or creditors raise with respect to the plan, which sometimes entails preparing a modified plan. Before confirmation, the lawyer may have to help the debtor respond to a motion for relief from stay or adequate protection filed by a creditor that holds a secured claim or by a lessor whose postpetition payments the debtor has failed to pay. The lawyer may need to attend the confirmation hearing to respond to objections and possibly put on evidence. Even though § 1324 says that there shall be a confirmation hearing in every Chapter 13 case, the actual practice varies widely among the bankruptcy courts; some courts have a confirmation hearing only if an objection to confirmation is filed, while other courts have a confirmation hearing in every case.

After confirmation, the lawyer may have to provide further services if the debtor is unable to complete the plan as proposed. Such services may include responding to motions to convert or dismiss, assisting the debtor in modifying the plan to deal with unanticipated changes in income or expenses, responding to a Chapter 13 trustee's or unsecured creditor's proposed modified plan increasing the plan payments if the debtor's income increases, and responding to creditor motions for relief from stay.

How much the debtor's attorney gets paid for a Chapter 13 case varies substantially depending on geographic location, the amount of work required, and the views of the judge(s) on the court regarding a reasonable fee. Sometimes lawyers are paid a flat fee for the entire case (usually in the range of $1,600–$5,000), or are paid a flat fee for all work through confirmation of the initial plan and hourly rates for work thereafter, or are paid their customary hourly rate for all services. The fee is often double or triple the amount of the average Chapter 7 legal fee in the community because of the greater complexity and duration of Chapter 13 cases.

Although the fees in Chapter 13 are usually higher than in Chapter 7, the payment terms are more attractive to the debtor. In Chapter 7, many attorneys require that the debtor pay the attorney fee in full before the case is filed, because they do not want to deal with the legal question of whether all or part of their fee would be discharged if not paid in advance and they do not want to face the practical problem of collecting from a debtor who was unable to pay many of her creditors. The same attorneys may be willing to accept payment of their fees over time through the Chapter 13 plan, because they know the Chapter 13 trustee will collect the money for their fees and their claim for fees will be a priority claim that must be paid in full before the debtor gets a bankruptcy discharge. The lawyer has to have his or her fees approved by the court as reasonable. Some courts establish a fee amount that will be approved without time records, because the court deems the amount inherently reasonable.

Problem 10–1: What Happens in Chapter 13 to the Debtor's Attorney's Claim for Fees?

You and your client have decided that Chapter 13 is her best alternative. Your client is short on cash and would like to pay your $1,500 fee over time. How will Chapter 13 treat your claim for fees? Consider §§ 330(a)(4)(B), 503(b)(2), 507(a)(1), 1322(a)(2), 1325(a)(1), and 1328(a)(1).[1]

---

1. Section 330(a)(4)(B) provides:

In a Chapter 12 or Chapter 13 case in which the debtor is an individual, the court may allow reasonable compensation to the debtor's attorney for representing the interests of the debtor in connection with the bankruptcy case based on a consideration of the benefit and necessity of such services to the debtor and the other factors set forth in this section.

Section 503(b)(2) provides:

(b) After notice and a hearing, there shall be allowed administrative expenses, other than claims allowed under section 502(f) of this title, including–. . . .

(2) compensation and reimbursement awarded under section 330(a) of this title;

Section 507(a)(1) provides:

(A) Allowed unsecured claims for domestic support obligations that, as of the date of the filing of the petition in a case under this title, are owed to or recoverable by a spouse, former spouse, or child of the debtor, or such child's parent, legal guardian, or responsible relative, without regard to whether the claim is filed by such person or is filed by a governmental unit on behalf of such person, on the condition that funds received under this paragraph by a governmental unit under this title after the date of the filing of the petition shall be applied and distributed in accordance with applicable nonbankruptcy law.

(B) Subject to claims under subparagraph (A), allowed unsecured claims for domestic support obligations that, as of the date of the filing of the petition are assigned by a spouse, former spouse, child of the debtor, or such child's parent, legal guardian, or responsible relative to a governmental unit (unless such obligation is assigned voluntarily by the spouse, former spouse, child, parent, legal guardian, or responsible relative of the child for the purpose of collecting the debt) or are owed directly to or recoverable by a governmental unit under applicable nonbankruptcy law, on the condition that funds received under this paragraph by a governmental unit under this title after the date of the filing of the petition be applied and distributed in accordance with applicable nonbankruptcy law.

4. UNDERSTANDING THE STATUTORY STRUCTURE OF CHAPTER 13

Chapter 13 of the Code consists of 18 statutory sections that control what an individual debtor with a regular income can do, and must do, in order to adjust her debts through the Chapter 13 process. In working through Chapter 13 legal issues, you should keep the following principles in mind. First, answering many problems will require consideration of more than one Code section. For instance, in order to begin to understand what the debtor must do to obtain relief under Chapter 13, one must consider both § 1322, which delineates what provisions a Chapter 13 plan can and must contain, and § 1325, which establishes the requirements for confirmation (court approval) of the plan. Second, remember that the provisions of Chapters 1, 3, and 5 of the Code are applicable in Chapter 13 cases. Therefore, in working through Chapter 13 problems, do not limit yourself to the statutory provisions you find in Chapter 13. Third, language identical to that used in a number of the Chapter 13 statutory provisions is found in other bankruptcy chapters. For instance, when trying to understand the requirements for confirmation imposed by § 1325, you may find similar language, and cases interpreting that language, in Chapters 11 and 12 (*e.g.*, compare §§ 1129(b)(2)(A)(i) and 1325(a)(5)(B)(ii)).

The following statutory overview will help you work through Chapter 13.

- **Eligibility for Chapter 13 Relief.** Chapter 13 permits an individual debtor with a regular source of income whose debts do not

---

(C) If a trustee is appointed or elected under section 701, 702, 703, 1104, 1202, or 1302, the administrative expenses of the trustee allowed under paragraphs (1)(A), (2), and (6) of section 503(b) shall be paid before payment of claims under subparagraphs (A) and (B), to the extent that the trustee administers assets that are otherwise available for the payment of such claims.

Section 1322(a)(2) is quoted on page 286.

Section 1325(a)(1) provides:

(a) Except as provided in subsection (b), the court shall confirm a plan if—

(1) the plan complies with the provisions of this chapter and with the other applicable provisions of this title;

Section 1328(a) provides:

(a) Subject to subsection (d), as soon as practicable after completion by the debtor of all payments under the plan, and in the case of a debtor who is required by a judicial or administrative order, or by statute, to pay a domestic support obligation, after such debtor certifies that all amounts payable under such order or such statute that are due on or before the date of the certification (including amounts due before the petition was filed, but only to the extent provided for by the plan) have been paid, unless the court approves a written waiver of discharge executed by the debtor after the order for relief under this chapter, the court shall grant the debtor a discharge of all debts provided for by the plan or disallowed under section 502 of this title, except any debt—

(1) provided for under section 1322(b)(5) of this title;

(2) of the kind specified in section 507(a)(8)(C) or in paragraph (1)(B), (1)(C), (2), (3), (4), (5), (8), or (9) of section 523(a) of this title; or

(3) for restitution, or a criminal fine, included in a sentence on the debtor's conviction of a crime; or

(4) for restitution, or damages, awarded in a civil action against the debtor as a result of willful or malicious injury by the debtor that caused personal injury to an individual or the death of an individual.

exceed certain limits to get bankruptcy relief by proposing and performing a plan.

- **Property of the Chapter 13 Estate.** While generally all the property described in § 541 becomes property of the estate in Chapter 13, property that the debtor acquires during the pendency of the Chapter 13, including earnings, is also property of the estate. § 1306. That section also tells us that the debtor retains possession of the property of the estate unless the plan or the confirmation order provides otherwise. *See* Unit 4.

- **Role of the Chapter 13 Trustee and Debtor.** Section 1302 establishes that the United States Trustee appoints a person who acts as the Chapter 13 trustee and establishes the duties of the Chapter 13 trustee. Sections 1303 and 1304 define the rights and powers of the debtor and tell us what happens to the business of a Chapter 13 debtor who is self-employed.

- **Administrative Provisions**. There is a co-debtor stay in Chapter 13 that, under certain circumstances, prevents creditors from pursuing collection from those who have co-signed consumer obligations for the debtor. § 1301. Section 1305 describes under what circumstances claims arising after the Chapter 13 case is filed can be treated as allowed claims in Chapter 13. Conversion of the Chapter 13 case to a different type of bankruptcy case or dismissal of the case are controlled by § 1307.

- **The Plan and Plan Payments**. The plan is the heart of the Chapter 13 case. It determines how much the debtor pays to the Chapter 13 trustee for disbursement to creditors and which creditors receive the money. The Chapter 13 debtor must file a plan. § 1321. Section 1322 delineates what a plan must contain, and what it can contain. That section must be read in conjunction with § 1325, which sets forth the confirmation requirements, because a plan that meets the requirements of § 1322 but cannot be confirmed accomplishes nothing. The circumstances under which the plan can be modified are controlled by § 1323 (pre-confirmation modification) and § 1329 (post-confirmation modification). Section 1326 establishes certain requirements regarding the plan payments and disbursement of those payments.

- **Confirmation of the Plan.** Section 1324 tells us that a confirmation hearing is held and any interested party can object to confirmation. The court confirms the plan if it meets the requirements of § 1325. Those requirements include that the debtor filed the case and proposed the plan in good faith, unsecured creditors receive at least as much as they would have if debtor had filed Chapter 7, the plan is feasible, the debtor has paid all her domestic support obligations that became due postpetition, the debtor has filed all required tax returns, and creditors with secured claims have their claims satisfied in one of the manners specified in the statute. Creditors do not get to vote whether to accept the plan. The effect of confirmation is controlled by § 1327. Section 1330 defines when an order of confirmation may be revoked.

- **Discharge**. Section 1328 controls the Chapter 13 bankruptcy discharge. It incorporates most, but not all, of the frequently applicable exceptions to discharge that apply in Chapter 7 cases.

B. ELIGIBILITY, DEADLINES AND TIMELINES (WHO CAN FILE AND WHAT HAPPENS WHEN?)

11 U.S.C. § 109(e)—[Chapter 13 Eligibility]

Only an individual with regular income that owes, on the date of the filing of the petition, noncontingent, liquidated, unsecured debts of less than $360,475 and noncontingent, liquidated, secured debts of less than $1,081,400, or an individual with regular income and such individual's spouse, except a stockbroker or a commodity broker, that owe, on the date of the filing of the petition, noncontingent, liquidated, unsecured debts that aggregate less than $360,475 and noncontingent, liquidated, secured debts of less than $1,081,400 may be a debtor under chapter 13 of this title.

Notice that there are two primary eligibility requirements. First, the debtor has to have a "regular income." Regular income is more than just wages. It can be social security, child support, earnings from a business or any other income. Second, the debtor's debts cannot exceed the limits specified in the statute. Notice that contingent or unliquidated debts are not counted in computing the total amount of the debts for eligibility purposes. This is true even though, as we learned in Unit 4.C., such debts are claims. "A debt is noncontingent 'if all events giving rise to liability occurred prior to the filing of the bankruptcy petition.' ... Whether debt is liquidated depends on 'whether it is subject to ready determination and precision in computation of the amount due.' A debt is subject to a ready determination when only a simple hearing is required, as compared to an extensive, contested evidentiary hearing." *In re Vaughn*, 276 B.R. 323 (Bankr. N.H. 2002).

Problem 10–2: Are These Debtors Eligible for Chapter 13?

1. Denny Crane is a partner in the law firm of Crane, Poole & Schmidt. Some years his partnership earnings are as high as $2,000,000. Some years as low as $500,000. Is Denny Crane eligible for Chapter 13 relief?

2. Denny Crane is being sued for malpractice. The complaint seeks damages of $1,000,000. Is Denny Crane eligible for Chapter 13?

3. Johnson (Debtor) owed Home State Bank (Bank) $470,000 secured by a mortgage on Debtor's home and owed $500,000 in unsecured claims. Johnson filed a petition under Chapter 7 of the Code and pursuant to 11 U.S.C. § 727, the Bankruptcy Court discharged Johnson. Even though Johnson has discharged his personal liability on his

promissory note to the Bank and on his unsecured claims, Bank still has its mortgage. Johnson is one year behind on his mortgage payments and Bank has initiated foreclosure proceedings. Johnson wants to keep his home, but it will take him three years to catch up his past due payments. Is Johnson eligible for Chapter 13?

———————

Chapter 13 is designed to move expeditiously and to keep costs to a minimum. The case starts when the debtor voluntarily files a Chapter 13 petition. Within 14 days after the petition is filed, the debtor is required to file her plan and schedules. Bankr. R. 1007(c) and 3015(b).[2] The debtor must start making the plan payments to the Chapter 13 trustee within 30 days after the case is filed. § 1326(a)(1).[3] A § 341(a) meeting of creditors is held between 21 and 50 days after the case is filed. Bankr. R. 2003(a).[4] Courts must hold a hearing on confirmation of the plan within 45 days after the § 341(a) meeting. § 1324(b).[5] Once the plan is confirmed, the Chapter 13 trustee may begin disbursing to creditors the payments the debtor has made under the plan. § 1326(a)(2).[6] Thus, in most Chapter 13 cases, the creditor payment plan is proposed, approved and the Chapter 13 trustee begins disbursing payments to creditors within four to six months after the debtor files her case.

The debtor does not receive a discharge until either the debtor makes all the payments required by her plan, or, the debtor qualifies for a hardship discharge. § 1328.[7] Depending on whether the debtor's income is above or below the median income and whether the debtor has any disposable income, the debtor will have to make payments for a minimum of either three years or five years. (§ 1325(b)(1) & (4)). As you can see, Chapter 13 cases last much longer than Chapter 7 cases.

---

2. Bankr. R. 3015 (b) provides:

The debtor may file a Chapter 13 plan with the petition. If a plan is not filed with the petition, it shall be filed within 14 days thereafter, and such time may not be further extended except for cause shown and on notice as the court may direct. If a case is converted to Chapter 13, a plan shall be filed within 14 days thereafter, and such time may not be further extended except for cause shown and on notice as the court may direct.

3. Section 1326(a)(1) provides:

Unless the court orders otherwise, the debtor shall commence making payments not later than 30 days after the date of the filing of the plan or the order for relief, whichever is earlier.

4. Bankr. R. 2003(a) provides:

Meeting of Creditors. ... In a Chapter 13 individual's debt adjustment case, the United States trustee shall call a meeting of creditors to be held no fewer than 21 and no more than 50 days after the order for relief. ...

5. Section 1324(b) provides:

The hearing on confirmation of the plan may be held not earlier than 20 days and not later than 45 days after the date of the meeting of creditors under section 341(a), unless the court determines that it would be in the best interests of the creditors and the estate to hold such hearing at an earlier date and there is no objection to such earlier date.

6. Section 1326(a)(2) provides:

A payment made [made by the debtor to the trustee] shall be retained by the trustee until confirmation or denial of confirmation of a plan. If a plan is confirmed, the trustee shall distribute any such payment in accordance with the plan as soon as is practicable. If a plan is not confirmed, the trustee shall return any such payment to the debtor [unless the payment has previously been paid to or is due to a personal property lessor or a creditor whose claim is secured by personal property], after deducting any unpaid claim allowed under section 503(b) of this title.

7. Section 1328(a) is quoted on page 235.

C. PLAN PAYMENTS (WHAT IS THE MINIMUM THAT THE DEBTOR HAS TO PAY?)

Section 1325, which sets forth the requirements for confirmation of a plan, sets a floor below which the debtor's total Chapter 13 plan payments cannot drop. There are two components to the floor. First, unless the debtor's plan pays the creditors in full, the debtor is often required to devote all of her "projected disposable income" to the plan for a three or five-year commitment period. § 1325(b). This is commonly referred to as the "best efforts test" or the "disposable income requirement." Second, creditors must receive at least as much as they would receive in a Chapter 7 case. § 1325(a)(4). This is commonly referred to as the "best interests test."

Sometimes a debtor will be required to pay more than the floor amount in order to confirm a plan, because Chapter 13 may impose requirements that can be met only if the debtor pays more. For instance, the debtor must pay priority claims in full, except support obligations owed to a government unit under certain circumstances, in order to confirm a plan. §§ 1322(a)(2) and (4). The most common types of priority claims that Chapter 13 debtors have are the costs of the Chapter 13 case (Chapter 13 trustee charges and debtor's attorney fees paid through the plan), support obligations and certain tax obligations. If the amount of the priority claims exceeds the amount that the debtor must pay to meet the best interests test and the disposable income requirement, effectively the minimum amount that the debtor must pay is the amount necessary to pay the priority claims.

A debtor sometimes will have to pay more than the floor amount to confirm a plan that accomplishes what the debtor wants to accomplish. If the debtor is behind on her house or car payments and she wants to keep the house or car, she will either need to cure the default though the plan payments (bring the house or car loan current) or will have to pay the entire debt through the plan. §§ 1322(b)(2)–(5) and 1325(a)(5). Some debts, such as most student loans, are excepted from discharge in Chapter 13 even though they are not entitled to priority. The debtor will often want to pay the nondischargeable debt in full through the Chapter 13 plan in order to avoid facing debt collection actions by creditors after getting to the end of the Chapter 13 case.

1. DISPOSABLE INCOME AND ITS IMPACT ON CHAPTER 13

How much disposable income a debtor has affects use of Chapter 13 in three distinct ways. First, it forces some debtors to proceed in Chapter 13 rather than Chapter 7. The bankruptcy court may dismiss as an abuse the case of a Chapter 7 debtor whose debts are primarily consumer debts. Abuse is presumed for debtors whose income equals or exceeds the applicable median income and who have the ability to pay a certain amount to unsecured creditors. § 707(b); *see* Unit 5.B. A consumer debtor who can afford to pay thus will likely be forced to use Chapter 13 if the debtor needs or wants a bankruptcy discharge.

Second, disposable income may affect the total amount the Chapter 13 debtor has to pay. If either the Chapter 13 trustee or a creditor with an allowed unsecured claim objects to confirmation of the debtor's payment plan, the court cannot approve the plan unless the debtor's proposed plan payments are not less than the debtor's projected disposable income and the payments continue for three years after the first plan payment is due if the debtor's income is below the median income or for five years if the debtor's income equals or exceeds the median income. §§ 1325(b)(1)(B)[8] & 1325(b)(4).[9] The minimum length of the plan is called the "commitment period." § 1325(b)(4).

Third, disposable income affects how much the debtor must pay to the unsecured creditors in particular. The court cannot approve a plan unless:

> the plan provides that all of the debtor's projected disposable income to be received in the applicable commitment period beginning on the date that the first payment is due under the plan will be applied to make payments **to unsecured creditors** under the plan.

§ 1325(b)(1)(B) (emphasis added).

---

8. Section 1325(b)(1)(B) provides:

(b)(1) If the trustee or the holder of an allowed unsecured claim objects to the confirmation of the plan, then the court may not approve the plan unless, as of the effective date of the plan—

. . .

(B) the plan provides that all of the debtor's projected disposable income to be received in the three year applicable commitment period beginning on the date that the first payment is due under the plan will be applied to make payments to unsecured creditors under the plan.

9. Section 1325(b)(4) provides:

(4) For purposes of this subsection, the "applicable commitment period"—

(A) subject to subparagraph (B), shall be—

(i) 3 years; or

(ii) not less than 5 years, if the current monthly income of the debtor and the debtor's spouse combined [is not less than the applicable median income] . . . [.]

(B) may be less than 3 or 5 years, whichever is applicable under subparagraph (A), but only if the plan provides for payment in full of all allowed unsecured claims over a shorter period.

2. WHAT IS PROJECTED DISPOSABLE INCOME?

Projected disposable income is projected income less projected allowable expenses. Determining the amount of the debtor's projected disposable income thus requires analysis of two distinct aspects of the debtor's finances: (a) **income** and (b) **expenses**. Calculating both income and expenses, and projecting those amounts for the duration of the plan, raises legal and factual issues.

In order to allow the Chapter 13 trustee, creditors, the court and the United States Trustee to analyze a debtor's projected disposable income, every individual debtor files as part of her bankruptcy schedules a Schedule I, which details the amounts and sources of the debtor's and the debtor's spouse's income, describes tax withholdings and lists dependents, and a Schedule J, which provides information about the debtor's household expenses. The following two pages contain an example of the budget information provided by Mr. and Mrs. 64 in the Chapter 13 case discussed in Unit 1.

B6I (Official Form 6I) (12/07)

In re _____   Case No. _____
                        Debtor(s)

SCHEDULE I - CURRENT INCOME OF INDIVIDUAL DEBTOR(S)

The column labeled "Spouse" must be completed in all cases filed by joint debtors and by every married debtor, whether or not a joint petition is filed, unless the spouses are separated and a joint petition is not filed. Do not state the name of any minor child. The average monthly income calculated on this form may differ from the current monthly income calculated on Form 22A, 22B, or 22C.

Debtor's Marital Status:	DEPENDENTS OF DEBTOR AND SPOUSE		
Married	RELATIONSHIP(S): daughter / daughter	AGE(S): 11 / 6	

Employment:	DEBTOR	SPOUSE
Occupation	Electrician/Foreman	app electrician
Name of Employer	Berg Electric	New Tech/les Inc
How long employed	4 yrs	4 months
Address of Employer		

INCOME: (Estimate of average or projected monthly income at time case filed)

	DEBTOR	SPOUSE
1. Monthly gross wages, salary, and commissions (Prorate if not paid monthly)	$ 5,655.00	$ 2,831.00
2. Estimate monthly overtime	$ 0.00	$ 0.00
3. SUBTOTAL	$ 5,655.00	$ 2,831.00
4. LESS PAYROLL DEDUCTIONS		
a. Payroll taxes and social security	$ 1,487.00	$ 845.00
b. Insurance	$ 0.00	$ 148.00
c. Union dues	$ 0.00	$ 0.00
d. Other (Specify):	$ 0.00	$ 0.00
	$ 0.00	$ 0.00
5. SUBTOTAL OF PAYROLL DEDUCTIONS	$ 1,487.00	$ 993.00
6. TOTAL NET MONTHLY TAKE HOME PAY	$ 4,168.00	$ 1,838.00
7. Regular income from operation of business or profession or farm (Attach detailed statement)	$ 0.00	$ 0.00
8. Income from real property	$ 0.00	$ 0.00
9. Interest and dividends	$ 0.00	$ 0.00
10. Alimony, maintenance or support payments payable to the debtor for the debtor's use or that of dependents listed above	$ 0.00	$ 320.00
11. Social security or government assistance (Specify):	$ 0.00	$ 0.00
	$ 0.00	$ 0.00
12. Pension or retirement income	$ 0.00	$ 0.00
13. Other monthly income (Specify):	$ 0.00	$ 0.00
	$ 0.00	$ 0.00
14. SUBTOTAL OF LINES 7 THROUGH 13	$ 0.00	$ 320.00
15. AVERAGE MONTHLY INCOME (Add amounts shown on lines 6 and 14)	$ 4,168.00	$ 2,158.00
16. COMBINED AVERAGE MONTHLY INCOME: (Combine column totals from line 15)	$ 6,326.00	

(Report also on Summary of Schedules and, if applicable, on Statistical Summary of Certain Liabilities and Related Data)

17. Describe any increase or decrease in income reasonably anticipated to occur within the year following the filing of this document:

B6J (Official Form 6J) (12/07)

In re _____   Case No. _____
                    Debtor(s)

SCHEDULE J - CURRENT EXPENDITURES OF INDIVIDUAL DEBTOR(S)

Complete this schedule by estimating the average or projected monthly expenses of the debtor and the debtor's family at time case filed. Prorate any payments made bi-weekly, quarterly, semi-annually, or annually to show monthly rate. The average monthly expenses calculated on this form may differ from the deductions from income allowed on Form 22A or 22C.

☐   Check this box if a joint petition is filed and debtor's spouse maintains a separate household. Complete a separate schedule of expenditures labeled "Spouse."

1. Rent or home mortgage payment (include lot rented for mobile home)	$	1,466.00
a. Are real estate taxes included? Yes ___ No _X_		
b. Is property insurance included? Yes ___ No _X_		
2. Utilities: a. Electricity and heating fuel	$	203.00
b. Water and sewer	$	145.00
c. Telephone	$	100.00
d. Other **Garbage (57), cable & internet (95), cell phone (230)**	$	382.00
3. Home maintenance (repairs and upkeep)	$	80.00
4. Food	$	752.00
5. Clothing	$	180.00
6. Laundry and dry cleaning	$	64.00
7. Medical and dental expenses	$	50.00
8. Transportation (not including car payments)	$	600.00
9. Recreation, clubs and entertainment, newspapers, magazines, etc.	$	150.00
10. Charitable contributions	$	0.00
11. Insurance (not deducted from wages or included in home mortgage payments)		
a. Homeowner's or renter's	$	40.00
b. Life	$	0.00
c. Health	$	50.00
d. Auto	$	250.00
e. Other **other insurance**	$	75.00
12. Taxes (not deducted from wages or included in home mortgage payments)		
(Specify) _____	$	0.00
13. Installment payments: (In chapter 11, 12, and 13 cases, do not list payments to be included in the plan)		
a. Auto	$	0.00
b. Other **les schwab tires**	$	50.00
c. Other _____	$	0.00
14. Alimony, maintenance, and support paid to others	$	0.00
15. Payments for support of additional dependents not living at your home	$	0.00
16. Regular expenses from operation of business, profession, or farm (attach detailed statement)	$	0.00
17. Other **personal care (65), housekeeping (74), child care (300)**	$	439.00
18. AVERAGE MONTHLY EXPENSES (Total lines 1-17. Report also on Summary of Schedules and, if applicable, on the Statistical Summary of Certain Liabilities and Related Data.)	$	5,076.00

19. Describe any increase or decrease in expenditures reasonably anticipated to occur within the year following the filing of this document:

20. STATEMENT OF MONTHLY NET INCOME

a. Average monthly income from Line 15 of Schedule I	$	6,326.00
b. Average monthly expenses from Line 18 above	$	5,076.00
c. Monthly net income (a. minus b.)	$	1,250.00

a.   Calculating Projected Income

For all Chapter 13 debtors, calculating projected income starts with the debtor's "current monthly income," a term defined by the Bankruptcy Code and discussed in the material on the means test that is discussed on pages 225–226. § 1325(b)(2)[10] Remember that the term focuses on money

---

10.   Section 1325(b)(2) provides:

For purposes of this subsection, the term "disposable income" means current monthly income received by the debtor (other than child support payments, foster care payments, or disability payments for a dependent child made in accordance with applicable nonbankruptcy law to the extent reasonably necessary to be expended for such child) less amounts reasonably necessary to be expended—

the debtor received in the six months before the bankruptcy filing, regardless of whether the debtor's finances have improved or gotten worse. If a debtor has recently had a substantial change in her wages, her "current monthly income" is likely to be significantly different than her income during her Chapter 13 plan.

The following two hypothetical debtors illustrate the point that probable future income is often different than current monthly income. Both debtors have a current monthly income of $6,000, because their income totaled $36,000 in the six calendar months before they filed.

- Debtor #1 earned $8,000 per month until she was laid-off two months before she filed bankruptcy. She then received a severance benefit of $2,000 per month for the next two months.

- Debtor #2 earned $5,000 per month until three months before bankruptcy, when she obtained a job paying $7,000 per month.

In calculating disposable income, should the court take into account any changes in the debtor's income, such as the two illustrated above? The following case explores the meaning of the term "projected disposable income" and whether the term "projected" allows adjustment of the amount of the debtor's income when the debtor's current (historic) monthly income is significantly different than the debtor's likely future monthly income.

HAMILTON v. LANNING

545 F.3d 1269 (10th Cir. 2008), cert. granted in part ___ U.S. ___, 130
S.Ct. 487, 77 USLW 3449, 78 USLW 3010 (U.S. Nov. 02, 2009)

Before MURPHY, Circuit Judge, BRORBY, Senior Circuit Judge, and TYMKOVICH, Circuit Judge.

BRORBY, Senior Circuit Judge.

This bankruptcy appeal presents a question of first impression in this circuit: What is the proper way to calculate the "projected disposable income" of an above-median Chapter 13 debtor under amendments to the bankruptcy code effected by the Bankruptcy Abuse Prevention and Consumer Protection Act of 2005, Pub.L. No. 109–8, 119 Stat. 23 (BAPCPA)? In this case, the United States Bankruptcy Court for the District of Kansas adopted the "forward-looking approach," which is the method adopted by the majority of bankruptcy courts and bankruptcy appellate panels (BAPs) that have considered the question. Under that approach, a

(A)(i) for the maintenance or support of the debtor or a dependent of the debtor, or for a domestic support obligation, that first becomes payable after the date the petition is filed; and

(ii) for charitable contributions (that meet the definition of "charitable contribution" under section 548(d)(3)) to a qualified religious or charitable entity or organization (as that term is defined in section 548(d)(4)) in an amount not to exceed 15 percent of the gross income of the debtor for the year in which the contributions are made; and

(B) if the debtor is engaged in business, for the payment of expenditures necessary for the continuation, preservation, and operation of such business.

Chapter 13 debtor's six-month, pre-petition "disposable income" (as defined by statute) is presumed to be the debtor's "projected disposable income" for purposes of establishing the monthly sum that the debtor must commit to repayment of unsecured creditors in order to advance a confirmable payment plan and overcome objections to it. The forward-looking approach permits the amount of projected disposable income to be rebutted upon a showing of special circumstances at the time of plan confirmation.

In the course of its analysis, the bankruptcy court rejected a different method, the "mechanical approach," which equates a Chapter 13 debtor's projected disposable income with the statutorily defined "disposable income" and then "projects" that amount over the length of the applicable commitment period. It does not permit adjustment to projected disposable income to account for special circumstances at the time of plan confirmation.

In affirming the bankruptcy court's decision, the Tenth Circuit BAP also adopted the forward-looking approach and its rebuttable presumption. *See In re Lanning,* 380 B.R. 17 (10th Cir. BAP 2007). For the reasons discussed below, we also adopt the "forward-looking approach." ...

I. Factual Background

... The debtor, Stephanie Kay Lanning ... filed a Chapter 13 petition on October 16, 2006, to address $36,793.36 in unsecured debt. Her annual gross income was $43,147 in 2004, and $56,516 in 2005. During the six-month period before filing her petition, Ms. Lanning took a buyout from her employer, Payless, that increased her monthly gross income to $11,990.03 in April 2006 and $15,356.42 in May 2006.

As part of her petition, Ms. Lanning filed Schedule I ("Current Income of Individual Debtor(s)"), which showed a monthly net income of $1,922 ($23,604 annually), apparently reflecting actual income from a job she started after leaving Payless. ...She also filed Schedule J ("Current Expenditures of Individual Debtor(s)"), which showed actual monthly expenses of $1,772.97 and, consequently, excess monthly income of $149.03. .. In addition, Ms. Lanning completed Form B22C (now denominated Form 22C), "Statement of Current Monthly Income and Disposable Income Calculation." ... Form B22C first requires a debtor to calculate "current monthly income" as an average of income for the six calendar months immediately preceding the month in which the petition is filed. ...Under this formula, Ms. Lanning's "current monthly income" was $5,343.70, which included the buyout from Payless. When that figure was annualized, her income ($64,124.34) was greater than the median income for a family of one in Kansas ($36,631.00), so she was required to complete the remainder of Form B22C, on which most expenses and other deductions are calculated by reference to standard sums issued by the Internal Revenue Service (National and Local IRS Standards). ...According to her Form B22C, Ms. Lanning's total monthly expenses were $4,228.71, leaving her with "Monthly Disposable Income Under [11 U.S.C.] § 1325(b)(2)" of $1,114.98. . . .

Based on the excess monthly income of $149 shown on Schedule J, Ms. Lanning proposed a repayment plan of $144 per month for thirty-six months ($5,184) as satisfaction of the $36,793.36 in unsecured debt. She moved the bankruptcy court to determine that 11 U.S.C. § 1325(b)(1)(B) did not require her to commit the $1,114.98 in monthly disposable income calculated on Form B22C (which included her buyout) to repayment of the unsecured creditors. Section 1325(b)(1)(B) is the primary statute involved in this case, and when, as here, a Chapter 13 debtor proposes a plan that contemplates less than full repayment of all allowed unsecured claims and there is an objection, that section conditions plan confirmation as follows:

> (b)(1) If the trustee or the holder of an allowed unsecured claim objects to the confirmation of the plan, then the court may not approve the plan unless, as of the effective date of the plan—
>
> . . .
>
> (B) the plan provides that all of the debtor's projected disposable income to be received in the applicable commitment period beginning on the date that the first payment is due under the plan will be applied to make payments to unsecured creditors under the plan.

11 U.S.C. § 1325(b)(1)(B) (emphasis added). (Footnote omitted.)

Although none of the unsecured creditors objected to the proposed plan, the Chapter 13 Trustee did, arguing that § 1325(b)(1)(B) provides a rigid formula for determining projected disposable income that is based on a debtor's historical monthly income as calculated on Form B22C. The Trustee proposed that a monthly payment of $756 (less than Ms. Lanning's Form B22C "monthly disposable income" of $1,114.98) for sixty months would repay the unsecured creditors in full, despite acknowledging that Ms. Lanning did not have the means to fund such a plan.

. . .

V. BAPCPA Amendments and Interpretive Judicial Decisions

The issue to be resolved is whether the "projected disposable income" referred to in § 1325(b)(1)(B) is calculated by mechanical application of the definitions of "disposable income" and "current monthly income" set forth in §§ 1325(b)(2) and 101(10A)(A)(i), respectively, or whether it is permissible to adjust the "monthly disposable income" calculated on Form B22C to account for a debtor's actual ability to fund a plan as of the effective date of the plan. "It is well established that when [a] statute's language is plain, the sole function of the courts-at least where the disposition required by the text is not absurd-is to enforce it according to its terms." *Lamie v. U.S. Trustee,* 540 U.S. 526, 534, 124 S.Ct. 1023, 157 L.Ed.2d 1024 (2004) (quotation omitted). Here, the statutory language may be plain, but it is unclear in its meaning. Thus, before turning to an analysis of the statutory language, we briefly will review the relevant changes Congress made (and did not make) when it enacted the BAPCPA, and then consider a number of judicial decisions representative of the two methods used to calculate "projected disposable income."

A. BAPCPA Amendments

In passing the BAPCPA, Congress left § 1325(b)(1)(B) substantially unchanged (for present purposes), the only differences being that the pre-BAPCPA version (1) referred to a "three-year period" rather than the "applicable commitment period" as the relevant time period over which the debtor's plan must apply "projected disposable income" to plan payments (now three years for below-median debtors and five years for above-median debtors); and (2) required all such "projected disposable income" to be "applied to make payments under the plan," 11 U.S.C. § 1325(b)(1)(B) (2000), rather than, more narrowly now, to make payments to the unsecured creditors. Thus, the relevant language of § 1325(b)(1)(B) is substantially the same now as it was before passage of the BAPCPA, i.e., that all "projected disposable income to be received in the applicable commitment period . . . will be applied to make payments." As the BAP pointed out, the pre-BAPCPA language meant that "projected disposable income" was the difference between a debtor's Schedule I income and her Schedule J expenses, subject to adjustment by the court if there was reason to believe that those schedules "did not accurately predict a debtor's actual ability to pay." *In re Lanning,* 380 B.R. at 24; *see also In re Nahat,* 315 B.R. 368, 378–79 (Bankr.N.D.Tex.2004).

Next, prior to passage of the BAPCPA, "disposable income" was defined as "income which is received by the debtor and which is not reasonably necessary to be expended" for the debtor's maintenance, support, charitable contributions, and business expenses. 11 U.S.C. § 1325(b)(2)(A) (2000). With the BAPCPA, Congress changed the definition of "disposable income" by tying it to a new term, "current monthly income," 11 U.S.C. § 1325(b)(2), and adding the definition of "current monthly income" that in relevant part, as noted above, looks at the debtor's six-month pre-petition income, *id.* § 101(10A)(A)(i). Finally, the BAPCPA added a new clause to § 1325(b) that, for above-median debtors, requires the use of the standardized expenses and deductions calculated on Form B22C as the "[a]mounts reasonably necessary to be expended" under § 1325(b)(2) (with the exception of charitable contributions under (b)(2)(A)(ii)). *See id.* § 1325(b)(3).

With this understanding of the relevant changes to the BAPCPA, we now turn to judicial decisions representative of the two interpretations of post-BAPCPA § 1325(b)(1)(B).

B. Courts adopting the "forward-looking approach"

The first court to address the issue appears to be *In re Hardacre,* 338 B.R. 718 (Bankr.N.D.Tex.2006).(Footnote omitted.) In *Hardacre,* the court expressed concern about the consequences when "current monthly income" derived from Form B22C is used as the sole determinant of the "income" side of the "projected disposable income" calculation. *Id.* at 722.

The court reasoned that a debtor expecting a significant increase in future income would file as quickly as possible, resulting in the commitment of less money to repay unsecured creditors than the debtor would actually be capable of paying during the commitment period. *Id.* Conversely, the court observed that a debtor who experiences a decrease in income after filing might not be able to confirm a plan because she would be unable to commit the amount of disposable income calculated on Form B22C. *Id.*

The *Hardacre* court offered three justifications in support of its conclusion that " 'projected disposable income' must be based upon the debtor's anticipated income during the term of the plan, not merely an average of her prepetition income." *Id.* First, noting the rule of statutory construction that requires a court "to presume that 'Congress acts intentionally when it includes particular language in one section of a statute but omits it in another,' "the court reasoned that "Congress must have intended 'projected disposable income' to be different than 'disposable income' "when it chose to define only the latter term. *Id.* at 723 (quoting *BFP v. Resolution Trust Corp.,* 511 U.S. 531, 537, 114 S.Ct. 1757, 128 L.Ed.2d 556 (1994)). Second, the court viewed the phrase "to be received" in § 1325(b)(1)(B) as an expression of congressional intent "to refer to the income actually to be received by the debtor during the commitment period, rather than the prepetition average income"; an alternative interpretation, the court said, would render "to be received" superfluous. *Id.* And third, the court considered § 1325(b)(1)'s prefatory language—"as of the effective date of the plan"—to be an indication that " 'projected disposable income' ... refers to income that a debtor reasonably expects to receive during the term of her plan." *Id.*

A number of other courts ... have applied *Hardacre*'s reasoning in adopting the forward-looking approach. (Citations and footnote omitted.)
. . .

C. Courts adopting the mechanical approach

To date, only one circuit court (other than a BAP) has adopted the mechanical approach. *See Maney v. Kagenveama (In re Kagenveama),* 541 F.3d 868 (9th Cir.2008). There the court reasoned:

> The substitution of any data not covered by the § 1325(b)(2) definition in the "projected disposable income" calculation would render as surplusage the definition of "disposable income" found in § 1325(b)(2). There can be no reason for § 1325(b)(2) to exist other than to define the term "disposable income" as used in § 1325(b)(1)(B). "If 'disposable income' is not linked to 'projected disposable income' then it is just a floating definition with no apparent purpose." *In re Alexander,* 344 B.R. 742, 749 (Bankr.E.D.N.C. 2006). The plain meaning of the word "projected," in and of itself, does not provide a basis for including other data in the calculation because "projected" is simply a modifier of the defined term "disposable income." Therefore, to give meaning to every word of § 1325(b),

"disposable income," as defined in § 1325(b)(2), must be "projected" in order to derive "projected disposable income."

Id. at 872–73. Regarding the pre-BAPCPA treatment of "projected disposable income," the court concluded that

> [a]ny change in how "projected disposable income" is calculated only reflects the changes dictated by the new "disposable income" calculation; it does not change the relationship of "projected disposable income" to "disposable income." Pre–BAPCPA, "projected disposable income" was determined by taking the debtor's "disposable income," under § 1325(b)(2)(A) & (B), and projecting that amount over the "applicable commitment period."

Id. at 873 (footnote omitted). The court refused to "read the word 'projected' to be synonymous with the word 'anticipated' in this context." *Id.* at 874.

In addition to *Kagenveama,* a number of bankruptcy courts have adopted the mechanical approach. (citations omitted). . . .

. . .

VI.   Analysis

As is evident from the foregoing discussion, each interpretation of the statutory language is not without problems. The difficulty with the forward-looking approach is that it renders the new definition of "disposable income," with its link to historic "current monthly income," nearly meaningless unless one reads a presumption into the statute—that the defined term "disposable income" is just the starting point—which can be rebutted by showing a substantial change in circumstances bearing on how much the debtor realistically can commit to repayment of unsecured creditors as of the effective date of the plan. This was the solution reached in the present case. It is compatible with the statutory language of § 1325(b)(1)(B), the new definition of disposable income, and the use of the means test to standardize an above-median Chapter 13 debtor's expenses, but requires a certain disregard of the notion that Congress knows how to create a presumption when it intends one, *see In re Kagenveama,* 541 F.3d at 874.

The main problem with the analysis in decisions adopting the mechanical approach is that little heed is given to three statutory phrases: "as of the effective date of the plan," 11 U.S.C. § 1325(b); "to be received in the applicable commitment period," *id.* § 1325(b)(1)(B); and "will be applied to make payments," *id.* "[A] cardinal principle of statutory construction [is] that a statute ought, upon the whole, to be so construed that, if it can be prevented, no clause, sentence, or word shall be superfluous, void, or insignificant." *TRW Inc. v. Andrews,* 534 U.S. 19, 31, 122 S.Ct. 441, 151 L.Ed.2d 339 (2001) (quotation omitted). We think that these textual problems, discussed below, outweigh the concern about implying a presumption.

Under § 1325(b)(1)(B), a bankruptcy court may not approve a Chapter 13 plan over objection unless "**as of the effective date of the plan**" the plan "provides that all of the debtor's projected disposable income **to be received in the applicable commitment period** beginning on the date that the first payment is due under the plan **will be applied to make payments** to unsecured creditors under the plan." (Emphasis added.) The first emphasized phrase, "as of the effective date of the plan," indicates that the court should determine, at that time, whether the plan meets the remaining requirements of subparagraph (b)(1)(B). The term "effective date" is not defined in the Bankruptcy Code, but for purposes of § 1325(b)(1), "the most logical interpretation . . . is the date of plan confirmation, as a chapter 13 plan is not binding on the debtor and other interested parties until it is confirmed." *In re Pak,* 378 B.R. at 265 (relying on 11 U.S.C. § 1327(a)), *abrogated on other grounds by In re Kagenveama,* 541 F.3d 868. The date of plan confirmation is practically certain to be later than the date on which the petition is filed, and it is the filing date that starts the backward-looking assessment of "current monthly income." Thus, determining whether or not a debtor has committed all projected disposable income to repayment of the unsecured creditors "as of the effective date of the plan" suggests consideration of the debtor's actual financial circumstances as of the effective date of the plan.

In turn, the remaining statutory requirements are subject to conflicting interpretations. As viewed by mechanical-approach courts, "projected" could mean that a plan simply must project the Form B22C disposable income over the applicable commitment period to determine the amount that "will be applied to make payments" to the unsecured creditors. *See, e.g., In re Kagenveama,* 541 F.3d at 872–73; *In re Hanks,* 362 B.R. at 499. Alternately, under the forward-looking approach, "projected" links "disposable income" and "to be received in the applicable commitment period," requiring the debtor to commit all "disposable income" (as defined by § 1325(b)(2) and its reliance on the definition of "current monthly income") that is "projected . . . to be received in the applicable commitment period." Under this reading, the debtor's actual circumstances at the time of plan confirmation are taken into account in order to "project" (in other words, to "forecast") how much income the debtor will actually receive during the commitment period, which, after deducting permitted expenses, then "will be applied to make payments" to the unsecured creditors, as the statute requires.

The second reading, i.e., the forward-looking approach, strikes us as the better one. As the *Hardacre* court said, Congress defined "disposable income," not "projected disposable income," meaning that "Congress must have intended 'projected disposable income' to be different than 'disposable income'"when it chose to define only the latter term for purposes of § 1325(b). *In re Hardacre,* 338 B.R. at 723. Unlike the Ninth Circuit in *Kagenveama,* we do not think the forward-looking approach leaves the definition of "disposable income" floating with no apparent purpose. Through its reliance on the statutory definition of "current monthly income," the definition of "disposable income" serves to "describe[ ] the sources of revenue that constitute income, as well as those that do not." *In re Hardacre,* 338 B.R. at 723.

Also, the forward-looking approach gives effect to the phrase "to be received in the applicable commitment period," which otherwise would be rendered superfluous. Under the mechanical approach, the amount "to be received in the applicable commitment period" would be a fiction if, as of the effective date of the plan, the debtor had no realistic expectation of earning enough to produce the amount of "disposable income" calculated on Form B22C. Furthermore, such a debtor could not get the plan confirmed due to infeasibility. *See id.* § 1325(a)(6). This undermines the importance given to historical income as a "better" predictor of "projected disposable income" in *In re Austin,* 372 B.R. at 679. (Footnote omitted.)

In addition, language used on Form B22C supports the forward-looking approach. Part VI of Form B22C is titled "Determination of Disposable Income Under § 1325(b)(2)." ... Similarly, the last line in Part VI of the form is termed "Monthly Disposable Income Under § 1325(b)(2)." *Id.* Although the form is subservient to the statute, (citation omitted), the absence of the word "projected" and any reference to the phrase "projected disposable income" are consistent with the forward-looking approach. (Footnote omitted.)

Legislative materials are of limited assistance in trying to divine the intent of Congress when it defined "disposable income" rather than "projected disposable income." Perhaps the best statement of the overarching purpose of the consumer aspects of the BAPCPA comes from a House Report issued by the Committee on the Judiciary just prior to enactment of the bill: "The heart of [BAPCPA's] consumer bankruptcy reforms consists of the implementation of an income/expense screening mechanism ('needs-based bankruptcy relief' or 'means-testing'), which is intended to ensure that debtors repay creditors the maximum they can afford." H.R.Rep. No. 109–31, pt. 1, at 2 (2005), *reprinted in* 2005 U.S.C.C.A.N. 88, 89. Commenting on this statement, one bankruptcy court has pointed out that "[t]he words 'maximum' and 'afford' tell the story. Congress intended that debtors pay the greatest amount within their capabilities. Nothing more; nothing less." *In re Kibbe,* 361 B.R. at 314. While the statement in the House Report is exceedingly general for our purposes and expresses the view only of the members of the Judiciary Committee, it is consistent with the forward-looking approach, which assists a Chapter 13 debtor to propose a confirmable plan and repay creditors the maximum she can afford-no more and no less.

. . .

Moreover, when an above-median debtor has Form B22C disposable income under the means test, she will not qualify for Chapter 7 protection. But when that debtor seeks Chapter 13 protection and no longer earns her prepetition income, she will be unable to confirm a plan over objection if bound to historical income and the mechanical approach to

§ 1325(b)(1)(B). If, as stated in *In re Hanks,* 362 B.R. at 500, Congress may have intended that such a debtor then could seek Chapter 11 protection, it appears the debtor would encounter the same bar to confirmation due to the application of the definition of "disposable income" in 11 U.S.C. § 1129(a)(15)(B).... Alternately, it could be that Congress intended to foreclose bankruptcy protection to such debtors altogether, but there is no obvious support for attributing such intent to Congress.

Finally, we note that the mechanical approach advocated by the Trustee would effectively foreclose bankruptcy protection to debtors like Ms. Lanning, who lack adequate income going into the commitment period to pay the amount of disposable income on Form B22C, while at the same time permitting above-median debtors who have greater income at the time of plan confirmation to pay less to unsecured creditors than they are able to. While the latter situation could be rectified by post-confirmation modification of the plan under 11 U.S.C. § 1329, the former situation cannot be addressed in this manner because the plan would be infeasible and therefore unconfirmable in the first place. A Chapter 13 debtor may modify the plan prior to confirmation under 11 U.S.C. § 1323(a), but any effort by the debtor to deviate from Form B22C "disposable income" through pre-confirmation modification begs the question of whether the forward-looking approach is proper or not.

VII. Conclusion

For the foregoing reasons, we hold that, as to the income side of the § 1325(b)(1)(B) inquiry, the starting point for calculating a Chapter 13 debtor's "projected disposable income" is presumed to be the debtor's "current monthly income," as defined in 11 U.S.C. § 101(10A)(A)(i), subject to a showing of a substantial change in circumstances. ... The judgment of the BAP is AFFIRMED.

QUESTIONS ABOUT LANNING

1. What are the advantages to creditors and to debtors of the "mechanical approach" to determining projected disposable income?

2. What are the advantages to creditors and to debtors of the "forward-looking approach" to determining projected disposable income?

3. What factors weigh in favor of selecting each of the two approaches?

b. Calculating Projected Expenses.

The starting point in determining what expenses the debtor is allowed to deduct from her monthly income is whether the debtor's income is above the median income for a household the size of debtor's household.

(1) Allowable Expenses for Debtors Whose Incomes do Not Exceed the Median Income

If the debtor's monthly income does is below or equals the applicable median income, reasonably necessary expenses of the debtor and the debtor's dependents are deducted in calculating disposable income. § 1325(b)(2).[11]

Notice that section 1325(b)(2) does not define the term "dependent" and does not provide courts with any guidance as to what standard of living to use in determining whether an expense is "reasonably necessary." This lack of statutory guidance, coupled with the inherently factual nature of the inquiry, has resulted in numerous interpretation problems with respect to what are reasonably necessary expenses.

Problem 10–3:   What Is a Reasonable Vehicle Expense?

Debtor is driving a two-year-old Lexus RX 350, which is a small luxury sport utility vehicle. Debtor does not drive the vehicle off the road, but feels safer in an all-wheel-drive vehicle during inclement winter weather. Debtor's car payments are $575 per month and will continue for another three years if paid according to the contract. The Chapter 13 trustee believes that the debtor could obtain necessary transportation at a lower cost.

(a) The Chapter 13 trustee objects to confirmation, arguing that debtor does not reasonably need the vehicle at all because, debtor could get to work and around town on the bus; a bus pass costs only $50 per month. This would increase debtor's disposable income by the $525 per month saved on payments plus the cost of insuring and maintaining the vehicle. Should the Chapter 13 trustee prevail? Is the answer any different depending on whether the debtor has children?

(b) After the Chapter 13 trustee loses this argument, he argues in the next case with similar facts that the debtor should be required to get a used vehicle, which would cost about half the amount that is still due on the Lexus, thereby increasing the debtor's disposable income by $275. Should the Chapter 13 trustee prevail?

Problem 10–4:   Are the Expenses of Children Who Are College Students Reasonably Necessary?

Debtors have a 20–year-old daughter who is a junior in college.

(a) Daughter is attending State University and debtors contribute $4,000 per year toward her tuition, books and room and board. The Chapter 13 trustee objects to this expense. The Chapter 13 trustee argues that the expense is not a reasonable expense because, under applicable state law, the daughter became an adult when she turned 18. The Chapter 13 trustee correctly points out that debtors have no legal obligation to support their daughter. Debtors argue that they have

---

11.   Section 1325(b)(2) is quoted on pages 243–244.

continuously supported their daughter, that $4,000 is a reasonable amount, and the fact that they are not legally obligated to support their daughter does not mean that she is not dependent on them for support. Should the court sustain the trustee's objection?

(b) Would your answer differ if the daughter were at Ivy League University and debtors were contributing $15,000 per year toward her support?

---

(2) Allowable Expenses for Debtors Whose Incomes Exceed the Median Income

If the debtor's household monthly income exceeds the median income, § 1325(b)(3) provides that "[a]mounts reasonably necessary to be expended . . . shall be determined in accordance with subparagraphs (A) and (B) of section 707(b)(2)," the means test formula discussed starting on page 225.

Recall that the means test calculates projected disposable income by permitting the deduction from income of four distinct types of expenses:

1. Living expenses, as determined by the Internal Revenue Service (IRS) standards;

2. Monthly secured debt payments;

3. Amounts required to pay priority debts in full;

4. Other administrative and special purpose expenses, including up to 10% of the projected Chapter 13 plan payments for administrative expenses, and most charitable contributions.

The IRS living expense standards are formulaic with respect to certain expenses. For example, as of November 1, 2009, all debtors with a four member household are allowed $1,370 for food, clothing, personal care and miscellaneous expenses, regardless of actual cost. Some debtors have expenses for these items that are higher, some are lower. Yet when calculating their disposable income, the means test formula requires that $1,370 be used.

One court candidly explained the impact of using the IRS expense formulas rather than actual expenses for above median-income debtors. "[U]sing means test expenses will result in some debtors . . . being forced to pay more than they can actually afford and others getting a windfall. . . ." *In re Becquer,* 407 B.R. 435 (Bankr. S.D. Fla. 2009).

Applying the IRS expense standards and the other deductions referenced in the means test in the context of Chapter 13 cases has caused significant interpretation problems with divergent results. The following problems explore a few of the common dilemmas.

Before working through the problems regarding allowable expenses, review the deductions allowed under the means test contained in § 707(b), in particular § 707(b)(2)(a)(ii)(I) and (II). Note that the above median debtor's monthly expenses "shall be the debtor's **applicable monthly expense amounts** specified under the National (IRS) Standards and Local (IRS) Standards, and the debtor's **actual monthly expenses**" for expenses that the IRS specifies as Other Necessary Expenses and that the debtor pays for certain non-dependent household or family members who are unable to pay such expenses themselves. (emphasis added). You can find current IRS expense standards by going to the following part of the United States Trustee's website, http://www.justice.gov/ust/eo/bapcpa/meanstesting.htm. After selecting the pertinent date the next screen will give you the necessary IRS Data for the means test.

Problem 10–5: Can an Above-Median Income Debtor Claim a Vehicle Ownership Expense Deduction If the Debtor Does Not Have a Car Payment?

The applicable Internal Revenue standards allow a maximum of $471 for the ownership cost of a vehicle if the debtor is making a payment to a creditor with a security interest in the debtor's vehicle or to a creditor who has leased the vehicle to the debtor. Debtor owns her car outright. The car is five years old and last year the debtor finished paying the creditor who financed the vehicle for her.

    (a) Outline the argument that the debtor would make in order to claim the $471 monthly ownership amount as a deduction in calculating her projected disposable income even though the debtor is not making a car payment.

    (b) What argument is the Chapter 13 trustee likely to make in response?

See, *In re Washburn*, 579 F.3d 934 (8th Cir.2009), and *In re Ransom*, 577 F.3d 1026 (9th Cir. 2009).

Problem 10–6: Can a Debtor Deduct a Secured Debt Payment if the Debtor's Chapter 13 Plan Provides for Surrender of the Collateral?

Debtor bought her house for $350,000 in 2006, just as housing prices peaked. Housing prices in the community where debtor lives have dropped by 40% and debtor's house is now worth only $210,000. Debtor owes $275,000 on her mortgage and her monthly payment is $1,476. She has decided to surrender her house as part of her Chapter 13 plan. It will be advantageous to debtor if she can treat the $1,476 as secured debt in calculating her projected disposable income.

    (a) What arguments can she make that she should be allowed to deduct the mortgage payment on her soon to be surrendered house as an expense in calculating her projected disposable income?

    (b) What arguments is the Chapter 13 trustee likely to make in response?

See, *In re Turner*, 574 F.3d 349 (7th Cir. 2009), *In re Washburn*, 579 F.3d 934, 940–942 (8th Cir. 2009).

In calculating projected disposable income, is the amount of expenses adjusted if the above median income debtor's anticipated expenses are different than the expenses allowed using the formula provided by the means test? The cases are divided on this point, with the majority concluding that Congress has determined that expenses should be calculated based upon the means test are the debtor's reasonably necessary expenses, rather than adjusting the means test expenses if projected actual expenses are different. *Compare, In re Demonica, 345 B.R. 895 (Bankr. N.D. IL. 2006)* (above-median income debtor must calculate expenses in accordance with the means test provisions referenced in § 1325(b)(3)), with, *In re McGillis, 370 B.R. 720 (Bankr. W.D. Mich. 2007)* (an above-median income debtor may only deduct expenses that the debtor actually expects to incur even when the applicable IRS expense amount is more than the debtor actually incurs).

3. THE PLAN MUST PROVIDE THAT CREDITORS RECEIVE AT LEAST AS MUCH AS THEY WOULD RECEIVE IN A CHAPTER 7 CASE (THE BEST INTERESTS TEST)

Section 1325(a)(4)[12] requires that the debtor's plan result in a distribution to creditors of at least as much as they would receive in a Chapter 7 case. The calculation of the amount required includes both the net amount that could be realized if the Chapter 7 trustee exercised her avoidance powers, *see* Unit 7.B.-F, plus the net amount that the Chapter 7 trustee would realize from the liquidation of the debtor's assets that are not fully exempt. In calculating the net amount the Chapter 7 trustee would realize, keep in mind that the Chapter 7 trustee may have to pay from the estate the cost of real estate brokers, auctioneers, attorneys, accountants and other professionals he hires to help him liquidate the estate. At a minimum, the Chapter 7 trustee will be paid for his services. The maximum Chapter 7 trustee compensation is established by § 326. All the probable Chapter 7 expenses are deducted before determining the amount, because costs of administration are paid before the creditors receive a distribution. These expenses can make a significant difference in how much the Chapter 13 debtor with non-exempt assets must pay.

Although the best interests test requires debtors to pay creditors not less than creditors would receive in Chapter 7, the payment terms are

---

12.   Section 1325(a)(4) provides:

(a) Except as provided in subsection (b), the court shall confirm a plan if—

(4) the value, as of the effective date of the plan, of property to be distributed under the plan on account of each allowed unsecured claim is not less than the amount that would be paid on such claim if the estate of the debtor were liquidated under chapter 7 of this title on such date[.]

often more affordable in Chapter 13. The debtor pays the sum due over the life of the plan, which we have learned will be three to five years. In Chapter 7, if the debtor wants to buy a non-exempt asset from the Chapter 7 trustee the Chapter 7 trustee will want to be paid for the asset in a lump sum or over a very short period of time, because it is the Chapter 7 trustee's duty to liquidate the assets expeditiously and make distributions to creditors.

Problem 10–6:   How Is the Best Interests Test Applied?

Debtors have the following non-exempt assets that a Chapter 7 trustee would likely claim:

(1) $25,000 in equity in their $90,000 house, and

(2) $2,000 in tax refunds.

In addition, debtors made an $8,000 loan repayment to Mr. Debtor's parents which the Chapter 7 trustee is likely to claim was a preferential transfer. Debtors do not want to have Mr. Debtor's parents sued by a bankruptcy trustee or be required to return the $8,000. How much will debtors have to pay creditors under their Chapter 13 plan to satisfy the requirement that creditors be paid at least as much as they would be paid in a Chapter 7 case and to avoid having to recover the preference from Mr. Debtor's parents?

For purposes of your answer, you can assume that:

(i) a Chapter 7 trustee would incur $7,000 in costs for the realtor and closing costs to sell debtors' house, and

(ii) the Chapter 7 trustee would be likely to incur at least $2,000 in legal fees to recover the $8,000 preference, and

(iii) the Chapter 7 trustee's compensation would be $7,250, based on the maximum compensation permitted by § 326(a).

D.   CARS AND HOUSES (HOW MUCH OF THE PLAN PAYMENT GOES TO PAY FOR THE CAR AND HOUSE?)

Most Chapter 13 debtors who have a house and one or more cars financed the purchase of those assets, and the creditor who advanced the money retains an interest in the house or car. In addition, the debtor often will have granted a second or third mortgage on her home as security for a debt consolidation loan, a home equity line of credit, or some other obligation. It is often the debtor's inability to pay one or more of these obligations with the resulting foreclosure or threatened repossession that prompts the debtor to seek legal help.

Chapter 13 provides the means by which the debtor can save her house and/or car, because Chapter 13 allows the debtor to cure defaults and, with respect to car loans, entirely restructure the payment obligation. Chapter 7 does not offer similar relief. Thus, many debtors trying to save their house or car use Chapter 13 rather than Chapter 7.

1. CHAPTER 13 PROVISIONS REGARDING THE TREATMENT OF CLAIMS SECURED BY CARS (AND OTHER ASSETS EXCEPT CLAIMS SECURED SOLELY BY THE DEBTOR'S PRINCIPAL RESIDENCE)

Section 1322(b)(2) and section 1325(a)(5) govern the treatment of secured claims in Chapter 13. In most Chapter 13 cases, the most significant secured claims are the (1) home mortgage and (2) the car loan. The Bankruptcy Code treats home mortgages separate from other secured claims and so will we.

Before reading sections 1322(b)(2) and 1325(a)(5) set out below and learning how Chapter 13 treats secured claims, it is important to remember what a secured claim is under section 506(a). As we learned earlier in Unit 4, a claim is secured if the creditor has a lien on property of the estate and that property of the estate has economic value. § 506(a). The amount of the secured claim, however, is limited by section 506(a) to the economic value of the lien on property of the estate. Thus, under section 506(a), a creditor who is owed $20,000 secured by a first lien on a debtor's car that is worth only $14,000 has a $14,000 secured claim and a $6,000 unsecured claim.

Under a 2005 amendment to the Bankruptcy Code a paragraph was added after section 1325(a)(9) making section 506(a) and the rule that a secured claim is limited to the value of the debtor's interest in the property inapplicable to certain secured claims against a Chapter 13 debtor. Please read this new paragraph carefully.

11 U.S.C. § 1325(a)

(9) . . . For purposes of paragraph (5), section 506 shall not apply to a claim described in that paragraph if the creditor has a purchase money security interest securing the debt that is the subject of the claim, the debt was incurred within the 910–day [sic] preceding the date of the filing of the petition, and the collateral for that debt consists of a motor vehicle (as defined in section 30102 of title 49) acquired for the personal use of the debtor, or if collateral for that debt consists of any other thing of value, if the debt was incurred during the 1–year period preceding that filing.

This amendment is commonly referred to as the "anti-strip down" provision or the "hanging paragraph" (or worse by some debtors' attorneys).

The claims of vehicle secured creditors that are the beneficiaries of this amendment are often called "910 claims."

The hanging paragraph prevents the Chapter 13 debtor who has financed the purchase of a vehicle for personal use within about 2 ½ years prior to bankruptcy, or financed the purchased of other personal property within a year of bankruptcy, from paying the secured creditor less than the full principal amount due on the debt if the debtor wants to retain the collateral. The following problem illustrates the impact of the hanging paragraph.

Problem 10–7:   How Is the Hanging Paragraph Applied?

Epstein (E) owns and operates a yard service as a sole proprietorship. E files for 13 bankruptcy. E is indebted to the following secured creditors: (a) $40,000 to A who has a security interest in a BMW that E bought 4 months before filing for bankruptcy; (b) $3,000 to B who has a security interest in a Kia that E bought his wife three years before filing for bankruptcy; (c) $22,000 to C who has a security interest in a truck that E bought two years before bankruptcy and uses only in yard service business, (d) $1,000 to Y who has a security interest in a used Yugo that E bought for his children to use 11 months before filing for bankruptcy. What is the amount of the secured claims of A, B, C, and Y? What, if any additional information do you need to answer this question?

Now that you know how to figure out the amount of a secured claim in Chapter 13, please read section 1322(b) to see what provisions a Chapter 13 plan can include changing the rights of holders of secured claims and then read section 1325(a)(5) to see what provisions of a Chapter 13 plan changing the rights of holders of secured claims the bankruptcy court will approve.

Section 1322(b) provides that the Chapter 13 plan may include one or more of the following provisions with respect to secured creditors.

11 U.S.C. § 1322(b)

[T]he plan may– . . .

(2) modify the rights of holders of secured claims, other than a claim secured only by a security interest in real property that is the debtor's principal residence, or of holders of unsecured claims, or leave unaffected the rights of holders of any class of claims;

(3) provide for the curing or waiving of any default; . . . .

(5) notwithstanding paragraph (2) of this subsection, provide for the curing of any default within a reasonable time and maintenance of payments while the case is pending on any unsecured claim or secured claim on which the last payment is due after the date on which the final payment under the plan is due[.]

Thus, the statute permits two approaches with respect to secured claims: (1) cure defaults and reinstate the original payment terms and (2) modify the claim.

First, curing the default. The debtor can cure the default and reinstate the original payment terms regardless of whether the creditor has accelerated the debt because of the debtor's default, *i.e.* declared the entire debt due and payable. If the original terms of the obligation extend beyond the duration of the Chapter 13 plan, which will usually be three to five years, the debtor may cure defaults during the Chapter 13 and then perform according to the original contract terms after the Chapter 13 case ends.

Second, modifying the payment terms. Think about how a debtor might want to change the payment terms of her car loans. Smaller monthly payments over a longer period of time? Lower interest rate? The seemingly endless possibilities that are presented by § 1322(b)(2), which permits modification of the secured claim (other than a claim secured solely by the debtor's principal residence), are limited by the requirements that must be met before the court can confirm the Chapter 13 plan. Section 1325(a)(5) provides that a plan cannot be confirmed unless:

(A) the holder of such claim has accepted the plan;

(B)(i) the plan provides that—

    (I) the holder of such claim retain the lien securing such claim;

    until the earlier of—

        (aa) the payment of the underlying debt determined under nonbankruptcy law; or

        (bb) discharge under section 1328; and

    (II) if the case under this chapter is dismissed or converted without completion of the plan, such lien shall also be retained by such holder to the extent recognized by applicable nonbankruptcy law; and

(ii) the value, as of the effective date of the plan, of property to be distributed under the plan on account of such claim is not less than the allowed amount of such claim; and

(iii) if—

    (I) property to be distributed pursuant to this subsection is in the form of periodic payments, such payments shall be in equal monthly amounts; and

    (II) the holder of the claim is secured by personal property, the amount of such payments shall not be less than an amount sufficient to provide to the holder of such claim adequate protection during the period of the plan; or

(C) the debtor surrenders the property securing such claim to such holder[.]

Thus, unless the creditor holding the secured claim agrees to the proposed treatment or the debtor surrenders the collateral to the creditor holding the security interest, the creditor must (1) retain its lien and (2) receive compensation the value of which equals the amount of the secured claim. The second provision requires that a debtor who is going to pay the secured claim over time pay interest at a sufficient rate that the present value of the stream of payments equals the secured claim. This requirement is imposed so that the creditor is not in any worse position than it would have been if it had been allowed to foreclose on its collateral. Periodic payments must be equal monthly payments.

The following example may help explain the logic behind this requirement. You are owed $60,000 by D, a Chapter 13 debtor. Which would you rather have—$60,000 in cash or D's promise to pay you $1,000 a month for 60 months?

Obviously, D's promise to pay $1,000 a month over 60 months does not have the same "present value" as $60,000 in cash. If you had the $60,000 in cash, you could either loan the $60,000 to another borrower who will pay you interest, or otherwise invest it. Moreover, there is a real risk that D will never make the 60 payments. In order for D's promise to pay over 60 months to have a present value of $60,000, the total payments must exceed $60,000—there must be some interest component.

This interest component is often referred to as cram down interest by judges and lawyers. But not by the Bankruptcy Code. Reread section 1325(a)(B)(ii) which uses the term "present value," instead of cram down interest. The Bankruptcy Code not only does not use the term "cram down" interest, but also does not provide any guidance as to how to figure out the appropriate rate of cram down interest so that periodic plan payments will have a "present value" equal to the amount of the secured claim.

In the next case, a divided Supreme Court provides some guidance with respect to cram down interest rates.

TILL v. SCS CREDIT CORP. (IN RE TILL)

541 U.S. 465 (2004)

Justice STEVENS announced the judgment of the Court and delivered an opinion, in which Justice SOUTER, Justice GINSBURG, and Justice BREYER join.

To qualify for court approval under Chapter 13 of the Code, an individual debtor's proposed debt adjustment plan must accommodate each allowed, secured creditor in one of three ways: (1) by obtaining the creditor's acceptance of the plan; (2) by surrendering the property securing the claim; or (3) by providing the creditor both a lien securing the claim and a promise of future property distributions (such as deferred cash payments) whose total "value, as of the effective date of the plan, . . . is not less than the allowed amount of such claim." . . . The third alternative is commonly known as the "cram down option" because it may be enforced over a claim holder's objection.... Associates Commercial Corp. v. Rash, 520 U.S. 953, 957, 117 S.Ct. 1879, 138 L.Ed.2d 148 (1997).

Plans that invoke the cram down power often provide for installment payments over a period of years rather than a single payment.... In such circumstances, the amount of each installment must be calibrated to ensure that, over time, the creditor receives disbursements whose total present value[4] equals or exceeds that of the allowed claim. The proceedings in this case that led to our grant of certiorari identified four different methods of determining the appropriate method with which to perform that calibration. Indeed, the Bankruptcy Judge, the District Court, the Court of Appeals majority, and the dissenting Judge each endorsed a different approach. We detail the underlying facts and describe each of those approaches before setting forth our judgment as to which approach best meets the purposes of the Code.

I

On October 2, 1998, petitioners Lee and Amy Till, residents of Kokomo, Indiana, purchased a used truck from Instant Auto Finance for $6,395 plus $330.75 in fees and taxes. They made a $300 down payment and financed the balance of the purchase price by entering into a retail installment contract that Instant Auto immediately assigned to respondent, SCS Credit Corporation. Petitioners' initial indebtedness amounted to $8,285.24—the $6,425.75 balance of the truck purchase plus a finance charge of 21% per year for 136 weeks, or $1,859.49. Under the contract, petitioners agreed to make 68 biweekly payments to cover this debt; Instant Auto—and subsequently respondent—retained a purchase money security interest that gave it the right to repossess the truck if petitioners defaulted under the contract.

On October 25, 1999, petitioners, by then in default on their payments to respondent, filed a joint petition for relief under Chapter 13 of the Code. At the time of the filing, respondent's outstanding claim amounted to $4,894.89, but the parties agreed that the truck securing the claim was worth only $4,000.... In accordance with the Code, therefore, respondent's secured claim was limited to $4,000, and the $894.89 balance was unsecured....

The proposed plan ... provided that petitioners would pay interest on the secured portion of respondent's claim at a rate of 9.5% per year. Petitioners arrived at this "prime-plus" or "formula rate" by augmenting the national prime rate of approximately 8% (applied by banks when making low-risk loans) to account for the risk of nonpayment posed by borrowers in their financial position. Respondent objected to the proposed rate, contending that the company was "entitled to interest at the rate of 21%, which is the rate ... it would obtain if it could foreclose on the

---

4. In the remainder of the opinion, we use the term "present value" to refer to the value as of the effective date of the bankruptcy plan.

vehicle and reinvest the proceeds in loans of equivalent duration and risk as the loan" originally made to petitioners. . . .

At the hearing on its objection, respondent presented expert testimony establishing that it uniformly charges 21% interest on so-called "subprime" loans, or loans to borrowers with poor credit ratings, and that other lenders in the subprime market also charge that rate. Petitioners countered with the testimony of an Indiana University–Purdue University Indianapolis economics professor, who acknowledged that he had only limited familiarity with the subprime auto lending market, but described the 9.5% formula rate as "very reasonable" given that Chapter 13 plans are "supposed to be financially feasible."[8] Moreover, the professor noted that respondent's exposure was "fairly limited because [petitioners] are under the supervision of the court." The bankruptcy trustee also filed comments supporting the formula rate as, among other things, easily ascertainable, closely tied to the "condition of the financial market," and independent of the financial circumstances of any particular lender. Accepting petitioners' evidence, the Bankruptcy Court overruled respondent's objection and confirmed the proposed plan.

The District Court reversed. It understood Seventh Circuit precedent to require that bankruptcy courts set cram down interest rates at the level the creditor could have obtained if it had foreclosed on the loan, sold the collateral, and reinvested the proceeds in loans of equivalent duration and risk. . . .

On appeal, the Seventh Circuit endorsed a slightly modified version of the District Court's "coerced" or "forced loan" approach. . . . [T]he majority held that the original contract rate should "serve as a presumptive [cram down] rate," which either the creditor or the debtor could challenge with evidence that a higher or lower rate should apply. . . .

Dissenting, Judge Rovner . . . advocated either the Bankruptcy Court's formula approach or a "straightforward . . . cost of funds" approach that would simply ask "what it would cost the creditor to obtain the cash equivalent of the collateral from an alternative source." . . .

II

The Code provides little guidance as to which of the rates of interest advocated by the four opinions in this case—the formula rate, the coerced loan rate, the presumptive contract rate, or the cost of funds rate—Congress had in mind when it adopted the cram down provision. That provision, 11 U.S.C. § 1325(a)(5)(B), does not mention the term "discount rate" or the word "interest." Rather, it simply requires bankruptcy courts to ensure that the property to be distributed to a particular secured creditor over the life of a bankruptcy plan has a total "value, as of the

---

8. The requirement of financial feasibility derives from 11 U.S.C. § 1325(a)(6), which provides that the bankruptcy court shall "confirm a plan if . . . the debtor will be able to make all payments under the plan and to comply with the plan." See infra, at 266.

effective date of the plan," that equals or exceeds the value of the creditor's allowed secured claim—in this case, $4,000. § 1325(a)(5)(B)(ii).

That command is easily satisfied when the plan provides for a lump-sum payment to the creditor. Matters are not so simple, however, when the debt is to be discharged by a series of payments over time. A debtor's promise of future payments is worth less than an immediate payment of the same total amount because the creditor cannot use the money right away, inflation may cause the value of the dollar to decline before the debtor pays, and there is always some risk of nonpayment. . . .

Three important considerations govern that choice. First, the Code includes numerous provisions that, like the cram down provision, require a court to "discoun[t] . . . [a] stream of deferred payments back to the[ir] present dollar value," Rake v. Wade, 508 U.S. 464, 472, n. 8, 113 S.Ct. 2187, 124 L.Ed.2d 424 (1993), to ensure that a creditor receives at least the value of its claim.[10] We think it likely that Congress intended bankruptcy judges and trustees to follow essentially the same approach when choosing an appropriate interest rate under any of these provisions. Moreover, we think Congress would favor an approach that is familiar in the financial community and that minimizes the need for expensive evidentiary proceedings.

Second, Chapter 13 expressly authorizes a bankruptcy court to modify the rights of any creditor whose claim is secured by an interest in anything other than "real property that is the debtor's principal residence." 11 U.S.C. § 1322(b)(2). . . . Thus, in cases like this involving secured interests in personal property, the court's authority to modify the number, timing, or amount of the installment payments from those set forth in the debtor's original contract is perfectly clear. Further, the potential need to modify the loan terms to account for intervening changes in circumstances is also clear: On the one hand, the fact of the bankruptcy establishes that the debtor is overextended and thus poses a significant risk of default; on the other hand, the postbankruptcy obligor is no longer the individual debtor but the court-supervised estate, and the risk of default is thus somewhat reduced.[12]

Third, from the point of view of a creditor, the cram down provision mandates an objective rather than a subjective inquiry. . . . That is,

---

10. See 11 U.S.C. § 1129(a)(7)(A)(ii) (requiring payment of property whose "value, as of the effective date of the plan" equals or exceeds the value of the creditor's claim); §§ 1129(a)(7)(B), 1129(a)(9)(B)(I), 1129(a)(9)(C), 1129(b)(2)(A)(ii), 1129(b)(2)(B)(I), 1129(b)(2)(C)(I), 1173(a)(2), 1225(a)(4), 1225(a)(5)(B)(ii), 1228(b)(2), 1325(a)(4), 1228(b)(2) (same).

12. Several factors contribute to this reduction in risk. First, as noted below, infra, at 1962, a court may only approve a cram down loan (and the debt adjustment plan of which the loan is a part) if it believes the debtor will be able to make all of the required payments. § 1325(a)(6). Thus, such loans will only be approved for debtors that the court deems creditworthy. Second, Chapter 13 plans must "provide for the submission" to the trustee "of all or such portion of [the debtor's] future . . . income . . . as is necessary for the execution of the plan," § 1322(a)(1), so the possibility of nonpayment is greatly reduced. Third, the Code's extensive disclosure requirements reduce the risk that the debtor has significant undisclosed obligations. Fourth, as a practical matter, the public nature of the bankruptcy proceeding is likely to reduce the debtor's opportunities to take on additional debt. Cf. 11 U.S.C. § 525 (prohibiting certain Government grant and loan programs from discriminating against applicants who are or have been bankrupt).

although § 1325(a)(5)(B) entitles the creditor to property whose present value objectively equals or exceeds the value of the collateral, it does not require that the terms of the cram down loan match the terms to which the debtor and creditor agreed prebankruptcy, nor does it require that the cram down terms make the creditor subjectively indifferent between present foreclosure and future payment. Indeed, the very idea of a "cram down" loan precludes the latter result: By definition, a creditor forced to accept such a loan would prefer instead to foreclose.[14] Thus, a court choosing a cram down interest rate need not consider the creditor's individual circumstances, such as its prebankruptcy dealings with the debtor or the alternative loans it could make if permitted to foreclose.... Rather, the court should aim to treat similarly situated creditors similarly, ... and to ensure that an objective economic analysis would suggest the debtor's interest payments will adequately compensate all such creditors for the time value of their money and the risk of default.

III

These considerations lead us to reject the coerced loan, presumptive contract rate, and cost of funds approaches. Each of these approaches is complicated, imposes significant evidentiary costs, and aims to make each individual creditor whole rather than to ensure the debtor's payments have the required present value....

IV

The formula approach has none of these defects. Taking its cue from ordinary lending practices, the approach begins by looking to the national prime rate, reported daily in the press, which reflects the financial market's estimate of the amount a commercial bank should charge a creditworthy commercial borrower to compensate for the opportunity costs of the loan, the risk of inflation, and the relatively slight risk of default.[18] Because bankrupt debtors typically pose a greater risk of non-payment than solvent commercial borrowers, the approach then requires a bankruptcy court to adjust the prime rate accordingly. The appropriate size of that risk adjustment depends, of course, on such factors as the circumstances of the estate, the nature of the security, and the duration

---

14. This fact helps to explain why there is no readily apparent Chapter 13 "cram down market rate of interest": Because every cram down loan is imposed by a court over the objection of the secured creditor, there is no free market of willing cram down lenders. Interestingly, the same is not true in the Chapter 11 context, as numerous lenders advertise financing for Chapter 11 debtors in possession. See, e.g., Balmoral Financial Corporation, http://www.balmoral.com/bdip.htm (all Internet materials as visited Mar. 4, 2004, and available in Clerk of Court's case file) (advertising debtor in possession lending); Debtor in Possession Financing: 1st National Assistance Finance Association DIP Division, http://www.loanmallusa.com/dip.htm (offering "to tailor a financing program ... to your business' needs and ... to work closely with your bankruptcy counsel"). Thus, when picking a cram down rate in a Chapter 11 case, it might make sense to ask what rate an efficient market would produce. In the Chapter 13 context, by contrast, the absence of any such market obligates courts to look to first principles and ask only what rate will fairly compensate a creditor for its exposure.

18. We note that, if the court could somehow be certain a debtor would complete his plan, the prime rate would be adequate to compensate any secured creditors forced to accept cram down loans.

and feasibility of the reorganization plan. The court must therefore hold a hearing at which the debtor and any creditors may present evidence about the appropriate risk adjustment. Some of this evidence will be included in the debtor's bankruptcy filings, however, so the debtor and creditors may not incur significant additional expense. Moreover, starting from a concededly low estimate and adjusting upward places the evidentiary burden squarely on the creditors, who are likely to have readier access to any information absent from the debtor's filing (such as evidence about the "liquidity of the collateral market," post, at 1973 (Scalia, J., dissenting)). Finally, many of the factors relevant to the adjustment fall squarely within the bankruptcy court's area of expertise.

Thus, unlike the coerced loan, presumptive contract rate, and cost of funds approaches, the formula approach entails a straightforward, familiar, and objective inquiry, and minimizes the need for potentially costly additional evidentiary proceedings. Moreover, the resulting "prime-plus" rate of interest depends only on the state of financial markets, the circumstances of the bankruptcy estate, and the characteristics of the loan, not on the creditor's circumstances or its prior interactions with the debtor. For these reasons, the prime-plus or formula rate best comports with the purposes of the Code. . . .

We do not decide the proper scale for the risk adjustment, as the issue is not before us. The Bankruptcy Court in this case approved a risk adjustment of 1.5%, and other courts have generally approved adjustments of 1% to 3%. Respondent's core argument is that a risk adjustment in this range is entirely inadequate to compensate a creditor for the real risk that the plan will fail. There is some dispute about the true scale of that risk— respondent claims that more than 60% of Chapter 13 plans fail, Brief for Respondent 25, but petitioners argue that the failure rate for approved Chapter 13 plans is much lower. We need not resolve that dispute. It is sufficient for our purposes to note that, under 11 U.S.C. § 1325(a)(6), a court may not approve a plan unless, after considering all creditors' objections and receiving the advice of the trustee, the judge is persuaded that "the debtor will be able to make all payments under the plan and to comply with the plan." Ibid. Together with the cram down provision, this requirement obligates the court to select a rate high enough to compensate the creditor for its risk but not so high as to doom the plan. If the court determines that the likelihood of default is so high as to necessitate an "eye-popping" interest rate, the plan probably should not be confirmed.

V

The dissent's endorsement of the presumptive contract rate approach rests on two assumptions: (1) "subprime lending markets are competitive and therefore largely efficient"; and (2) the risk of default in Chapter 13 is normally no less than the risk of default at the time of the original loan. Although the Code provides little guidance on the question, we think it highly unlikely that Congress would endorse either premise.

. . .

Even more important, if all relevant information about the debtor's circumstances, the creditor's circumstances, the nature of the collateral, and the market for comparable loans were equally available to both debtor and creditor, then in theory the formula and presumptive contract rate approaches would yield the same final interest rate. Thus, we principally differ with the dissent not over what final rate courts should adopt but over which party (creditor or debtor) should bear the burden of rebutting the presumptive rate (prime or contract, respectively).

Justice SCALIA identifies four "relevant factors bearing on risk premium[:] (1) the probability of plan failure; (2) the rate of collateral depreciation; (3) the liquidity of the collateral market; and (4) the administrative expenses of enforcement." Post, at 1973. In our view, any information debtors have about any of these factors is likely to be included in their bankruptcy filings, while the remaining information will be far more accessible to creditors (who must collect information about their lending markets to remain competitive) than to individual debtors (whose only experience with those markets might be the single loan at issue in the case). Thus, the formula approach, which begins with a concededly low estimate of the appropriate interest rate and requires the creditor to present evidence supporting a higher rate, places the evidentiary burden on the more knowledgeable party, thereby facilitating more accurate calculation of the appropriate interest rate.

If the rather sketchy data uncovered by the dissent support an argument that Chapter 13 of the Code should mandate application of the presumptive contract rate approach (rather than merely an argument that bankruptcy judges should exercise greater caution before approving debt adjustment plans), those data should be forwarded to Congress. We are not persuaded, however, that the data undermine our interpretation of the statutory scheme Congress has enacted.

The judgment of the Court of Appeals is reversed, and the case is remanded with instructions to remand the case to the Bankruptcy Court for further proceedings consistent with this opinion.

It is so ordered.

Justice THOMAS, concurring in the judgment.

This case presents the issue of what the proper method is for discounting deferred payments to present value and what compensation the creditor is entitled to in calculating the appropriate discount rate of interest. Both the plurality and the dissent agree that "[a] debtor's promise of future payments is worth less than an immediate payment of the same total amount because the creditor cannot use the money right away, inflation may cause the value of the dollar to decline before the debtor pays, and there is always some risk of nonpayment." Ante, at 1958; post, at 1968. Thus, the plurality and the dissent agree that the proper method for discounting deferred payments to present value should take into account each of these factors, but disagree over the proper starting point for calculating the risk of nonpayment.

I agree that a "promise of future payments is worth less than an immediate payment" of the same amount, in part because of the risk of nonpayment. But this fact is irrelevant. The statute does not require that the value of the promise to distribute property under the plan be no less than the allowed amount of the secured creditor's claim. It requires only that "the value . . . of property to be distributed under the plan," at the time of the effective date of the plan, be no less than the amount of the secured creditor's claim. 11 U.S.C. § 1325(a)(5)(B)(ii) (emphasis added). Both the plurality and the dissent ignore the clear text of the statute in an apparent rush to ensure that secured creditors are not undercompensated in bankruptcy proceedings. But the statute that Congress enacted does not require a debtor-specific risk adjustment that would put secured creditors in the same position as if they had made another loan. It is for this reason that I write separately.

. . .

II

The allowed amount of the secured claim is $4,000. . . . The statute then requires a bankruptcy court to identify the "property to be distributed" under the plan. Petitioners' Amended Chapter 13 Plan (Plan) provided:

> "The future earnings of DEBTOR(S) are submitted to the supervision and control of this Court, and DEBTOR(S) shall pay to the TRUSTEE a sum of $740 per month in weekly installments by voluntary wage assignment by separate ORDER of the Court in an estimated amount of $170.77 and continuing for a total plan term of 36 months unless this Court approves an extension of the term not beyond 60 months from the date of filing the Petition herein." App. to Pet. for Cert. 77a.

From the payments received, the trustee would then make disbursements to petitioners' creditors, pro rata among each class of creditors. The Plan listed one priority claim and four secured claims. For respondent's secured claim, petitioner proposed an interest rate of 9.5%. . . . Thus, petitioners proposed to distribute to respondent a stream of cash payments equaling respondent's pro rata share of $740 per month for a period of up to 36 months. . . .

Although the Plan does not specifically state that "the property to be distributed" under the Plan is cash payments, the cash payments are the only "property" specifically listed for distribution under the Plan. Thus, although the plurality and the dissent imply that the "property to be distributed" under the Plan is the mere promise to make cash payments, the plain language of the Plan indicates that the "property to be distributed" to respondent is up to 36 monthly cash payments, consisting of a pro rata share of $740 per month.

The final task, then, is to determine whether petitioners' proposed 9.5% interest rate will sufficiently compensate respondent for the fact that instead of receiving $4,000 today, it will receive $4,000 plus 9.5% interest over a period of up to 36 months. Because the 9.5% rate is higher than the risk-free rate, I conclude that it will. I would therefore reverse the judgment of the Court of Appeals.

Justice SCALIA, with whom THE CHIEF JUSTICE, Justice O'CONNOR, and Justice KENNEDY join, dissenting.

My areas of agreement with the plurality are substantial. We agree that, although all confirmed Chapter 13 plans have been deemed feasible by a bankruptcy judge, some nevertheless fail.... We agree that any deferred payments to a secured creditor must fully compensate it for the risk that such a failure will occur.... Finally, we agree that adequate compensation may sometimes require an " 'eye-popping' "interest rate, and that, if the rate is too high for the plan to succeed, the appropriate course is not to reduce it to a more palatable level, but to refuse to confirm the plan.

Our only disagreement is over what procedure will more often produce accurate estimates of the appropriate interest rate. The plurality would use the prime lending rate—a rate we know is too low—and require the judge in every case to determine an amount by which to increase it. I believe that, in practice, this approach will systematically undercompensate secured creditors for the true risks of default. I would instead adopt the contract rate—i.e., the rate at which the creditor actually loaned funds to the debtor—as a presumption that the bankruptcy judge could revise on motion of either party. Since that rate is generally a good indicator of actual risk, disputes should be infrequent, and it will provide a quick and reasonably accurate standard.

. . .

QUESTIONS ABOUT TILL

1. The Supreme Court approved the Tills using Chapter 13 to reduce the interest rate on their automobile loan from the contract rate of 21% to 9.5% (prime plus 1.5% for risk of nonpayment). Who gets the benefit of the money that will be saved by the reduced interest rate?

2. After *Till* does the debtor or the creditor have the burden of proving how much the risk adjustment should be? Is this appropriate? Why?

3. What factors may be relevant to determining the size of the risk adjustment?

4. Will the *Till* decision impact the determination of the appropriate interest rate in bankruptcy cases other than cases under Chapter 13? Compare footnotes 10 and 14 of the opinion.

Problem 10–8:   What Interest Rate Does Debtor Have to Pay the Car Lender?

1.   Debtor owns a five-year-old car worth $6,500. Debtor owes EZ Finance $6,500 secured by the car. Debtor proposes the following payments for EZ in her plan: $6,500 amortized over the remaining 5 years of her plan with interest at 8%. Prime rate is currently 6.5%. EZ objects to the interest rate proposed and the five year payout arguing that they are not adequate to compensate it for the risk of default. The car already has been driven 90,000 miles and EZ argues that it is not realistic that the car will last another five years. EZ complains that it currently charges 22% interest to borrowers with credit histories similar to debtor, which is similar to the rate established in the loan agreement between debtor and EZ. Should EZ prevail?

2.   Is you answer any different if EZ financed Debtor's purchase of the car 900 days before Debtor filed for Chapter 13?

3.   Is your answer any different if Debtor had a prior Chapter 13 case, which was dismissed a year ago because debtor failed to make required plan payments?

4.   Is your answer any different if EZ had originally provided debtor with 0% financing?

To review Chapter 13 and car loans, Chapter 13 balances the rights of creditors and debtors. The debtor gets the benefit of more time to pay and the opportunity to keep the automobile; the creditor gets sufficient payments so that the creditor is no worse off than if bankruptcy had not intervened. The challenge in maintaining this balance is in the detail of determining the value of the creditor's collateral if the hanging paragraph provision does not apply and the appropriate rate of interest. The next problem illustrates what we learned about valuation of collateral in Unit 4.

Problem 10–9:   Review: How Should the Car Lender's Collateral Be Valued?

Debtor purchased an old pick-up truck to use in her business three months before bankruptcy for $7,000. The dealer included a 30–day warranty as part of the purchase. Debtor paid $500 down and dealer financed the remaining $6,500 balance. Debtor filed Chapter 13 before she made her first payment. Her plan values the truck and proposes to pay dealer $4,500 to satisfy the secured debt. Debtor argues that she overpaid because she was desperate and the truck is not worth any more than $4,500. The plan will pay off the obligation in the same three years as originally agreed between the parties. The wholesale value of the truck is $3,000, the private-party value of the truck is $4,500, and its retail value is $6,000. You represent the dealer, who objects to the proposed valuation and only being paid $4,500 on account of its secured claim. What arguments do you make? How would your arguments change if the debtor purchased the truck for personal use rather than business use? Remember the Supreme Court's decision in *Rash* on page 48 of the text, particularly footnote 6, § 506(b)(2) and the provision immediately following § 1325(a)(9), both of which were added by the 2005 amendments to the Bankruptcy Code.

---

2. SPECIAL RULE FOR CLAIMS SECURED SOLELY BY THE DEBTOR'S PRINCIPAL RESIDENCE

The plan cannot modify the claim of a creditor secured only by an interest in the debtor's principal residence. § 1322(b)(2). Thus, the debtor generally cannot bifurcate a partially secured mortgage claim into a secured claim and an unsecured claim and cannot modify the interest rate, the required postpetition payments (except a balloon payment as discussed below), or other monetary or nonmonetary obligations imposed by the security agreement.

That does not mean that the debtor cannot use Chapter 13 creatively to solve her home mortgage problem. As long as the debtor can maintain current payments, the debtor may choose to sell or refinance the home during the Chapter 13. In the process the debtor may be able to raise money to cure a default or to pay other creditors.

One question that had led much litigation was the question of when was it too late for the debtor to cure defaults in her home mortgage. The question was legislatively answered in 1994 through adoption of § 1322(c)(1), which provides:

(c) Notwithstanding subsection (b)(2) and applicable nonbankruptcy law–

(1) a default with respect to, or that gave rise to, a lien on the debtor's principal residence may be cured under paragraph (3) or (5) of subsection (b) until such residence is sold at a foreclosure sale that is conducted in accordance with applicable nonbankruptcy law; [.]

In most states, real property lien foreclosures take several months. At any time before the foreclosure sale occurs, the debtor can file Chapter 13 and cure the default and reinstate the loan.

Another frequent area of litigation is with respect to § 1322(b)(2) which provides that a plan may:

(2) modify the rights of holders of secured claims, other than a claim secured only by a security interest in real property that is the debtor's principal residence, or of holders of unsecured claims, or leave unaffected the rights of holders of such claims.

This provision contains what is commonly referred to as an "anti-modification rule with respect to debtor's principal residence."

An important issue is whether a creditor who has a security interest in the residence, but whose claim is wholly unsecured under the Code because the residence has insufficient value to secure any part of the obligation, is protected by this anti-modification rule. The majority of the courts that have considered the question, including all six federal courts of appeals that have considered the issue, focus on the requirement that the creditor hold a secured claim. Under § 506(a), a creditor has a secured claim only if it has a security interest in the debtor's property and that security has actual value. If the security interest does not have actual value, the anti-modification rule does not apply. The minority view interprets § 1322(b)(2) to prohibit modification of the claim of any creditor whose debt is secured solely by the debtor's residence, regardless of whether the security interest has actual value. To understand the point, consider the following factual scenario:

Debtor has a residence worth $150,000.

Debtor owes Bank $155,000 secured by a first mortgage on her residence.

Debtor owes Finance Co. $25,000 secured by a second mortgage on her residence.

Under the majority view, debtor can avoid the mortgage of Finance Co. and treat Finance Co. as an unsecured creditor. Avoidance of the mortgage is commonly called "stripping off" the mortgage. Under the minority view, debtor must pay Finance Co. in full because of the anti-modification provision of § 1322(b)(2), although debtor may cure any default over the life of the plan.

3. CAN THE DEBTOR CURE THE HOME MORTGAGE BALLOON PAYMENT OVER TIME?

Some home loans have a balloon payment rather than having affordable monthly payments for the duration of the loan. For instance, a loan may have payments established based on what it would take to pay the loan over 30 years, but the entire balance is due five years after the date the loan is made. Such a required payoff is commonly referred to as a balloon payment (or, in darker circles, a "bullet" payment).

Section 1322(c)(2) allows debtors to use Chapter 13 for relief if they cannot pay the balloon payment in full when due, notwithstanding the general anti-modification rule. Section 1322(c)(2) provides:

(c) Notwithstanding subsection (b)(2) and applicable nonbankruptcy law– . . .

(2) in a case in which the last payment on the original payment schedule for a claim secured only by a security interest in real

property that is the debtor's principal residence is due before the date on which the final payment under the plan is due, the plan may provide for the payment of the claim as modified pursuant to section 1325(a)(5) of this title.

This section allows the debtor to pay the balloon through the plan. Because no regular monthly payment is due if the entire debt has come due, the debtor may not be required to make monthly payments or to make payments as large as originally required by the contract prior to the balloon, if the creditor is otherwise adequately protected. The debtor may be able to use Chapter 13 to obtain time to refinance or sell the property with a balloon payment.

Problem 10–10: Home Mortgage Problems

1. Debtor owes Friendly Bank $70,000 secured by a mortgage on debtor's principal residence, which is worth $100,000. Debtor is $6,000 behind on her payments to Friendly. Although debtor's plan will cure the arrearage, the plan does not provide for any payments on the arrearage for two years. Interest on the $6,000 arrearage will be paid at a rate that meets the legal requirements of Chapter 13. At the end of two years the Debtor's plan provides that Friendly's arrearage plus interest will be paid in a single payment through the refinance or sale of the debtor's residence. Debtor wants to use her plan payments to pay her high-interest-rate car loan before paying Friendly. Friendly objects, arguing that secured creditors should be treated equally and it is not fair to make it wait two years for its payment. The judge overrules Friendly's objection. What rationale justifies the judge's decision?

2. Debtor, facing foreclosure on her mortgage a little more than two years ago, refinanced the loan through EZ Finance. Unfortunately, EZ's terms were onerous. Debtor's interest rate increased from 7% to 12%, she paid $5,000 in loan and closing costs, which she borrowed from EZ, and she agreed to repay the entire balance in two years. The house is worth $100,000 and debtor owes EZ $75,000. In order to make the monthly payments to EZ, debtor moved in with relatives and rented out her home. Using the rents and her other income, debtor made the monthly payments due to EZ. She has no ability to pay the balloon. She could sell her house, but she cannot complete a sale before EZ completes its foreclosure. Debtor consults you regarding whether she should accept EZ's offer to refinance again at a cost of another $5,000. How do you advise debtor? What do you tell debtor about bankruptcy?

E. DIFFERENCES IN THE TREATMENT OF LEASED HOUSES AND CARS v. MORT-GAGED HOUSES AND CARS

Debtors often are parties to leases at the time they file Chapter 13. Many debtors rent the premises where they live. Some debtors lease rather than purchase automobiles.

As we learned in greater detail in Unit 8 on the treatment of leases and executory contracts, Section 365 of the Code forces the any bankruptcy trustee who wants to be assured of retaining the benefits of a lease to assume the lease and, upon assumption, promptly cure any defaults. Such defaults may be cured through the plan. Section 1322(b)(7) gives the Chapter 13 debtor the power to assume or reject leases and executory contracts in the debtor's plan.

A debtor who does not want to retain the leased property will "reject" the lease. As long as the debtor rejects the lease without assuming it, the lessor will have a prepetition claim for any lease amounts due at the time of filing and any damages arising from the breach of the lease. The lessor will also have the right to recover the leased property. The lessor's rejection claim will be an unsecured claim, unless the lessor has a security interest in assets of the debtor securing performance of the lease. The consequences of assumption and rejection are discussed in greater detail in Unit 8.

Chapter 13 debtors who want to keep leased property usually assume the lease and cure the defaults. This option is potentially far less flexible than the treatment of secured claims. Recall, with respect to secured claims, the debtor does not have to pay more than the value of the collateral (except with respect to the claims secured solely by the debtor's principal real property residence, personal vehicle purchase-money debts incurred within 910 days of bankruptcy and personal property purchase-money secured debt incurred within one year of bankruptcy). In addition, under certain circumstances, the debtor may be able to repay the secured debt at an interest rate that is lower than the contract rate. If the debtor has a leased vehicle and wants to keep it, she cannot "cram down" the debt to the value of the collateral and cannot alter the charge for the use of the money effectively imbedded in the lease payment. Finally, with respect to secured claims, there is no requirement that the debtor promptly cure defaults. Thus, the debtor who has leased her house and automobile will have to cure any defaults more quickly than if she had purchased them and was behind in performing her mortgage and automobile purchase payment obligations.

Problem 10–11: Differences in Leasing and Lending in Chapter 13

1. You are interviewing a debtor in your office about her financial and legal problems. She tells you that she makes $250 per month payments on her car. What questions do you ask debtor so that you can properly advise her?

2. You represent a debtor who has leased a two-year-old car worth $15,000, with a monthly lease payment of $400. Debtor is three payments behind. When the lease matures in one year, the debtor has the choice of returning the car or purchasing it for $17,000. Debtor needs a car to get to work and would like to keep her leased car. She can afford to pay the current lease payments, but she wants to pay the minimum she can toward curing the lease arrears because of her tight family budget. What terms will you propose that you think will allow debtor to retain her leased car? If the debtor assumes the lease through the plan, what rights and obligations will she have when the lease matures in one year?

   What could the debtor do differently in her plan if she had purchased the same car instead of leasing it, and her monthly payments under the purchase contract were the same amount as the lease payments?

F. CLASSIFICATION OF UNSECURED CLAIMS (CAN THE DEBTOR PAY SOME UNSECURED CLAIMS MORE THAN OTHERS?)

Chapter 13 debtors often want to pay certain unsecured claims in full. The following are a few of the reasons that a debtor might want to make sure that certain creditors are paid in full. First, some debts are excepted from the Chapter 13 discharge. § 1328(a). Student loans are the most common example of debts that fall in this category. The debtor will want to pay the nondischargeable debt during the Chapter 13; otherwise the debtor will be forced to repay whatever remains of the nondischargeable debt, including postpetition interest, after completing the Chapter 13 case. The debtor wants a complete, not a partial, fresh start after making Chapter 13 payments for three to five years. Second, in order to get a loan or other credit, many debtors had to have someone who was more creditworthy guarantee payment of the obligation. If the debtor does not pay that obligation, the co-signer, who is often a parent or other relative, will have to pay the debt. In order to maintain family harmony, the debtor does not want this to happen. Third, some debtors who have committed crimes are on probation or parole and have obligations under a criminal sentence to pay restitution for the benefit of the crime victim as a condition of avoiding imprisonment. If the debtor fails to make the restitution payments as ordered, the criminal court may require the debtor to go to jail.

A debtor who wants to make sure that one or more of her creditors are paid in full will often not have enough money to pay all the unsecured creditors in full. Chapter 13 provides two primary plan mechanisms through which the debtor can potentially accomplish the goal of paying some unsecured creditors in full even if that is better treatment than provided to the rest of the unsecured creditors.

First, section 1322(b)(1) provides that the plan may:

> designate a class or classes of unsecured claims, as provided in section 1122 of this title, but may not discriminate unfairly against any class so designated; however, such plan may treat claims for a consumer debt of the debtor if an individual is liable on such consumer debt with the debtor differently than other unsecured claims[.]

Examination of § 1122, which is referenced in § 1322(b)(1), tells us that the "plan may place a claim or an interest in a particular class only if such claim or interest is substantially similar to the other claims or interests of such class." § 1122(a). If a plan classifies claims, the plan must "provide the same treatment for each claim within a particular class." § 1322(a)(3). Using these provisions, the debtor may confirm a Chapter 13 plan that divides the unsecured creditors into more than one class and treats the classes differently, provided that, if more than one claim is included within a particular class, the claims are "substantially similar" and the separate classification does not discriminate unfairly.

Second, if the debtor were to pay obligation(s) that the debtor wants to treat preferentially according to the established contractual payment schedule and the final payment would not be made until after completion of the Chapter 13 plan payments, the debtor has an alternative approach available. Section 1322(b)(5) provides that a plan may:

> provide for the curing of any default within a reasonable time and maintenance of payments while the case is pending on any unsecured claim or secured claim on which the last payment is due after the date on which the final payment under the plan is due[.]

This allows the debtor to cure any default and pay the balance according to the contractual terms. If the debtor chooses this approach, the debtor will not be done paying the debt upon completion of the Chapter 13 plan because, by definition in the statute, the debt must have payments due after completion of the plan.

The opportunity to classify separately unsecured claims does not alter any of the other requirements for confirmation of a Chapter 13 plan. The debtor's plan still must meet the "best interests" test of § 1325(a)(4). In other words, each creditor, including those in the class receiving poorer treatment, must receive at least what the creditor would have received in a Chapter 7 case. In Chapter 7 cases, all nonpriority unsecured creditors are generally treated the same. § 726(a)(2)–(3). Thus, if the debtor had a Chapter 7 case in which the Chapter 7 trustee would have distributed $5,000 to the unsecured creditors and that distribution would have resulted in unsecured creditors receiving payment of 25% of their claims, the debtor cannot confirm a Chapter 13 plan that distributes $5,000 to unsecured creditors by paying the entire $5,000 to the class of unsecured creditor(s) the debtor wants to pay and nothing to the other class of unsecured creditors. That plan will not satisfy the "best interests" test imposed by § 1325(a)(4).

The propriety of such separate classification can be determined either before confirmation on motion after notice and hearing, Bankr. R. 3013, or as part of the hearing on confirmation at which the court must decide whether the plan complies with the legal requirements.

IN RE WILLIAMS

253 B.R. 220 (Bankr. W.D. Tenn. 2000)

JENNIE D. LATTA, Bankruptcy Judge.

The court scheduled status conferences in each of the referenced Chapter 13 cases which propose to separately classify and preferentially treat student loan claims. No objections to the proposed classifications were raised by any creditor or the standing Chapter 13 trustee. Nevertheless, the bankruptcy judge has an independent obligation to determine whether a plan fulfills the requirements for confirmation under Chapter 13.

The issue before the court is whether a plan that proposes to separately classify and fully repay nondischargeable student loan debt unfairly discriminates against other unsecured creditors who will receive only partial repayment of their dischargeable claims. For the reasons set forth below, the court determines that the proposed plans are not capable of confirmation because they discriminate unfairly against general unsecured creditors. . . .

I. BACKGROUND FACTS

In each of these cases, the debtor proposes to pay 100% of his or her student loan claim over the life of the plan. Each of the plans is expected to terminate after 60 months. Two of the plans specify no distribution to the other unsecured creditors, but leave that percentage to be determined by the Chapter 13 trustee after the bar date for filing proofs of claim has passed. The other three plans propose paying a specified percentage to the general unsecured creditors: the Kings propose to pay 15%, Mr. Williams to pay 20%, and the Hunters to pay 25%. . . .

II. ANALYSIS

Section 1322(b)(1) provides in pertinent part that a debtor's plan may "designate a class or classes of unsecured claims, as provided in section 1122 of [title 11], but may not discriminate unfairly against any class so designated." Section 1122 requires that a claim or interest be placed in a particular class only if the claim or interest is substantially similar to other claims or interests of that class, but permits dissimilar claims to be classified together for administrative convenience. See 11 U.S.C. § 1122(a) and (b). Implicit in section 1122 is the requirement that claims be sufficiently dissimilar to warrant separate classification. . . . In Chapter 11 cases where confirmation of the plan requires the acceptance of the plan by at least one class of impaired claims, a reasonable limitation upon a debtor's ability to separately classify claims prevents inappropriate "gerry-mandering" to obtain an accepting class. Chapter 13 does not provide for acceptance of the plan by the vote of creditors, thus the only purpose served by a separate designation of unsecured claims in Chapter 13 is discrimination in treatment. Discrimination between classes of unsecured claims generally takes the form of a difference in the percentage of payment or the order of distribution. Discrimination is said to be unfair when there is no valid reason to prefer one group of unsecured claims over another. . . . If there is no valid reason for discrimination, there is also no valid reason for separate classification in Chapter 13. . . .

George Stevenson, the standing Chapter 13 trustee, . . . argues that section 1322(b)(1) requires that a specially designated class of unsecured creditors not be treated worse than general unsecured creditors, but does not prohibit better treatment of the designated class. Mr. Stevenson is correct in one sense—section 1322(b)(1) does not prohibit better treatment of a designated class. Mr. Stevenson is incorrect in another sense because designation of one class necessarily involves designation of a second class. As was shown, in Chapter 13 the only purpose for such designation is discrimination in treatment. After secured claims and administrative expenses are provided for, the balance of payments under a Chapter 13 plan are divided among the unsecured claims. To discriminate in favor of one class of unsecured claims necessarily results in discrimination against another class of unsecured claims. What is required is that the discrimination not be unfair.

In these cases, the debtors propose to separately classify their student loan claims from other unsecured claims, and to pay their student loan claims "100%." Ms. Haten, Mr. and Mrs. King, and Mr. and Mrs. Hunter propose to pay interest on the student loan claims as well. The debtors, as proponents of the plans, bear the burden of proving that the proposed classification does not discriminate unfairly. . . . This court has previously quoted with approval the comments of Bankruptcy Judge Barbara Sellers concerning separate classification of claims in Chapter 13 cases:

> Any classification of unsecured claims must pass a test of fairness unless that classification involves consumer debts for which co-signers were obtained. Unlike Chapter 11, unsecured creditors in Chapter 13 are not afforded an opportunity to vote. Further, unless their claims are unusually large, such creditors generally lack economic incentive to object to confirmation of a low dividend plan. Therefore, the primary burden for scrutinizing the differing treatment of separately

classified unsecured claims in Chapter 13 falls, first on the Chapter 13 trustee, and then on the court.

In re Riggel, 142 B.R. 199, 202 (Bankr.S.D.Ohio 1992).

Four factors must be considered in determining whether a proposed classification scheme is proper:

1.   Whether the discrimination has a reasonable basis;

2.   Whether the debtor can carry out the plan without such discrimination;

3.   Whether the classification has been proposed in good faith; and

4.   The nature of the treatment of the class discriminated against.[1]

. . .

The debtors have put forth a number of justifications for the separate classification of their student loan debts. The primary reason offered for the separate classification is that the student loan claims, unlike the general unsecured claims, are not dischargeable in bankruptcy. See 11 U.S.C. § 523(a)(8).[2] Related to this is the argument that the debtors will not receive the benefit of a fresh start if they are not allowed to fully repay their student loans during the pendency of their plans. The debtors argue that the remedies available to student loan creditors, such as wage garnishment and set off of income tax refunds distinguishes these claims from other general unsecured claims. The trustee argues that the fact that Congress has rendered student loans nondischargeable except in cases of undue hardship demonstrates a strong public policy in favor of full repayment of student loans. Another distinction between student loans and other unsecured loans is the length of the period for repayment of most student loans. Pursuant to section 1322(b)(5), if the last payment on the student loan is due after the final payment under the plan is due, the plan may provide for the curing of any default and the maintenance of ongoing payments. This treatment can only be accomplished through separate classification of the student loan claim.

The court agrees that there are a number of reasonable bases for separately classifying student loan claims from other general unsecured claims. The more important and difficult question is what degree of discrimination in the treatment of student loan claims is necessary and appropriate. The determination of unfair discrimination lies within the discretion of the bankruptcy judge and is to be made on a case by case basis. . . .

---

1. This is the test most commonly used by courts to determine whether proposed discrimination is unfair. . . .

2. Section 1322(a)(2) provides:

(a) The plan shall—

(2) provide for the full payment, in deferred cash payments, of all claims entitled to priority under section 507 of this title, unless the holder of a particular claim agrees to a different treatment of such claim.

11 U.S.C. § 1322(a)(2).

A. Interest Payments

The first type of discrimination proposed by three of the debtors is the payment of interest on their student loan claims, but not on other unsecured claims. Creditors are not entitled to include unmatured (or "post-petition") interest as part of their claims in bankruptcy proceedings. See 11 U.S.C. § 502(b)(2); . . . In order to be confirmed, a Chapter 13 plan . . . is not required to provide for the payment of interest on priority claims (including administrative claims) or general unsecured claims. . . . 11 U.S.C. §§ 1322(a)(2),[3] . . . The student loan creditor cannot compel the payment of post-petition interest on its claim from the bankruptcy estate, but may compel the payment of interest from the debtor after completion of the Chapter 13 plan because interest on nondischargeable debts is nondischargeable. . . .

The debtors in these cases argue that their interest in a fresh start justifies the payment of interest on their student loan claims, but not on other unsecured claims. The debtors want to emerge from their Chapter 13 cases with a full discharge of all their debts, including their student loan debts. . . . The court does not believe that the debtors' interest in a fresh start should override the requirement of fairness in distribution.[6] After completion of their Chapter 13 plans, these debtors should be left with very little ongoing debt, and should be able to structure an appropriate agreement for the repayment of interest accrued on their student loans during the pendency of their Chapter 13 plans.

In the alternative, the Bankruptcy Code itself provides one approved method of preferring student loan claims over other unsecured claims. Section 1322(b)(5) . . . provides for the curing of any default within a reasonable time and maintenance of payments on unsecured claims on which the last payment is due after the final payment under the plan is due. Many student loan claims will have remaining terms that extend beyond a three-to five-year plan. The maintenance of ongoing payments necessarily involves the payment of post-petition interest. Pre-petition interest will be included in the creditor's proof of claim consisting of the arrearage to be paid (cured) within a reasonable time. Through this method, a debtor should be able to fully repay student loan arrearages during the plan, and reestablish the original loan repayment schedule. This type of discrimination is specifically contemplated and sanctioned by the Bankruptcy Code. . . . Because the Bankruptcy Code contemplates the curing of any default within a reasonable time, a debtor may pay 100% of a student loan arrearage while paying less than 100% of other unsecured claims, so long as the degree of discrimination is necessary to the debtor's success under the plan. . . .

3. Section 1322(a)(2) provides:

(a) The plan shall–

(2) provide for the full payment, in deferred cash payments, of all claims entitled to priority under section 507 of this title, unless the holder of a particular claim agrees to a different treatment of such claim [.]

6. A debtor cannot expect an unfettered fresh start when one of the debtor's debts is nondischargeable. . . .

B. Acceleration of Student Loans

1. The Hunters

The Hunters' proposed plan contemplates full repayment of their student loan even though under its original terms the loan would not be repaid until at least 2007. The Hunters borrowed funds under the PLUS program ... to enable their son to attend Alabama State University. The son did not complete his studies and has not been able or has not offered to assist his parents in repaying the loan. The Hunters propose to pay 100% of their PLUS loan during their five year plan, but only 25% of their other unsecured debt. In effect, the Hunters propose that their unsecured creditors subsidize their son's educational efforts. The Hunters do not wish to file a Chapter 7 case because they have equity in their home. Mr. Hunter receives military disability income of $1,476 per month. Mrs. Hunter plans to retire from teaching school and expects to receive a retirement income of $1,695 per month. The ongoing payments on the PLUS loan would be $121.30 per month. Mr. Hunter testified that Mrs. Hunter is retiring upon the advice of her doctor, ... but the Hunters have not sought a hardship discharge[10] with respect to their PLUS loan nor apparently have they sought disability relief from their lender. Absent the establishment of a hardship under section 523(a)(8), the court does not find it reasonable that the debtors expect to receive a fresh start after five years through this Chapter 13 plan, when they originally agreed to and expected a ten-year repayment term for their PLUS loan.

... The Hunters argue that leaving a student loan unpaid after the completion of a Chapter 13 case is an "unnecessary impairment of the Debtors' right to a 'fresh start' after bankruptcy," citing In re Whittaker, 113 B.R. 531 (Bankr.D.Minn.1990); In re Boggan, 125 B.R. 533 (Bankr. N.D.Ill.1991); and In re Tucker, 159 B.R. 325 (Bankr.D.Mont.1993). The court in In re Whittaker permitted the payment of a child support arrearage in full before the payment of general unsecured claims. Boggan and Tucker provide that the nondischargeability of student loan claims provides a reasonable basis for a debtor to prefer student loan claims through his Chapter 13 plan so long as the general unsecured creditors receive at least what they would have received in Chapter 7. This court agrees with the conclusion of Whittaker, and would permit the Hunters to cure the arrearage on their PLUS loan in full through their plan, even if that would result in a greater percentage being paid on the student loan arrearage than that being paid to general unsecured creditors. What the Hunters propose however, is more akin to prepayment of an ongoing child support obligation rather than the curing of an arrearage. The Whittaker opinion does not support such treatment. The court has reviewed the Boggan and Tucker opinions. Unfortunately, neither of them provides information concerning the remaining term of the student loans at issue. Thus the court cannot determine whether payment in full of the student

---

10. Section 523(a)(8) provides that a student loan may be discharged if the debtor can prove that repayment of the loan would cause an undue hardship on the debtor or his dependents....

loans in those cases resulted in an acceleration of the repayment of those loans such as is proposed by the Hunters. This court does not believe that acceleration of the Hunters' PLUS loan is necessary to the success of their plan, or that such treatment is fair to the general unsecured creditors. . . .

2. Annette Haywood Burton

. . . Ms. Burton proposes to pay 100% of this loan and a percentage to be determined after all proofs of claim are filed to other general unsecured creditors. Assuming a repayment period of ten years, it would appear that this loan, which was obtained in 1998, would qualify as a long term obligation for treatment under section 1322(b)(5). For the reasons stated earlier, the court does not believe that it is fair to permit the acceleration of student loans through a Chapter 13 plan at the expense of other unsecured creditors. . . .

C.   Greater Percentage

Assuming that the remaining debtors have student loans for which the last payment is due before the last payment under their proposed plans (i.e., that section 1325(b)(5) does not apply), the third type of discrimination proposed for student loans in these cases is the payment of 100% of these claims while other unsecured claims are paid a much lower percentage. Neither Ms. Haten nor the Kings have articulated a need for such discriminatory treatment other than their desire to emerge from their Chapter 13 plans debt free. In the clear majority of reported cases, the courts have concluded that the nondischargeability of a student loan by itself is not enough to permit debtors to pay student loans in full while the other general unsecured creditors receive less than 100% of their claims. . . . Clearly plans could be proposed by Ms. Haten and the Kings that would provide the same percentage repayment to all unsecured creditors, with the balance of the student loan claims surviving the completion of the Chapter 13 plans. Neither Ms. Haten nor the Kings introduced proof of any special circumstances that would prevent them from completing payment of their student loans after the conclusion of their Chapter 13 plans.

Both Ms. Haten and the Kings, through their attorney, assert that in a Chapter 7 liquidation, there would be no assets available for distribution to unsecured creditors. These debtors have left open the percentage to be paid to general unsecured creditors pending the bar date for filing proofs of claim, but they assert that payment of any amount to these creditors will satisfy the best interest of creditors test. Mr. Fox asserts that so long as the Chapter 13 plan proposes to pay more to general unsecured creditors than they would have received under Chapter 7, discrimination in favor of student loan creditors is fair. The court does not agree. . . .

Chapter 13 is a strictly voluntary provision for the repayment of debts. The court must assume that the debtors in these cases chose Chapter 13 over Chapter 7 because of some perceived advantage to themselves. The debtors cannot, therefore, ignore the requirements for confirmation of a

Chapter 13 plan, including the requirement that the plan not discriminate unfairly among classes of unsecured creditors.

Both of the student loans in these cases are relatively small. TSAC filed a proof of claim in the amount of $1,586.10 in Ms. Haten's case. USAF filed a proof of claim in the amount of $2,151.67 in the Kings' case. On the one hand, this means that an amendment to the plan to provide for the same percentage to be paid to the student loan creditor as to other creditors would result in a rather small increase in the percentage to be paid to other unsecured creditors. On the other hand, the size of these claims also means that it would be relatively easy for the debtors to complete the repayment of their student loans after completion of their plans. Again the court cannot determine the remaining length of the original loan terms in these cases. If these are long term debts the court would permit the debtors to maintain ongoing payments and cure any arrearage over the life of the plan. If these loans are now short term obligations, the court will permit the debtors to discriminate in favor of the student loan creditors so long as the percentage to be paid on the student loan claims is no more than 30 percentage points in excess of the percentage to be paid to general unsecured claims. That is, if the debtor proposes to pay 100% of his student loan claim, he must propose to pay at least 70% of his general unsecured claims. Such discrimination will be considered fair by the court. The debtors bear the burden of showing unique circumstances to support a greater degree of discrimination.

D. Preferential Payment

A final type of discrimination proposed for student loans in these cases is the full repayment of the student loan claims before the payment of general unsecured claims. In an unrelated case, Mr. Stevenson, the standing Chapter 13 trustee, has testified that in this district those claims classified as "Class I, unsecured," are paid in full before general unsecured creditors receive any distribution.... The court is aware from personal experience that a substantial number of Chapter 13 cases fail within the first 18 months. Unlike claims for child and spousal support, student loan claims do not enjoy a statutory priority for distribution. It was in the 1990 amendments to the Bankruptcy Code that student loans were made nondischargeable in Chapter 13.... In 1994, child and spousal support obligations were given seventh priority in distribution.... Had Congress intended that student loans also enjoy priority of distribution, it could have specifically provided for it.... The effect of classifying student loan claims as Class I unsecured is to give such claims priority of distribution. Even if a debtor were to propose 100% repayment to general unsecured creditors, if those creditors are not paid concurrently with student loans, they may in fact receive no distribution at all. There is nothing to prevent the debtors from making enough plan payments to pay their student loans in full and then voluntarily dismissing their cases with no distribution to general unsecured creditors. This imposes an unfair risk on the general unsecured creditors and will not be permitted.... None of the debtors in these cases, except perhaps the Hunters, have articulated any reason for paying their student loan debts before their other unsecured debts.[14]

III. CONCLUSION

Section 1322(b)(1) is a creditor protection device.... It was not intended as a means for debtors to focus solely upon their interests and does not justify unfair discriminatory treatment.... The court is aware that there are substantial protections available to student loan debtors outside the bankruptcy process.... The filing of a Chapter 13 case should be a last resort, and indeed provides little relief when the debtor's primary problem is a nondischargeable student loan....

To ensure equity of distribution the court provides the guidelines contained in this opinion. Of course, the determination of whether a particular plan discriminates unfairly is to be made on a case by case basis, and the court invites debtors with unique circumstances to seek a hearing. This judge will not confirm Chapter 13 plans that provide for the payment of interest to student loan creditors, but not to other unsecured creditors; that accelerate the repayment of student loans at the expense of general unsecured creditors; that provide for repayment of 100% of student loan claims when other unsecured claims are not paid at least 70%; or that provide for the repayment of student loans before other unsecured claims are paid. This judge will permit arrearages on student loans to be paid in full, even though other unsecured claims will not be paid in full, if the student loan is treated as a long term debt pursuant to section 1325(b)(5). Finally, the court encourages debtors to seek discharge of their student loans under section 523(a)(8) in appropriate circumstances....

Problem 10–12:   Should Separate Classification of the Debt Due the Family Doctor Be Approved?

Debtor has $25,000 in unsecured nonpriority debt, which includes $2,500 owed to the family doctor. Debtor wants to pay the long-time family doctor in full, because she is concerned that, if she does not, the doctor might not continue to provide the same excellent care, which has included after-hours house calls, in the future. If debtor is allowed to classify the doctor's claim separately and pay it 100%, debtor can afford to pay other creditors only 10% of their claims during the three-year Chapter 13 plan debtor will propose. If the classification is not allowed, the unsecured creditors will received payment of 20% of their claims.

(a) Should the court approve the separate classification?

14. For example, this court routinely permits debtors to preferentially repay traffic court tickets and costs to enable the debtors to reestablish their driver's licenses. The court believes that this treatment furthers the purposes of Chapter 13 by permitting debtors to drive to and from work in order to support themselves and make payments called for by their plans.

(b) If the answer is no, would the answer differ if debtor's child has a serious medical problem and needs continuing care from the doctor?

(c) If the answer is no, should the classification be permitted if debtor proposes to extend the duration of the plan by one year and to pay the doctor 100% and the other unsecured nonpriority creditors 20%?

Problem 10–13: Should the Court Allow the Debtor to Cure a Default on the Long-Term Car Loan and Pay the Auto Lender in Full, Even Though the Auto Lender Is Undersecured?

Debtor obtained a car loan more than 910 days before bankruptcy. She is $4,000 in arrears on the obligation. The auto lender is undersecured. Debtor owes $20,000 to the auto lender, but the car is worth only $15,000. Debtor proposes a three-year plan that will allow the debtor to cure the $4,000 arrearage during the first year of the plan and pay the auto lender the remaining balance according to the contract terms. The remaining unsecured creditors will receive 25% payment on their claims. The Chapter 13 trustee objects on the basis that the plan unfairly discriminates in favor of the auto lender. Debtor responds by arguing that his budget is tight and he wants to get current on his auto loan in case he is unable to complete his plan. He must have a car to retain his job. Should the court approve the separate classification?

Problem 10–14: Should the Court Approve Separate Classification of Criminal Restitution or Traffic Fines?

A year before filing Chapter 13, debtor was convicted of criminal manslaughter because he ran over and killed a pedestrian while driving under the influence of alcohol. The incident prompted debtor to come to terms with his alcoholism. He has joined Alcoholics Anonymous and has been sober for one year. Part of his criminal sentence was the requirement that he pay $75,000 in restitution for the benefit of the victim's family. If he fails to pay the restitution, his probation can be terminated and he may have to report to prison. Debtor owes $50,000 in other unsecured debt. Debtor proposes a five-year Chapter 13 plan that will pay his restitution in full and nothing to his other unsecured creditors. One of the unsecured creditors objects to the proposed classification and disparate treatment, arguing that the creditors should not bear the burden of debtor's criminal sentence. Debtor responds by arguing that, unless the separate classification and treatment is permitted, he will go to prison and none of his creditors will receive anything. Should the court approve the separate classification?

G. USE OF CHAPTER 13 TO DEAL WITH A DEMANDING TAX COLLECTOR

As we learned in Unit 9, certain debts are excepted from discharge in an individual Chapter 7 case. The most common tax debts excepted from the individual debtor's Chapter 7 discharge are certain income tax liabilities. § 523(a)(1).

Chapter 13 takes a different approach than Chapter 7. Rather than except the pertinent tax obligation from discharge, as required by the following three Bankruptcy Code sections, Chapter 13 requires the debtor to pay these common tax debts, which are priority debts, in full.

Section 1322(a)(2) provides:

The plan shall– . . .

> (2) provide for the full payment, in deferred cash payments, of all claims entitled to priority under section 507 of this title, unless the holder of a particular claim agrees to a different treatment of such claim; . . . .

Section 507(a) provides:

> The following expenses and claims have priority in the following order: . . . .

>> (8) Eighth, allowed unsecured claims of governmental units, only to the extent that such claims are for–

>>> (A) a tax on or measured by income or gross receipts—

>>>> (i) for a taxable year ending on or before the date of the filing of the petition for which a return, if required, is last due, including extensions, after three years before the date of the filing of the petition;

>>>> (ii) assessed within 240 days, plus any time plus 30 days during which an offer in compromise with respect to such tax that was made within 240 days after such assessment was pending, before the date of the filing of the petition; or

>>>> (iii) other than a tax of a kind specified in section 523(a)(1)(B) or 523(a)(1)(C) of this title, not assessed before, but assessable, under applicable law or by agreement, after, the commencement of the case;
>>>> . . .

>>> (D) an employment tax on a wage, salary, or commission of a kind specified in paragraph (3) of this subsection earned from the debtor before the date of the filing of the petition, whether or not actually paid before such date, for which a return is last due, under applicable law

or under any extension, after three years before the date of the filing of the petition; . . .

The income tax debts are not excepted from discharge.[15] *Consequently, they are discharged in a Chapter 13 case even though they are not discharged in other types of bankruptcy cases.*

As illustrated by the following problem, Chapter 13 can often be used by an individual debtor to deal effectively with unpaid tax debts.

Problem 10–15:   How Much Will a Chapter 13 Debtor Have to Pay the Tax Collector and Over How Long a Period Can the Debtor Stretch Out the Payments?

Before bankruptcy, debtor, as a sole-proprietor, operated a store selling low-carbohydrate foods. After a couple of good years, the business started losing money rapidly when regular grocery stores started offering low-carbohydrate foods in every department. Debtor had spent the money earned during the good years rather than saving it, because debtor thought the good times would continue. Debtor owes the Internal Revenue Service $12,000 for two-year-old income taxes. The IRS has told debtor that any payment plan it will work out informally must be completed within one year and she must pay interest at 8% per annum. Debtor is now working as a clerk in a retail store and she can afford to pay the IRS only $250 per month after paying her family living expenses. If debtor files Chapter 13, how much will she have to pay the IRS? Will she have to pay interest on the IRS debt? How long will debtor have to complete her payments to the IRS? [Hint regarding whether interest is required. Compare the language of § 1322(a)(2) above with § 1325(a)(5)(B)(ii) discussed in the *Till* case at page 261 above which provides:

   (5) with respect to each allowed secured claim provided for by the plan—

      (B) . . . (ii) [the plan provides that] the value, as of the effective date of the plan, of property to be distributed under the plan on account of such claim is not less than the allowed amount of such claim[.]]

H. USE OF CHAPTER 13 BY DEBTORS WHO OPERATE A BUSINESS

Chapter 13 can be used by self-employed debtors. Often the source of the financial distress for such individuals is business debts. Chapter 13 provides a relatively prompt and inexpensive way to deal with business

---

15. The statute that applies to the discharge granted to a Chapter 13 debtor who completes her plan, § 1328(a), is quoted in footnote 1 on page 235. The income tax debts are included in § 523(a)(1)(A) which is not included in the exceptions to the Chapter 13 discharge if the debtor completes her plan.

debts. Let's look at how filing Chapter 13 affects the ability of the debtor to operate her business and how some of the common types of business debts are dealt with by Chapter 13 debtors.

Section 1304 contains special provisions applicable to only Chapter 13 debtors who are engaged in business. It provides, in part:

(a) A debtor that is self-employed and incurs trade credit in the production of income from such employment is engaged in business.

(b) Unless the court orders otherwise, a debtor engaged in business may operate the business of the debtor and, subject to any limitations on a trustee under sections 363(c) and 364 of this title and to such limitations or conditions as the court prescribes, shall have, exclusive of the trustee, the rights and powers of the trustee under such sections.

The business Chapter 13 debtor may use property of the estate other than cash collateral in the ordinary course of business. § 363(c). The debtor may incur ordinary unsecured debt postpetition in the ordinary course of business. § 364(a). These Bankruptcy Code sections allow many business debtors who file Chapter 13 to continue operating their businesses with no disruption and with no court or Chapter 13 trustee permission or orders. Note that the ability to continue operating is limited; the debtor cannot engage in transactions outside the ordinary course of business and cannot incur postpetition debt that is either secured or outside the ordinary course of business, without complying with the applicable subsection of § 363 or § 364.

In analyzing whether an individual business debtor with financial problems can effectively use Chapter 13, the first step is to figure out whether the debtor's business produces enough income after payment of all current business expenses to pay the debtor's living expenses and Chapter 13 plan payments. To aid in this analysis, the business Chapter 13 debtor must complete and file a Schedule D–2, which sets forth the projected business gross receipts and expenses. On the following page is an example of a Schedule D–2 from an actual case.

```
                    UNITED STATES BANKRUPTCY COURT
                         DISTRICT OF OREGON

In re                    )                              CLERK U.S. BANKRUPTCY COURT
                         ) Case No.  302-36662-elp13         DISTRICT OF OREGON
SINDELAR, Sally Loujean, )         EX. D-2
                         ) FINANCIAL REVIEW OF DEBTOR'S    JUL 2 6 2002
                         )    NONFARMING BUSINESS
                         ) [File With the Statement of Affairs in Chapter 12
                         ) and 13 Cases If Debtor Earns Any Income
                         ) From Operation of a NONFARMING Sole
                         ) Proprietorship Business or Debtor or an Insider
Debtor(s)                ) Owns 20% or More of a NONFARMING Corporation]
```

(NOTE: ONLY INCLUDE information directly related to the NONfarming business operation. This information is to be from the corporate books where necessary. If an item of Income or Expense does not apply indicate with "N/A.")

ATTACH COPY OF SCHEDULE C FROM PRIOR YEAR'S TAX RETURN (OR EXPLAIN ABSENCE).

INDICATE ACCOUNTING METHOD USED: XX Cash Basis ____Accrual Basis
BUSINESS NAME, ADDRESS AND PHONE NUMBER: Sindelar Foster Care, PO Box 17478, Portland, OR 97217

NATURE AND STARTING DATE OF BUSINESS AND PERCENTAGE OF OWNERSHIP: Adult Foster Care - 1986 - 100%

PROJECTED ANNUAL BUSINESS INCOME:
1. Gross Sales or Receipts $ 807,147.00
2. Returns and Allowances   (   )
3. Less Cost of Goods Sold   (   )
4. Other Income
5. Gross Income $ 807,147.00

PROJECTED ANNUAL BUSINESS EXPENSES (DO NOT Include Payments Paid Through Plan):
6. Advertising
7. Car and Truck Expenses   2,100.00
8. Commissions and Fees
9. Secured Debt Including Interest (attach list)
10. Employee Benefits (other than on line 14) HEALTH INS.   48,000.00
11. Insurance (other than health)   1,020.00
12. Legal and Professional Services   12,000.00
13. Office Expenses   2,208.00
14. Pension/Profit-Sharing Plans
15. Rent or Leases
    a. Vehicles, Machinery, Equipment (attach list)
    b. Other Business Property (attach list) 3 HOMES   48,192.00
16. Repairs and Maintenance   14,200.00
17. Supplies (if not included in line 3) INCLUDES FOOD 30,780.00
18. Taxes and Licenses
    a. Payroll Taxes   142,116.00
    b. Income/Self-Employment Tax   15,996.00
    c. Other Taxes/Licenses   1,200.00
19. Travel   300.00
20. Meals and Entertainment
21. Utilities   20,348.00
22. Wages   408,000.00
23. Other expenses (list separately):

24. Total Expenses $ 746,460.00
PROJECTED ANNUAL NET INCOME (line 5 less line 24) $ 60,687.00
ESTIMATED AVERAGE NET MONTHLY INCOME $ 5,057.25
(Attach explanation if not same as amount listed on Schedule I for the question "Regular income from operation of business ...")
Exhibit D-2 (8/1/99)

The debtor's living expenses are calculated on Schedule J, an example of which was included on page 243.

Business debt will fall into three primary categories. The first category is secured debt and lease obligations. We already learned on pages 258–273 what can be done with respect to secured debt and on pages 274–275 what the plan can and must provide with respect to leases. The second category is unsecured debt. We know from pages 256–257 that the debtor must pay unsecured creditors not less than they would receive in a

Chapter 7 case. In addition, unless the debtor is paying unsecured creditors in full, the plan must provide that all the debtor's projected disposable income for 36 months or 60 months, depending upon whether the debtor's income is below the median income, be paid to the unsecured creditors if the Chapter 13 trustee or an unsecured creditor objects. Sometimes the debtor will chose to pay unsecured creditors more than the minimum required. The third primary category of business debt is tax debt.

If the debtor's business is not generating sufficient net income to pay the debtor's living expenses and required plan payments, the debtor will have to do one or more of the following (a) make changes to the business operations that increase the receipts and income, (b) cut the business expenses, and/or (c) reduce the debtor's living expenses. All that can be done through the Chapter 13 plan is financial restructuring. All the financial restructuring in the world will not do the debtor any good if the business is not any good. Put another way, some businesses do not make money even if you take away all the debt. A debtor who owns such a business cannot use Chapter 13 to save the business unless she can make changes in the business that make the business sufficiently profitable to allow it to pay its restructured debt and the debtor's living expenses.

Thus, Chapter 13 will not provide effective relief to all eligible Chapter 13 business debtors with financial problems. It is part of the attorney's role as counselor to help the business debtor figure out whether Chapter 13 will help.

Problem 10–16:   Chapter 13 Business Debtor

Sally Smith operates two foster homes that care for elderly disabled people. At the time of bankruptcy, she has three employees who work in the foster homes. When she filed her case she had $225,000 in secured claims, consisting of a $120,000 mortgage on one of the foster homes, a $100,000 mortgage on the other foster home and a $5,000 debt secured by equipment worth $8,000 that is used in the two homes. The equipment has a remaining useful life of 5 years. Sally has $15,000 in mortgage arrearages and $102,000 in unsecured debt. Sally has lost money each of the last two years operating the foster homes. She has developed a business plan to turn her finances around by converting one of the homes to a day care facility for people with Alzheimer's. Although the new day care operation will need $3,000 worth of furniture and equipment, Sally expects that can raise the $3,000 by selling furniture from the foster care home she is going to close. Because it will take some time to build the day care business, she projects that for the first year she can pay $600 per month in plan payments, thereafter she can pay $1,000 per month. Can Sally keep operating her foster care business after filing? Will filing Chapter 13 prevent Sally from selling the furniture? From buying new furniture and equipment? From opening the new day care business? Can Sally pay lower monthly payments at the beginning of her plan? If Sally tells her lawyer that she needs to skip her plan payment each January because she has extraordinary expenses that month for licensing fees, what would the lawyer advise Sally?

I. WHAT DOES THE REQUIREMENT THAT THE CASE BE FILED IN GOOD FAITH AND THE PLAN BE PROPOSED IN "GOOD FAITH" MEAN?

Section 1325(a) requires that the debtor both file the petition in good faith and propose the plan in good faith. The term "good faith" is vague. Courts have not developed a consistent approach, let alone one that produces predictable outcomes, as to how to determine good faith. Because of the vagueness and breath of "good faith," creditors frequently assert that the debtor does not satisfy the "good faith" requirements.

Some courts use a general standard, such as good faith which is determined by the "totality of the circumstances" or requires "honesty of intention." Other courts either supplement the general standard with, or, rely instead on, a list of factors. One frequently cited list of the factors is:

1. The amount of the proposed payments and the amount of the debtor's surplus;

2. The debtor's employment history, ability to earn and likelihood of future increases in income;

3. The probable or expected duration of the plan;

4. The accuracy of the plan's statements of debts, expenses and percentage repayment of unsecured debt and whether any inaccuracies are an attempt to mislead the court;

5. The extent of preferential treatment between classes of creditors;

6. The extent to which secured claims are modified;

7. The type of debt sought to be discharged and whether any such debt is nondischargeable in Chapter 7;

8. The existence of special circumstances such as inordinate medical expenses;

9. The frequency with which the debtor has sought relief under the Bankruptcy Reform Act;

10. The motivation and sincerity of the debtor in seeking Chapter 13 relief; and

11. The burden which the plan's administration would place upon the trustee.

In re Estus, 695 F.2d 311, 317 (8th Cir. 1982).

Problem 10–17: Do the Following Chapter 13 Cases Meet the Good Faith Requirements?

1. Above-median income debtor has filed chapter 13. Her actual expenses are $500 per month less than her reasonably necessary expenses calculated using the applicable portions of the means test. Debtor's Chapter 13 plan only proposes to pay unsecured creditors $200 per month, which will only pay 30% of their claims. The Chapter 13 trustee objects to confirmation on the basis that the plan is not proposed in good faith because the debtor could afford to pay unsecured creditors $500 per month. How should the court rule? Why?

2. This is debtor's third Chapter 13 case in eighteen months. Her first case was dismissed after she failed to appear at her § 341(a) meeting of creditors because her car broke down. Her second case was dismissed because she fell behind in her plan payments because she was temporarily unemployed. Debtor proposes a plan that is similar to the plan in her second case. Has debtor proposed the plan in good faith? Is your answer any different if each of the three cases was filed on the eve of the foreclosure on debtor's home mortgage?

3. The recent dissolution of Debtor's marriage resulted in Debtor being ordered to pay his ex-spouse $50,000 to equalize the division of property. Debtor's lawyer explains to debtor that debts arising from property division in a dissolution are not dischargeable in a Chapter 7 case, but they are dischargeable in a Chapter 13 case. Debtor does not want to pay the $50,000 because he is mad at his ex-spouse and he considered the award unfair. Debtor files Chapter 13 and proposes a 60–month plan. The plan payments are only enough to pay for debtor's car, priority taxes, mortgage arrears and his legal fees. Debtor's ex-spouse objects on the basis that the debtor has neither filed the case in good faith nor proposed the plan in good faith. Will the ex-spouse prevail? Would the outcome be any different if Debtor agreed to the terms of the dissolution decree rather than having the $50,000 obligation created by a judge's decision?

J. WHAT OTHER REQUIREMENTS MUST THE DEBTOR SATISFY TO CONFIRM A PLAN?

Section 1308 requires that the debtor file all tax returns due for the four years preceding the bankruptcy. The court cannot confirm the debtor's plan unless the debtor has filed the required tax returns. § 1325(a)(9). This is a helpful requirement because without the tax returns it is difficult to determine the amount of debtor's priority tax debt which must be paid before the plan can be completed.

In addition, a debtor who has an obligation to pay a domestic support obligation must have paid all support due postpetition before the court can confirm the debtor's plan. § 1325(a)(8). This prevents debtors from paying their Chapter 13 plan payments while falling behind in their support obligations.

K. HOW DO CHAPTER 13 CASES END?

The objective of most debtors who file Chapter 13 is to obtain a discharge from the unsecured debts that the debtor did not pay through the plan. Before a Chapter 13 debtor can receive a discharge, the debtor must satisfy three requirements. First, the debtor must perform the plan or satisfy the requirements for a hardship discharge discussed below. Second, the debtor must complete a personal financial management course. § 1328(g). Third, if the debtor is required to pay a domestic support obligation, the debtor must certify that the debtor has paid in full the domestic support obligations due postpetition and the full amount of the prepetition domestic support obligations due under the Chapter 13 plan. § 1328(a).

The debtor will not receive a discharge if the debtor received a discharge in a Chapter 7, 11 or 12 case filed within four years preceding the filing of the Chapter 13, or in a earlier Chapter 13 case filed within two years preceding the filing of the current case. § 1328(f).

If the debtor satisfies the prerequisites and has not received a discharge in an earlier bankruptcy within the pertinent period, the Chapter 13 debtor can receive a discharge of any debts not paid through the plan, except those that are nondischargeable under § 1328, in one of two ways. First, a Chapter 13 debtor can complete payments under his plan and be granted a discharge under § 1328(a). Second, if the debtor is unable to complete her plan payments for reasons beyond her control, but has paid creditors at least what they would receive in a Chapter 7 case, the debtor may be granted a "hardship" discharge under § 1328(b).

Approximately two-thirds of Chapter 13 debtors never receive a discharge. Their cases are either dismissed or converted, usually to Chapter 7.

Many of the debtors who fail to complete their plans do so because of unanticipated adverse financial circumstances such as loss of a job, reduction in employment income, or unexpected medical or other expenses. For some debtors, the failure to complete the plan is the result of happier circumstances, such as an increase in income that allows them to pay creditors in full without a Chapter 13 case, or bringing their house, car, or other secured debt payments current, thereby eliminating the financial problem that brought them to Chapter 13 in the first instance.

L. CHAPTER 13 v. CHAPTER 7 (WHAT DIFFERENCE WILL IT MAKE IF A DEBTOR USES CHAPTER 13 RATHER THAN CHAPTER 7?)

Some debtors use Chapter 13 because they want to repay their creditors. In such cases, the creditors often receive far more than if the debtor had filed Chapter 7. Sometimes the Chapter 13 debtor is able to repay her creditors in full. The Chapter 13 debtor, particularly one who repays a substantial portion of her debt, often feels good about the repayment and may feel that there is less stigma in using Chapter 13 than in using Chapter 7.

Notwithstanding the potentially disparate treatment of creditors under the two chapters, the law does not require credit reporting agencies to distinguish between Chapter 7 and Chapter 13 on the debtor's credit reports. Both types of cases remain on the debtor's credit record for 10 years from the time the case is filed.

Chapter Choice.

The following hypothetical illustrates why a debtor might be better served by filing a Chapter 13 case than a Chapter 7 case, and reviews the difference in outcome between the two chapters.

Joe has had a job for the last two months working in a warehouse earning $17.31 per hour ($36,000 per year). Prior to that time he earned about $28 per hour ($57,600 per year) as a unionized truck driver. He lost his job as a truck driver and could not find a comparable job. He is divorced and lives by himself. Joe came to see you last week about filing bankruptcy and describes his situation as follows:

Joe's Earnings During Preceding Six Calendar Months

October	$3,000
September	$3,000
August	$4,800
July	$4,800
June	$4,800
May	$4,800
Total	$25,200 ($4,200 per month average)

Median Family Income in Oregon, where Joe lives, is $42,495 per year for a one earner household like Joe's.

Joe's Monthly Expenses (and the relevant IRS expense standards) are as follows:

Expense	Actual Amount	IRS Allowance
Home Mortgage	$1,100	$862 (county where Joe resides)
Other housing expenses—Utilities & Phone ($150), real estate taxes ($100), home maintenance ($50)	$350	$409
Food, clothing and personal expenses including recreation	$300	$517
Vehicle Payment (current interest rate 15%)	$416	$489
Vehicle Operating Expenses	$200	$211
Unreimbursed health expenses	$60	$60
Income and payroll taxes	$500	$500
Total	$2,810	$3,048

Joe's assets and liabilities are as follows:

Assets:

	Value
House	$ 100,000.00
Ford Pickup—debt incurred 3 years ago	$ 9,000.00
Household Goods	$ 2,000.00
Clothes & Personal Items	$ 1,000.00
401(k) Account	$ 10,000.00
Cash and Bank Accounts	$ 175.00

Liabilities:

	Amount
Bank (1st Lien on House) (Includes $3,600 Arrearage)	$ 70,000.00
Bank (Secured by Truck)	$ 12,000.00
IRS (Income Taxes from year before chapter 13 filed; timely return was filed)	$ 2,700.00
IRS (income taxes from 4 years ago for which a timely return was filed)	$ 5,000
Credit Card Debt (Unsecured)	$ 25,000.00
Former Spouse (Child Support–Unsecured)	$ 4,000.00
Former Spouse (Property Division–Unsecured)	$ 19,000.00

Exemptions

Joe has the following exemptions available:

Home Equity	$15,000
Vehicle	$3,000
Household Goods	$3,000
Clothes and Personal Items	$1,750
Retirement benefits, including 401(k)	unlimited

Problem 10–18:   If Joe Files Chapter 13, How Much Will He Have to Pay His Creditors?

1.   Calculate how much Joe can afford to pay in plan payments. In calculating the amount you should assume that Joe will pay his $1,100 current monthly mortgage payment directly to the mortgage company and will pay his other debt obligations, including the $3,600 arrearage on his mortgage, as part of his plan payment.

2.   What is the minimum amount that Joe will have to pay his unsecured creditors? To answer this question calculate both:

A.   Joe's disposable income. Query, will this amount potentially be affected by the date on which Joe files bankruptcy? If your answer is yes, what will you advise Joe to do?

B.   The amount Joe must pay unsecured creditors to satisfy the best interests test.

3.   What is the total amount of the priority claims that Joe has to pay through his plan? How much will his plan have to provide for priority claims?

4.   Joe wants to keep his house and his truck.

A.   Truck. How much total principal and at what rate of interest will he have to pay Bank to keep his truck? You can assume that prime rate is 9% and that the rate charged to borrowers with a credit history like Joe's is 22%.

B.   Over what period of time will Joe have to pay back the arrearage on his home mortgage?

Problem 10–19: What Benefits Did Joe Get From Filing Chapter 13 Rather Than Chapter 7?

1.   With respect to his house.

2.   With respect to his truck.

3. With respect to his past-due income tax obligation and his past-due child support obligation.

4. With respect to his obligation to his former spouse for property division.

———————

UNIT 11

LEGAL ISSUES TO WATCH FOR
IN CHAPTER 11 CASES

■ ■ ■

In the previous two units of the book the focus was on the fresh start for and rehabilitation of individuals. While we don't completely abandon individuals in this unit, we now shift our focus to the intersection of bankruptcy and business.

More specifically, our focus will be on operating businesses. Businesses like Chrysler that make and sell stuff; businesses like Circuit City that sell stuff that others make; businesses like Delta Airlines that sell services.[1]

Let's start with the basic, obvious, yet important notion that some operating businesses have more economic value if kept together rather than taken apart. Not only are there instances in which the sum of the business parts is "worth more" than the business parts individually, there is also a human component in keeping an operating business together, in the form of jobs for individuals and communities.

As we have seen in Unit 2, creditors have the ability to dismantle their business debtors through state court collection procedures. And, recall from Unit 9, that Chapter 7 similarly dismantles business debtors through the trustee's liquidation of property of the estate.

---

1. We know that Chrysler, Circuit City and Delta are (or were) really big businesses.–business that in the heated jargon of today would be identified with "Wall Street", rather than "Main Street." And, we know that most people working through this Unit will later work primarily with "Main Street" business clients.

Most Chapter 11 cases involve "Main Street" businesses. While most Chapter 11 "Main Street" business cases do not involve most of the complicated legal issues considered in this Unit, the lawyers involved in these Main Street cases need to know Chapter 11. But cf. Douglas G. Baird & Robert K. Rasmussen, *The End of Bankruptcy*, 55 Stan.L.Rev. 751 (2002)("The typical case is the electrical subcontractor who uses the bankruptcy forum to cut a deal with the IRS while keeping other creditors at bay. Marginally competent owner-managers, bureaucratically inept tax collectors, small-time landlords and suppliers, and unsophisticated workers and tort victims populate this world. The business is run out of small office with little in the way of hard assets and few long-term employees. To the extent we understand the law of corporate reorganization as providing a collective forum in which creditors and their common debtor fashion a future for a firm that would otherwise be tort apart by financial distress, we may safely conclude that its era has come to an end.")

So what is to be done with a business that is worth more together than apart? Can the additional, going concern value be preserved? Yes. The Code preserves a business's going concern value in Chapter 11 which is entitled "Reorganization." As stated by the Supreme Court in *United States v. Whiting Pools, Inc.*, 462 U.S. 198, 203 (1983), "[b]y permitting reorganization, Congress anticipated that the business would continue to provide jobs, to satisfy creditors' claims, and to produce a return for its owners.... Congress presumed that the assets of the debtor would be more valuable if used in a rehabilitated business than if 'sold for scrap.' "[2]

But how do businesses "reorganize" in bankruptcy? As written, the statutory goal of Chapter 11 is court approval ("confirmation") of a plan of debt restructuring and repayment. To facilitate confirmation, the Code allows a Chapter 11 plan to do things that cannot be done under state law or under Chapter 7.

Under state law, non-assenting creditors are not in any way bound to a plan of debt restructuring and repayment. If D has 26 creditors and all of the creditors except N agree to a plan of restructuring, N is not bound by its provisions. N can still act unilaterally to collect its claim. And N's unilateral collection actions often prevent D from making the distributions to the other 25 creditors as provided in the plan of restructuring,

While all creditors are bound by the distribution scheme in Chapter 7, so is the debtor. The Chapter 7 debtor is not able to dictate the amount and form of distribution to specific creditors. The provisions of Chapter 7, and not the debtor, determine who gets what. Recall section 726(a) and (b).

In Chapter 11, unlike Chapter 7, the provisions of the plan, not the provisions of the Bankruptcy Code, determine who gets what. And, in Chapter 11, unlike state law, the provisions of the plan will be binding on nonassenting creditors if the plan is approved by the requisite majorities of creditors and the bankruptcy court. *Cf.* section 1141(a)("provisions of a confirmed plan bind ... any creditor ... whether or not ... such creditor ... has accepted the plan.")

While confirmation of a Chapter 11 debt restructuring and repayment plan is the statutory goal for a Chapter 11 case, most Chapter 11 cases do not end in confirmation of such a plan. Empirical studies report that less than 1/3 of the bankruptcy cases that begin with the filing of a Chapter 11 petition end with the confirmation of a Chapter 11 plan of debt restructuring and repayment.

---

2. A corporate reorganization is a combination of a municipal election, an historical pageant, an anti-vice crusade, a graduate school seminar, a judicial proceeding, and a series of horse trades, all rolled into one—thoroughly buttered with learning and frosted with distinguished names. Here the union of law and economics is celebrated by one of the wildest ideological orgies in intellectual history. Men work all night preparing endless documents in answer to other endless documents, which other men read in order to make solemn arguments.

THURMAN W. ARNOLD, THE FOLKLORE OF CAPITALISM 230 (1937).

Questions

1. Is the liquidation value of a business ever greater than the going concern value of that business?

2. Who cares whether the going concern value of a business is greater than its liquidation value? Are there ever creditors who don't care whether the going concern value of one of their business debtors is greater than its liquidation value?

3. Is a Chapter 11 case a "success" if it ends in a confirmed plan of debt restructuring and repayment?

For now, let's think about how Chapter 11 cases begin, rather than how Chapter 11 cases end. It is important to understand that work on a Chapter 11 case begins before a Chapter 11 petition is filed.

Generally, an operating business considers filing for Chapter 11 relief because the income that the business generates from its operations is not sufficient to pay its debts as they come due. This insufficient cash flow may be due to operational problems,[3] marketing problems,[4] and/or financial problems.[5] The business needs a plan, a business plan, for solving these problems and the time, funding, and creditor support necessary to implement that business plan. Businesses start addressing these needs even before filing for bankruptcy—especially the need for additional short term funding to enable the business to continue operating while it implements this business plan.[6]

Increasingly, businesses also address the need for creditor support before filing for bankruptcy. You read more and more about "pre-arranged", "pre-negotiated" and "pre-packaged" bankruptcy cases. For example,

> Chelsea Emery, Reader's Digest Plans To File For Bankruptcy, August 19, 2009, Reuters, 2009 WLNR 16170098
>
> Reader's Digest Association Inc., whose namesake magazine has been a staple of dentists' offices for generations, said Monday it planned to

---

3. E.g., moving manufacturing facilities overseas to cut costs and the kayaks manufactured in the new Kazakhstan plant leak.

4. E.g., trying to sell road maps and former customers are now using GPS navigational systems

5. E.g., buying a business and, unduly optimistic about the business's future, borrowing too much and promising to repay too soon.

6. Remember that

— this is a business whose operations pre-bankruptcy are not generating sufficient income to pay its existing debts as they come due;

— a business's filing for bankruptcy typically reduces income from business operations as some businesses and individuals are reluctant to buy from or otherwise deal with a company that filed for bankruptcy;

— section 362 only prevents creditors from collecting existing debts; the automatic stay does not require creditors to continue extending credit.

file for Chapter 11 bankruptcy for its US businesses as part of a pre-arranged plan with lenders to cut debt by 75 percent . . . . .

The bankruptcy would take the form of a prearranged filing, which comes after a company has already reached deals with lenders to reduce debt. The deal, if approved by a bankruptcy court, would allow Reader's Digest to slash its debt load to $550 million, from the current $2.2 billion.

The arrangement would also allow the company to reduce its annual interest payments on remaining debt to less than $80 million from about $145 million, said president and chief executive officer Mary Berner in an interview.

"Our deal has already been negotiated and hammered out with a majority of our creditors," said Berner. The arrangement "doesn't affect our employees, it doesn't affect the vast majority of vendors, it doesn't mean we'll do mass layoffs, it doesn't mean we're going to be selling off assets. It's business as usual." . . .

The company expects to file its petition in bankruptcy court within 15 days, said chief financial officer Thomas Williams, and the firm hopes to conclude the restructuring process within 45 to 90 days, said Berner. . . .

Under the plan, the company will work with lenders to swap a portion of its $1.6 billion in senior secured debt for equity, and transfer company ownership to the lender group.

The agreement, which is subject to court approval, also includes a commitment from some members of the senior lender group to provide $150 million in debtor-in-possession financing, which would help fund operations during the reorganization phase.

JPMorgan Chase will lead the team DIP lenders, said Williams. Other lenders include GE Capital and Eaton Vance, among others.

Holders of about 60 percent of the dollar value of the bank debt support the proposed restructuring plan, according to a source familiar with the negotiations, who declined to be named since they were not cleared to speak on the matter.

Later in this Unit, there will be more to read about the legal issues raised by "pre-packaged" Chapter 11 plans, i.e., Chapter 11 plans negotiated with creditors before the Chapter 11 petition is filed.

For now, think about the legal documents that must be reviewed and prepared in every Chapter 11 case, Remember the bankruptcy petition is to be accompanied by schedules listing the debtor's assets, contracts, creditors, leases. In a large case like Circuit City or Reader's Digest, it is going to take some time to prepare these schedules. And, in large cases like Circuit City and Reader's Digest, the petition and schedules are also accompanied by pleadings requesting various "first day orders."

The term "first day orders" is not used in the Bankruptcy Code but is regularly used by bankruptcy attorneys and judges. Lynn Harrison, III and James Drew, outstanding bankruptcy attorneys with the firm Curtis, Mallet–Prevost, Colt & Mosle, provide the following explanation of "first day orders:" "First day orders are orders which typically are presented to the court on or shortly after the petition date. First day orders are usually sought by debtors to address pressing issues, extend certain early deadlines set by the Bankruptcy Code, and generally minimize disruptions early in the case.

Examples of typical first day orders include those approving, among other things:

1.   Joint administration of cases;

2.   Extension of deadline to file schedules and statement of financial affairs;

3.   Preparation of consolidated matrix of creditors and security holders;

4.   Extension of deadline to provide utilities with adequate assurance, and setting utility procedures;

5.   Payment of employee claims, and approving continuation of employee programs (such as pensions, worker's compensation benefits, year-end bonuses, 401(k), etc.);

6.   Continuation of debtor's cash management system;

7.   Waiver of investment and deposit guidelines set forth in section 345 of the Bankruptcy Code;

8.   Establishment of reclamation claim procedures;

9.   Retention of professionals;

0.   Establishment of procedures for monthly compensation and reimbursement of professionals;

11.   Assumption or rejection of executory contracts and unexpired leases, or to extend time to decide whether to assume or reject;

12.   Use of cash collateral or debtor-in-possession financing; and

13.   Payment of certain pre-petition claims, such as those of employees, tax authorities, or particularly important vendors, among others." Lynn P. Harrison & James V. Drew, *First Day Orders: A Survey of Critical Vendor Motions and Recent Developments*, 915 PLI/Comm 335 (2009).

A. BEGINNING A CHAPTER 11 CASE FOR AN OPERATING BUSINESS

1. PAYING CRITICAL VENDORS

IN RE KMART CORP.

359 F.3d 866 (7th Cir. 2004)

EASTERBROOK, Circuit Judge.

On the first day of its bankruptcy, Kmart sought permission to pay immediately, and in full, the pre-petition claims of all "critical vendors." (Technically there are 38 debtors: Kmart Corporation plus 37 of its affiliates and subsidiaries. We call them all Kmart.) The theory behind the request is that some suppliers may be unwilling to do business with a customer that is behind in payment, and, if it cannot obtain the merchandise that its own customers have come to expect, a firm such as Kmart may be unable to carry on, injuring all of its creditors. Full payment to critical vendors thus could in principle make even the disfavored creditors better off: they may not be paid in full, but they will receive a greater portion of their claims than they would if the critical vendors cut off supplies and the business shut down. Putting the proposition in this way implies, however, that the debtor must prove, and not just allege, two things: that, but for immediate full payment, vendors would cease dealing; and that the business will gain enough from continued transactions with the favored vendors to provide some residual benefit to the remaining, disfavored creditors, or at least leave them no worse off.

Bankruptcy Judge Sonderby entered a critical-vendors order just as Kmart proposed it, without notifying any disfavored creditors, without receiving any pertinent evidence (the record contains only some sketchy representations by counsel plus unhelpful testimony by Kmart's CEO, who could not speak for the vendors), and without making any finding of fact that the disfavored creditors would gain or come out even. The bankruptcy court's order declared that the relief Kmart requested—open-ended permission to pay any debt to any vendor it deemed "critical" in the exercise of unilateral discretion, provided that the vendor agreed to furnish goods on "customary trade terms" for the next two years—was "in the best interests of the Debtors, their estates and their creditors". The order did not explain why, nor did it contain any legal analysis, though it did cite 11 U.S.C. § 105(a)....

Kmart used its authority to pay in full the pre-petition debts to 2,330 suppliers, which collectively received about $300 million. This came from the $2 billion in new credit (debtor-in-possession or DIP financing) that the bankruptcy judge authorized, granting the lenders super-priority in post-petition assets and revenues. Another 2,000 or so vendors were not deemed "critical" and were not paid. They and 43,000 additional unsecured creditors eventually received about 10¢ on the dollar, mostly in stock of the reorganized Kmart. Capital Factors, Inc., appealed the critical-vendors order immediately after its entry on January 25, 2002. A little more than 14 months later, after all of the critical vendors had been paid and as Kmart's plan of reorganization was on the verge of approval, District Judge Grady reversed the order authorizing payment. 291 B.R. 818 (N.D.Ill.2003). He concluded that neither § 105(a) nor a "doctrine of necessity" supports the orders. . . .

Section 105(a) allows a bankruptcy court to "issue any order, process, or judgment that is necessary or appropriate to carry out the provisions of" the Code. This does not create discretion to set aside the Code's rules about priority and distribution; the power conferred by § 105(a) is one to implement rather than override. . . . Every circuit that has considered the question has held that this statute does not allow a bankruptcy judge to authorize full payment of any unsecured debt, unless all unsecured creditors in the class are paid in full. . . . We agree with this view of § 105. "The fact that a [bankruptcy] proceeding is equitable does not give the judge a free-floating discretion to redistribute rights in accordance with his personal views of justice and fairness, however enlightened those views may be." . . .

A "doctrine of necessity" is just a fancy name for a power to depart from the Code. Although courts in the days before bankruptcy law was codified wielded power to reorder priorities and pay particular creditors in the name of "necessity," today it is the Code rather than the norms of nineteenth century railroad reorganizations that must prevail. Today the Bankruptcy Code of 1978 supplies the rules. Congress did not in terms scuttle old common-law doctrines, because it did not need to; the Act curtailed, and then the Code replaced, the entire apparatus. Answers to contemporary issues must be found within the Code (or legislative halls). Older doctrines may survive as glosses on ambiguous language enacted in 1978 or later, but not as freestanding entitlements to trump the text. . . .

So does the Code contain any grant of authority for debtors to prefer some vendors over others? Many sections require equal treatment or specify the details of priority when assets are insufficient to satisfy all claims. E.g., 11 U.S.C. §§ 507, 1122(a), 1123(a)(4). Appellants rely on 11 U.S.C. §§ 363(b), 364(b), and 503 as sources of authority for unequal treatment. Section 364(b) reads: "The court, after notice and a hearing, may authorize the trustee to obtain unsecured credit or to incur unsecured debt other than under subsection (a) of this section, allowable under section 503(b)(1) of this title as an administrative expense." This authorizes the debtor to obtain credit (as Kmart did) but has nothing to say about how the money will be disbursed or about priorities among creditors . . . . . Section 503, which deals with administrative expenses, likewise is irrelevant. Pre-filing debts are not administrative expenses; they are the antithesis of administrative expenses. Filing a petition for bankruptcy effectively creates two firms: the debts of the pre-filing entity may be written down so that the post-filing entity may reorganize and continue in business if it has a positive cash flow. . . . Treating pre-filing debts as "administrative" claims against the post-filing entity would impair the ability of bankruptcy law to prevent old debts from sinking a viable firm.

That leaves § 363(b)(1): "The trustee [or debtor in possession], after notice and a hearing, may use, sell, or lease, other than in the ordinary course of business, property of the estate." This is more promising, for satisfaction of a pre-petition debt in order to keep "critical" supplies flowing is a use of property other than in the ordinary course of administering an estate in bankruptcy. Capital Factors insists that § 363(b)(1) should be limited to the commencement of capital projects, such as building a new plant, rather than payment of old debts—as paying vendors would be "in the ordinary course" but for the intervening bankruptcy petition. To read § 363(b)(1) broadly, Capital Factors observes, would be to allow a judge to rearrange priorities among creditors (which is what a critical-vendors order effectively does), even though the Supreme Court has cautioned against such a step.... Yet what these decisions principally say is that priorities do not change unless a statute supports that step; and if § 363(b)(1) is such a statute, then there is no insuperable problem. If the language is too open-ended, that is a problem for the legislature. Nonetheless, it is prudent to read, and use, § 363(b)(1) to do the least damage possible to priorities established by contract and by other parts of the Bankruptcy Code. We need not decide whether § 363(b)(1) could support payment of some pre-petition debts, because this order was unsound no matter how one reads § 363(b)(1).

The foundation of a critical-vendors order is the belief that vendors not paid for prior deliveries will refuse to make new ones. Without merchandise to sell, a retailer such as Kmart will fold. If paying the critical vendors would enable a successful reorganization and make even the disfavored creditors better off, then all creditors favor payment whether or not they are designated as "critical." This suggests a use of § 363(b)(1) similar to the theory underlying a plan crammed down the throats of an impaired class of creditors: if the impaired class does at least as well as it would have under a Chapter 7 liquidation, then it has no legitimate objection and cannot block the reorganization.... For the premise to hold true, however, it is necessary to show not only that the disfavored creditors will be as well off with reorganization as with liquidation—a demonstration never attempted in this proceeding—but also that the supposedly critical vendors would have ceased deliveries if old debts were left unpaid while the litigation continued. If vendors will deliver against a promise of current payment, then a reorganization can be achieved, and all unsecured creditors will obtain its benefit, without preferring any of the unsecured creditors....

Doubtless many suppliers fear the prospect of throwing good money after bad. It therefore may be vital to assure them that a debtor will pay for new deliveries on a current basis. Providing that assurance need not, however, entail payment for pre-petition transactions. Kmart could have paid cash or its equivalent. (Kmart's CEO told the bankruptcy judge that COD arrangements were not part of Kmart's business plan, as if a litigant's druthers could override the rights of third parties.) Cash on the barrelhead was not the most convenient way, however. Kmart secured a $2 billion line of credit when it entered bankruptcy. Some of that credit could have been used to assure vendors that payment would be forthcoming for all post-petition transactions. The easiest way to do that would have been to put some of the $2 billion behind a standby letter of credit on which the bankruptcy judge could authorize unpaid vendors to draw. That would not have changed the terms on which Kmart and any of its vendors did business; it just would have demonstrated the certainty of payment. If lenders are unwilling to issue such a letter of credit (or if they insist on a letter's short duration), that would be a compelling market signal that reorganization is a poor prospect and that the debtor should be liquidated post haste.

Yet the bankruptcy court did not explore the possibility of using a letter of credit to assure vendors of payment. The court did not find that any firm would have ceased doing business with Kmart if not paid for pre-petition deliveries, and the scant record would not have supported such a finding had one been made. The court did not find that discrimination among unsecured creditors was the only way to facilitate a reorganization. It did not find that the disfavored creditors were at least as well off as they would have been had the critical-vendors order not been entered. For all the millions at stake, this proceeding looks much like the Chapter 13 reorganization that produced In re Crawford, 324 F.3d 539 (7th Cir.2003). Crawford had wanted to classify his creditors in a way that would enable him to pay off those debts that would not be discharged, while stiffing the creditors whose debts were dischargeable. We replied that even though classification (and thus unequal treatment) is possible for Chapter 13 proceedings, see 11 U.S.C. § 1322(b), the step would be proper only when the record shows that the classification would produce some benefit for the disfavored creditors. Just so here. Even if § 362(b)(1) [sic] allows critical-vendors orders in principle, preferential payments to a class of creditors are proper only if the record shows the prospect of benefit to the other creditors. This record does not, so the critical-vendors order cannot stand.

AFFIRMED.

QUESTIONS ABOUT KMART

1.   Who objected to the bankruptcy judge's entering the critical vendors order in the *Kmart* case? Who should have objected?

2.   Assume that (1) Kmart paid its employees on the second and fourth Friday of each month and (2) Kmart filed its bankruptcy petition on the second Wednesday of the month. Would Judge Easterbrook affirm a first day order authorizing payments to employees for the work they had done prepetition?

3.   Recall that in Unit 6 we learned that Congress, in 2005, added an administrative expense priority, section 503(b)(9), for vendors who delivered

goods within 20 days before the bankruptcy filing. Would Judge Easterbrook today affirm a first day order authorizing payment to vendors who had delivered goods within 20 days of filing?

4. "Since *Kmart*, it appears that critical vendor motions are still being filed and approved with some regularity (at least in Delaware and the Southern District of New York)." Lynn P. Harrison & James V. Drew, *First Day Orders: A Survey of Critical Vendor Motions and Recent Developments*, 915 PLI/Comm 335 (2009). As we will learn in Unit 12. a business debtor can file for bankruptcy relief in the state in which it is incorporated. After *Kmart*, will a business headquartered in Illinois but incorporated in Delaware file its Chapter 11 petition in Delaware instead of Illinois?

2. DECIDING WHETHER THERE WILL BE A DEBTOR IN POSSESSION OR TRUSTEE

Judge Easterbrook's *Kmart* opinion uses the terms "debtor" and "debtor in possession." So have other cases that we have read. In all likelihood, so has your law professor. What is a "debtor in possession" and how is a "debtor in possession" different from a "debtor?"

Only the filing of a Chapter 11 case creates a "debtor in possession." A debtor in possession is the debtor in a Chapter 11 case in which a trustee has not been appointed so that the debtor remains in possession of property of the estate. With possession of property of the estate, the debtor in possession is able to continue to operate the business after the Chapter 11 petition has been filed.[7]

The House Report accompanying a draft of the Bankruptcy Code provides the following justification for the Chapter 11 debtor in possession:

> [V]ery often the creditors will be benefitted by continuation of the debtor in possession, both because the expense of a trustee will not be required, and the debtor, who is familiar with his business, will be better able to operate it during the reorganization case. A trustee frequently has to take time to familiarize himself with the business before the reorganization can get under way. Thus, a debtor continued in possession may lead to a greater likelihood of success in the reorganization. Moreover, the need for reorganization of a public company today often results from simple business reverses, not from any fraud, dishonesty, or gross mismanagement on the part of the debtor's management. Even if the cause is fraud or dishonesty, very frequently the fraudulent management will have been ousted shortly before the filing of the reorganization case, and the new management, very capable of running the business, should not be ousted by a trustee because of the sins of former management.

7. Sections 1107, 1108 and 363 provide the statutory basis for the debtor in possession's operation of a business after it files for Chapter 11 relief.

... [F]acilitation of the reorganization to the benefit of the debtor and the creditors, militates against the appointment of a trustee.... Debtors' lawyers that participated in the development of a standard for the appointment of a trustee were adamant that a standard that led to too frequent appointment would prevent debtors from seeking relief under the reorganization chapter, and would leave the chapter largely unused except in extreme cases. One of the problems that the Bankruptcy Commission recognized in current bankruptcy and reorganization practice is that debtors too often wait too long to seek bankruptcy relief. Too frequent appointment of a trustee would exacerbate that problem, to the detriment of both debtors and their creditors.

H. Rep. 595, 95th Cong., 1st Sess. 232–34 (1977).

Section 1104 provides that a party in interest can request the bankruptcy court to order the appointment of a trustee in a Chapter 11 case to replace the debtor in possession. If a trustee is appointed, he or she will take possession of property of the estate and take over the management of the debtor's business operation, sections 1106, 1108. For the reasons set out in the excerpt from the 1977 House Report, requests for the appointment of a Chapter 11 trustee are unusual, if not rare.

3. APPOINTING A CREDITORS' COMMITTEE

The Bankruptcy Code contemplates that there will be a Chapter 11 creditors' committee acting on behalf of all unsecured creditors, section 1102. Bankruptcy courts' websites provide the following explanation of creditors' committees:

"Creditors' committees can play a major role in chapter 11 cases. The committee is appointed by the U.S. trustee and ordinarily consists of unsecured creditors who hold the seven largest unsecured claims against the debtor. 11 U.S.C. § 1102. Among other things, the committee: consults with the debtor in possession on administration of the case; investigates the debtor's conduct and operation of the business; and participates in formulating a plan. 11 U.S.C. § 1103. A creditors' committee may, with the court's approval, hire an attorney or other professionals to assist in the performance of the committee's duties. A creditors' committee can be an important safeguard to the proper management of the business by the debtor in possession." http://www.uscourts.gov/bankruptcycourts/bankruptcybasics/chapter11.html#committee

Problem 11–1: Serving on Creditors' Committees

1. In the *Kmart* case, did the debtor in possession consult with the creditors' committee before deciding to pay critical vendors?

2. Your client, Samsung, second largest unsecured creditor of Circuit City with a claim of more than $116,000,000, asks you to explain the advantages and disadvantages of its serving on the Circuit City creditors' committee.

3.   Your client C is a member of the creditors' committee in the Acme Corp. bankruptcy case. H, a hedge fund, offers to buy C's $1,000,000 unsecured claim for $300,000. C does not believe that unsecured claims will receive 30 cents on the dollar from Acme Corp. Advise C as to whether it can sell its claim to H.

4.   Jersey Jiffy Marts LLC, (JJM), a Chapter 11 debtor, owns and operates three convenience stores in New Jersey. JJM owes Beverage Distributor Center, Inc. (BDC), the Pepsi distributor for New Jersey, $33,000. BDC has the third largest unsecured claim in the JJM bankruptcy case. Do you think that there will be a creditors' committee in the JJM bankruptcy? An active creditors' committee?

———————

As the above questions suggest, (1) most Chapter 11 cases do not have an active creditors' committee and (2) much of the "action" in a Chapter 11 case occurs without consulting a creditors' committee. For example, Kmart's decision to pay critical vendors was made before a creditors' committee had been appointed.

4.   OBTAINING DEBTOR IN POSSESSION FINANCING

Kmart's payment of $300 million to critical vendors was made from "DIP financing," Recall from the *Kmart* opinion that the $300 million "came from the $2 billion in new credit (debtor-in-possession or DIP financing) that the bankruptcy judge authorized." Don't you think that Kmart "consulted" with its DIP lender, General Electric Capital Corporation, before filing a motion to pay $300 million of the $2 billion borrowed from General Electric Capital Corporation to critical vendors? We need to learn more about dip financing.

a.   Understanding Bankruptcy Code Provisions That Encourage Extending Credit to a Debtor in Possession

Why would a vendor sell goods on credit to a business in bankruptcy? Why would a lender make a loan to a business in bankruptcy? The short answer to these questions is "to make money."

A more complete answer to questions about why extend credit to a business in bankruptcy involves a comparison of the risks of not being paid with the compensation for that risk. An understanding of the risks of extending credit to a business in bankruptcy begins with an understanding of section 364(a) which empowers the debtor in possession to "obtain unsecured credit and incur unsecured debt in the ordinary course of business allowable under section 503(b)(1) of this title as an administrative expense" and section 364(b) which provides that the bankruptcy court, "after notice and a hearing, may authorize the trustee to obtain unsecured credit or to incur unsecured debt other than under subsection

(a) of this section, allowable under section 503(b)(1) of this title as an administrative expense.''

We considered administrative expenses in Unit 6. We know that administrative expenses have priority over all unsecured claims other than "domestic support obligations" and that business entity debtors will not owe "domestic support obligations." There are four more things that you need to know about administrative expenses in Chapter 11 before applying section 364(a): (1) Section 1129(a)(9)(A) requires that a Chapter 11 plan provide for payment of all administrative expenses in full, in cash, on confirmation of the plan; (2) most Chapter 11 cases do not end in a confirmed Chapter 11 plan; many bankruptcy cases that are filed as Chapter 11 cases are converted to Chapter 7 cases; (3) when a Chapter 11 case is converted to Chapter 7, section 726(b) requires that the administrative expenses incurred in the Chapter 7 part of the case be paid in full before the administrative expenses incurred in the Chapter 11 part of the case can be paid; and (4) section 364(c), which we will consider next, empowers the court to grant qualifying post-petition creditors a priority over administrative expenses.

Problem 11–2: Applying Section 364(a) to Vendors

Your client, C, sells dairy products on credit to D, a group of supermarkets. C bills D monthly. D files a Chapter 11 petition. Should C continue to sell dairy products to D on credit? If so, should C first obtain bankruptcy court approval?

———————

Generally, an administrative priority is sufficient incentive for vendors to continue selling goods on credit. However, generally, an administrative expense priority is not sufficient incentive for lenders to make new loans. Debtors in possession who need more financing (which are virtually all debtors in possession) need to be able to offer lenders more than an administrative expense priority.

Under section 364(c), a debtor in possession needing additional financing can offer a DIP lender (1) priority over any or all other administrative expenses, (2) a lien on property that is not subject to a lien (lien on unsecured property) and/or (3) a junior lien on property already subject to a lien. Section 364(c) is set out below:

11 U.S.C. § 364(c)

(c) If the trustee is unable to obtain unsecured credit allowable under section 503(b)(1) of this title as an administrative expense, the court, after notice and a hearing, may authorize the obtaining of credit or the incurring of debt—

> (1) with priority over any or all administrative expenses of the kind specified in section 503(b) or 507(b) of this title;

(2) secured by a lien on property of the estate that is not otherwise subject to a lien; or

(3) secured by a junior lien on property of the estate that is subject to a lien

---

Problem 11–3: Obtaining DIP Financing Under Section 364(c)

Notice that section 364(c) requires "notice and hearing." What does the court want to hear at a hearing to approve debtor in possession financing under section 364(c)?

Think about the section 364(c)(2) phrase "property of the estate not otherwise subject to a lien." How does an operating business in Chapter 11 still have "property of the estate not subject to a lien"? If you were running a business wouldn't you exhaust every credit possibility before filing for bankruptcy? Wouldn't you subject all of the business's property to liens in order to borrow as much as possible?

Understanding why operating businesses that have filed for Chapter 11 bankruptcy generally have "property of the estate not otherwise subject to a lien" requires understanding (1) proceeds and floating liens under Article 9 of the Uniform Commercial Code and (2) section 552 of the Bankruptcy Code. Under section 552(a), "property acquired ... by the debtor after the commencement of the case is not subject to any lien resulting from a security agreement entered into by the debtor before the commencement of the case." Section 552(b) carves out an exception: "[I]f the debtor and an entity entered into a security agreement before the commencement of the case and if the security interest created by such security agreement extends to property of the debtor acquired before the commencement of the case and to proceeds, product, offspring, or profits of such property, then such security interest extends to such proceeds, product, offspring, or profits acquired by the estate after the commencement of the case ... , except to any extent that the court, after notice and a hearing and based on the equities of the case, orders otherwise."

Problem 11–4: "Property of the Estate Not Otherwise Subject to a Lien"

In 2009 SP entered into a loan agreement with G & L Marble Co., a company that quarries, processes and sells natural stones and tiles. The loan agreement granted SP a security interest in "all of G & L Marble's inventory of processed granite slabs and tiles, now owned or later acquired." In 2010, G & L Marble Co. filed a Chapter 11 petition. Does G & L Marble Co have "property of the estate not otherwise subject to a lien"?

If a debtor in possession is unable to obtain needed financing under section 364(c), then the debtor in possession (and you) need to look to section 364(d) set out below.

11 U.S.C. § 364(d)

(d)(1) The court, after notice and a hearing, may authorize the obtaining of credit or the incurring of debt secured by a senior or equal lien on property of the estate that is subject to a lien only if—

    (A) the trustee is unable to obtain such credit otherwise; and

    (B) there is adequate protection of the interest of the holder of the lien on the property of the estate on which such senior or equal lien is proposed to be granted.

(2) In any hearing under this subsection, the trustee has the burden of proof on the issue of adequate protection.

———

Do you understand section 364(d)? Professor George Triantis explains section 364(d) as follows: "Under 364(d), the court may authorize later-in-time priority that is senior to a prepetition security interest in the debtor's assets. . . . In order to 'prime' prepetition security interests [and other liens] in this manner, the debtor must show not only that the firm is unable to obtain credit otherwise but also that the interest of the prepetition secured party is adequately protected. Adequate protection requires that the prepetition secured party's financial position is somehow preserved. A debtor who applies for DIP financing is unlikely to have either the liquid or unencumbered assets with which to provide adequate protection. Rather, the debtor often asserts that the secured party will realize the indubitable equivalent of its interest in the collateral because of the profitability of the proposed investment of new capital. The debtor argues that the primed creditor either will be paid periodically from the value created or will continue to enjoy a substantial equity cushion in its collateral as a result. The court's assessment of the profitability of the proposed use of new funds and continuation of the firm has been pivotal in many cases." George J. Triantis, *Financial Slack Policy and the Law of Secured Transactions*, 29 Journal of Legal Studies 35 (2000).

Do you now understand section 364(d)? Apply section 364(d) in the following problem.

Problem 11–5: Obtaining a Section 364(d) "Priming Lien"

D, a Chapter 11 debtor, owns and operates a regional chain of motels. D owes F $100,000,000, and F has a first mortgage on all of D's motels. D needs $20,000,000 to remodel and refurnish the motels,. F is unwilling to loan D the $20,000,000. S is willing to loan D the $20,000,000 if it receives a first lien on all of D's motels. D files a motion with the bankruptcy court asking the court to approve (1) S's making a $20,000,000 loan to D and (2)

D's granting S a mortgage on all of its motels that will have priority over F's existing mortgage. As either F's or S's attorney, what, if any, witnesses would you bring to the section 364(d)(hearing)?

The prior problem focuses on people who are a part of the DIP lending process, Now let's focus on the documents involved. As Problem 11–5 indicates, DIP lending involves a motion seeking bankruptcy court approval of the dip financing agreement. We need to learn more about DIP financing agreements.

B. UNDERSTANDING DIP FINANCING AGREEMENTS

SHAPIRO v. SAYBROOK MFG. CO. (IN RE SAYBROOK MFG. CO.)

963 F.2d 1490 (11th Cir. 1992)

Cox, Circuit Judge:

Seymour and Jeffrey Shapiro, unsecured creditors, objected to the bankruptcy court's authorization for the Chapter 11 debtors to "cross-collateralize" their pre-petition debt with unencumbered property from the bankruptcy estate. The bankruptcy court overruled the objection and also refused under the Bankruptcy Code to grant a stay of its order pending appeal. The Shapiros appealed to the district court which dismissed the case as moot under section 364(e) because the Shapiros had failed to obtain a stay. We conclude that this appeal is not moot and that cross collateralization is not authorized under the Bankruptcy Code. Accordingly, we reverse and remand.

I.   Facts and Procedural History

Saybrook Manufacturing Co., Inc., and related companies (the "debtors"), initiated proceedings seeking relief under Chapter 11 of the Bankruptcy Code on December 22, 1988. On December 23, 1988, the debtors filed a motion for the use of cash collateral and for authorization to incur secured debt. The bankruptcy court entered an emergency financing order that same day. At the time the bankruptcy petition was filed, the debtors owed Manufacturers Hanover approximately $34 million. The value of the collateral for this debt, however, was less than $10 million. Pursuant to the order, Manufacturers Hanover agreed to lend the debtors an additional $3 million to facilitate their reorganization. In exchange, Manufacturers Hanover received a security interest in all of the debtors' property—both property owned prior to filing the bankruptcy petition and that which was acquired subsequently. This security interest not only protected the $3 million of post-petition credit but also secured Manufacturers Hanover's $34 million pre-petition debt.

This arrangement enhanced Manufacturers Hanover's position vis-a-vis other unsecured creditors, such as the Shapiros, in the event of liquidation. Because Manufacturers Hanover's pre-petition debt was undersecured by approximately $24 million, it originally would have shared in a pro rata distribution of the debtors' unencumbered assets along with the other unsecured creditors. Under the financing order, however, Manufacturers Hanover's pre-petition debt became fully secured by all of the debtors' assets. If the bankruptcy estate were liquidated, Manufacturers Hanover's entire debt—$34 million pre-petition and $3 million post-petition—would have to be paid in full before any funds could be distributed to the remaining unsecured creditors.

Securing pre-petition debt with pre-and post-petition collateral as part of a post-petition financing arrangement is known as cross-collateralization. The Second Circuit aptly defined cross-collateralization as follows:

> [I]n return for making new loans to a debtor in possession under Chapter XI, a financing institution obtains a security interest on all assets of the debtor, both those existing at the date of the order and those created in the course of the Chapter XI proceeding, not only for the new loans, the propriety of which is not contested, but [also] for existing indebtedness to it.

Otte v. Manufacturers Hanover Commercial Corp. (In re Texlon Corp.), 596 F.2d 1092, 1094 (2d Cir.1979).

Because the Second Circuit was the first appellate court to describe this practice in In re Texlon, it is sometimes referred to as Texlon-type cross-collateralization. Another form of cross-collateralization involves securing post-petition debt with pre-petition collateral. This form of non-Texlon-type cross-collateralization is not at issue in this appeal. The Shapiros challenge only the cross-collateralization of the lenders' pre-petition debt, not the propriety of collateralizing the post-petition debt.

The Shapiros filed a number of objections to the bankruptcy court's order on January 13, 1989. After a hearing, the bankruptcy court overruled the objections. The Shapiros then filed a notice of appeal and a request for the bankruptcy court to stay its financing order pending appeal. The bankruptcy court denied the request for a stay on February 23, 1989.

The Shapiros subsequently moved the district court to stay the bankruptcy court's financing order pending appeal; the court denied the motion on March 7, 1989. On May 20, 1989, the district court dismissed the Shapiros' appeal as moot under 11 U.S.C. § 364(e) because the Shapiros had failed to obtain a stay of the financing order pending appeal, rejecting the argument that cross-collateralization is contrary to the Code. The Shapiros then appealed to this court.

II. Issues on Appeal

1. Whether the appeal to the district court and the appeal to this court are moot under section 364(e) of the Bankruptcy Code because the Shapiros failed to obtain a stay of the bankruptcy court's financing order.

2. Whether cross-collateralization is authorized under the Bankruptcy Code.

III. Contentions of the Parties

The lenders argue that this appeal is moot under section 364(e) of the Bankruptcy Code. That section provides that a lien or priority granted under section 364 may not be overturned unless it is stayed pending appeal. Even if this appeal were not moot, the Shapiros are not entitled to relief. Cross-collateralization is a legitimate means for debtors to obtain necessary financing and is not prohibited by the Bankruptcy Code.

The Shapiros contend that their appeal is not moot. Because cross-collateralization is not authorized under bankruptcy law, section 364(e) is inapplicable. Permitting cross-collateralization would undermine the entire structure of the Bankruptcy Code by allowing one unsecured creditor to gain priority over all other unsecured creditors simply by extending additional credit to a debtor....

V. Discussion

A. Mootness

We begin by addressing the lenders' claim that this appeal is moot under section 364(e) of the Bankruptcy Code. Section 364(e) provides that:

> The reversal or modification on appeal of an authorization under this section to obtain credit or incur debt, or of a grant under this section of a priority or a lien, does not affect the validity of any debt so incurred, or any priority or lien so granted, to an entity that extended such credit in good faith, whether or not such entity knew of the pendency of the appeal, unless such authorization and the incurring of such debt, or the granting of such priority or lien, were stayed pending appeal.

The purpose of this provision is to encourage the extension of credit to debtors in bankruptcy by eliminating the risk that any lien securing the loan will be modified on appeal.

. . .

By its own terms, section 364(e) is only applicable if the challenged lien or priority was authorized under section 364.... We can not decide if this appeal is moot under section 364(e) until we decide the central issue in this appeal–whether cross collateralization is authorized under section 364. Accordingly, we now turn to that question.

B. Cross–Collateralization and Section 364

Cross-collateralization is an extremely controversial form of Chapter 11 financing. Nevertheless, the practice has been approved by several bankruptcy courts....

The issue of whether the Bankruptcy Code authorizes cross-collateralization is a question of first impression in this court. Indeed, it is essentially a question of first impression before any court of appeals. Neither the lenders' brief nor our own research has produced a single appellate decision which either authorizes or prohibits the practice.

. . .

The Second Circuit expressed criticism of cross-collateralization in In re Texlon. The court, however, stopped short of prohibiting the practice altogether. At issue was the bankruptcy court's ex parte financing order granting the lender a security interest in the debtor's property to secure both pre-petition and post-petition debt. The court, in an exercise of judicial restraint, concluded that:

> In order to decide this case we are not obliged, however, to say that under no conceivable circumstances could "cross-collateralization" be authorized. Here it suffices to hold that ... a financing scheme so contrary to the spirit of the Bankruptcy Act should not have been granted by an ex parte order, where the bankruptcy court relies solely on representations by a debtor in possession that credit essential to the maintenance of operations is not otherwise obtainable.

In re Texlon, 596 F.2d at 1098. Although In re Texlon was decided under the earlier Bankruptcy Act, the court also considered whether cross-collateralization was authorized under the Bankruptcy Code. "To such limited extent as it is proper to consider the new Bankruptcy Act, which takes effect on October 1, 1979, in considering the validity of an order made in 1974, we see nothing in § 364(c) or in other provisions of that section that advances the case in favor of 'cross-collateralization.' "In re Texlon, 596 F.2d at 1098 (citations omitted).

Cross-collateralization is not specifically mentioned in the Bankruptcy Code. We conclude that cross-collateralization is inconsistent with bankruptcy law for two reasons. First, cross-collateralization is not authorized as a method of post-petition financing under section 364. Second, cross-collateralization is beyond the scope of the bankruptcy court's inherent equitable power because it is directly contrary to the fundamental priority scheme of the Bankruptcy Code.

Section 364 authorizes Chapter 11 debtors to obtain secured credit and incur secured debt as part of their reorganization. . . .

By their express terms, sections 364(c) & (d) apply only to future—i.e., post-petition—extensions of credit. They do not authorize the granting of liens to secure pre-petition loans.

. . .

Given that cross-collateralization is not authorized by section 364, we now turn to the lenders' argument that bankruptcy courts may permit the practice under their general equitable power. Bankruptcy courts are indeed courts of equity, 11 U.S.C. § 105(a), and they have the power to adjust claims to avoid injustice or unfairness. Pepper v. Litton, 308 U.S.

295, 60 S.Ct. 238, 84 L.Ed. 281 (1939). This equitable power, however, is not unlimited.

. . .

Section 507 of the Bankruptcy Code fixes the priority order of claims and expenses against the bankruptcy estate. 11 U.S.C. § 507. Creditors within a given class are to be treated equally, and bankruptcy courts may not create their own rules of superpriority within a single class. Cross-collateralization, however, does exactly that. As a result of this practice, post-petition lenders' unsecured pre-petition claims are given priority over all other unsecured pre-petition claims. . . .

. . . We disagree with the district court's conclusion that, while cross—collateralization may violate some policies of bankruptcy law, it is consistent with the general purpose of Chapter 11 to help businesses reorganize and become profitable. Rehabilitation is certainly the primary purpose of Chapter 11. This end, however, does not justify the use of any means. Cross-collateralization is directly inconsistent with the priority scheme of the Bankruptcy Code. Accordingly, the practice may not be approved by the bankruptcy court under its equitable authority.

VI.   Conclusion

Cross-collateralization is not authorized by section 364. Section 364(e), therefore, is not applicable and this appeal is not moot. Because Texlon-type cross-collateralization is not explicitly authorized by the Bankruptcy Code and is contrary to the basic priority structure of the Code, we hold that it is an impermissible means of obtaining post-petition financing. The judgment of the district court is REVERSED and the case is REMANDED for proceedings not inconsistent with this opinion.

REVERSED and REMANDED.

QUESTIONS ABOUT SAYBROOK

1.   Facts of the case

1.1   Who objected? Why did the debtor agree to the cross-collateralization? Why didn't the creditors' committee object?

1.2   To borrow from Clara Peller and Rod Tidwell, "where is the money?" The bankruptcy court approved the $3,000,000 dip loan in 1988. The United States Court of Appeals for the Fifth Circuit reversed and remanded in 1992. Where was the $3,000,000 in 1992?

2.   Vocabulary

2.1   *Texlon*-type cross collateralization. What is "*Texlon*—type cross collateralization"? S has a security interest in all of D's personal property. D files for bankruptcy. S agrees to provide post-petition financing for D under section 364 if all of its post-petition advances are secured by both D's postpetition assets and D's pre-petition assets. Is that cross-collateralization? Is that *Texlon*-type cross-collateralization?

2.2   Cash collateral. Recall that in *Saybrook*, "the debtors filed a motion for the use of cash collateral and for authorization to incur secured debt." What is "cash collateral" and why did the debtor file a motion to use cash collateral as a part of its dip financing motion? Professor Jack Ayer, a former bankruptcy judge; Michael L. Bernstein, a bankruptcy partner at Arnold & Porter; and Jonathan Friedland, a bankruptcy partner at Kirkland & Ellis answer these questions:[8]

> [I]n chapter 11, the DIP can continue to operate its business without a court order until the judge orders otherwise. But lawfulness is only one issue; practicalities are another. The ordinary debtor won't make it to lunchtime without some operating income.... [C]hances are that all of it [operating income] was pledged, pre-petition, to secured creditor(s).

> Security agreements typically give the secured creditor a first-priority security interest in all of the debtor's (a) inventory, (b) accounts receivable and (c) proceeds of inventory or accounts receivable. In the ordinary course, this works fine: Inventory becomes accounts, which becomes cash, which becomes new inventory and so forth. But now in chapter 11, it means the creditor has its hands on the debtor's throat: The debtor can't do anything without cash, and he can't touch the encumbered cash or cash equivalents (cash collateral) without the permission of the secured creditor or a court order.

> Bankruptcy Code section 363(c) provides that the DIP may use "cash collateral" only with (a) creditor consent or (b) a court order. In a contested hearing, the pre-petition lender has the burden to prove the "validity, priority or extent" of its interest in cash collateral. The debtor has the burden of proving that the pre-petition lender is "adequately protected." ... [Recall that "adequate protection" is explained in section 361 and Unit 4.]

> Negotiated cash-collateral orders are fairly common. This is predictable for several reasons. First, use of cash is essential to preserve going-concern value. Thus, there is typically a strong unity of interest on this matter between a debtor and its pre-petition lender, even where there are other disagreements. Second, courts tend to understand the need, and so are inclined to allow cash collateral use. Finally, a lender can enhance its position by negotiating certain terms into an "agreed" cash-collateral order.

> This last point requires amplification: A pre-petition lender is also often the DIP lender in a chapter 11 case. Thus, a single motion often combines a request to use cash collateral with a request to incur DIP financing. A common tactic of such pre-petition lenders/DIP financiers is to characterize a contemplated DIP financing that includes permission to use cash collateral as purely a DIP financing. However, bankruptcy courts understand that different rights ought to inure to a lender who makes a truly

8.   John D. Ayer, Michael L., Bernstein & Jonathan Friedland, *Obtaining DIP Financing and Using Cash Collateral*, American Bankruptcy Institute Journal, September, 2004, 23–SEP AMB-KRIJ 16.

new advance of funds as opposed to a lender who is merely permitting the use of cash collateral.

Did the bankruptcy court in *Saybrook* understand that different rights ought to inure to a lender who makes a truly new advance of funds as opposed to a lender who is merely permitting the use of cash collateral? Did the Eleventh Circuit understand? Do you understand?

Problem 11–6:   Review of Cash Collateral Financing Under Section 363 and Debtor in Possession Financing Under Section 364

1. D, an operating business, is not generating sufficient cash from its business operations to pay its debts. D is considering Chapter 11. D has prepared a business plan based on D's using cash generated from business operations and D's obtaining an additional $10,000,000 in DIP financing. D owes F $40,000,000, and F has a first lien on all of D's assets. Representing F, under what terms would you agree to D's use of cash collateral?

2. Same facts as #1. Representing D, what alternatives do you have to acceding to F's demands?

3. Same facts as #1. Representing, X, a DIP lender, under what terms would you agree to making a DIP loan to D?

You might get some ideas of what F or X will ask for in Problem 11–6 by looking again to Circuit City. In the Circuit City Chapter 11 case, a group of banks generally (and cleverly) referred to as "Bank Group" had a first lien on all of Circuit City's assets, and Bank Group provided the "DIP Financing." In his testimony to Congress, the attorney for the Circuit City Creditors' Committee provided this description of the DIP Financing: "The face amount of the 'new' DIP Financing offered by the Bank Group was $1.1 billion.... At the first day hearing on the interim DIP Financing, Circuit City's counsel advised the Bankruptcy Court that when all was said and done there would be $50 million of actual, additional availability to Circuit City ... In order to receive the additional $50 million of availability, Circuit City had to give to the Bank Group, among other things, the following:

— $30,000,000 in fees and expenses (for $50,000,000 of additional availability); ...

— Circuit City had to ready their businesses for sale by early March 2009 [remember that the Circuit City Chapter 11 case was filed in November 2008]. A default would arise otherwise.

— Circuit City was prohibited from seeking to prime the Bank Group's claims."[9]

————————

While the Circuit City Chapter 11 case did not result in a sale of the business, many other "high profile" (and "no profile") Chapter 11 cases have ended in a sale of the business. So, we need to know more about selling an operating business in Chapter 11.

C. SELLING AN OPERATING BUSINESS IN CHAPTER 11 USING SECTION 363

THE CHANGING FACE OF BANKRUPTCY

CFO Magazine, August 11, 2009, 2009 WLNR 16169064

Chrysler emerged from bankruptcy 45 days after it filed its Chapter 11 petition using what is known as a Section 363 sale. Now other companies that succumb to Chapter 11 protection may want to follow, and in fact many already have. Since the beginning of the year, General Motors, Midway Games, Nortel, and Tropicana Atlantic City Casino and Resort have all initiated 363 sales.

Unlike traditional bankruptcies, a petitioner that files a 363 transaction—which is named for the bankruptcy code provision under which it falls—does not submit a reorganization plan to the court. Rather, the company arranges to sell assets to a buyer in an expedited process that does not require buy-in from the debtor or its shareholders . . . . .

In some cases, all parties agree that a 363 sale makes sense. The classic time-sensitive example involves a bankrupt vegetable wholesaler that runs out of money to pay its growers for the broccoli, lettuce, and spinach that sit rotting in boxcars while Chapter 11 proceedings drag on. The faster the company emerges from bankruptcy and pays its creditors, the faster the veggies make it to grocery-store shelves. . . .

While there is no central repository that tracks 363 sales, there is reason to believe these accelerated transactions are becoming more popular. The number of Chapter 11 filings rose 69%, year-over-year, for the 12–month period ending March 31, 2009, according to the U.S. Bankruptcy Courts. That "sheer number of bankruptcies," combined with the lack of availability of debtor-in-possession financing, probably means that more 363 sales are being completed, posits Douglas Pugliese, managing director at valuation consultancy Marshal & Stevens. "Companies are going straight into liquidation" because there is not enough DIP financing in the market, Pugliese tells CFO.com. . . .

———

9. Testimony of Richard M. Pachulski before the Subcommittee on Commercial and Administrative Law of the House Judiciary Committee, 111 Congress, 1st Session, for Hearings on "Circuit City Unplugged: Why Did Chapter 11 Fail to Save 34,000 Jobs?"

Another reason for the increase in 363 sales is lender impatience. Tight credit markets have forced lenders to be stingy with respect to giving borrowers more time before declaring them in default. While lenders won't be "irrational," and will continue to rework credit terms for most commercial customers, says Carson, the time horizon for working out new payoff schedules has shrunk from about a year down to three months. That's because banks and other lenders know they may be able to quickly recoup some of their investment through an accelerated bankruptcy process or liquidation ...

Section 363 sales are also popular because the expedited process keeps bankruptcy costs at bay, and lenders are keen on that feature. Paying fees to creditor committees, lawyers, advisers, and consultants for their work to strip out debt from the balance sheet is a relatively expensive proposition. And it can be hard to convince lenders that a company needs to spend time and money to work out operational issues while still in Chapter 11 ...

Also, complex capital structures are forcing companies to spend more time—and money—in Chapter 11 limbo, and a 363 sale helps avoid that financial purgatory. Twenty years ago, companies raised debt through fairly straightforward bank borrowing, bond issues, and trade credit. Today, bank debt is often structured with first and second liens; companies then add mezzanine debt, and bonds are often issued in first-tier and subordinated tranches. Carson contends that the layering of debt leads to prolonged infighting among creditors, as they jockey for position in the bankruptcy pecking order to determine which creditor gets paid off first ...

Problem 11–7: Overview of Section 363(b) Sale Issues

1. D, owner and operator of fifteen dry cleaning plants, is a Chapter 11 debtor. While in Chapter 11, D negotiates for the sale of all of its assets to X, another owner and operator of dry cleaning plants. Under the terms of the asset purchase agreement ("APA"), X will acquire all of D's assets in exchange for 40% of X's stock. X is not publicly traded; experts retained by D's creditors' committee have valued the X stock at $8,000,000. Under section 363(b), the sale to X must be approved by the bankruptcy court after notice and hearing. Warren Buffett[1] appears at the hearing and offers to pay $6,000,000 in cash for twelve of the eleven dry cleaning plants. What should the bankruptcy court do? Should the bankruptcy court consider which deal the creditor's committee prefers? Should the creditors' committee's preference be controlling?

2. If the bankruptcy court orders the sale of the nine cleaning plants to Warren Buffett, what, if anything, can X do? Can you make a reasoned

---

1. We are all big Buffett fans (although "Buffett" causes one of us to think of pina coladas and another, who is not particularly strong at spelling, to think of tables laden with food) and hope that Mr. Buffett life goes on much longer than the "life" of this book.

argument for X's recovering its due diligence expenses from D's bankruptcy estate? A winning argument?

3. In light of (1) and (2) above, what provisions should X include in its next APA?

4. Same facts as (1) except that your client M has a pre-bankruptcy mortgage on all of D's cleaning plants to secure payment of the $7,000,000 that D owes M. In advising M, is section 363(f) helpful? Is section 363(k) helpful?

———————

The next case provides not only an overview of section 363 sale issues but also a review of section 364 debtor in possession financing issues.

IN RE ON–SITE SOURCING, INC.

412 B.R. 817 (Bankr. E.D. Va. 2009)

MAYER, Bankruptcy Judge.

The issue before the court is the extent to which a chapter 11 debtor may substitute a § 363 sale for a chapter 11 plan. The debtor reached too far in this case. While the sale will be approved, those portions that are a substitute for a chapter 11 plan will be excised. This memorandum opinion supplements the oral ruling of the court disallowing the proposed unsecured creditors trust. In order to fully appreciate the § 363 sale proposal, it is necessary examine the debtor's pre-petition sales efforts, the debtor's pre-petition debt structure and the debtor-in-possession's post-petition financing.

Background

Pre-Petition Sales Efforts

On-Site Sourcing, Inc., filed a voluntary petition in bankruptcy pursuant to chapter 11 of the Untied States Bankruptcy Code on February 4, 2009, at 8:53 p.m. Over the next five hours the debtor filed twelve additional pleadings. The one at issue, a motion to approve auction procedures and the sale of substantially all of the debtor's assets (Docket Entry 10), was filed just after midnight, at 12:47 a.m., on February 5, 2009.[2] That morning, the court granted the debtor's motion for an expedited hearing on its first day motions which included the motion to approve the auction procedures and the sale of substantially all of the debtor's assets. The hearing was set for the following day, February 6, 2009.

———————

2. The breadth of the motion is captured, in part, by its title: "Motion of the Debtors for Entry of Orders (I)(A) Establishing Bid Procedures Related to the Sale of Substantially All of the Debtors' Assets, (B) Scheduling a Hearing to Consider the Sale, (C) Approving the Form and Manner of Notice of Sale by Auction, (D) Establishing Procedures for Noticing and Determining Cure Amounts and (E) Granting Related Relief; and (II)(1) Approving Asset Purchase Agreement and Authorizing the Sale Free and Clear of All Liens, Claims, Encumbrances and Interests, (2) Authorizing the Assumption and Assignment of Certain Executory Contracts and Unexpired Leases and (3) Granting Related Relief."

It was immediately obvious from the papers filed in the case and the statements of counsel in court that this case was filed to facilitate Integreon Discovery Solutions (DC), Inc.'s purchase of substantially all of the debtor's assets. It appears that nothing would have prevented a non-bankruptcy UCC sale but the parties sought a § 363 sale instead. The essence of the case and the events leading to the filing of the petition are captured in the debtor's sale motion. The debtor stated:

"8.   By 2008, the Debtors could no longer service their secured debt and entered into several forbearance agreements and amended credit facilities to negotiate revised repayment terms. In late 2008, still significantly leveraged and facing continued revenue decreases, the Debtors were facing liquidation. As part of a final offer to their secured lenders, the Debtors, along with their advisors, solicited potential purchasers of the business. After speaking to a number of potential buyers, both strategic and financial, as well as investment bankers and business brokers, the Debtors engaged in further discussions with six interested parties (the 'Other Interested Parties'). These marketing efforts resulted in a competitor, Integreon Managed Solutions, Inc., agreeing to assume the role of the Debtors' secured lenders and negotiate the possible sale of the business. The secured debt (in a principal amount of approximately $35,000,000) was assigned to Integreon by the Debtors' former secured lenders in early 2009. The bankruptcy case was filed in order to pursue the highest and best offer for the sale of the Debtors' business operations.

9.   Ultimately, the Debtors' discussions and negotiations with Integreon prior to and after the assignment of the Debtors' secured debt to Integreon resulted in the proposed asset purchase agreement (the 'APA') described herein. Based on the Debtors' consultations with its financial advisors and other relevant considerations, the Debtors believe that it is in the best interest of the Debtors, their estates, creditors and other stakeholders to enter into the APA. In particular, the APA or a similar transaction would allow a significant portion of the Debtors' business to continue operations as a going concern thereby maintaining the important services the Debtors provide to their customers and, most importantly, preserving many of the jobs of the employees of the Debtors."

. . .

DIP Financing Motion

One of the first day motions was a debtor-in-possession financing motion. Not surprisingly, the proposed DIP lender was Integreon. Integreon was the sole pre-petition secured creditor. The debt, while secured by a lien on almost all of the debtor's assets, was significantly undersecured. The debt was about $35 million, but Integreon proposed to pay and the debtor proposed to accept $28 million for substantially all of the debtor's assets as a going concern. As the sole secured creditor with a lien on assets worth less than its debt, it controlled the debtor's ability to obtain financing from any other source . . . As the prospective purchaser of the debtor's assets as a going concern, it was in Integreon's best interests to assure that the debtor continued in operation. And that required post-petition funding.

The proposed DIP loan contained many provisions generally frowned upon and frequently rejected by most bankruptcy courts. Integreon proposed to loan the debtor $40 million even though the debtor only needed about $1 million, less receipts, to operate during the pendency of the sale of substantially all of its assets to Integreon, a period that was intended to be 30 to 60 days. The proposed loan term capped this period at 90 days. The $40 million was to be used to pay-off Integreon's pre-petition secured debt and replace it with post-petition debt. The provision would have promoted Integreon's pre-petition $7 million unsecured portion of its debt to an administrative claim.[3] In *821 addition, Integreon was to be paid a lending fee of 0.75%, or $300,000, on the $40 million loan. It was to have a lien on all assets of the debtor, including all recoveries under chapter 5 of the Bankruptcy Code. It was to have priority and super-priority liens on all collateral over all other liens and claims under § 364(d). All obligations under the DIP loan were to be allowed administrative expense claims with a priority under § 364(c)(1) over any and all other administrative expenses of the kind specified or ordered pursuant to any provision of the Bankruptcy Code, including, but not limited to, §§ 105, 326, 328, 503(b), 507(a), 507(b) and 726. The effect of the proposed DIP loan was to foreclose the possibility of any other creditor receiving any distribution from the debtor, including all administrative claimants.

Certain administrative claimants were protected by proposed carve-outs. Integreon agreed that court fees, the United States Trustee's fees, fees incurred by a chapter 7 trustee not to exceed $50,000, a premium on directors and officers tail insurance not to exceed $30,000, and certain professional fees not to exceed $50,000 after a carve-out trigger notice would be carved-out from its lien and administrative claim.

The remedy in the event of a default under the proposed DIP loan, including the maturity of the loan in 90 days, was immediate and assured. The automatic stay would immediately terminate without further order of the court and Integreon could immediately utilize its remedies under the DIP loan documents.

The Sale Motion

The Sale Motion was filed with the petition and the DIP Financing Motion. The debtor and Integreon sought a prompt sale which would have

---

3. Bankruptcy Code § 506(a)(1) provides that an allowed secured claim is a secured claim only to the extent of the value of collateral and is an unsecured claim as to the balance. The DIP Financing Motion requested, in addition to a blanket lien on all of the debtor's assets, Bankruptcy Code § 364(c) protection which would also make Integreon's DIP loan an administrative claim with priority over any and all administrative expenses provided in §§ 503(b) and 507(b). This protection is important only if a DIP loan is not fully covered by the proposed collateral. Here, the "new" post-petition loan is clearly as undersecured as the "old" pre-petition loan. The effect would be to convert the pre-petition unsecured loan into a post-petition superpriority administrative claim. If the other unsecured creditors had even a glimmer of hope of receiving any distribution before the proposed DIP loan, they certainly had none under the proposed DIP loan. Integreon's pre-petition unsecured claim would be paid ahead of them as a post-petition superpriority administrative claim.

effectively prevented any individual creditor from undertaking any meaningful review and analysis of the proposed sale. The sale did not proceed as quickly as anticipated, however, and the Unsecured Creditors Committee was able to become involved.

The terms of the proposed sale benefitted Integreon and could have, had there been any other realistic interest, chilled the bidding. The Sale Motion proposed a break-up fee to Integreon of $560,000 plus additional expenses not to exceed $250,000.[5] Integreon's initial bid was to be $28,000,000. The minimum bid for any qualified bidder was $28,810,000 so that the break-up fee and expenses would be covered if there were another successful bidder. Thereafter, the bidding increment was $500,000. The sale was to be free and clear of all interests and claims.

Modifications to the Proposed Sale Obtained by Unsecured Creditors Committee

The Unsecured Creditors Committee ultimately supported the sale on modified terms. The proposed modifications provided that Integreon would forgive its deficiency claim; that certain assets would be excluded from the sale, specifically, tax refunds and chapter 5 causes of action against officers and directors (except three key employees that Integreon intended to retain) and 35% of all other chapter 5 causes of action. The pre-sale budget line for the Committee's attorneys was increased from $115,000 to $225,000, which Integreon agreed to pay. In addition, a general unsecured creditors trust was to be established. Integreon agreed to fund the trust with a lump sum payment of $132,500, a one-half interest in all tax refunds and the immediate payment of the Committee's professional's carve-out.

The United States Trustee objected to some of the proposed modifications. The sale was approved without the general unsecured creditors trust and without the releases for the three key employees. The funds that Integreon was to have paid to the trust were paid to the debtor.

No plan of reorganization has been filed. It appears from the comments of counsel that a plan, if it is filed, will be a liquidating plan and that there are no significant assets remaining to be liquidated after the consummation of the sale to Integreon.

Discussion

The difficulty with this case is not the decision to sell the debtor's assets in bankruptcy rather than through a non-bankruptcy UCC sale or

---

5. Break-up fees can serve a useful purpose in bankruptcy auctions. But merely reciting the theoretical benefits in a motion does not insure that they inure to the benefit of the estate. One frequently proffered benefit is that the breakup fee encourages a reluctant prospective bidder to perform its due diligence and make the first bid, thereby opening a vigorous auction. If it is not the successful bidder, it is compensated for its efforts and reimbursed for its expenses, the compensation being justified by opening the auction in circumstances where there may have been no other reasonable bid. This is not the situation in this case. Integreon made its decision to purchase On–Site's electronic discovery business when it purchased the bank's note and the subordinated debt. It committed to the acquisition at that moment. It needed no other incentive to open the bidding. Indeed, it appears to have actively cooperated with the debtor in filing the case and seeking a quick § 363 sale. The break-up fee purchased nothing in this case.

the skill of the attorneys in identifying their client's interests and endeavoring to maximize them, but in recognizing the proper line between sales under § 363 before the confirmation of a chapter 11 plan and sales under § 1123(a)(5)(D) after confirmation of a chapter 11 plan. There are substantial differences in the procedures between the two sale methods and the creditor protections available. They are concisely stated in In re Gulf Coast Oil Corp.:

A § 363(b) sale is generally viewed as quicker. Only a motion and a hearing are required, and most courts apply a "business judgment test" to determine whether to approve the sale. By contrast, confirmation of a chapter 11 plan usually involves (i) preparation, court approval, and distribution of a disclosure statement, (ii) voting by creditors to accept or to reject the plan, and (iii) determination by the Court of whether the plan meets statutory confirmation standards. In re Gulf Coast Oil Corp., 404 B.R. 407, 415 (Bankr.S.D.Tex.2009).

. . .

Judge STEEN explains the development of the jurisprudence of chapter 11 § 363(b) sales in the Fifth Circuit in In re Gulf Coast Oil Corp. The discussion generally reflects the development of the law throughout the United States. . . . The debtor in possession or trustee in a chapter 11 case must consider its fiduciary duties to all creditors and interest holders before seeking approval of a transaction under § 363(b).

• The movant must establish a business justification for the transaction and the bankruptcy court must conclude, from the evidence, that the movant satisfied its fiduciary obligations and established a valid business justification.

• A sale, use, or lease of property under § 363(b) is not per se prohibited even though it purports to sell all, or virtually all, of the property of the estate, but such sales (or proposed sales of the crown jewel assets of the estate) are subject to special scrutiny.

• Parties that oppose § 363(b) transactions on the basis that they constitute a sub rosa chapter 11 plan must articulate the specific rights that they contend are denied by the transaction.

• Although the bankruptcy court need not turn every § 363(b) hearing into a mini-confirmation hearing, the bankruptcy court must not authorize a § 363(b) transaction if the transaction would effectively evade the "carefully crafted scheme" of the chapter 11 plan confirmation process, such as by denying §§ 1125, 1126, 1129(a)(7), and 1129(b)(2) rights.

• If the bankruptcy court concludes that such rights are denied, then the bankruptcy court can only approve the transaction if it fashions an appropriate protective measure modeled on those which would attend a reorganization plan.

• Transactions that explicitly release all (or virtually all) claims against the estate, predetermine the structure of a plan of reorganization, and explicitly obligate parties to vote for or against a plan are not authorized under § 363(b) Id. at 422.

The court considered these and other factors in approving the proposed sale in this case, but required certain provisions to be excised. The excised provisions all furthered a sub rosa plan of reorganization. None, especially the proposed unsecured creditors trust, had a good business reason . . .

The payment to the proposed general unsecured creditors trust was removed. This provision was inserted at the insistence of the Unsecured Creditors Committee. . . . The provision effectively predetermines, in significant part, the structure of an as yet to be drafted plan of reorganization and effectively evades the "carefully crafted scheme" of the chapter 11 plan confirmation process. In re Gulf Coast Oil Corp., 404 B.R. at 422 (quoting Pension Benefit Guaranty Corp. v. Braniff Airways, Inc. (In re Braniff Airways, Inc.), 700 F.2d 935, 940 (5th Cir.1983)).

The general unsecured creditors trust provision is contrary to the scheme of distribution envisioned in both a chapter 7 and chapter 11 liquidation. It would assure that the general unsecured creditors are paid in advance of the administrative and priority claims. At oral argument, the Committee's counsel candidly admitted that the purpose was to assure that the general unsecured creditors received a distribution. He admitted that if there were insufficient funds to pay all administrative expenses and priority claims, some administrative or priority claimants would go unpaid while the unsecured creditors received a distribution. The chapter 7 liquidation scheme is a matter of consideration because conversion of this case to chapter 7 and payment of creditors under § 726 is likely. Moreover, the chapter 7 liquidation scheme provides a comparison against which this chapter 11 liquidation plan may be compared. . . .

The end result of the proposed consideration for the general unsecured creditors trust would have been to divert a part of the proceeds of the sale of the debtor's assets to the general unsecured creditors to the detriment of administrative expense and priority creditors and thereby allow the general unsecured creditors to avoid some of the vicissitudes of the chapter 11 process or a conversion to chapter 7. All of this violates the protections chapter 11 seeks to provide for creditors, particularly administrative expense and priority creditors. They are effectively deprived of their rights under § 1129(a)(7) and (a)(9), their right to adequate information to make an informed decision on a proposed chapter 11 plan under § 1125, and their right to object to a proposed chapter 11 plan under § 1126. . . .

The court is satisfied that the overall sale was in the best interests of the debtor and that the debtor exercised its sound business judgment in proposing the sale. However, the court cannot give any significant weight to the debtor's business judgment as exercised by the inclusion of the general unsecured creditors trust or the release of the three key employees. The remedy was, with the consent of the debtor, Integreon and the

Unsecured Creditors Committee, to excise these provisions and approve the sale without them.

Conclusion

The 363(b) sale of substantially all of the assets of the debtor to Integreon was approved by the court despite the fact that it was for all practical purposes the predetermined purchaser. The debtor's pre-petition sales efforts and the absence of money in the credit market satisfied the court that this was the best deal-and the only one-available. Integreon came into the court with an exceptionally strong position as the sole pre-petition secured creditor with a significant undersecured claim. It sought additional leverage in the DIP Financing Motion. Much of the requested relief in the DIP Financing Motion, such as the roll-up of the pre-petition debt into a single post-petition debt was denied. The excesses in the Sales Motion were eliminated, such as the unnecessary break-up fee. The Unsecured Creditors Committee was successful in obtaining a major concession, the forgiveness of any deficiency claim. Whether this will be worth anything is unknown at this time, but without the concession, the unsecured creditors' claims would have been significantly diluted by Integreon's huge unsecured deficiency claim.

The principal relief denied was the Unsecured Creditors Committee's provision for a general unsecured creditors trust. That was excised from the sale for the reasons set out above.

QUESTIONS ABOUT ON-SITE

1. Do you understand the facts?

    1.1 What is the APA? Who are the parties to the APA? When was the APA negotiated?

    1.2 The opinion tells us "The secured debt (in a principal amount of approximately $35,000,000) was assigned to Integeron by the Debtors' former secured lenders in early 2009." What does "assigned" mean?

2. Do you understand the law?

    2.1 What provision of the Bankruptcy Code supports the Debtors' sale of all of its assets to Integeron?

    2.2 What does "notice and hearing" in section 363(b) require? More specifically, how many hearings are required to complete a section 363(b) sale? Does the bankruptcy court hold a hearing to approve sale procedures such as break-up fees and a later, separate hearing to approve the sale?

    2.3 Was it important that "The Unsecured Creditors Committee ultimately supported the sale on modified terms"? Was it important that "The United States Trustee objected to some of the proposed modifications [to the proposed sale]"?

    2.4 What facts indicate that a section 363(b) transaction constitutes a "sub rosa plan"?

2.5   Recall that Integeron was not only the buyer but also the DIP lender. Jane Vris, a New York bankruptcy partner in the Vinson & Elkins law firm, explains that "DIP financing can come into play in a 363 sale because section 363(k) generally allows a secured creditor to 'credit bid' its claim at any 363 sale, unless the court prohibits it. 11 U.S.C. § 363(k). Thus, a section 364(c) or 364(d) DIP lender (or syndicate of lenders), in general, may avail itself of section 363(k) to essentially leverage its loan to acquire the debtor's business."[10] Is that what happened in the *On-Site Sourcing* case?

2.6   Judge Mayer predicts that "conversion of this case to chapter 7 and payment of creditors under section 726 is likely." Judge Mayer also tells us that "distribution would be determined in a confirmed chapter 11 plan." Why would a section 363 sale be followed by either "conversion of this case to chapter 7 or (2) a confirmed chapter 11 plan"? In *On-Site Sourcing,* what would be the differences, if any, between "conversion of this case to chapter 7" and a "confirmed chapter 11 plan"?

D. UNDERSTANDING THE CHAPTER 11 PLAN PROCESS—AN OVERVIEW

In Chapter 7 cases, the Code expressly answers the questions: "who gets what?" and "when?" Section 726(a) provides for the distribution of "property of the estate" and, in numbered paragraphs, sets out the order of distribution; section 726(b) then mandates that if there is not sufficient property of the estate to pay all of the claims in one of the section 726(a) kinds of clams, then "payment . . . shall be made pro rata among claims of the kind specified in each such particular paragraph of section 726(a)." Section 704 requires that, in Chapter 7 cases, distributions to creditors to be made "as expeditiously as is compatible with the best interests of the parties in interest."

The only way for a debtor to vary the baselines set by section 726 and section 704 is the Chapter 11 plan. In Chapter 11 cases, it is the plan that answers the questions "who gets what?"and "when?" And, the answer provided by a Chapter 11 plan can be much more "creative" than Chapter 7 answers.

First, distributions in a Chapter 11 plan are not limited to "property of the estate." Chapter 11 distributions can be cash, notes, and/or equity securities. Second, distributions to creditors in a Chapter 11 plan are not required to be made "pro rata among claims of the kind specified in [section 726(a)]." The "classes" of claims in a Chapter 11 plan can be very different from the kinds of claims in section 726 and the distribution can vary among the various classes of claims.

It is the confirmed Chapter 11 plan that determines which if any creditors get paid in full in cash and what if anything other creditors

---

10.   Jane Vris, An Introduction to DIP Financing, Practising Law Institute (November–December 2009), 918 PLI/Comm 319.

receive. And, whatever the confirmed Chapter 11 provides will be binding on the debtor and all creditors.

Although a Chapter 11 plan will be binding even on creditors who oppose the plan, the approval of the plan by the requisite number of creditors is the most important part of the Chapter 11 plan process. What a Chapter 11 plan provides and what a bankruptcy judge will confirm turns largely on what the requisite majorities of the creditors approve.

While "expeditiously" is a part of the Chapter 7 distribution process, the word "expeditiously" is seldom used in connection with the Chapter 11 plan process. It often takes more than a year to obtain confirmation of a Chapter 11 plan.

The plan process begins with the drafting of a plan. Generally, the debtor in possession prepares the Chapter 11 plan.[11]

Section 1123 is entitled "Contents of the Plan." While compliance with section 1123 is important, making the requisite number of creditors "happy" is even more important. Accordingly, the contents of a Chapter 11 plan are governed not only by section 1123 but also by what the requisite number of creditors under section 1126 will accept.

The plan proponent files not only the plan but also a "disclosure statement" providing "adequate information" to enable a hypothetical "reasonable investor" to make an informed judgment about the plan. The process for obtaining creditor approval of a Chapter 11 plan is like the federal securities laws that you learned in your business enterprises course in that it is premised on disclosure: the creditors of a business in Chapter 11 (like the stockholders of a public corporation) can make decisions only if provided with adequate information. After the court determines that the disclosure statement contains "adequate information," the process of soliciting creditor approval of the plan begins.

Critical to an understanding of creditor approval of Chapter 11 plans is an understanding of classes of claims in Chapter 11. Creditors vote by class. A Chapter 11 plan can divide creditors into classes. While all claims within the same class must be treated the same, different classes of claims can be treated differently. For example, Markell Markets' Chapter 11 plan might place all unsecured vendors that Markell Markets intends to continue to buy from in one class and provide that claims in that class receives cash and place all unsecured vendors that Markell Markets does not intend to continue to buy from in another class and provide that class receives notes.

Creditors votes are counted by class. In the Markell Markets hypothetical from the prior paragraph, the votes of the class of unsecured vendors that Markell Market plans to continue to buy from will be counted separately from the votes of the class of unsecured vendors that Markell Markets does not plan to continue to buy from. A class of claims

---

11. Section 1121(b) provides that "Except as otherwise provided in this section, only the debtor may file a plan until 120 days after the order for relief under this chapter."

has accepted a plan when more than 1/2 in number and at least 2/3 in amount of the allowed claims actually voting on the plan approve the plan. Generally, the debtor in possession "massages" the plan provisions so that the plan is accepted by the requisite majorities of each class.

Even if every single creditor enthusiastically votes to accept the plan, the court must still determine whether the plan meets the requirements for confirmation in section 1129(a). And, even if one or more classes of claims does not approve the plan by the requisite majorities, the court can still confirm the plan if it meets not only the requirements of section 1129(a) but also the requirements of section 1129(b). That is called a cram down.

Section 1129(b) "cram down," like section 1121 "exclusivity," section 1124 "impairment," section 1122 "gerrymandering," section 1111(b) "election," and section 1129(b)(2)(C) "new value," are generally left to an advanced course in corporate reorganization. If you, like Markell's students, have drawn the "short straw"[12] and have a professor who wants to cover that stuff in the basic bankruptcy course, read on. The rest of you can skip to page 416.

E. REALLY UNDERSTANDING THE CHAPTER 11 PLAN PROCESS— A MUCH CLOSER VIEW

1. PREPARING THE PLAN

a. Who and When?

Section 1121 answers the question of who can file a plan. In reading section 1121 notice that:

- the debtor at any time in any chapter 11 case can file a plan [section 1121(a)];
- only the debtor can file a plan unless either a trustee has been appointed [section 1121(c)(1)] or statutory time deadlines have expired [section 1121(c)(2),(3), 1121(d)].

And, in reading section 1121 and the following problems, think about what "exclusivity" is and why it is important.

---

11 U.S.C. § 1121

(a) The debtor may file a plan with a petition commencing a voluntary case, or at any time in a voluntary case or an involuntary case.

(b) Except as otherwise provided in this section, only the debtor may file a plan until after 120 days after the date of the order for relief under this chapter.

---

12. Literally, Nickles, not Markell would be the "short straw." Markell is more the "thick straw."

(c) Any party in interest, including the debtor, the trustee, a creditors' committee, an equity security holders' committee, a creditor, an equity security holder, or any indenture trustee, may file a plan if and only if—

  (1) a trustee has been appointed under this chapter;

  (2) the debtor has not filed a plan before 120 days after the date of the order for relief under this chapter; or

  (3) the debtor has not filed a plan that has been accepted, before 180 days after the date of the order for relief under this chapter, by each class the claims or interests of which are impaired under the plan.

(d)(1) Subject to paragraph (e) on request of a party in interest and after notice and a hearing, the court may for cause reduce or increase the 120–day period or the 180–day period referred to in this section. . . .

  (2)(A) The 120–day period specified in paragraph (1) may not be extended beyond a date that is 18 months after the date of the order for relief under this chapter.

  (B) The 180–day period specified in paragraph (1) may not be extended beyond a date that is 20 months after the date of the order for relief under this chapter.

Problem 11–8: *Plan Exclusivity*

1. D Corp. files a Chapter 11 petition on April 5. The debtor files its Chapter 11 plan thirty days later. What is the first date that another party in interest can file a competing plan (without seeking an order under section 1121(d) shortening time)?

2. D Co files a Chapter 11 petition on December 7. A Chapter 11 trustee is appointed on January 15. Can the trustee file a Chapter 11 plan? Can D Co. still file a Chapter 11 plan? Can a creditor of D Co. file a Chapter 11 plan? Can there be more than one plan filed?

3. Megacorp files its chapter 11 case on January 1, 2011. On June 1, 2012, it files its fifth request to extend the exclusive periods found in Section 1121 so that Megacorp will be the only entity that can file a plan up to and including October 1, 2012. The evidence, such as it is, before the court indicates that such an extension would be in the best interests of creditors and the estate. May the court grant the motion?

---

b.   What Is in the Chapter 11 Plan?

Section 1123 is entitled "contents of the plan." Section 1123 is, however, only one of the sections that governs what is in the plan. While compliance with section 1123 is essential, it is also essential to remember that a Chapter 11 plan will be effective only if it is approved by the requisite number of creditors and by the court. Accordingly, in the "real world", the answer to "what is in the Chapter 11 plan" is controlled not only by section 1123 but also by what the requisite number of creditors will accept (section 1126) and what the court will confirm (section 1129).

(1) Importance of Concept of Class of Claims

The concept of classification of claims is the best example of the relationship of sections 1123 and 1126 and 1129. First, section 1123(a)(1) requires that a Chapter 11 plan designate classes of creditor claims. These different classes may be treated differently (although section 1123(a)(4) requires the same treatment for all claims within the same class). Accordingly, it would seem from section 1123 that Congress believed that a debtor might want to create different classes of claims for economic reasons. It might, for example, pay vendors who are not in the business of making long-term loans (such as trade creditors) more quickly than lenders who are in the business of extending credit (such as banks).

Second, while Section 1129(a) requires that all classes consent to the plan,[13] class consent doesn't require unanimity. Rather, section 1126 establishes the test for determining whether a class accepts a plan: acceptance occurs when creditors holding more than one-half of the total number of claims voting accept the plan, and the number so accepting also hold claims worth at least two-thirds of the amount of claims voting (11 U.S.C. § 1126(c)). This test applies separately to each class of claims. Accordingly, it would seem from section 1126 and 1129 that a debtor might want to create different classes of claims for voting reasons—for example, placing a dissenting creditor with a large claim in a separate class.

(2) Definition of Class of Claims

We did not leave out the Code's definition of "class" or "class of claims" No Code section provides these definitions.

11 U.S.C. § 1122

(a) Except as provided in subsection (b) of this section, a plan may place a claim or an interest in a particular class only if such claim or interest is substantially similar to the other claims or interests of such class.

(b) A plan may designate a separate class of claims consisting only of every unsecured claim that is less than or reduced to an amount that the

---

13. There is an important exception to this called "cramdown," but we will get to that later. In any event, even in cramdown, section 1129(a)(10) requires at least one consenting impaired class.

court approves as reasonable and necessary for administrative convenience.

Problem 11–9:   Classification of Secured Claims

1. D Co.'s creditors include F who has a first mortgage on Blackacre, and S who has a second mortgage on Blackacre. D Co. also has many unsecured lenders and vendors. Can D Co.'s plan place all its creditors in the same class? Can D Co.'s plan put both F's claim and S's claim in the same class? What statutory language controls the answers to these questions?

2. All of D Inc.'s creditors are unsecured except for S. S is owed $2,000,000 and has a lien on D Inc.'s assets that have a value of no more than $1,500,000. Can D Inc.'s Chapter 11 plan put S in one class all of its other creditors in another class?

---

(3)   Classification of Secured Claims

IN RE KECK, MAHIN & CATE

241 B.R. 583 (Bankr. N.D. Ill. 1999)

RONALD BARLIANT, Bankruptcy Judge.

Keck, Mahin & Cate ("Keck" or "the Debtor") was once a leading Chicago law firm with as many as 350 attorneys and 10 offices. In the 1990s, however, the firm's fortunes began to decline and it was never able to recapture its past glory.... In 1997, more than a century after the firm began in the practice of law, Keck ceased the representation of clients and continued only in a wind-up capacity. Apparently Keck was unable to wind-up its affairs to the satisfaction of all its creditors, however, because five trade creditors filed an involuntary bankruptcy petition against the firm under chapter 7 of the United States Bankruptcy Code on December 16, 1997. On December 31, 1997, upon Keck's request, the case was converted to chapter 11. Presently before the Court is the confirmation of the Third Amended Joint Chapter 11 Plan ("the Plan"), proposed jointly by Keck and the Official Committee of Unsecured Creditors.

The Plan enjoys broad support by creditors and former partners, but is opposed by . . . a former partner, who (in common with other partners) holds a secured claim . . .

Class III consists of the secured claims of partners who lent the Debtor approximately $4,625,000 to pay a portion of the Bank Group's secured loan ("the Sub–Debt Holders"). The loans are secured by security interests, subordinated only to the Bank Group's security interests, in virtually all of the Debtor's assets. The only such asset of any importance is accounts receivable. Since the Bank Group has been satisfied, the Sub–Debt Holders' lien is now senior. Based on alleged inequitable conduct of the Debtor and its partners, the Creditor's Committee and a major creditor have contended that the Sub–Debt claims should be equitably subordinated....

Mr. Dennis O'Dea is a Non–Participating Partner of the Debtor and the lone rejecting member of Class III ..., Mr. O'Dea also argues that his Sub–Debt claim should be separately classified. "[A] plan may place a claim ... in a particular class only if [it] is substantially similar to the other claims of such class." § 1122(a). Commonly, each secured claim is placed in a separate class. But that is because usually each such claim is secured by distinct rights to property of the estate. Secured creditors typically have either liens on different assets, or, if their liens are on the same asset, one has a higher priority than the other. In this case, however, each Sub–Debt claim is secured by a common interest in the same collateral, and each Sub–Debt Holder has the same right to pro rata payment from that collateral. Hence, each Sub–Debt Holder is in the same relationship to the Debtor and its assets as all other Sub–Debt Holders. Therefore, these claims are substantially similar, and, accordingly, Mr. O'Dea's objection to their classification in a single class is overruled....

Problem 11–10: Reasons for Classification of Unsecured Claims

1. X Corp.'s Chapter 11 plan provides for two classes of unsecured claims: (1) claims under $3,000; and (2) claims above $3,000. Under this plan, each class (1) claim will be paid in full in cash on the effective date of the plan and each class (2) claim will be paid 90% of its amount owed over a nine-year period. What is the probable reason for classification?

2. Z's Chapter 11 plan provides for two classes of unsecured claims: (1) vendor claims; and (2) lender claims. Under the plan, each class (1) claim will be paid 50% of its amount over a one-year period, and each class (2) claim will be paid 70% of its amount over a five-year period. What is the probable reason for the classification?

3. Same facts as #2 except that the plan provides to treat claims in each class the same: 60% of the amount owed over a three-year period. What is the probable reason for the classification?

(4) Classification of Unsecured Claims for Economic Reasons

IN RE DOW CORNING CORP.

280 F.3d 648 (6th Cir.), cert. denied, 537 U.S. 816 (2002)

BOYCE F. MARTIN, JR., Chief Circuit Judge.

Years after Dow Corning Corporation filed a petition for reorganization under Chapter 11 of the Bankruptcy Code, and following extensive and vigorous negotiations, the third proposed plan of reorganization for Dow was submitted to the bankruptcy court. The bankruptcy court confirmed the Amended Joint Plan of Reorganization for Dow and the district court affirmed the bankruptcy court's Confirmation Order. Certain claimants who voted against the Plan appealed. The second issue presented is whether the Plan's classification of foreign claimants complies with the Bankruptcy Code's classification requirements. For the following reasons we AFFIRM the bankruptcy court's determination regarding the Plan's classification.

I.

For nearly thirty years, Dow was the predominant producer of silicone gel breast implants, accounting for almost fifty percent of the entire market. In addition, Dow supplied silicone raw materials to other manufacturers of silicone gel breast implants.

In the 1980s, certain medical studies suggested that silicone gel may cause auto-immune tissue diseases such as lupus, Scleroderma and rheumatoid arthritis. In 1992, the Food and Drug Administration ordered that silicone gel implants be taken off the market and Dow ceased manufacturing and marketing its silicone implants. Soon thereafter, tens of thousands of implant recipients sued Dow and its two shareholders, the Dow Chemical Company and Corning, Incorporated, claiming to have been injured by auto-immune reactions to the silicone in their implants. . . .

Dow filed a petition for reorganization under Chapter 11 of the Bankruptcy Code. . . .

Under the Plan, a $2.35 billion fund is established for the payment of claims asserted by (1) personal injury claimants, (2) government health care payers, and (3) other creditors asserting claims related to silicone-implant products liability claims. The $2.35 billion fund is established with funds contributed by Dow's products liability insurers, Dow's shareholders and Dow's operating cash reserves. . . .

Under the Plan, claimants who choose to settle are channeled to the Settlement Facility, a legal entity created by the Plan and authorized to negotiate payments out of funds set aside for that purpose. Claimants who choose to litigate are channeled to the Litigation Facility, a legal entity created by the Plan that is essentially substituted for Dow as a defendant in the claimant's lawsuit.

The Plan divides claims and interests into thirty-three classes and subclasses. Classes 6.1 and 6.2 are composed of foreign breast-implant claimants who are given the opportunity to either settle or litigate their claims. Settlement payments to foreign breast implant claimants are between 35% and 60% of the amounts to be paid to domestic breast-implant claimants....

For the following reasons we hold that the Plan's classification of foreign claimants meets the Code's requirements.

Under the Plan, a foreign claimant is defined as someone who (1) is not a United States citizen, (2) is not a resident alien, or (3) did not have his or her medical procedure performed in the United States. Plan §§ 1.67. The Plan creates two classes for foreign claimants. Class 6.1 consists of claimants who are from a country that either (1) belongs to the European Union, (2) has a common law tort system, or (3) has a per capita Gross Domestic Product of greater than 60% of the United States's per capita Gross Domestic Product. Class 6.2 consists of claimants from all other countries. Class 5 generally consists of domestic breast-implant claimants. Class 6.1 claimants receive settlement offers of 60% of analogous domestic claimants' settlements, and Class 6.2 receive settlements of 35% of the domestic claimants' settlements. Members of both classes retain the option to litigate against the Litigation Facility for the full value of the claim should they deem the settlement offer inadequate.

The various groups of foreign claimants argue that their claims are not worth less than those of the domestic tort claimants and, therefore, should not be classified separately from domestic claims. The issue is whether the Plan improperly classifies the foreign claimants separately from domestic claimants. For the following reasons we hold that the separate classification is not improper.

The Bankruptcy Code provides that "a plan may place a claim or an interest in a particular class only if such claim or interest is substantially similar to the other claims or interests of such class." 11 U.S.C. § 1122(a). This circuit has recognized that section 1122(a), "by its express language, only addresses the problem of dissimilar claims being included in the same class." In re U.S. Truck Co., 800 F. 2d 581, 585 (6th Cir. 1986). Section 1122(a) does not demand that all similar claims be in the same class. To the contrary, the bankruptcy court has substantial discretion to place similar claims in different classes. We have observed that "Congress incorporated into section 1122.... broad discretion to determine proper classification according to the factual circumstances of each individual case."

In this case, the bankruptcy court determined that the evidence supported the factual assumptions upon which the classifications are based, and that given those facts, the Plan's classifications are proper. For example, the bankruptcy court found the testimony of three widely recognized expert witnesses helpful.... Id. They offered quantitative evidence demonstrating that the highest tort awards in various other countries were significantly lower than in the United States. For example, one expert witness testified that the highest non-pecuniary award in injury cases in Australia is approximately $230,000. The bankruptcy court found these witnesses credible, in contrast to the foreign claimants' witnesses, who the court found to be "unhelpful."

Based on such evidence, the bankruptcy court found that "without question, the evidence on the record shows that tort recoveries in the United States tend to be significantly higher than those in foreign jurisdictions." Though the foreign claimants point to countervailing considerations, their arguments, at best, show that there was conflicting evidence on the factual assumptions underlying the classification scheme. The foreign claimants have not shown that the facts used to support the separate classifications for foreign and domestic claimants were clearly erroneous.

Second, the various groups of foreign claimants contend that their claims are more valuable than claims originating from other countries in their respective classes. They argue that the various claims in their class are not "substantially similar" as required by section 1122(a). They further argue that by giving identical consideration to class members whose claims are of different value, they are not being treated the same as other members of their class in violation of the Code's requirement that claimants within a class be treated equally. 11 U.S.C § 1123(a)(4).

This issue, therefore, turns on whether the Plan improperly places foreign claims that are not "substantially similar" in the same class. For the following reasons we find that the bankruptcy court's determination that the claims within a given class are "substantially similar" is not clearly erroneous.

The bankruptcy court relied on the testimony of a leading expert in comparative law methodology, Basil Markenisis, who pointed to legal, economic, and cultural factors supporting the bankruptcy court's conclusion that the claims within each class are "substantially similar." Markenisis discussed (1) the availability of social safety nets in other countries, (2) other countries' reliance on judges as opposed to juries, (3) limitations on punitive damages, (4) unavailability of contingency fees, (5) limitations on strict liability doctrines, (6) cultural factors, (7) reluctance to use lawyers, especially in the Far East, and (8) reliance upon semi-official medical reports in Europe. The bankruptcy court concluded, based on such evidence, that the claims are "substantially similar." Though the foreign claimants offer countervailing considerations, they have offered no evidence to indicate that the facts relied upon by the bankruptcy court were clearly erroneous. Moreover, we note that all foreign claimants retain the right to pursue full payment of their claims in the Litigation Facility. The fact that foreign claimants maintain the litigation option further supports the finding that the Plan does not treat claims that are in the same class unequally.

IV.

For the reasons set forth above, we AFFIRM the bankruptcy court's determination that the Plan's classification of foreign claimants meets the Bankruptcy Code's requirements. In addition, we AFFIRM the district court's determination that, when there are "unusual circumstances," the bankruptcy court may enjoin non-consenting creditors' claims against a non-debtor to facilitate a Chapter 11 plan of reorganization. However, we REMAND this case to the district court for those matters needing additional findings.

QUESTIONS ABOUT DOW CORNING AND CLASSIFICATION OF CLAIMS

1. Note that the Plan divides claims into "thirty-three classes and subclasses." What is the legal difference between a "class" of claims and a "subclass" of claims?

2. Did the bankruptcy court find that all of the foreign breast implant claims are substantially similar?

3. Did the bankruptcy court find that foreign breast implant claims are not substantially similar to the domestic breast implant claims?

---

(5) Review of What We Have Done with Classifications of Claims and Preview of What We Will Do Later with Classification of Claims

Dow Corning applied sections 1123(a)(1) and 1122 to a plan that created multiple classes of unsecured claims for financial reasons—to distribute less to foreign tort claimants. Later, we will again apply sections 1123(a)(1) and 1122 to a plan that created multiple classes of unsecured claims for plan confirmation reasons—to satisfy the requirements of section 1129(a)(10) that at least one "impaired" class accepted the plan.

---

2. OBTAINING CREDITOR APPROVAL ("ACCEPTANCE")

The late Professor MacLachlan described a business reorganization under the bankruptcy laws as a "composition in bankruptcy." James MacLachlan, *BANKRUPTCY* 371 (1956). More recently (but not recently) a prominent bankruptcy lawyer, J. Ronald Trost wrote that "Reorganization plans are essentially contracts between the debtor and its creditors." J. Ronald Trost, *Business Reorganizations Under Chapter 11 of the New Bankruptcy Code*, 34 Bus. Law. 1309, 1327 (1979).

You need to question what you read. Particularly if it was written either by a guy who changes the spelling of his last name[14] or someone who uses his first initial and middle name.[15]

A Chapter 11 plan is similar to a composition, similar to a contract, in that it will be necessary to obtain consent from at least some creditors. A Chapter 11 plan is different from a composition or any other form of contract in that it binds not only the creditors who agree to it but other creditors as well. The binding nature of the plan requires extra steps to ensure that its fairness—to provide an index of fairness other than consent. The first such step is regulation of the manner in which consent is obtained.

---

a. Disclosure of Adequate Information Before Creditors Vote

In Chapter 11, creditors assent to a plan by voting to accept the plan. While Chapter 11 does not require that all creditors consent to the plan, it contemplates that creditors will receive "adequate information" about the plan and have the opportunity to vote on the plan.

Note section 1125's phrase: "adequate information." According to legislative history, "The premise underlying ... Chapter 11 ... is the same as the premise of the securities laws. If adequate disclosure is provided to all creditors and stockholders whose rights are to be affected, then they should be able to make an informed judgment of their own, rather than having the court or the Securities and Exchange Commission inform them in advance whether the proposed plan is a good plan." H. Rep. 595, 93d Cong., 1st Sess. 226 (1977). Accordingly, a bankruptcy court does not review the substantive merits of a Chapter 11 plan before the plan is submitted to creditors and stockholders for vote. Instead, the bankruptcy court reviews the adequacy of the information about the plan provided to creditors and stockholders.

Section 1125(b) requires the creditors and stockholders be provided with "a written disclosure statement approved after notice and hearing by the court as containing adequate information." "Adequate information" is defined in section 1125(a). Although courts acknowledge that what constitutes "adequate information" varies from case to case, several courts have developed checklists.

---

11 U.S.C. § 1125(b)

(b) An acceptance or rejection of a plan may not be solicited after the commencement of the case under this title from a holder of a claim or

---

14. Professor MacLachlan changed the spelling of his name from "McLaughlin" when he was older even than your senior author, "correcting an error made in Scotland about 1835." J. HANNA & J. MACLACHLAN, CASES AND MATERIALS ON CREDITORS' RIGHTS, at viii n.1 (4th ed. 1951)

15. Remember G. Gordon Liddy, H. Howard Hunt, L. Ron Hubbard and P. Diddy Combs.

interest with respect to such claim or interest, unless, at the time of or before such solicitation, there is transmitted to such holder the plan or a summary of the plan, and a written disclosure statement approved, after notice and a hearing, by the court as containing <u>adequate information</u>.... (emphasis added)

---

11 U.S.C. § 1125(a)

(a) In this section–

(1) "adequate information" means information of a kind, and in sufficient detail, as far as is reasonably practicable in light of the nature and history of the debtor and the condition of the debtor's books and records, including a discussion of the potential material Federal tax consequences of the plan to the debtor any successor to the debtor, and a hypothetical investor typical of the holders of claims or interests in the case, that would enable a hypothetical reasonable investor typical of holders of claims or interests such a hypothetical investor of the relevant class to make an informed judgment about the plan, but adequate information need not include such information about any other possible or proposed plan and in determining whether a disclosure statement provides adequate information, the court shall consider the complexity of the case, the benefit of additional information to creditors and other parties in interest, and the cost of providing additional information.

Numerous courts have prescribed a list of disclosures which typically should be included in a disclosure statement. For example, in *In re Scioto Valley Mortgage Co.*, 88 B.R. 168 (Bankr. S.D. Ohio 1988) the court adopted a 19–point list of types of information that may be required in a disclosure statement:

1. The circumstances that gave rise to the filing of the bankruptcy petition;

2. A complete description of the available assets and their value;

3. The anticipated future of the debtor;

4. The source of the information provided in the disclosure statement;

5. A disclaimer, which typically indicates that no statements or information concerning the debtor or its assets or securities are authorized, other than those set forth in the disclosure statement;

6. The condition and performance of the debtor while in Chapter 11;

7. Information regarding claims against the estate;

8.   A liquidation analysis setting forth the estimated return that creditors would receive under Chapter 7;

9.   The accounting and valuation methods used to produce the financial information in the disclosure statement;

10.   Information regarding the future management of the debtor, including the amount of compensation to be paid to any insiders, directors, and/or officers of the debtor;

11.   A summary of the plan of reorganization;

12.   An estimate of all administrative expenses, including attorneys' fees and accountants fees;

13.   The collectibility of any accounts receivable;

14.   Any financial information, valuations or pro forma projections that would be relevant to creditors' determinations of whether to accept or reject the plan;

15.   Information relevant to the risks being taken by the creditors and interest holders;

16.   The actual or projected value that can be obtained from avoidable transfers;

17.   The existence, likelihood and possible success of non-bankruptcy litigation;

18.   The tax consequences of the plan; and

19.   The relationship of the debtor with affiliates.

Several reported decisions have used this checklist.

Another bankruptcy judge prepared a different list—a list of the causes of delay and expense in Chapter 11. He included disclosure statements on the list, stating:

> The process of preparing a disclosure statement and then dealing with the objections and the hearing is an expensive and time consuming process. It is especially troubling in those circumstances in which the creditor objects to the disclosure statement in a strategic effort to improve its treatment under the plan. Regardless, the process can adversely impact the debtor in two ways. First, it can result in substantial fees for attorneys and accountants. Second, it can result in a substantial diversion of the management time from the debtor's business and the reorganization process. . . . The suspicion is that in the average small to medium size chapter 11 case, the time and money spent on this process is largely wasted because creditors are not interested in all of the disclosures that are presently required and thus they do not read the disclosure statement.

See Honorable Steven Rhodes, *Eight Statutory Causes of Delay and Expense in Chapter 11 Bankruptcy Cases*, 67 Am. Bankr. L.J. 287, 316–17 (1993).

Problem 11–11:   What Is Disclosed?

1. Perris Pizza, Inc. has filed its Chapter 11 plan and disclosure state-
    ment. C, a creditor, objects to the disclosure statement because it fails
    to mention articles in Business Week, Forbes and the Wall Street
    Journal that are critical of Perris Pizza, Inc.'s business plan and
    management team. What should be the result?

2. Nickles Stores has filed its Chapter 11 plan and disclosure statement.
    The creditors' committee objects to the disclosure statement because
    it fails to mention that (i) WalMart has expressed an interest in
    buying Nickles Stores. and (ii) the creditors' committee would prefer
    that WalMart own Nickles Stores. What should be the result?

Problem 11–12:   Who Discloses?

1. If in the Nickles Stores case exclusivity has ended, and the creditors
    committee files its own plan, providing for the sale of Nickles Stores
    to WalMart, will the creditors' committee have to file a disclosure
    statement?

2. D files a plan and disclosure statement in its Chapter 11 case, and the
    court approves the disclosure statement. The creditors' committee is
    opposed to the plan and wants to send material to creditors urging
    them to vote against the plan. Does section 1125 require that the
    creditors' committee submit its solicitation material to the bankrupt-
    cy court for approval? Is section 1121 relevant to your answering this
    question about section 1125?

b. Prepackaged Plans

In some cases, parties have been negotiating long and hard before the
bankruptcy case is even filed. A majority of creditors may have agreed to a
sensible workout plan, but some creditors may be "holding out," trying to
use their leverage as holdouts to extract special deals for their particular
consent. In such cases, if all the work and disclosure is done before the
filing, it would be economic waste for the parties to ignore what has gone
on.

The Bankruptcy Code recognizes this. It allows the solicitation and
voting to occur pre-petition. Once the case is filed, the plan proponent
usually immediately files the plan and all disclosure materials, and asks
for a joint hearing on the plan and disclosure statement. Section 1126(b)
then permits the votes so solicited to count if "the solicitation of such
acceptance or rejection was in compliance with any applicable nonbankruptcy law, rule, or regulation governing the adequacy of disclosure in
connection with such solicitation; or . . . if there is not any such law, rule,
or regulation, such acceptance or rejection was solicited after disclosure to

such holder of adequate information, as defined in section 1125(a) of this title." *In re Pioneer Finance Corp.*, 246 B.R. 626, 630 (Bankr. D. Nev. 2000) (describing the difference between a prepackaged plan and a prenegotiated plan). See also section 1125(g).

Prepackaged plans are typically used when the debtor has relatively constant amounts of debt, such as the bonds or debentures of publicly-traded companies. It does not work well when the debt is trade debt, widely disbursed and constantly changing.

How can a "pre-pack" not work well? What can go wrong with a "pre-pack"? A fair amount. As we have seen, one of the great benefits for debtors in bankruptcy is the automatic stay of section 362. The stay stops unilateral collection efforts by creditors while the debtor regroups. But by definition, the negotiation of a pre-pack occurs before the filing, and hence before the effectiveness of the automatic stay. This skews negotiating leverage somewhat.

Problem 11–13: Problems With a Pre–Pack

Jonas, Inc. sells garments on a wholesale basis to retailers such as K–Mart, Wal–Mart and the like. Due to an ill-advised leveraged buyout several years ago, it is currently in a precarious financial situation. It believes that it can survive if it gathers together its creditors (consisting of trade creditors who shipped goods to Jonas on unsecured credit, and the bondholders who received their bonds in the leveraged buyout).

At the meeting, things don't go well. Jonas is proposing to pay trade creditors in full, and to issue new bonds in exchange for the old bonds–but the new bonds will be only 80% of face amount of the old bonds, will carry a lower (but market) interest rate, and will be repayable over a 15–year period. As it now stands, the bonds are due in three years.

Several bondholders balk at the package. They leave the meeting, and the next Jonas hears of them they have sued on their bonds, and have sought a pre-judgment attachment of all of Jonas' inventory.

1. What can Jonas do? Does it matter if the bondholders who sued hold only 2% of the outstanding bond issue?

2. Would it matter if instead of the bondholders, the dissident creditors were trade creditors (who would otherwise stand to be paid in full if the pre-pack goes through)? If they were disgruntled insiders suing over their severance package?

3. If Jonas just pays the dissident bondholders, what do you think the reaction will be from the other bondholders? The trade creditors?

Another risk of a prepackaged plan is that the bankruptcy court will not approve of the pre-filing solicitation. "A proponent of a prepackaged plan takes a substantial risk that, at the confirmation stage of the case, the Court may determine that the proposed disclosure statement or process of solicitation are inadequate." *In re Colorado Springs Spring Creek Gen. Imp. Dist.*, 177 B.R. 684, 691 (Bankr. D. Colo. 1995). There is some guidance here, in that most prepackaged plans, to the extent that ask for changes in securities, are subject to federal and state securities laws. Again, see section 1125(g).

---

c. Connection Between Creditor Acceptance Requirements and Court Confirmation Requirements

You can not understand Chapter 11's provisions with respect to creditor voting (i.e.,"acceptance") without some understanding of Chapter 11's provisions with respect to bankruptcy judge approval (i.e., "confirmation".)

Chapter 11 contemplates not only a vote on the plan by the debtor's creditors and stockholders, but also a review of the plan by the bankruptcy court. A bankruptcy judge has the statutory power to confirm a Chapter 11 plan that has not received the necessary majorities; a bankruptcy judge has the power not to confirm a plan that has been accepted by all holders of claims and interests.

Section 1128 requires the bankruptcy court to hold a hearing on confirmation and give the parties in interest notice of the hearing so that they might raise objections to confirmation. Section 1129 contains the confirmation standards.

Subject to the limited exceptions of section 1129(c) and (d), a plan that has been accepted by the requisite majorities of every class of claims and interests must be confirmed by the bankruptcy court if the enumerated requirements of section 1129(a) are satisfied. A plan that has been accepted by the requisite majorities of at least one class of "impaired" claims but not every class can still be confirmed by the bankruptcy court but only if the plan satisfies the requirements of section 1129(b) as well as the requirements of section 1129(a)(1)–(7) and (9)–(16).

Let's wait to deal with the specific confirmation requirements of section 1129(a) and (b) until we know more about the specifics of the creditor acceptance requirements. More specifically, we need to know how to determine whether the requisite majorities of a class have accepted the plan.

d. The Math of Counting Creditors' Votes

Section 1126(c) and section 1126(d) ,set out below, deal with the questions of how many creditors and how many shareholders must accept the plan. Please read these provisions. Note that section 1126 focuses on classes of claims and classes of interests. Section 1126 does not require that each and every member of a class of claims or interests accept a

Chapter 11 plan. Under section 1126(c), a class of claims has accepted a plan when more than one-half in number and at least two-thirds in amount of those actually voting on the plan accept the plan. Under section 1126(d), a class of interests (think equity securities) has accepted a plan when two-thirds in amount of those actually voting on the plan accept the plan.

"One-half." "Two-thirds." If you can still do fractions (½, ⅔), you can do the math of counting acceptances under section 1126.

---

11 U.S.C. § 1126(c), (d)

(c) A class of claims has accepted a plan if such plan has been accepted by creditors, other than any entity designated under subsection (e) of this section, that hold at least two-thirds in amount and more than one-half in number of the allowed claims of such class held by creditors, other than any entity designated under subsection (e) of this section, that have accepted or rejected such plan.

(d) A class of interests has accepted a plan if such plan has been accepted by holders of such interests, other than any entity designated under subsection (e) of this section, that hold at least two-thirds in amount of the allowed interests of such class held by holders of such interests, other than any entity designated under subsection (e) of this section, that have accepted or rejected such plan.

Problem 11–14: Means and Methods of Voting

1. Flintco has ten unsecured creditors, each of which is owed $10 (for a total debt of $100). They are all classified together for purposes of Flintco's plan. Does the class accept or reject the plan under the following scenarios:

    (a) Five creditors turn in ballots. Three vote in favor of the plan, and two reject it.

    (b) Six creditors turn in ballots. Four vote in favor of the plan, and two reject it.

    (c) Only one creditor turns in a ballot, and votes in favor of the plan.

    (d) No creditor turns in a ballot.

2. Assume the facts in Problem 1, above except now the ten creditors are owed money as follows: Two creditors are owed $30 each, and the remaining eight creditors are owed $5 each (again for a total of $100 in debt). Does the class accept or reject the plan under the following scenarios:

    (a) All creditors turn in ballots. The two creditors holding $30 claims each vote in favor of the plan; all other creditors reject it.

    (b) All creditors turn in ballots. The two creditors holding $30 claims each vote in favor of the plan, as do two creditors holding $5 claims. All other creditors reject it.

    (c) All creditors turn in ballots. All eight creditors owed $5 vote in favor of the plan; the two other creditors reject it.

    (d) All creditors turn in ballots. Seven of the eight creditors owed $5 and one of the creditors owed $30 vote in favor of the plan; the remaining two creditors (one with a $30 claim and one with a $5 claim) vote to reject.

    (e) The following are the only votes cast: One creditor holding a $30 claim votes to accept; one creditor holding a $5 claim votes to reject.

    In law school hypotheticals, professors get to make up numbers: "Two creditors are owed $30 each." Lawyers in practice do not enjoy that luxury. Often, as in the next case, the validity and/or amount of a claim is disputed. In reading the next case, consider section 1126(a) set out below and remember what we learned about claims in section 502 and Unit 6.

11 U.S.C. § 1126(a)

    (a) The holder of a claim or interest allowed under section 502 of this title may accept or reject a plan. . . .

STONE HEDGE PROP. v. PHOENIX CAPITAL CORP. (IN RE STONE HEDGE PROP.)

191 B.R. 59 (Bankr. M.D. Pa. 1995)

John J. Thomas, Bankruptcy Judge:

Confronting the court are legal issues concerning valuation under Federal Rule of Bankruptcy Procedure 3012 and temporary allowance under Federal Rule of Bankruptcy Procedure 3018. Motions to value the claim and to temporarily allow a claim have been filed by Phoenix Capital Corporation, ("Phoenix"), in conjunction with the presentation of separate plans of reorganization filed by the Debtor as well as Phoenix.

    Significantly, Phoenix is the principal secured creditor of the Debtor having filed a proof of claim in the amount of Two Million Five Hundred Ninety–Two Thousand Seven Hundred Eighty–Nine and 36/100 Dollars ($2,592,789.36). The Debtor not only disputes the validity of the claim by way of a separate adversary filed against Phoenix, it vehemently opposes the temporary allowance of Phoenix's claim and a determination that Phoenix's claim is secured to any extent. . . .

    A review of the history of the Debtor's relationship with Phoenix would be helpful.

Stone Hedge Properties is a Pennsylvania general partnership organized in 1988 and situate in Wyoming County, Pennsylvania. The principals of Stone Hedge Properties are members of the Kenia family who decided that the best way to maximize the value of their family farm was to convert it into an eighteen-hole golf course. Financing for that endeavor was secured through PNC Bank. Prior to the bankruptcy, the Debtor and PNC Bank agreed that the debt should be restructured but, unfortunately, the restructuring resulted in creating an obligation that the Debtor could not afford to meet on a regular basis.

On June 7, 1993, the Debtor filed for relief under Chapter Eleven of the United States Bankruptcy Code. On June 23, 1993, PNC Bank sold its paper, then representing approximately Two Million Three Hundred Fifty Thousand Dollars ($2,350,000.00) in debt, to Phoenix for a negotiated consideration of One Million Three Hundred Fifteen Thousand Dollars ($1,315,000.00). Principals of Phoenix were former employees of a PNC Bank subsidiary that was servicing the PNC mortgage. Phoenix was formed for the purpose of acquiring distressed assets for investment.

Phoenix maintains that its debt, for plan purposes, should now be valued at the face amount of the mortgage together with accrued interest, attorney's fees and costs. They further maintain that the collateral securing this debt, i.e. the golf course and its equipment, as well as the housing development which abuts Stone Hedge, should be valued at no more than Two Million Eighty Thousand Dollars ($2,080,000.00) in accordance with the testimony of their expert, John Carl Shultz, Jr. This would make Phoenix significantly undersecured. This obviously would have a significant impact on the ability of the Debtor to confirm their plan pursuant to the criteria suggested in the case of In Re John Hancock Mutual Life Insurance Co., 987 F.2d 154 (3rd Cir. 1993).

The Debtor argues just as strenuously that the Phoenix claim should not be allowed to any extent because of the inequities apparent from the restructuring of the loan and the subsequent assignment of that loan to an entity composed of former employees of the bank. They further argue that should this court allow the claim to any extent, it should be limited to the consideration paid by Phoenix for the mortgage, i.e. One Million Three Hundred Fifteen Thousand Dollars ($1,315,000.00), and not the actual balance due the mortgage of Two Million Three Hundred Fifty Thousand Dollars ($2,350,000.00).

The Debtor further argues that, regardless of the amount to which Phoenix is allowed, the value of the collateral at issue; the golf course, the land development and the equipment, is Four Million Five Hundred Thousand Dollars to Five Million Dollars ($4,500,000.00—$5,000,000.00) and, therefore, Phoenix is fully collateralized. . . .

Phoenix has asked that we value their collateral under Federal Rule of Bankruptcy Procedure 3012 and temporarily allow their claim under Federal Rule of Bankruptcy Procedure 3018. The interplay of Code Sections 1126 and 502 typically require adjudication of the Motion for

Temporary Allowance in order to afford the creditor some substantive input in the plan adjudication. 11 U.S.C. § 1126(a) indicates that a holder of a claim allowed under Section 502 may accept or reject a plan. Section 502(a) indicates that a claim is deemed allowed unless a debtor objects. A creditor whose claim is objected to is therefore disenfranchised from voting on the plan unless the objection is adjudicated prior to plan voting or a mechanism, such as temporary allowance, is provided for. Since claims litigation is often drawn out, thereby defeating one of the essential purposes of the Code, i.e. expedited and efficient administration of the bankruptcy estate, the bankruptcy rules provide that, for voting purposes only, the court can temporarily allow a claim in such an amount as the "court deems proper".

At the outset, we wish the parties to make no mistake that we are not, at this juncture, dealing with an estimation issue under 11 U.S.C. § 502(c), which appears to confine itself to "contingent or unliquidated" claims for distribution purposes.

In essence, the Phoenix claim is a liquidated claim specific in dollar amount but apparently subject to a contingent and unliquidated counterclaim that may offset Phoenix's claim or, in fact, exceed it. . . .

In conjunction with this dispute between the parties, Phoenix contemporaneously with its Motion for Temporary Allowance, requested that the court value its claim. . . .

Federal Rule of Bankruptcy Procedure 3001(f) indicates that an executed and filed proof of claim constitutes prima facie evidence of the validity and amount of the claim. Nevertheless, the Debtor need only present evidence supporting its objection to shift the burden of proving the claim to the claimant, who bears the ultimate burden of proving the claim. . . .

We view the following factors as critical in considering whether we shall temporarily allow the Phoenix claim and, if allowed, the degree to which we make such allowance: (1) the manner in which the claim was initially scheduled by the Debtor; (2) the proof of claim filed by the creditor; and (3) the objection (adversary counterclaim) of the Debtor.

Since our principal consideration must be an accommodation of the underlying purpose of the Code, we first must identify what that purpose is. "The fundamental purpose of reorganization is to prevent a debtor from going into liquidation, with an attendant loss of jobs and possible misuse of economic resources." National Labor Relations Board v. Bildisco & Bildisco, 465 U.S. 513, 528, 104 S. Ct. 1188, 1197, 79 L. Ed. 2d 482 (1984) citing H.R.Rep. No. 95–595, p. 220 (1977).

The statutory scheme advancing the reorganization contemplates that both secured and unsecured creditors will have a "weighted" influence in the eventual program by which a debtor solves its financial dilemma.

Since both the Debtor's plan and the Phoenix plan recognize the possibility that the Phoenix claim would eventually be allowed, we recognize no fundamental concern in temporarily allowing the Phoenix claim to some degree. Additionally, the Debtor recognizes the PNC claim (now held by Phoenix) as undisputed, liquidated and non-contingent in its original schedules. No one, including the Debtor, has argued that there was a lack of consideration for the PNC–Stone Hedge loan. Rather, the Debtor argues that Phoenix should not be allowed to reap an exorbitant profit from its One Million Three Hundred Fifteen Thousand Dollar ($1,315,000.00) investment when it may have benefitted from "insider" information. To a limited degree, and in a context that only permits this court to cursorily examine that issue, the Debtor's point is well-made and there is a possibility that some part of the Phoenix claim will be disallowed.

The courts have long considered that bankruptcy courts were essentially courts of equity and the proceedings in those courts were inherently proceedings in equity. Pepper v. Litton, 308 U.S. 295, 304, 60 S. Ct. 238, 244, 84 L. Ed. 281 (1939). Since we sit as a court of equity in passing on the allowance of claims (Id. at p. 307 and 245), then necessarily we sit as same in passing on the temporary allowance of claims. While it violates no elemental principal to award a claimant the profits attendant to its good investment, we cannot help but be mindful of the allegations of surreptitious conduct suggested by the Debtor. While such allegations alone are insufficient to deny temporary allowance of the entire claim, it does cause this court to hesitate allowing this claim in a manner never originally contemplated by the parties, i.e. as unsecured. When this bankruptcy was filed, the Debtor posited in its schedules that Phoenix was totally secured. When it filed its chapter eleven plan, it adopted the same premise. When Phoenix proposed its chapter eleven plan, it considered itself fully secured. Presumably, when the prepetition creditors of the Debtor dealt with Stone Hedge, they considered PNC Bank, predecessor of Phoenix, to be fully secured. Although we have yet to consider the valuation of this collateral, we herein conclude that the claim of Phoenix should be temporarily allowed up to the value of its collateral or its debt, whichever is the lesser, and denied for any amount in excess thereof. This would allow Phoenix to vote as a secured creditor, which was their historical posture, but not as an unsecured creditor, a position never anticipated by any party prior to the case. Of course, all parties recognize that the impact of this decision affects only the voting on the plan and is not any indication of the eventual disposition of the pending adversary action between the parties.

Next, we must address the valuation of the collateral. [After reviewing the testimony of various appraisers, the court concluded as follows:]

This discussion allows us to find that the value of the Phoenix collateral, pursuant to its Motion to value same, totals Two Million Five Hundred Sixty–Seven Thousand Dollars ($2,567,000.00). Having already determined to temporarily allow Phoenix's claim as secured up to the value of its collateral or the amount of its debt, whichever is less, and having concluded that insufficient cause has been demonstrated at this juncture to reject the Phoenix proof of claim of Two Million Five Hundred Ninety–Two Thousand Seven Hundred Eighty–Nine and 36/100 Dollars

($2,592,789.36), we conclude that the claim of Phoenix should be temporarily allowed as a secured claim in the total amount of Two Million Five Hundred Sixty–Seven Thousand Dollars ($2,567,000.00). To the extent that this renders the balance of their claim, i.e. Twenty–Five Thousand Seven Hundred Eighty–Nine and 36/100 Dollars ($25,789.36), unsecured, the court will deny the Motion to temporarily allow any part of Phoenix's claim as unsecured for the reasons enunciated earlier in this opinion. . . .

Furthermore, since we temporarily conclude that Phoenix is not over-collateralized, they have shown no entitlement to accruing interest on their claim at this juncture. We accordingly issue the preliminary injunction without any requirement by Stone Hedge to make regular payments to Phoenix. . . .

---

e. "Non-Votes"

Some holders of claims and interests do not vote. For example, section 1126(f) provides that a class of claims that is not "impaired under a plan" does not vote; such an unimpaired class is "conclusively presumed" to have accepted the plan. Accordingly, we need to know more about the meaning of "impaired under a plan." We need to read section 1124 set out below and apply section 1124 to Problem 11–15.

---

11 U.S.C. § 1124

[A] class of claims or interests is impaired under a plan unless, with respect to each claim or interest of such class, the plan—

(1) leaves unaltered the legal, equitable, and contractual rights to which such claim or interest entitles the holder of such claim or interest; or

(2) notwithstanding any contractual provision or applicable law that entitles the holder of such claim or interest to demand or receive accelerated payment of such claim or interest after the occurrence of a default—

(A) cures any such default that occurred before or after the commencement of the case under this title, other than a default of a kind specified in section 365(b)(2) of this title;

(B) reinstates the maturity of such claim or interest as such maturity existed before such default;

(C) compensates the holder of such claim or interest for any damages incurred as a result of any reasonable reliance by such holder on such contractual provision or such applicable law; and

(D) does not otherwise alter the legal, equitable, or contractual rights to which such claim or interest entitles the holder of such claim or interest.

Problem 11–15: Applying Impairment

1. All of the claims in Class 3 of X Co.'s plan are based on notes, payable over 10 years at 6% interest. The plan proposes to pay Class 3 claims over 3 years at 6.5% interest. Are Class 3 claims impaired under section 1124?

2. The claim in Class 2 is a 20–year note, secured by Blackacre. Prior to filing for Chapter 11 relief, the debtor defaulted on this mortgage note. That default triggered an acceleration so that the entire debt is now due and payable and triggered a default interest rate of 11%. What does the plan have to provide so that Class 2 will not be impaired under section 1124?

3. The claims in Class 4 are unsecured claims by vendors If the plan provides for payment in full of Class 4 on the effective date of the plan, is Class 4 impaired? If the plan provides for payment in full of Class 4 within 30 days of the effective date, is Class 4 impaired? Is it relevant that Chapter 11 debtor could have paid Class 4 on the effective date—that any impairment is "artificial"?

Just as a class that loses nothing by a plan does not vote because its acceptance is conclusively presumed, a class that loses everything does not vote because its rejection is conclusively presumed.

While insolvency is not a requirement for the use of Chapter 11, most business debtors that use Chapter 11 are insolvent. Insolvency for business debtor generally means that, if the debtor's assets were all sold, there would not be sufficient proceeds to pay all creditors, let alone any equity holders. In short, the equity interests are 'out of the money.' But if a plan recognizes the consequences of insolvency, and eliminates all equity interests, those equity interests are not e allowed to vote on the plan? See section 1126(g)("a class is deemed not to have accepted a plan if such plan provides that the claims or interests of such class do not entitle the holders of such claims or interests to receive or retain any property under the plan on account of such claims or interests.")

We have just considered sections 1126(f) and (g) which precludes entire classes of claims or interests from voting. Section 1126(e) which we consider next throws out the vote of a single creditor from counting.

Please read section 1126(e), set out below. Note that section 1126(e) uses the word "designate", instead of the phrase "throw out." More important, section 1126 uses the phrase "good faith" as the test for determining whether a vote should be designated instead of counted.

What does good faith mean? Creditors usually vote according to their economic self-interest, and that assumption is built into section 1126(c)'s test for whether a class has accepted. Is a creditor's vote "not in good faith" if it does not vote according to its economic self-interest? What if the creditor irrationally hates the debtor's management? Or, what if the creditor's vote is in its economic self-interest but not in the economic best interest of the debtor or other creditors? For example, what if the creditor is a competitor who would love nothing more than the economic death of the debtor? In dealing with such questions, bankruptcy judges generally look to and cite from the *Figter* case below.

11 U.S.C. § 1126(e)

(e) On request of a party in interest, and after notice and a hearing, the court may designate any entity whose acceptance or rejection of such plan was not in good faith, or was not solicited or procured in good faith or in accordance with the provisions of this title.

FIGTER LTD. v. TEACHERS INS. & ANNUITY ASS'N (IN RE FIGTER LTD.)

118 F.3d 635 (9th Cir. 1997)

FERNANDEZ, Circuit Judge:

Figter Limited, a Chapter 11 debtor and owner of Skyline Terrace, an apartment complex, appeals from the district court's affirmance of the bankruptcy court's decision that Teachers Insurance and Annuity Association of America (Teachers), the holder of a $15,600,000 promissory note secured by a first deed of trust on Skyline Terrace, bought twenty-one unsecured claims in good faith and that it could vote each one separately. We affirm.

BACKGROUND

Figter filed a voluntary petition under Chapter 11 of the Bankruptcy Code. It owns Skyline Terrace, a 198–unit residential apartment complex located in Los Angeles. Teachers is a creditor. It holds a $15,600,000 promissory note executed by Figter. The note is secured by a first deed of trust on Skyline Terrace and by $1,400,000 of cash on hand. In fact, Teachers is Figter's only secured creditor and is the only member of Class 2 in a reorganization plan proposed by Figter. The plan contemplates full payment of Teachers' secured claim, but at a disputed rate of interest.

Thus, under Figter's plan, Teachers' claim is not impaired. The plan calls for the impairment of Class 3 unsecured claims by payment at only 80% of their face value.

Teachers has opposed Figter's reorganization plan from its inception because, among other things, that plan contemplates the conversion of Skyline Terrace Apartments into condominiums, with payment to and partial releases by Teachers as the units sell. That could easily result in a property that was part condominium and part rentals, if the plan ultimately fails in operation.

[After the court found that Teachers' claim was fully secured,] Teachers purchased twenty-one of the thirty-four unsecured claims in Class 3 at one hundred cents on the dollar, for a total purchase price of $14,588.62. Teachers had made the same offer to all of the Class 3 claim holders, but not all accepted it. The offer remained open. . . . As a result, Figter's plan is unconfirmable because it is unable to meet the requirements of 11 U.S.C. § 1129(a)(10); there will not be an impaired, consenting class of claims. That will preclude a "cram down" of Teachers' secured claim under 11 U.S.C. § 1129(b). Figter has appealed in an attempt to avoid that result. . . .

DISCUSSION

Figter asserts that Teachers should be precluded from voting its purchased Class 3 claims because it did not buy them in good faith. Figter also asserts that even if the claims were purchased in good faith, Teachers cannot vote them separately, but is limited to one total vote as a Class 3 creditor. If Figter were correct in either of its assertions, it could obtain Class 3 approval of its plan and enhance its chances of cramming down Teachers' Class 2 claims. But Figter is not correct.

A. Good Faith.

The Bankruptcy Code provides that "on request of a party in interest, and after notice and a hearing, the court may designate any entity whose acceptance or rejection of [a] plan was not in good faith, or was not solicited or procured in good faith or in accordance with the provisions of this title." 11 U.S.C. § 1126(e). In this context, designate means disqualify from voting. The Bankruptcy Code does not further define the rather murky term "good faith." That job has been left to the courts.

The Supreme Court brought some clarity to this area when it decided Young v. Higbee Co., 324 U.S. 204, 65 S. Ct. 594, 89 L. Ed. 890 (1945). In Young, the Court was discussing the predecessor to § 1126(e) when it declared that if certain persons "had declined to accept [the] plan in bad faith, the court, under section 203 could have denied them the right to vote on the plan at all." Id. at 210–11, 65 S. Ct. at 598 (footnote omitted). It went on to explain that the provision was intended to apply to those "whose selfish purpose was to obstruct a fair and feasible reorganization in the hope that someone would pay them more than the ratable equivalent of their proportionate part of the bankrupt assets." Id. at 211, 65 S.

Ct. at 598. In other words, the section was intended to apply to those who were not attempting to protect their own proper interests, but who were, instead, attempting to obtain some benefit to which they were not entitled. While helpful, those reflections by the Court do not fully answer the question before us. Other courts have further illuminated the area.

If a person seeks to secure some untoward advantage over other creditors for some ulterior motive, that will indicate bad faith. But that does not mean that creditors are expected to approach reorganization plan votes with a high degree of altruism and with the desire to help the debtor and their fellow creditors. Far from it.

> If a selfish motive were sufficient to condemn reorganization policies of interested parties, very few, if any, would pass muster. On the other hand, pure malice, "strikes" and blackmail, and the purpose to destroy an enterprise in order to advance the interests of a competing business, all plainly constituting bad faith, are motives which may be accurately described as ulterior.

In re Pine Hill Collieries Co., 46 F. Supp. 669, 671 (E.D. Pa. 1942). That is to say, we do not condemn mere enlightened self interest, even if it appears selfish to those who do not benefit from it. See id.

Thus, if Teachers acted out of enlightened self interest, it is not to be condemned simply because it frustrated Figter's desires. That is true, even if Teachers purchased Class 3 claims for the very purpose of blocking confirmation of Figter's proposed plan. That self interest can extend even further without being an ulterior motive. It has been held that a creditor commits no wrong when he votes against a plan of a debtor who has a lawsuit pending against the creditor, for that will not, by itself, show bad faith. It has also been held that no bad faith is shown when a creditor chooses to benefit his interest as a creditor as opposed to some unrelated interest. And the mere fact that a creditor has purchased additional claims for the purpose of protecting his own existing claim does not demonstrate bad faith or an ulterior motive. "As long as a creditor acts to preserve what he reasonably perceives as his fair share of the debtor's estate, bad faith will not be attributed to his purchase of claims to control a class vote." In re Gilbert, 104 B.R. 206, 217 (Bankr. W.D. Mo. 1989).

Courts, on the other hand, have been sensitive to situations where a company, which was not a preexisting creditor, has purchased a claim for the purpose of blocking an action against it. They have seen that as an indication of bad faith. The same has been true where creditors were associated with a competing business and desired to destroy the debtor's business in order to further their own. And when the debtor had claims against itself purchased by an insider or affiliate for the purpose of blocking a plan, or fostering one, that was seen as a badge of bad faith. Figter would have us add that in a single asset bankruptcy, claim purchasing activities, like those of Teachers, are in bad faith. It cites no authority for that, and we see no basis for establishing that as a per se rule.

In short, the concept of good faith is a fluid one, and no single factor can be said to inexorably demand an ultimate result, nor must a single set of factors be considered. It is always necessary to keep in mind the difference between a creditor's self interest as a creditor and a motive which is ulterior to the purpose of protecting a creditor's interest. Prior cases can offer guidance, but, when all is said and done, the bankruptcy court must simply approach each good faith determination with a perspicacity derived from the data of its informed practical experience in dealing with bankrupts and their creditors.

Here, the bankruptcy court did exactly that. It decided that Teachers was not, for practical purposes, the proponent of an alternate plan when it sought to purchase the Class 3 claims. Nor, it found, did Teachers seek to purchase a small number of claims for the purpose of blocking Figter's plan, while injuring other creditors, even if it could do that in some circumstances. Rather, Teachers offered to purchase all Class 3 claims, and only some of those claimants' refusals to sell precluded it from doing so. Moreover, Teachers was a lender, not a competing apartment owner. It acted to protect its interests as Figter's major creditor. It reasonably feared that it could be left with a very complex lien situation, if Figter went forward with its plan. Instead of holding a lien covering the whole of the property, it could have wound up with separate fractured liens on various parts of the property, while other parts were owned by others. That could create a very undesirable mix of owners and renters and of debtors and nondebtors. Added to that was the actual use of cash, which was collateral for the debt owed to Teachers. It cannot be said that Teachers' concerns were irrational.

Based on all that was before it, the bankruptcy court decided that in this case Teachers was a creditor which acted in a good faith attempt to protect its interests and not with some ulterior motive. We cannot say that it erred in making that ultimate determination.

B. Voting.

Figter's fallback position is that even if Teachers did act in good faith, it must be limited to one vote for its twenty-one claims. That assertion is answered by the language of the Bankruptcy Code, which provides that:

> A class of claims has accepted a plan if such plan has been accepted by creditors. . . . that hold at least two-thirds in amount and more than one-half in number of the allowed claims of such class held by creditors . . . that have accepted or rejected such plan.

11 U.S.C. § 1126(c) (emphasis added). That language was interpreted in Gilbert, 104 B.R. at 211, where the court reasoned:

> The formula contained in Section 1126(c) speaks in terms of the number of claims, not the number of creditors, that actually vote for or against the plan. . . . Each claim arose out of a separate transaction, evidencing separate obligations for which separate proofs of claim were filed. Votes of acceptance . . . are to be computed only on

the basis of filed and allowed proofs of claim.... [The creditor] is entitled to one vote for each of his unsecured Class X claims.

That same view was iterated in Concord Square Apartments of Wood Cty, Ltd. v. Ottawa Properties, Inc. (In re Concord Square Apartments of Wood Cty., Ltd.), 174 B.R. 71, 74 (Bankr. S.D. Ohio 1994), where the court held that a creditor with "multiple claims, has a voting right for each claim it holds." We agree. It would not make much sense to require a vote by creditors who held "more than one-half in number of the allowed claims" while at the same time limiting a creditor who held two or more of those claims to only one vote. If allowed claims are to be counted, they must be counted regardless of whose hands they happen to be in....

Of course, that is not to say that a creditor can get away with splitting one claim into many, but that is not what happened here. Teachers purchased a number of separately incurred and separately approved claims (each of which carried one vote) from different creditors. There simply is no reason to hold that those separate votes suddenly became one vote, a result which would be exactly the opposite of claim splitting.

Therefore, the bankruptcy court did not err.

CONCLUSION

Figter hoped to obtain approval of a reorganization plan, which would require Teachers to thole what it saw as a diminution of its creditor's rights. Those hopes were dashed when Teachers bought up most of the Class 3 claims in an effort to protect its own Class 2 claim. Because the bankruptcy court determined that Teachers acted to protect its valid creditor's interest, rather than for ulterior motives, it held that Teachers had acted in good faith. That precluded designation of Teachers' purchased claims. The bankruptcy court also determined that Teachers could vote each of its twenty-one claims separately; it was not limited to a single vote. The district court affirmed those decisions. Because the bankruptcy court did not err in either its factual or its legal determinations, we agree with the district court and affirm the decision.

AFFIRMED.

_____

QUESTIONS ABOUT FIGTER

1. What facts were important to the bankruptcy court's decision? Was it important that "Teachers did not pursue its plan"? That Teachers offered to purchase all Class 3 claims?

2. The leading case disallowing the vote of purchased claims is *In re Allegheny International, Inc.*, 118 B.R. 282 (Bankr. W.D. Pa. 1990). In *Allegheny*, Japonica Partners, a coalition of investment bankers who were not prepetition creditors of the debtor, purchased enough claims to block the debtor's plan and thereby open the way for confirmation

of its own competing plan. Japonica's plan contemplated converting its purchased debt into a controlling stock interest in the debtor. The bankruptcy court held that Japonica's votes rejecting the debtor's plan were cast in bad faith. Is *Figter* distinguishable from *Allegheny*?

---

3.   OBTAINING COURT APPROVAL ("CONFIRMATION") OF A CHAPTER 11 PLAN UNDER SECTION 1129(a)

Section 1129(a) contains sixteen separate confirmation requirements. We have already looked at the creditor voting requirement of section 1129(a)(8): the requisite majorities of each impaired class has accepted the plan. Now let's consider the four other most considered confirmation requirements in section 1129(a): good faith, 1129(a)(3); the "best interests" test, 1129(a)(7); feasibility, 1129(a)(11) and payment of administrative and tax claims, 1129(a)(9).

a.   Good Faith

11 U.S.C. § 1129(a)(3)

(a) The court shall confirm a plan only if all of the following requirements are met:....

> (3) The plan has been proposed in good faith and not by any means forbidden by law.

IN RE DOW CORNING CORP.

244 B.R. 673 (Bankr. E.D. Mich. 1999)

AMENDED OPINION ON GOOD FAITH

ARTHUR J. SPECTOR, Chief Judge.

The Debtor and the Official Committee of Tort Claimants negotiated and on November 9, 1998 filed a Joint Plan of Reorganization.... [On July 30, 1999], the Court issued its Findings of Fact and Conclusions of Law on the matter of the confirmation of the Plan. This opinion is one of several which will serve to supplement and explicate some of the findings and conclusions....

A number of parties objected to confirmation of the Plan on the ground that the Proponents failed to satisfy the requirements of § 1129(a)(3). For the reasons which follow, the Court finds that the Plan was filed in good faith and not by any means forbidden by law.

The Bankruptcy Code does not define the term "good faith." Courts have taken a variety of approaches when applying it. This is not surprising, however, for it is difficult to place precise boundaries around such a fuzzy concept. Laguna Assoc. Ltd. Partnership v. Aetna Cas. & Surety Co. (In re Laguna Assoc. Ltd. Partnership), 30 F.3d 734, 738 (6th Cir. 1994)("[G]ood faith is an amorphous notion, largely defined by factual inquiry." (quoting In re Okoreeh–Baah, 836 F.2d 1030, 1033 (6th Cir. 1988))).

Several courts borrow the concept of good faith from jurisprudence under §§ 362(d)(1) and 1112(b) of the Bankruptcy Code. Those sections focus primarily on the debtor's pre-petition conduct. By the time a case reaches the plan confirmation stage, pre-petition behavior is largely irrelevant. Instead, when considering whether a plan satisfies the § 1129(a)(3) requirement, the focus of the court must be on the plan itself. This issue is whether the plan "will fairly achieve a result consistent with the objectives and purposes of the Bankruptcy Code."

One court explained the rationale for this standard this way:

[§ 1129(a)(3)] reads as follows: "The court shall confirm a plan only if all of the following requirements are met: (3) The plan has been proposed in good faith and not by any means forbidden by law." 11 U.S.C. § 1129(a)(3) (emphasis added). Thus, it is the plan's proposal which must be (a) in good faith and (b) not by a means forbidden by law.

[T]he purpose of 1129(a)(3) was to insure that the proposal of a plan of reorganization was to be done in good faith and not in a way that was forbidden by law. Indeed one commentator, in comparing Section 1129(a)(3) with its predecessor sections under the Bankruptcy Act, has indicated that the focus of 1129(a)(3) is upon the conduct manifested in obtaining the confirmation votes of a plan of reorganization and not necessarily on the substantive nature of the plan.

In re Sovereign Group, 1984–21 Ltd., 88 B.R. 325, 328 (Bankr.D.Colo. 1988) (citing 5 Collier on Bankruptcy ¶ 1129.02 (15th ed.1984))....

Moreover, in our view, placing the amorphous concept of good faith outside the confines of all of the other elements for confirmation of the plan, even outside § 1129(b)'s cramdown requirements, is intended to allow courts to utilize their gut feeling about a plan's effects:

We have always been reluctant to seize upon "good faith" as an easy way out of confirming a difficult or questionable plan. We believe that a finding of lack of good faith in proposing a plan ought to be extraordinary and should not substitute for careful analysis of other elements necessary for confirmation. Haines, Good Faith: An Idea Whose Time Has Come and Gone, Norton Bankruptcy Law Adviser (April 1988). However, we also believe that a court of equity must use all of its senses to determine whether a proposed course is fair and equitable. A bankruptcy judge is more than a pair of ears to hear the argument and a pair of eyes to read the law. Furthermore, the mind, which may tell us intellectually that there is nothing technically "illegal" in a particular course of action, is not always the final arbiter. Sometimes a bankruptcy judge's nose tells him/her that something doesn't smell right and further inquiry is warranted. (Others may call this "common sense.") As a human being, a bankruptcy judge may allow the heart to influence a decision even though, as a judge, he/she should beware not to let emotions stand in the way of justice. Sometimes, a bankruptcy judge's stomach may turn, when he/she is preparing to sign a particular judgment or order. This queasiness is reflective of the judge's sense that for some, perhaps inarticulable, reason, it just isn't right to grant the relief requested. In the context of plan confirmation in bankruptcy cases, when this is the way the judge feels, it may be because the plan has not "been proposed in good faith." In short, the reading of the law should be tempered by the judge's sense of equity—what is just in the circumstances of the case. If there are objective facts to support this feeling, perhaps the plan should not be confirmed.

In re John P. Timko et al., No. 87–09318 (unpublished) (Bankr.E.D.Mich. July 22, 1988). For a plan where this test is put to use see In re Barr, 38 B.R. 323, 325 (Bankr.E.D.Mich.1984) (Bernstein, J.) ("At this stage the maxim 'be just before being generous' is called to mind. Mr. E. Barr's generosity to his family members would, if approved by this Court, result in a discharge of close to one million dollars of unsecured debts. That is simply unacceptable when for all practical purposes the Debtors continue to manage their same business. No amount of refined (or strained) analysis can still the moral outrage that the Debtors' plan triggers. At some point, a court of equity has to say, no, this cannot be.... If 'good faith' is to have any moral significance, the Debtors' plan cannot be found to be deserving of that appellation."). Thus, courts frequently do and ought to reject sloppy reliance on good faith to cover all sorts of more specific objections covered by specific confirmation standards.

Applying this standard to facts of the instant case after carefully reviewing the Plan and the entire record, the Court finds that the Proponents of the Plan have met their burden of showing that the Plan was proposed and formulated in "good faith" under § 1129(a)(3). The Plan was proposed in a legitimate effort to rehabilitate a solvent but financially-distressed corporation, besieged by massive pending and potential future product liability litigation against it—an articulated policy objective of chapter 11. A plan proposed as a means to resolve tort liability claims does not violate the § 1129(a)(3) "good faith" confirmation requirement. The evidence is clear that the legal costs and logistics of defending the worldwide product liability lawsuits against the Debtor threatened its vitality by depleting its financial resources and preventing its management from focusing on core business matters. The Debtor "is a real company with real debt, real creditors and a compelling need to reorganize in order to meet these obligations" and is therefore, exactly the type of debtor for which chapter 11 was enacted. As testified by Tommy Jacks, Arthur B. Newman, Scott Gilbert and Ralph Knowles, the Plan was the result of intense arm's-length negotiations between parties represented by competent counsel who were guided by an experienced Court-appointed mediator and the findings and recommendations of highly qualified experts. The Plan incorporates procedures to effectively resolve the multitude of tort claims that drove the Debtor into bankruptcy and will allow the Debtor to emerge from bankruptcy as a viable corporation with the ability to pay its creditors the full amount to which they are entitled, to continue providing a return for its stockholders, to pay taxes to the federal government and to innumerable state and local governments, and to provide jobs for its employees. This is exactly the result envisioned by the drafters of chapter 11.

The Official Committee of Unsecured Creditors ("U/S CC") was among the parties who objected on good-faith grounds. Its arguments are basically no more than attempts to revisit and reargue objections it made to the Plan under other provisions. Its claim that the Plan unjustly enriches the Debtor's shareholders at the expense of the unsecured commercial creditors by not paying them according to their legal entitlements is just another way of arguing that the commercial creditors are entitled to postpetition interest at their contract rate. This issue has already been disposed of in two other opinions by this Court.

Similarly, the U/S CC's § 1129(a)(3) objection, based on the allegedly improper so-called "third-party releases" is and will be more appropriately addressed and disposed of in another separate opinion of the Court.

Likewise, the U/S CC's § 1129(a)(3) objection based on the Plan's payment of allegedly invalid and unenforceable claims merely reiterated the arguments it made under its § 502(b) objection. That objection was overruled in yet another separate opinion.

Like the other objections, the U/S CC's fourth and fifth objections, arguing that the process by which the Plan was formulated and proposed was "inequitable, unconscionable and impermissible" and that the Plan "contains inequitable, unconscionable and impermissible terms and conditions" rely on arguments made in support of objections under §§ 1129(a)(1), (2), and (7), as well as other arguments that were separately decided by the Court, and will be discussed in greater detail in an opinion to be released in the future. In essence, the U/S CC argues that the Plan as formulated and proposed is inequitable because it treats the unsecured commercial creditors less favorably than a previous plan by not paying them postpetition interest at their contract rate. This objection was sustained in this Court's opinion on cramdown of Class 4 and is rendered moot by the Plan's self-correcting mechanism. Moreover, the "good-faith" determination under § 1129(a)(3) is to be made with regard only to the plan proposed to be confirmed and without regard to any prior plans.

Therefore, because the Court has disposed of all the U/S CC's objections on which its § 1129(a)(3) objection is based, and because the Plan advances the policy objectives of chapter 11, § 1129(a)(3) is satisfied.

McCORMICK v. BANC ONE LEASING CORP. (IN RE McCORMICK)

49 F.3d 1524 (11th Cir. 1995)

Before ANDERSON and CARNES, Circuit Judges, and RONEY, Senior Circuit Judge.

PER CURIAM:

The debtor appeals the denial of his Chapter 11 reorganization plan for lack of good faith in an order which simply stated that "The Debtor's invocation of his Fifth Amendment privilege in connection with this case demonstrates that the Plan of Reorganization was not filed in good faith." The debtor had invoked the Fifth Amendment and refused to testify in a related adversary proceeding. The district court affirmed without opinion. This appeal comes without the benefit of a brief from the appellee.

On the simple issue presented by this appeal, we hold that the debtor's assertion of the Fifth Amendment in a related adversary proceeding, standing alone, when all other aspects of his Chapter 11 Plan of Reorganization are consistent with the goals of the Bankruptcy Code, is not sufficient evidence of bad faith to merit the denial of his plan.

In order to be confirmed, a Chapter 11 reorganization plan must be submitted in good faith and not by any means forbidden by law. 11 U.S.C. § 1129(a)(3). While the Bankruptcy Code does not define the term, courts have interpreted "good faith" as requiring that there is a reasonable likelihood that the plan will achieve a result consistent with the objectives and purposes of the Code.

Where the plan is proposed with the legitimate and honest purpose to reorganize and has a reasonable hope of success, the good faith requirements of section 1129(a)(3) are satisfied.

The focus of a court's inquiry is the plan itself, and courts must look to the totality of the circumstances surrounding the plan, keeping in mind the purpose of the Bankruptcy Code is to give debtors a reasonable opportunity to make a fresh start.

Other than the debtor's refusal to testify in a related adversary proceeding, the totality of the circumstances surrounding Timothy McCormick's proposed reorganization plan would seem to negate any specific showing of bad faith. McCormick, who filed an individual, voluntary petition for relief under Chapter 11 of the Bankruptcy Code, complied with all necessary financial and other disclosure requirements. McCormick timely filed the required schedules and statement of financial affairs, and he testified at the meeting of creditors. The bankruptcy court approved the disclosure statement. The debtor secured the necessary number of the ballots by creditors in favor of the plan.

McCormick proposed to distribute approximately $23,000 to his creditors along with another $200 per month for 36 months. Apparently,

McCormick could have filed a Chapter 7 petition, liquidating all his assets and obtaining a discharge, leaving his creditors in worse condition than under the Chapter 11 plan.

There is no doubt that the Fifth Amendment privilege extends to bankruptcy proceedings. In Chapter 7 liquidation cases, the Bankruptcy Code provides that absent a grant of immunity, the debtor is free to invoke his Fifth Amendment privilege and still receive a discharge from his debts. 11 U.S.C. § 727(a)(6)(B).

The Bankruptcy Code does not dictate nor have we found any other court to have held that a bankruptcy court may deny confirmation of a reorganization plan solely because the debtor refused to testify on the basis of the privilege against self-incrimination in a related proceeding during the pendency of a Chapter 11 case.

While his case was proceeding, one of McCormick's creditors, First Interstate Credit Alliance, Inc., filed a separate adversary proceeding against McCormick seeking to declare a debt non-dischargeable under section 523 of the Code. During a related deposition, McCormick asserted his Fifth Amendment privilege against self-incrimination and refused to testify. Notably, McCormick and First Interstate later agreed to a compromise on the dispute. The bankruptcy court entered an order approving the compromise. Prior to the final confirmation hearing, after McCormick filed the necessary disclosure statement and proposed reorganization plan, three creditors, Advanta Leasing Corporation, Banc One Leasing Corporation, and First Interstate, filed objections to the confirmation claiming McCormick's plan was not proposed in good faith, as required by section 1129(a)(3) of the Bankruptcy Code. Only Advanta cited as its reason for objecting to the plan McCormick's assertion of the Fifth Amendment during the course of the proceedings. The bankruptcy court concluded that McCormick's failure to testify in some of the proceedings was contrary to the goals of the Bankruptcy Code and was evidence he did not propose the plan in good faith.

As long as McCormick's failure to testify at the First Interstate deposition did not impede the basic bankruptcy administration of his case, however, assertion of his Fifth Amendment privilege alone cannot be the basis for denying confirmation of his plan.

It may well be that the bankruptcy court may have denied McCormick's confirmation for reasons additional to his refusal to testify in the First Interstate deposition, or that his refusal impeded the administration of the Chapter 11 plan in a way not disclosed by this record. If so, that issue may be addressed on remand. Being unable to find support in this record for the bankruptcy court's finding of bad faith under section 1129(a)(3) of the Bankruptcy Code on the refusal to testify alone, however, we must vacate the decision of the district court and remand for further proceedings consistent with this opinion. . . .

Vacated and Remanded.

Problem 11–16: Good Faith and Conflicting Allegiances

Before it filed for chapter 11 bankruptcy, Perris Air, Inc. agreed to its lenders' demands that it bring in a 'workout' specialist to run the company. Frank Bestwin was chosen by the management of Perris Air from a short list of three acceptable persons provided by the lender.

Frank has a deal with Perris Air for compensation that is fair and consistent with other similar air carriers. He also has a deal with the lenders to pay him a $1 million "success fee" upon confirmation of any plan in which the lenders are paid in full.

Frank develops such a plan. The unsecured creditors' committee does not care for it. Do they have a valid objection under 11 U.S.C. § 1129(a)(3)?

---

b. The Chapter 7 Test: AKA, The "Best Interests Of Creditors"

Recall that Chapter 11 is premised on the notions that the going concern value of a business will be greater than its liquidation value and that through the Chapter 11 plan negotiation process this going concern value premium will be allocated between a business's creditors and its owners. Accordingly, it is only reasonable for section 1129(a)(7) to require each creditor receive a distribution that is at least equal to what it would have received "if the debtor were liquidated under chapter 7."

11 U.S.C. § 1129(a)(7)

(a) The court shall confirm a plan only if all of the following requirements are met: . . . .

(7) With respect to each impaired class of claims or interests—

(A) each holder of a claim or interest of such class—

(i) has accepted the plan; or

(ii) will receive or retain under the plan on account, of such claim or interest property of a value, as of the effective date of the plan, that is not less than the amount that such holder would so receive or retain if the debtor were liquidated under chapter 7 of this title on such date; . . . .

IN RE SIERRA–CAL

210 B.R. 168 (Bankr. E.D. Cal. 1997)

OPINION

CHRISTOPHER M. KLEIN, Bankruptcy Judge:

The issue, which appears to be a question of first impression, is whether in plan confirmation proceedings the mandatory disallowance of certain claims pursuant to 11 U.S.C. § 502(d) should be imposed when calculating the hypothetical chapter 7 liquidation required by the "best interests" test.

This court concludes that § 502(d), which mandatorily disallows claims of creditors who received avoidable transfers or who owe the estate, does apply in the "best interests" test analysis under 11 U.S.C. § 1129(a)(7)(A)(ii). A plan of reorganization fails the "best interests" test when it purports to give any value to a creditor who has a claim disallowable under § 502(d) at the expense of creditors and interest holders who are not under a § 502(d) disability and who would receive a distribution in a hypothetical chapter 7 liquidation in which § 502(d) is enforced.

This court further concludes that a plan proponent has an affirmative duty under 11 U.S.C. § 1125 to disclose all known § 502(d) disabilities, even if that means that the plan proponent must confess or inform against affiliates, insiders, and friends.

The confirmation of such a plan, assuming adequate disclosure, could occur only if either: (1) the § 502(d) disability is removed by reversing all avoidable transfers and disgorging all funds owed to the trustee; or (2) all affected creditors and interest holders actually accept the plan.

FACTS

Sierra–Cal is a debtor in possession that operated a hotel ("lodge") in South Lake Tahoe, California, until it was sold for $2,750,000 in a combination of cash and secured notes.

The estate now consists of about $440,000 on deposit in the registry of the court plus the stream of income on $325,000 in secured notes that are payable over ten years.

The first deed of trust, all outstanding taxes, and expenses of sale were previously extinguished by payment through escrow. The plan of reorganization provides for liquidating the remaining debt.

The remaining secured debt is owed to insiders, all of whom have relationships that center about Carl R. Corzan, who is the debtor corporation's president. Corzan, directly and through affiliates and relatives, owns or controls about 91.2 percent of the debtor corporation's shares.

CRC Trust, an affiliate that owns 25.5 percent of the debtor corporation, holds a deed of trust securing a debt of about $293,000. The plan proposes to pay CRC Trust in full from the sale proceeds on deposit in the registry of the court.

SCF, Inc. ("SCF"), another Corzan entity that owns 18.5 percent of the debtor, has two secured claims. One is a junior deed of trust securing a debt of about $223,000 that would be paid $90,000 on the effective date of the plan, with the balance paid over ten years. The other is a personal property security interest on furnishings and equipment securing a debt listed as $66,000, the outstanding balance of which would be paid on the effective date of the plan.

SCF's personal property security interest is not supported by a financing statement that has been recorded in accordance with Article 9 of the Uniform Commercial Code and, hence, is avoidable under the bank-ruptcy trustee's "strongarm" power. This debt has also been reduced by more than $28,000 during the course of this chapter 11 case, at least $10,000 of which was paid by the debtor without court authorization and, accordingly, is also avoidable by a bankruptcy trustee as an unauthorized postpetition transfer.

The plan was modified to treat the personal property claim as unsecured after the pertinent facts were disclosed for the first time during Corzan's testimony at the confirmation hearing. The debtor conceded that the security interest could not withstand a trustee's "strongarm" avoiding power and that there had been avoidable postpetition transfers.

Unsecured claims that are not disputed are approximately $7,500. The objecting creditor, a lessee of the debtor whose lease was rejected early in the case, has a disputed unsecured claim in excess of $175,000. The unsecured claims will be paid from a percentage of net revenues in annual payments over a period of seven years with interest at 8 percent.

The various Corzan entities will retain their ownership interests.

DISCUSSION

I.

The initial focus is on § 1129(a)(7), which is an essential element for confirmation of a plan of reorganization that cannot be finessed by a "cram down" under § 1129(b).

The primary method of satisfying § 1129(a)(7) is the "best interests" test prescribed by § 1129(a)(7)(A)(ii) that contrasts the plan distributions with distributions in a hypothetical chapter 7 liquidation. The key issue presented here is the application of the § 502(d) disability in the context of the "best interests" test.

The alternative method of satisfying § 1129(a)(7) with respect to an impaired class is actual acceptance by each creditor who would do better in a chapter 7 liquidation than under a chapter 11 plan.[6]

---

6. Since § 1129(a)(7) applies only to impaired classes, it can be bypassed entirely by leaving the pertinent class unimpaired.

A

The "best interests" test permits a plan to be confirmed without actual acceptance by each holder of a claim or interest that would be impaired by the plan if each holder "will receive or retain under the plan on account of such claim or interest property of a value, as of the effective date of the plan, that is not less than the amount that such holder would so receive or retain if the debtor were liquidated under chapter 7 of this title on such date." 11 U.S.C. § 1129(a)(7)(A)(ii).

The "best interests" concept is a cornerstone of the theoretical underpinnings of chapter 11. It stands as an "individual guaranty to each creditor or interest holder that it will receive at least as much in reorganization as it would in liquidation." 7 COLLIER ON BANKRUPT-CY ¶ 1129.03[7] (Lawrence P. King et al. eds., 15th. ed. rev. 1997) ("COLLIER");

The "best interests" test must be satisfied even with respect to claims that are not eligible to vote because they are contingent or disputed.

If a prompt chapter 7 liquidation would provide a better return to particular creditors or interest holders than a chapter 11 reorganization, then a reorganization is inappropriate and a chapter 11 plan should not be confirmed.

Applying the "best interests" test requires the court to conjure up a hypothetical chapter 7 liquidation that would be conducted on the effective date of the plan.

The hypothetical liquidation entails a considerable degree of speculation about a situation that will not occur unless the case is actually converted to chapter 7. It contemplates valuation according to the depressed prices that one typically receives in distress sales. 7 COLLIER ¶ 1129.03[7] [b][iii]. It requires estimation of disputed and contingent claims and of chapter 7 administrative expenses. Id. And it requires application of the chapter 7 distribution scheme, taking into account such matters as subordinations (11 U.S.C. § 510) and recoveries from general partners (11 U.S.C. § 723) that would be applied in a chapter 7 liquidation. M. Long Arabians, 103 B.R. at 216–17. One such matter, as this court now holds, is mandatory disallowance of claims. See 7 COLLIER ¶ 1129.03[7][c].

Liquidation value and expenses of administration are less speculative in this instance than in most because the estate has been reduced to $715,000 in notes and cash: two secured notes have a present value of $275,000; $440,000 is on deposit in the registry of the court. After deducting remaining expenses of administration of $40,000, about $675,000 would be available to be distributed to creditors and interest holders.

The total nominal claims are about $768,000, of which the unsecured claims are $182,500, including the $175,000 disputed claim of the objecting creditor that, the court estimates, has a value of $87,500.[11] Thus, for

---

11. Estimating the disputed claim for the limited purpose of the "best interests" test's hypothetical liquidation calls for application of straightforward expected value analysis, based on

purposes of the hypothetical liquidation, unsecured claims are $95,000 and total nominal secured claims are about $675,000.

The question becomes the order in which claims would be paid in a hypothetical chapter 7 liquidation.

B

Mandatory claim disallowance under § 502(d) is one Bankruptcy Code provision that applies in chapter 7 liquidations. It requires that the court disallow "any claim" of any entity from which property is recoverable by a trustee, or that is the transferee of an avoidable transfer, unless and until the property is turned over and the transfer is paid.

The § 502(d) disallowance is in the nature of an affirmative defense to a proof of claim and does not provide independent authority for affirmative relief against the creditor. Parker N. Am. Corp. v. Resolution Trust Corp. (In re Parker N. Am. Corp.), 24 F.3d 1145, 1155 (9th Cir.1994). As an affirmative defense, § 502(d) can even be asserted when an affirmative recovery from the creditor under the pertinent avoiding statute would be time-barred.

Formally, § 502(d) operates as a temporary disability. It is temporary in the sense that the disallowance ceases when the creditor disgorges the property in question. Nevertheless, it can be crippling in at least three respects.

First, the disability is mandatory. The statutory language "the court shall disallow" leaves no latitude for the court once the predicate rights are determined.

Second, while actual adjudication of the avoidance status of the creditor ultimately is necessary, the mere assertion of a prima facie § 502(d) defense is sufficient to place the claim in a status in which it is neither allowed nor disallowed. See Katchen v. Landy, 382 U.S. 323, 330, 86 S.Ct. 467, 473, 15 L.Ed.2d 391 (1966) (Bankruptcy Act § 59g).

Third, because the focus is on the creditor and not on the specific claim, a small avoidable transfer may require disallowance of all the creditor's claims, even a large secured claim, until the avoidable transfer is disgorged. See id. at 330 n. 5, 86 S.Ct. at 473 n. 5. Thus, in this instance, the two avoidance issues involving the $66,000 personal property interest (defeat of secured status under "strongarm" power and unauthorized postpetition transfers) would also prevent payment on the $323,000 deed of trust.

1

No reported decision appears to focus upon the question whether § 502(d) must be applied when calculating the hypothetical liquidation under the "best interests" test for chapter 11 plan confirmation. Nevertheless, the straightforward language of the Bankruptcy Code makes

the court's analysis of the record of the case, reflecting a "50–50" likelihood of success on the merits. Specifically, the probability of success is .5. Accordingly, the expected value (Expected Value = Probability x Claim) is .5 x $175,000 = $87,500....

§ 502(d) a provision that affects the distribution scheme in a chapter 7 liquidation.

The description of the hypothetical liquidation in legislative history of § 1129(a)(7)(A)(ii) does not directly mention § 502(d). The legislative history does, however, cite subordinations under § 510 as an example of how the hypothetical liquidation sweeps in the complexities of the chapter 7 liquidation scheme, including the specialized rules regarding partnership and community property distributions. The leading treatises and commentators similarly omit mention of § 502(d).

But it is generally agreed that all provisions applicable in a chapter 7 liquidation are to be taken into account when the court determines what sums would be paid to whom in a hypothetical liquidation.

If an actual chapter 7 liquidation were to occur on the date of the hypothetical liquidation, it is beyond cavil that a creditor who is under a § 502(d) disability would receive nothing.

Since the central focus of the "best interests" test for plan confirmation is on what would occur in an actual chapter 7 liquidation, this court holds that any applicable § 502(d) disability must be taken into account in the test's hypothetical liquidation.

2

The "best interests" analysis in plan confirmation being hypothetical, it is not necessary (as would be required in an actual liquidation) to adjudicate the creditor's § 502(d) status before imposing the § 502(d) disability.

In computing the hypothetical chapter 7 liquidation, the court is entitled to view the entire record of the case and to engage in rational speculation about what would occur in a chapter 7 liquidation. Among other things, the court can hypothesize that certain claims would evoke the objection of a chapter 7 trustee and can speculate about the likely fate of such objections, bearing in mind the protective purpose of the "best interests" test.

3

The § 502(d) disability applies to SCF on two counts, based upon this court's assessment of the record, for purposes of a hypothetical liquidation.

The testimony of the debtor's principal at the confirmation hearing established that at least $10,000 of estate funds had been used postpetition without authority in partial payment of SCF's $66,000 prepetition claim, which warrants an inference of transfers avoidable under § 549. And the testimony established that SCF's personal property security interest securing the $66,000 claim is unrecorded, which warrants an inference of avoidability pursuant to the trustee's § 544 "strongarm" power.

In a hypothetical liquidation, a competent chapter 7 trustee would be able to recover against SCF under § 544 and § 549. Hence, SCF is subject to the § 502(d) disability for two, independent reasons.

If SCF were not subject to the § 502(d) disability, the unsecured claims would be paid about 56 percent of their total in a chapter 7 liquidation.[18] Since the present value of the payments promised to unsecured creditors would provide payment of between 90 and 100 percent of the unsecured claims, the "best interests" test would have been satisfied in the hypothetical scenario.

SCF, however, is under a § 502(d) disability, which requires that all of its claims be disallowed in the hypothetical chapter 7 liquidation. In consequence, the unsecured claims would be paid in full and would, pursuant to § 726(a)(5), receive interest at the legal rate from the date of the filing of the petition, after which funds would be returned to owners pursuant to § 726(a)(6).

Since the plan does not propose to pay sums that have a present value that reflects interest at the legal rate from the date of the filing of the petition, the "best interests" test is not satisfied when the § 502(d) disability is imposed.

4

The debtor orally modified the plan at the close of the confirmation hearing in an attempt to cure the defect by providing that SCF would be paid the balance on its personal property security interest as an unsecured claim. This modification does not, however, surmount the hurdle.

a

Merely treating the unpaid balance of the personal property security interest as an unsecured claim does not cure the § 502(d) disability for two reasons. First, the avoidable underlying security agreement must have been actually revoked in order to comply with § 502(d). Second, the modification does not reverse the unauthorized postpetition transfers that are avoidable under § 549 and that form an independent basis for the § 502(d) disability.

b

Nor does the oral modification enable the plan to pass the "best interests" test under § 1129(a)(7)(A)(ii).

Treating the $66,000 personal property claim as an unsecured claim would mean that $119,000 would be available to pay unsecured claims of $161,000. A dividend of 74 percent is less than the full payment plus interest that unsecured creditors would otherwise receive in the hypothetical liquidation.

---

18. Present value of funds available on liquidation $675,000—$40,000 expenses of administration—$293,000 CRC secured claim—$223,000 SCF secured real estate claim—$66,000 SCF secured personal property claim = $53,000 available to pay on unsecured claims of $95,000 (55.8%).

The same result would apply if the plan were further modified to treat SCF's real property claim as unsecured. In that event $342,000 would be available to pay claims of $384,000. An 89 percent dividend is still less than full payment plus interest.

Hence, the modification that occurred orally on the record at the confirmation hearing is inadequate.

C

[The court then denied approval of the disclosure statement for failure to provide a liquidation analysis that complied with the above analysis.]

Problem 11–17: *The Holdout*

Airtime, Inc. has proposed a Chapter 11 plan which pays its unsecured creditors 50¢ on the dollar. 95% of its unsecured creditors, in number and amount, have voted in favor of the plan. The sole negative vote is Delay, Inc., which comes to you for advice. Delay's management shows you a spreadsheet that indicates that if Airtime were liquidated in chapter 7, creditors would receive 55¢ on the dollar. Does Delay have a valid objection to plan confirmation?

What if the 55¢ calculation did not take into account the chapter 7 trustee's 3% fee, which would bring the proposed distribution down to 49%? What if the difference between Delay's calculations and Airtime's calculations is in the present value each places on patent technology owned by Airtime, a technology all agree is at least three years away from producing profits?

---

c. Feasibility

Section 1129(a)(11) does not use the term "feasibility." Judges applying section 1129(a)(11), including Judge Morris Sheppard "Buzz" Arnold in the next case, use that term in applying section 1129(a)(11).

11 U.S.C. § 1129(a)(11)

(a) The court shall confirm a plan only if all of the following requirements are met:....

> (11) Confirmation of the plan is not likely to be followed by the liquidation, or the need for further financial reorganization of the debtor or any successor to the debtor under the plan, unless such liquidation or reorganization is proposed in the plan.

DANNY THOMAS PROPERTIES II LTD. PARTNERSHIP v. BEAL BANK, S.S.B. (IN RE DANNY THOMAS PROP. II LTD. PTSHP.)

241 F.3d 959 (8th Cir. 2001)

Before BEAM and MORRIS SHEPPARD ARNOLD, Circuit Judges, and DOTY, District Judge.

MORRIS SHEPPARD ARNOLD, Circuit Judge.

Danny Thomas Properties II Limited Partnership (DT/II) and Danny Thomas Properties III Limited Partnership (DT/III; collectively, the debtors) each own a portion of the Le Marquis apartment complex in North Little Rock, Arkansas. When the debtors filed separate petitions for relief under the federal bankruptcy laws, Beal Bank, the debtors' primary creditor, objected to their plans of reorganization.

The bankruptcy court refused to "cram down" the plans, that is, to confirm them over Beal's objections, because the court found that the plans did not establish that future liquidation or further reorganization was unlikely, see § 1129(a)(11). The district court affirmed the decision of the bankruptcy court, the debtors appealed, and we affirm.

I.

During the late 1980s and early 1990s, the debtors experienced numerous financial difficulties that required them to restructure their loan agreements with the United States Department of Housing and Urban Development (HUD), their primary lender at the time. In 1995, Beal purchased the debtors' mortgage loans from HUD. Later that year, the debtors became financially unable to meet their obligations to Beal, and in response to foreclosure proceedings brought by Beal, they petitioned for protection pending reorganization under the federal bankruptcy laws. The debtors have continued to operate Le Marquis since that time as debtors-in-possession.

The debtors filed reorganization plans that proposed to pay off Beal's claim, currently valued at approximately $2,220,000, based on a 30-year amortization schedule but requiring installment payments for the first 10 years and then a balloon payment for the balance. The plans also described the debtors' strategy for ensuring successful reorganization. As part of that strategy, the debtors proposed to establish maintenance reserve accounts into which each debtor would place $50,000 per year for five years to cover future maintenance costs for Le Marquis.

The debtors also included, however, so-called "drop dead" provisions in their reorganization plans as a secondary guarantor of the plans' success. In these provisions, the debtors consented to the initiation of immediate foreclosure proceedings against Le Marquis should the debtors fail to cure a default within 45 days of receiving notice from Beal of the default. In the event of an ongoing bankruptcy proceeding, moreover, the plans gave Beal the right to obtain an ex parte order.

II.

Before a bankruptcy court may "cram down" a reorganization plan over the objections of a creditor, the court must determine that the plan is "fair and equitable," see § 1129(b)(1). With respect to a secured creditor, such as Beal, this requirement means that the creditor must receive payments with a present value that equals the value of the secured claim. See § 1129(b)(2)(A)(i)(II).

The provision allowing a "cramdown" also requires that the bankruptcy court find that the plan meets various requirements specified in § 1129(a). One of these requirements is a finding by the court that "[c]onfirmation of the plan is not likely to be followed by the liquidation, or the need for further financial reorganization, of the debtor or any successor to the debtor under the plan, unless such liquidation or reorganization is proposed in the plan," see § 1129(a)(11). This statutory provision establishes what is commonly known as the "feasibility" requirement, and as a practical matter it requires the court to find that the plan is "workable" before it may be confirmed. See In re Monnier Brothers, 755 F.2d 1336, 1341 (8th Cir.1985).

The debtors contend that the "drop dead" provisions make the reorganization plans feasible as a matter of law. They maintain that the "drop dead" provisions amount to liquidations and that because these liquidations are contemplated within the plans, the requirements of § 1129(a)(11) are automatically met. Beal contends that the provisions do not provide for liquidations, as that term is used in the bankruptcy laws, but are merely agreements by the debtors to consent to foreclosure proceedings.

We agree with Beal that the "drop dead" provisions do not amount to liquidations for purposes of § 1129(a)(11). "Liquidation in or out of bankruptcy means the end of a [debtor's] existence," Maytag Corp. v. Navistar International Transportation Corp., 219 F.3d 587, 591 (7th Cir.2000). The "drop dead" provisions here do not contemplate the end of the debtors' existence, but merely allow Beal to foreclose on their primary asset. It is true that foreclosure by Beal would leave the debtors as nearly-empty shells, but the debtors would nonetheless continue to exist and would be free to pursue new opportunities. The "drop dead" provisions are, therefore, more closely akin to clauses that permit a sale of assets, an action that is contemplated by the bankruptcy laws as a proper part of a reorganization plan. See § 1123(a)(5)(D); see also 7 Collier on Bankruptcy ¶ 1123.02[4] (Lawrence P. King ed., 15th ed. rev.2000). Because the provisions offered by the debtors do not provide for liquidations, the language is entitled to no special significance under § 1129(a)(11), and thus the provisions certainly cannot make the reorganization plans feasible as a matter of law.

Even if the "drop dead" provisions amounted to liquidations, we could not accept the debtors' contention that providing for liquidation in the event of a default in a reorganization plan renders a plan feasible as a matter of law. Were we to do so, a bankruptcy court would be required to find that even the most implausible of reorganization plans is feasible so long as the plan provided that the debtor would liquidate if the plan failed. To require the court to confirm a reorganization plan merely because it allows future liquidation would eliminate the courts' duty under § 1129(a)(11) to protect creditors against " 'visionary schemes,' " In the Matter of Pizza of Hawaii, Inc., 761 F.2d 1374, 1382 (9th Cir.1985), quoting what is now 7 Collier on Bankruptcy ¶ 1129.03[11] (Lawrence P. King ed., 15th ed. rev.2000). We therefore reject the debtors' contention that their plans are feasible as a matter of law.

We recognize that in certain situations a plan may be rendered feasible by the inclusion of a provision similar to the "drop dead" provisions involved in this case. See, e.g., In the Matter of 203 North LaSalle Street Partnership, 126 F.3d 955, 962 (7th Cir.1997), rev'd on other grounds, Bank of America National Trust and Savings Association v. 203 North LaSalle Street Partnership, 526 U.S. 434, 437, 458, 119 S.Ct. 1411, 143 L.Ed.2d 607 (1999); In the Matter of T–H New Orleans Limited Partnership, 116 F.3d 790, 803–04 (5th Cir.1997); and In re Nite Lite Inns, 17 B.R. 367, 370 (Bankr.S.D.Cal.1982). Each of these cases involved a reorganization plan proposing that in the event of a default a particular asset would be sold to cover the creditor's secured claim. Rather than declaring the plans feasible as a matter of law, however, the court in each of these cases examined the facts supporting the plans and found them to be feasible because the liquidation alternative guaranteed payment of the secured claim. These cases thus fail to support the debtors' contention that the inclusion of the "drop dead" provisions makes their plans feasible as a matter of law. The debtors show merely that such provisions are entitled to be considered by a bankruptcy court when evaluating a plan's prospects for success.

III.

Having rejected the argument that the debtors' plans are feasible as a matter of law, we turn to a review of the bankruptcy court's determination that they were in fact not feasible. While a reorganization plan's "[s]uccess need not be guaranteed," In re Monnier Brothers, 755 F.2d at 1341, the bankruptcy court cannot approve a plan unless it has at least a reasonable prospect for success. See id. With respect to Beal, a secured creditor, the debtors must show, as we have said, that it is reasonably likely that the plan will result in full payment of Beal's secured claim. The debtors bear the burden of establishing the feasibility of their plans by a preponderance of the evidence.

We first address the reorganization plan that DT/III proposed. The bankruptcy court found that in year 1 of the plan DT/III will be responsible for an interest payment to Beal of approximately $169,700, a payment on a claim for past-due management company fees of approximately $4,900, and other miscellaneous claims totaling approximately $24,600, for a total of approximately $199,200. Combining this total with the $50,000 payment, noted earlier, that DT/III promises to make to its maintenance reserve account, the court found that DT/III will need approximately $249,200, at a minimum, in net operating income to meet its obligations. DT/III does not seriously dispute these numbers other than to contend that the plan proposes to make no payments to the management company unless there is sufficient cash flow to do so. While the bankruptcy court questioned whether any management company would work for free, we give DT/III the benefit of the doubt and assume that it would require an approximate total of only $244,300 in net operating income to meet its year 1 obligations.

During the confirmation hearing, DT/III's own expert witness testified that DT/III's net operating income during year 1 would be approximately $196,700 if management fees resulting from year 1 operations were paid, and approximately $221,300 without payment of the fees. Even if we assume that no management fees will be paid, DT/III's projected net operating income is approximately $23,000 less than needed to fund DT/III's plan during the first year. DT/III fails to address this testimony on appeal, but instead cites other projections showing an increase in revenue based upon its belief that both rental and occupancy rates will increase.

Feasibility determinations must be "firmly rooted in predictions based on objective fact," In re Clarkson, 767 F.2d 417, 420 (8th Cir.1985). After carefully reviewing the record, however, we believe that DT/III's projections have little basis in anything other than sheer speculation. At the very least, they do not convince us that the bankruptcy court clearly erred in accepting the testimony of DT/III's expert and concluding on the basis of that testimony that DT/III will operate at a deficit during the first year of its reorganization plan.

We also find no error in the bankruptcy court's determination that DT/III will operate at a significant loss throughout the life of its proposed plan. DT/III's initial deficit will prevent it from being able to fund its maintenance reserve account fully, thus limiting its ability to perform the maintenance required to keep the property at its current value. The bankruptcy court concluded that Le Marquis is an aging property that will continue to deteriorate without regular maintenance, a conclusion that the record amply supports. Common sense dictates that the deterioration of the property is likely to have two important effects on the success of DT/III's reorganization plan: First, the property will probably be less attractive to potential tenants, with a resulting decrease in either rental prices or occupancy rates, and, second, as the property deteriorates it will continue to become less valuable as collateral for Beal's claim. These difficulties are likely to be exacerbated in the later years of the plan, for which a finding of feasibility is already much more difficult for a court to make because of the hazards involved in estimating future income. The failure to fund the maintenance reserve accounts fully therefore makes it highly unlikely that DT/III's reorganization plan will succeed.

We do not believe that the "drop dead" provisions of the reorganization plan can save this otherwise infeasible plan, unlike the similar provisions in 203 North LaSalle Street, T–H New Orleans, and Nite Lite Inns, because nothing in the record indicates that Le Marquis will remain more valuable than Beal's secured claim during the life of the plan. While the bankruptcy court did not make a specific finding as to the value of Le Marquis, DT/III's reorganization plan does note that, at this time, a foreclosure sale would not bring an amount greater than the amount of Beal's secured claim. Combining this admission with the bankruptcy court's finding that the property will deteriorate, DT/III becomes unable to show that the execution of the "drop dead" provisions will fully satisfy Beal's claim. We thus detect no error in the bankruptcy court's determination that the plan was not feasible.

DT/II's reorganization plan is virtually identical to DT/III's plan. Since DT/II's plan suffers from the same infirmities as the DT/III plan does, we conclude that the bankruptcy court did not err by finding that DT/II's plan was not feasible.

IV.

For the foregoing reasons, we affirm the judgments of the district court.

Problem 11–18:   Factors Affecting Feasibility

1. Dingus Marketing is a real estate development company currently in chapter 11. It has filed a plan and disclosure statement which show that for the 18 months following plan confirmation, reorganized Dingus will lose money. The same projections, however, assume that real estate prices are rising (which seems to be the case), and that they will be able to refinance or sell properties at the 18–month mark to pay any shortfalls. Is the plan feasible? Would it help if the plan gave the secured lenders the absolute right to foreclose in 18–months?

2. Take the facts in #1 above, but now add that the lenders have produced expert testimony that the real estate market will be flat over the next 18 months. Dingus' expert disagrees, and sees at least a 8% annual increase. If both experts are equally credible, has Dingus met its obligation to show feasibility? Just how much better does Dingus' expert have to be?

---

d.   Paying Administrative Claims and Tax Claims in Full

This should be largely review. We covered the section 507 administrative expense priority in Unit 6. And, in covering section 364 earlier in this Unit, we learned that payment of administrative claims is a confirmation requirement.

11 U.S.C. § 1129(a)(9)

(a) The court shall confirm a plan only if all of the following requirements are met:....

(9) Except to the extent that the holder of a particular claim has agreed to a different treatment of such claim, the plan provides that—

(A) with respect to a claim of a kind specified in section 507(a)(1) or 507(a)(2) of this title, on the effective date of the plan, the holder of such claim will receive on account of such claim cash equal to the allowed amount of such claim;...., and

(C) with respect to a claim of a kind specified in section 507(a)(8) of this title, the holder of such claim will receive on account of such claim regular installment payments in cash—

(i) of a total value, as of the effective date of the plan, equal to the allowed amount of such claim; and

(ii) over a period ending not later than 5 years after the date of the order for relief under section 301, 302, or 303; and

(iii) in a manner not less favorable than the most favored nonpriority unsecured claim provided for by the plan (other than cash payments made to a class of creditors under section 1122(b)); and

(D) with respect to a secured claim which would otherwise meet the description of an unsecured claim of a governmental unit under section 507(a)(8), but for the secured status of that claim, the holder of that claim will receive on account of that claim, cash payments, in the same manner and over the same period, as prescribed in subparagraph (C).

Problem 11–19: Questions About Administrative Priority

1. Which of the following kinds of claims are covered by section 507(a)(1), such that section 1129(a)(9) requires them to be paid in full on the plan's effective date?

   (a) Post-petition trade credit (goods or services bought on credit after the filing)?

   (b) Debtor-in-Possession financing under Section 364?

   (c) Claims of the attorneys for the official committee of creditors holding unsecured claims?

   (d) Claims of the debtor in possession's attorneys?

   (e) Damages payable to third-parties due to an uninsured post-petition fire that destroyed an adjoining building to the debtor in possession's headquarters?

2. Debtor has significant unpaid and unsecured tax claims. May it pay such claims:

(a) Over a ten-year period?

(b) Over a three-year period, if it also is paying its general unsecured creditors (by way of a separate class) over five years?

(c) What result in (b) if the plan provides that the unsecured creditor class were to be paid in three years, and the class of tax claims were to be paid in five years?

(d) Does it matter if the tax claim is secured?

(e) May the interest rate on the payout be the general market rate used for all other classes of creditors? See 11 U.S.C. § 511.

---

e. The "Other" Section 1129(a) Confirmation Requirements

Again, there are sixteen separate confirmation requirements in section 1129(a). And, we have looked only at five of the sixteen—voting, good faith, the "best interests" test, feasibility, and payment of administrative and tax claims,

That leaves eleven others. Some of these are for "special debtors," such as section 1129(a)(6), which requires approval of any regulatory agency with jurisdiction over the debtor. Some are the product of political wrangling for "special interests," such as Section 1129(a)(12), which requires the estate to be current in its United States Trustee payments, and Section 1129(a)(13), which requires estates to be current in benefits covered by Section 1114. Others apply only to individuals (paragraphs (14) and (15) and will be discussed later).

Of the remaining seven, four speak directly to public policy concerns. Section 1129(a)(10) requires the consent of at least one impaired, non-insider class.[11] Sections 1129(a)(4) and 1129(a)(5) require disclosure and approval of compensation paid to plan proponents and those proposed to be post-confirmation management. Section 1129(a)(16) provides that debtors who are non-profit entities may not override nonbankruptcy law restrictions on such entities.

That leaves two—Sections 1129(a)(1) and 1129(a)(2), which require, respectively, that the plan and the plan proponent comply with chapter 11 and title 11. That seems redundant, doesn't it? Doesn't everyone and every plan have to comply with the Code? Well, many hot battles are waged under these sections. How so? Read on.

---

11. This requirement would seem to be superfluous given Section 1129(a)(8)'s requirement that each class consent, but we will see that paragraph (8)'s requirement can be relaxed in "cramdown," which is explored in the next section.

IN RE DOW CORNING CORP.

280 F.3d 648 (6th Cir.), cert. denied, 537 U.S. 816 (2002)

BOYCE F. MARTIN, JR., Chief Circuit Judge.

Years after Dow Corning Corporation filed a petition for reorganization under Chapter 11 of the Bankruptcy Code, and following extensive and vigorous negotiations, the third proposed plan of reorganization for Dow was submitted to the bankruptcy court. The bankruptcy court confirmed the Amended Joint Plan of Reorganization for Dow and the district court affirmed the bankruptcy court's Confirmation Order. Certain claimants who voted against the Plan appealed. The first principal issue presented here is whether a bankruptcy court may enjoin a non-consenting creditor's claims against a non-debtor to facilitate a reorganization plan under Chapter 11 of the Bankruptcy Code. For the following reasons, we AFFIRM the district court's conclusion that, under certain circumstances, a bankruptcy court may enjoin a non-consenting creditor's claim against a non-debtor to facilitate a Chapter 11 plan of reorganization. However, the factual findings of the bankruptcy court do not demonstrate that such an injunction is appropriate in this case. Therefore, we REMAND to the district court.

For nearly thirty years, Dow was the predominant producer of silicone gel breast implants, accounting for almost fifty percent of the entire market. In addition, Dow supplied silicone raw materials to other manufacturers of silicone gel breast implants.

In the 1980s, certain medical studies suggested that silicone gel may cause auto-immune tissue diseases such as lupus, Scleroderma and rheumatoid arthritis.... Soon thereafter, tens of thousands of implant recipients sued Dow and its two shareholders, the Dow Chemical Company and Corning, Incorporated, claiming to have been injured by auto-immune reactions to the silicone in their implants.... Dow filed a petition for reorganization under Chapter 11 of the Bankruptcy Code....

Under the Plan, a $2.35 billion fund is established for the payment of claims asserted by (1) personal injury claimants, (2) government health care payers, and (3) other creditors asserting claims related to silicone-implant products liability claims. The $2.35 billion fund is established with funds contributed by Dow's products liability insurers, Dow's shareholders and Dow's operating cash reserves. As a quid pro quo for making proceeds available for the $2.35 billion fund, section 8.3 of the Plan releases Dow's insurers and shareholders from all further liability on claims arising out of settled personal injury claims, and section 8.4 permanently enjoins any party holding a claim released against Dow from bringing an action related to that claim against Dow's insurers or shareholders. Plan §§ 8.3, 8.4....

The bankruptcy court confirmed the Plan, but construed the non-debtor release and injunction provisions to apply only to consenting creditors. Although the bankruptcy court determined that it has authority under the Bankruptcy Code to enjoin a non-consenting creditor's claims against non-debtors, it decided, based on non-bankruptcy law, that such injunctions are inappropriate as applied to non-consenting creditors, and construed the Plan accordingly. The district court affirmed the bankruptcy court's Confirmation Order but reversed the bankruptcy court's interpretation of the release and injunction provisions of the Plan. The district court interpreted the non-debtor release and injunction provisions of the Plan to apply to all creditors, consenting and non-consenting. . . .

The first issue we are asked to decide is whether a bankruptcy court has the authority to enjoin a non-consenting creditor's claims against a non-debtor to facilitate a reorganization plan under Chapter 11 of the Bankruptcy Code. This is a question of first impression in this Circuit.

The Bankruptcy Code does not explicitly prohibit or authorize a bankruptcy court to enjoin a non-consenting creditor's claims against a non-debtor to facilitate a reorganization plan. However, bankruptcy courts, "as courts of equity, have broad authority to modify creditor-debtor relationships." United States v. Energy Resources Co., 495 U.S. 545, 549, 110 S.Ct. 2139, 109 L.Ed.2d 580 (1990). For example, section 105(a) of the Bankruptcy Code grants a bankruptcy court the broad authority to issue "any order, process, or judgment that is necessary or appropriate to carry out the provisions of this title." 11 U.S.C. § 105(a). This section grants the bankruptcy court the power to take appropriate equitable measures needed to implement other sections of the Code.

Consistent with section 105(a)'s broad grant of authority, the Code allows bankruptcy courts considerable discretion to approve plans of reorganization. Energy Resources Co., 495 U.S. at 549, 110 S.Ct. 2139. Section 1123(b)(6) permits a reorganization plan to "include any . . . appropriate provision not inconsistent with the applicable provisions of this title." 11 U.S.C. § 1123(b)(6). Thus, the bankruptcy court, as a forum for resolving large and complex mass litigations, has substantial power to reorder creditor-debtor relations needed to achieve a successful reorganization. For example, under the doctrine of marshaling of assets, "[t]he bankruptcy court has the power to order a creditor who has two funds to satisfy his debt to resort to the fund that will not defeat other creditors." In re A.H. Robins Co., 880 F.2d 694, 701 (4th Cir.1989). Moreover, it is an "ancient but very much alive doctrine . . . [that] . . . a creditor has no right to choose which of two funds will pay his claim." Id. Likewise, when a plan provides for the full payment of all claims, enjoining claims against a non-debtor so as not to defeat reorganization is. consistent with the bankruptcy court's primary function.

For the foregoing reasons, such an injunction is "not inconsistent" with the Code, and is authorized by section 1123(b)(6).

Nevertheless, some courts have found that the Bankruptcy Code does not permit enjoining a non-consenting creditor's claims against a non-debtor. . . . These courts primarily rely on section 524(e) of the Code, which provides that "the discharge of the debt of the debtor does not affect the liability of any other entity on, or the property of any other entity for, such debt." 11 U.S.C. § 524(e). However, this language explains the effect of a debtor's discharge. It does not prohibit the release of a non-debtor.

The bankruptcy court concluded that non-debtor releases were authorized by section 1123(b)(6), but were precluded by a non-bankruptcy law limitation on the bankruptcy court's equity power. In re Dow Corning Corp., 244 B.R. at 744. We disagree. The bankruptcy court cited Grupo Mexicano de Desarrollo v. Alliance Bond Fund, Inc., 527 U.S. 308, 322, 119 S.Ct. 1961, 144 L.Ed.2d 319 (1999), for the proposition that a court's use of its general equity powers "is confined within the broad boundaries of traditional equitable relief." The Grupo Mexicano Court explained that, "the equity jurisdiction of the federal courts is the jurisdiction in equity exercised by the High Court of Chancery in England at the time of the adoption of the Constitution and the enactment of the original Judiciary Act, 1789." Based upon this principle, the Grupo Mexicano Court vacated an injunction preventing a toll road operator from dissipating, transferring, or encumbering its only assets to the prejudice of an unsecured note holder because traditional equity jurisprudence did not allow such remedies until a debt had been established. The bankruptcy court, applying the Grupo Mexicano analysis, concluded that non-consensual, non-debtor releases were also unprecedented in traditional equity jurisprudence, and therefore exceeded the bankruptcy court's equitable powers.

The district court rejected this argument on the grounds that the releases were authorized by "sufficient statutory authority under the Bankruptcy Code." For the following reasons, we agree with the district court. In Grupo Mexicano, the Supreme Court distinguished its own holding from that in United States v. First National City Bank, 379 U.S. 378, 85 S.Ct. 528, 13 L.Ed.2d 365 (1965). 527 U.S. at 326, 119 S.Ct. 1961. First National approved an injunction preventing a third-party bank from transferring any of a taxpayer's assets. The Grupo Mexicano Court distinguished that holding on the grounds that the First National case "involved not the Court's general equitable powers under the Judiciary Act of 1789, but its powers under the statute authorizing tax injunctions." Thus, because the district court had a statutory basis for issuing such an injunction, it was not confined to traditional equity jurisprudence available at the enactment of the Judiciary Act of 1789. The statute in First National gave courts the power to grant injunctions "necessary or appropriate for the enforcement of the internal revenue laws." 26 U.S.C. § 7402(a) (1964). Similarly, the Bankruptcy Code gives bankruptcy courts the power to grant injunctions "necessary or appropriate to carry out the provisions of [the Bankruptcy Code]." 11 U.S.C. § 105(a). We conclude that due to this statutory grant of power, the bankruptcy court is not confined to traditional equity jurisprudence and therefore, the bankruptcy court's Grupo Mexicano analysis was misplaced.

Because we determine that enjoining a non-consenting creditor's claim against a non-debtor is "not inconsistent" with the Code and that Grupo Mexicano does not preclude such an injunction, we turn to when such an injunction is an "appropriate provision" of a reorganization plan pursuant to section 1123(b)(6). Because such an injunction is a dramatic measure to be used cautiously, we follow those circuits that have held that enjoining a non-consenting creditor's claim is only appropriate in "unusual circumstances.". In determining whether there are "unusual circumstances," our sister circuits have considered a number of factors, which are summarized in our holding below. We hold that when the following seven factors are present, the bankruptcy court may enjoin a nonconsenting creditor's claims against a non-debtor: (1) There is an identity of interests between the debtor and the third party, usually an indemnity relationship, such that a suit against the non-debtor is, in essence, a suit against the debtor or will deplete the assets of the estate; (2) The non-debtor has contributed substantial assets to the reorganization; (3) The injunction is essential to reorganization, namely, the reorganization hinges on the debtor being free from indirect suits against parties who would have indemnity or contribution claims against the debtor; (4) The impacted class, or classes, has overwhelmingly voted to accept the plan; (5) The plan provides a mechanism to pay for all, or substantially all, of the class or classes affected by the injunction; (6) The plan provides an opportunity for those claimants who choose not to settle to recover in full and; (7) The bankruptcy court made a record of specific factual findings that support its conclusions.

For several reasons, the record produced by the bankruptcy court in this case does not support a finding of "unusual circumstances" such that we can endorse enjoining non-consenting creditors' claims against a non-debtor.

QUESTIONS ON DOW CORNING

1. Just where in the Code is the term "unusual circumstances"?

2. Sections 1129(a)(1) and (a)(2) require compliance with title 11 and chapter 11. What about Dow's plan arguably did not comply with either of these two statutes?

3. Can you use Dow Corning to confirm a plan for the corner drugstore that has a provision enjoining banks from pursuing the officers and directors of the drugstore post-confirmation for the unpaid portion of any pre-petition debt? Would it matter if the officer and directors had each given the banks a personal guaranty?

4. OBTAINING COURT APPROVAL ("CONFIR-MATION") OF A PLAN UNDER SECTION 1129(b) ("CRAM DOWN")

Sometimes not all classes will consent. As in *Keck, Mahn*, a single secured creditor may comprise a single class and have interests significantly different than the remaining creditors. Or a sufficient minority of creditors may have ulterior motives to shut down the debtor (think of a class of unsecured creditors containing a significant minority of creditors who hold antitrust claims against the debtor, or who are competitors of the debtor).

What can a debtor in possession, or other plan proponent who wants the plan confirmed do if there is a non-assenting class of claims? The answer is found in Section 1129(b)(1). It reads "if all of the applicable requirements of subsection (a) of this section other than paragraph (8) are met with respect to a plan ... the court ... shall confirm the plan ... if...."

As a consequence, there are two plan confirmation alternatives:

- by the court's finding that all of the requirements of section 1129(a), including section 1129(a)(8) have been satisfied; or

- by the court's finding that all of the requirements of section 1129(a) except section 1129(a)(8), and that all of the other requirements of section 1129(b) have been satisfied.[12]

Looking to section 1129(b) to confirm notwithstanding a non-asseting class is commonly called a "cram down" or a "cramdown."[13] Even though neither "cram down" nor "cramdown" appears in the Bankruptcy Code, everyone uses the term. Even the novelist Richard Dooling.

RICHARD DOOLING, WHITE MAN'S GRAVE 4

7–9 (1995)

Randall lived and breathed the Bankruptcy Code, and intimidated anybody who crossed him by quoting it chapter, section, and verse. The famous biologist James Watson lived and breathed the problem of DNA until the structure of the double helix was revealed to him in a dream. Descartes nodded off and discovered the order of all the sciences in a dream. The nineteenth-century chemist Friedrich August Kekulé von

---

12. Remember, one of the requirements of section 1129(a) is section 1129(a)(10)'s requirement that "at least one class of claims that is impaired under the plan has accepted the plan." Accordingly, the court can use this second, 1129(b) alternative to plan confirmation only if there is at least one class that has accepted the plan. We referred to this confirmation requirement above in note 11.

13. "Cramdown" and "cram down" and "cram-down" are used interchangeably. Indeed, the Supreme Court has used both the "cramdown" and "cram-down" in the same sentence. Blanchette v. Connecticut General Ins. Corp., 419 U.S. 102, 167 (1974) (Douglas, J., dissenting).

Stradonitz dreamed of a serpent swallowing its tail, and woke up to discover the closed carbon ring structure of the benzene molecule. When Randall Killigan slept, he dreamed sections of the U.S. Bankruptcy Code, and woke up to discover money—lots of it—eagerly paid by clients who had insatiable appetites for his special insights into the Code. . . .

The attorneys representing all the major creditors in the WestCo Manufacturing case had arrayed themselves around a conference table, with their associates sitting demurely behind them, notepads and pens at the ready. The table was studded with notebook computers, briefcases, pitchers of ice water, notepads, cellular phones, and glasses fogging in the sunlight pouring in from the bay windows. Randall took his place at the head of the table and prepared to divide the spoils of WestCo Manufacturing among the lawyers for the various classes of creditors.

In primitive societies, the dominant male of the tribe apportioned the kill according to the skill and valor of the members of the hunting party. As far as Killigan was concerned, nothing much had changed for twentieth-century man, except that the weapons had become rules—complex and abstract rules—and the warriors were now lawyers. The kill was relatively bloodless (except for the occasional unhinged, atavistic client who showed up now and again on the six o'clock news dragging a lawyer around in a noose of piano wire attached to a shotgun). In Randall's hands, the U.S. Bankruptcy Code was a weapon, anything from a blazing scimitar to a neutron bomb, depending upon how much destruction he was being paid to inflict on his client's adversaries. International corporate behemoths—like WestCo—were weakened strays bleeding money, suffocated by debt, and falling behind the pack, where they could be picked off, dropped in the crosshairs of Randall's scope rifle, and plundered like carcasses rotting in the sun.

But bankruptcy law went far beyond the hunt, for the kill was always followed by brutal, expensive combat among the contending classes of creditors. Sure, passions ran high at Troy when Agamemnon took Achilles' beautiful sex slave for himself, but a bondholder who's being asked to take out-of-the-money warrants instead of principal plus interest at 14 percent is something else. Blood and gore. Section 1129 of the Code coyly referred to it as "plan confirmation," but when things went awry every bankruptcy lawyer in the country called the process "cram down," and for a good reason. After months or years of acrimonious, adversarial proceedings, one supreme warrior eventually emerged with a plan of reorganization, which he crammed down the throats of the vanquished creditors, so the spoils could be distributed to the victorious. . . .

---

a. Gerrymandering and Section 1129(a)(10)

We look at section 1129(b) only if all of section 1129(a) requirements other than section 1129(a)(8) have been satisfied. Section 1129(a)(10) requires that at least one class of impaired claims accept the plan Putting this all together, section 1129(b) applies only if there is at least one impaired class that did not accept the plan. But at least one impaired class must accept before you can apply section 1129(b) You can't use the cramdown power if no class consents to the plan. Section 1129(a)(10) creates pressure on how plan proponents create their classes. As the *U.S. Trucks* case, below, tell us, section 1129(a)(10) creates "gerrymandering."

11 U.S.C. § 1122(a)

[A] plan may place a claim or an interest in a particular class only if such claim or interest is substantially similar to the other claims or interests of such class.

11 U.S.C. § 1129(a)(10)

(a) The court shall confirm a plan only if all of the following requirements are met: . . . .

(10) If a class of claims is impaired under the plan, at least one class of claims that is impaired under the plan has accepted the plan, determined without including any acceptance of the plan by any insider.

IN RE U.S. TRUCK CO., INC.

800 F.2d 581 (6th Cir. 1986)

CORNELIA G. KENNEDY, Circuit Judge.

The Teamsters National Freight Industry Negotiating Committee (the Teamsters Committee), a creditor of U.S. Truck Company, Inc. (U.S. Truck)—the debtor-in-possession in this Chapter 11 bankruptcy proceeding—appeals the District Court's order confirming U.S. Truck's Fifth Amended Plan of Reorganization. The Teamsters Committee complains that the plan does not satisfy three of the requirements of 11 U.S.C. § 1129 . . .

Section 1129 contains two means by which a reorganization plan can be confirmed. The first way is to meet all eleven of the requirements of subsection (a), including (a)(8) which requires all impaired classes of claims or interests to accept the plan. The other way is to meet the requirements of subsection (b), which, first, incorporates all of the requirements of subsection (a), except for that contained in subsection (a)(8), and, second, imposes two additional requirements. Confirmation under subsection (b) is commonly referred to as a "cram down" because it permits a reorganization plan to go into effect over the objections of one or more impaired classes of creditors. In this case, U.S. Truck sought approval of its plan under this "cram down" provision. . . .

The Teamsters Committee's first objection is that the plan does not meet the requirement that at least one class of impaired claims accept the plan, see 11 U.S.C. § 1129(a)(10), because U.S. Truck impermissibly gerrymandered the classes in order to neutralize the Teamsters Committee's dissenting vote.

In this case, U.S. Truck is using its classification powers to segregate dissenting (impaired) creditors from assenting (impaired) creditors (by putting the dissenters into a class or classes by themselves) and, thus, it is assured that at least one class of impaired creditors will vote for the plan and make it eligible for cram down consideration by the court. We agree with the Teamsters Committee that there must be some limit on a debtor's power to classify creditors in such a manner. The potential for abuse would be significant otherwise. Unless there is some requirement of keeping similar claims together, nothing would stand in the way of a debtor seeking out a few impaired creditors (or even one such creditor) who will vote for the plan and placing them in their own class.[8] . . .

The District Court noted three important ways in which the interests of the Teamsters Committee differ substantially from those of the other impaired creditors. Because of these differences, the Teamsters Committee has a different stake in the future viability of the reorganized company and has alternative means at its disposal for protecting its claim. The Teamsters Committee's claim is connected with the collective bargaining process. In the words of the Committee's counsel, the union employees have a "virtually unique interest." These differences put the Teamsters Committee's claim in a different posture than the Class XI claims. The Teamsters Committee may choose to reject the plan not because the plan is less than optimal to it as a creditor, but because the Teamsters Committee has a noncreditor interest—e.g., rejection will benefit its members in the ongoing employment relationship. Although the Teamsters Committee certainly is not intimately connected with the debtor, to allow the Committee to vote with the other impaired creditors would be to allow it to prevent a court from considering confirmation of a plan that a significant group of creditors with similar interests have accepted. Permitting separate classification of the Teamsters Committee's claim does not automatically result in adoption of the plan. The Teamsters Committee is still protected by the provisions of subsections (a) and (b), particularly the requirements of subsection (b) that the plan not discriminate unfairly and that it be fair and equitable with respect to the Teamsters Committee's claim. In fact, the Teamsters Committee invokes those requirements, but as we note in the following sections, the plan does not violate them.

---

8. We need not speculate in this case whether the purpose of separate classification was to line up the votes in favor of the plan. The debtor admitted that to the District Court. . . .

QUESTIONS ABOUT U.S. TRUCK

1. In *U.S. Truck*, the Sixth Circuit states that "there must be some limit on a debtor's power to classify creditors in such a manner." Why? What is the Sixth Circuit's "limit"? Is the Sixth Circuit's limit on classifying claims to satisfy section 1129(a)(10) different from the limit suggested by the National Bankruptcy Review Commission in 1997: "Section 1122 should be amended to provide that a plan proponent may classify legally similar claims separately, if, upon objection, the proponent can demonstrate that the classification is supported by a 'rational business justification.'" Nat'l Bankruptcy Rev. Comm'n, Bankruptcy: The Next Twenty Years, The National Bankruptcy Review Commission Final Report, Recommendation 2.4.16, at 567 (1997).

2. In *U.S. Truck*, the Sixth Circuit upheld the confirmation of a U.S. Truck Chapter 11 plan that classified the union's unsecured claim for the debtor's breach of its collective bargaining agreement separate from other unsecured claims. If U.S. Truck's Chapter 11 plan had included the union's claim in the same class as other unsecured claims, would the Sixth Circuit have upheld a bankruptcy court's confirmation of that plan over the objection of some other unsecured creditor?

3. Most of the reported cases on classifying as gerrymandering involve single asset real estate cases in which:

- the debtor owns a building or land;

- the building or land is subject to a mortgage;

- the amount secured by the mortgage is much greater than the value of the building or land;

- the deficiency claim of the mortgage holder is much greater than all of the other unsecured claims combined;

- the holder of the mortgagor is voting both its secured claim and its unsecured claim against confirmation of the plan.

In these cases, the debtor can meet the requirement of section 1129(a)(10) only by classifying the deficiency claim separate from other unsecured claims. In these cases, court commonly consider the "1111(b) election" and the "new value corollary/exception" and section 1129(b)(1) "unfairly discriminates" and other stuff we are fixing to cover.

---

b. "Not Discriminate Unfairly" and Section 1129(b)(1)

Before we look at the additional requirements of section 1129(b), let's think about we have already seen (and not seen). We have seen that sections 1122 and 1123 provide for Chapter 11 plan's classification of claims with different treatment for different treatment. So, obviously we will see "discrimination" among the various classes in a Chapter 11 plan.

We have not however seen the word "discriminate" in any of the section 1129(a) confirmation standards. We only see the phrase "discriminate unfairly" in section 1129(b), set out below (and in the *Sentry* case that Markell insist we include).

To summarize then, a plan's discrimination among classes is only an issue when (1) a class of claims does not accept the plan and (2) that class is unfairly discriminated against that class.

11 U.S.C. § 1129(b)(1)

[I]f all of the applicable requirements of subsection (a) of this section other than paragraph (8) are met with respect to a plan, the court, on request of the proponent of the plan, shall confirm the plan notwithstanding the requirements of such paragraph if the plan does not discriminate unfairly, ... , with respect to each class of claims or interests that is impaired under, and has not accepted, the plan.

Problem 11–20: "Not Discriminate Unfairly"

1. D's Chapter 11 plan has two classes of unsecured claims: Class V, which includes the unsecured claims of "critical vendors" and Class O which includes all other unsecured claims. The plan proposes to pay Class V claims in full within three months of the effective date of the plan and pay Class O claims 10% of the amount owed, over a three year period. If Class V accepts the plan and Class O does not, can the court still confirm the plan?

2. Same facts as #1 except that 75% of the claims (in number and amount) in Class O accept the plan. Can the court confirm the plan?

IN RE SENTRY OPERATING CO. OF TEXAS, INC.

264 B.R. 850 (Bankr. S.D. Tex. 2001)

WESLEY W. STEEN, Bankruptcy Judge.

In this contested matter, the Court must decide whether to confirm a chapter 11 plan over the objection of a class of unsecured creditors that has rejected the plan. These creditors argue ... that a chapter 11 plan cannot be confirmed over their rejection and objection if it proposes to pay them a lesser percentage than it proposes to pay other creditors of equal rank. The Court concludes that ... the plan proponents have not met their burden to prove that the class definitions are drawn sufficiently narrowly and have not met their burden to prove that the plan does not discriminate unfairly.

The SCI–L debt is secured by a lien and security interest in all assets involved in these cases.

. . .

Summary of Classification of Claims, Plan Treatment, and Acceptance/Rejection

	Accept/ Reject	Number–% Voting for	Claims–% Voting for	Amount to be paid	Percent of claim to be paid
Class 1, SCI–L	Impaired, Insider, Accepts			Approx. $21 million (Note 1)	61%
Class 2, Priority	Unimpaired			Approx. $4,440	100%
Class 3, Unsecured Trade Creditors	Impaired, Accepts	100%	100%	Approx. $400,000	100%
Class 4, Other Unsecured Creditors	Impaired	20% (See Note 2)	11% (See Note 2)	Approx. $100,000	1% (Note 3)
Class 5, Ford Motor Credit	Unimpaired			Approx. $66,443	100%
Class 6, Stillwater National Bank	Unimpaired			Approx. $66,443	100%
Class 7, Equity	Deemed to reject			Nothing	

Note 1: SCI–L will receive all of the value of the company ($23 million) less approximately $1.5 million to be used to fund other payments under the plan.

Note 2: For reasons set forth below, the Court concludes that the votes of the Stumpff group should not be counted but the Subordinated Investor votes should be counted. Debtors counted and recounted the Class 4 votes, but even after the recount the report was admittedly incorrect. The percentages related in the table are reasonably close to the correct count based on the Court's determination that the votes of Subordinated Investors should be counted, but not the votes of the Stumpff group.

Note 3: $100,000 divided among total claims of $10,469,737.51 listed for class 4 in Debtor's revised vote tally.

. . .

Bankruptcy Code Section 1129(b) does not define "discriminate unfairly." In this case, the issue is whether the Plan discriminates unfairly by proposing to pay a greater percentage distribution to Class 3 creditors than it pays to Class 4 creditors, even though both have equal rank under state law and under the distribution priorities of the Bankruptcy Code. It is clear that the Plan discriminates between the two groups of creditors since it proposes to pay one set 1% of their claims and it proposes to pay the other group 100%. The Plan proponents argue that SCI–L has a lien on all assets and therefore the Plan does not discriminate unfairly because Class 4 has no legal right to a distribution. They argue that SCI–L is merely giving up part of its entitlement, and that Class 4 has no legal right to complain. . . .

In general, the Bankruptcy Code is premised on the rule of equality of treatment. Creditors with claims of equal rank are entitled to equal distribution. But § 1129(b) obviously permits some discrimination, since it only prohibits unfair discrimination. The task is to determine what constitutes "fair" discrimination.

A very persuasive historical analysis and proposed test is presented by Bruce A. Markell, entitled A New Perspective on Unfair Discrimination in Chapter 11 (hereafter "Markell"). In that article, Markell observes that:

> . . . [U]nfair discrimination is best viewed as a horizontal limit on nonconsensual confirmation . . . Just as the fair and equitable requirement regulates priority among classes of creditors having higher and lower priorities, creating inter-priority fairness, so the unfair discrimination provision promotes intra-priority fairness, assuring equitable treatment among creditors who have the same level of priority.

Markell proposes the following test:

In particular, I propose that a Chapter 11 plan is presumptively subject to denial of confirmation on the basis of unfair discrimination, even though it provides fair and equitable treatment for all classes, when there is (1) a dissenting class; (2) another class of the same priority; and (3) a difference in the plan's treatment of the two classes that results in either (a) a materially lower percentage recovery for the dissenting class (measured in terms of the net present value of all payments), or (b) regardless of percentage recovery, an allocation under the plan of materially greater risk to the dissenting class in connection with its proposed distribution.

Under this test, the Plan is "presumptively subject to denial of confirmation." However, Markell suggests that the presumption can be overcome by proof of one of two exceptions.

The plan proponent may overcome the presumption based on different percentage recoveries by showing that a lower recovery for the dissenting class is consistent with the results that would obtain outside of bankruptcy, or that a greater recovery for the other class is offset by contributions from that class to the reorganization.

At first blush, the first exception might seem to cover this Plan: "a lower recovery for the dissenting class is consistent with the results that would obtain outside of bankruptcy." But nowhere in the article does Markell suggest that a secured lender may simply purchase the assent of an unsecured class by giving up part of its claim. Markell seems to suggest that the "results that would obtain outside of bankruptcy" has to do with pre-petition status of creditors and their legitimate expectations about relative rights and likelihood of payment. His example of appropriate discrimination between trade claims in one class and deficiency claims of a non-recourse secured creditor in another class. The discrimination is justified in this example because outside of bankruptcy the non-recourse creditor has no expectations of recovery on its deficiency claim. Since any recovery in bankruptcy is more than the creditor would get outside of bankruptcy, discriminatory treatment may not be unfair.

In the Plan, there is no such justification for gross discrimination between the percentage payouts to Classes 3 and 4. Class 3 contains some small creditors whose continued work with the funeral homes would probably provide some value. However, Class 3 contains many more national creditors (some of them very large) who appear to be paid for reasons other than preservation of value. Thus there does not appear to be sufficient "contribution to preservation of value through the plan" that justifies a payout differential. Although there are equity investors in Class 4 who might be paid differently based on expectations and inside information, there are also ex-proprietors of small funeral homes in Class 4 who sold businesses to the Debtor and did not share control or insider information. While a deferred payout and possibly risk differential among the different kinds of creditors in this case might be justified, a 99% payout differential is not justified. Adopting the Markell proposal, the Court concludes that the plan discriminates unfairly.

Even more persuasive is the interrelationship of creditor protections evidenced in the statutory confirmation requirements. Bankruptcy Code § 1129(a)(7) protects all creditors in all classes against receiving less than what they would receive in liquidation, even if their class were to accept the plan. The "fair and equitable" requirement of 1129(b) protects each class of creditors against involuntary loss of their priority status, vis a vis other classes of different rank. The "does not discriminate unfairly" requirement in § 1129(b) protects each class of creditors against involuntary loss of their equal distribution rights vis a vis other creditors of equal rank.

To accept SCI–L's argument that a secured lender can, without any reference to fairness, decide which creditors get paid and how much those creditors get paid, is to ... read section 1129(b) requirements out of the Code. If the argument were accepted with respect to § 1129(b) "unfair discrimination requirement," there is no logical reason not to apply it to the § 1129(b) "fair and equitable" requirement, or to the § 1129(a)(10) requirement that at least one class has accepted the plan. To accept that argument is simply to start down a slippery slope that does great violence to history and to positive law. There are devices at law, such as foreclosure, in which the secured lender is not required to negotiate with unsecured creditors, to obtain consent of at least one class of impaired creditors, or to be fair. But the advantage of an equity receivership, and its descendant the chapter 11 reorganization, is (among others) (i) that going concern value is preserved or enhanced, (ii) that the debtor (in this case in league with the secured lender) is left in possession and control of the business to decide how to restructure it, (iii) that executory contracts can be assumed or rejected, (iv) that preferences and fraudulent conveyances can be recovered, and (v) that all other creditors are held at bay under an automatic stay while the plan is formulated and implemented. The Bankruptcy Code establishes the price of these powerful equitable tools (when any class of creditors is impaired) as negotiation to win over the acceptance of an impaired class and treatment of all non-accepting classes fairly, equitably, and without unfair discrimination. SCI–L proposes to obtain the benefits of equitable tools without paying the price. The statute has no provision for that, and the Court is unwilling to read these requirements out of the Code.

The Court, at this point, is not required (or able) to define the limits of "unfair discrimination" in this case. The plan, as indicated above, fails to meet other confirmation requirements. The fact that Class 4 creditors would receive nothing in a liquidation might or might not be influential under the right circumstances. All that the Court need determine at this stage is that the dire financial consequences of foreclosure is not sufficient to sustain a finding that the proposed discriminatory Plan treatment of Class 4 is fair and equitable.

CONCLUSION

The plan does not meet all of the confirmation requirements of Bankruptcy Code Section 1129. Therefore, by separate order issued this date, plan confirmation is denied. To consider additional orders for the expedient and economical prosecution of this case, the Court will conduct a status conference under Bankruptcy Code § 105(d).

NOTES ON SENTRY

1. Under the rationale of *Sentry*, could a plan separately classify tort and trade creditors into different unsecured classes, and then pay each 100% on the dollar, albeit with the trade creditor class being paid off in six months and the tort class being paid off in six years? Is that unfair discrimination? What if the plan not only proposes differences in the timing of the payout, but also different payouts, such as 100% to the "necessary" trade creditors, but only 10% to the tort claimants.

2. The "Markell test" has been challenged as too soft and too uncertain. See The Committee on Bankruptcy and Corporate Reorganization of the Association of the Bar of the City of New York, *Making the Test for Unfair Discrimination More "Fair": A Proposal*, 58 Bus. Lawyer 83 (2002); Markell,

of course, has replied. Bruce A. Markell, *Slouching Towards Fairness: A Reply to the ABCNY's Proposal on Unfair Discrimination*, 58 Bus. Lawyer 109 (2002).

---

c. "Fair and Equitable" and Section 1129(b)

The most important phrase in section 1129 is "fair and equitable." In order for a plan to be cram downed on a class, that plan must be fair and equitable as to that class. To determine whether a plan is "fair and equitable" to a non-assenting class, it is helpful to look to section 1129(b)(2), which contains a series of non-exclusive examples of fair and equitable treatment. And to apply these examples in section 1129(b)(2), it is necessary to know whether the non-assenting class is a class of secured claims or a class of unsecured claims or interests.

---

(1) Cram Down of Secured Claims

Let's do cram down of secured claims first. Assume that there was a secured claim class that did not accept the plan. In determining whether to confirm the plan notwithstanding the non-assenting secured class, the court will look to section 1129(b)(2)(A).

---

11 U.S.C. § 1129(b)(2)(A)

(2) For the purpose of this subsection, the condition that a plan be fair and equitable with respect to a class includes the following requirements:

(A) With respect to a class of secured claims, the plan provides—

(i)(I)   that the holders of such claims retain the liens securing such claims, whether the property subject to such liens is retained by the debtor or transferred to another entity, to the extent of the allowed amount of such claims; and

(II) that each holder of a claim of such class receive on account of such claim deferred cash payments totaling at least the allowed amount of such claim, of a value, as of the effective date of the plan, of at least the value of such holder's interest in the estate's interest in such property;

(ii) for the sale, subject to section 363(k) of this title, of any property that is subject to the liens securing such claims, free and clear of such liens, with such liens to attach to the proceeds of such sale, and the treatment of such liens on proceeds under clause (i) or (iii) of this subparagraph; or

(iii) for the realization by such holders of the indubitable equivalent of such claims.

———————

Generally, the legal issues in a Chapter 11 cram down of a secured claim under section 1129(b)(2)(A) are similar to the legal issues in a Chapter 13 cram down of a secured claim under section 1325(a)(5): the value of the collateral *(Rash)* and the interest rate to be paid *(Till)*. Only in Chapter 11, however, can the holder of a secured claim make a "section 1111(b) election" and a section 1111(b) election affects the application of section 1129(b)(2)(A).

Section 1129(b)(2)(A) uses the phrase "secured claims" and then refers to "secured claims" repeatedly as "such claims" or "such claim." We have repeatedly cited to section 506 when referring to "secured claims." But section 1111(b) also is relevant, and thus we must look at the election given certain secured creditors in section 1111(b).

Section 506(a) determines what is a "secured claim" for most purposes under the Bankruptcy Code. If, for example, D has filed a Chapter 7 case and it owes S $1,000 and the debt is secured by property with a value of $700, then under section 506(a) S has a secured claim of $700. S would also have an unsecured claim of $300, unless the loan was non-recourse.

Section 1111(b), applicable only in Chapter 11 cases, changes section 506(a) in two ways that can be important in applying section 1129(b)(2)(A) to a nonassenting secured class whose collateral is not sold during the case or under the plan. In particular:

- Section 1111(b)(1)(A) gives even the secured creditor with a nonrecourse claim the same rights as a secured creditor with a recourse claim.

- Section 1111(b)(2) enables any nonassenting secured class whose collateral is not sold during the case to elect to have its claim allowed and treated as a secured claim for the full amount of the debt rather than a lower amount measured by its collateral's value (as section 506 generally requires.)

Look again at the above example (D owed S $1,000 and the debt is secured by property with a value of $700). Under section 1111(b)(2), S could elect to have its full $1,000 debt simply treated as a secured claim.

After reading this example, the benefits of making a section 1111(b) election should seem obvious. After carefully reading section 1129(b)(2)(A) and remembering what you have learned about the plan approval process, the costs of a section 1111(b) election should be equally obvious.

———————

Problem 11–21: Understanding Section 1129(b)(2)(A)(i)(I) With No Section 1111(b) Election

1. D Co. a Chapter 11 debtor, owes S $1,000,000. The debt is based on a note which provides for interest at 10% and 20 equal monthly payments of interest and principal. D Co.'s payment of the note is secured by a first mortgage on Blackacre. Assume the following facts:

   • Blackacre has a value of $700,000; and

   • D Co. intends to retain Blackacre; and

   • S has not made a section 1111(b) election; and

   • every class of claims other than the S secured claim class has accepted the plan.

   Will the court cram down a plan that pays S $700,000 on the confirmation date?

2. Same assumed facts as #1. Will the court cram down a plan that pays S $350,000 six months after the effective date of the plan and $350,000 more six months later? Why not?

3. Same assumed facts as #1. Will the court cram down a plan that pays S $350,00 six months after the effective date of the plan and $350,000 more six months with interest?

4. Would your answers to #1 and #3 change if S made a section 1111(b) election?

Give us (and section 1111(b)) one more chance.

Examine sub-clause (II) of section 1129(b)(2)(A) with the following example in mind: an overall debt to S of $1,000, and collateral worth $750. If S does not elect under Section 1111(b)(2), then S will have a secured claim of $750, and an unsecured deficiency claim of $250, even if S's claim was non-recourse under non-bankruptcy law. If S elects under Section 1111(b)(2), then S loses any deficiency, but S gets a $1,000 secured claim.

Will S get a Chapter 11 plan distribution worth $1,000 as of the date of confirmation? No. Sub-clause (II) only requires that S get "deferred cash payments" totaling $1,000. So the undiscounted stream of payments to S only has to add up to $1,000. The value of such "deferred cash payments," however, have to have a "value, as of the effective date of the plan," not of the allowed amount of the claim—$1,000—but "the value of the such holder's [S's] interest in the estate's interest in such property," or $750.

How can this work? This can be done by giving the creditor a note in the full amount of the allowed claim that bears a below market interest rate. Thus, it will not have a present value equal to its face amount (it would have to have a market rate of interest to have a value equal to its face), but something lesser.

Problem 11–22: *Electing and Cramming*

1. C has a $1 million nonrecourse note from D. The note is secured by D's plant. The bankruptcy court acting pursuant to Bankruptcy Rule 3012 has valued the plant at $700,000. D's Chapter 11 plan provides that C will receive a $1 million note, secured by the plan. The note will mature in four years and, until maturity, will bear an annual interest rate of 3.5%. D makes a section 1111(b) election and votes against the plan. Can the court confirm the plan?

2. Same facts as #1 except that the court confirms the plan and one year after confirmation, D sells the plant for $900,000. Who gets the proceeds? How much of the sale proceeds would C have received if it had not made the section 1111(b) election?

3. Trick question: Same facts as #1 except that:

    ● the debt was a recourse debt; and

    ● the plan proposes to sell the property for $700,000 and pay the proceeds of the sale to S in full satisfaction of S's secured claim.

    Can S make the section 1111(b) election and block plan confirmation because it is not receiving the full amount of its secured claim?

4. Harder question. D owns an apartment building. D owes $3,000,000 to your client S; the debt is secured by the apartment building. S believes that the apartment building has a value of $2,000,000. D owes other, unsecured creditors a total of $400,000. D has filed for Chapter 11 relief. Do you advise S to make a section 1111(b) election? What, if any, additional information, do you need to advise S? Cf. Bankr. R. 3014.

Problem   11–23: Replacement   Collateral   and   Section *1129(b)(2)(A)(i)(III)*

D Co., a Chapter 11 debtor, owes S $5,000,000. S has a first mortgage on Blackacre. Advise D Co. as to whether the court will cram down a plan that sells Blackacre to T free and clear of S's mortgage and grants S a first mortgage on Redacre.

Problem 11–24: *Stock Plans and Section 1129(b)(2)(A)*

D Co., a Chapter 11 debtor, owes S $20,000,000. The debt is secured by all of D Co.'s buildings and equipment. D Co. wants to use its stock to satisfy S's secured debt. S is unwilling to agree to any Chapter 11 plan that replaces its secured debt with stock. Advise D Co. as to how to determine the amount of its stock that it will have to issue to S so that a court will cram down a plan that replaces S's secured debt with stock.

---

(2) Cram Down of Unsecured Claims

Lawyers and judges (but not the Bankruptcy Code) use the phrase "absolute priority" to describe section 1129(b)(2)(B)'s standard for "fair and equitable" treatment of unsecured claims.

11 U.S.C. § 1129(b)(2)(B)

(2) [T]he condition that a plan be fair and equitable with respect to a class includes the following requirements:

(B) With respect to a class of unsecured creditors—

. . .

(ii) the holder of any claim or interest that is junior to the claims of such class will not receive or retain under the plan on account of such junior claim or interest any property.(emphasis added)

Who is "junior" to an unsecured creditor?: Under the Bankruptcy Code, as under corporate codes, stockholders are "junior:" to unsecured creditors. Accordingly, the absolute priority rule of section 1129(b)(2)(B) requires payment in full to each non-assenting class of unsecured claims before distributions to stockholders. Saying the same thing another way, a plan can not be crammed down on unsecured creditors unless stockholders lose all of their stock.

Problem 11–25: Applying Section 1129(b)(2)(B)(i) to Plans That Distribute Cash to the Non-Assenting Class

D Co.'s Chapter 11 plan provides that each holder of a class 7 unsecured claim will receive a note for the full amount of its claim. The note is payable in 7 years with 4.3% interest. D Co.'s shareholders will receive all of the stock of the reorganized D Co. If class 7 is a non-assenting class, will the court confirm the plan under section 1129(b)(2)(B)(i)? What, if any, additional information do you need to answer this question?

Problem 11–26: Applying Section 1129(b)(2)(B)(I) to Plans That Distribute Stock to the Non-Assenting Class

D Co.'s Chapter 11 plan provides that 49% of the stock of the reorganized D Co. will be distributed to holders of unsecured class 7 claims and that the other 51% of the stock will be distributed to D Co.'s existing shareholders. If class 7 is a non-assenting class, will the court confirm the plan under section 1129(b)(2)(B)? Again, what, if any, additional information do you need to answer this question?

By making a new capital contribution, can the existing shareholders of a Chapter 11 corporation keep their stock even though a non-assenting class of claims has not been paid value? In the next case, *203 North LaSalle*, Justice Souter considers but does not directly answer this question.

BANK OF AMERICA v. 203 N. LaSALLE ST. PARTNERSHIP

526 U.S. 434 (1999)

Justice SOUTER delivered the opinion of the Court.

The issue in this Chapter 11 reorganization case is whether a debtor's prebankruptcy equity holders may, over the objection of a senior class of impaired creditors, contribute new capital and receive ownership interests in the reorganized entity, when that opportunity is given exclusively to the old equity holders under a plan adopted without consideration of alternatives. We hold that old equity holders are disqualified from participating in such a "new value" transaction by the terms of 11 U.S.C. § 1129(b)(2)(B)(ii), which in such circumstances bars a junior interest holder's receipt of any property on account of his prior interest.

I

Petitioner, Bank of America National Trust and Savings Association (Bank), is the major creditor of respondent, 203 North LaSalle Street Partnership (Debtor or Partnership), an Illinois real estate limited partnership. The Bank lent the Debtor some $93 million, secured by a nonrecourse first mortgage on the Debtor's principal asset, 15 floors of an office building in downtown Chicago. In January 1995, the Debtor defaulted, and the Bank began foreclosure in a state court.

In March, the Debtor responded with a voluntary petition for relief under Chapter 11 of the Bankruptcy Code, 11 U.S.C. § 1101 et seq., which automatically stayed the foreclosure proceedings, see § 362(a). The Debtor's principal objective was to ensure that its partners retained title to the property so as to avoid roughly $20 million in personal tax liabilities, which would fall due if the Bank foreclosed. The Debtor proceeded to propose a reorganization plan during the 120–day period when it alone had the right to do so, see 11 U.S.C. § 1121(b); see also § 1121(c) (exclusivity period extends to 180 days if the debtor files plan within the initial 120 days). The Bankruptcy Court rejected the Bank's motion to terminate the period of exclusivity to make way for a plan of its own to liquidate the property, and instead extended the exclusivity period for cause shown, under § 1121(d).

The value of the mortgaged property was less than the balance due the Bank, which elected to divide its undersecured claim into secured and unsecured deficiency claims under § 506(a) and § 1111(b). Under the plan, the Debtor separately classified the Bank's secured claim, its unsecured deficiency claim, and unsecured trade debt owed to other creditors. See § 1122(a). The Bankruptcy Court found that the Debtor's available assets were prepetition rents in a cash account of $3.1 million and the 15 floors of rental property worth $54.5 million. The secured claim was valued at the latter figure, leaving the Bank with an unsecured deficiency of $38.5 million.

So far as we need be concerned here, the Debtor's plan had these further features:

(1) The Bank's $54.5 million secured claim would be paid in full between 7 and 10 years after the original 1995 repayment date.

(2) The Bank's $38.5 million unsecured deficiency claim would be discharged for an estimated 16% of its present value.

(3) The remaining unsecured claims of $90,000, held by the outside trade creditors, would be paid in full, without interest, on the effective date of the plan.

(4) Certain former partners of the Debtor would contribute $6.125 million in new capital over the course of five years (the contribution being worth some $4.1 million in present value), in exchange for the Partnership's entire ownership of the reorganized debtor.

The last condition was an exclusive eligibility provision: the old equity holders were the only ones who could contribute new capital.

The Bank objected and, being the sole member of an impaired class of creditors, thereby blocked confirmation of the plan on a consensual basis. The Debtor, however, took the alternate route to confirmation of a reorganization plan, forthrightly known as the judicial "cramdown" process for imposing a plan on a dissenting class.

There are two conditions for a cramdown. First, all requirements of § 1129(a) must be met (save for the plan's acceptance by each impaired class of claims or interests, see § 1129(a)(8)). Critical among them are the conditions that the plan be accepted by at least one class of impaired creditors, see § 1129(a)(10), and satisfy the "best-interest-of-creditors" test, see § 1129(a)(7). Here, the class of trade creditors with impaired unsecured claims voted for the plan, 126 F.3d, at 959, and there was no issue of best interest. Second, the objection of an impaired creditor class may be overridden only if "the plan does not discriminate unfairly, and is fair and equitable, with respect to each class of claims or interests that is impaired under, and has not accepted, the plan." § 1129(b)(1). As to a dissenting class of impaired unsecured creditors, such a plan may be found to be "fair and equitable" only if the allowed value of the claim is to be paid in full, § 1129(b)(2)(B)(i), or, in the alternative, if "the holder of any claim or interest that is junior to the claims of such [impaired unsecured] class will not receive or retain under the plan on account of such junior claim or interest any property," § 1129(b)(2)(B)(ii). That latter condition is the core of what is known as the "absolute priority rule."

The absolute priority rule was the basis for the Bank's position that the plan could not be confirmed as a cramdown. As the Bank read the rule, the plan was open to objection simply because certain old equity holders in the Debtor Partnership would receive property even though the Bank's unsecured deficiency claim would not be paid in full. The Bankruptcy Court approved the plan nonetheless, and accordingly denied the Bank's pending motion to convert the case to Chapter 7 liquidation, or to dismiss the case. The District Court affirmed, as did the Court of Appeals.

The majority of the Seventh Circuit's divided panel found ambiguity in the language of the statutory absolute priority rule, and looked beyond the text to interpret the phrase "on account of "as permitting recognition of a "new value corollary" to the rule.

We granted certiorari to resolve a Circuit split on the issue. The Seventh Circuit in this case joined the Ninth in relying on a new value corollary to the absolute priority rule to support confirmation of such plans.... The Second and Fourth Circuits, by contrast, without explicitly rejecting the corollary, have disapproved plans similar to this one. We do not decide whether the statute includes a new value corollary or exception, but hold that on any reading respondent's proposed plan fails to satisfy the statute, and accordingly reverse.

II

The terms "absolute priority rule" and "new value corollary" (or "exception") are creatures of law antedating the current Bankruptcy Code, and to understand both those terms and the related but inexact language of the Code some history is helpful. The Bankruptcy Act preceding the Code contained no such provision as subsection (b)(2)(B)(ii), its subject having been addressed by two interpretive rules. The first was a specific gloss on the requirement of § 77B (and its successor, Chapter X) of the old Act, that any reorganization plan be "fair and equitable." The reason for such a limitation was the danger inherent in any reorganization plan proposed by a, debtor, then and now, that the plan will simply turn out to be too good a deal for the debtor's owners.... Hence the pre-Code judicial response known as the absolute priority rule, that fairness and equity required that "the creditors ... be paid before the stockholders could retain [equity interests] for any purpose whatever." Northern Pacific R. Co. v. Boyd, 228 U.S. 482, 508, 33 S.Ct. 554, 57 L.Ed. 931 (1913)....

The second interpretive rule addressed the first. Its classic formulation occurred in Case v. Los Angeles Lumber Products Co., in which the Court spoke through Justice Douglas in this dictum:

> "It is, of course, clear that there are circumstances under which stockholders may participate in a plan of reorganization of an insolvent debtor.... Where th[e] necessity [for new capital] exists and the old stockholders make a fresh contribution and receive in return a participation reasonably equivalent to their contribution, no objection can be made....

> "[W]e believe that to accord 'the creditor his full right of priority against the corporate assets' where the debtor is insolvent, the stockholder's participation must be based on a contribution in money or in money's worth, reasonably equivalent in view of all the circumstances to the participation of the stockholder." 308 U.S., at 121–122, 60 S.Ct. 1.

... [T]he Case observation ... never rose above the technical level of dictum in any opinion of this Court.... Hence the controversy over how weighty the Case dictum had become, as reflected in the alternative labels for the new value notion: some writers and courts (including this one) have spoken of it as an exception to the absolute priority rule ... while others have characterized it as a simple corollary to the rule....

Which of these positions is ultimately entitled to prevail is not to be decided here, ... [Even if the Court recognized a new value corollary, the] Bank's objection would require rejection of the plan at issue in this case. It is doomed, we can say without necessarily exhausting its flaws, by its provision for vesting equity in the reorganized business in the Debtor's partners without extending an opportunity to anyone else either to compete for that equity or to propose a competing reorganization plan. Although the Debtor's exclusive opportunity to propose a plan under § 1121(b) is not itself "property" within the meaning of subsection (b)(2)(B)(ii), the respondent partnership in this case has taken advantage of this opportunity by proposing a plan under which the benefit of equity ownership may be obtained by no one but old equity partners. Upon the court's approval of that plan, the partners were in the same position that they would have enjoyed had they exercised an exclusive option under the plan to buy the equity in the reorganized entity, or contracted to purchase it from a seller who had first agreed to deal with no one else. It is quite true that the escrow of the partners' proposed investment eliminated any formal need to set out an express option or exclusive dealing provision in the plan itself, since the court's approval that created the opportunity and the partners' action to obtain its advantage were simultaneous. But before the Debtor's plan was accepted no one else could propose an alternative one, and after its acceptance no one else could obtain equity in the reorganized entity. At the moment of the plan's approval the Debtor's partners necessarily enjoyed an exclusive opportunity that was in no economic sense distinguishable from the advantage of the exclusively entitled offeror or option holder. This opportunity should, first of all, be treated as an item of property in its own right. . . . While it may be argued that the opportunity has no market value, being significant only to old equity holders owing to their potential tax liability, such an argument avails the Debtor nothing, for several reasons. It is to avoid just such arguments that the law is settled that any otherwise cognizable property interest must be treated as sufficiently valuable to be recognized under the Bankruptcy Code. Even aside from that rule, the assumption that no one but the Debtor's partners might pay for such an opportunity would obviously support no inference that it is valueless, let alone that it should not be treated as property. And, finally, the source in the tax law of the opportunity's value to the partners implies in no way that it lacks value to others. It might, indeed, be valuable to another precisely as a way to keep the Debtor from implementing a plan that would avoid a Chapter 7 liquidation.

Given that the opportunity is property of some value, the question arises why old equity alone should obtain it, not to mention at no cost whatever. The closest thing to an answer favorable to the Debtor is that the old equity partners would be given the opportunity in the expectation that in taking advantage of it they would add the stated purchase price to the estate. But this just begs the question why the opportunity should be exclusive to the old equity holders. If the price to be paid for the equity interest is the best obtainable, old equity does not need the protection of exclusiveness (unless to trump an equal offer from someone else); if it is not the best, there is no apparent reason for giving old equity a bargain. There is no reason, that is, unless the very purpose of the whole transaction is, at least in part, to do old equity a favor. And that, of course, is to say that old equity would obtain its opportunity, and the resulting benefit, because of old equity's prior interest within the meaning of subsection (b)(2)(B)(ii). Hence it is that the exclusiveness of the opportunity, with its protection against the market's scrutiny of the purchase price by means of competing bids or even competing plan proposals, renders the partners' right a property interest extended "on account of" the old equity position and therefore subject to an unpaid senior creditor class's objection.

It is no answer to this to say that the exclusive opportunity should be treated merely as a detail of the broader transaction that would follow its exercise, and that in this wider perspective no favoritism may be inferred, since the old equity partners would pay something, whereas no one else would pay anything. If this argument were to carry the day, of course, old equity could obtain a new property interest for a dime without being seen to receive anything on account of its old position. But even if we assume that old equity's plan would not be confirmed without satisfying the judge that the purchase price was top dollar, there is a further reason here not to treat property consisting of an exclusive opportunity as subsumed within the total transaction proposed. On the interpretation assumed here, it would, of course, be a fatal flaw if old equity acquired or retained the property interest without paying full value. It would thus be necessary for old equity to demonstrate its payment of top dollar, but this it could not satisfactorily do when it would receive or retain its property under a plan giving it exclusive rights and in the absence of a competing plan of any sort. Under a plan granting an exclusive right, making no provision for competing bids or competing plans, any determination that the price was top dollar would necessarily be made by a judge in bankruptcy court, whereas the best way to determine value is exposure to a market. This is a point of some significance, since it was, after all, one of the Code's innovations to narrow the occasions for courts to make valuation judgments, as shown by its preference for the supramajoritarian class creditor voting scheme in § 1126(c). In the interest of statutory coherence, a like disfavor for decisions untested by competitive choice ought to extend to valuations in administering subsection (b)(2)(B)(ii) when some form of market valuation may be available to test. the adequacy of an old equity holder's proposed contribution.

Whether a market test would require an opportunity to offer competing plans or would be satisfied by a right to bid for the same interest sought by old equity is a question we do not decide here. It is enough to say, assuming a new value corollary, that plans providing junior interest holders with exclusive opportunities free from competition and without benefit of market valuation fall within the prohibition of § 1129(b)(2)(B)(ii).

The judgment of the Court of Appeals, accordingly, is reversed, and the case is remanded for further proceedings consistent with this opinion.

It is so ordered.

---

5. AFTER CONFIRMATION

A Chapter 11 case does not end with confirmation. After confirmation, the debtor continues operating its business (providing the plan does not call for liquidation) and makes the payments provided for in the plan.

Even though confirmation requires a finding that the plan is feasible, the debtor may encounter problems in paying or otherwise performing pursuant to the provisions of the plan. Postconfirmation problems raise questions about the effects of confirmation.

Section 1141 is entitled "Effect of Confirmation." Please read section 1141 and determine the effect of confirmation of the Chapter 11 plan in the following problems.

---

11 U.S.C. § 1141

(a) Except as provided in subsections (d)(2) and (d)(3) of this section, the provisions of a confirmed plan bind the debtor ... and any creditor ... whether or not ... such creditor ... has accepted the plan.

(b) Except as otherwise provided in the plan or the order confirming the plan, the confirmation of a plan vests all of the property of the estate in the debtor. . . .

(d)(1) Except as otherwise provided in this subsection, in the plan, or in the order confirming the plan, the confirmation of a plan-

(A) discharges the debtor from any debt that arose before the date of such confirmation, and any debt of a kind specified in section 502(g), 502(h), or 502(i) of this title, whether or not-

(i) a proof of the claim based on such debt is filed or deemed filed under section 501 of this title;

(ii) such claim is allowed under section 502 of this title; or

(iii) the holder of such claim has accepted the plan; and

. . .

(3) The confirmation of a plan does not discharge a debtor if—

(A) the plan provides for the liquidation of all or substantially all of the property of the estate;

(B) the debtor does not engage in business after consummation of the plan; and

(C) the debtor would be denied a discharge under section 727(a) of this title if the case were a case under chapter 7 of this title.

Problem 11–27: *If the Debtor Does Not Make Plan Payments*

1. D's Chapter 11 reorganization plan provides for the continuation of business operations and the issuance of notes to holders of unsecured claims. The notes are to be for 40% of the amount owed and are to be payable over five years. The plan is confirmed. What are the rights of X, an unsecured creditor who voted against the plan? Of Y, an unsecured creditor who did not file a proof of claim?

2. Same facts as #1. What are the rights of D's unsecured creditors if D defaults on its new payment obligations? Is D protected by the automatic stay? By the confirmation order?

3. D's Chapter 11 plan provides for the sale of all of its assets to Newco and the issuance of Newco notes to holders of unsecured claims. The notes are to be 40% of the amount owed and are to be payable over five years. The plan is confirmed. What are the rights of D's unsecured creditors against D? What if D is a corporation? *See* sections 1141(d)(3) and 727(a)(1).

4. D's Chapter 11 plan that provides for monthly payments to creditors for two years is confirmed. D is able to make the first three payments. Because of an unexpected deep drop in sales, D is not able to make the fourth payment. How can D modify its payment obligations under the confirmed plan? Section 1127(b) prohibits modification after "substantial consummation." *See* section 1101(c). If D can not modify its confirmed

Chapter 11, can D file another Chapter 11 petition, i.e., use "Chapter 22?" *Cf.* section 109(d), (g).

F. NON–CONSENSUAL DISMISSAL OR CONVERSION TO CHAPTER 7

11 U.S.C. § 1112(b)

(b)(1) Except as provided in paragraph (2) of this subsection, subsection (c) of this section, and section 1104(a)(3), on request of a party in interest, and after notice and a hearing, the court may absent unusual circumstances specifically identified by the court that establish that the requested conversion or dismissal is not in the best interests of creditors and the estate, the court shall convert a case under this chapter to a case under chapter 7 or dismiss a case under this chapter, whichever is in the best interests of creditors and the estate, if the movant establishes cause,

(2) The relief provided in paragraph (1) shall not be granted absent unusual circumstances specifically identified by the court that establish that such relief is not in the best interests of creditors and the estate, if the debtor or another party in interest objects and establishes that—

> (A) there is a reasonable likelihood that a plan will be confirmed within the timeframes established in sections 1121(e) and 1129(e) of this title, or if such sections do not apply, within a reasonable period of time; and

> (B) the grounds for granting such relief include an act or omission of the debtor other than under paragraph (4)(A)—

>> (i) for which there exists a reasonable justification for the act or omission; and

>> (ii) that will be cured within a reasonable period of time fixed by the court.

(3) The court shall commence the hearing on a motion under this subsection not later than 30 days after filing of the motion, and shall decide the motion not later than 15 days after commencement of such hearing, unless the movant expressly consents to a continuance for a specific period of time or compelling circumstances prevent the court from meeting the time limits established by this paragraph.

(4) For purposes of this subsection, the term "cause" includes—

> (A) substantial or continuing loss to or diminution of the estate and the absence of a reasonable likelihood of rehabilitation;

> (B) gross mismanagement of the estate;

> (C) failure to maintain appropriate insurance that poses a risk to the estate or to the public;

> (D) unauthorized use of cash collateral substantially harmful to 1 or more creditors;

(E) failure to comply with an order of the court;

(F) unexcused failure to satisfy timely any filing or reporting requirement established by this title or by any rule applicable to a case under this chapter;

(G) failure to attend the meeting of creditors convened under section 341(a) or an examination ordered under rule 2004 of the Federal Rules of Bankruptcy Procedure without good cause shown by the debtor;

(H) failure timely to provide information or attend meetings reasonably requested by the United States trustee (or the bankruptcy administrator, if any);

(I) failure timely to pay taxes owed after the date of the order for relief or to file tax returns due after the date of the order for relief;

(J) failure to file a disclosure statement, or to file or confirm a plan, within the time fixed by this title or by order of the court;

(K) failure to pay any fees or charges required under chapter 123 of title 28;

(L) revocation of an order of confirmation under section 1144 of this title, and denial of confirmation of another plan or a modified plan under section 1129 of this title;

(M) inability to effectuate substantial consummation of a confirmed plan;

(N) material default by the debtor with respect to a confirmed plan;

(O) termination of a confirmed plan by reason of the occurrence of a condition specified in the plan; and

(P) failure of the debtor to pay any domestic support obligation that first becomes payable after the date of the filing of the petition.

Section 1112(a) provides that the bankruptcy court "shall" dismiss or convert a Chapter 11 case if the movant establishes "cause." Section 1112(b)(4) sets out sixteen examples of "cause."

Although section 1112(a) uses the verb "shall," conversion or dismissal is not mandatory if one of the sixteen grounds for cause listed in section 1112(b)(4) is established. There is a thicket of qualifying language.

The first qualifier is in section 1112(b)(1). The mandatory duty to convert, dismiss or appoint a trustee is excused if there are "unusual circumstances specifically identified by the court that establish that the requested conversion or dismissal is not in the best interests of creditors and the estate."

The second qualifier is found in section 1129(b)(2). It applies if there are:

[1] unusual circumstances specifically identified by the court that [2] establish that such relief is not in the best interests of creditors and the estate [3] if the debtor or another party in interest objects and [4] establishes that—[5] (A) there is a reasonable likelihood that a plan will be confirmed with the timeframes [established in chapter 11], [6] or if such sections do not apply, within a reasonable period of time; and [7] (B) the grounds for granting such relief include an act or omission of the debtor other than under paragraph (4)(A) [regarding substantial or continuing loss, and the absence of a reasonable likelihood of rehabilitation] [8] (i) for which there exists a reasonable justification for the act or omission; and [9] that will be cured within a reasonable period of time fixed by the court. [The bracketed numbers are not in section 1129(b)(2).]

So, conversion, dismissal or appointment of a trustee can be avoided by showing that a confirmable plan is imminent, and that the omission or act that lead to the creation of cause was somehow justifiable, but is not likely to happen again.

Problem 11–28: Struggling to Stay in

1. Flapdoodle, Inc. is a Chapter 11 debtor in possession. The Office of the United States Trustee has filed a motion under section 1112(b) seeking to dismiss the case because Flapdoodle's management failed to show for two scheduled meetings with their office. Flapdoodle responds by saying that it just forgot; after all, it got into Chapter 11 because it didn't manage its time well. What discretion does the judge have with respect to this motion?

2. Flapdoodle again. This time the motion is by a creditor who complains that Flapdoodle was a month late in filing its schedules and statement of affairs. Flapdoodle again concedes it was late and has no good excuse. It does point out, however, that the papers were filed, and that six months have passed since it complied with all filings. What discretion does the judge have with respect to this motion?

Re-read section 1112(b)(4). Notice that section 1112(b)(4) [like section 361] uses the verb "includes." The section 1112(b)(4) list of "causes," however, is non-exclusive. The following case is a good example of what else might found to be "cause."

IN RE SGL CARBON CORP.

200 F.3d 154 (3d Cir. 1999)

SCIRICA, Circuit Judge.

The issue on appeal is whether, on the facts of this case, a Chapter 11 bankruptcy petition filed by a financially healthy company in the face of potentially significant civil antitrust liability complies with the requirements of the Bankruptcy Code. In this case, the Official Committee of Unsecured Creditors of SGL Carbon Corporation appeals the District Court's order denying its motion to dismiss SGL Carbon's Chapter 11 bankruptcy petition on bad faith grounds.

This case also presents the threshold issue whether we will adopt a "good faith" requirement for Chapter 11 petitions. We will. After undertaking the fact intensive analysis inherent in the good faith determination, we conclude that SGL Carbon's Chapter 11 petition lacks a valid reorganizational purpose and, therefore, lacks the requisite good faith. We will reverse.

I.

SGL Carbon is a Delaware corporation that manufactures and sells graphite electrodes used in steel production. In 1997, the United States Department of Justice commenced an investigation of alleged price-fixing by graphite electrode manufacturers, including the SGL Carbon Group.[2] Soon thereafter, various steel producers filed class action antitrust lawsuits in the United States District Court for the Eastern District of Pennsylvania against SGL Carbon and other graphite electrode manufacturers. The District Court consolidated the cases into a single class action and certified a class under Fed. R. Civ. P. 23(b)(3) consisting of all United States purchasers of graphite electrodes between 1992 and 1997. Many class members opted out of the class before the November 28, 1998 opt-out deadline and subsequently filed or threatened to file separate antitrust lawsuits. Since the class certification, six complaints have been filed in federal district court and one complaint has been filed in a Canadian court.

In June 1998, SGL Carbon's German parent SGL AG recorded a charge in Deutschmarks of approximately $240 million as its "best estimate" of the SGL Carbon Group's potential liability in the criminal and civil antitrust litigation.[4]

---

2. In May 1999, SGL AG (SGL Carbon's parent) and its chairman Robert Koehler each pled guilty to several criminal antitrust charges and agreed to pay fines of $135 million and $10 million respectively. It is important to note that the guilty pleas and the payment of the criminal fines by the parent company occurred after the filing of the Chapter 11 petition and the District Court's denial of the motion to dismiss.

4. Although the record does not reflect the amount by which the $240 million reserve was increased by SGL AG subsequent to its guilty plea and accompanying fine, the parties have indicated that the reserve was increased. It is significant that, at the time of SGL Carbon's Chapter 11 petition, the $240 million reserve was in place and untouched.

On December 16, 1998, at the direction of SGL AG, SGL Carbon filed a voluntary Chapter 11 bankruptcy petition in the United States District Court for Delaware. In SGL Carbon's Disclosure Statement, in a section addressing "Factors Leading to [the] Chapter 11 Filing," SGL Carbon only discussed the antitrust litigation. The bankruptcy filing contained a proposed reorganization plan under which only one type of creditor would be required to accept less than full cash payment for its account, namely the antitrust plaintiffs who obtained judgments against SGL Carbon. Under the plan, potential antitrust judgment creditors would receive credits against future purchases of SGL Carbon's product valid for 30 months following the plan's confirmation. The proposed plan also bars any claimant from bringing an action against SGL Carbon's affiliates, including its parent SGL AG, "based on, relating to, arising out of, or in any way connected with" their claims against SGL Carbon.

The next day, on December 17, in a press release, SGL Carbon explained it had filed for bankruptcy "to protect itself against excessive demands made by plaintiffs in civil antitrust litigation and in order to achieve an expeditious resolution of the claims against it." The press release also stated:

> SGL CARBON Corporation believes that in its case Chapter 11 protection provides the most effective and efficient means for resolving the civil antitrust claims.
>
> . . .
>
> "SGL CARBON Corporation is financially healthy," said Wayne T. Burgess, SGL CARBON Corporation's president. "If we did not face [antitrust] claims for such excessive amounts, we would not have had to file for Chapter 11. We expect to continue our normal business operations."
>
> . . . .
>
> However, because certain plaintiffs continue to make excessive and unreasonable demands, SGL CARBON Corporation believes the prospects of ever reaching a commercially practicable settlement with them are remote. After much consideration, SGL CARBON Corporation determined that the most appropriate course of action to address the situation without harming its business was to voluntarily file for chapter 11 protection . . . . .

Contemporaneous with the press release, SGL AG Chairman Robert Koehler conducted a telephone conference call with securities analysts, stating that SGL Carbon was "financially healthier" than before and denying the antitrust litigation was "starting to have a material impact on [SGL Carbon's] ongoing operations in the sense that . . . [it was] starting to lose market share." He also stated that SGL Carbon's Chapter 11 petition was "fairly innovative [and] creative" because "usually Chapter 11 is used as protection against serious insolvency or credit problems, which is not the case [with SGL Carbon's petition]."

Two weeks after SGL Carbon filed its petition and issued the press release, the United States Trustee formed a nine member Official Committee of Unsecured Creditors. Eight of the committee members are antitrust plaintiffs; two of the eight serve as class representatives and the other six have opted out of the class. In January 1999, the Committee filed a motion to dismiss SGL Carbon's bankruptcy petition on the grounds that it was a "litigation tactic designed to frustrate the prosecution of the civil antitrust claims pending against [SGL Carbon] and preserve[SGL Carbon's] equity from these claims." In re SGL Carbon Corp., 233 B.R. 285, 287 (D. Del. 1999).

The District Court held a hearing on the motion on February 17, 1999. Neither side presented witnesses. The evidence was entirely documentary or deposition testimony, including the deposition of SGL Carbon's Vice President Theodore Breyer, who directs the company's graphite electrode business in the United States. In his deposition, Breyer testified that SGL Carbon was financially healthy, having no overdue debts when it filed its Chapter 11 petition. Breyer stated that he recommended filing for bankruptcy because he believed SGL Carbon "could not expeditiously settle with the [antitrust] plaintiffs" absent Chapter 11 protection. Acknowledging that bankruptcy protection was the "sole reason" SGL AG's Executive Committee had authorized the Chapter 11 petition, Breyer testified that he believed filing for Chapter 11 would "change the negotiating platform" with plaintiffs and "increase the pressure on ... plaintiffs to settle."

The District Court denied the Committee's motion to dismiss on April 23, 1999 assuming, without deciding, that 11 U.S.C. § 1112(b) imposes a duty of good faith upon bankruptcy petitioners. It further assumed this duty requires the proposed reorganization to further what it characterized as Chapter 11's purpose: " 'to restructure a business's finances so that it may continue to operate, provide its employees with jobs, pay its creditors and produce a return for its stockholders.' " SGL Carbon Corp., 233 B.R. at 288 (quoting H.R. Rep. No. 595 (1977) reprinted in 1978 U.S.C.C.A.N. 6179). The court made no findings that SGL Carbon filed for bankruptcy for reasons other than to improve its negotiating position with plaintiffs. But the court concluded the petition furthered the purpose of Chapter 11 because plaintiffs' litigation was imperiling SGL Carbon's operation by distracting its management, was potentially ruinous and could eventually force the company out of business. The court explained that

> the distractions of the litigation pose a serious threat to the continued successful operations of [SGL Carbon]. Further, the potential liability faced by [SGL Carbon] could very well force it out of business. Consistent with the policies and purposes of Chapter 11 which encourage early filing so as to increase the possibility of successful reorganization, the Court will not allow [SGL Carbon] to wait idly by for impending financial and operational ruin, when [SGL Carbon] can take action now to avoid such a consequence.

SGL Carbon Corp., 233 B.R. at 291.

The Committee has appealed.

II.

. . .

A.

The threshold issue is whether Chapter 11 petitions may be dismissed for "cause" under 11 U.S.C. § 1112(b) if not filed in good faith. Although we have not squarely addressed this issue, we implied in First Jersey Nat'l Bank v. Brown (In re Brown), 951 F.2d 564 (3d Cir. 1991), that Chapter 11 imposes a good-faith obligation. In Brown, we considered evidence of bad faith in reviewing the dismissal of a Chapter 11 petition, but concluded "the evidence . . . of bad faith . . . was not strong enough for us to say that it was established as a matter of law." Id. at 572. Because Brown focused on the adequacy of the record for making a good faith/bad faith determination, we did not expressly address whether "bad faith" constituted cause for dismissal. In this case, we make clear what we implied in Brown—Chapter 11 bankruptcy petitions are subject to dismissal under 11 U.S.C. § 1112(b) unless filed in good faith.

Four factors guide our adoption of a good faith standard—the permissive language of § 1112(b), viewed in light of its legislative history; the decisions of our sister courts of appeals; the equitable nature of bankruptcy; and the purposes underpinning Chapter 11.

We begin with 11 U.S.C. § 1112(b), which allows the court to dismiss or convert a Chapter 11 petition for cause. . . . As many courts and commentators have noted, this language neither requires nor prohibits imposition of a "good faith" requirement on Chapter 11 petitions. But we have noted the provision that "cause" "includes" the ten enumerated factors strongly suggests those factors are not exhaustive and that a court may consider whether other facts and circumstances qualify as "cause." See Brown, 951 F.2d at 572; 7 Collier on Bankruptcy at 1112–20. That interpretation of § 1112(b) is strengthened by the statute's legislative history, which provides in part:

> [The] list [contained in § 1112(b)] is not exhaustive. The court will be able to consider other factors as they arise, and to use its equitable powers to reach an appropriate result in individual cases.

H.R.Rep. No. 595, at 405, reprinted in 1978 U.S.S.C.A.N. 5963, 6362. The Bankruptcy Code's rules of construction, which provide that "include" and "including" are not limiting terms, also support an expansive reading of § 1112(b). See 11 U.S.C. § 102(3). Section 1112(b), by its terms, therefore, does not preclude consideration of unenumerated factors in determining "cause." . . .

B.

Having determined that § 1112(b) imposes a good-faith requirement on Chapter 11 petitions, we consider whether SGL Carbon's Chapter 11 petition was filed in good faith.

The requisite fact intensive inquiry requires determining where SGL Carbon's petition falls along the spectrum ranging from the clearly acceptable to the patently abusive. We first review the District Court's findings of fact and then examine the totality of facts and circumstances to determine whether they support a finding of good faith.

i.

As discussed in part I, the District Court found SGL Carbon's Chapter 11 petition was filed in good faith for two reasons: first, because the distractions caused by the antitrust litigation "posed a serious threat to [SGL Carbon's] continued successful operations," and second, because the litigation might result in a judgment that could cause the company "financial and operational ruin," SGL was required to file when it did. SGL Carbon, 233 B.R. at 291. Although mindful of the careful consideration given by the able District Court, we believe each of these findings of fact was clearly erroneous.

Although there is some evidence that defending against the antitrust litigation occupied some officers' time, there is no evidence this "distraction" posed a "serious threat" to the company's operational well being. At his deposition, Theodore Breyer testified the antitrust litigation consumed a significant portion of his time. But Breyer also noted the Carbon/Graphite Business Unit had met all of its financial targets during the nine months preceding filing. Additionally, Breyer testified that only his business unit was heavily involved in the antitrust litigation, recognizing that any management distraction effecting the rest of SGL Carbon resulted from the bankruptcy filing and not the antitrust litigation. As noted, SGL AG and SGL Carbon officers insisted the company was financially healthy despite the litigation. In addition, SGL AG's Chairman denied that the litigation was having a "material negative impact on [SGL Carbon's] operations." In light of all the evidence, we believe the District Court's finding to the contrary is mistaken.

We also find clearly erroneous that SGL Carbon's Chapter 11 petition was filed at the appropriate time to avoid the possibility of a significant judgment that "could very well force [SGL Carbon] out of business." There is no evidence that the possible antitrust judgments might force SGL Carbon out of business. To the contrary, the record is replete with evidence of SGL Carbon's economic strength. At the time of filing, SGL Carbon's assets had a stipulated book value of $400 million, only $100,000 of which was encumbered. On the date of the petition, SGL Carbon had $276 million in fixed and non-disputed liabilities. Of those liabilities, only $26 million were held by outsiders as the remaining liabilities were either owed to or guaranteed by SGL AG. Although SGL Carbon's parent, SGL AG, recorded a $240 million charge on its books as "its best estimate of the potential liability and expenses of the SGL Carbon Group in connection with all civil and criminal antitrust matters," SGL Carbon is only one part of the SGL Carbon Group covered by the reserve. Furthermore, at the time SGL Carbon filed its petition, that is, before SGL AG paid its $135 million criminal fine, the $240 million reserve was untouched. In documents accompanying its petition, SGL Carbon estimated the liquidation value of the antitrust claims at $54 million. In contrast, no evidence was presented with respect to the amount sought by the antitrust plaintiffs beyond SGL Carbon's repeated characterization of their being "unreasonable."

Whether or not SGL Carbon faces a potentially crippling antitrust judgment, it is incorrect to conclude it had to file when it did. As noted, SGL Carbon faces no immediate financial difficulty. All the evidence shows that management repeatedly asserted the company was financially healthy at the time of the filing. Although the District Court believed the litigation might result in a judgment causing "financial and operational ruin" we believe that on the facts here, that assessment was premature. A Chapter 11 petition would impose an automatic stay on all efforts to collect the judgment and would allow the company the exclusive right to formulate a reorganization plan under which the amount of the judgment could be adjusted to allow the company to reorganize. SGL Carbon has offered no evidence it could not effectively use those protections as the prospect of such a judgment became imminent.[13] The District Court's finding that the petition had to be filed at that particular time to avoid financial ruin and therefore was made in good faith is clearly contradicted by the evidence.

The District Court was correct in noting that the Bankruptcy Code encourages early filing. See SGL Carbon, 233 B.R. at 291. It is well established that a debtor need not be insolvent before filing for bankruptcy protection. It also is clear that the drafters of the Bankruptcy Code understood the need for early access to bankruptcy relief to allow a debtor to rehabilitate its business before it is faced with a hopeless situation. Such encouragement, however, does not open the door to premature filing, nor does it allow for the filing of a bankruptcy petition that lacks a valid reorganizational purpose.

SGL Carbon, therefore, is correct that the Bankruptcy Code does not require specific evidence of insolvency for a voluntary Chapter 11 filing. But SGL Carbon cites no case holding that petitions filed by financially healthy companies cannot be subject to dismissal for cause. At any rate, as we explain more fully, SGL Carbon's ability to meet its debts is but one of many factors compelling the conclusion it did not enter Chapter 11 with a valid reorganizational purpose.

We do not hold that a company cannot file a valid Chapter 11 petition until after a massive judgment has been entered against it. Courts have

---

13. The Texaco Corporation's use of the bankruptcy protections is instructive. See In re Texaco, Inc., 84 B.R. 893 (Bank. S.D.N.Y. 1988). Texaco resorted to bankruptcy only after suffering an $11 billion judgment. Even saddled with such a large judgment, bankruptcy provided Texaco a means of reorganizing and continuing as a going concern.

allowed companies to seek the protections of bankruptcy when faced with pending litigation that posed a serious threat to the companies' long term viability. In those cases, however, debtors experienced serious financial and/or managerial difficulties at the time of filing. In Cohoes, the Court of Appeals for the Second Circuit found a good faith filing, in part, because "it [was] clear that Cohoes[the debtor] was encountering financial stress at the time it filed its petition. . . . " 931 F.2d at 228. In Bible Speaks, pending litigation had already had an adverse effect on the debtor's financial well being as it was experiencing "a cash flow problem which prevented it from meeting its current obligations," compounded by an inability to obtain financing. 65 B.R. at 426. In Johns–Manville, the debtor was facing significant financial difficulties. A growing wave of asbestos-related claims forced the debtor to either book a $1.9 billion reserve thereby triggering potential default on a $450 million debt which, in turn, could have forced partial liquidation, or file a Chapter 11 petition. Large judgments had already been entered against Johns–Manville and the prospect loomed of tens of thousands of asbestos health-related suits over the course of 20–30 years.

For these reasons, SGL Carbon's reliance on those cases is misplaced. The mere possibility of a future need to file, without more, does not establish that a petition was filed in "good faith." See, e.g., In re Cohoes Indus. Terminal Inc., 931 F.2d at 228 ("Although a debtor need not be in extremis in order to file [a Chapter 11] petition, it must, at least, face such financial difficulty that, if it did not file at that time, it could anticipate the need to file in the future."). SGL Carbon, by its own account, and by all objective indicia, experienced no financial difficulty at the time of filing nor any significant managerial distraction. Although SGL Carbon may have to file for bankruptcy in the future, such an attenuated possibility standing alone is not sufficient to establish the good faith of its present petition.

    ii.

. . .

Despite those differing approaches, several cases hold that a Chapter 11 petition is not filed in good faith unless it serves a valid reorganizational purpose. . . . The In re Marsch Court articulated the relationship between the good faith determination and the dismissal of petitions filed merely for tactical advantage:

> The term "good faith" is somewhat misleading. Though it suggests that the debtor's subjective intent is determinative, this is not the case. Instead, the "good faith" filing requirement encompasses several, distinct equitable limitations that courts have placed on Chapter 11 filings. Courts have implied such limitations to deter filings that seek to achieve objectives outside the legitimate scope of the bankruptcy laws. Pursuant to 11 U.S.C. § 1112(b), courts have dismissed cases filed for a variety of tactical reasons unrelated to reorganization.

In re Marsch, 36 F.3d at 828 (citations omitted).

It is easy to see why courts have required Chapter 11 petitioners to act within the scope of the bankruptcy laws to further a valid reorganizational purpose. Chapter 11 vests petitioners with considerable powers—the automatic stay, the exclusive right to propose a reorganization plan, the discharge of debts, etc.—that can impose significant hardship on particular creditors. When financially troubled petitioners seek a chance to remain in business, the exercise of those powers is justified. But this is not so when a petitioner's aims lie outside those of the Bankruptcy Code. See United Sav. Ass'n v. Timbers of Inwood Forest Assocs., Ltd. (In re Timbers of Inwood Forest Assocs., Ltd.), 808 F.2d 363, 373 (5th Cir. 1987) (en banc), aff'd, 484 U.S. 365, 98 L. Ed. 2d 740, 108 S. Ct. 626 (1988) (stating that if Chapter 11 plan does not have a rehabilitative purpose, the "statutory provisions designed to accomplish the reorganizational objectives become destructive of the legitimate rights and interests of creditors"); In re Little Creek, 779 F.2d at 1072 (explaining that Chapter 11 powers should be given only to debtors with "clean hands"); Furness, 35 B.R. at 1009 ("Chapter 11 was designed to give those teetering on the verge of a fatal financial plummet an opportunity to reorganize on solid ground and try again, not to give profitable enterprises an opportunity to evade contractual or other liabilities."); see also 7 Collier on Bankruptcy at 1112–22 (stating that dismissal is appropriate when costs of Chapter 11 are not justified).

Courts, therefore, have consistently dismissed Chapter 11 petitions filed by financially healthy companies with no need to reorganize under the protection of Chapter. Those courts have recognized that if a petitioner has no need to rehabilitate or reorganize, its petition cannot serve the rehabilitative purpose for which Chapter 11 was designed.

The absence of a valid reorganizational purpose and the consequent lack of good faith by SGL Carbon is evident here. SGL Carbon's financial disclosure documents give no indication the company needed to reorganize under Chapter 11 protection. Prior to filing, SGL Carbon had assets of $400 million and liabilities of only $276 million, or a net worth of $124 million. In addition, there is no evidence that SGL Carbon had difficulty meeting its debts as they came due, that it had any overdue debts, or that it had defaulted on any debts. Nor is there any evidence that SGL had any difficulty raising or borrowing money, or otherwise had impaired access to the capital markets.

Statements by SGL Carbon and its officials confirm the company did not need to reorganize under Chapter 11. As discussed, in a press release issued when SGL Carbon filed its petition, the company's president insisted SGL Carbon was "financially healthy" and that its "normal business operations" would continue despite bankruptcy. In addition, SGL AG's Chairman Robert Koehler stated in a conference call with securities analysts that SGL Carbon was experiencing "healthy and growing success" and denied that the class action antitrust litigation was materially interfering with SGL Carbon's operations or its customer relationships. Koehler added that unlike most Chapter 11 cases, SGL Carbon's petition did not involve "serious insolvency or credit problems." SGL Carbon Vice President Theodore Breyer acknowledged in his deposition that SGL Carbon had no defaults nor any financial distress when it filed for Chapter 11.

An examination of the reorganization plan SGL Carbon filed simultaneously with its Chapter 11 petition also suggests the petition was not motivated by a desire to reorganize or rehabilitate SGL Carbon's business. Under the proposed plan, all creditors—including SGL Carbon's parent SGL AG—other than civil antitrust judgment creditors are to be paid in full in cash. Antitrust judgment creditors, by contrast, would be required to accept limited-time credits to purchase SGL Carbon's products. The plan's differing treatment of creditors suggests SGL Carbon's petition was not filed to reorganize the company but rather to put pressure on antitrust plaintiffs to accept the company's settlement terms. . . .

Based on the facts and circumstances of this case, we conclude SGL Carbon's Chapter 11 petition lacks a valid reorganizational purpose and consequently lacks good faith making it subject to dismissal "for cause" under 11 U.S.C. § 1112(b).

. . .

For the reasons stated, we will reverse the judgment of the District Court and remand to the District Court so that it may dismiss SGL Carbon's Chapter 11 petition.

QUESTIONS ABOUT *SGL CARBON*

1. If SGL had not issued any press releases, or spoken to any securities analysts after its filing, would the result have been any different?

2. What does *SGL Carbon* tell you about whom an operating business should tell that it is "fixing to" file for Chapter 11?

G. SPECIAL TYPES OF CHAPTER 11 CASES

The Bankruptcy Code has special rules for certain categories of Chapter 11 debtors. The changes are based mainly on the debtor's status. For example, if the Chapter 11 debtor is a "small business" debtor, or a "single asset real estate" debtor, or an individual, then Chapter 11 has some different rules.

1. SMALL BUSINESS CASES

You need to be able to answer two questions about small business cases: (1) what is a small business Chapter 11 case, and (2) how is a small business Chapter 11 case different from other Chapter 11 cases.

A small business Chapter 11 case is a Chapter 11 case involving a debtor that comes within the Bankruptcy Code's definition of "small business debtor." Obviously, that is stating the obvious. Except that wasn't obvious prior to 2005. Before the 2005 legislation, debtors that came within the section 101 definition could choose whether they were "small business debtors." Now debtors that come within the statutory definition are "small business debtors."

That definition in section 101 focuses primarily on the amount of debt and not the size of the business operations. The amount of the debtor's earnings is irrelevant.

More specifically, in order to be a "small business debtor" the debtor must meet two requirements:

(1) debt not more than $2,343,300 [This includes both secured and unsecured debt; it does not include contingent or unliquidated debt.]

(2) person engaged in "commercial or business activities" other than simply "owning or operating real property."

There is a third requirement for being a "small business debtor" that is beyond the debtor's control: either the U.S. Trustee has not appointed a creditors' committee or the committee is "not sufficiently active and representative to provide effective oversight."

A small business debtor Chapter 11 case is different from other Chapter 11 cases in that

(1) United States Trustee has additional oversight duties, as described in section 1116 and 28 U.S.C. § 586, and

(2) a small business debtor has additional reporting requirements detailed in section 308 and other duties set out in section 1116, and

(3) the plan process can be simpler because section 1125(f) permits courts to

- determine that a plan itself provides adequate information so that no disclosure statement is necessary;

- approve a standard form disclosure statement;

- combine approval of the disclosure statement with confirmation.

(4) time periods and deadlines are different

- 180 days of debtor exclusivity, section 1121(c);

- 300–day deadline for filing plan and disclosure statement, section 1121(c);

- 45 days after filing for confirmation of the plan, section 1129(e).

Problem 11–29: Well Meaning But Disorganized Debtors

1. Fumblerule, Inc. is a small business debtor in a small business case. You have told it the deadline to file schedules but the same disorganization

that caused Fumblerule to file has caused it to miss the deadline. It comes into your office on the due date with a hopeless mass of papers and asks what it can do to get the deadline extended. What do you say?

2. Fumblerule again. It got away with late filing its schedules and now has filed its plan, some six months into the case. The plan has angered some of its creditors because it asks them to take bigger discounts than Fumblerule had previously indicated would be necessary. When you filed the plan, you immediately discovered that you'll have to amend it if you have any chance of obtaining a consenting class of creditors. Trouble is, it looks like you won't be able to meet with the creditors until next month. If you do meet with them 30 days after filing the plan, and want to amend the plan on file, what concerns might you have, especially if there are some creditors out there who still will object to the plan?

---

2. SINGLE ASSET REAL ESTATE CASES

The phrase "single asset real estate" is a part of the language of section 101 and of section 362 and part of the language of bankruptcy judges and lawyers. The phrase "single asset real estate" is not, however, a phrase that actually appears in Chapter 11.

The definition of "single asset real estate" in section 101(51B) is straightforward:

- single property or project;
- real property;
- no substantial other business.

There is no dollar limit in the section 101(51B) definition of "single asset real estate." An entity created to own Rockefeller Center could be a single asset real debtor.

Again there is no special language in Chapter 11 governing single asset real estate debtors. That language is in section 362(d). Under section 362(d)(3), the single asset real estate debtor will have to pay its lenders for the privilege of staying in Chapter 11; that is, section 362(d)(3) requires to stay current on monthly interest payments to secured creditors. As an alternative to paying interest, the debtor can avoid termination of the stay and foreclosure by getting a confirmable plan on file within 90 days.

The stay provision for single asset real estate cases in section 362(d)(3) needs to be read together with section 1121. Even though section 1121 provides for an initial 120–day exclusivity period, in a single asset real estate Chapter 11, the deadline is sometimes 90 days, not 120 days. In a single asset real estate case, lenders secured by the real property are entitled to stay relief 90 days after the bankruptcy filing unless the debtor has filed a plan and that plan has a reasonable possibility of being confirmed within a reasonable time or the debtor is making monthly payments to those lenders.

And, even though there is no other statutory basis for treating Chapter 11 cases involving a real estate debtor differently than other Chapter 11 cases, a distinct body of Chapter 11 single asset real estate case law has developed. Facts common to these cases include

- debtor's only asset is a piece of real estate, i.e., a shopping center, office building, apartment complex, raw land;

- debtor's only secured creditor and only significant creditor is the lender that holds the mortgage on the real estate;

- that lender is seriously undersecured;

- the amount of the mortgage lender's unsecured claim is substantially larger than the claims of all other unsecured creditors combined.

In sum, the typical single asset real estate case is a dispute between a debtor and one creditor over one asset. For some law professors and judges, such single asset real estate cases raise a bankruptcy policy question: should bankruptcy be used to resolve a dispute between a debtor and only one of its creditors?

Problem 11–30: Review of Single Asset Real Estate Debtors and Small Business Debtors

1129 Partners owns a small apartment complex. It owes $1.75 million to First Bank, $25,000 to its management company, and $500,000 in notes to its partners. It is in default on the First Bank loan. If 1129 Partners files for Chapter 11 relief, will it be governed by the SARE rules, the small business rules, both or neither?

3. INDIVIDUAL CHAPTER 11 CASES

A Chapter 11 case in which the debtor is an individual is like a Chapter 13 case in many major respects. For example, section 1123(a)(8) and 1129(a)(15), like section 1325(b), impose a "best efforts" kind of test, requiring commitment of "disposable income" to plan payments; and section 1141(d)(5), like section 1328(a), defers discharge until completion of plan payments.

There are of course also important differences between Chapter 13 cases and individual Chapter 11 cases. For example, there is no creditor voting in Chapter 13 but debtors in Chapter 11 must solicit creditors for their votes after obtaining approval of a disclosure statement.

The next opinion, written by co-author Markell, but selected and edited by your favorite co-author Epstein, explores some other obvious and non-obvious similarities and differences between individual Chapter 11 cases and Chapter 13 cases.

IN RE SHAT

424 B.R. 854 (Bankr. Nev. 2010)

OPINION ON ABSOLUTE PRIORITY RULE

BRUCE A. MARKELL, United States Bankruptcy Judge.

Martin and Anjanette Shat ("Debtors") filed for bankruptcy protection under chapter 11 on November 5, 2008. On August 20, 2009, they filed their Third Amended Plan of Reorganization ("Plan") which the court orally confirmed on October 13, 2009.

The only contested issue at the confirmation hearing was whether the "absolute priority" rule of 11 U.S.C. § 1129(b)(2)(B)(ii) applies to individual chapter 11 debtors after passage of the Bankruptcy Abuse Prevention and Consumer Protection Act of 2005, Pub.L. No. 109–8 (2005) ("BAPCPA"). This court holds that it does not.

I. Facts

The Debtors run a dry cleaning business, known as Flair Cleaners, which they own as a sole proprietorship. It is profitable. They also invested in several residential rental properties. Those are not so profitable.

The Debtors' Plan classifies their creditors into eight classes. Three of these classes are for creditors holding unsecured claims: one for a prior domestic support obligation; one for mortgage lenders' deficiencies; and one for creditors holding credit card claims.

Seven of the eight classes either accepted the plan or did not vote. The eighth class was Class V, which the Plan labeled as "Miscellaneous General Unsecured Creditors (Credit Card Creditors), With Claims Totaling to Approximately $85,000." Under the Plan, creditors in this class were to be paid "10% of their allowed claims without interest over 5 years." Only one member of this class voted, and it rejected the plan.[3] This dissenting unsecured creditor did not make any objection under 11 U.S.C. § 1129(a)(15) or file any other objection to the Plan.[4]

---

3. The creditor rejecting the Plan was Discover Financial Services. It held an unsecured claim of $10,683.09. Its solitary negative vote meant that Class V rejected the Plan, because Section 1126(c) requires creditors holding "at least two-thirds in amount and more than one-half in number of the allowed claims of such class" to vote in favor in order to accept. 11 U.S.C. § 1126(c).

4. A plan proponent need only satisfy the disposable income test of Section 1129(a)(15) if "the holder of an allowed unsecured claim objects to the confirmation of the plan...." Id. (emphasis supplied). Here, the dissenting creditor simply cast a ballot rejecting the Plan. It did not file any other document or pleading. This is insufficient to invoke Section 1129(a)(15).

Doing nothing more than casting a rejecting ballot might indicate an objection to the plan, but it is also consistent with the belief that the plan is legally sufficient, coupled with an acknowledgment by the creditor that it will be bound by the decision of a majority of creditors in its class or by an appropriate cramdown.

In contrast, an objection requires more-at a minimum, the objector must affirmatively take a position the plan proposed is objectionable on some legal ground; for example, that it is not proposed in good faith, or that the proposed payment does not return to the creditor its statutory

The Plan provided that, upon confirmation, "the Debtors shall be revested with their assets, subject only to outstanding liens which are not modified or avoided by the Debtors...."

II. "Fair and Equitable" and the Absolute Priority Rule

A. Confirmation Generally

As a general matter, a plan of reorganization can be confirmed in one of two ways. If all sixteen paragraphs of Section 1129(a) are satisfied, a plan can be confirmed consensually under Section 1129(a). If, however, a plan proponent satisfies all paragraphs of Section 1129(a) other than the voting requirement of paragraph (8), then the court may still confirm the plan as long as the plan is, among other things, "fair and equitable."[6] This second, nonconsensual, method of confirmation is colloquially referred to as "cramdown."[7]

B. Historic Treatment of Individual Chapter 11 Debtors and Confirmation

Given Class V's rejection, the Debtors bore the burden of proving that the Plan was "fair and equitable" in order to confirm their Plan Before 2005, the Bankruptcy Code provided that a plan was "fair and equitable" as to unsecured creditors if it met the following test:

> *2 (i) the plan provides that each holder of a claim of such class receive or retain on account of such claim property of a value, as of the effective date of the plan, equal to the allowed amount of such claim; or
>
> (ii) the holder of any claim or interest that is junior to the claims of such class will not receive or retain under the plan on account of such junior claim or interest any property.

11 U.S.C. § 1129(b)(2)(B) (before taking into account changes made by BAPCPA).

---

entitlement. As a result, Section 1129(a)(15) does not apply in this case because the dissenting creditor did not also file or otherwise assert any objection to the Plan.

6. "[I]f all of the applicable requirements of subsection (a) of this section other than paragraph (8) are met with respect to a plan, the court, on request of the proponent of the plan, shall confirm the plan notwithstanding the requirements of such paragraph if the plan does not discriminate unfairly, and is fair and equitable, with respect to each class of claims or interests that is impaired under, and has not accepted, the plan." 11 U.S.C. § 1129(b)(1).

7. Courts use "cramdown" and "cram down" and "cram-down" interchangeably to refer to nonconsensual confirmation. Indeed, Justice Douglas once combined different forms in the same paragraph. Blanchette v. Connecticut Gen. Ins. Corps., 419 U.S. 102, 167, 95 S.Ct. 335, 42 L.Ed.2d 320 (1974) (Douglas, J., dissenting). The hyphenated version appears to have been the first locution used by a court. New England Coal & Coke Co. v. Rutland R.R. Co., 143 F.2d 179, 189 n. 36 (2d Cir.1944). The earliest print references to the term use either the two-word or the hyphenated form. Compare Robert T. Swaine, Present Status of Railroad Reorganizations And Legislation Affecting Them, Am. Bar Ass'n, Proceedings Of The Section On Comm. Law 15, 15 (1940) (two-word form) and Warner Fuller, The Background and Techniques of Equity and Bankruptcy Railroad Reorganizations—A Survey, 7 Law & Contemp. Probs. 377, 389, 390 (1940) (hyphenated form).

Before BAPCPA, most courts applied this provision equally to individual and nonindividual debtors;[8] that is, courts held that these provisions applied to humans and corporations alike. . . . This reasoning had the effect of preventing individual debtors from keeping a business under a chapter 11 plan if they did not pay their unsecured creditors in full. Accordingly, had the Debtors filed their case before 2005, their Plan likely could not have been confirmed.

C. BAPCPA Amendments to 11 U.S.C. § 1129(b)(2)(B)(ii)

As part of BAPCPA, however, Congress amended Section 1129(b)(2)(B)(ii) with respect to individual chapter 11 debtors. The statute now reads as follows, with the provisions added by BAPCPA in italics:

> (ii) the holder of any claim or interest that is junior to the claims of such class will not receive or retain under the plan on account of such junior claim or interest any property, except that in a case in which the debtor is an individual, the debtor may retain property included in the estate under section 1115, subject to the requirements of subsection (a)(14) of this section.

This clause obviously modifies the absolute priority rule stated in subparagraph (ii). The question is, how extensive is this modification? Specifically, may the Debtors in this case retain their dry cleaning business without paying their unsecured creditors in full? To answer these questions requires an examination of the history of the BAPCPA amendment, and an examination of the role of the absolute priority rule in individual chapter 11 reorganizations.

1. History of the 2005 Amendments Relating to Individual Chapter 11 Debtors

. . .

2. The General Effect of the 2005 Amendments on Individual Chapter 11 Debtors

This analysis indicates that, although not entirely free from doubt, it appears that Congress inserted the individual chapter 11 provisions to ensure no easy escape from means testing. The template for this effort was to adopt and adapt as much of chapter 13 as possible with respect to individual debtors in chapter 11. Again, these changes to chapter 11 were:

- redefining property of the estate in chapter 11 under Section 1115 along the lines of property of the estate under Section 1306;

- changing the mandatory contents of a plan pursuant to Section 1123(a)(8) to resemble Section 1322(a)(1);

- adding the disposable income test of Section 1325(b) to Section 1129(a)(15);

---

8. Along the way, however, it took a Supreme Court decision to decide definitively that individual debtors—that is, debtors made of flesh and blood—could even file under chapter 11. Toibb v. Radloff, 501 U.S. 157, 160–61, 111 S.Ct. 2197, 115 L.Ed.2d 145 (1991).

- delaying the discharge until the completion of all plan payments as in Section 1328(a);

- permitting a discharge for cause before all payments are completed pursuant to Section 1141(d)(5), similar to the hardship discharge of Section 1328(b); and

- the addition of Section 1127(e) to permit the modification of a plan even after substantial consummation for purposes similar to Section 1329(a)....

What remains is a sort of hybrid chapter 13, in which many of the provisions of chapter 13 sit uneasily in chapter 11.[33]

III.　Analysis of Amended Section 1129(b)(2)(B)(ii)

As indicated above, before 2005, the authorities were pretty much in agreement that the absolute priority rule applied to individuals in chapter 11. That meant that a individual debtor could not retain any property if his or her creditors were not paid in full. After 2005, however, this changed. By the process outlined above, Congress decreed that, even in cramdown, an individual "debtor may retain property included in the estate under Section 1115, subject to the requirements of subsection (a)(14) of this section."

A.　The Scope of the Amendment

This shifts the focus to the meaning of this added language, and that inquiry starts with Section 1115. Section 1115, also added in 2005, in turn provides that property of the estate is different for an individual chapter 11 debtor than other chapter 11 debtors. Section 1115 states:

(a) In a case in which the debtor is an individual, property of the estate includes, in addition to the property specified in section 541—[34]

> (1) all property of the kind specified in section 541 that the debtor acquires after the commencement of the case but before the case is closed, dismissed, or converted to a case under chapter 7, 12, or 13, whichever occurs first; and

> (2) earnings from services performed by the debtor after the commencement of the case but before the case is closed, dismissed, or converted to a case under chapter 7, 12, or 13, whichever occurs first.

---

33. A good example is the addition of the disposable income test in Section 1129(a)(15). In chapter 13, the disposable income test is a protection designed to overcome objections that creditors may not vote on a chapter 13 plan; one rationale is that if a debtor is providing all of his or her projected disposable income to the payment of his or her debts, no rational creditor could object. But when this test was imported into chapter 11, the plan proponent was not excused from also balloting its unsecured creditors under Section 1129(a)(8). So a plan proponent faces the possibility that it can have an accepting class of unsecured creditors, but still have to meet the disposable income test of paragraph (15) due to the objection of just one of those creditors.

34. "The commencement of a case ... creates an estate. Such estate is comprised of all the following property, wherever located and by whomever held ... Except as provided in subsections (b) and (c)(2) of this section, all legal or equitable interests of the debtor in property as of the commencement of the case." 11 U.S.C. § 541(a).

Section 1115 thus defines property of the estate for an individual chapter 11 debtor via a two-step process. Initially, Section 1115 creates a baseline estate of all the property covered by Section 541. It then adds to that one class of property excluded for other chapter 11's by Section 541(a)(6): postpetition income from services.

So far, so good. But other than postpetition income from services, what else, if anything, changes? That depends on what the meaning of the ambiguous phrase in Section 1129(b)(2)(B)(ii) that an individual debtor may retain "property included in the estate under section 1115."[35]

If "included" means only property which is added by Section 1115, then Section 1129(b)(2)(B)(ii) has a very narrow meaning: it refers only to postpetition income from services-and not to property originally specified in Section 541. Section 1115, however, itself includes Section 541(a) property. Thus, "included" could refer to all property Section 1115 itself references, and this would then be a reference to the superset of Section 541(a) property and the debtor's postpetition service income. Put another way, if Section 1115 entirely supplants Section 541 by specifically incorporating it and adding to it, the "included" has a very broad meaning, essentially exempting individuals from the absolute priority rule as to unsecured creditors. . . .

Given the relatively straightforward reading of the statute supporting the broader reading, and the general rehabilitative aim of chapter 11, the court understands the phrase "in addition to the property specified in section 541" to mean that Section 1115 absorbs and then supersedes Section 541 for individual chapter 11 cases. This construction, in turn, leads to the position that Section 1129(b)(2)(B)(ii)'s exception extends to all property of the estate, including such things as prepetition ownership interest of nonexempt property. This conclusion is supported by the revisions in 2005 to bring individual chapter 11's more in line with chapter 13. It is also supported by the few cases to examine the topic. . . .

Although relatively straightforward, and uniformly adopted by courts, the broad reading is not without problems. It essentially reads the absolute priority rule out of individual chapter 11 cases, but does so in a convoluted manner-arguably indicative that Congress did not fully appreciate the effect of the language it chose.[42] . . .

But counterarguments to these objections are powerful. While "the absolute priority rule has long been a feature of American bankruptcy

---

35. Section 1115(a)(1) also added "all property of the kind specified in Section 541 that the debtor acquires after the commencement of the case," but this would seem to be at least partially duplicative of Sections 541(a)(6) and (7), which already add "proceeds, products, offspring, rents or profits of property of the estate" and "[a]ny interest in property that the estate acquires after commencement of the case." An argument exists that Section 1115(a)(1) brings into the estate gifts to the debtor (as opposed to the estate) through the language including "all property of the kind specified in Section 541 that the debtor acquires after the commencement of the case. . . ."

42. As stated by one commentator in a related context, "Congress appears to have thought about the problem in its amendment to Bankruptcy Code § 1129(b)(2)(B)(ii) although it may not have thought about the problem enough." Richard I. Aaron, Bankruptcy Law Fundamentals § 12.23.1 (2009).

law," Bank of New York Trust Co., NA v. Official Unsecured Creditors' Comm. (In re Pacific Lumber Co.), 584 F.3d 229, 244 (5th Cir.2009), it is not sacrosanct. Chapter 13 has no absolute priority rule,[45] and as noted above, most of the changes effected by BAPCPA to individual chapter 11 debtors were part of an overall design of adapting various chapter 13 provisions to fit in chapter 11. . . .

Here, given the host of change to chapter 11 with respect to individuals, all made with the goal of shaping an individual's chapter 11 case to look like a chapter 13 case, and the relatively simple wording used in both Section 1129(b)(2)(B)(ii) and Section 1115, this court concludes that the broader interpretation is the proper one.

IV. Conclusion

Although the Plan was rejected by a class of unsecured creditors, and does not pay such creditors in full, it may still be confirmed. Changes in 2005 to 11 U.S.C. § 1129(b)(2)(B)(ii) modified the absolute priority rule as set forth above to allow these Debtors to keep their business. Accordingly, the Plan is confirmed. The court will enter a separate order confirming the Plan using Official Form 15.

---

45. Chapter 13 has no "fair and equitable" requirement for confirmation. 11 U.S.C. § 1325(b)(1). The same is true for chapter 12. Id. § 1225(b)(1).

Before 1952, individual debtors under chapter XI of the Bankruptcy Act had to propose plans that were "fair and equitable." H.R. Rep. No. 82–2320, at 21 (1952). Congress deleted the "fair and equitable" requirement from chapter XI in 1952. Act of July 7, 1952, Pub.L. No. 82–456, § 35, 66 Stat. 420, 433 (1952). As the accompanying House Report stated, "the fair and equitable rule . . . cannot be realistically applied in a Chapter XI [action]. . . . Were it so applied, . . . no corporate debtor where the stock ownership is substantially identical with management could effectuate an arrangement except by payment of the claims of all creditors in full." H.R.Rep. No. 82–2320; see also S. Rep. No. 82–1395, at 11–12 (1952).

UNIT 12

WHERE DOES ALL OF THIS HAPPEN, AND WHO MAKES IT HAPPEN?

■ ■ ■

In the main, the substantive law of bankruptcy is in title 11 of the United States Code. Questions of judicial power over bankruptcy-related matters are, in the main, answered in title 28 of the United States Code.

The question of which court has the power to adjudicate the litigation that arises in bankruptcy can be an important one. Many attorneys who represent parties with claims against the bankrupt or parties against whom the bankrupt has claims prefer to litigate in some forum other than the bankruptcy court. Some believe that the bankruptcy judge has a pro-debtor bias; others are simply more comfortable or more familiar with state court procedures; others prefer state court for reasons of delay—a state court generally has a larger backlog of cases than a bankruptcy court so that filing in state court delays any litigation.

In considering the question of which court has the power to adjudicate the litigation that arises in bankruptcy, it is helpful to consider the kinds of matters that can arise in bankruptcy.

Some matters will involve only bankruptcy law. For example, D files a Chapter 7 petition. The Chapter 7 trustee alleges that D's payment of $40,000 to C a month before bankruptcy is recoverable by the estate under section 550 as a section 547 voidable preference. C contends that the $40,000 payment is protected from avoidance as a section 547(c)(2) ordinary course of business payment.

Other matters will involve both bankruptcy law and nonbankruptcy law. For example, D files a Chapter 7 petition. C files a secured claim that describes its Article 9 security interest. The bankruptcy trustee takes the position that C's security interest is invalid because it was not properly perfected. If this is litigated, it will probably involve both the Bankruptcy Code's avoidance provisions and the Uniform Commercial Code's perfection provisions.

And, still other matters will not involve substantive bankruptcy law. For example, *D*, Inc., a Chapter 11 debtor, files a breach of contract claim against *X*.

A. HISTORY

The allocation of judicial power over bankruptcy matters has been, and still is, one of the most controversial bankruptcy issues. A general familiarity with prior statutory schemes and prior controversies is helpful to understanding the present situation.

1. 1898 ACT

Under the Bankruptcy Act of 1898, bankruptcy courts had limited jurisdiction. This jurisdiction was commonly referred to as "summary" jurisdiction. (The phrase summary jurisdiction is somewhat misleading. First, it incorrectly implies that under the Bankruptcy Act of 1898, bankruptcy courts had a second, non-summary form of jurisdiction. Bankruptcy courts had only summary jurisdiction; other courts had plenary jurisdiction. Second, it incorrectly implies that in resolving controversies, the bankruptcy judge always conducted summary proceedings.)

Summary jurisdiction extended to (1) *all* matters concerned with the administration of the bankruptcy estate and (2) *some* disputes between the bankruptcy trustee and third parties involving rights to money and other property in which the bankrupt estate claimed an interest. The tests for which disputes with third parties were within the bankruptcy judge's summary jurisdiction turned on issues such as whether (1) the property in question was in the actual possession of the bankrupt at the time of the commencement of the case, (2) the property in question was in the constructive possession of the bankrupt at the time of the commencement of the case, and (3) the third party actually or impliedly consented to bankruptcy court jurisdiction.

There was considerable uncertainty over which disputes were within the summary jurisdiction of the bankruptcy court. This uncertainty gave rise to considerable litigation.

2. 1978 CODE

To eliminate this uncertainty, Congress in 1978 decided to create a bankruptcy court with pervasive jurisdiction. For apparently political reasons, Congress also decided that this bankruptcy court should *not* be an Article III court.

As you recall from your Constitutional Law course in law school or civics course in high school, Article III of the Constitution vests the judicial power of the United States in the United States Supreme Court and such inferior tribunals as Congress might create. To insure the independence of the judges appointed under Article III (the so-called constitutional courts), Article III provides them with certain protections. These include tenure for life, removal from office only by congressional impeachment, and assurance that their compensation will not be diminished. The constitutional courts created under Article III include the United States Supreme Court, the United States Courts of Appeal, and the United States District Courts. The United States Customs Court (now the Court of International Trade) is also an Article III court; its judges may be, and often are, assigned to hear cases in the district courts and the courts of appeal.

Congress, in the exercise of its legislative powers enumerated in Article I of the Constitution, may create other inferior federal tribunals— the so-called legislative courts. Judges of these legislative courts need not be granted tenure for life. In addition, they can be removed by mechanisms other than congressional impeachment, and their salaries are subject to congressional reduction. Historically, these Article I legislative courts and their judges have been granted jurisdiction over limited and narrowly defined subject matters, like the Tax Court. In other instances, jurisdiction has been limited to narrowly defined geographical territories, such as the territorial courts, the District of Columbia courts, etc.

In amending title 28 in 1978, Congress gave bankruptcy judges none of the protections found in Article III of the Constitution. Nevertheless, the 1978 amendments to title 28 gave bankruptcy judges much of the power and responsibilities of an Article III judge. Since bankruptcy debtors can be just about any kind of individual or business entity, this meant that litigation in the bankruptcy courts could deal with almost every facet of business and personal activity.

3.   MARATHON PIPELINE DECISION

The 1978 grant of pervasive jurisdiction to a non-Article III bankruptcy court was successfully challenged in the *Marathon* case. *Northern Pipeline Const. Co. v. Marathon Pipe Line Co.*, 458 U.S. 50 (1982).

In that case, Northern Pipeline, a Chapter 11 debtor, filed a breach of contract lawsuit against Marathon Pipeline in bankruptcy court. There was no question as to whether the bankruptcy court had jurisdiction over this lawsuit under the jurisdictional statute enacted in 1978, 28 U.S.C. § 1471(c). Marathon Pipeline did, however, question whether section 1471(c) conferred Article III judicial power on non-Article III courts in violation of the separation of powers doctrine and filed a motion to dismiss. A divided Supreme Court sustained Marathon's challenge.

The Court in *Marathon* was so divided that there was no majority opinion. Justice Brennan's opinion was joined by three other justices. Additionally, two justices concurred in the result. The holding of these six is perhaps best summarized in footnote 40 of Justice Brennan's plurality opinion which indicates that (1) the 1978 legislation does grant the bankruptcy court the power to hear Northern Pipeline's breach of contract claim, (2) the bankruptcy court, a non-Article III court, cannot constitutionally be vested with jurisdiction to decide such state law claims, and (3) this grant of authority to the bankruptcy court is not severable from the remaining grant of authority to the bankruptcy court.

After *Marathon*, Congress was urged to solve the constitutional dilemma by establishing bankruptcy courts as Article III courts. Congress rejected this solution. Instead, Congress in 1984[1] made the bankruptcy court a part of the federal district court, conferred jurisdiction in bankruptcy on the district court, and allocated judicial power in bankruptcy matters between the federal district judge and the bankruptcy judge.

It is easy for a law professor or law student to criticize the provisions allocating judicial power over bankruptcy matters. It is more difficult (but probably more important) for a lawyer or law student to understand how these provisions operate.

B. PROVISIONS IN TITLE 28 ALLOCATING JUDICIAL POWER OVER BANKRUPTCY

In understanding the present law allocating judicial powers over bankruptcy matters, it is necessary to understand three separate sections in title 28: (1) § 151, (2) § 1334, and (3) § 157. By understanding these three provisions you will understand that (1) bankruptcy courts are a part of the United States District Court but bankruptcy judges are different from district court judges, (2) bankruptcy cases are different from bankruptcy proceedings, (3) bankruptcy cases can be handled by either bankruptcy judges or federal district judges (depending on withdrawal of the reference), but not by state court judges and (4) bankruptcy proceedings can be tried by bankruptcy judges or federal judges (depending on withdrawal of the reference) or even state court judges (depending on where the lawsuit was filed and removal and abstention). To understand even more, please read the following descriptions of the three key sections in title 28:

1. Bankruptcy Court as Part of the District Court
28 U.S.C. § 151

In each judicial district, the bankruptcy judges in regular active service shall constitute a unit of the district court to be known as the bankruptcy court for that district. Each bankruptcy judge, as a judicial officer of the

---

1. In the two-year gap between the 1982 *Marathon* decision and the 1984 legislation, the allocation of judicial power over bankruptcy was governed by an Emergency Rule adopted by all district courts.

district court, may exercise the authority conferred under this chapter with respect to any action, suit, or proceeding and may preside alone and hold a regular or special session of the court, except as otherwise provided by law or by rule or order of the district court.

Section 151 refers to a bankruptcy judge and a bankruptcy court as a "unit" of the district court. It is important to keep this reference in mind when reading other sections in title 28 dealing with the allocation of judicial power in bankruptcy matters. When the term "district court" appears in section 1334 or section 157, it could be referring to the United States district judge and/or the bankruptcy judge. After all, the bankruptcy judge is a part of the district court—a "unit" of the district court.

---

2.   *Grants of Jurisdiction to the District Court*[2]
28 U.S.C. § 1334(a), (b)

(a) Except as provided in subsection (b) of this section, the district courts shall have original and exclusive jurisdiction of all cases under title 11.

(b) Except as provided in subsection (e)(2), and notwithstanding any Act of Congress that confers exclusive jurisdiction on a court or courts other than the district courts, the district courts shall have original but not exclusive jurisdiction of all civil proceedings arising under title 11, or arising in or related to cases under title 11.

Section 1334(a) vests original and exclusive jurisdiction in the district court over all cases arising under the Bankruptcy Code. "Case" is a term of art used in both the Bankruptcy Code and the Bankruptcy Rules. "Case" refers to the entire Chapter 7, 9, 11, 12 or 13—not just some controversy that arises in connection with it.

The term "case" is to be distinguished from the term "proceeding." A specific dispute that arises during the pendency of a case is referred to as a "proceeding." Section 1334(b) provides that the district courts have original but not exclusive jurisdiction over all civil proceedings, "arising under title 11, or arising in or related to cases under title 11."

"Proceedings" include "contested matters," motions brought in the main bankruptcy case and "adversary proceedings," lawsuits. Section 1334(b) grants the district court original but not exclusive jurisdiction over three types of "civil proceedings":

---

2.   Section 1334(c) which deals with abstention will be separately considered later in this unit.

(1) "Arising Under" Title 11

This involves adjudication of rights or obligations created by the Bankruptcy Code. For example, stay relief. A further example: preference litigation.

(2) "Arising in" A Title 11 Case

This covers matters peculiar to bankruptcy but based on rights or obligations created by the Bankruptcy Code. For example, allowance or disallowance of claims. A further example: assumption or rejection of executory contracts.

(3) "Related to" A Title 11 Case

This covers matters that impact on the bankruptcy case. While it is not a "catch-all," it certainly catches a lot. In *Celotex Corp. v. Edwards*, 514 U.S. 300 (1995), the Supreme Court held that entry of an injunction prohibiting a judgment creditor from executing on a supersedeas bond of a third party surety of the debtor was "related to." In so ruling, the Supreme Court stated:

> The jurisdiction of the bankruptcy courts, like that of other federal courts, is grounded in, and limited by, statute. Title 28 U.S.C. § 1334(b) provides that "the district courts shall have original but not exclusive jurisdiction of all civil proceedings arising under title 11, or arising in or related to cases under title 11." The district courts may, in turn, refer "any or all proceedings arising under title 11 or arising in or related to a case under title 11 . . . to the bankruptcy judges for the district." 28 U.S.C. § 157(a). Here, the Bankruptcy Court's jurisdiction to enjoin respondents' proceeding against Northbrook must be based on the "arising under," "arising in," or "related to" language of §§ 1334(b) and 157(a).
>
> Respondents argue that the Bankruptcy Court had jurisdiction to issue the Section 105 Injunction only if their proceeding to execute on the bond was "related to" the Celotex bankruptcy. Petitioner argues the Bankruptcy Court indeed had such "related to" jurisdiction. Congress did not delineate the scope of "related to"[5] jurisdiction, but its choice of words suggests a grant of some breadth. The jurisdictional grant in § 1334(b) was a distinct departure from the jurisdiction conferred under previous Acts, which had been limited to either possession of property by the debtor or consent as a basis for jurisdiction. We agree with the views expressed by the Court of Appeals for the Third Circuit in Pacor, Inc. v. Higgins, 743 F.2d 984 (1984), that "Congress intended to grant comprehensive jurisdiction to the bank-

---

5. Proceedings "related to" the bankruptcy include (1) causes of action owned by the debtor which become property of the estate pursuant to 11 U.S.C. § 541, and (2) suits between third parties which have an effect on the bankruptcy estate. See 1 Collier on Bankruptcy P 3.01[1][c] [iv], p. 3–28 (15th ed. 1994). The first type of "related to" proceeding involves a claim like the state-law breach of contract action at issue in Northern Pipeline Constr. Co. v. Marathon Pipe Line Co., 458 U.S. 50, 102 S.Ct. 2858, 73 L.Ed.2d 598 (1982). The instant case involves the second type of "related to" proceeding.

ruptcy courts so that they might deal efficiently and expeditiously
with all matters connected with the bankruptcy estate," id., at 994,
and that the "related to" language of § 1334(b) must be read to give
district courts (and bankruptcy courts under § 157(a)) jurisdiction
over more than simple proceedings involving the property of the
debtor or the estate. We also agree with that court's observation that
a bankruptcy court's "related to" jurisdiction cannot be limitless.[6]

We believe that the issue whether respondents are entitled to immediate execution on the bond against Northbrook is at least a question
"related to" Celotex's bankruptcy. Admittedly, a proceeding by respondents against Northbrook on the supersedeas bond does not
directly involve Celotex, except to satisfy the judgment against it
secured by the bond. But to induce Northbrook to serve as surety on
the bond, Celotex agreed to allow Northbrook to retain the proceeds
of a settlement resolving insurance coverage disputes between Northbrook and Celotex. The Bankruptcy Court found that allowing respondents—and 227 other bonded judgment creditors—to execute immediately on the bonds would have a direct and substantial adverse effect
on Celotex's ability to undergo a successful reorganization. It stated:

> [I]f the Section 105 stay were lifted to enable the judgment
> creditors to reach the sureties, the sureties in turn would seek to
> lift the Section 105 stay to reach Debtor's collateral, with corre-
> sponding actions by Debtor to preserve its rights under the
> settlement agreements. Such a scenario could completely destroy
> any chance of resolving the prolonged insurance coverage dis-
> putes currently being adjudicated in this Court. The settlement of
> the insurance coverage disputes with all of Debtor's insurers may
> well be the linchpin of Debtor's formulation of a feasible plan.
> Absent the confirmation of a feasible plan, Debtor may be liqui-
> dated or cease to exist after a carrion feast by the victors in a race
> to the courthouse.

In re Celotex, 140 B.R. 912, 915 (1992) (Celotex II).

In light of these findings by the Bankruptcy Court, it is relevant to note
that we are dealing here with a reorganization under Chapter 11, rather
than a liquidation under Chapter 7. The jurisdiction of bankruptcy courts
may extend more broadly in the former case than in the latter.

---

6. In attempting to strike an appropriate balance, the Third Circuit in Pacor, Inc. v. Higgins,
743 F.2d 984 (1984), devised the following test for determining the existence of "related to"
jurisdiction:

The usual articulation of the test for determining whether a civil proceeding is related to
bankruptcy is whether the outcome of that proceeding could conceivably have any effect on the
estate being administered in bankruptcy.... Thus, the proceeding need not necessarily be
against the debtor or against the debtor's property. An action is related to bankruptcy if the
outcome could alter the debtor's rights, liabilities, options, or freedom of action (either
positively or negatively) and which in any way impacts upon the handling and administration of
the bankrupt estate. Id., at 994 (emphasis in original; citations omitted). The First, Fourth,
Fifth, Sixth, Eighth, Ninth, Tenth, and Eleventh Circuits have adopted the Pacor test with
little or no variation.

3. *Role and Power of the Bankruptcy Court*

28 U.S.C. § 157(a), (b)

(a) Each district court may provide that any or all cases under title 11 and any or all proceedings arising under title 11 or arising in or related to a case under title 11 shall be referred to the bankruptcy judges for the district.[7]

(b)(1) Bankruptcy judges may hear and determine all cases under title 11 and all core proceedings arising under title 11, or arising in a case under title 11, referred under subsection (a) of this section, and may enter appropriate orders and judgments, subject to review under section 158 of this title.

   (2) Core proceedings include, but are not limited to—

   (A) matters concerning the administration of the estate;

   (B) allowance or disallowance of claims against the estate or exemptions from property of the estate, and estimation of claims or interests for the purposes of confirming a plan under chapter 11, 12, or 13 of title 11 but not the liquidation or estimation of contingent or unliquidated personal injury tort or wrongful death claims against the estate for purposes of distribution in a case under title 11;

   (C) counterclaims by the estate against persons filing claims against the estate;

   (D) orders in respect to obtaining credit;

   (E) orders to turn over property of the estate;

   (F) proceedings to determine, avoid, or recover preferences;

   (G) motions to terminate, annul, or modify the automatic stay;

   (H) proceedings to determine, avoid, or recover fraudulent conveyances;

   (I) determinations as to the dischargeability of particular debts;

   (J) objections to discharges;

   (K) determinations of the validity, extent, or priority of liens;

   (L) confirmations of plans;

   (M) orders approving the use or lease of property, including the use of cash collateral;

   (N) orders approving the sale of property other than property resulting from claims brought by the estate against persons who have not filed claims against the estate;

---

7. Every district—yes, every district—has entered a local order referring bankruptcy matters to the bankruptcy court as anticipated by this provision. The provision in effect in New Mexico is typical: "IT IS ORDERED that all cases under Title 11 and all proceedings arising under Title 11 or arising in or related to a case under Title 11 are referred to the bankruptcy judges for the district to the extent permitted by law." Misc. Order No. 84–0324 (N.M., July 1, 1984). Just so you don't think it is only small states that have this short order, the general order of reference for the Southern District of New York has identical language. Gen. Order No. 61 (S.D.N.Y., July 10, 1984).

(O) other proceedings affecting the liquidation of the assets of the estate or the adjustment of the debtor-creditor or the equity security holder relationship, except personal injury tort or wrongful death claims; and

(P) recognition of foreign proceedings and other matters under chapter 15 of title 11.

Clearly, section 1334 confers jurisdiction over bankruptcy matters to the district court. It is equally clear that most federal district judges have neither the time nor the inclination to exercise this jurisdiction. Accordingly, section 157 empowers the district judge to refer bankruptcy matters to a bankruptcy judge.

The title of section 157 is "Procedures." As this title suggests, section 157 is not a jurisdictional provision. It does not confer jurisdiction on the bankruptcy judge. Rather, it deals with procedure—the role that the bankruptcy judge, a unit of the district court under section 151, is to play in exercising the jurisdiction conferred by section 1334 on the district court.

Section 157 differentiates between "core" and "noncore" proceedings. A nonexclusive list of core proceedings is set out in section 157(b)(2).

Obviously, if a matter is not a core proceeding, it is a "noncore proceeding." "Noncore proceeding" is neither defined nor illustrated in the statute. In noncore proceedings, the bankruptcy judge still can hold the trial or hearing, but generally[8] cannot issue a final judgment. She instead submits proposed findings of fact and law to the district court for review, section 157(c)(1).

The bankruptcy judge is empowered to determine whether a matter is a core proceeding or a noncore proceeding, section 157(b)(3). Remember that a determination that a proceeding is noncore does not mean that the matter is withdrawn from the bankruptcy judge. Remember that a bankruptcy judge can hear noncore proceedings and prepare proposed findings of facts and law.

---

4. Centralizing Litigation (or Not): Removal From and Remand Back to Other Courts

28 U.S.C. § 1452

(a) A party may remove any claim or cause of action in a civil action other than a proceeding before the United States Tax Court or a civil

---

8. The bankruptcy judge can enter a final order or judgment in a noncore matter only if the parties consent, 28 U.S.C. § 157(c)(2). To help assist the parties in knowing when the bankruptcy judge may enter a final order, the Bankruptcy Rules require the parties' pleading to state that a matter is core or noncore, and to state affirmatively that they do not consent to entry of a final judgment by the bankruptcy court. BANKR. R. 7008(a).

action by a governmental unit to enforce such governmental unit's police or regulatory power, to the district court for the district where such civil action is pending, if such district court has jurisdiction of such claim or cause of action under section 1334 of this title.

(b) The court to which such claim or cause of action is removed may remand such claim or cause of action on any equitable ground. An order entered under this subsection remanding a claim or cause of action, or a decision to not remand, is not reviewable by appeal or otherwise....

Occasionally, there may be litigation pending in state court that could be heard more quickly or more efficiently in bankruptcy court. If that is the case, *any* party (not just the debtor) can remove the action to bankruptcy court. Not only that, but unlike normal removal to federal court, a party need not remove the entire action; individual causes of action may be removed to federal bankruptcy court. All that is required is that the action be within the large scope of section 1334.

This right of removal is not absolute. The rules require that in most cases removal occur within 90 days of the order for relief. BANKR. R. 9027(a)(2)(A). Even if timely, section 1452(b) gives a broad right of remand on "any equitable ground." And if the bankruptcy court orders remand, that's determinative. The statute pretty clearly provides that "[a]n order entered ... remanding a claim or cause of action, or a decision to not remand, is not reviewable by appeal or otherwise."

In many mass tort cases, the debtor will remove pending tort cases pending against it in the various state courts. It also sometimes happens that pending non-bankruptcy cases that involve a non-dischargeable claim will be removed—a creditor suing an individual debtor being sued for fraud might, for example, remove the state court fraud case and then amend it to include a non-dischargeability count.

If you think that all of this—core, noncore, "related to" and removal—is a lot for a non-Article–III court to handle, you are not alone. Congress provided for a safeguard to ensure that, in proper cases, the Article III District Court can still hear the case.

———————

5. *The Constitutional Escape Hatch—Withdrawal of the "Reference"*

As we saw above, every district has entered an order authorized by section 157(a) that "refers" all bankruptcy matters within the scope of section 1334 to the bankruptcy court for that district. But to preserve at least the pretense that district courts still are the residual keepers of Article III jurisdiction over bankruptcy, there has to be some way to get the case or parts of it "back" to the district court. In that way, the district judge can retain ultimate control over the role of the bankruptcy judge, and ensure that matters that require an Article III judge will get one.

———————

28 U.S.C. § 157(d)

(d) The district court may withdraw, in whole or in part, any case or proceeding referred under this section, on its own motion or on timely motion of any party, for cause shown. The district court shall, on timely motion of a party, so withdraw a proceeding if the court determines that resolution of the proceeding requires consideration of both title 11 and other laws of the United States regulating organizations or activities affecting interstate commerce.

Section 157(d) authorizes the district judge to withdraw a case or proceeding from a bankruptcy judge. The first sentence of section 157(d) provides for permissive withdrawal "for cause shown." Under the second sentence of section 157(d), withdrawal of the reference is mandatory if "resolution of the proceeding requires consideration of both Title 11 and other laws of the United States regulating ... interstate commerce."

In applying this provision, most courts disregard the "plain language" quoted above. The plain language of section 157(d) indicates that withdrawal of the reference is mandatory only if both the Bankruptcy Code and another federal statute must be construed to resolve the proceeding. Under the statute's "plain language," a district court would be required to withdraw the reference only in actions involving both bankruptcy and nonbankruptcy law—not in matters involving nonbankruptcy law alone. And, under the statute's plain language, the bankruptcy court would have to abstain on all matters that involve both bankruptcy law and a nonfederal statute regulating interstate commerce, regardless of how simple and straight forward the application of the other statute.

Because the "plain language" of section 157(d)'s second sentence plainly does not work, most courts have ignored the literal language of section 157(d) for mandatory withdrawal. Instead, these courts require that the reference be withdrawn if an action involves a "substantial and material" consideration of a nonbankruptcy federal statute regulating interstate commerce, regardless of whether the action also involves consideration of the Bankruptcy Code.

Withdrawal of the reference from the district court to the bankruptcy judge is also mandatory for (1) claims for wrongful death or other personal injuries, 28 U.S.C. § 157(b)(5), or (2) matters in which a party has a right to a jury trial unless the district court has authorized the bankruptcy judge to conduct the jury trial and the parties have consented, 28 U.S.C. § 157(c).

Remember that withdrawal under section 157(d) merely moves a matter from the bankruptcy judge to the federal district judge. Withdrawal under section 157(d) does not move a matter to a state court. That requires abstention.

---

6. *Abstention*

28 U.S.C. § 1334(c)

(c)(1) Except with respect to a case under chapter 15 of title 11, Nothing in this section prevents a district court in the interest of justice, or in the interest of comity with State courts or respect for State law, from abstaining from hearing a particular proceeding arising under title 11 or arising in or related to a case under title 11.

(2) Upon timely motion of a party in a proceeding based upon a State law claim or State law cause of action, related to a case under title 11 but not arising under title 11 or arising in a case under title 11, with respect to which an action could not have been commenced in a court of the United States absent jurisdiction under this section, the district court shall abstain from hearing such proceeding if an action is commenced, and can be timely adjudicated, in a State forum of appropriate jurisdiction.

Abstention under section 1334(c) moves litigation from bankruptcy court to a state court. In considering and applying the abstention provisions of section 1334(c), it is important to recall the jurisdictional provisions of section 1334(b). As you learned from your readings in constitutional law and/or federal courts, a federal court with jurisdiction over a matter or controversy must exercise that jurisdiction except under unusual circumstances. And, as you learned from reading this book, Congress provided for broad, pervasive bankruptcy jurisdiction in section 1334(b) to eliminate the costly litigation over jurisdiction that occurred under the Bankruptcy Act of 1898. As a result, some of the matters covered by the jurisdictional grant in section 1334(b) are not really bankruptcy matters, but are matters that would be better left to other courts. Section 1334(c) empowers the bankruptcy judge to leave such matters to other courts by abstaining.

Section 1334(c)(1) provides for permissive abstention. Section 1334(c)(2) provides for mandatory abstention.

C. OPERATION OF THE JURISDICTIONAL PROVISIONS OF THE PRESENT LAW

IN RE TOLEDO
170 F.3d 1340 (11th Cir. 1999)

ANDERSON, Circuit Judge:

Carmen Sanchez filed the instant adversary proceeding against the trustee of the bankruptcy estate ("Estate") of Orlando and Maria Toledo, the debtors themselves, and the Continental National Bank of Miami ("Bank"). The bankruptcy court invalidated the Bank's mortgage on real estate owned by a partnership of which the debtors and Sanchez were the partners. The district court affirmed the bankruptcy court, applying the deferential standards of review applicable to "core" proceedings under the Bankruptcy Code. The Bank appeals. The issues presented for review are (i) whether the bankruptcy court had jurisdiction to hear this adversary proceeding, and (ii) if so, whether the district court was correct in treating it as a core proceeding rather than as a non-core proceeding requiring *de novo,* plenary review. For the reasons stated below, we hold that the bankruptcy court had jurisdiction, but that this was a non-core matter necessitating plenary review by the district court.

In 1988, Orlando and Maria Toledo, debtors in the underlying bankruptcy case, formed a partnership with Tomas and Carmen Sanchez called the Latin Quarter Center Partnership ("Partnership"). Each of the four partners held an equal one-fourth share. The purpose of the partnership was to hold, develop, and deal in certain contiguous parcels of real estate in downtown Miami ("Partnership Property"). No formal partnership agreement was ever entered into, but Orlando Toledo, acting alone, generally managed and acted on behalf of the partnership. Shortly after the Partnership came into being, Tomas Sanchez died, and his wife Carmen Sanchez (plaintiff in the instant adversary proceeding) succeeded to his 25% share, so that she then owned a total 50 interest in the Partnership. Orlando Toledo continued to act as managing partner and Carmen Sanchez was uninvolved in Partnership affairs.

In April of 1989, Orlando Toledo encountered personal financial difficulties. In order to assuage the Bank's concern about its position as one of his creditors and to induce it not to foreclose on a mortgage it held on his Key Biscayne personal residence, Toledo purported to convey a mortgage on the Partnership Property to the Bank to secure Toledo's personal indebtedness to the Bank in the approximate amount of $1,100,000. This was done without Sanchez' consent or knowledge. In taking this action, Toledo claimed to be acting in the capacity of a general partner as an agent for the Partnership. If the mortgage was valid, the Partnership Property thereby became a guarantee for Toledo's personal debt. Toledo also convinced McDonald's Corp., which had a $275,000 pre-existing purchase money mortgage on the Partnership Property, to subordinate its mortgage to the one newly granted to the Bank.

Orlando Toledo's financial outlook did not improve, and the Bank eventually obtained a judgment of foreclosure on both the Partnership Property and Toledo's Key Biscayne personal residence (which secured the same indebtedness) in Dade County circuit court in November 1992.... On January 11, 1993, the day before the scheduled foreclosure sale of the Key Biscayne residence, Orlando and Maria Toledo filed for Chapter 11 and thereby averted the sale.

Soon after the commencement of the bankruptcy case, a private sale of the Partnership Property to McDonald's Corp. was negotiated by Toledo, the Estate, and the Bank under supervision of the bankruptcy court.... The parties, apparently assuming that the bankruptcy court's stamp of approval was necessary in order to consummate the sale, applied to the court for approval even though the Partnership Property was not property of the Estate. Acting under purported authority of 11 U.S.C. § 363(f), Judge Weaver approved the sale in an order dated April 12, 1993.[3] . . .

Meanwhile, Sanchez filed the instant adversary complaint in the bankruptcy court against the trustee of the Estate, the debtors them-selves, and the Bank (i) to determine entitlement to the proceeds of the sale of the Partnership Property to McDonald's Corp., and (ii) to contest the validity of the Bank's lien. The action was styled as a "Complaint to Determine Validity, Priority, and Extent of Lien and Ownership Interest." After four evidentiary hearings in which extensive testimony was taken from Orlando Toledo, employees of the Bank, and others, Judge Cristol of the bankruptcy court accepted Sanchez' argument and ordered that (i) the Bank had had no valid lien on the Partnership Property because it knew Toledo was conveying the mortgage for improper, non-partnership pur-poses, and (ii) the Bank must pay to Sanchez the $200,000 it had previously received from the sale of the Partnership Property. The bank-ruptcy court noted that it had jurisdiction under 28 U.S.C. § 1334, but never specifically confronted the question whether the adversary proceed-ing was core or non-core under 28 U.S.C. § 157. By issuing an order that purported to be final and binding, rather than submitting proposed findings of fact and conclusions of law to the district court, the bankruptcy court indicated that it viewed the proceeding as a core one of which it had full, plenary authority to dispose.

Appealing to the district court, the Bank argued that (i) the bankrupt-cy court lacked subject matter jurisdiction to hear the adversary proceed-ing filed by Sanchez; (ii) the bankruptcy court erred in finding that the Bank knew Toledo lacked authority to mortgage the Partnership Property for personal purposes; . . . . The district court held that the bankruptcy court had subject matter jurisdiction and that the matter was a core matter. It then found, applying the "clearly erroneous" standard of review to the bankruptcy court's fact findings (the appropriate standard of review for bankruptcy court orders regarding core matters), that Toledo lacked authority to mortgage the Partnership Property for his personal purposes, and that the Bank was aware thereof. . . . Consequently, the district court affirmed the bankruptcy court's judgment.

On appeal to this court, the Bank argues first that the bankruptcy court lacked jurisdiction to entertain the adversary proceeding under 28 U.S.C. § 1334. Second, it argues that, even if the bankruptcy court had

---

3. Section 363(f) of the Bankruptcy Code provides that "[t]he trustee may sell property under subsections (b) and (c) of this section free and clear of any interest in such property of an entity other than the estate" upon certain conditions. It is questionable whether § 363(f) gives a bankruptcy court power to order or approve a sale of property that belongs only to an entity in which the estate holds an interest, and not to the estate itself. However, the validity of the sale order is not presently before this Court, and at any rate, it appears that the sale of the Partnership Property was a voluntary transaction, on favorable terms to the seller, to which all of the parties consented. Thus, we do not consider any issues relating to Judge Weaver's sale order.

jurisdiction, such jurisdiction was in the nature of a non-core proceeding limiting the bankruptcy court's adjudicative powers. Third, the Bank reiterates its various substantive arguments as to why the bankruptcy court erred in its determination of the merits under Florida law; however, in light of our conclusion that this was a non-core proceeding, it is unnecessary for us to reach those issues.

The first question is whether the bankruptcy court had jurisdiction to entertain the instant adversary proceeding under 28 U.S.C. § 1334. Section 1334(b) provides that "the district courts shall have original but not exclusive jurisdiction of all civil proceedings arising under title 11, or arising in or related to cases under title 11." This provision creates jurisdiction in three categories of proceedings: those that "arise under title 11," those that "arise in cases under title 11," and those "related to cases under title 11." The bankruptcy court's jurisdiction is derivative of and dependent upon these three bases. The instant adversary proceeding did not "aris[e] under" or "aris[e] in" a case under the Bankruptcy Code. "Arising under" proceedings are matters invoking a substantive right created by the Bankruptcy Code. The "arising in a case under" category is generally thought to involve administrative-type matters. Hence, the only one of the three categories of proceedings over which the district court is granted jurisdiction in § 1334(b) that is potentially relevant to the instant case is proceedings "related to cases under title 11."

The Bank claims that the dispute between Sanchez and the Bank over entitlement to the proceeds of the Partnership Property was not related to Toledo's underlying bankruptcy case and had no effect on Toledo or the Estate, and therefore the bankruptcy court had no jurisdiction to adjudicate that dispute. Blending the concepts of jurisdiction and the core versus non-core dichotomy, the district court held that the bankruptcy court had jurisdiction because the dispute was a "core proceeding" under 28 U.S.C. § 157(b)(2)(K).[6]

As both parties acknowledge, *Miller v. Kemira, Inc. (In re Lemco Gypsum, Inc.)*, 910 F.2d 784 (11th Cir.1990), is the seminal case in this Circuit on the scope of the bankruptcy court's "related to" jurisdiction. In *Lemco Gypsum*, this Court adopted the following liberal test from *Pacor, Inc. v. Higgins*, 743 F.2d 984 (3d Cir.1984), for determining jurisdiction over an adversary proceeding:

The usual articulation of the test for determining whether a civil proceeding is related to bankruptcy is whether the outcome of the proceeding could conceivably have an effect on the estate being administered in bankruptcy. The proceeding need not necessarily be against the debtor or the debtor's property. An action is related to bankruptcy if the outcome could alter the debtor's rights, liabilities,

---

6. Although whether something is a core proceeding is analytically separate from whether there is jurisdiction, by definition all core proceedings are within the bankruptcy court's jurisdiction. Core proceedings are defined in 28 U.S.C. § 157(b)(1) as "proceedings arising under title 11, or arising in a case under title 11," which is a subset of the cases over which jurisdiction is granted in § 1334(b).

options, or freedom of action (either positively or negatively) and which in any way impacts upon the handling and administration of the bankrupt estate.

The key word in the *Lemco Gypsum/Pacor* test is "conceivable," which makes the jurisdictional grant extremely broad.

In the instant case, Sanchez was seeking a judicial determination of the extent and priority of liens and other interests in the Partnership Property so that the proceeds of the sale earlier approved by Judge Weaver's order could be distributed appropriately.... [I]f the Bank's mortgage was held invalid, as actually occurred, the Bank would have to look entirely to the Key Biscayne residence (or, more precisely, to what remained from the proceeds of the residence after satisfaction of BankAtlantic's first mortgage thereon) for satisfaction of its $1.8 million indebtedness. To the extent the value to which it was entitled from the residence was insufficient to satisfy this debt, the Bank would become an unsecured creditor causing the funds available for unsecured claims to be spread more thinly. A conceivable effect on the Estate thus exists in the possible partial satisfaction and consequent downward adjustment of the claim filed against the Estate by the Bank....

Having found that the district court had jurisdiction over the adversary proceeding, we turn next to the question whether the district court correctly referred to it as a core proceeding under 28 U.S.C. § 157(b). If it was a core proceeding, the district court correctly applied normal, deferential standards of appellate review to the bankruptcy court's disposition of it. *See* 28 U.S.C. § 158(a); Fed. R. Bankr.P. 8013. If it was a non-core proceeding, the bankruptcy court could only submit proposed findings of fact and conclusions of law, not a final order or judgment, and the district court was obligated to conduct a *de novo* review of those matters to which the Bank objected. *See* 28 U.S.C. § 157(c)(1) ("In [a non-core] proceeding, the bankruptcy judge shall submit proposed findings of fact and conclusions of law to the district court, and any final order or judgment shall be entered by the district judge after considering the bankruptcy judge's proposed findings and conclusions and after reviewing de novo those matters to which any party has timely and specifically objected."); Fed. R. Bankr.P. 9033 (specifying the exact procedures to be followed by the district court in such cases).

Congress created the distinction between core and non-core proceedings in the Bankruptcy Amendments and Federal Judgeship Act of 1984 ("1984 Act"), in order to avoid the constitutional problems, identified in *Northern Pipeline Constr. Co. v. Marathon Pipe Line Co.,* 458 U.S. 50, 102 S.Ct. 2858, 73 L.Ed.2d 598 (1982), associated with the expansive bankruptcy court jurisdiction permitted under prior law.[9] 28 U.S.C. § 157(b)(2)

9. In *Northern Pipeline,* the Supreme Court held that allowing bankruptcy courts to hear a state-law breach-of-contract action was an impermissible delegation of the Article III powers reserved to the federal judiciary. The adjudication of state-created "private rights" was seen as too far removed from the "core" of the federal bankruptcy power, i.e., the restructuring of debtor-creditor relations.

lists fourteen specific types of actions that are considered core proceedings, *id.* § 157(b)(2)(A)-(N), and provides a fifteenth, catch-all category for "other proceedings affecting the liquidation of the assets of the estate or the adjustment of the debtor-creditor or the equity security holder relationship," *id.* § 157(b)(2)(O). The statutory list provides that it is not intended to be exhaustive of the entire universe of core proceedings.

The district court held that the instant case was a core proceeding under 28 U.S.C. § 157(b)(2)(K), which applies to "determinations of the validity, extent, or priority of liens." This reliance on § 157(b)(2)(K) was misplaced. The district court apparently reasoned that since the purpose of the instant adversary proceeding was to obtain a judicial determination of the validity of the Bank's mortgage, which is a lien on real estate, it fit the language of subsection (b)(2)(K). However, the case law on (b)(2)(K) indicates that it encompasses only proceedings to determine the validity, extent, or priority of liens *on the estate's or the debtor's property.* Here, the real property on which the disputed mortgage existed belonged to the non-debtor Partnership, not to the Toledos or the Estate. The Estate owned a 50% interest in the Partnership, but no direct interest in the Partnership Property. Thus, § 157(b)(2)(K) is no basis for calling the instant proceeding a "core proceeding."

The distinction between property belonging to a partnership of which the debtor was partner, and property belonging to the debtor-partner, is well-established in bankruptcy law. ... The only partnership property before the court during an individual's bankruptcy is the partner's personal property interest in the partnership, which consists of the individual's interest, if any, in the partnership assets after an accounting and payment of partnership debts out of the property belonging to the partnership. The Partnership Property never entered the Estate in the instant case.

Nor do any of the other types of core proceedings appearing in § 157(b)'s list fit the instant adversary proceeding. To the extent that the literal wording of some of the types of proceedings might conceivably seem to apply, it should be remembered that engrafted upon all of them is an overarching requirement that property of the estate under § 541 be involved. Here, of course, the property in question was owned by the Partnership, not by Toledo himself.

Because the list in the statute is non-exhaustive, it is not the end of our inquiry whether the adversary proceeding was core. The most helpful explanation of what is a core proceeding, accepted almost universally by the courts, is found in the Fifth Circuit's decision in *Wood v. Wood (In re Wood)*, 825 F.2d 90 (5th Cir.1987):

> If the proceeding involves a right created by the federal bankruptcy law, it is a core proceeding; for example, an action by the trustee to avoid a preference. If the proceeding is one that would arise only in bankruptcy, it is also a core proceeding; for example, the filing of a proof of claim or an objection to the discharge of a particular debt. If the proceeding does not invoke a substantive right created by the

federal bankruptcy law and is one that could exist outside of bankruptcy it is not a core proceeding; it may be *related* to the bankruptcy because of its potential effect, but under section 157(c)(1) it is an "otherwise related" or non-core proceeding.

In *Wood,* the adversary proceeding in question was an action by a shareholder of a corporation of which the bankruptcy debtor was the only other shareholder, to obtain redress for allegedly improper stock issued to and dividends received by the debtor-shareholder or the estate. The Fifth Circuit held that under the above test this adversary proceeding was not a core proceeding because it was "simply a state contract action that, had there been no bankruptcy, could have proceeded in state court." Although the court had subject matter jurisdiction pursuant to the "related to" prong of § 1334(b), it was not a core proceeding.

Wood's interpretation of § 157 rested heavily on the ostensible purpose of the 1984 Act, i.e., "to conform the bankruptcy statutes to the dictates of *Marathon* [v. *Northern Pipeline*]." The Fifth Circuit's test breathes life into the terms "core" and "non-core" by construing them in light of the constitutional concerns that prompted the enactment of the statute. In fact, it appears that the use of the word "core" was itself borrowed from Justice Brennan's reference in the plurality opinion to "the core of the federal bankruptcy power." What the Supreme Court, and by extension Congress, was concerned about was the plenary adjudication by bankruptcy courts of proceedings "related only peripherally to an adjudication of bankruptcy." Hence, the issue before us ultimately depends on whether the instant case was of the type with respect to which the *Northern Pipeline* Court rejected giving bankruptcy courts full adjudicative power.

. . . Sanchez' action to determine the validity, priority, and extent of liens on the Partnership Property did not invoke a substantive right created by bankruptcy law, and could clearly occur outside of bankruptcy.[11] Indeed, actions similar to the instant case are filed in state court all the time.

The linguistic structure of § 157 lends further support to this conclusion. Subsection (b)(1) equates core proceedings with those "arising under title 11, or arising in a case under title 11," whereas subsection (c)(1) makes "non-core" proceedings synonymous with "otherwise related to" proceedings. "The phrases 'arising under' and 'arising in' are helpful

---

11. *Wood* is especially instructive because its facts are roughly analogous to those in the instant case. In *Wood,* the complaint filed in the bankruptcy court concerned the debtors' post-petition wrongful issuance of stock and payment of dividends (the debtors were controlling shareholders and directors of the corporation) to themselves, which violated the plaintiff's right as an equal shareholder. By comparison, the instant case concerns a debtor-partner's alleged manipulation of a partnership to exploit its property to secure personal debts, to the detriment of the other partner. In both cases, the right that the plaintiffs sought to vindicate involved a wrongful manipulation of the property of an entity other than the debtor (i.e., a corporation or partnership), and was essentially a state-law right based on principles of contract and/or fiduciary duty. Neither case is one involving a right created by bankruptcy law, or one which would arise only in bankruptcy. Rather, both cases invoke purely state-law rights and could exist outside bankruptcy.

indicators of the meaning of core proceedings." "Arising under" means that a proceeding invokes a cause of action, or substantive right, created by a specific section of the Bankruptcy Code. "Arising in" describes administrative matters unique to the management of a bankruptcy estate. For example, as the *Wood* court explained, the filing of a claim against a bankruptcy estate triggers a core proceeding under § 157(b)(2)(B), but only because it "invoke[s] the peculiar powers of the bankruptcy court." However, the administrative act of filing such a claim must be distinguished from the state-law right underlying the claim, which "could be enforced in a state court proceeding absent the bankruptcy" and is noncore. In the instant case, the adversary proceeding sought to vindicate state-created common-law rights but did not utilize any process specially established by the Bankruptcy Code. Clearly, Sanchez' adversary proceeding neither "arose under" nor "arose in" the Bankruptcy Code as those terms of art have been understood, and therefore it must necessarily fall within the residual category of "otherwise related," i.e., non-core matters.

In conclusion, we hold that there was "related to" jurisdiction over the adversary proceeding under 28 U.S.C. § 1334, but that it was a non-core proceeding under 28 U.S.C. § 157. Because the district court mistook it for a core proceeding, it exercised only "clearly erroneous" review of the bankruptcy court's findings of fact and "abuse of discretion" review of the bankruptcy court's application of waiver and estoppel, despite the Bank's specific objections to those findings and applications.[12] We remand with instructions to the district court to treat the bankruptcy court's findings of fact and conclusions of law entered at the October 13, 1994, hearing, and the accompanying February 23, 1995, and June 7, 1995 "judgments" granting Sanchez relief, as merely proposed findings of fact and conclusions of law, and to conduct the *de novo* review contemplated by § 157(c)(1) and Bankruptcy Rule 9033. The judgment of the district court is

VACATED AND REMANDED.

QUESTIONS ABOUT *TOLEDO*

1. **"Related to" jurisdiction precedent:** In finding "related to" jurisdiction over an action to determine the validity of a lien on a nondebtor's property because the existence of that lien would affect the amount of the lienor's claim against the estate, the Eleventh Circuit relied on its earlier decision in *Lemco Gypsum* which relied on *Pacor* which had been relied on by the Supreme Court in *Celotex*. Why didn't the Eleventh Circuit in *Toledo* simply rely on the Supreme Court's decision in *Celotex*?

---

12. It is evident from the tone of the district court's opinion that its review of certain issues was highly deferential to the bankruptcy court. For example, it stated that "there is a valid basis for the relief granted by the bankruptcy court to avoid an injustice to override the application of res judicata and collateral estoppel." District Court Order at 8. On remand, the district court should undertake a fresh, independent analysis of these issues.

2. **Related to jurisdiction problem**: D's Chapter 11 plan provided for the sale of all of its assets to X, free and clear of liens and claims, including claims based on successor liability. The bankruptcy court confirmed the plan and entered an order expressly providing that the sale to X would not be subject to successor liability claims. The amount X paid D was distributed to D's creditors, D went out of business, and the Chapter 11 case was closed. A year later, P sued X, alleging successor liability. X asked the bankruptcy court to reopen D's bankruptcy case and enjoin P from proceeding with her successor liability suit. Does the bankruptcy court have jurisdiction?

3. **Core/non-core Statutory Language**: What statutory language supports the district court's core proceeding determination? What statutory language supports the Circuit Court's non-core ruling?

D. JURY TRIALS

Having a powerful, centralized court to handle all matters involving the debtor in a bankruptcy case may be a good idea, but might there be cases in which constitutional considerations require something different?

Jury trial is a cherished right enshrined in the Seventh Amendment to the Constitution. And the Supreme Court has held that when an estate representative seeks to obtain the liability of a party who has not participated in the bankruptcy, and a jury traditionally (or at least by 1791) established that liability, the defendant is entitled to a trial by jury. *See Granfinanciera, S.A. v. Nordberg*, 492 U.S. 33 (1989) (fraudulent transfer cause of action recognized at law at the time of the adoption of the constitution, and thus defendant in such an action entitled to a jury).

Does this mean that every time a trustee wants to sue on a preference or a fraudulent transfer, the court has to empanel a jury? Can bankruptcy courts even conduct jury trials?[13] Read on.

LANGENKAMP v. CULP
498 U.S. 42 (1990)

PER CURIAM.

This case presents the question whether creditors who submit a claim against a bankruptcy estate and are then sued by the trustee in bankruptcy to recover allegedly preferential monetary transfers are entitled to jury trial under the Seventh Amendment. This action was brought by petitioner Langenkamp, successor trustee to Republic Trust & Savings Company and Republic Financial Corporation (collectively debtors). Debtors were

---

13. We'll answer this question first. Yes.... Well, maybe. Congress has given bankruptcy courts the power to hold jury trials only if the local district court specifically permits such trials, and if the parties expressly consent. 28 U.S.C. § 157(e).

uninsured, nonbank financial institutions doing business in Oklahoma. Debtors filed Chapter 11 bankruptcy petitions on September 24, 1984. At the time of the bankruptcy filings, respondents held thrift and passbook savings certificates issued by debtors, which represented debtors' promise to repay moneys the respondents had invested.

Within the 90–day period immediately preceding debtors' Chapter 11 filing, respondents redeemed some, but not all, of debtors' certificates which they held. Thus, upon the bankruptcy filing, respondents became creditors of the now-bankrupt corporations. Respondents timely filed proofs of claim against the bankruptcy estates. Approximately one year after the bankruptcy filing, the trustee instituted adversary proceedings under 11 U.S.C. § 547(b) to recover, as avoidable preferences, the payments which respondents had received immediately prior to the September 24 filing. A bench trial was held, and the Bankruptcy Court found that the money received by respondents did in fact constitute avoidable preferences.... The United States District Court for the Northern District of Oklahoma affirmed.... On appeal, the United States Court of Appeals for the Tenth Circuit upheld the District Court's judgment on three grounds, but reversed on the issue of the holders' entitlement to a jury trial on the trustee's preference claims. *In re Republic Trust & Savings Co.,* 897 F.2d 1041 (1990). Relying on our decisions in *Granfinanciera, S.A. v. Nordberg,* 492 U.S. 33, 109 S.Ct. 2782, 106 L.Ed.2d 26 (1989), and *Katchen v. Landy,* 382 U.S. 323, 86 S.Ct. 467, 15 L.Ed.2d 391 (1966), the Tenth Circuit correctly held that "those appellants that did not have or file claims against the debtors' estates undoubtedly [were] entitled to a jury trial on the issue whether the payments they received from the debtors within ninety days of the latter's bankruptcy constitute[d] avoidable preferences." The Court of Appeals went further, however, concluding:

> "Although some of the appellants did file claims against the estates because they continued to have monies invested in the debtors at the time of bankruptcy, ... we believe they likewise are entitled to a jury trial under the rationale of *Granfinanciera* and *Katchen.* Despite these appellants' claims, the trustee's actions to avoid the transfers, consolidated by the bankruptcy court, were plenary rather than a part of the bankruptcy court's summary proceedings involving the 'process of allowance and disallowance of claims.' "

Petitioner contends that the Tenth Circuit erred in holding that those creditors of the debtors who had filed claims against the estate were entitled to a jury trial. We agree.

In *Granfinanciera* we recognized that by filing a claim against a bankruptcy estate the creditor triggers the process of "allowance and disallowance of claims," thereby subjecting himself to the bankruptcy court's equitable power. If the creditor is met, in turn, with a preference action from the trustee, that action becomes part of the claims-allowance process which is triable only in equity. *Ibid.* In other words, the creditor's claim and the ensuing preference action by the trustee become integral to the restructuring of the debtor-creditor relationship through the bankruptcy court's *equity jurisdiction*. As such, there is no Seventh Amendment right to a jury trial. If a party does *not* submit a claim against the bankruptcy estate, however, the trustee can recover allegedly preferential transfers only by filing what amounts to a legal action to recover a monetary transfer. In those circumstances the preference defendant is entitled to a jury trial.

Accordingly, "a creditor's right to a jury trial on a bankruptcy trustee's preference claim depends upon whether the creditor has submitted a claim against the estate." *Id.*, at 58, 109 S.Ct., at 2799. Respondents filed claims against the bankruptcy estate, thereby bringing themselves within the equitable jurisdiction of the Bankruptcy Court. Consequently, they were not entitled to a jury trial on the trustee's preference action. The decision by the Court of Appeals overlooked the clear distinction which our cases have drawn and in so doing created a conflict among the Circuits on this issue. For this reason we grant the petition for certiorari, reverse the judgment of the Court of Appeals for the Tenth Circuit, and remand for further proceedings consistent with this opinion.

It is so ordered.

QUESTIONS ABOUT LANGENKAMP

1. What does *Langenkamp* say about the standard wisdom that a creditor should always file a proof of claim?

2. Now put the above question to practical use. What should a creditor do if it wants a jury trial and it is owed, say, $50,000, but believes that it likely received preferential payments during the reachback period of $100,000? Should it file a proof of claim? Is there any different result if the numbers are reversed; that is, if it is owed $100,000, but received preferences of $50,000? *See also* section 502(d).

E. VENUE

So once you determine that a bankruptcy court has the power to hear and decide a matter, who (or what) decides where it is to be heard? It is a big country, after all, and, there are big bankruptcy cases.

---

8 U.S.C. § 1408

[A] case under title 11 may be commenced in the district court for the district—

(1) in which the domicile, residence, principal place of business in the United States, or principal assets in the United States, of the person or entity that is the subject of such case have been located for the one hundred and eighty days immediately preceding such commencement, or for a longer portion of such one-hundred-and-eighty-day period than the domicile, residence, or principal place of business, in the United States, or principal assets in the United States, of such person were located in any other district; or

(2) in which there is pending a case under title 11 concerning such person's affiliate, general partner, or partnership.

Problem 12–1: Venue and Change of Venue in Business Cases

G Inc. owns and operates a chain of grocery stores in Alabama, Arkansas, Louisiana and Mississippi. G Inc. also owns all of the stock of GS Inc., a small chain of health food stores in California, Nevada, Oregon and Washington. G Inc. is incorporated in Delaware. GS Inc. is incorporated in New York. The chief executive office of both G Inc. and GS Inc. is in Piggott, Arkansas.

On January 15, GS Inc. files a Chapter 11 petition in New York. Later that same day, G Inc. files a Chapter 11 petition in New York. On January 29, a group of creditors of G Inc.'s retain your firm to get G Inc.'s bankruptcy case moved from the Southern District of New York to Arkansas. Where are you going to file a change of venue motion? Should the court grant the motion? Will the court grant the motion?

Of course, the venue for a *case* can be different from the venue for a *proceeding*. The presumption in title 11 cases is that all proceedings and matters will be heard in the same court as the main case. 11 U.S.C. § 1409(a). This sometimes causes hardship—if a small vendor to Circuit (say its janitorial service at its Las Vegas stores) was paid $6,000 just before Circuit City's Chapter 11 filing and the Circuit City Creditors' Committee attorneys are asserting that the $6,000 payment was a preference and demanding its return, does the Las Vegas janitorial service have to hire Virginia lawyers and litigate in Virginia to establish its ordinary course defense?

Section 1409(b) tries to take some of the sting out of this situation. It provides that efforts to collect consumer debts of less than $15,000 or any debts against non-insiders can be brought only where the defendant resides.

F. APPEALS

Appeals from bankruptcy decisions are probably more complicated than they should be. Under the statute, the basic appeal right is to the district court of which the bankruptcy court is a unit. 28 U.S.C. § 158(a). Some circuits, such as the Ninth and the Tenth, have taken advantage of the congressional authorization to create "Bankruptcy Appellate Panels," which consist of three bankruptcy judges drawn from districts other than the district from which the appeal arises. 28 U.S.C. § 158(b). The jurisdiction of such "BAPs," as they are called, is wholly consensual; although the consent is usually assumed unless there is an affirmative election made to go to the district court. 28 U.S.C. § 158(c).

Once the district court or the BAP decides the appeal, there is a further level of appeal to the circuit court. And for that leg of the appeal (from the district court or BAP to the circuit), it is pretty much standard federal appellate process. 28 U.S.C. § 158(d).

G. FOREIGN CASES

As economic problems become more global, more international problems will crowd the docket of the United States bankruptcy courts.

In 2005, Congress took a large step towards establishing an international set of protocols for bankruptcies that touch more than one country. The 2005 Act added a new chapter to the Bankruptcy Code—Chapter 15— and in so doing radically changed the law regarding bankruptcies that affect the United States and other countries. This chapter is essentially an adoption of a model law on cross-border insolvencies promulgated in 1997 by the United Nations Commission on International Trade Law (UNCITRAL).[14]

Europe has its own cross-border protocol, which came into effect on May 31, 2002. EC Regulation 1346/2000.

1. CHAPTER 15 OVERVIEW

In essence, a case under Chapter 15 is commenced by a petition filed by a foreign representative seeking "recognition" of a foreign insolvency

---

14. These changes apply only to bankruptcy cases that are filed on or after October 17, 2005. A different and more limited provision, previously codified at Section 304 of the Bankruptcy Code, applied to cases before that date.

The discussion of Chapter 15 in the House Report, H.R. REP. 109–31, 109TH CONG., 1ST SESS. 105–119 (2005), is an adaption and expansion of the official UNCITRAL commentary. The full text of UNCITRAL's convention and commentary, together with a current list of adoptions, can be found at: http://www.uncitral.org/uncitral/en/uncitral_texts/insolvency/1997Model.html.

proceeding. This description contains several defined terms; in short, something like a bankruptcy trustee in a foreign case will have standing to commence a proceeding in the United States to protect assets here for administration and distribution in the foreign insolvency proceeding. If the court recognizes the foreign proceeding under the principles set down in Chapter 15, the automatic stay and certain other protections of the Bankruptcy Code will apply. Chapter 15 is designed to encourage coordination among courts and estate representatives in different countries in the interest of avoiding inconsistent decisions that may hinder restructuring efforts.

Chapter 15 accomplishes these goals through four sets of provisions: (i) those related to the recognition of a foreign representative; (ii) those detailing the effects of recognition of a foreign representative; (iii) those which attempt to foster inter-court cooperation; and (iv) those which have effect in all cases.

2. CHAPTER 15 AND RECOGNITION OF THE "FOREIGN REPRESENTATIVE"

Chapter 15 is the vehicle by which "foreign representatives" can protect and obtain assets located in this country that relate to, or are owned by, a debtor with a case pending in another country. Section 101(24) defines "foreign representative" as follows:

> (24) The term "foreign representative" means a person or body, including a person or body appointed on an interim basis, authorized in a foreign proceeding to administer the reorganization or the liquidation of the debtor's assets or affairs or to act as a representative of such foreign proceeding;

This definition in turn incorporates the revised definition of "foreign proceeding," found in section 101(23), which states:

> (23) The term "foreign proceeding" means a collective judicial or administrative proceeding in a foreign country, including an interim proceeding, under a law relating to insolvency or adjustment of debt in which proceeding the assets and affairs of the debtor are subject to control or supervision by a foreign court, for the purpose of reorganization or liquidation;

Foreign representatives have significant powers under Chapter 15. But to invoke them, the foreign representative must be "recognized." Indeed, a Chapter 15 case is commenced by the filing of a petition to be recognized by a foreign representative, section 1504. Ultimate recognition, however, is governed by section 1515, which provides:

§ 1515. Application for recognition

(a) A foreign representative applies to the court for recognition of a foreign proceeding in which the foreign representative has been appointed by filing a petition for recognition.

(b) A petition for recognition shall be accompanied by—

(1) a certified copy of the decision commencing such foreign proceeding and appointing the foreign representative;

(2) a certificate from the foreign court affirming the existence of such foreign proceeding and of the appointment of the foreign representative; or

(3) in the absence of evidence referred to in paragraphs (1) and (2), any other evidence acceptable to the court of the existence of such foreign proceeding and of the appointment of the foreign representative.

(c) A petition for recognition shall also be accompanied by a statement identifying all foreign proceedings with respect to the debtor that are known to the foreign representative.

(d) The documents referred to in paragraphs (1) and (2) of subsection (b) shall be translated into English. The court may require a translation into English of additional documents.

Basically, the foreign representative files documents issued by a foreign court or tribunal, that have been translated into English, and which establish that he or she is the authorized representative of a foreign insolvency proceeding. Once satisfactory documents have been produced, recognition is essentially automatic, section 1517.

---

3. THE EFFECTS OF RECOGNITION OF A FOREIGN REPRESENTATIVE

Once a foreign representative is recognized, many substantive provisions of the Bankruptcy Code automatically apply. For example, with respect to any property in the United States,

- the automatic stay applies.

- the administrative provisions regarding sale of the property (including the ability to sell free and clear of liens and other interests) apply, as does section 549 with respect to unauthorized post-petition transfers.

- the foreign representative may operate the debtor's business under sections 363 and 552.

In addition, the foreign representative may apply for additional powers, which may include the taking of examinations (although not mentioned by name, this presumably covers examinations under Rule 2004) and any other power a trustee might have *except* for the commencement of avoidance powers actions (other than those under Section 549), section 1521.

The foreign representative may, however, commence a separate case under any other applicable chapter, section 1511, and once that case is commenced, the foreign representative has standing to pursue avoidance powers actions, such as preference actions under section 547 and fraudulent transfer actions under section 548, in that domestic case, section 1523.

4. PROVISIONS DESIGNED TO FOSTER INTER–COURT COOPERATION

Subchapters IV and V of Chapter 15 (11 U.S.C. § 1525 to 1532) contain a series of provisions designed to authorize and simply court-to-court communications with respect to bankruptcy cases pending in more than one country. The provisions authorize direct communication with a foreign court (section 1524(b)), and the entry of protocols or other agreed means of communication in a particular case (section 1527). Finally, there are provisions which attempt to coordinate a number of filings in affect countries, primarily by designation of one countries as a "foreign main proceeding" (which is to be where the debtor's "center of main interests"—something akin to a chief executive office, section 1502(4), is located.)

As an example, if a United States debtor has property in Mexico, a United States trustee can commence a proceeding in Mexico to recover it (since Mexico has adopted the very same convention). The two courts–United States and Mexico–would then each be authorized to communicate with each other to make the process more efficient. Similarly, a Mexican *sindico* would then be able to commence a Chapter 15 case in the United States if the debtor in his or her case had assets in the United States. The courts would still be able to communicate with one another.

5. PROVISIONS WHICH AFFECT ALL CASES

Under new Section 103(k), some provisions of Chapter 15 affect all title 11 cases–that is, they apply in Chapter 7, 9, 11, 12 and 13 cases. They are:

- section 1505, which empowers the court to authorize a trustee or examiner under any other case to act in a foreign case in any manner permitted by foreign law;
- section 1513, which removes any and all disabilities of foreign creditors to appear in any pending case under title 11 to the extent that such disabilities are based upon their status as foreign creditors;

- section 1514, which applies to the claims of foreign creditors in domestic title 11 cases. Among other things, this provision requires notice to be given individually to creditors with foreign addresses if practical, and requires that notification of a domestic title 11 case contain certain notices regarding the time limits and the content of proofs of claim. Finally, the section requires additional time to file proofs of claim be given to creditors with foreign addresses, with such additional time being reasonable under the circumstances, section 1514(d).

- section 1509, which applies even if a title 11 case is not pending, allows foreign representatives to commence Chapter 15 proceedings, and if they do, to then have the capacity to sue or be sued in any court in this country (including state courts). This includes a foreign representative's right, upon recognition, to apply to a non-bankruptcy court for such relief as is consistent with comity and cooperation.

INDEX

References are to Pages

References are to Pages

†